Completely Morgan

Four-wheelers from 1968

Other books of interest to enthusiasts available from Veloce -

Alfa Romeo Owner's Bible
by Pat Braden
Alfa Romeo Tipo 6C, 1500, 1750 & 1900
by Angela Cherrett
Alfa Romeo Modello 8C 2300
by Angela Cherrett
Alfa Romeo Giulia Coupé GT & GTA
by John Tipler
Biggles!
by Peter Berresford Ellis & Jennifer Schofield
British Car Factories from 1896 - A Complete Survey
by Paul Collins & Michael Stratton
Bubblecars & Microcars Colour Family Album
by Andrea & David Sparrow
Bugatti 57 - The Last French Bugatti
by Barrie Price
Car Bodywork & Interior: Care & Repair
by David Pollard
Car Security Manual
by David Pollard
Citroën 2CV Family Album
by Andrea & David Sparrow
Citroën DS Family Album
by Andrea & David Sparrow
Cobra: The Real Thing!
by Trevor Legate

Completely Morgan: Four-Wheelers 1936-1968
by Ken Hill
Daimler SP250 'Dart'
by Brian Long
Fiat & Abarth 124 Spider & Coupé
by John Tipler
Fiat & Abarth 500 & 600
by Malcolm Bobbitt
Lola T70
by John Starkey
Mazda MX5/Miata Enthusiast's Workshop Manual
by Rod Grainger & Pete Shoemark
Mini Cooper: The Real Thing!
by John Tipler
Nuvolari: When Nuvolari Raced
by Valerio Moretti
Pass the MoT
by David Pollard
The Prince & I - My Life with the Motor Racing Prince of Siam (biography of racing driver 'B.Bira')
by Princess Ceril Birabongse
Rover P4 Series-60, 75, 80, 90,100,105,110
by Malcolm Bobbitt
Standard & Standard-Triumph - The Illustrated History
by Brian Long
Total Tuning for the Classic MG Midget/A-H Sprite
by Daniel Stapleton

First published in 1994 by Veloce Publishing Plc., Godmanstone, Dorset DT2 7AE, England. Fax 0300 341065

ISBN 1 874105 34 0

© Ken Hill and Veloce Publishing Plc 1994

Readers with ideas for automotive books, or books on other transport or related hobby subjects are invited to write to the editorial director of Veloce Publishing at the above address.

British Library Cataloguing in Publication Data -
A catalogue record for this book is available from the British Library.

Typesetting (Bookman, 9pt), design and page make-up all by Veloce on Apple Mac.

Printed and bound in England.

IMPORTANT NOTE. While the author has prepared the practical information in this book with diligence and care, it is possible that it contains errors or omissions. It is not possible to foresee every possible area of personal danger or possibility of mechanical damage and warn readers accordingly. The author, publisher and retailers therefore accept no responsibility for personal injury or mechanical damage which is in any way related to the use of this publication. If you use the practical information contained within this book, you accept full personal responsibility for the consequences.

Completely Morgan

Four-wheelers from 1968

Ken Hill

VELOCE PUBLISHING PLC
PUBLISHERS OF FINE AUTOMOTIVE BOOKS

ACKNOWLEDGEMENTS

No book of this type can be written without the unstinted co-operation of many people.

Firstly, I must again record my sincere thanks to Peter Morgan, Charles Morgan and the staff of the Morgan Motor Company for their unfailing assistance with the provision of the works' production records, photographs and a mass of material from their archives.

I am also indebted to Michael Ware and Linda Springate of the National Motor Museum for placing their expertise, library and records at my disposal and to Sarah Joselin LBIPP, LMPA for her expert photographic advice and assistance.

Thanks to Motor Racing Publications, Motorbooks International and Shire Publications Ltd who kindly allowed me to use previously published material.

Sincere thanks to The Morgan Plus 4 Club, The Morgan Sports Car Club and John H Sheally II for invaluable assistance and permission to use original copyright material. Also to T W Barney, Chief Technical Editor of Glass's Guide Service Ltd, for supplying and granting permission to reproduce the copyright Technical Data Sheets, and Lucas after-sales service for assistance in compiling the electrical data and wiring diagrams.

In addition, a very special thank you to Mike Duncan, Jerry Willburn and John Worrall for all their advice and assistance, and for sharing their technical expertise which helped so much in compiling the technical chapter. Also, thanks are due to Richard Tipping.

Many of the photographs used in this book originated from members of the Saga Travel Club, who responded so wonderfully to my request for information and photographs. In all, over 320 people have contacted me and lent over 200 photographs from family albums. It is impossible to list them all individually, but I wish to place on record my grateful thanks to them all.

I have obtained information from notes left by the late Dick Pritchard. The material had been collected by him over forty or more years and the exact origin of much of it is unknown. I know that he assembled material from most motoring magazines, including *Light Car & Cycle Car*, *Motor Cycle*, *Motor Cycling*, *Autosport*, *Motor Sport*, *Motor* and *Autocar*, all of which he read regularly. In addition I have collected information over the past twenty years from magazines, Morgan clubs and Morgan owners from all over the world. In many cases it is now impossible to establish the exact source of certain material, photographs and information, and therefore I offer my heartfelt thanks to all such writers, magazines and photographers.

Finally, as usual, I'd like to thank my wife, Janet, who has once again helped me so much in the research and compilation of this book.

Ken Hill

CONTENTS

INTRODUCTION

Over the past eighty years, hundreds of thousands - if not millions - of words have been written about the Morgan sports car and the Morgan Motor Company Limited, a few thousand of which, over the last thirteen years, were contributed by me.

Throughout this period I have continued with my research into Morgan history. This research, along with information gathered from Peter Morgan and my numerous Morgan friends worldwide, has created a necessity to add to, or correct, some previously-published material. The majority of my previous work remains accurate, though much of it is now out of print. Some parts of this book are therefore direct reprints of this previously-published information.

The chapters covering maintenance and practical tips have been greatly enlarged, although it is not intended they be regarded as workshop manual information but rather to act as a basic guide to practical Morgan ownership.

It is impossible to cover every practical subject and fact relating to Morgans; in writing this book I have endeavoured to incorporate as much information as possible within the limitations of size. Much of its content has never before been available to the Morgan owner.

To own a Morgan, no matter what age or model, is to become a member of the worldwide 'Morgan brotherhood'. This fraternity has no rules or regulations, no committees, no annual membership dues, no divisions based on the number of wheels or type of radiator, no geographical or political boundaries, and its members are united by a common love. In fact, the only qualification needed is the exposure to - and contracting of - the incurable disease 'Morganitis'.

If you have read this far, I am sorry to inform you that you have just shown the first symptoms. Welcome to the wonderful world of Morgans!

Ken Hill
Brockenhurst, England

Publisher's note on photo reproduction
As Ken Hill points out in his acknowledgements, many of the photographs used to illustrate this work have come from private photo albums. Of course, this means that the originals are a little fuzzy and of poor tonal balance; nevertheless, because of the unique and rare nature of this material, we have reproduced such pictures in this publication. We hope you will agree that the inclusion of these otherwise delightful photographs is worthwhile.

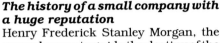

I
MULTUM IN PARVO

The history of a small company with a huge reputation

Henry Frederick Stanley Morgan, the man who was to guide the destiny of the Morgan Motor Company Limited for almost fifty years, was born at Morton Jeffries Court - the Manor House of the village of Morton Jeffries in Herefordshire, England - on August 11, 1881 to Florence and the Reverend Prebendary Henry George Morgan (known as George to his family), who had succeeded his father Henry George as Rector of Stoke Lacy in 1871. It was in this tranquil setting that Harry, or 'HFS', as he was to become known throughout the motoring world, spent his early childhood, in company with his younger sisters, Freida, Ethel and Dorothy.

HFS was educated at Stone House, Broadstairs, and then at Marlborough College. However, as with most public schools of this period, conditions were austere and the food frequently almost inedible. Slowly young Harry became undernourished and his health began to suffer, becoming so ill that his parents removed him from the college.

Amongst his many talents was a natural ability for art, which he had obviously inherited from his father, an accomplished amateur artist. Shortly after he was withdrawn from Marlborough, his parents took him to Italy. It is not certain if this was to help speed his recovery or an attempt to encourage his artistic talent. The first reason is the more likely because, in spite of his family's religious background, HFS felt no call to join the church, nor did his parents try to force him to do so: with what was, for the time, very forward thinking, his parents allowed him to choose freely between art and engineering. He chose

the latter and continued his education at the Crystal Palace Engineering College in South London. Whilst there, he was allowed to design, develop and build all manner of things. One of the best of these was a bicycle which he designed and built himself, which proved to be almost invincible in the College races and established a new speed record.

HFS's father was devoted to his children and would often fly in the face of public opinion if he felt it right for them. At that time it was very much frowned upon for a clergyman's son to go into trade. He was in later years, after his son had established himself as a car manufacturer, to become a familiar sight in his top hat, watching, with ill-concealed pride, the performance of Morgan cars in competitive events. When his son left engineering college at the age of 18, he secured for him an apprenticeship to William Dean and subsequently C J Churchward, the chief engineers of the Great Western Railway at Swindon, where HFS worked in the drawing office for seven years.

By this time, Britain's railway companies had become a productive training ground for car people. At the same time as HFS was at Swindon, W O Bentley was serving his apprenticeship at the Doncaster works of the Great North Railway, the same company which, a few years earlier, had enabled Henry Royce to develop his engineering skills at its Peterborough works.

For most motorists, memories of their first attempt to drive a car tend to be of a pounding heart and feeling of thankfulness when it was all over and they, their car and everything around them were still intact. But for HFS it was to be rather different. His first drive in 1899 was in a 3 1/2hp Benz which he

Henry Frederick Stanley ('HFS') Morgan 1881-1959. Founder of the Morgan Motor Company Limited.

The dream becomes reality

At the end of his apprenticeship, HFS was offered permanent employment in the Swindon works but decided instead to leave the GWR and open a garage in the area of his home. After some thought and research, he decided on Malvern Link as the right location and opened the garage in partnership with his close friend Leslie Bacon. Initially, It was far from plain sailing. Motor cars were still regarded as noisy, smelly nuisances, and for a clergyman's son to be selling them was beyond belief. He was to receive many rude letters; HFS silenced the writers by displaying their correspondence in the garage window!

The business soon began to flourish and they were able to acquire agencies for Wolseley and Darracq cars. In addition, he started a bus service with a 15-seater 10hp Wolseley from Malvern Link to the Wells and from Malvern to Gloucester. This, however, was not too successful and eventually the bus was sold and they started a car-hire business, which did well.

Before long HFS was able to devote more time to his experiments with design. He started work on a new type of car with another very good friend, W Stephenson-Peach, the engineering master of Malvern College and a direct descendant of George Stephenson who, in 1814, designed the famous 'Rocket' locomotive. About this time HFS bought a 7hp twin-cylinder Peugeot engine with the intention of installing it in a motorcycle, but he was becoming increasingly attracted to the idea of three-wheeled transport. This led him to construct a machine which was neither a motorcycle nor a car, but something halfway between the two - a cyclecar.

There can be little doubt that with-

had hired from an unsuspecting Mr Marriot, the first motor trader in Hereford. All went well until he started to descend the 1-in-6 gradient of a hill between Bromyard and Hereford and the Benz took charge and ran away with him. He emerged intact, but the damage to the Benz was to cost his father £28.

However, Mr Marriott could not have been too put out by the incident as he continued to hire cars to HFS from time to time over the next two years until young Morgan had saved enough money to buy a motor vehicle of his own - an Eagle Tandem. The Eagle, a three-wheeler, was driven by a water-cooled 8hp de Dion engine. It had a motorcycle-style rear wheel, with a car-type front axle. A wickerwork passenger seat was sited between the front wheels.

This vehicle was to stimulate HFS's interest in the design and development of the three-wheeler. The Eagle was also to give him his first conviction for a motoring offence when he exceeded the 12mph speed limit. In 1902 the Eagle was replaced by a four-wheeler, a 7hp two-cylinder car called The Little Star, which was purchased with part of the £200 that his godfather had left him on becoming of age.

out the facilities of Malvern College's engineering machinery, HFS would not have had time to build the experimental car and run his business. In all it took a little under a year for the car to be built, with completion early in 1909. The prototype was a three-wheeled vehicle of very simple design. The main chassis member was a single large diameter tube, which had the clutch mounted at the front end, the bevel-box at the rear and the propshaft running through the centre. Further tubing was used for bracing from the bevel box to the centre pins of the front wheels. These front wheels were mounted on a unique design of independent front suspension. Two other tubes, mounted parallel and running longitudinally, completed the chassis and also acted as exhaust pipes, with silencers mounted on the front of each. The drive to the rear wheel was by chain, via two speeds, high and low, which were engaged through a simple dog clutch arrangement, and a lever next to the bevel-box. The bevel-box also served as the seat. Braking was obtained by foot and/or hand pressure to levers which operated constricting bands mounted on each side of the rear wheel. Steering was by means of a tiller. The bodywork was minimal, with a bucket seat of sorts, a front-mounted fuel tank and a mudguard over the rear wheel only.

Mounted at the front was the previously mentioned 7hp Peugeot engine.

The prototype's good power-to-weight ratio, combined with the rigid frame and ingenious independent front suspension, have remained part of the Morgan hallmark ever since. These features ensured a remarkable performance for such a small vehicle when it was run for the first time; its first outing on public roads was to Shelsley Walsh, not to compete in the hill-climb but simply to raise interest.

Although built primarily for his own use, HFS soon found he was being approached by others with requests for him to make similar cars: so great was this pressure that he began to think in terms of the possibility of manufacturing cars as a business. Yet again, Reverend George Morgan was completely supportive of his son's endeavour and provided the necessary capital to equip the garage with the few machine tools necessary for HFS to start production on a limited basis.

With the information gained from driving the prototype around Malvern, HFS was able to incorporate one or two improvements to these production cars, which included the fitting of tie bars to the crosshead at the front of the vehicle, and silencers modified to the 'coffee pot' design which was to become so well known.

Having patented his design (the

The twin-cylinder 1910 Olympia Show car had an 8hp engine and tiller steering; Morgan offered a steering wheel for an extra charge.

As a result of comments received at the Motor Cycle Show debut, Morgan constructed a two-seater prototype, considerable improvements to which were made before the 1911 show.

patent drawings were produced by a bright young man called John Black, later Sir John Black, who was to contribute to Morgan history again 28 years later in his role as head of the Standard Motor Company) and spurred on by his local success, HFS and his partner formed the Morgan Company and decided to exhibit at the First International Motor Cycle Show at Olympia, London in November 1910. They displayed two versions of the car - one fitted with a 4hp JAP 85.5mm x 85mm single- cylinder engine and the other with a twin-cylinder 8hp version of the same engine and a bare chassis. Both cars were single-seaters and were fitted with tiller steering. Although the cars and their unique design attracted a lot of attention and good press coverage, the number of orders received - 30 in all - was disappointing, and Leslie Bacon decided to withdraw from the partnership. However, he remained friends with HFS for the whole of his life and Peter Morgan remembers going to stay with him on holiday.

This could well have been the end of the Morgan company if help had not come from an entirely unexpected quarter. The managing director of Harrods, the famous London store, was one Richard Burbridge, who was far-seeing enough to recognize that, in spite of its primitive design, the Morgan Runabout had great potential. In return for being granted the first dealership, the Knightsbridge store injected much-needed capital into the business and guaranteed orders. Encouraged by these developments HFS decided to carry on. It became obvious that he must do two things if he was to succeed. First and foremost, he must prove his product in competition (a principle still practised by the family today) and, secondly, he

had to build a two-seater version of his design. This he did in ample time for the Motor Cycle Show at Olympia in November 1911. There, on Stand 127, he exhibited:

Two-seater, fitted with hood and screen, price £96.00
8hp two-seater, price 85 guineas
8hp Torpedo single-seater, price 85 guineas
8hp single-seater, tiller steering, price 85 guineas
8hp two-seater chassis, price 80 guineas

The steering on all but the one mentioned was by wheel. The combination of early competition successes and the two-seater version of the car ensured an amazing number of orders were taken at the show. A caption associated with a contemporary drawing of the two-seater read, '*The Morgan Magnet attracts all young couples by its double seating accommodation*'. After the show, *Motor Cycling* commented '*The interest displayed in the Morgan Runabouts was phenomenal. As all our readers know, these machines have competed with unqualified success in all the big trials of the last 18 months, gaining a reputation of which the makers may justly be proud*'.

So great was the demand that it far

outstripped the production capacity of his little works and HFS was obliged to seek a tie-up with a major manufacturer. Fortuitously, as it turned out, every company he approached turned him down, and so, with the help of deposits accepted from potential buyers, he had to buy more machine tools and make further extensions to the additional premises which his father had financed the previous year in order that the initial production of Morgan Runabouts could begin.

Behind every great man ...
1912 was to be a momentous year for HFS with three major events taking place. This was the year in which the Morgan Motor Company Limited was formed and it made a small but significant profit - £1314. It was also the year when, in June, he married Ruth Day, the daughter of the Reverend Archibald Day, vicar of St Mattias, Malvern Link. He had met Ruth at a dance at the Grand Hotel in Malvern, which later became the Malvern Girls' College. It has often been said that behind every great or successful man, there is a strong woman. By all accounts Ruth was certainly this. Besides being very attractive, she was also capable, giving practical advice and encouragement whenever necessary.

Ruth Morgan was HFS's passenger in trials. Here, at Brooklands during the 1921 Auto Cycle Union Six Day Trial, she stands behind her husband. On the left is EB Ware, chief experimental engineer of JAP Engines.

In the early years, Ruth accompanied HFS on many trials and competitions, acting as a very good 'bouncer' on the steep hills. Somehow she still managed to fit into this busy schedule time to have five children; four girls, Sylvia, Stella, Brenda and Barbara (known as Bobbie), and one son, Peter. In the case of Peter it would be true to say that he was born to competition; press reports of the period tell of Ruth acting as trials passenger to HFS less than three months before his birth. As far as is known, she never drove in competitions herself but did own a variety of different cars as her own personal transport, including a Fiat, Alvis 12/50, Alvis Speed 20 and a Hillman Minx.

Ruth made a great impact on the motor sporting scene and, following her death in 1956, a magazine editor wrote: 'With sorrow I heard of the death recently of Mrs HFS Morgan. In the early days of the Morgan three-wheeler, HFS, piloting one of his own cars, was seldom absent from any big trial, and his wife was always at his side. In a personal letter I received from Mr Morgan he said, "You will remember how keen she was and how much she helped me in trials work".

'Only those who took part in them can remember the severe conditions under which those trials were often run, and to sit quietly and stoically in an open three-wheeler, come rain or snow, beside a skilful driver was often in the nature of a major ordeal. Mrs Morgan took it all in her stride, and always there was a welcoming smile and a helping hand for those with whom she came in contact. HFS achieved many successes; the glory was always with his passenger to whom he owed so much.'

Keeping the pot boiling

The chairman of the Morgan Motor Company Limited was Preb H George Morgan. He was to become a familiar figure at Brooklands, in his long coat and top hat, and many other events where his son was competing or attempting to break records. Completely dedicated to the company (though he had made a small personal fortune by investing in gold shares on the stock market), Morgan Senior was not unknown to write, under a pseudonym, controversial letters to the motoring press, to stimulate public interest in the marque. Should this bring little or no response, he would answer himself, in a manner best likely to stimulate debate, using another pseudonym. What is not generally known is that he also wrote several articles, in particular for Light Car or Light Car & Cyclecar magazines. With an excellent head for figures, he kept the company's books for several years and still found time to indulge his hobby as an artist. (An excellent self-portrait hangs in the entrance hall of the Morgan factory). George Morgan died on November 10, 1936, aged 84. Many of the motoring magazines printed tributes to him, with the Light Car & Cyclecar magazine heading its obituary, 'A Pioneer Passes Away'.

On the formation of the company HFS had become managing director, but on the death of his father he succeeded him as chairman. George Goodall, who had become works manager in January 1927, was joined by his son Jim in 1936, although it was not until 1938 that George was appointed managing director. At about this time HFS established a new home at Bray in Berkshire, and handed over the day-to-day running of the factory to George Goodall, although he still visited the factory once a week. George Goodall did an excellent job and the move made for a far more relaxed life for HFS.

George Goodall, works manager of the Morgan Motor Company, was known as 'Uncle George'. Here is is having fun on a Brough Superior 11-50 at Brooklands in 1935.

From little acorns ...

Continued outstanding successes in all forms of competition by HFS and an increasing band of private owners ensured the expansion of the company. At this time motor manufacturers had to make 95% of all the parts for their product as there were very few outside manufacturers of components. Slowly, the signs of increased productivity began to show at the Malvern Link works. The machine shops were extended, albeit only a little, and various storage and painting sheds were erected behind the main works. These were not large affairs at all. For example, the painting was carried out by hand using brushes, a practice which continued up to the outbreak of war in 1939, and did not require a large factory area. For several years after the war, painting was by sprayed coach paint for speed but the rubbing down and build-up of paint was still labour intensive

Profits increased. The published figures were £4797 in 1913 and £10,450 in 1914. The latter figure was somewhat reduced from what it might have been, due to the outbreak of war.

When the First World War began, sales had never been higher, with almost 1000 cars being built in 1913. These included export sales to France, Russia, India and North and South America. As with all engineering works, a major part of the company's production had to be made over to the production of shells and other munitions for the war effort. To avoid any possibility of profiteering from the government contracts, a fixed profit allowance - generous by any standards - was legislated. When one considers that in addition to this the government also supplied, or helped substantially with the cost of, new machinery, there can be

Morgan chassis frames and the people who made them, at the Worcester Road works, 1912.

little wonder the company continued to make increased profits throughout the war years.

Throughout the war very limited car production was maintained and the repair shop remained open. Experiments and improvements continued which included the production of an experimental four-wheeled model which, for various reasons, was discontinued. As the war drew to an end, HFS realized that the sooner he could get his factory back into full production after peace was declared, the greater number of cars he could sell in the postwar rush. So successful was he with this that the factory was back into full production long before any of his major

Pickersleigh Road in the early 1920s - the erecting and finishing shop.

Coach painters take a lunch break - Pickersleigh Road, circa 1922.

competitors.

Besides careful planning and foresight, the other factors which helped with this success was, without doubt, the simplicity of the cars' design and construction and the fact that the vehicle was not dependent on any single engine manufacturer (a status which the factory still strives to maintain today).

All vee-twin engines have a basic banjo-shaped crankcase. It is therefore only necessary to fabricate a simple baseplate, drilled out to match both sets of mounting holes, engine and chassis front tubes to give the car its power source. Although engines were not plentiful at this time, HFS was able to buy enough to keep production at maximum rate and eventually to build up sufficient stocks to sustain production when the depression arrived and engines became difficult to obtain.

The immediate postwar boom in demand for mechanized transport was caused by the war itself. Before 1914, most people had never driven in or on a motor vehicle of any type; the war was to change all that. Ordinary men and women were trained to drive all manner of vehicles, and when they returned to civilian life they wanted to be able to continue driving. Secondhand motorcycles and cyclecars were almost unobtainable and, as with all cases where demand far outstrips supply, prices shot up. In the three years immediately after the war the cost of a new Morgan was greater pro-rata than at any other time in its history. At the declaration of war, the highest priced car was £98. At the 1920 Motor Cycle Show the cheapest was £206, and at the 1932 Show the lowest price was back down to the prewar figure of £98.

Immediately after the war, produc-tion became severely restricted by the small size of the factory in Worcester Road. In April 1919 HFS was walking through the turning shop and, whilst passing a capstan lathe, slipped on a small patch of grease. Instinctively, he threw out his right hand to save himself and caught it in the machinery. As a result of this accident the first two fingers of his right hand had to be amputated. A new site in Pickersleigh Road was purchased, which HFS opened on October 16, 1919, three weeks before Peter Morgan was born on November 3, 1919.

The new premises were used for the finishing work of painting and trimming. The production of the chassis with all its associated machinery continued at the Worcester Road factory. The part-completed cars were then loaded on a Crossley lorry and transported to Pickersleigh Road. This was not an efficient or convenient arrangement, and by 1922 a major building programme was underway. Early in 1923 the whole factory was relocated to the new site, with the exception of the machine shop which was not moved until 1929. To mark the occasion, HFS held a party for over 500 people in one of the new buildings. In his speech he praised his workforce for their loyalty and hard work in spite of all the disruptions and a call for increased productivity.

Just how prosperous the company and HFS had become is reflected in the fact that purchasing the new site and building the factory was achieved without loans. In 1925 his family moved to a much larger house in Malvern Link named Fern Lodge, which is now Seaford Court School. Also in 1921 he purchased a Rolls-Royce 40/50 to replace his Prince Henry Vauxhall. It is not certain whether this Rolls-Royce was bodied at the Morgan works. However, in 1932 HFS arrived at the Motor Cycle Show at Olympia in a Rolls-Royce Phantom II, which was fitted with an all-weather body built in the Morgan factory. A report in *Light Car & Cyclecar* magazine went as follows: *'I happened to call there whilst it was in the course of construction, and very odd it looked in a shop filled with three-wheeler bodies. Mr Morgan designed the body himself, and had no difficulties in getting it accepted for guarantee purposes by the hyper-critical Rolls-Royce engineers'.*

After the Morgan success in the French Cyclecar Grand Prix in July 1913 demand for the car increased enormously, particularly in France. It was reported that the Paris agent sold 150 examples in 1914 and placed an order for 500 in 1915. Postwar, the demand for small, reasonably-priced cars remained high, both here and in France. In 1914 HFS granted a licence to Roger Darmont (later Darmont et Badelogue) to build Morgan cars in Paris. The success of the Darmont Morgan was assured when Paul Houel scored a memorable victory in the Cir-

Pickersleigh Road paint shop, 1929/30. The mottled dashboard of the family model in the foreground was introduced in 1929. On the left, halfway down the workshop, is a delivery van.

cuit de L'Eure on August 16, 1919.

The Depression and mass-production

The postwar boom could not last forever and by 1923 it was over. It was followed by the General Strike and Depression of the mid-to-late 1920s and early 1930s, which were to have a devastating effect on the manufacturers of light cars and cyclecars, both three and four-wheelers, in Britain and on the Continent. The less well-off were the main purchasers of this type of vehicle, and it was these people who were most affected by the new economic climate. Moreover, mass-production was on the increase, with both Austin and Morris joining Ford in being able to produce cars on a continuous line system. The

prices of all light cars and cyclecars fell steadily throughout the 1920s as their manufacturers attempted to compete with mass-production. Many went bankrupt. Morgan survived because of numerous factors: the loyalty of the workers, who did not strike; stocks of engines of different makes, which avoided supply problems when strikes affected their production; continued competition and record-breaking successes and, above all, the shrewd business acumen of HFS. Unlike so many of his competitors, he slowly reduced his production and lowered his prices. At the same time he realized that he must also make his product even more attractive to the now limited market. By careful planning and correct

timing he was able to introduce several improvements through these lean years, matching them against those introduced by the mass-production companies. Most of the improvements, such as front-wheel brakes, electric lighting, and self-starters, were at first offered as optional extras and later adopted as standard fittings.

Litigation

In November 1921, Charles J Fox, a piano manufacturer, purchased what was left of the British Anzani Engine Company. S F Edge of the AC company had bought a large shareholding in the company and then after a few months withdrew AC's order of Anzani engines and changed the AC's power unit to a

Morgan-bodied Rolls-Royce; this 1935 Phantom II was the second of the marque that HFS owned. He designed its body, which was built at the Morgan works. Note the Morgan stork mascot, replacing the Spirit of Ecstasy, also used on his earlier Rolls-Royce 40/50.

Old-time timepiece: the punch clock that was used for years to 'clock in' employees at the Morgan factory.

Cubitt engine. In this way he effectively killed off the Anzani competition but ensured that AC and Cubitt (he was a major shareholder in both) made a good profit. Fox named his new company the British Vulpine Engine Company Limited and continued to produce exactly the same range of engines as before, but in much reduced numbers.

In June 1926 the Vulpine company went into liquidation. It was claimed that this was due to the fact that Lea Francis had cancelled its or-

ders for the side-valve engine. This was true but Lea Francis was taking so few engines per month that the stoppage would have had little effect on the profits of the company. The real reason was the result of a lawsuit that Fox had taken out against the Morgan Motor Company. What had happened was that because of market uncertainty HFS had refused to place orders a year in advance for any of the engines used in his cars. He ordered his engines 100 at a time from JAP, Blackburne and Anzani. In this way he was also able to play off one company against the other and obtain the best possible terms. Vulpine, in order to remain competitive, had to reduce its prices. One of the

ways in which this was achieved was by reducing the quality of the steel used in the manufacture of the exhaust valve. This resulted in a large number of broken exhaust valves on Morgans during the guarantee period. Vulpine only replaced the valves. However, Morgan customers demanded and got the replaced valves fitted free, in accordance with the Morgan Motor Company's guarantee which, of course, meant that HFS was losing money every time. When he contacted Vulpine about this, Fox refused even to discuss the matter, saying *'HFS wanted a cheap engine and he got it.'* So HFS cancelled his contract with Vulpine and Fox took Morgan to court for breach of contract. He lost the

Morgan Three-wheelers replaced motor cycle and sidecar combinations for police patrols. Here, two 1933 Family models are delivered to the Newport Monmouthshire Police by Alex Thom, the Newport motor agent.

case and also had costs awarded against him. This litigation ruined the Vulpine company and Fox had no option but to go into liquidation. Once again HFS's shrewdness as a businessman had saved the company from financial disaster.

Demise of the three-wheeled cyclecar

In 1931 Morris introduced the first '£100 motorcar', closely followed by the two other mass-producers, although it was rumoured that the companies sold below cost to stay in contention. I recently asked Peter Morgan if this had ever happened in the Morgan Motor Company. He replied that it certainly never has whilst he has been in charge and, as far as he knew, had never happened in his father's time, although profit margins had at times been reduced to the minimum to enable the company to stay competitive.

Amongst the other ploys used by the company to maintain its position in the market was the clever use of advertising. The Morgan Motor Company produced a new advertisement on average every two weeks which listed the

major competition or record-breaking achievements of the marque for the previous fortnight. Many other companies employed the same basic idea, but their cars were not achieving the same success as the Morgan.

HFS also realized he must continue to exploit that part of the market which had served him so well in the past. He knew there was a huge potential market for his cars with the family man; his advertisement for the family model invariably included the words *'Speed, comfort, economy and reliability combined'*, with the latest competition results. As mass-production cars began to take more of the market, the emphasis of the company's advertising shifted to *'tax, economy, comfort, cost'* and comparisons with motorcycles and cars.

The extent of the postwar boom, the subsequent depression and the effect that it had worldwide can be gauged by these figures: in John Bolster's

A cartoon of HFS which appeared in the Junior Car Club Gazette in the early 1930s.

French Vintage Cars he states that in the early 1920s there were at least 350 light car and cyclecar manufacturers in the Paris suburbs alone. By 1929 there were just 23. In Britain in the early 1920s, there were at least 25 three-wheeler manufacturers. At the 1929 Motor Cycle Show 11 exhibited; in 1931 six; 1933 just three and by 1936 only one - the Morgan.

The major cost-saving derived by buying a three-wheeler was its low taxation, and this was used to maximum effect in Morgan advertising. Until 1920, taxation of motor vehicles was based roughly on a guinea per 4 horsepower, in addition to a petrol tax of 3d per gallon. On January 21, 1921, the Motor Taxation Act, which taxed private cars at £1 per horsepower, was enacted. This was calculated by using a complicated RAC formula, which in simple terms reckoned 1 horsepower to be equal to 2 square inches (12.9sq cm) of piston area. This was known as the 'Treasury Rating' and is basically why so many long-stroke engines were designed in the 1920s and 1930s. Three-wheelers of the Morgan type were taxed regardless of engine size, provided that they weighed less than 8 hundredweight (406kg) at a flat rate of £4 per annum. This compared to £9 for an air-cooled Rover, £7 for a Jowett and £8 for an Austin 7, all classed as four-wheeler light cars. An independent report showed that, based on an annual mileage of 6000 (9650km), the difference in fuel costs between the three-wheeler and the three light cars was approximately £1 10s to £2. Oil consumption was very similar. Tyre life on the three-wheeler was less than on the four-wheeler, with its more evenly distributed load, but the extra wear was more than balanced by the cost of the additional wheel and tyre. The three-wheeler was also less expensive to garage. The report found that the running costs of the four vehicles, which took into consideration petrol, oil, tyres, insurance and a club subscription (JCC), were as follows: Morgan £54 12s 3d; Rover £68 15s 5d; Jowett £65 18s 0d; Austin £65 14s 0d. A saving of almost £1 per month to the three-wheeler owner was a great deal in those days!

Only three companies came anywhere close to seriously challenging Morgan's supremacy in three-wheelers. In 1933 Raleigh had produced a true three-wheeler with a four-seater open body. Then, in 1935, it offered the Safety Seven Saloon. The first attempt at a 'passenger saloon' was really an extended van fitted with windows and a side opening door in the centre of the nearside. There was no door on either side for the driver. Although Sir Harold Bowden had serious ideas of attacking Morgan sales, the whole enterprise failed completely and he was pleased to sell out his car division to T L Williams, who then made commercial vehicles at Tamworth under the name of Reliant.

In 1929, BSA entered the market with a good-looking three-wheeler powered by an 1100cc overhead valve, vee-twin Hotchkiss engine. It was fitted with an attractive two-seater or family body, electric starter, car-type controls and all-round weather protection equipment; truly a car on three wheels. It performed well on the road and in competition, and nearly 2000 examples were produced. In 1933 the company introduced a water-cooled, four-cylinder 60mm x 95mm, 1100cc-engined car, still with front-wheel-drive, but within a year had added a fourth wheel and named the model the Scout. By the end of 1935 all three-wheeler construction had ceased.

The Morgan's most serious and successful competitor was without doubt the Coventry Victor. This company was very well known as an engine manufacturer which, in 1926, started making its own car. The car followed the 'proper' car layout, with a horizontally-opposed twin-cylinder water-cooled engine mounted in a conventional manner immediately behind the radiator, through which projected the starting-handle shaft. A plate clutch with fabric universal joints at each end conveyed the drive to a bevel-box, bolted at the rear to the channel-section crossmember. It was produced in various forms, including a family model and, eventually, a fully enclosed version, the Avon Bodied Sports Coupé. It continued in production until 1938, albeit only in very limited numbers for the last two years.

Both Raleigh and BSA produced a commercial van version of their three-wheelers and these sold well. HFS decided to join in the battle for this part of the market with his own van. It was not

Immediately after the war sheet steel was at a premium and many Morgans were bodied by other companies. This Woody Drop Head Coupé is one example; it's a 1949 4/4 with a Standard Special engine.

at all successful and only around 40 were produced over five years.

HFS was a very shrewd businessman, as has already been illustrated, and his interpretation of the market trend in the early 1930s was brilliant. At the 1933 Motor Cycle Show (a show was not held in 1932 so HFS staged his own at the Malvern works, where he exhibited eight models to invited guests) he introduced the F-type model which was a complete departure from his original ideas. By producing a three-wheeler model which was more in line with the design of a 'proper' motor car, with a water-cooled side-valve Ford engine mounted in a Z-section chassis behind an inverted vee-shaped radiator, he was within one easy step of another major development.

Demand for the Morgan three-wheeler was dropping fast. In 1929 total production consisted of 444 Family models; 297 Aeros; 140 De Luxe; 108 Super Sports; 11 vans; 1 box carrier and 1 Convertible Family, making a total of 1002. By 1934, this was down to 659 and in 1935 to just 286. The introduction of the F-type did little to stem the decline; it was obvious that the motoring public was turning away from three-wheelers.

Way back in 1915, HFS had experimented with a four-wheeled ver-

sion of his car, but had abandoned the idea. Now was the time to rethink the whole concept. The design and layout of the F-type lent itself to easy conversion into a four-wheeler. After building three experimental cars, the new four-wheeled Morgan was announced at Christmas 1935. In keeping with his maxim that his cars must prove themselves in competition, HFS entered the final prototype in the London-Exeter Trial and timed the announcement to coincide with this. Although production of the new model did not commence until March 1936, the company produced 130 in the period to the end of December. By then, annual three-wheeler production was down to just 137 units.

Predictions

In October 1926, *Light Car & Cyclecar* magazine asked prominent persons in the motor trade to predict what light cars would be like in 10 years' time. Most of the predictions made by HFS came true, but he did not employ many of them in his own cars. Of all the opinions published, his was the closest to what actually happened:

"Mr H F S Morgan, who has forgotten more about cyclecars than most other people in the world have ever learned,

expresses views with which many will agree.

"My convictions are that the next 10 years will not see any startling changes in the design of light cars. Price will still be, as it is now, the most important factor and will prevent the use of eight-cylinder engines and four-wheel-drive which, no doubt, will become popular with those who can afford the luxury.

"The popular car for 1936 will probably have a lower chassis than those used today and larger wheels. A four-seated body with really good all-weather equipment will be in demand and glass side screens will be used instead of celluloid. Steel press work will be very largely used instead of wood, this method bringing the total weight to about 12cwt. Shock absorbers will be discarded; a better springing will have been achieved by improved designs.

"The engine will be about 9hp RAC rating. Overhead valves will be used, operated by an overhead camshaft. The engine will turn over at 3000rpm and the petrol consumption with be 40mpg.

"Superchargers will certainly not be used on the cheap light car. The gearbox will remain much as it is at present, also the back axle, except that it is possible that worm drive will be-

come popular.

"Hydraulic four-wheeler brakes may possibly be used and a single electrical instrument will serve for starting, lighting and ignition. The cost of such a car will be about £150 complete."

The final death knell for light cars and cyclecars, both three and four-wheelers, was sounded in 1936. On April 28, Neville Chamberlain, the Chancellor of the Exchequer, announced that the government intended to abolish the Road Fund Tax on all motor vehicles in 1937. Although this did not actually happen, it was too late to save all but a handful of manufacturers. By 1939, Morgan's output of three-wheelers was down to 29, whereas the production of the 4-4 model was 234 and increasing steadily at the outset of the Second World War.

Once again successes in competition played a big part in the increase of orders, particularly in the 24-hour race at Le Mans and the RAC Rally. Clearly, the timely introduction of the 4-4 saved the company from going the same way as Morgan's three-wheeler competitors. The company was financially buoyant as it entered the war.

Early in 1939 HFS pondered the question whether it would not be better for the company to manufacture its own engines rather than buying them in. To this end he commissioned a small overhead-cam engine to be designed by a Mr Hatch who, at that time, was working in the engine design department of AJS. (The Morgan factory still have the original drawings of this engine.) With the benefit of hindsight, it was to be a good thing for the postwar survival of the company that various factors - such as the offer from the Standard Motor Company to produce a special 1267cc engine just for Morgan -

delayed any further development of this engine.

The war years

Almost immediately war was declared, Morgan's machine shops were made over to the manufacture of essential precision parts for the Oerlikon gun and various hydraulic undercarriage components, gauges and compressor parts for aircraft. There was to be no production of cars at all in this war, although the repair shop, offices and stores did operate for some time on a very limited basis. Part of the factory was rented out to HFS's old friend, John Black, of the Standard Motor Company, who built carburettors there. The remainder was rented to Sir Alan Cobham, and it was here he developed his brainchild, in-flight refuelling. For a large part of the war the various buildings housed several complete aircraft, including a Lancaster bomber. During this time the head of security for the factory complex was Charles (Reg) Lisseman. It was he who earned the doubtful distinction of being the man who refused entry to no less a person than Winston Churchill because he did not have the correct pass. The matter was soon sorted out and the great man made his official inspection. It was obvious, however, that all Lisseman's superiors were very upset over the incident and were going to deal severely with him when the visit was over. However, as he was leaving, Churchill made a point of congratulating Lisseman on his efficiency!

At the end of the war, the Morgan company was in good financial shape as a result of the rentals and the government's fixed profit payments for the production of parts for military equipment. However, the return to car pro-

duction was to be totally different from that achieved after the First World War, for a number of reasons. The removal of the tenants could not take place overnight and was delayed until the middle of 1946. The slow return of the workforce was another important factor. The armed forces were kept at a high level of readiness, due to the continuing war in the Far East and the occupation and policing of Europe. It was therefore to be almost 18 months before the workforce was complete again.

As they returned, the workers were employed in re-organizing the factory. Financially, the machine shop was able to support the wage bill and cost of reorganization by the continued production of aircraft parts. (The company remained licensed to produce aircraft parts until 1960.)

During the war the government installed almost 100 machines which, due to the fastidiousness of HFS, were still in excellent condition when the war ended. Eventually, HFS was able to purchase most of them at a very reasonable price, so helping to reduce the overall cost of re-equipping the factory for car production.

Production re-starts

Throughout this period a few cars were built from spare parts stored during the war and a few chassis were also produced from the limited amount of parts available. These were fitted with whatever body the purchasing garage could invent. Some of these were excellent, whereas others left a lot to be desired ... Alternatively, they were sent away for bodying by another company. Amongst those companies used for this purpose were Motorists of North West London and Peamore Garage, Exeter, the main reason for which was the

Peter Morgan was an accomplished competition driver. Here he is in September 1948 competing in a TT replica.

limited availability of sheet steel. Allocation was based mainly on the respective company's ability to export its products.

Morgan's orders far exceeded anything they could hope to produce. In order to obtain more steel, and then to get back into full production as soon as possible, the company established overseas agencies in America and France. Morgan had exported cars on a fairly regular basis before the war, either directly or through exporting agents. Now the government slogan for British Industry was 'Export or Die'. By 1950 the company had more than doubled its exports and by the mid-1950s they amounted to over 66 per cent.

Overseas markets now had little interest in three-wheelers and sales in the home market were very low. Reluctantly, HFS decided to end production of the three-wheeler. On March 31, 1952 the last F4 model Morgan - no. F1296, Ford engine no. C61153, gearbox no. XC85 - and on July 29, 1952 the last F Super - no. F1301, Ford engine no. C611562 and gearbox no. XC107 - left the factory to go to Morgan agent Bennett's of Southampton.

Standard's Sir John Black, who had the reputation of being a very hard man in business, remained friends with HFS. It was therefore mainly on a personal basis that the Standard Motor Company supplied engines to Morgans. Just before the war, the Triumph Motor

Company had gone bankrupt, and in 1946 Sir John Black acquired the remains of the company, with Triumph becoming a subsidiary of Standard. In 1951 Sir John Black made an exceptionally good offer to buy out the Morgan concern: he was searching for a quick means of entry into the lucrative sports car market in America. The Morgan company was financially sound enough to resist this takeover bid and, eventually, Sir John developed Triumph to produce the very successful TR series, the engine of which Morgan adopted for the Plus 4 model with such outstanding success. Again, the supply of the TR engine was a personal deal between Sir John and HFS. Then, early in 1954, Sir John resigned as managing director of Standard. Officially this was due to the effects of a serious motor accident, but it is believed that fellow directors on the Standard-Triumph board demanded his resignation because of his dictatorial attitude. This led to a reduction in the supply of engines to Morgans for a while, until a change of policy at Standard-Triumph reinstated the supply, this time with the more powerful TR3 engine.

Family links maintained
HFS's son Peter Morgan was educated initially at Link School, Malvern, and then at the famous Oundle Public School in Northamptonshire. On leaving Oundle in 1936 he had a choice of

continuing his education at engineering college or university. Selecting the former, he went to Chelsea College of Automobile Engineering, where he stayed until the outbreak of war. Initially, he went to Admiralty House and attempted to enlist into the Royal Navy as an artificer but was rejected. He was then interviewed for the Army and was selected for the Royal Army Service Corps, where he became a workshop officer for a motor coach company. Posted overseas, he went from the Royal West African Frontier Force Workshop to Nairobi, where he remained until the end of the war. He was released from the Army in late 1946, having reached the rank of captain, and joined the family company as development engineer, draughtsman

Peter Morgan

Morgan's chief tester, Charlie Curtis, long retired, with the author's Le Mans Replica.

- and a member of the board of directors.

Peter Morgan took over as managing director when George Goodall died in 1958 and, when in the following year his father died, aged 78, he became chairman.

Peter learnt to drive before the war and on his father's insistence graduated to racing, through trials and rallies. The competition results reflect his competence.

After the death of his father, Peter Morgan's additional responsibilities meant he had little spare time available to continue competition driving but he did return to trials for a short while, driving the prototype Plus 4 Plus.

Over the years Peter Morgan has enjoyed various hobbies and interests; he played golf, had a miniature railway layout in his garden, enjoyed ski-ing and, until his faithful Red Setter, Kerry, died in 1986, did a lot of walking. He still enjoys gardening, which he finds relaxing, but his lifelong hobby is stamp collecting, specializing in the Seychelles in particular, and postal history.

HFS's farewell

The content of HFS's will reflected his love for his family and his sense of fairness, both of which had been very obvious during his life. Handwritten on two sheets of paper it read: 'I have made this will as simple as possible and hope it will give my dear family the least possible trouble ... 'I bequeath to my son, Peter, rather more than his sisters, as he has the trouble and worry of running my old business (now under the control of my family), which may have to be sold owing to the increasing difficulty of running a private business. I have had a long and happy life, and words cannot express my thanks to my children, in-laws, and grandchildren for their love and kindness to me. May you all live long in happiness together. God bless you all.'

In all, he left £250,287 (duty £146,349). This meant that the business was left in trust to his four daughters and his son, with Peter Morgan and Major Kendall appointed trustees and Peter Morgan in charge of the company. It was obvious that if the Morgan Company was to survive, there had to be an all-out effort to increase production and sales and reduce costs. To this end, Peter Morgan called a meeting of the entire staff and explained the position; with typical loyalty they responded to meet the challenge.

Saved by the chequered flag

In 1961 Morgan's main market, the United States of America, endured depression and the factory was forced to reduce production whilst exploring other export markets. The company did amazingly well to survive at all during this period. Its saviours were really two new models plus the outstanding success of Chris Lawrence in the Le Mans 24-Hour race. This led to the production of the Plus 4 Super Sports, tuned by Lawrence, and the introduction of an entirely new concept in Morgan design, the Plus 4 Plus. Whereas the former was an unqualified success , the Plus 4 Plus did not sell well, although its revolutionary design helped to draw the attention of the motoring press and public alike.

As the company's finances began to recover, the family felt that it was time to arrange a redistribution of capital shares. In order to achieve this, it was necessary for the company to lose its limited liability status for a few years. During this period the official designation of the company was 'Peter Morgan trading as The Morgan Motor Company'. In 1970 the business was re-formed as a limited company. It was whilst in this state of flux that the company took the decision to introduce the Plus 8.

Although the development and introduction of this model was ridiculously inexpensive in terms of the motor industry in general, for Morgan it was very expensive, and financed completely from its own reserves. The new model was well received by press and public alike, and proved an excellent investment.

Expansion

Another indication of the company's improved financial stability came in 1972 when it made its largest investment since the Second World War. Peter Morgan had become increasingly aware of overcrowding within the factory due, in the main, to the increased complexity of the cars and the greater time needed to complete each one. The adjoining factory site and building came on to the market, but was really far too large for the company's requirements. However, when, after a considerable time the site remained unsold, Peter Morgan realized he could purchase it at a very reasonable price. This he did and moved the trim, wiring, final finish and test departments into the largest building, situated furthest from the

Gas powered: Morgan Plus 8s imported to the USA are converted to run on propane gas by Isis Imports of San Francisco.

main entrance. The remainder of the site he rented out to provide the company with a steady income. Yet again the company was able to finance the whole deal without need of outside assistance.

Postwar depression

In the mid-1960s there was renewed interest in the marque. All through the 1970s the demand and orders increased, as did the wait for delivery. This trend has continued and, except for a period in the early 1980s when Britain and most of Europe went through an economic depression, delivery dates of about five years have been the norm. Had it not been for the American market, there can be little doubt that the company would have collapsed in the late 1950s, a time when nearly 85 per cent of production was exported to the USA. In 1961 there was a great recession in the Californian aircraft industry and not only did it hit the prosperity of those who were directly involved, it also spread throughout the whole country.

So dramatically did sports car sales drop in the USA that MG and Triumph agents were reduced to holding weekly auction sales in an attempt to reduce their stocks. Morgan's New York agent, Fergus Motors, cancelled an entire shipment. It just so happened that when the cancellation was received at the factory, Peter Morgan and his wife were taking their first ever holiday in America. The factory cabled him at his hotel and told him the bad news. Peter ordered the shipment be dispatched and immediately went to New York to see if his personal intervention could improve matters. His strategy worked; he persuaded the agent to accept delivery and whilst he was in the US met a large

number of American enthusiasts.

Back in England, production had to be cut by one car a week. This does not sound very much but it did represent about 14 per cent of total output. Slowly, the market improved but it was almost two years before production and sales returned to their previous levels.

Several valuable lessons were learnt from this episode. The company needed to broaden its markets to avoid ever again being too dependent on sales to one country. Also, it was vital for

Peter Morgan to be available to visit wherever possible enthusiasts of the marque around the world.

Emission and safety controls (USA)

Throughout the initial development of the Plus 8 everything had been done to incorporate all the foreseeable requirements of the new motor vehicle regulations introduced in the United States in the late 1960s. However, Morgan was forced to drop out of the US market by the end of 1971. The main

reason for this was the increasingly tough exhaust emission control standards which caused Rover to pull out of America at the same time, and automatically forced Morgan out as well. Other requirements such as 5mph 'no damage' bumpers and seatbelt warning buzzers also caused problems. These devices and necessary technology would eventually become available to Morgan as introduced by the major manufacturers; however, there was always a delay.

When the supplies of Morgans to the United States stopped, one American enthusiast, Bill Fink, who, from 1969, had traded in Morgan parts, repairs and the sale of second-hand Morgans, was determined to find a way to import Morgan cars. From the inquiries he made of the Department of Transport and all the other relevant governmental departments, he discovered that any car powered by propane gas was exempt from the emission control regulations. Having successfully overcome the most serious of all the legal requirements, he set about investigating ways to overcome the remainder. He worked out that if some of the modifications were carried out at the factory during construction, then he would be able to complete the work in the United States, making each car acceptable for resale. In 1973 he was in a position to approach Peter Morgan, who eventually agreed with his basic

ideas, and promised to supply him with up to 24 cars a year, although bureaucratic delays meant it was not until 1976 that Fink sold his first car.

For these special US cars, some of the work was carried out at the factory - telescopic gas-filled shock absorbers, mounted behind reinforced front and rear bumpers, to comply with the 5mph head and tail end impact legislation; four-seater size windscreen; special steel reinforcing hoop bolted to the chassis behind the dashboard.

On the car's arrival in the United States, steel beams were fitted into the doors to meet the side impact regulations; in addition, a rear roll-over bar, inertia reel seat belts, padded sun visors and seatbelt warning alarm were all fitted. The interior was coated with a flameproof fluid.

The conversion of the engine required a special 18-gallon fuel tank with the filler valve neatly hidden under the spare wheel mounting, sealed fuel lines and a vaporizer and a lock-off to stop the supply when the engine was switched off. The inlet manifold and carburettors were changed. Finally, a 45-page dossier, with full written and photographic evidence of all the modifications carried out, had to be prepared for each car.

In 1986 another American enthusiast, Win Sharples from Virginia, successfully obtained permission to import Morgans into the United States,

and was granted an agency by the Morgan Motor Company. All the modifications previously listed above also had to be carried out by his company.

In Canada the exhaust emission control laws are not so strict as in the United States, as a result of which the fuel injected Ford XR3 and Rover engines comply with regulations. All other modifications as required for the American market do apply and all new Morgans imported to Canada must be modified by Chris Charles, the authorized distributor. New Morgans can now be purchased in either the United States or Canada. However, the extensive modifications necessary always mean that the numbers sold will not approach those of the 1950s or 1960s.

Exports worldwide
Learning from the near-disaster of the 1960s, Peter Morgan has slowly broadened the company's overseas sales. The main European outlet is West Germany which has two distributors and now accounts for 30-35 per cent of the company's export sales. All the western European countries have a Morgan distributor but a problem is that in recent years Europe has also seen the introduction of tougher rules and regulations governing motor vehicles. The result of this is that it is now impossible to buy a new Morgan in Switzerland, Denmark and Sweden.

Dealing with the legislation around the world is a complicated matter. For example, in Japan, the Morgan distributor has to send all his imported cars to a specialist company for modifications so that they meet the emission control regulations. But before a 4/4 is exported to Japan the works has to fit the car with wider wings than normal to

HFS competes at Angle Bank in July 1923 in a wide-track, flat-sided Aero model, fitted with an 8 valve Anzani engine.

comply with the local wire wheel regulations. In all, at the time of writing there are a total of 15 European distributors; two in the USA; one in Canada and five in the rest of the world. Exports account for approximately 35 per cent of total production. It therefore follows that the home market must be buoyant to sustain production levels.

The welcome mat
The factory's 'open door' policy, whereby prospective owners, or even just the inquisitive, are shown around the works, and the friendly nature of all the employees, are important aspects in promoting sales. So is the buyer's personal choice of car specification when his or her turn on the four to five year waiting list eventually arrives.

Campaign agents
Throughout the three-wheeler era, many Morgan distributors proved the car in competition. Such men as Frank Boddington (Worcester), Freddie James (Sheffield), Jack Sylvester (Nottingham), FG Cox (Bristol), Horrocks (Bolton), Jim Hall (Stevenage), Roger Darmont (Paris), 'Joe' Huxham (Bournemouth), Billie Elce, Harold Holmes, Stanley McCarthy and Arthur Maskell (London) competed in all manner of competitions from trials to circuit racing.
With the introduction of the four-wheeler, much of the distributor competition participation faded away and motorsport was left mainly to the works. The most spectacular exception to this rule was Chris Lawrence who, although not an official distributor, was a works concessionaire. Then, around the late 60s, the distributors began to get involved again; John McDonald, Rob Wells, Bruce and John Stapleton, Mike Duncan, John Brittan, service

agent Rick Bourne and other Morgan specialists have all been highly successful, particularly in racing. Their exploits are well covered in this and other books and it's as well to remember that by their skills and expertise they have promoted the marque wherever they have appeared.

Additional promotion for the marque has come from a large number of specialist companies who are able to offer the Morgan owner not only a spares service, but tuning, preparation and complete rebuilds to the highest possible standards.

Morgan Owners' Clubs around the world also help to create the reassurance and spirit of camaraderie so important to most Morgan owners.

Although he loved competing in sporting trials, HFS Morgan was basically of a nervous disposition. He dis-

Charles Morgan with Plus 8 at St Moritz for the 100th Anniversary of the Cresta Run in 1985. The Sotheby Cup races were part of the celebrations.

The next generation. Xan Morgan in a racing Three-wheeler with father Charles at Silverstone.

liked racing and speed events, but realized he must compete in them to prove his product. His most outstanding achievement in those early days must have been on November 23, 1912 when he came within yards of achieving the magic average of a mile a minute for an hour at the Brooklands race track, and won the Cyclecar Trophy.

HFS's nervousness was not inherited by either his son, Peter, or his grandson, Charles. Peter Morgan always maintains that the war spoilt his racing career; in the few races in which he did compete he showed great promise. Charles had no such interruptions, other than the different locations in the world where his work took him. He was very successful on the race track, as can be seen in the competition chapter, winning the 1978 British Production Sports Car Championship.

The next generation

Charles Peter Harry Morgan was born on July 29, 1951, schooled first at The Elms Preparatory School, Malvern, and then Oundle like his father, and went on to Sussex University, where he read the history of art, gaining a Bachelor of Arts Honours degree. On leaving university he worked for a year as a bookseller with Idea Books Limited, and then joined Independent Television News as a cameraman. This work took him to many remote and far-off places such as Vietnam, Kampuchea and Afghanistan, where he made an award-winning documentary programme about the guerrillas.

Although his father never placed any pressure on Charles to join the company, he was obviously very pleased when Charles did decide to join him full-time. In 1979 Charles married Vivien Lipschitz who, on January 8,

1985, gave birth to a son, Xan. Later Charles and Vivien went their separate ways.

Charles married his present wife, Jane, in 1990.

For relaxation, Charles loves motor racing, gardening, studying architecture and the Cresta Run. The last interest came about as a result of photography and directing a film, made for the St Moritz Tobogganing Club as part of the celebrations of 100 years of the Cresta Run in 1985. Whilst making the film he fell in love with the whole concept and was allowed by the Cresta Club to try it out a few times. They were so impressed by his skillful performances and keenness that they made him a member there and then, something which normally takes years to achieve.

Visiting the factory

Many authors, myself included, have tried to put into words the feelings and

impressions they experience when they step into the visitors' waiting room at the factory for the very first time. One, in 1966, even went so far as to write 'it has a dinginess that could almost be considered studied. The manure-coloured paintwork is lustreless with age.' Things have improved since those days; the paintwork has been renewed, and a glass display counter installed, but the walls are still covered with display boards listing, in hand painted lettering, the competition achievements of the three-wheelers, plus various framed photographs. Entering, one gets the impression of stepping through a time warp, back to the 1920s.

The factory is an enigma. From initial impressions, you might expect the workforce and management to be of comparable age to the premises. Nothing could be further from the truth, with the average age in 1985 of the whole workforce being just 34. This clearly indicates that Peter Morgan and his board of directors are not afraid of

The Morgan factory at Malvern Link - mecca for all true sports car enthusiasts.

change or of young ideas.

There have been many subtle changes in recent years which have ensured an on-going supply of skilled staff on the shop floor. The biggest of these has been the removal of the foremen from the piecework bonuses scheme. They are no longer required to work full-time at their various trades and now spend a great deal of their time in on-the-job training and leadership. In this way their skills are handed down to an up-and-coming team of young men. Many of the skilled trades necessary to build a Morgan, such as tinsmithing and coachbuilding, are fast dying in outside industry. It is not that there is a lack of suitable young men to train, it is that these skills are no longer generally required, due to the continuing change to automation.

It is not just on the shop floor that the influx of young men is occurring. Obviously, the youngest member of the board of directors is Charles Morgan, but at the next level of senior management, Peter Morgan's assistant, Mark Aston, whose job description would be almost impossible to write due to his numerous and diverse responsibilities, has only just turned 30, while Derek Day's deputy in the sales department, Mark Read, was only 29 when this was written.

Litigation

In July 1980 an incident occurred in the USA which could have brought about the complete collapse of the Morgan company. A 1967 Morgan, which had been illegally imported into America from Canada, was stationary in traffic when it was rammed from behind by a small truck. The small truck was, in turn, rammed by a 55-ton gravel truck. As a result of the impact a fire ensued and the Morgan driver's hands were quite badly burnt. In 1983, solicitors acting on behalf of the injured driver included in their litigation lawsuit an allegation that the Morgan was partly responsible for the injury, due to the design and location of its petrol tank. It took the company's legal representatives almost 10 hours to present the technical evidence to the court, which in the end accepted that the claim was almost completely unjustified. No legal defence is cheap and American legal costs are notoriously high. The action cost the company almost £150,000, an amount, although large, was minute in comparison to what it could have been if the court had held that the company was wholly or partly responsible.

75 years young

1984 was to mark the 75th anniversary of the Morgan and also Peter Morgan's 65th birthday. The celebrations of the anniversary were to bring together more Morgans than had ever been seen in one place, with well over 1000 cars converging on Eastnor Castle on the final day of the 10-day of celebrations. For those of us who were involved in the organization in any way, there was a feeling of immense honour and satisfaction; to have taken part was to have gained a place in the unique history of the oldest one-family motor car manufacturer in the world. Media coverage was enormous, with over 120 magazines and newspapers worldwide publishing some form of tribute; then there was also coverage on local, national and international radio and television. Morganeers from all over the world made lasting friendships.

A few years ago a motoring magazine published an article on the Morgan which posed the question 'Morgan's Raison d'Etre?' If its author was at the 75th, his question was answered. The article ended, 'Dr Johnson once said "The ultimate end to all employments is to produce amusement". Morgans are sheer fun to drive, and they produce more amusement than a train load of Playboy bunnies.'

II

FOUR-WHEELERS IN COMPETITION

1968: Amongst the big boys

When the Daytona Continental 24-hour race came to an end the afternoon of February 4, the applause for the winning Porsche 907 was little more than that which greeted the Morgan Plus 4 crossing the finishing line at the other end of the field. George Waltman had had the effrontery to enter the Morgan in the GT class at Daytona, where its main rivals were 7.3-litre Chevrolet Corvette Stingrays. He caused quite a stir as, wearing regulation racing kit but with a red scarf flying in the wind, he plodded steadily on as, one-by-one, faster cars dropped out, and was eventually classified last of the 30 survivors out of 63 entries. The winning Porsche covered 673 laps at an average speed of 106.97mph, whereas the Morgan completed just 339 laps at 53.69mph. Nevertheless, bearing in mind that the little car was being lapped every other lap, it was a remarkable piece of endurance driving.

In a very different environment David Way set a new class record of 37.9 seconds with his 4/4 to win his class in the BARC South Wales Centre's hillclimb at Pontypool Park on September 29.

To round off another interesting year for Morgan drivers the MCC announced that its coveted Triple Baddeley award - only presented to a driver who has cleared every section in the classic Lands End, Exeter and Edinburgh Trials - had been won by Roger Bricknall and his Plus 4.

1969

The first event of significance in which a Plus 8 competed was the 10-lap Morgan handicap race at the Bentley DC's annual Silverstone meeting. As usual, the race was a great success,

victory going this time to Jim Tucker and his fully race-tuned Plus 4, which overtook Adam Bridgeland's new Plus 8 on the last lap. Harvey Postlethwaite attempted to take Becketts sideways in his twin-cam 4/4 and recovered to finish the race fourth on the road, which meant that he was third in the official results because Brian Jenkins, who had crossed the line ahead of him, had incurred a penalty for jumping the start in his Plus 4 Super Sports.

There must have been many occasions when a car has not won a race because of brake failure but, for a change, on October 18 John Stapleton had the distinction of winning his class in the production sports car race at the Guards Motor Show 200 meeting at Brands Hatch with the brakes of his Plus 4 jammed on!

Newcomer David Way proved himself a vigorous competitor in his 4/4: in his first full season of hillclimbing he finished third overall in the Castrol/BARC Hillclimb Championship.

1970

David Way was back in action again with his successful hillclimbing 4/4, and a time of 42.15 seconds at Gurston Down gave him a class victory in the fourth round of the Castrol/BARC Hillclimb Championship.

One of the highlights of the Mini Se7en Club's race meeting at Brands Hatch on June 14 was the battle in the 10-lap modified sports car race between a TVR Vixen and Irvine Laidlaw's 4/4. Although the TVR won the race, throughout Laidlaw continually slipstreamed the leader, trying time after time to find a way past, but the Morgan simply hadn't sufficient power to hold its rival down the straights.

During the Bugatti OC's invitation

One of the most notable lady racing drivers in the Morgan world during the 1970s & '80s was Mary Lindsay (nee Smith). Here, she is seen competing in her very first race at the Bentley Drivers Club Silverstone meeting in August 1970, being chased by Adam Bridgland (Plus 8) through Woodcote.

hillclimb at Prescott on July 5, Andy Duncan's run in 56.58 seconds with his twin-cam-engined 4/4 earned him a lot of applause, while the following weekend at the Midland AC's Shelsley Walsh meeting he managed to break the 40 seconds barrier with the same car. However, the first sub-40 second time by a Morgan - 39.41 seconds - had been recorded earlier by Ray Meredith in his, by now, ageing Plus 4. (During the same meeting one driver stopped the clock at 44.44 seconds in - yes, you've guessed it - a Morgan 4/4!) On the same day at a hillclimb organized by the BARC at Pontypool, Dennis Parsons won his class with a time of 38.47 seconds, which put him 0.19 seconds ahead of a Porsche.

1971

In May, the South West Centre of the BARC ran a qualifying round of the Castrol/BARC Hillclimb Championship at Gurston Down, where Bevel Harrison clinched the class victory with his second-run time of 43.70 seconds with his 4/4. To confirm his liking for this hill he returned to Gurston Down on June 27 to score another class win, although at the slightly slower time of 44.29 seconds. Bevel made quite a name for himself in hillclimbing this year; his successes included class wins at Pontypool on June 20, Shelsley Walsh early in July and once again at Gurston

The Canadian Sports Car Championship 1971 was won by 'G.B.' Sterne, the Canadian west coast Morgan agent in those days. He is seen here leading from Dr. Grant Hill and Al Allinson through one of the bends at the Westwood Racing Circuit in British Columbia.

Down in October.

London Morgan main agent, John Stapleton, took part in a marvellous 10-lap race for modified sports cars at Mallory Park on August 29, his Plus 8 being matched against a 4.7-litre Sunbeam Tiger and a 4.2-litre Jaguar E-type at the front of the field. During a race-long battle with the Jaguar, some spectacular driving by John had the Morgan out-cornering the E-type round the outside at the Esses and he held on to finish in second place behind the winning Tiger, setting the fastest lap at a speed of 87.41mph.

1972: Road & track

At the BRDC's race meeting at Silverstone on Easter Monday, Robin

Gray entertained the crowd with a fine display of sideways driving through the corners with his Plus 8 and was rewarded with a class win in the 15-lap modified sports car race.

Although it was rare by this time to see a fully-equipped road car fitted with road tyres competing in a hillclimb, this did not stop Alex Robinson from winning his class in the BARC/Castrol Hillclimb Championship meeting at Prescott, in early April, with a respectable time of 58.78 seconds.

Adam Bridgland scored another class win for his collection at the Romford Enthusiasts' CC race meeting at Snetterton on May 14, with his Plus 8, but Alex Robinson's car did not perform too well in the same race and

Frank Gillam (Plus 4) pushes it to the limit in the 750 Club's Six-hour Relay race in September 1973. He was a member of the second Morgan team which, although placed third for much of the race, dropped to finish in eleventh place after the rain. The other Morgan team won the event.

finished well down the field.

Another hillclimb success came the way of a road-equipped Morgan when Bill Holt's Plus 8 recorded a time of 39.17 seconds at the Midland AC's meeting at Shelsley Walsh, scoring a class win on July 9, one week after Ruth Atkinson and J A Gregson had taken their Morgans to first and second places in their class in the Rodney Whiteley Trial organized by the Airedale and Pennine MC.

The combined classes race at the Romford Enthusiasts' CC meeting at Snetterton on September 17 brought a good Morgan result, despite very heavy rain. It looked as though Brian Haslam would have it all his own way in his Plus

8, but Adam Bridgeland, who seemed to be revelling in the wet conditions, fought his way through into second place by the fourth lap. When Brian had a quick spin at the hairpin he rushed by into first place. A supercharged Alfa Romeo had gone through into second place while Brian was spinning but he fought back well and repassed the Italian car, making it Morgans first and second.

1973: Records galore

This was the year Chris Lawrence made a welcome return to racing, when he competed in the first round of a new championship for thoroughbred cars, sponsored by Charles Spreckley

Industries, which took place at Silverstone in March. He celebrated his comeback with a class victory and second place overall behind a Jaguar XK 120.

In the 750 MC's annual six-hour relay race at Silverstone, the Morgan team, 'Libra Morgan Grinders', consisting of the Plus 4s of Aubrey Brocklebank and Nigel Still, received 55 credit laps. Skillfully managed by Mike Rudd, the team won the event and collected the *Cars and Car Conversions* Trophy and associated awards. The second Morgan team finished in 11th position, having slipped from third place in the later stages of the race.

Robin Gray borrowed Chris Lawrence's Plus 4 for the Charles Spreckley thoroughbred cars race at the BRDC Silverstone meeting on October 6 and had the crowd on its feet with some magnificent driving. An Austin-Healey 3000 had gone into the lead at the start,

Team 'Anglemog' pose in the sunshine before the start of the 1974 Six-hour Relay race. Left-right are Allan Samuels (Plus 4 four-seater); Peter Joiner (Plus 8); Adam Bridgland (Plus 8); Bob Chaplin (4/4) and Mary Smith (4-4 Series I). The race was abandoned after two-and-a-half hours due to torrential rain.

Cyril Charlesworth with his wife Joyce as 'Bouncer' tackles the 'Blue Hills Mine' in the 1975 MCC Lands End Trial.

but Robin found a way past it around the outside at Woodcote and remained in front until the Healey went by again down Hangar Straight on the fifth lap. Robin kept up the pressure and the Healey spun off at Club on the next lap, allowing Gray to regain the lead and hang on to win by just a second from a Triumph TR3, with a Jaguar XK 120 a further 0.4 seconds away in third place. Robin's winning speed was 90.33mph and his fastest lap 91.63mph - a magnificent effort.

This was a great year for Chris Lawrence's Plus 4, which collected four 2-litre class records for thoroughbred sports cars, the first being at Brands Hatch on June 3 when Chris lapped in 1 min 3.8 sec for a record speed of 69.97mph. Then came Brian Cuttings' lap in 1 min 12.2 sec, 80.18mph with the car on the Silverstone Club circuit on July 29; next was Chris' lap of Thruxton on September 16 in 1 min 42.0 sec, 83.15mph and, finally, on October 6 Robin Gray used the car to lap the Silverstone Grand Prix circuit in 1 min 55.0 sec, at a speed of 91.63mph.

1974

Robin Gray continued his winning form with really great racing. In pouring rain at the BARC meeting at Mallory Park he had a race-long dice with an XK 120 and a TR3. On the penultimate lap of the 10-lap race he managed to snatch the lead by driving through on the inside of the Esses. In spite of the conditions he also set a new lap record.

One of the high spots of the BRSCC North West Centre's meeting at Oulton Park on July 14 was the great battle between John Britten in his Plus 8 and Colin Blower in his Lotus Europa in the production sports car race - the class victory going to John by barely a bon-

net-length.

Morgan successes during 1974 included five new lap records, beginning on April 28 when Robin Gray lapped Mallory Park in his Plus 4 in 1 min 3.4 sec, 76.66mph; on May 12 he used his Plus 8 to take the Snetterton class record at 1 min 15.0 sec, 91.37mph; on May 27 John Northcroft drove round Castle Combe in his Plus 8 in 1 min 24.6 sec, 78.30mph; Robin Gray took another record when he was timed at Cadwell Park on June 2 at 1 min 42.0 sec, 79.41mph and, finally, John Britten went round the Brands

Hatch club circuit on September 8 in 1 min 0.2 sec, 73.18mph.

1975: Washed out

This was again to be Robin Gray's year in his Lawrence-tuned Plus 8. Another Morgan man, Chris Alford with his Britten Minster-tuned 4/4, also provided Morgan enthusiasts with plenty to cheer about.

Rain stopped play in the 750 MC's six-hour relay race after two-and-a-half-hours of racing. By then, the heavy rain and poor visibility had caused the track to become littered with shunted

Mary Lindsay (nee Smith) proves just how keen she was on racing when she returned early from her honeymoon to take part in the 1975 Bentley Drivers Club Meeting at Silverstone. This time she drove her brother's rare 1953 Interim Radiator Plus 4 (in fact, the first one, chassis no. T3000) and is seen here firmly 'shutting the door' on Leigh Sebba in his 4/4.

cars and it was proving altogether too hazardous for marshals and drivers alike. After a meeting of team managers, the race was halted and it was decided to base the results on the positions at the time of abandonment, which gave a class win to the Middlesex Polytechnic Libre Morgan team of Rob Wells and Bryan Harvey in 4/4s and Bill Hopkins and Charles Morgan in Plus 8s.

The season ended with a fine Morgan double, Robin Gray being announced the winner of the over-3-litre class in the Miller Organs Modified Sports Car Championship, and Chris Alford being declared the BRSCC Production Sports Car Champion, having only twice failed to win his class in this contest.

1976

For several months Charles Morgan had been gaining useful racing experience with his Plus 8 and on July 25 at the BRSCC meeting at Cadwell Park he demonstrated his progress by finishing the production sports car race in second place behind Chris Meek's Lotus Europa and ahead of the best-placed TVR.

At the 40th anniversary Bentley DC meeting at Silverstone on August 28, the first all-comers handicap race became a Morgan benefit, the marque taking the first four places, led by Bob Nicholls in his turbocharged Plus 8, who was chased across the line so closely by Charles Morgan in his works Plus 8 they were credited with identical times. Malcolm Hayward in another Plus 8 was only 0.8 seconds further behind and fourth was the Plus 4 SLR of Aubrey Brocklebank. Charles Morgan also set the fastest lap at 1 min 17.0 sec, 75 .18mph.

Robin Gray led the Morgan SCC's 10-lap scratch race from start to finish. He was followed across the line by Bruce Stapleton, Peter Garland and Charles Morgan, all of them in Plus 8s. Stapleton then took part in another all-comers handicap race, which he led all the way to win by just 1 second from a 3.5-litre Alvis Silver Eagle Special.

Although Morgan drivers failed to win a championship this season, they finished the year with honour. Chris Hampshire was runner-up to Chris Alford (TVR) in the £2000-3000 class of the Euro-Burgess Southern League Production Sports Car Championship, and Tony Brewer and his 4/4 was runner-up to Alford in the Direct Tapes Championship. Despite an early season crash at Oulton Park, Robin Gray still finished third in the BARC Modified Sports Car Championship.

1977: Sportsmanship & protests

This was the year of the Silverstone Production Sports Car Championship, staged at several circuits throughout the season, which developed into a bitter feud between a Lotus Europa driven by Chris Meek and various Morgans, but mainly Charles Morgan in a Plus 8, Bill Wykeham in his Morris Stapleton Plus 8 and Rob Wells. Chris Meek's Europa came out on top in many of the races, although his tactics both on and off the track left a lot to be desired ...

In a race at Snetterton, Rob Wells and Bill Wykeham finished second and fourth, split by Colin Blower's TVR. Victory went to Chris Meek's Europa after a controversial incident on the third lap when the Lotus literally pushed Bill Wykeham's car off the track and into the fields, and then cut across the track to bump Rob Wells' car off as well.

In June 1976 the Morgan Motor Company, in conjunction with John MacDonald, developed a special Plus 8 (chassis no. R8112) with a view to competing in the Le Mans 24-hour race. The car was fitted with a specially imported Tranco Buick engine and special gearbox. It was finished in black with red leather upholstery, wire wheels, 8 inch V15 Avon 205/70 VR15 tyres, centre lock hubs, alloy rear brake drums, alloy body and wings and aluminium floor boards, roll cage, seat belts and dual circuit servo brakes. However, the project had to be shelved due to a change in the fuel efficiency competition regulations. The car is now owned by Swedish Morgan enthusiast, Leif Barryd, of Stockholm.

That no protests were lodged is an indication of the sporting attitude that previously prevailed in this class of racing.

The next day Rob had his revenge when he won a championship race over 10 laps at Silverstone and Meek's Lotus ran out of track at Copse, leaving a TVR to take second place. The two met again at Donington on September 11, when Wells was barged off the track at Redgate and later ran into the sand at Old Hairpin in his efforts to make up the lost ground. Bob Stuart then took up the Morgan challenge but lost his third place when the radiator of his Plus 8 boiled. Meek went on to win and, again, Wells decided not to protest, although an MGB driver decided to challenge Meek's driving but had his protest turned down.

A week later the battle was re-

Rob Wells in the slightly bent works Plus 8, MMC 11, passes Stewart Halstead's works TVR at Mallory Park in 1977.

joined at Snetterton; at Riches on lap 6 Rob Wells' car was elbowed off the track yet again. The Lotus had been chasing the Plus 8s of Wells and Wykeham and Blower's TVR and, having passed the TVR as Blower was searching for a way through back markers, it hit Wells' car, causing it to spin: Rob had to walk back to the pits. Next time round Blower pulled into his pit, conferred with Rob and withdrew from the race while, by some superb driving, Bill Wykeham managed to outwit Meek and hold on to the lead at the chequered flag, though the two were credited with the same time. Several protests flew around afterwards but apparently none was upheld.

By now protests were thoroughly marring these events and things got so bad at Donington on October 2 that 16 drivers, allegedly tired of Meek's constant questioning of the legality of their cars and of his own driving tactics, refused to race if he was allowed to start. It was all smoothed out at a meeting before a BRSCC official; the protests were withdrawn and the race took place, with Meek emerging the winner from Wykeham. However, it was clear that the RAC would have to step in and restore some order to the production sports car scene.

The final round of the series took place at Donington on October 20, but Wykeham and Wells were not present and Meek's race ended in mechanical failure.

1978: Charles Morgan wins his spurs
The second round at Donington on April 9 was to be a memorable race for Charles Morgan. Drama began for him on the front row of the grid when he noticed a leaking fuel line a few minutes from the start which he managed to

repair in time and shot off into the lead, only to be outbraked by Blower's TVR and Wykeham's Plus 8 on the approach to the Park chicane. By lap 4 the two leaders were hard at it, first one and then the other taking turns to set the pace until, on lap 9 with one to go, the TVR passed the Morgan on Starkey's straight. Bill tried to counter-attack by under-braking into Park, the two cars touched and they both spun off. Charles

Morgan, who had been keeping in touch, was able to slip through to claim his first-ever race win in his Plus 8. Colin recovered first to claim second place in front of Bill, who had set a new class record at 1 min 28.0 sec, 80.07mph.

Throughout the season Charles Morgan was to do battle with Colin Blower's TVR, with the honours being divided fairly evenly after some really exciting racing.

The contrasting Plus 8s of Rob Wells (no. 2) and John Lindsay coming out of the hairpin at Mallory park in August 1978.

Alan Kennedy in his 4/4 Modsports signals his intention to come into the pits during the 1978 Six-hour Relay race at Silverstone.

The highly popular 750 MC six-hour relay race, held on this occasion at Donington on October 7, produced a magnificent result for Morgan drivers. The Anglemog Saxon team and the Anglemog Viking team each scored 264 laps, one more than the third-placed Chanton 750F team - the Saxons also narrowly won the handicap challenge award.

On October 21 night racing returned to Britain at Snetterton, when a two-hour race was split into two parts, the second taking place in darkness. The 22 entries were divided into modified saloon, production saloon and production sports car categories.

Failure of the marshals' telephone system brought the first race to an end after 35 minutes, but the night race ran its full distance and in the final order Bill Wykeham and Bruce Stapleton were placed third overall and won their category, while Anthony Palmer was placed second in the category; all were in Plus 8s.

The following weekend Snetterton provided the scene for a runaway victory in a members' handicap race organized by the Combined One Make CC for Norman Stechman and his Plus 8 while, a long way behind, Mary Lindsay and her Plus 8 were beaten by only 0.6 seconds into second place by a Porsche 914S.

It had been a very good year for Morgans in the production sports car field, and when the points were totted

up Charles Morgan was the overall winner of the DB Motors Championship, and Bruce Stapleton sixth overall and third in his class. In the Aleybars Championship, Bill Wykeham was second overall and a class-winner, with Charles Morgan taking third place in the class.

1979: international long-distance racing

For the new season DB Motors shared joint sponsorship with *Cars and Car Conversions* for one production sports car championship, while the CAV name was linked to another. The opening round of the DB/CCC contest took place at Thruxton on April 1, when Rob Wells in his Libra Motive Plus 8 and Colin Blower in his TVR had an exciting battle for the lead, their positions changing constantly until, finally, Rob managed to cross the line 0.3 seconds ahead.

The same drivers dominated the CAV race at the BRSCC meeting at Snetterton on Easter Sunday, Rob never seriously challenged this time and winning by 4 seconds. At the DB/CCC round at Brands Hatch a week later, the same finishing order persisted for the third time, the gap being 1.83 seconds.

One round of the CAV Championship was held at Cadwell Park on July 22. Charles Morgan was a comfortable class winner and finished sixth overall in a race in which production sports

cars competed against Modsports cars and special saloons. Charles then went on to Snetterton on July 29, where he celebrated his birthday with another easy win, averaging 82.13mph and finishing 16.6 seconds ahead of the field.

The following weekend the Plus 8, which he had shared with Rob Wells and which had proved so reliable, blew up at Silverstone. For the Mallory Park round on August 26, Charles was lent Malcolm Paul's car, which he used to good effect, finishing second to John Kent's TVR after a long scrap to maintain his challenge in the championship.

When a Plus 8 lined up on the starting grid at Brands Hatch on August 5 for the ninth round of the World Championship of Makes, it was the first time that a Morgan had appeared in a long-distance international sports car race since 1968. It was the Stapleton Motors car which had been built to the specification worked out by Bruce Stapleton and Bill Wykeham and homologated into Group 4. John Spero joined Brian Classic and Bill Wykeham to share the driving, Bruce Stapleton having to step down at the last moment because of a family tragedy. Mike Wykeham acted as team manager and Bruno Pericardi was technical adviser.

The car ran like clockwork in the race, apart from one very alarming moment when Bill Wykeham heard a sound like a gunshot, followed by a rumbling brake pedal as he descended Dingle Dell. An unscheduled pit stop

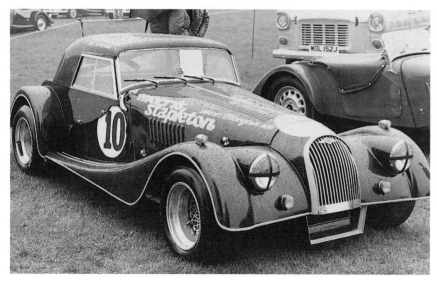

1979 was the first time a Morgan appeared in a long distance international race since 1968. It finished 18th out of 32 starters and more than justified the Stapleton brothers' faith in their specially-built car. It is seen here parked next to the author's Le Mans Replica at Mog'79.

failed to diagnose the cause and so the drivers continued, using high gears as much as possible and with minimum braking. Strangely, their times continued to fall, so the 'Easy' sign was held out and the car came home 18th of the 32 starters and eighth in Group 4, having beaten four Porsches and a BMW amongst the finishers. It was a magnificent effort.

The final round of the CAV Championship took place at the BRSCC Midland Centre's championship finals meeting at Mallory Park, although all the classes had already been decided. Charles Morgan ended his season in fine style, winning easily at 86.47mph and equalling the class lap record at 88.04mph. Malcolm Paul was unable to recover from a bad start and could only finish fourth.

The Plus 8 which Charles Morgan and Rob Wells shared for the two championships had served them very well indeed, Charles being the CAV champion in Class A and finishing third overall with 48 points, while Rob was DB Motors/CCC Champion in Class A and second overall with 31 points.

1980: 24-hour racing in Britain

At the start of the year Phillip Young and Tony Ambrose entered a Plus 8 in the Monte Carlo Rally and did well until the third special stage when a mishap

John Smith in the first Interim Radiator Plus 4 holds off a determined challenge from Charles Pilbeam's 'F' Super at Woodcote in the 1979 Bentley Drivers Club Silverstone meeting.

put them out of the rally.

A newcomer to the Morgan racing scene was Steve Cole. Driving his special works-built ProdSports Plus 8, tuned by Rob Wells at Libra Motive, he used this season to get used to the car and the circuits around the country. In his first race at Donington at the start of the season he finished third behind Colin Blower's apparently unbeatable 3-litre TVR Convertible and John Kent's TVR, but just one second ahead of Malcolm Paul in a Plus 8.

For the rest of the season he met with varying success, whilst learning a great deal. At Mallory Park in April he had a great overall and class win in the 10-lap CAV Production Sports Car Championship race, setting the fastest lap on the way. He and Malcolm Paul always had close battles wherever they raced, with the honours being roughly even by the end of the season.

Derek Wright in his 4/4 started the season well by winning his class in the Dutton Forshaw Hillclimb Championship at Castle Howard in March. However, he does not appear to have sustained this form for the rest of the

One of the rare occassions when Charles Morgan's works Plus 8 was stationary long enough to be photographed. It is seen here on display at the MSCC's Mog'79 event.

June 21 / 22, 1980: Britain's first ever 24-hour race - the Willhire - was held at Snetterton. Mary Lindsay is seen here taking her stint of driving the MSCC Team Car, a Plus 8. The team finished third overall and were First Sports Car team.

season as his name does not appear in any other published results.

This was the year when Britain started its own 24-hour race. Held at Snetterton and sponsored by Willhire, the race attracted a large entry, including five Morgans.

The first of these was the works-entered Plus 8, MMC 11, the only Morgan entry which could be regarded as a truly race-prepared car. Driven by Charles Morgan, Rob Wells and Norman Stechman, it was the only one to experience any serious trouble. Well into the race a fault developed in the rear axle, which, in order for the car to finish the race, required parts to be stripped from Peter Morgan's car in the car park.

The other four cars can only be described as basic shopping cars which had received the minimum of tuning. One of these was another single entry from Morris Stapleton Motors, driven by a four-driver crew of Bruce Stapleton, Bill Wykeham, Richard Down and John Spero. This was, in fact, Vivien Morgan's shopping car, which enjoyed a trouble-free race, covering 1732.97 miles and winning the much coveted Commander's Cup.

The final three cars were a team entered by the Morgan Sports Car Club consisting of a 1969 Plus 8 driven by Mary Lindsay, a Plus 8 driven by Patrick Keen, which was really his wife's shopping car, and another 1969 Plus 8 driven by Mike Duncan. By clever pit management they were able to have one car racing, one being serviced and one in reserve. Mike Duncan's car developed an oil leak, and Patrick Keen's suffered brake trouble, both of which were easily repaired. Mary Lindsay's car did not miss a beat and the team finish an excellent third.

1981

During the winter Steve Cole succeeded in obtaining sponsorship from Lyster Oil for the forthcoming season. From the very first race it was obvious that the class championship would be fought out between Steve and Tony Lanfranchi in a Porsche 911C, with Malcolm Paul always in close contention. The closest race was at Mallory Park, the track where Steve had won the previous year. On the straight the Porsche would pull out 15 to 20 yards on the Morgan, but at the next corner the Morgan outbraked him, with the two cars coming out side-by-side. As Cole said in an interview later, 'We swapped a lot of paintwork in that race'. At the end of an exciting season Cole was runner-up to Lanfranchi in the championship.

Rob Wells made a welcome return to ModSport racing this year in the STP Modified Sports Car Championship. Always in contention, he achieved several class wins and fastest lap times throughout the season.

In April at Donington Park, former Production Sports Car Champion, Charles Morgan, returned to the racing scene to do battle with reigning BRDC Champion, Colin Blower, in his TVR, in the DB Motors Production GT Championship. Pressed hard from the start,

The last race in the 1981 Modsports Championship was held at Thruxton and was won by Rob Wells, seen here leading the Fiat X1/9 of Steve Soper and the Davrian of Steve Roberts.

Blower was forced into a mistake which allowed the works Plus 8 to take the lead and finish almost 10 seconds ahead of the next-placed car.

This was to be the first full racing season for Patrick Keen in his recently-purchased ex-Le Mans Plus 4 Super Sports, TOK 258. He entered his car in the British Thoroughbred Sports Car Championship and, after a very successful series of races in which he broke the lap record at Silverstone, he found himself sharing the lead in the championship on level points. All depended on the result of the final race at Brands Hatch.

Just before the start the heavens opened and, in teeming rain, the race was started. On the first lap Keen had to take avoiding action when an Aston Martin spun off the track in front of him. By the time he recovered, three cars had slipped through on the inside. Driving a well-judged race, he held his position, leaving his challenge for the last lap. Then, just as he was about to mount his final charge, two of the lead-

ing cars touched and, in the resulting mêlée, all three of the leading cars spun off. Keen was able to pick his way through the debris and win the class, becoming overall champion in his first full season.

Inspired by the brilliant third place achieved the previous year, the Morgan Sports Car Club entered almost the same team again for the second 24-hour race at Snetterton, the car of Patrick Keen being substituted by one belonging to Mike Robson with co-driver David Saunter. The team was named MSCC/Bulldog. The race went well for many hours, the only problems being a loose wire which caused some amazing illuminations on David Saunter's car and Peter Garland experiencing rear axle trouble, but both faults were corrected without too much trouble.

Soon after 8am, however, Mike Duncan's car developed a serious oil leak and Mary Lindsay took his place on the track. Suddenly, her car began to handle in a strange manner and then, as it was coming into Coram, it

spun and rolled two or three times before coming to rest upside down on the grass. Luckily, Mary was not seriously hurt but she was very shaken. The accident was due to a broken half-shaft.

Quick thinking by the pit manager meant that only half a lap was lost before the next car was sent out. This was David Saunter, who was also involved in an accident which resulted in his car being written-off. The remaining car, driven by Mike Robson, was put on the track and, in spite of a broken throttle cable which was quickly exchanged, it finished the race. The final result after so many mishaps was a well-deserved sixth place.

The two other Morgan entries in the race did well, with the car driven by the team of Norman Stechman, Malcolm Harrison, Mike Ridley and Francois Duret winning the Commander's Cup. The works car driven at the time by Charles Morgan also lost a wheel out on the track, but he managed to drive it back to the pits on the brake drum,

36

Rob Wells leads the pack of Rob Cox (Black Brick), Mark Hales (Marcos) and Paul Edwards (Porsche) in a Modsports race at Mallory Park in August 1981.

have another stub axle fitted and finish in seventh place.

1982: 24-hours again

Over the winter Cole's car received extensive improvements' it was fitted with the latest Rover engine, 15 inch wheels and a set of very hard rear shock absorbers and was sent to Hesketh Racing for final tuning.

The first race of the season at Silverstone in March set the scene for the forthcoming season, when Cole finished just ahead of Malcolm Paul's Plus 8, the two cars being separated by only 0.18 seconds. The race was a continuous battle between the two Morgans, Lanfranchi's Porsche and Pete Hall's Lotus Esprit Turbo.

Cole continued his success throughout the season and would have had the championship won before the last race if it had not been for the equally successful season of Ian Jacob in his Matra-Simca Bagheera in Class C of the championship. Everything rested on the result of the 15th and

final race of the championship at Brands Hatch in October. The pouring rain greatly affected Cole's performance and he finished down the field in fourth place overall, but Jacob could only manage to finish fourth in his class. When all the mathematics were completed, Cole had won 12 of the 15 races in the Lucas-CAV Championship and taken the overall championship title by just two points!

For this season the Thoroughbred Championship included both modified and unmodified cars in the same class. However, this did not deter Patrick Keen from defending his championship. After a hard and very strenuous season he lost the overall position but did win his class championship.

This was the last year that teams would be allowed to enter the Snetterton 24-hour race. The MSCC/Bulldog team this year consisted of John and Mary Lindsay, Richard Caswell, Mike Duncan, Peter Garland and Jim Deacon. Due to the loss of several minutes when Deacon's car stopped out on the

circuit and he had to have a petrol pump ferried out to him to change there on the side of the track, the race was almost trouble-free. However, this incident cost the team several places and they only managed to finish 10th out of 20 starters.

Morgan's honour was more than upheld by Rob Wells, Chris Alford and Malcolm Paul driving MMC 11. They took the lead after two hours and finished well ahead of their nearest rival, completing a record 970 laps. The team also gave Morgan its third consecutive win of the Commander's Cup.

The other Morgan entry was a Plus 8 driven by Norman Stechman's team which, for many hours, ran second to MMC 11, but was forced to retire due to serious mechanical trouble on the Sunday morning. Some time after the race, the result was disputed due to a technicality, but even this could not take away the joy of Rob Wells' team.

1983

For this season Cole and his sponsors

The Bulldog Team Plus 8 makes a pit stop during the night at the 1983 Willhire 24-hour Race at Snetterton. It finished fifth overall.

decided to concentrate their efforts on attempting to win the Donington GT Championship, having socred several wins in this contest the previous season.

All went well for Cole in spite of very strong opposition from Blower, Meek and Kent: at the three-quarter stage, he had won every race in the championship. Then, out of the blue, came an opportunity which he could hardly refuse - he was offered a drive in a single-seater in a Formula Ford 2000 race. The problem was that this race clashed with the date of the next round of the championship. After a lot of soul-searching, he decided to take the risk and go for this once-in-a-lifetime opportunity and drive the single-seater.

However, while the cat is away, the mice do play, and Cole's closest rival won his class in that round of the championship, meaning that the championship would be decided by whoever finished in the highest place in the final race of the series. Typically, the only race of the season that Cole did not win was this one; he finished in third place which meant that he had lost the overall championship by one point. However, as a consolation, he did win the Class A Donington GT Championship.

With the regulations changed, the 24-hour race at Snetterton included only two Morgan entries. These were Norman Stechman's Allied Rubber Products team and the Bulldog Morgan team.

The latter used Jim Deacon's car this year and, after a trouble-free race, finished fifth overall. But the Stechman team could only manage 14th.

1984

As, from 1985, only saloon cars would be eligible to compete in the 24-hour race at Snetterton, 1984 was the last year that Morgans were able to take part in this event.

Two Plus 8s were entered and by the early hours of Sunday morning it was looking like a repeat of 1982, with the works Plus 8, MMC 11, driven by the team of Rob Wells, Chris Alford and Charles Morgan leading the field. But it was not to be. First, brake problems cost them first place, and then a faulty

terminal on the alternator failed to respond to repair and the car eventually came to a halt out on the circuit with a completely depleted battery.

The Bulldog team consisted of John and Mary Lindsay, Mike Duncan and Bob Cook driving the now rebuilt Plus 8 of Mary Lindsay. All the careful rebuilding paid off, with the only trouble being a leaking rear oil seal which cost them a 30-minute pit stop. In spite of this they finished 12th out of 36 starters and were in front of three Porsche 911s.

During the winter Patrick Keen had managed to obtain sponsorship from Hire-a-Tool Company and had fitted his car with a new Lawrencetune cylinder head. The Thoroughbred Championship again placed modified and unmodified cars together in the same races and for the same championship, which resulted in some very close and high-speed racing.

Throughout the season Keen engaged in battle two Healeys driven by Richard Brightman and Phil Eggington. The championship was to be decided on the result of the last race of the

MMC 4 (nee MMC 3) in current specifications, with KLM air filters and improved front air dam, is driven here by Rob Wells in the 1983 Bentley Drivers' Club meeting at Silverstone.

John H. Sheally II track tests the works experimental fuel-injected, aluminium, rack and pinion steering Plus 8 at Silverstone in 1984.

series: Patrick Keen would be overall champion if he won his class and if Mike Wilds failed to finish. However, it was not to be Keen's title. Due to an incident when Wild's Aston Martin tore off its sump, flooding the track with oil, the race was stopped. The results were determined on the positions of the cars on the track at the end of the fourth lap. Unfortunately, at this stage, Brightman was still ahead of Keen, and even though Keen had managed to avoid the oil and Brightman had spun out of the race on it, the championship was Brightman's. However, Keen did manage to become

The Morgan Challenge Race Series, Mallory Park heat held in June 1985. Line astern are David Haith (Plus 8); Mary Lindsay (Plus 8); Leigh Sebba, (Plus 8) and Andy Garlick (Plus 4). This was the year that Mary Lindsay won the challenge race series and became overall MSCC Champion after 15 years of competition driving.

The MGCC held the 1985 Kimber Trail in November. Here, Mary Lindsay tries to prove that her Plus 8 is really a Three-wheeler, whilst husband, John, looks over the passenger door in an attempt to find out where the ground has gone.

class champion.

1985: Stop ... and go, go, go!

Strategy can play a big part in racing, as Steve Cole proved in the first round of the 4th Cheshire Cats Trophy Race at Oulton Park on April 20.

Cole, in his Plus 8, was on pole position at the start of the 100-mile race. By the end of the first lap he had lost the lead to Robin Gray in a Caterham 7 and, to everyone's dismay, pulled into the pits at the end of the lap. After a short stop he rejoined the race, albeit in last place, with the car running exceedingly well. Slowly, Cole worked his way up through the field and, by lap 30, took the lead.

From there on he was never seriously challenged and went on to win by just over 7 seconds. Knowing that all competitors must make one compulsory pit stop during the race, he had elected to make his at the end of lap 1, and drive the rest of the race non-stop. A very successful ploy - which also meant that he turned in the fastest lap in 1 min 35.8 sec, 88.53mph. In the same race, Richard Casswell, in his 1600cc 4/4, finished fourth overall and won his class at an average speed of 80.40mph.

A week later, Richard Comber took his 1938 short-wheelbase, Coventry-Climax-engined 4-4 (the ex-works trials car used by Jim Goodall, BWP 47) to Donington Park to compete in a 5-lap handicap race. Although he finished only 11th out of 24 finishers, his was a very good performance against many larger-engined vehicles.

The MSCC Morgan Challenge Race over 10 laps at Lydden Hill, Kent, at the 750 MC meeting proved a runaway victory for Peter Garland in his modified Plus 8. He finished a full 40 seconds ahead of the field. The real battle went on behind him for the whole race, with Leigh Sebba and Dave Freeman having a great dice to finish second and third respectively with only 0.5 seconds separating them. Fourth-placed Mary Lindsay was only a further 0.7 seconds behind. Fifth and sixth places were 9.5 seconds slower, both Andy Garlick and Barry Sumner being credited with the same time. Garland at 72.28mph, Sebba at 68.70mph and Sumner at 66.54mph all established lap records in their respective classes.

Many Morgan drivers were involved in more than one championship series this season. One of these was Grahame Bryant who set up a lap record of 77.95mph in the *Sporting Cars* Magazine Roadgoing Sports Car Series at Brands Hatch on August 10, winning the race by a 5 second margin. However, he was forced to retire with engine trouble in the next round of the championship. At the end of the season he became 1985 Class C Champion in this series.

On the trials front it was not a particularly good year for Morgan drivers. George Proudfoot, in his 1938 4/4, was the only one to win a first class award in any of the three MCC events. His award was won in the Edinburgh Trial held at the beginning of October.

1986

At Brands Hatch on April 26 Grahame Bryant was in a hurry when he competed in the second round of the *Sporting Cars* Magazine Sports Car Championship, as he had to dash off to Silverstone for a Giroflex Porsche race on the same day. However, he was delayed when the race had to be stopped and re-run due to a multiple pile-up in the heavy rain. In spite of the weather he powered away to lead throughout the race, finishing almost 17 seconds in front of the second-placed Caterham 7, winning at an average speed of 69.65mph and putting in the fastest lap of 70.95mph. Incidentally, he made Silverstone in time for the Porsche race but finished well down the field.

In the next round of the championship, Bryant repeated his win, but this

Wall-to wall-racing Morgans at Castle Coombe in 1987. Left to right are Rob Wells, Grahame Bryant, David Raeside, Tony Morgan-Tipp, Bob Stuart and Peter Garland, all in Plus 8s.

time the second-placed Caterham 7 was only 1.6 seconds behind him.

On May 26 the 750 Motor Club held a race meeting at Snetterton. In the 10-lap Combined One Make Car Clubs Handicap Race, James Deacon in his Plus 8 had a race-long battle with a Triumph TR4, winning by 2.6 seconds at an average speed of 83.64mph. In the same race David Haith and Leigh Sebba, both in Plus 8s, were placed fourth and sixth, respectively.

The next round of the *Sporting Cars* Championship, held at the same meeting, saw no less than four Morgans entered.

Making a rare but nonetheless welcome return to the track was Rob Wells in the Libra Motive Plus 8. Rob had lost none of his old skills, finishing 37.5 seconds ahead of James Deacon in another Plus 8. Leigh Sebba and David Haith finished fifth and tenth respectively.

Wells also competed in the next race for Modified Sports Cars but could only manage only third place behind a Marcos GT and a Turner Mk 3.

The Bentley Drivers' Club meeting at Silverstone every August is always a popular one with Morgan competitors, as they have their own race and can also compete in the Allcomers event.

This year, the Morgan-only race was one in the new Morgan Sports Car Club Challenge, Applied Handicap series. The race was won by Grahame Bryant, but only just; less than a second separated him from Peter Garland in another Plus 8. The two cars battled it out for most of the race, with Garland putting in the fastest lap at 92.92mph.

The Allcomers race over 8 laps proved to be even more exciting, with Grahame Bryant winning by inches from an MGB GT V8. So close were they

that they were credited with the same times. In third place, less than 3 seconds behind, was Peter Garland who, once again, put in the fastest lap with a speed this time of 92.18mph.

When the final round of the *Sporting Cars* championship was held on October 26 at Snetterton, the title still had not been decided. The championship hung on the final positions of Grahame Bryant in his Plus 8 in Class C and Paul Lucas with a Triumph Spitfire in Class A. If Bryant failed to win his class, the championship went to Lucas, if *he* won *his* class.

Complicated mathematics were involved, but this is a sign of a good championship. When the race was over, both men had won their respective classes, with a total of 90 points. However, the overall champion was Grahame Bryant because of his number of overall wins through the series, including the final one.

Once again the MCC Edinburgh Trial in October proved to be a good one for Morgan, with Geoff Margetts and George Proudfoot both winning first class awards.

1987

On March 29 at the Scottish Motor Racing Club meeting at Ingliston, John MacDonald had a race-long battle in the 12-lap Historic Sports Car race. Just 0.04 seconds separated his Plus 4 from the winning Frazer-Nash.

In the first round of the MSCC race series held at Snetterton on April 5, the superior power of Grahame Bryant's Plus 8 put him in the lead from the start, but Rob Wells took him around the outside at Riches. However, Wells' lead did not last for long and at the Esses Bryant re-took the lead and was not headed again throughout the race.

Behind him Wells and Jim Deacon battled it out, finishing second and third with only 0.7 seconds separating them. The remainder of the field, including an SLR, swapped and changed places throughout the race.

Later in the month, Peter Garland, in his Plus 8, won his class in the first round of the Guyson USA British Hillclimb Championship held on April 20 at Loton Park. The same weekend Stuart Adamson in a Plus 4 set up a new class record of 60.3 seconds in the Strathclyde Park Grampian Scottish Hillclimb Championship.

In the GB Roadgoing Sports Cars race at Mallory Park over 10 laps on May 3, Grahame Bryant had a lights-to-flag win and established a new class record of 89.50mph. Second was Tony Morgan-Tipp in another Plus 8.

Bryant repeated his runaway win in the next race in the series held at Brands Hatch, setting a new class record for the course of 86.55mph. Second place went to Peter Garland after he had come out on top at about the halfway stage in his private battle with a Caterham 7.

In the Historic Handicap race at Knockhill at the end of May, John MacDonald in his Plus 4 shot into the lead from the start and had no difficulty in staying out front for the whole race.

Grahame Bryant was making a habit of winning his own trophies and setting class records in the process. Yet again he had a start-to-finish win in the 10-lap race which he sponsored - the GB Roadgoing Sports Car race. This time the race was at Donington Park.

Peter Garland made two superb climbs to win his class at the Prescott Short Course hillclimb event on June 28. He also set a new class record, bettering his brother Nigel's previous

One of America's leading Morgan fanatics is John H. Sheally II. He is a consistent winner of events in his Cosworth-engined 4/4; this time at the Southside Speedway in Richmond, Virginia in July 1987.

record. A week later at at Shelsley Walsh hillclimb he achieved yet another class win and set another record.

For the first time in years, Grahame Bryant suffered a mechanical failure on his car when a fault developed in the rear axle, making him a non-starter at the Donington Park round of the MSCC race series. At the green light, Jim Deacon, Tony Morgan-Tipp and Rob Wells shot off from the front row of the grid and it was Deacon who came out of Redgate in the lead. However, by the end of lap 1, Wells was leading. Thenceforth he was harrassed by Morgan-Tipp but held on to win by 0.7 seconds. Deacon finished a lonely third, almost 35 seconds ahead of the chasing pack.

Yet again Peter Garland won his class in the Shell Oils Midland Hillclimb Championship event held at Prescott on July 19, whilst Mike Hall in a Plus 8 also won his.

In the MSCC race at Silverstone on August 29, Grahame Bryant once again led the entire race, in spite of the extra drag of a rear-facing video camera. This, more than likely, recorded Tony Morgan-Tipp's very spectacular 'moment' at Woodcote, whilst attempting to stay in touch with the leader. Rob Wells was running on road tyres instead of the

leading two cars' slicks but finished a long way clear of the rest of the field.

On September 26 Bryant made an uncharacteristic error in his calculations in the 10-lap Core Lion Developments Trophy Race. Well in the lead and with the chequered flag in sight, his engine died. The car rolled to a halt

Peter Askew's 4/4, which finished sixth overall in this Bentley Drivers' Club meeting Morgans only race at Silverstone in 1988. It was the first 4/4 home and was beaten only by the much larger Plus 8s.

amid speculation that some terrible mechanical disaster had overtaken it. The truth was far simpler - Grahame had miscalculated and had run out of fuel! This let through Tony Morgan-Tipp to win, with Rob Wells second and Peter Garland third. Rick Bourne won Class B with Andy Garlick and Mike

Rob Wells at the limit at Donington in 1988.

Duncan close behind. Class C was won by Chas Windridge.

At Cadwell Park on October 3, Bryant made no mistakes. He was never seriously challenged and finished a full 18 seconds ahead of the field, setting a new lap record of 74.02mph in the process.

He recorded another victory at Mallory Park on October 11 when he romped home 26 seconds ahead of the second-placed Porsche 911S in the 12-lap Roadgoing Sports Car race.

On October 17 at Snetterton, the BF Goodrich Morgan Plus 8 team, consisting of Grahame Bryant, Rob Wells, David Raeside and Tony Morgan-Tipp, won the 750 Motor Club's Six Hour Relay Race. The team should have consisted of five cars, but the back axle of Peter Garland's car failed in practice

and there was insufficient time to repair it before the race. Halfway through the fourth hour the race was red-flagged, when a member of the MGA team rolled three times at Riches. It was restarted after 53 minutes, but the organizers decided to shorten the race to only five hours. Not that this in any way affected the final result - the Morgan team was increasing its lead by a lap every hour.

This was to be a very special year for Barry Sumner on the trials scene. He started the year with a class win in the Lands End Trial, 'cleaning' every hill. The Morgans of Barry Sumner, Dave Sapp and Geoff Margetts all won first class awards.

This success was repeated in the Exeter Trial later in the year, although the 1987 team championship was to elude them when Dave Sapp had a

mishap in the Edinburgh Trial in October managed just a second class award. Geoff Margetts won another first to take the Gold Medal Triple Award for the year. Barry Sumner once again 'cleaned' every hill and therefore won the Triple Baddeley Award - the only car driver to receive the award this year.

1988: SLRs at home & away

The first round of the MSCC Challenge Race Series was held at Snetterton on April 10. For reasons best known to the organizers and the club officials concerned, the Morgan race was combined with the Lotus Challenge race series.

From the start the battle for the lead was between the Plus 8s of Rob Wells and Grahame Bryant. At the end of lap 2 Bryant was shadowing Wells

43

and by the halfway mark managed to get past as the Wells car developed a misfire. Bryant pulled away steadily to win by 11 seconds at an average speed of 86.57 mph.

Behind these two cars, David Raeside, in a Plus 8, had a race-long battle with Richard Smith (Caterham 7) and Jon Woodward (Lotus Sunbeam). Raeside was able to move to the front on the straights, but the opposition went ahead as they braked for the Esses. On the last lap Raeside left it just a little too late and ended up on the escape road, allowing Woodward and Smith to finish third and fourth respectively.

Later in the meeting Wells and Bryant battled it out again in the Road Going Sports Car Race, but this time Bryant had changed cars and was driving his Porsche Carrera.

Wells had apparently cured the misfire and led from the green light and, by halfway, was 5 seconds clear. However the misfire developed again, enabling Bryant to close the gap, but Wells managed to hold him off, finishing just 0.2 seconds in front.

The following week Brian Hopkins in a Plus 4 had a convincing 6 seconds win over a Vixen, a Brooklands Riley and a Jaguar XK120 in the Lothian Chemical Company Historic Handicap 10-lap race at Ingliston, organized by the Scottish Motor Racing Club.

In the next round of the MSCC Challenge Race Series held at Oulton Park on May 2, Rob Wells made a rare error when he incurred a 10 second penalty for jumping the start. However, he gave a great display of wet weather driving skills which resulted in a re-sounding victory. This race also contained a rare SLR Morgan driven by Tony Howard.

The vintage racing season in the USA began with the Historic Motorcar Racing Association at Sears Point during the Sonoma Classic held on May 14 & 15.

There were nine racing groups with Morgans entered in three different grids. In Group 3 six Morgans raced against Corvettes, Porsches, Twin Cam MGAs, a 250 Ferrari and various Alfas, Lancias and MGBs. The Morgan entries performed well, finishing in the following positions:- 6th John Butks (4/4); 8th Tony Kearney (Plus 4 Super Sports); 11th Bill Cathey (Plus 4); 12th Ed DeMayo; 15th Gerry Medeiray (4/4) and 20th Dick Delafield (Plus 4).

In Group 7 Bill Fink entered his SLR and Greg Solow his Plus 4, and in Group 8 Bill Fink entered the prototype Plus 8 . For Morgan enthusiasts it was great to see so many cars competing so well, and those Americans who had never seen Morgans racing were treated to a show of the fine competitive ability of the marque.

Those race-goers who left the Bentley Drivers' Club meeting at Silverstone because of the onset of heavy rain, missed the last and best race of the day. This year the meeting also included one race in the MSCC Challenge Race Series and was the last in the series.

Over thirty Morgans took the field with the first three cars on the grid being within 0.8 seconds of each other in practice. The race, however, did not live up to the potential of these three fastest cars. Grahame Bryant's Plus 8 leapt away at the start and was never seriously challenged. Late in the race Rob Wells put in the fastest lap in an effort to catch Bryant, but with so much machinery about he just could not find a way through and settled for second place.

In the Allcomers race Rob Wells treated those spectators who stayed to a fine display of wet weather driving, having a great battle with the AC Cobra of John Atkins. By lap three he had managed to establish a big enough lead to hold off the power advantage of the AC on the straights. On lap 5 Atkins made a spectacular exit from the race. The Cobra of Bruce Channor made a desperate attempt to catch Wells, but Wells held on to the chequered flag.

On October 29 at Silverstone the 750 Motor Club held the Birkett Four Hour Relay Race for roadgoing cars.

In this event there are two competitions being fought out on the track at the same time, with all teams competing for both prizes. The first is the handicap race where the organizers hope that they have got the sums right as all of the competing teams - from the Austin 7s to the mid-engined Ultimas - should have covered roughly the same distance, allowing for the credit laps given to the smaller engined cars.

The second event is a scratch race where the winner is the team which travels the furthest in the four hour race period. Because of Morgan's success in this event in 1987, the team of Rob Wells, Grahame Bryant, David Raeside and Peter Garland (all 3.9-litre Plus 8s) stood very little chance in the handicap section, having to start from scratch with no credit laps. However, after a hard fought race, the team was declared "Winners on the Road". The 'Back of the Grid Club' team of Peter Sergeant (Plus 8), George Hodkinson (4/4 TC), David James (Plus 4) Ian Doolan (4/4) John Milbank (4/4 TC) and Kevin Laidlaw were very much after the handicap race honours, but a broken throttle cable put paid to their chances.

This was yet another good competition year for Morgans, with Chas Windridge in his Plus 4 winning the Historic Sports Car Club Classic Championship Class 'A'. He also won the John Bull Shipping Trophy for the best novice in the race series.

The Morgan Sports Car Club Challenge Race Series Championship was once again won by Chris Daddy with a total of 442.60 points. He competed in only four races in the series but the rules of the Championship state that the best four results in the series to count.

1989: Playing in the sand
The first round of the Milbank Trucks - Morgan Challenge Race Series this year was held on April 16 at Cadwell Park. The race turned out, as before, to be several races within the race proper, with the various classes having their own battles. This, of course, made for interesting racing for spectators and particularly for the drivers of the big Plus 8s. However, further interest arose from the fact that the faster of the 4/4s was pressing the Plus 8s in the corners, as the big boys braked a lot earlier than the 4/4s and were not nearly as fast through the bends. Of course, on the straights superior power meant that the 8s leapt away again. Peter Garland led for most of the race but failed to complete lap 8 due to a broken transmission, which left Rob Wells to romp home the winner by over 90 seconds. This impressive margin included the fastest lap of the day and a new lap record. Second was Ian Allwood (Plus 8) and third Chas Windridge (Plus 4).

The next round was held on April 30 at Donington Park. At the start of the race everything looked normal as the cars approached Redgate. Suddenly,

David Watson in a 4/4 jumped from ninth to second as he, in his excitement, either forgot to brake or experienced complete brake failure. The ensuing chaos, as the whole field endeavoured to avoid one another, had to be seen to be believed. When the dust had settled, five cars were left stranded in the sand. The race was stopped, cars recovered and inspected and the race restarted.

The ensuing race turned out to be very entertaining, with Kevin Laidlaw (Plus 8) and Chas Windridge (Plus 8) finishing only 0.4 seconds apart, with third-placed Bill Gledhill (Plus 8) only 1.6 seconds behind them.

On June 25 at Snetterton the 750 Motor Club held a nine race programme. Only one Morgan, the Plus 8 of Peter Garland, was entered in any race. However, Peter Garland romped home a full 13 seconds ahead of the second-placed Lotus in the ten lap G.B. Roadgoing Sports Car race. Peter became Class C Champion with seven wins from seven starts.

On September 24 the penultimate race in the MSCC Challenge Race series was held at Thruxton. It was to prove to be a very close one for the top three Plus 8 exponents - Rob Wells, Peter Garland and Grahame Bryant - with all three lapping at over 90mph. Such was the speed of these cars that they finished the 10 lap race whilst the rest of the field were on either laps 6 or 7. The eventual winner was Rob Wells and second Grahame Bryant, who set the fastest lap of over 94 mph.

The last round of the series was held at the Bentley Drivers' Club Meeting at Silverstone the following weekend. Yet again the race provided excitement for competitors and spectators alike. When all the mathematics were

completed Rob Wells was the worthy champion with Kevin Laidlaw and Ian Allwood close behind.

1990: Three & four wheels race together
The first race in the MSCC Challenge Race series was held at Cadwell Park in near perfect weather. The whole circuit was not in use that day, so the competitors had to negotiate an almost reciprocal hairpin bend, complete with a dip in the middle. The total number of Morgans entered meant that the organisers were able to hold two Morgan-only events. The split was perfect with the modified Plus 8s (Classes A & B) in the first race.

In Class A for modified Plus 8s Peter Garland led from start to finish, but not without having to fight off determined attacks by Rob Wells and Mathew Wurr. This was the order in which they finished: Class B was won by Grahame Walker with Kevin Laidlaw and Craig Jones taking the next two places. The German dentist, Dr Klaus Nesbach, who had come over especially for the event, drove a spirited race but was forced to retire later on with mechanical failure.

In the second race were Classes C & D (standard Plus 8s and modified and standard Plus 4 and 4/4 models). The Class C race was appropriately won by the sponsor, John Milbank, who had a super drive to win by a full 16 seconds, while Class D was won by Keith Morris.

The Morgan Club of Holland held a well-organized race meeting at the Zandvoort track on May 26. This was one of those very rare occasions when both three-and four-wheelers formed up on the same starting grid. Practice was to see Barry Sumner's Flat Radiator Plus 4 spinning on lap 1, luckily

without damage. Dave Watson was forced to retire on lap 3 with the Lotus twin-cam making very expensive noises. Dr. Klaus Nesbach managed to just pip Rob Wells for the fastest practice lap, but was immediately put out of the race when his engine dropped a rod through the sump.

Whilst all this was going on the three-wheeler boys were buzzing around the track pumping out those exciting smells of yesteryear, Castrol R and Methanol. Their times placed Bill Turner (1933 Super Sports) between Leigh Sebba (Plus 8) and Barry Sumner (Plus 4), and Greg Bibby (1933 Super Sports) between Dave Watson (4/4 TC) and Mary Lindsay (Plus 8).

From the green light Rob Wells roared off into the lead and stayed there until the finish, with Rick Bourne, Kevin Laidlaw, Mary Lindsay and the rest of the four-wheelers having a great battle. The three-wheelers were set off after a 10 second delay and immediately set about getting in touch with the rest of the pack. On lap 8 Bill Turner was closing fast on Mary Lindsay, when his engine's main bearing failed, the engine seized and the back wheel locked up as he was entering a tight left-hander. The car turned over with Bill still inside. The pace car was immediately out on the track, whilst Bill extracted himself, unaided from the in-

verted car. Surprisingly, he suffered only bruising and a bloodied nose, but his leathers were not as good as new.

Wreckage removed, the pace car left the track and the race continued. The top six places remained unchanged but Chas Reynolds (1933 Super Sports) overtook Mary Lindsay with Greg Bibby just on her tail.

On Sunday August 26 six Morgans competed in the South West Morgan Hillclimb Championship heat at Gurston Down. In perfect weather the crowd was treated to a display of some fine driving. The only true dispute of the day was over the time given for Graham Dunn's first run of the afternoon. A time of 40.02 seconds was displayed on the public timing board, the same time as that recorded by the commentator. However, the official result listed a time of 44.02 seconds. To prove the point Graham made a second run of 40.09 seconds and was promptly offered a third run, which he declined. The point had been made and the new time broke the long-standing record of Stephen Lindsay.

The Morgan Challenge Race Series Championship this year turned out to be a very close contest between Rob Wells and Peter Garland.

Garland had won the Cadwell Park and Donington rounds, and Wells the next two at Snetterton and Brands

Hatch. At the start of the next round the scores were Wells 105.10 and Garland 104.49, setting the stage for a great battle. As it was, Garland got clear of Wells as they worked their way through the back markers, with Wells taking the wrong line at the new exit onto the club straight. This resulted in Garland winning by 5 seconds to go into the championship lead by a fraction of a point, and also to win the Maurice Stapleton Trophy.

In the Allcomers Scratch Race which, by tradition, is always the last race of the day, Garland's engine suddenly decided it wanted to do it's own thing, by throwing con rods in every direction. Sparks flew from under the car and it burst into flames at the end of the long club straight. No one was hurt but the car needed a lot of work if it was to be ready for the next round of the championship.

Surprisingly, Garland's car was ready and back on the grid for the final round of the championship at Thruxton, and needed to win by two seconds to clinch the title. However, in pouring rain it was to be Wells who spent longer on the tarmac than Garland. An excursion into the long grass by Garland towards the end of the race assured Wells of a race win and also the championship for the second year running.

4/4S

4/4 '1600'
February 1968 - March 1982

Ford introduced the Mark II version of the Cortina in August 1966, which had restyled bodywork but was still fitted with the Mark I's 'Kent' engine.

A new version of this power unit was developed for the Cortina and announced at the 1967 Motor Show. The capacity was now 1599cc and it was fitted with a crossflow cylinder head; the carburettor and inlet manifold were mounted on the left-hand side, whereas previously they had been mounted on top of the exhaust manifold on the right. By February 1968 the engine was made available to Morgan and a new 4/4 model was introduced. By using the new Ford 'three rail' gearbox, as fitted on the new Cortina GT model, Morgan

had to make very few alterations to the chassis to accommodate the new engine and transmission unit.

At the same time, Ford developed a GT version of the engine which was also made available to Morgan. Designated 2737E by Ford, it had the same modification as did the Series V Competition engine, but with the refinement of a lightened flywheel, plus a plastic cooling fan, which all helped to reduce weight. The power difference between the two engines was quite astonishing, though - 95.5bhp at 5500rpm instead of 74bhp at 4750rpm.

This extra power meant that Morgan was able once again to offer a four-seater version. The first of these was chassis no. B1732, built in September 1968. For an additional cost of

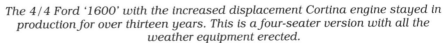

The 4/4 Ford '1600' with the increased displacement Cortina engine stayed in production for over thirteen years. This is a four-seater version with all the weather equipment erected.

only £80 including tax, the GT engine could be had and demand for these cars far exceeded that of the standard version by four to one. By May 1971 the demand for the GT version was such that the company phased out the standard engine.

As from chassis B2381 (May 1971) all cars produced were fitted with the uprated Ford 2265E, and all engine numbers were prefixed with the letter 'A'. When Ford replaced the 2737E engine with the 2265E single overhead-camshaft engine for their Series III Cortina GT, Morgan followed suit.

New exhaust emission control laws introduced in America in 1970 effectively lost Morgan its main export market - the same market which had saved the company in the 1950s and 1960s. But they had been prepared and introduced modifications so that their cars complied with the (less severe) requirements of European countries, in particular West Germany. This market developed so well that by the mid-1970s it had become the company's major export destination.

In 1980, the West German government announced that, as from April 1982, it would be implementing stricter exhaust emission regulations. This news coincided with the appearance of a completely new engine and transmission from Ford, transversely-mounted for the front-wheel-drive Escort. Although Ford assured Morgan that they were going to continue production of the conventional in-line engine for the foreseeable future, the implications were only too obvious; reluctantly, the Morgan company had to decide to end production of the 4/4 1600. It stopped as the new German regulations were

introduced.

4/4 Series 1600 Fiat (Factory listed as 4/4 T/C)
November 1981 - November 1985
4/4 Series 1600 Ford CVH
March 1982 - November 1991
4/4 Series 1600 Ford EFI
November 1991 - February 1993

Once again Morgan had to find an engine which was suitable to power the 4/4 range. After careful research they settled on the 1585cc Fiat twin-cam, coupled with Fiat's own five-speed gearbox, as used in the Fiat Abarth rally car. This was a well-tried and proven engine that had been used in various forms since 1966.

No sooner had the company committed itself to the Fiat engine than the Ford CVH engine unexpectedly became available. By coincidence, a senior Ford executive had a 4/4 on order, so that when Morgan made the announcement of the new model, he realized he would have to take delivery of a car fitted with a Fiat engine. He therefore immediately set to work with Morgan to devise a method whereby the new four-cylinder CVH (Compound Valve-angle Hemispherical combustion chamber) transverse engine could be adapted for use in the conventional in-line installation.

Actually, this required only limited modification: the sump was exchanged for the more tapered Cortina equivalent; a Capri bellhousing and a Morgan-designed flywheel meant that it could be combined with the Cortina four-speed gearbox. The following year the gearbox was replaced by the new five-speed Ford gearbox which had been designed for the Ford Sierra and Capri. This, however, necessitated reshaping

the bulkhead and designing new engine mountings. Finally, a slightly larger radiator was fitted to improve the cooling. It all worked exceptionally well, so Morgan decided to produce the 4/4 model with optional engines.

The Morgan factory was soon to discover that the side-by-side production of the two variants of the same model did not make for efficient working. Management agonised about it but decided that the Fiat-engined 4/4 would be discontinued at the end of the current stock. They also concluded that, after a 15-year absence, a new version of the Plus 4 should be introduced.

A few months later, production was threatened when the company which supplied Morgan with their steering boxes gave notice it had decided that the limited production required to meet Morgan's orders was no longer financially viable. In conjunction with Jack Knight Developments, Morgan quickly had designed and then put into production its own rack-and-pinion steering system. Although this system was a distinct improvement, it was expensive, adding almost £250 to the cost of the car, and was only offered as an option for the Plus 8, never for any other model.

However, it was not to be very long before a French company named Gemmer commenced production of a re-circulating ball-type steering box. This proved to be suitable for use in the 4/4 at very little extra cost to the basic price.

In November 1991 Ford phased out the CVH engine and introduced a fuel injected version of the same engine. The change had no effect on Morgan's production other than it enabled them to fit a catalytic converter so that the car could run on unleaded fuel.

The Fiat 1600 twin-cam fitted snugly into the 4/4's engine compartment, with the carburettor carrying a specially-made inlet chamber connecting to the re-positioned air filter.

Completed rolling chassis of the Ford CVH-engined 4/4 and the Rover-engined Plus models await transfer to the bodyshop for the next stage of construction. No mechanical handling here - the cars are pushed from workshop to workshop by specially-employed porters.

Ford CVH engines lined up on the floor in the Morgan works, awaiting installation in the 4/4s. You can see why Morgan engines are not fitted in number sequence.

The new Ford 1800 engines mounted in their allocated chassis, with others on delivery pallets waiting to be fitted.

There's very little room to spare under the bonnet of the new Ford 1800 4/4, either nearside (right) or offside (far right).

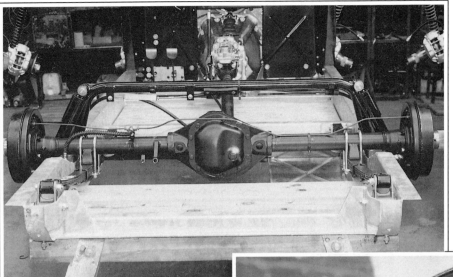

A standard rear axle was adopted for use on all models from 1993.

A new standard braking system for all models was introduced in 1993. The rear brakes are self-adjusting and the hand brake operated by cable which is suspended on a rear shock absorber.

The model continued unchanged until February 1993 when Ford introduced the new 1800cc engine.

4/4 Series Ford 1800 engine
August 1993 - and continuing

The ending by Ford of production of their 1600 CVH EFI engine heralded the end of another in the Morgan 4/4 series. It was to be almost six months from the end of production 4/4 Series 1600 CVH before all the 'sorting' of the new Ford 1800 engine was completed and the new 4/4 model could officially go into production. When it did, it was allocated the chassis prefix letter 'D' rather than 'Z' as the latter could be mistaken for a figure '2'. Chassis

At the same time the front caliper was changed for the four-pot variety and the caliper bracket was modified to accommodate the new calipers.

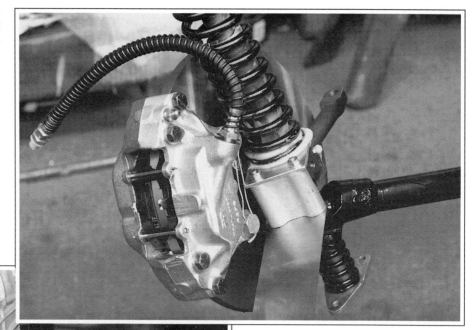

As well as the new design brakes, the system on all models was now servo-assisted. As can be seen, the servo unit only just clears the master cylinder. The pedal operating assembly has been modified.

A new damper has been fitted between the universal joints on the steering shaft of Plus 4 and Plus 8 models with the hole in the valence changed to accommodate it. A spacer is used under the bottom front bolt of the steering bracket between the bracket and the chassis to angle the steering box for the new shaft.

number D8720 was allocated to the works experimental car.

At the same time another important decision was taken by Morgan that this model would only be produced as a two-seater and the production of the four-seater car would be confined to the Plus 4 two-litre Rover T16-engined series. A similar situation existed in the 1950s and 60s when all four-seater Morgans were only available in the larger-engined Plus 4 format. It was not until the introduction of the 4/4 1600 'Cross Flow' series that the 4/4 four-seater was re-introduced after it had ended with the demise of the Standard Special engined Series I 4/4.

IV

PLUS 4s

Plus 4 Fiat-engined
April 1985 - January 1987

When, in 1984, Fiat offered Morgan a 2-litre, fuel-injected engine, Maurice Owen, Morgan's research and development engineer, saw in it the opportunity to create an alternative intermediate model, which would fall between the basic 4/4 and the high-performance Plus 8.

Experiments carried out with one of the engines showed that the Morgan chassis required only the minimum of alterations to accommodate it. Owen had developed a new fuel tank for use with the fuel-injected Rover Vitesse V8 engine in the Plus 8. In addition, the wiring harness, which had been developed for the more complicated electrics of the Vitesse injection system, was appropriate for this new model. The

five-speed Fiat Abarth rally car gearbox, as used in the 1600 version of the 4/4, completed the power-train.

This engine developed 122bhp, more power than was appropriate for the 4/4 designation. The company therefore decided it would revive one of the most respected models in Morgan history - the Plus 4.

However, all Fiat-engined Plus 4s registered in the UK are named as 4/4s in the log book (V5), as the model was never Type Approved. Therefore, the 'Certificates of Newness' from the factory could not carry the Plus 4 designation - although a Plus 4 cowl badge was fitted to the cars.

The revived Morgan Plus 4 was fitted with 6 inch Cobra wire wheels, with Avon tyres as standard. This made it, at the time, the only car in the world

The Fiat-engined Plus 4, based on the 1600 4/4 model, was available with either two- or four-seater bodywork.

The 2-litre Fiat engine was a tight fit under the Morgan bonnet. This is an early version with a twin-choke Weber carburettor; later models had fuel injection.

twin-cam engine fitted with a 36/38 DCOE Weber twin-choke carburettor. Later, Fiat changed the engine to fuel injection which, without much difficulty, Morgan was able to adopt as standard.

The Fiat-engined model remained in production until January 1987, when supplies of this engine and gearbox became totally unavailable, as did all spare parts. The fuel-injected version of the engine was never offered in the UK in a production Fiat.

Plus 4 Rover M16 & T16-engined M16 engine - January 1989-November 1992.
T16 engine-September 1992-To date and continuing.

Wherever possible the Morgan Motor Company has used British engines to power its three- and four-wheeler production models. It became necessary to depart from this tradition when suitable British engines were not available.

Although the Fiat-engined 4/4s and Plus 4s sold well enough, they were somehow inappropriate to a marque which is the epitome of the true British sports car.

The tradition of British engines was reinstated when the Rover Group introduced its award-winning M16 'lean burn', 16-valve, fuel-injected, 2-litre engine. The Morgan Company was able to negotiate a supply of these engines converted for 'in line' installation .

After the engines had been converted, a problem was encountered with the marriage of the engine to the Rover 75mm, five-speed gearbox, as fitted to the Plus 8. This was overcome by using Sherpa van components, primary shaft and flywheel. Modifications were made to the bell-housing, scuttle and chassis

Morgan's new dashboard, introduced in early 1990, has VDO instruments on a polished wood panel. Speedometer and rev counter are somewhat larger than in recent years, the odometer reads to six figures and, among the supplementary dials at the centre, the oil pressure gauge reads in bar.

with low profile tyres fitted to wire wheels: the wings had to be slightly widened to accommodate them. At the same time, this wider wheel and wing style was offered as an extra on the 4/ 4 models and was designated 'the Plus 4 body style'.

The first of the new models was delivered in April 1985 and, in all, 15 Plus 4s were produced with the 2-litre

crossmembers to accommodate the new engine.

Rather than create a brand new model designation for the new car, which was to be in addition to the range rather than a replacement model, it was once again decided to use Plus 4. This time the model was Type-Approved and there was no problem with registration of the cars in the UK. As Morgan said in its press release on the model, 'The Morgan Plus 4 is re-born with a British 16-valve, 2-litre engine'.

As far as I have been able to trace, no new Morgan model had ever had an official press launch before the introduction of this new model at Brands Hatch circuit on Tuesday May 3, 1988. When questioned about this at the launch, Charles Morgan said, ' Well, there have been so many rumours and stories about the new car that we thought we would use the occasion to announce that production has now started'.

The first prototype - a specially-constructed four-seater - was produced on chassis number M7, 300, registration number D955 AWP. Aluminium-bodied, the car was basically a marriage between a two- and four-seater 4/4 body. The front of the car, up to and including the modified scuttle and windscreen, was two-seater with a Plus 8 cowl; the rear a modified four-seater body. The result was a very acceptable combination, so successful it is doubtful that more than a handful of Morgan enthusiasts noticed the amalgamation. This car was finished in opalescent white, with pale blue interior, dark blue tonneau cover and a burr-wood dashboard. Peter Morgan would not agree to this body being adopted for the production four-seater as it made the car too low; the body on the production four-seater is therefore higher.

The second prototype was built on chassis number M7, 400, registration number E766 FUY. This is a two-seater which has wider wings to cover the 6 inch Cobra wire wheels now fitted as standard (this body was eventually offered as an option on the 4/4). The second prototype had a steel body and was finished in dark metallic blue, with a red interior, tonneau cover and red wire wheels.

The first production version, chassis number M7, 494, was finished in British Racing Green, with cream interior, chrome wire wheels and wooden dashboard.

The new engine was designed to minimize exhaust emissions and to

A new 16-valve Rover twin-cam engine at the works, awaiting fitment in the new Plus 4.

provide excellent fuel economy (35mpg claimed). It also accepted unleaded petrol. The combustion chamber in the aluminium head is shaped to produce a swirl effect, which maximizes the amount of fuel actually burnt. A large-bore exhaust manifold and aluminium silencer comply with the most stringent legal noise limits in Europe.

The new Plus 4 was available with either aluminium or steel bodywork, with galvanized or epoxy powder-coated chassis and fireproof vinyl or leather upholstery. Other extras available included burr-walnut or burr-ash veneer dashboard, mohair hood and tonneau cover, and a choice of no less than 30,000 different paint finish combinations.

The published price for the car on introduction was £13,500 (two-seater) and £14,500 (four-seater.) A running change from the M16 to the modified T16 series was made in autumn 1992 and by November production of the M16-engined Plus 4 ended. This was also in good time for the introduction of rules requiring three-way exhaust catalysts on all new cars from January 1993. The T16 also took the place of the M16 in Rover's 800 saloon.

When fitted with all its ancillaries the T16 engine was a lot wider than the M16. This necessitated moving it further back in the chassis which, in turn, resulted in better weight distribution. It also meant that the factory was then able to use the same chassis for both the Plus 4 and the Plus 8.

In spite of the increased engine width the overall dimensions of the bodywork remained the same but the power output was reduced slightly from 138 to 134bhp. The model is also offered with an optional 'Low Line' body, which is the same body as that previously named 'Wide Body'. If fitted with this body the car has to have low profile tyres on painted or chrome wire wheels.

By April 1993, the price of the Rover-engined two-seater Plus 4 was £19,153.

V

PLUS 8s

Plus 8
October 1968-to date and continuing

In the mid-60s it was becoming increasingly obvious that the four-cylinder Triumph TR engine was obsolescent. Standard Triumph had to develop a new engine to replace the TR series or give up the sports car section of the market.

Their answer was to design and produce a completely new six-cylinder engine for a new TR5 model. Standard Triumph gave HFS Morgan an assurance that they would continue to produce the TR4A engine for Morgan. However, it was soon clear that the comparatively small number of engines required by Morgan would make prohibitive the cost of keeping their factory tooled up. History was repeating itself, just as with the free-standing headlamps and integral radiators in 1953.

The physical size of the TR5 six-cylinder unit was such that it was completely impractical to adopt it for use in the Morgan chassis. The obvious alternative was the Ford V6, but this posed some of the same problems as the Standard Triumph unit, when offered up in the Morgan chassis - it was too tall and too heavy. Also, to use the V6 would mean that Morgan would be entirely dependent on one company for all its engine requirements, which would place the company at the mercy of Ford with regard to any price increases or conditions they might try to impose, and expose them to disruptions caused by Ford's industrial disputes.

Somehow, Morgan had to continue to produce a high-powered model, capable of maintaining the sporting tradition of the company. The search for an alternative power unit was on.

In May 1966, Peter Wilks, a director of Rover Cars Limited, made what was supposedly a social call on Peter Morgan at the Malvern factory. During the conversation, Wilks intimated that Rover would very much like to enter the sports car market, and tentatively asked if Morgan might be receptive to some sort of takeover by Rover. Thanking him for the enquiry, Peter Morgan replied that he had no intention of selling the company but if, at some time in the future, he changed his mind then he would be pleased to consider Rover's offer.

Later at the same meeting, the two men discussed the new V8 engine, for which Rover had recently acquired the rights to develop and build from Buick (General Motors). Peter Morgan had already heard and read a great deal about this V8: light and compact, it looked a possible answer to his problem but he knew that Rover had never been known to supply its engines to other motor manufacturers, so he had dismissed the idea. Seizing the opportunity, Peter Morgan tentatively suggested that he would be very interested in using the engine in a new Morgan model. To his amazement, Wilks told him that there was a distinct possibility Rover would be willing to supply.

Coincidentally, during the previous few months Maurice Owen, a motor racing engineer from nearby Upton-on-Severn, had periodically approached Peter Morgan to ask if the factory wanted any 'special' developments carried out. Each time Peter Morgan had said 'No'. However, by the time the V8 was in the offing, Morgan production capacity was almost at maximum, so they did not have the experienced staff available to take on the development of a new prototype. Peter Morgan therefore arranged an interview with Maurice Owen at the factory to discuss the basic idea with

The prototype Plus 8 had two bulges in the bonnet to allow room for the dashpots of the SU carburettors. Note the wire-spoked wheels; only three cars were fitted with these before they were introduced as an optional extra in 1993. Before the model went into production a completely new wheel design was necessary to handle the torque generated by the V8 engine.

him, decided that he was ideal for the job and invited him to join the Morgan Motor Company.

Owen's previous employers, the Laystall Racing Team, had just been wound up, so within a very short time Owen was installed in the research and development department at Morgan. In keeping with everything else in the Morgan factory, this department was a small, brick-built building at the rear of the works; no clinically-tiled workshop with the latest electronic equipment for Morgan, just an ordinary concrete floor workshop with a few storage racks and a workbench.

Owen was soon able to establish that the idea of a Morgan V8 was feasible, but further development was hampered because they had only a non-working mock-up of the Rover engine. By devious means, Morgan acquired an example of the Buick original which, with the help of Rover's engineers, was modified to bring it up as close as possible to the physical and mechanical specifications of the engine which Rover would eventually produce.

In fact, it was to be 1967 before Rover actually started production of this engine. The main difference between General Motors' Buick V8 and the Rover version was that Rover sand-

cast the engine block as opposed to die-casting, and they also stiffened the webs of the main bearings. Other minor alterations were made, but none of them had any adverse effect on Morgan's research findings. The development was conducted in the utmost secrecy, with the majority of the Morgan staff not knowing what Maurice Owen was working on.

Amazingly, few changes were needed to turn a Plus 4 chassis into a working test bed. The major modifications were to increase the width and length by 2 inches (and increase the body size by the same amount) and to replace the traditional wooden floor with a steel one which ran from the pedal board to the seat-mounting points. This effectively stiffened the chassis and meant that it would meet the new safety regulations being implemented in America.

Due to these regulations, and the size of the engine, a new type of steering column was needed; an adapted AC Delco-Saginaw collapsible column was used. Owen's team carefully sifted through the complex American legal language so that all the regulations which applied to Morgan were incorporated into the new model during the design stage - rocker-type switches,

padded dashboard, and so on.

The Moss gearbox as used on the Plus 4 was adapted to fit the engine, as was the rear axle, but it was necessary to modify the rear suspension to avoid axle tramp. Using his racing experience, Owen designed and built special bucket seats to fit the car. These are made for Morgan by Restall. To keep the costs down, Plus 4 body panels were used, so this led to the prototype having two rather sexy bulges on the top of the bonnet to allow clearance for the dashpots of the two SU carburettors. However, before production started, alterations were made which adversely affected the overall appearance of the new model.

As he had worked on the project ever since its concept without any interference from Peter Morgan, it was only fitting that the prototype Plus 8, chassis number R7000, registration number OUY 200E, should be driven by its creator, Maurice Owen, when it made its maiden drive on public roads. This was done just after midnight on the morning of February 17, 1967. Later that day Owen and Peter Morgan drove the car in the surrounding countryside and were delighted with the results: the car's handling and performance far exceeded their expectations.

This early Plus 8 dates from 1970 and is owned by John H Sheally II in America. The chromed steel bumpers were later changed to aluminium with a brushed finish.

By the end of the month the whole project was placed in jeopardy by the politics and financial manoeuvring among the big companies. Rover was in financial difficulties with the design, development, tooling-up and production of several new models, the V8, and other experimental projects, coming on top of the costly takeover of Alvis in 1965. At the end of 1966 Rover accepted an offer made by Leyland Motors to buy them out, and by March 1967 the takeover was complete.

It was inevitable that some changes in policy would occur. Obviously, one of the questions raised was the need and/or advisability of supplying the Rover V8 engine to Morgan, but this was low on the list of priorities for attention. Because of this, there was no way in which Peter Morgan would be able to launch his new model at the 1967 Motor Show, as he had hoped to do. Any attempt to force the issue with Leyland could have proved disastrous.

Whilst pondering on his next course of action, Peter Morgan received an invitation to lunch with Harry Webster, the technical director of Standard Triumph of Coventry (Standard Triumph having been taken over by Leyland Motors in 1961). After lunch, he was given a conducted tour of the Triumph engine factory, and was shown the complete range, including the new V8 engine which was being developed for the Stag. The tour completed, Peter was asked if he would be interested in adopting any of the engines for use in a new Morgan model. Having carried out all the research and development of the Rover unit, he told Standard Triumph that he wished to continue with it - provided that he could get a supply of engines.

Within a few weeks of this visit, Peter Morgan was asked to go and see Sir George Farmer, financial controller of Leyland Motors, who informed him that, without permission from General Motors, Morgan could not use the Rover version of the V8. By enlisting the aid of a Plus 4 owner who happened to be on the board of directors of General Motors, Peter Morgan was granted the necessary permission within weeks. However, this speedy response was not matched by that from Leyland, who further delayed the decision on supplying the engine. The whole business had reached an impasse ...

By October, Peter Morgan realized that unless he took some direct action, Leyland Motors management would continue to leave the matter in abeyance. With his usual astuteness, he invited Harry Webster and George

Plus 8 chassis mounted on trestles, with engines, rear axles and other components ready for assembly. The chassis on the right has a galvanized finish, now offered as an option by the Morgan works.

*Plus 8 engines and transmissions
waiting to be assembled at the
Morgan works.*

Turnbull of Triumph-Rover (by this time the two companies were working closely together as a result of the reorganization after the takeover) to the Morgan factory. Here, he gave them both demonstrations of, and allowed them to drive, the prototype Plus 8. The strategy worked and, before they left, both Webster and Turnbull gave assurances that the original agreement between Rover and Morgan was definitely on and that supplies of the engine would start immediately after the launch of the Rover 3.5 model in April 1968.

Immediately after that an intensive development programme was begun under the direction of Maurice Owen. The factory was prepared for the manufacture of the new model. Several improvements were implemented as a result of the information they had gathered from the prototype. They concluded that the tremendous performance required far better stopping power; a more powerful servo-assisted braking system was developed and installed.

Because of the increased fuel consumption of the larger engine, a bigger fuel tank had to be accommodated. The car was far too powerful to be run on spoked wheels although, of course, the first prototype did, so for the production cars cast alloy wheels were designed. So that the car conformed to the new US regulations, it was necessary to incorporate a more complex electrical system. This included such items as an alternator, twin spotlights, three windscreen wipers and hazard warning lights.

All these items were incorporated into the next two experimental cars. The first was chassis number R7001, registration number MMC 11, which was Peter Morgan's personal car, and which is now in the Heritage Motor

Museum at Syon Park near London. The second was chassis number R7002, registration number AB 16 (which is now on Peter Morgan's personal Ferrari); it was eventually sold to Peter's son-in-law, Lord Colwyn. For many years Maurice Owen used the original prototype as his personal transport, but eventually it was sold to America.

Unbelievable as it may seem, the total development cost of the most powerful model ever produced by Morgan did not exceed £14,000. Add to this the cost of stocking and preparing the factory and we arrive at a figure of about £40,000. There can be no realistic comparison between this figure and the millions spent by major companies in developing a new model.

Before the V8 was officially announced in October at the 1968 Earls Court Motor Show, the prototypes had been loaned to the motoring press for appraisal. Their reports appeared in the issues published to coincide with the Motor Show. The new car received some exciting headlines: 'A true but primitive sports car' (*Motor Sport*); 'New for '69 - Vee-8 Morgan, powerful Rover engine in traditional Morgan' (*Autocar*). Of them all, the one that I liked the most was the one word title used by Michael Bowler who, at that time, was writing for *Motor* - 'Transmogrification'. It means, 'to transform in a magical or surprising manner'. How true! Of all the models introduced by the Morgan

Motor Company, none has been so startlingly different in performance as the Plus 8.

Plus 8 Sports Lightweight
October 1975 - January 1977

In January 1974 Rover had to reduce the compression ratio of their V8 engines, due to new emission control regulations in Europe which, of course, adversely affected the Morgan Plus 8. The reduction meant that the power output dropped from 160bhp to 143bhp in stages as the compression ratio was lowered: initially 10:1 (5-star fuel); then 9.5:1 (155bhp); then 9.25:1 (143bhp). The latter had a drastic affect on the Plus 8's performance.

Meanwhile, owners of aluminium-bodied Plus 8s (aluminium bodies had been offered as an option for several years), who wished to enter Production Sports Car races, were failed by the scrutineers. This was because the bodies were only available at extra cost and therefore did not meet the requirements of the class regulations.

In an attempt to improve the performance of the revised engine, the Morgan factory introduced the Sports Lightweight model. The new model was bodied entirely in aluminium except for the scuttle and cowl, and this made the car considerably lighter. To reduce the overall height, and to facilitate the use of a larger variety of tyres, 14 inch diameter wheels were fitted. To provide

The prototype fuel-injection-engined Plus 8 outside the Morgan factory.

room for the 6 inch rims of the new wheels, it was necessary to widen the wings. The track was therefore increased to 4ft 4in at the front and 4ft 5in at the rear. All these modifications helped to return the Plus 8's performance near to original.

The Sports Lightweight was introduced at the Motor Show in October 1975 and was offered at the same price as the normal Plus 8, so removing any doubts a scrutineer may have had about extra costs. Although production ended in January 1977, the model had by this time been produced in sufficient quan-

tity to qualify under the second part of the competition regulations, which cover minimum production numbers. When the production of this model ended, the aluminium body was retained and

adopted as standard for all side and rear panels on normal production Plus 8s.

During the 15 months of the Sports Lightweight's production, Rover had

The Plus 8 Sports Lightweight was fitted with a roll-over bar as standard. The 'Revolution' one-piece wheels are a works approved alternative. The bumpers are not original, and are colour-coded (black) to the car. The original bumpers had a curved section and were fitted with overriders.

The 14-inch diameter wheels were fitted to reduce the height, and the wings widened to make room for the 6-inch rims and the increase in front and rear tracks.

The facia of the Sports Lightweight is based on the normal layout but with a rev counter immediately in front of the driver. As this car was raced, an oil temperature gauge was fitted to the right of the facia and a 'deadman's switch' electrical cut-out is located on the far right.

carried out extensive modifications to their engines in an attempt to re-establish the engine's original power output. This, coupled with the fitting of two specially-designed four-branch exhausts with an extra resonator on each, helped to reduce noise levels, and the power was put back up to 155bhp.

With the introduction of the uprated engine (Rover SD1), production of the Sports Lightweight ended. Although only 19 were produced, the model had served its purpose well.

Plus 8 Four-seater & Drop Head Coupé Automatic

At the time of writing, at least four examples of the four-seater Plus 8 exist but only one of them was produced at the factory. It was built as a works experiment and as a special favour for Eric White of Allon White & Son (Cranfield) Ltd, a Morgan main agent.

The other cars were constructed by or for their owners and at least one of them is as a result of a rear-end accident.

The factory-produced Plus 8 four-seater is far more than just a graft of a 4/4 four-seater body on to a Plus 8 chassis. The changes in specifications include a larger fuel tank, larger seats (which were fixed) and changes to the rear timbers, bulkhead and the steering shaft measurements. It is also fitted with twin-servo, twin-circuit brakes.

When it was completed, the works found that there were three main rea-

The only works-produced Plus 8 four-seater was built experimentally and was subsequently sold to a Morgan main agent for personal use. The wide-section tyres and tow bar contribute to the unfamiliar appearance.

Another unique Morgan is this automatic transmission Plus 8 Drop Head Coupé which, again, was built as an experiment. After extensive testing it was decided not to put the car into production because of potential limited demand and because the extra weight adversely affected performance. This car has since been used as Mrs Jane Morgan's personal transport. The registration number is JM 53. Here, it is seen at the works undergoing repairs after being involved in an accident.

sons for not putting either this or the other experimental car, the automatic-transmission Drop Head Coupé, into production. (The Drop Head Coupé is still owned by the company and used exclusively by Mrs Jane Morgan, Peter Morgan's first wife). First, by introducing another variation to the range it would have meant a reduction in production (a four-seater taking longer to produce) at a time when the factory was keen to maximize production to help reduce the long customer waiting lists.

Secondly, a four-seater model would have to be a compromise in handling characteristics because, whenever a third or fourth passenger was carried, much more of the weight would be over the rear wheels. Although not so critical in the 4/4 model, the greatly increased power and torque of the Plus 8 caused the balance of the car to change with the passenger load.

Finally. it was obvious that there would be only a limited demand for such cars and that sales could not

justify the cost involved.

Although perfectly legal at the time of production, the Drop Head Coupé was constructed with front-opening (rear-hinged) doors, which regulations no longer permit. This problem has been overcome by Morgan restorer Bob Harper who, with the co-operation of the factory, has designed and built a Plus 8 Drop Head Coupé with conventional front-hinged doors.

Morgan Plus 8 injection two-seater Drop Head Coupé. This car offers the combination of a new Plus 8 Injection engine and the older coupé body style used by Morgans during the 1950s and 1960s. The Morgan Motor Company supplied a rolling chassis, rebuilt from a 1971 Plus 8. It was then stripped again, virtually all items were sandblasted and powder coated, and then reassembled using stainless steel fasteners. The engine was stripped and bored to 3.9-litres and uprated to 240bhp, all this work being undertaken by J.E. Motors of Coventry. The wooden bodyframe was designed and built by Harpers and all the main bodywork carried out by Syd Cochrane of Harpers restoration. The bodyframe was completely panelled in aluminium.

The main difference between this coupé and the older models is in the use of later instrumentation and interior design, this coupé being fitted with de-misters, a fresh-air heater, two-speed wipers and all Plus instrumentation. The biggest difference is in the door construction; all other Morgan coupés are rear-hinged whereas Bob Harper's car has its doors hinged on the front pillar, a particularly difficult task as the front pillar slopes at 70 degrees.

Bob Harper's next project is to build a Plus 8 Injection four-seater coupé for his expanding family.

Above & top right: Beneath a lockable flap the narrow-neck petrol filler leads to a small pipe on an experimental Plus 8 being exported to America for Bill Fink in 1989. The car was fitted with a low-compression Rover Eagle 3.9-litre lean-burn engine.

The interior of the experimental car; the many modifications included new-type screen washers.

Morgan

VI

RESTORATION, PREPARATION & PRACTICAL TIPS

Before undertaking any of the practical work described in this chapter it is essential to read the safety and working procedure notes in this chapter and those given as an appendix to this book.

It is not my intention to deal with the dismantling and reassembly of every small part of all Morgan models, a task which would fill several books. Instead, I will confine myself to useful general methods, highlight common pitfalls and advise on the standard of finish for which an owner should aim.

Restoration is not a task to undertake without a lot of thought about what is involved. How many times does one come across an advertisement which reads: 'For sale ... insufficient time to restore', or, 'insufficient funds force sale'? Basically, one has to consider (a) the work involved, (b) the time involved, (c) the space required, (d) whether you are capable of carrying out the work or obtaining assistance from specific firms and, (e) can you afford the costs involved? If, having considered all these points, you still want to go ahead, I advise you to read and study every available book on the subject before you begin.

Remember, too, that a successful restoration job has invariably benefited from (a) a firm plan of action (b) patience (c) a tolerant partner (d) willing and reasonably strong friends to assist when required (e) the will to succeed against all setbacks (f) ample working and storage space (g) a good camera or an ability to sketch accurately (h) good tools of the right size (i) an electric drill (j) electric lighting and power points in the garage/workshop.

Safety - general
Whilst on the subject of accidents when restoring, never work under a car that is jacked off the ground without using axle stands. Never attempt to lift something by yourself that is too heavy or awkward for you. Always use protective clothing and, where necessary, masks and goggles. Always ensure that your power points really are power points and are correctly earthed. Check all power tools, inspection lights, etc, and ensure that they have good wiring and that they, too, are properly earthed. Never smoke or allow others to smoke in or near the garage, workshop or place where you are working. Always read, and read again, the manufacturer's instructions on any product you use and obey them. Always store inflammable material and products well away from the garage and the house.

Personal safety
Service work can be a very satisfying experience, but it can also become a hazard if procedures are not followed in a responsible manner. There is absolutely no place for poor workmanship; lives are endangered by slipshod procedures. If you are not willing or able to do the best work on your vehicle, leave it to someone else.

Store petrol in approved containers and use it only for its intended use as fuel; it is not a cleaning fluid. Store it in an outbuilding a way from your work area. Locate a fire extinguisher of the foam or carbon dioxide type (in a handy location in your garage) so that it can be used for petrol or oil fires. Make sure it works. If you are going to run a vehicle indoors, see that you have a flexible pipe connected to the exhaust and vented to the outdoors. Carbon monoxide is a silent and deadly killer; if you feel at all drowsy, get out into the fresh air.

• JACKS
Jacking up the car is probably more the cause of serious injury than anything else. Jacks - bumper, hydraulic, bottle - are for raising the car and nothing else: if you need to get under the car use axle stands standing on concrete.

Once the car is up on the stands, push it a couple of times to be sure it is solid. Driving the car up onto ramps is another good way to raise it, as long as you do not have to remove the wheels. This is about as secure as you can get, but be careful driving up; 'slow and easy' is the message here. When two wheels are off the floor, block the others to prevent the car from rolling.

• UNDER THE BONNET
Fans and fan belts are dangerous, not only to fingers but also to anything hanging in the vicinity, like cords from inspection lamps, timing lights and jump cables, not to forget loose clothing.

Both radiators and exhaust manifolds can cause serious burns and spark plug and coil wires, while not likely to do permanent damage, will certainly bite. Batteries can explode! When using jump leads, connect to the dead battery first, then to the positive side of the good battery. Finally, connect the negative terminal as far from the dead battery as possible.

• EYES
When grinding or buffing, use a face shield or safety glasses. This sort of protection will prevent not only dirt from getting into your eyes but also battery acid, brake fluid, coolant and gasoline and is an excellent habit to get into when working around cars.

• BATTERY
Do not smoke when working in the engine compartment; the battery produces explosive gases which can cause an explosion. It is a good idea to disconnect the battery earth strap when working under the bonnet.

The battery electrolyte can cause serious skin and eye burns, so use rubber gloves and eye protection. If you do come into contact with this acid, flush with cold water and then neutralize with a mixture of baking soda and water. Do the same for battery acid on the car's finish.

If you remove the battery from the car, do not store it on the cement floor but on a shelf where it will not be knocked over or exposed to sparks or flames.

• TOOLS
Keep your tools clean and in good condition. Worn sockets, for instance, can lead to very sore knuckles when they slip. Greasy tools do the same. Replace worn and broken tools and try to use the right tool for the job (when needed, the closest tool always becomes a hammer!)

• YOURSELF
The most important safety item is YOU! Slow down and think, 'If I do this, how many different things can happen? If any of these things do happen, will the result cause me injury?' Be safety conscious all the time and remember that accidents can happen to you and not just someone else. With just a bit of planning and foresight, you can enjoy service work. Remember the ABC - **A**lways **B**e **C**areful.

• GARAGE DOORS
If you have ever had a garage door spring break then you know the power involved. Run a light steel cable through the middle of the new spring to prevent a repeat performance. A friend once used heavy electrical wire but it snapped with the spring. Use steel cable securely fastened with clamps at both ends and eliminate the risk of a lot of grief.

• ACIDS
Do not use acids to remove rust from critical heat-treated parts such as axles, spindles, springs, etc, because of the danger of hydrogen embrittlement. And, for goodness sake, never use the old Pyrene fire extinguishers: carbon tetrachloride plus an open flame creates deadly phosgene gas.

• FIRST AID
Have a fully-stocked first aid kit readily available in the garage so that you can treat burns and cuts immediately. Know what it contains and how to use it. Always remember to replace used items.

Preparation for restoration
Before dismantling, some careful photography can save you hours of work at a later stage. It is advisable to take as many photographs - or make sketches of the car and its components - as possible, which should be taken from every angle to assist with correct reassembly. Photographs should also be taken at every stage of dismantling. Remember to make a list of the photos as they are taken and do so in a logical sequence. If possible, try to locate a member of the specialist club who has an identical model; most owners will be only too happy to allow you to take a series of photographs of their car and to

give you various tips (some good, some bad ...). If possible, take these photographs in the same sequence as those of your own car; this will assist you when making comparisons.

Next, ensure that you have ample boxes and containers to store the components and nuts and bolts from each particular section. You will also need labels to mark the containers; the self-adhesive type which can be purchased in most newsagents or deep-freeze centres are ideal. Remember to stick them on the side that will face forward when placed on shelves, not on the lid, as invariably there will be another container on top of the one you need.

Before you begin stripping components, be sure the car is situated in such a way that when it comes to removing the body you can do so without first having to remove the garage roof! Another common fault is to remove the wheels first which, of course, restricts every other job that requires changing the position of the car.

Dismantling

It is advisable first to dismantle the car into the minimum number of sections, each of which should be left complete until such time as you are ready to concentrate on that section by further dismantling, then cleaning, making good, painting and reassembling the various components.

Start by removing the spare wheel(s) and vulnerable parts like mirrors, headlamps, headlamp bar, side lamps, pass light, rear light and number plates - anything, in fact, that can easily be damaged. Remember to label the wiring so that you can identify it later and, if possible, disconnect wires at snap connectors. In general, first off is last on, so take care to store these items in a safe place where they cannot be damaged by other pieces falling on them.

Next, the windscreen, complete with wipers and motor (where applicable). This is best stored in the loft, under the bed or in the blanket chest. The most difficult section of the car, as far as handling and storing is concerned, is the bonnet, which should now be removed. The best method is to free both ends from their fixing points, then apply a liberal amount of penetrating oil to the centre hinge, no matter which type is used on your car. If it is the centre pin type, hammer it with a brass punch from one end and, as soon as enough appears the other end to get a grip with the mole wrench, slowly remove the pin by twisting it first one way, then the other. The centre looped spine type can be removed in the same manner, but care must be taken to avoid crimping the rolled edges. The bonnet is then in two manageable sections. A point arises here as to whether one should remove the bonnet fasteners ready to be sent off with other parts for re-chroming. From experience I have found it is better to send only a small number of pieces at a time to the plating works to minimize the chances of losing small but valuable parts. Therefore, leave them on until you are ready to work on the bonnet. This, too, should be stored in a safe place as the panels are very easily dented or bent; one suggestion is to secure them over the rafters of the garage.

Then comes removal of the radiator. First, drain it by removing the drain tap at the bottom, replacing the tap as soon as draining is completed. Unless you are extremely lucky, the hoses will have become vulcanized to inlet and outlet pipes. The best method is to put a hacksaw through the hoses (not the stubs!); at least then you are not tempted to put them back on when you replace the radiator, only to find they are cracked or that they burst as soon as you refill the cooling system with water. Store in a safe place (under the spare bed again?)

Wings and running boards are the next items for removal. First jack the side of the car to be worked on and insert axle stands front and rear as a safety precaution. Next, remove the front and rear wheels but do not store them as they are going back on again. Follow the line of fixing screws along the wing edge and remove every other one, repeating this until all the screws are removed. If they are very rusty, they can be removed by careful use of a chisel. Replace the wheels, remove the axle stands and jack and lift the other side, repeating the complete operation.

All seats and carpets can now be removed, and this is an ideal time to take the battery out, too. Unless it is fairly new, make no attempt to save it, but if it is new, try to use it whilst the restoration is carried out; if it is to be of any use to you afterwards it must be charged and discharged regularly.

When dismantling any component always remember to replace the nut on the bolt from which it came, and wherever possible replace the bolt in its corect hole. This way, when it comes to putting everything back together you will know the correct size of bolt required should the original bolt need replacing.

Body removal

Before the body is removed be sure that it is completely free of all encumbrances. For example, the petrol fillers should be disconnected and, dependent upon which model you are restoring, the method will vary; a close examination of the filler and how it connects to the fuel tank will reveal the easiest way. It is not essential to drain the fuel tank at this stage as the drain plug is situated on the base of the tank, but whether or not you drain it you must plug the filler hole of the tank. Follow the fuel lines leading to the fuel pump and if these are fastened to the body by clips they should be disconnected.

The wiring should be cut away or disconnected and the ends marked appropriately. A new loom is by far the best course of action as there is no easy way of establishing the condition of the insulation throughout the whole system.

Next to be dealt with are the bulkhead and dashboard. If it is possible to detach them from the body it is better to do so; to be able to work on the wiring and other instrument connections without the encumbrance of the body is so much easier and quicker. On some models, where the dashboard is a part of the body, it may be necesary to remove the steering wheel and steering column before attempting to lift the body.

Check the whole body to see that nothing is attached to or passing through any part of it which would hinder or prevent the body removal from the chassis. If everything is clear, locate and loosen the nuts holding the body to the chassis. More than likely some of the nuts will be rusty and the coach bolts will turn with their nuts. There are several ways of dealing with this. First, give the bolts a good soaking with penetrating oil, then try tapping the head of the coach bolt further into the wood. However, if the nut is very rusty the whole thing will probably still turn. Another method is to cut a slot in

the head of the coach bolt, wide and deep enough to take a screwdriver, but by far the best solution is to saw through the nut at the side or straight down the centre of the bolt, cutting the nut in half. In this way you avoid damaging the wood or metal behind the nut. If the nut is held in place by a split-pin as well, another alternative is to drill through the head of the coach bolt and use a tool of the 'Easyout' type to hold it. This type of tool is a tapered left-hand coarse tap made of hardened steel and can be supplied in different sizes; provided you drill the pilot hole to the correct size and hold the tool in a tap wrench it will grip nearly any rusted bolt. It is also invaluable for getting out broken bolts and studs. As a last resort, a sharp chisel and a 2lb hammer works wonders. If the last method is adopted, care must be taken to chisel on the nut side of the chassis, not at the end against the wooden frame. Always try to split the nut, rather than cut the bolt.

Now, after a final check, you are ready to remove the body. Firstly, obtain the assistance of four friends, one for each corner of the body (it is possible to lift the body with two people, but four is safer). Make sure that you have already prepared sufficient space in which to store the body and that access to the storage space has also been cleared: there is nothing worse than lifting the body, not knowing which way to move and then one of your helpers dropping and damaging his corner in the confusion. It will be a great help if you can arrange for the body to be rested across three or four trestles about 3ft to 3ft 6in in height. This saves moving the body again and is a convenient working height. While your assistants are manhandling the body, your own task should be to give them clear, positive instruc-

tions and, at the same time, adjust the position of the trestles so that the body will rest on them squarely, securely and correctly balanced. Having done this, you can then move on to removal of the flooring.

Marking components
I think at this point I should devote a paragraph or two to the marking of relative parts. There are two methods frequently used but neither is good practice and, where possible, should be avoided. The first is differing numbers of centre punch marks and the second hacksaw blade marks. Recently I assisted a friend in restoring a 1930 Lagonda and marking the place from where the halfshafts had been drawn was a total of 18 centre punch marks on both surfaces. It took some time to count them all, and just to help matters the opposite side had 17 punch marks. The simplest and cheapest method is to invest in a set of letter and number stamps, which may still be useful when you have completed the restoration; a set embracing A-Z and 0-9 provides you with a huge number of permutations.

First of all, ask yourself whether a particular part needs to be marked at all. If it does, then be sure to select a point for your punch where the component is least stressed. Also avoid placing it too close to the edge of a flange, as it will raise the metal on the face and you will spend hours trying to obtain a perfect mating surface; never allow a punch mark to spoil a working surface. By all means use the letter or number punches when necessary, but remember there are very few components that require such marking; masking tape of suitable size is ideal for the remainder.

Cleaning components

Most people restoring cars seem to want to remove the accumulated oil and grease from components as soon as possible, but this is not a good idea as the covering can be an effective rust preventer. Only degrease a particular part when you are ready to start work on restoring it. The same may be said about draining the engine, gearbox and rear axle: leave them until you are ready to work on them.

Most areas of the country these days are covered by a travelling steam-degreasing company; they are not unduly expensive and can completely degrease a rolling chassis in under two hours. Before deciding to use such a service it is, of course, advisable to ensure that you have somewhere accessible where you can roll the chassis and where the resulting mess will not cause total war with your wife or neighbours!

The easiest manual method to adopt is to first scrape with an old knife or paint scraper and then, using an old paint brush, liberally apply paraffin (not petrol), washing off with a pressure hose or wiping off with an old rag. It cannot be over-emphasized how much care must be taken when working with petrol, paraffin, cellulose and any other preparations which have a high flash-point. I remember someone who for three years spent every minute of his spare time restoring his car. The time arrived to attempt to start it but, try as he might, it just would not fire. He then obtained some ether-based 'Easy Start' solution, but liberal applications of this in the carburettor still did not obtain the desired result. Meanwhile, unbeknown to him, one of the petrol feed unions was leaking. He then removed a plug and earthed it by holding it against

the block, turning the engine over to check the spark. There was a spark! Result - his car, garage and workshop were completely destroyed and he spent nearly two years in hospital. You just cannot be too careful.

Paint removal

Chemical paint removers, of course, are convenient to use in the garage. However, chemical paint removers do not deal with rust, which will require special treatment, first with a wire brush (hand or powered) and then with rust inhibitors, although from experience I have found that no matter how thorough you are, somehow you never manage to remove all the rust. If you can afford to have the part sand-blasted you will save a lot of time and end up with a far more efficient job (if your classified telephone directory cannot help, remember that specialist service firms are often listed or advertised in car enthusiasts' magazines). However, this treatment is not recommended for Morgan body panels, due to the distortions which can be created by the process. By far the best way is to have the part chemically and professionally stripped in caustic soda vats, which is not nearly as expensive as you may think.

Replacement of worn or broken parts

To the amateur, this is the most worrying part of restoration, especially if he has no skills with a lathe or other machines. This is where the help of the specialist clubs can be so useful.

Most clubs have a spares register (the Morgan Sports Car Club being no exception), whose job is to locate new or secondhand spares and arrange for the special manufacture of otherwise unobtainable parts, providing there is

sufficient demand from club members. When you discover a worn or broken part, do not panic; if you are restoring a Morgan you will find that the vast majority of parts can be replaced with the help of the spares registrar or by companies who specialize in Morgans.

Other sources of supply are the numerous autojumbles which are so much a part of the classic car scene nowadays; not so many years ago an almost complete Coventry-Climax engine came my way for £35: it is amazing what can be found.

For the location of parts, services and materials covering all aspects of car restoration, I can also recommend the *Directory of Specialist Firms and Services* published by the British magazine *Classic Cars*.

Body panels that are damaged can be dealt with by a motor body shop that specializes in accident repairs, while damaged ash frames can be entrusted to any good carpenter and joiner, although in some cases the Morgan Motor Company may still have replacements in stock. Boat builders, of course, are a good source of well-seasoned ash for the frame and can also supply marine standard plywood for floors, scuttles, etc.

Restoration standards

No matter how much is written on a practical subject, there can be no substitute for experience. Remember that in restoring your car you will require skills in which, like as not, you have had little, if any, previous experience. By comparison the car manufacturer, or the professional restoration company is fortunate; they tend to employ people for various individual aspects of the job, which they do day-in, day-out, having first been taught their particular

Morgan

trade by highly-skilled colleagues.

Do not be deterred by lack of experience. Amazing results have been obtained by sheer determination, hard work and patience. In offering the advice which follows I hasten to add that I do not see myself as an expert, nor do I claim that my advice is always based on the accepted correct way of tackling a particular job. But at least it is the result of watching and talking to talented experts; in applying their techniques, my own restoration work has led to many concours successes.

No matter what material you are working with - wood, metal, paint - the following basic rules must apply: (a) there are no short cuts; (b) never rush, no matter how slow you are or how long it takes to achieve a good standard; (c) never settle for second best; (d) have in your mind's eye the standard you are attempting to achieve; (e) never lose patience with a particular job: if you feel you are doing so, leave it and return to it later. There is always plenty of other work to be done.

Before dealing with specific methods and materials, I think I should point out that over-restoring is just as bad as under-restoring. Do not have parts chromium-plated or polished if, when the car left the works new, they were painted. Examples of over-restoration are chromium-plated exhaust manifolds and downpipes which were never chromium-plated when new; radiator header and floorboards made of mahogany or sapelia and then French-polished top and bottom. Chromium-plated steering gear is another popular example of 'restoring' a car to a finish it didn't have in the first place.

Paintwork
The question of whether to have the chassis, wheels, steering parts, rear axle, etc, stove-enamelled is a thorny one. If it is well done it produces a marvellous finish, but should it subsequently become chipped it can never be touched-in to look correct. Also, if stone chips go unnoticed, rust will spread under the enamelling. There is also the question of cost - stove-enamelling is not cheap.

On the other hand, really good finishes can be obtained using brushed-on coach paint or sprayed cellulose paint, providing you are patient and rub down well with varying grades of wet-or-dry abrasive paper between each coat. Whilst on the subject of rubbing-down paintwork, remember to use a rubbing-down pad or block for the wet-or-dry, also to continually rinse the paper to prevent clogging.

In an effort to remove a lot of the tedium of the job of painting a chassis and other so-called 'blackwork', a professional restorer will often use a twin-pack acrylic commercial vehicle chassis paint. First the chassis is cleaned and shot-blasted, then etch-primed and sprayed with a high-build primer. This is hand rubbed to a reasonably flat finish and then sprayed with the two-pack acrylic paint which gives a high-gloss finish comparable to any obtained by the usual slow and laborious methods. The more up-to-date method is to have the 'blackwork' epoxy powder-coated, which is the modern alternative to wet paint stove-enamelling. In this process, the part is electrically charged to become polarized and is then sprayed with minute plastic particles which have the opposite charge. Because opposite poles attract, the part becomes completely covered with an even coating of the powder. The part is then baked to provide a finish which, beside being very good-looking, is also very durable and chip-resistant. The process uses a wide range of plastics, epoxies, polyesters and polyurethanes, depending on the part to be coated. It can be carried out in a wide range of colours and finishes, including full gloss, matt, plain and metallic.

When painting the bodywork, start by applying several coats of rust inhibitor before using a filler coat. When you have applied the filler coat, cover it completely with a very thin coat of matt black, then rub it down gently. In this way you will discover all the high and low spots which must be dealt with before you go on to the primer and colour coats. Small indentations can be dealt with by using cellulose stopper which, when hardened, is rubbed down level with the surrounding metal or paint surface. Larger dents which cannot be reached by a panel-beater can be filled with plumber's lead; any plumber should be able to do the job for you if you cannot yourself. High spots, depending on size, can be flattened with the aid of a rubber mallet applied either to the spot or, if it is large, from the outer edges of the high spot, working towards the middle. Remember to hold a supporting pad or block to the underside of the metal and do not strike it too heavily.

Brass and copper
This should first be cleaned with fine wire wool and then polished with metal polish until all scratch marks disappear. Always renew any old brittle or badly-dented brass or copper tubing; nothing looks worse than a copper pipe wound in a close spiral, or bent to accommodate a change of direction, on which the bends have become flattened. Any good tool shop can supply bending springs

which will avoid this.

Another solution is to anneal the pipe by heating to a cherry red and plunging it into cold water, which will soften the metal. Then block one end of the pipe with a small cork and fill the pipe with sand and seal. The bends can then be made without fear of flats being formed. When finished, empty out the sand and wash the pipe thoroughly under running water to ensure that not a single particle is left inside; blowing out with compressed air is insufficient as the sand tends to stick to the walls of the pipe.

Aluminium finishes

It is possible to obtain a finish on aluminium that can be mistaken for chromium-plating, but it involves hours of work. It is advantageous, wherever possible, to remove the part and work on it on a bench or table. The final finish that can be obtained must, by necessity, depend on the condition of the aluminium before you begin. Oxidized aluminium will have small pinhead-size holes over the surface. The depth of these will vary greatly, and the number that can be removed is largely dependent upon the thickness of the metal. It is better to leave some of the holes rather than reduce the thickness to such a level that the casting becomes fragile.

If the metal is in poor condition, begin by lightly filing the casting and then progress to the gentle use of engineer's scrapers. Then, by the use of emery cloth of diminishing grades of coarseness, or wet-or-dry paper impregnated with liquid metal polish, continue the polishing until you reach the desired standard. Care should be taken at all times to follow as closely as possible the grain of the metal. When you have achieved the standard required,

polish finally with a small amount of metal polish such as 'Autosol' and shine with a soft duster.

Some castings should not be polished at all, particularly on sides exposed to the weather, such as the bottom of the sump. With these parts simply remove the forge marks by fettling with files and scrapers and finish off by wiping with a clean rag soaked in petrol (taking all necessary precautions to avoid a fire and skin contamination).

Pieces such as the base of SU petrol pumps, AC mechanical petrol pumps and carburettors look far better with a satin finish. This is best obtained by having them lightly bead-blasted, which has the added advantage of getting clean all those little crevices that are so hard to reach. Bead-blasting can also produce very good results on the exposed castings mentioned in the previous paragraph.

Remember that the largest proportion of any charge in connection with outside work is labour; therefore do as much preparatory work as you can before sending the part to a specialist firm.

Dashboard

The hardest part of dashboard restoration is obtaining the right type of well-seasoned timber. Boat-builders, timber yards and even undertakers are possible sources, but by far the cheapest way may be to visit auctions, house contents sales, or secondhand furniture dealers. It may take a little searching but you should find an old table, chest of drawers, bookcase, or even an old wooden fireplace surround. Any of these can usually be bought for a small sum, and by careful selection you will find a piece of ash, oak, teak, walnut or some

other hardwood which is well-seasoned and can be cut to the size you require. However, be sure to inspect the item carefully before you buy it; woodworm, rot or cracks must be avoided for obvious reasons.

Having found your piece of wood, strip off the old paint or varnish - this can be done with any proprietary brand of chemical paint remover but be careful to scrape the old varnish off without damaging the wood. Then cut out the oblong you require and, using the remains of the old dashboard as a template, carefully mark out the exact shape you need. If the dashboard is missing completely, here is one of the instances when your photographic or sketching ability comes in handy. Having marked out the correct shape, and using an electric jigsaw, carefully cut round your marked-out shape, remembering to cut outside the line. The average saw cut is 0.12in-0.19in thick, and if you follow your marked line you will be that much out in the size you require.

The next stage is to cut the various holes, but always practise on a spare piece of wood before beginning work on the actual dashboard. If you think that you are unable to carry out this work, a carpenter or joinery shop should be able to tackle it for you. Also, they can usually be persuaded to machine-sand the surfaces for you, even if you have cut the shape yourself. This can save you hours of rubbing-down with sand-paper of diminishing grades of coarseness to achieve a good finish.

Next comes the staining, which can be done with wood dyes obtainable at most hardware stores. However, by far the cheapest method is to buy a few pence worth of permanganate of potash from your chemist, which is mixed into a thin paste and applied with a pad made of cotton wool about 2 inches square. Apply the paste using a gentle circular motion and, having covered the wood, allow to dry thoroughly before gently rubbing down with very fine sandpaper. (When staining it is advisable to wear a pair of old rubber kitchen gloves to avoid staining your hands). Repeat if necessary until you obtain the desired colour.

The next stage is to paint the wood with a half-and-half mixture of white spirit and clear polyurethane varnish. Allow to dry thoroughly and then rub down well with fine sandpaper. The next coat should be undiluted polyurethane clear varnish. Two coats should be sufficient, but however many coats you use remember to rub down well with fine sandpaper between each one. The final coat should be left for several days before any other type of polishing is carried out. In practice, I have found that the finish obtained is so good that extra polishing is quite unnecessary.

The metal base of the dashboard is easiest made from 16-18 gauge aluminium sheeting, which must be polished, matt-finished or painted, according to the original specification of your car. A useful tip to remember when working with new aluminium rolled section, be it flat sheet, rounded or angled, is to wipe over with 'Jenolite' before polishing or painting. The reason is that part of the process of manufacture is to cover the rollers with lanolin. The 'Jenolite' removes this and leaves the surface clean. Castings of the same metal should not require this treatment as lanolin is not used in the manufacturing process. Some aluminium sheeting is coated with a plastic film before it leaves the factory; it is usually light blue in colour and can be removed with the aid of the manufacturer's recommended solvent.

Exhaust systems
Regardless of the type of finish you require, the only effective method to obtain the correct prepared surface is sand-blasting, which removes all the rust and old finishes, not only from the flat surfaces, but also from all the small indentations which will never be reached using a wire brush, even if it is powered.

The types of finishes vary from vitreous enamelling to brush-painted exhaust paints. In my opinion one of the best finishes is provided by using a VHT paint which is obtainable from most automobile paint shops. This is the paint that was developed for the re-entry module on all the manned moon rockets, which is capable of withstanding heat far in excess of anything that your engine will produce. However, one of its disadvantages is that if the system is sand-blasted before the paint is applied (it is supplied in aerosol form) it must be baked on. Although this can be done by running the engine, the result is usually unsatisfactory, and if you cannot find a company with a kiln the best method is to use a butane gas blow-lamp (not a paraffin lamp, as this leaves stains). Heat the system all over, slowly raising the temperature until it is red hot (dull cherry red), and then allow to cool. It is also advisable to apply the spray as best you can to the inside of the system as well.

Once it has been baked on, it protects the system very effectively from the ravages of the weather and road salts. It also has the capability of being restored back to its original colour by a hard brushing with a nail or scrubbing brush soaked in washing-up liquid, rinsed off with water, which should be done when the system is cold. A word of warning: most VHT paints are soluble in paraffin, even after they have been heat-cured. A more lasting and, arguably, better finish can be obtained by having the system 'aluminized' after sand-blasting and the VHT paint then baked on.

Whilst on the subject of exhaust systems, one must mention that stainless steel exhausts are now being supplied by various after-market manufacturers. There is a great deal to be said for them and they should not be dismissed without investigation. Originally, they were rather expensive, but now, in many cases, they are actually cheaper than the factory mild steel units.

The question of chromium-plating the manifold, *etc*, must be considered but, again, this is very expensive and has the tendency to 'blue'. In respect of originality, only a very few Morgans were ever supplied with such a 'luxury' as this; they were mainly the four-branch manifolds as fitted to the TT and Le Mans Replicas.

Electrical equipment and wiring
As mentioned earlier in the chapter, it is by far the safest policy to discard the old wiring. Depending upon the model being restored, it is possible that a replacement wiring harness will be available; here is where the club register could be of assistance to you. If not, and if you feel unable to carry out the work yourself, make contact with one of the specialist firms who advertise in motoring magazines.

Here are a few wiring tips that could be of use to you: (a) always solder the ends of wires into a solid piece to stop fraying; (b) where applicable, always solder connectors to the wires (terminals fitted to wire ends without without the special crimping tools always produce high-resistance joints and often work loose); (c) always use rubber grommets where cables pass through holes in metal; (d) ensure good connections and especially good earthing points (an intermittent or poor earth connection can produce the most peculiar faults which will take hours to locate); (e) always use junction boxes of a recognized manufacture (these can be obtained in all sizes); and lastly (f) use snap connectors (push-fit) at convenient places to assist cable runs. Always leave 2-3 inches spare on a run to avoid breakages due to vibration of taut cables.

Attention must be drawn to the fact that the lighting regulations may have altered since your car was manufactured. Try a visit to your nearest reference library, which should hold copies of the lighting regulations. Alternatively, the local police station or an approved vehicle testing centre should be able to advise you.

Upholstery

The complete re-upholstering of a car is a very difficult job for the amateur and should, in the main, be left to the professional coachtrimmer and upholsterer. However, if the leather is not damaged and only looking sorry for itself, it can be brought back to its original lustre quite easily.

First, wash the leather with warm water, glycerine or non-caustic soap, or preferably with a proprietary cleaner, such as 'Connolly's Concentrated Cleaner', according to the manufacturer's instructions. If necessary, use a small tooth or nail brush, which is not too hard, to clean the ingrained dirt away from the seams and crevices. Try

not to soak the leather and always ensure that the temperature of the water is no more than hand-hot. When dry, use a leather reviver and polish with a good leather polish.

The world-renowned firm of leather merchants, Connolly Brothers (Curriers) Limited, of London, are always most helpful and, in addition to supplying all the necessary cleaners and revivers, have a very good leaflet on the subject of renovation of leather and other car trimmings.

Fuel tank

Never use a blowlamp or any other form of naked flame on or near a fuel tank. Nor should you smoke or have naked lights anywhere near it, no matter how many years may have passed since the tank last had fuel in it.

All fuel tanks fitted to Morgans are made of tinned steel and, if old, generally have a considerable amount of rust inside. First remove the tank from the chassis and wash out repeatedly with water until all the loose rust is removed. The tank should then be dried immediately. This is best done by first draining and then standing it in the sun. Remember to turn it end for end and side to side at regular intervals.

When the tank is thoroughly dry, remove the old paint with the aid of a chemical paint remover. Do not scrape the paint off dry as this removes the tinning as well as the paint. Dents, if any, can only be removed by unsoldering (with a soldering iron) the end giving best access to the dent, then hammering out the dent and resoldering the end plate back into place.

Carefully examine the tank for pin holes and cracks. The most likely place to find pin holes are on the bottom of the tank, especially if at any time it has

stood with water in it. In this case it will be extremely thin and the best course is to solder a plate over the area. Cracks, of course, can be soldered providing they are not too wide.

When you have completed any necessary repairs, the best way of testing the tank for leaks is by sealing the inlet and outlet pipes with corks or rubber bungs, one of which should be drilled down the centre and an old inner tube valve inserted through it. Then, with the aid of a foot pump, pressurize the tank to 5psi (no more than that and never use a compressor!). Then immerse the tank in water, check for any air bubbles, mark their positions and remove and dry the tank. After depressurizing the tank, clean the area with a scraper and emery cloth before soldering.

Soldering on an object of this size requires a large iron which will not cool down too quickly. If you feel that you cannot manage this work, a good tinsmith will do it for you and even, if necessary, make a complete new tank to the original design using the original filler neck and other fittings.

Useful tips

Cleaning fuse clips: everyone who has tried knows just how difficult it is to clean corrosion off the little clips that hold the fuses: you just cannot get at the inside with a file, emery cloth or sandpaper.

Take a 0.25in wooden dowel (a pencil will do, but it must be a round one) and cut it to the length of a fuse. Glue fine emery cloth or sandpaper around the dowel. Drill a small hole in the side and insert a 2in nail as a handle. (Do not hammer the nail into the dowel without drilling as the wood will split).

Insert the dowel into the fuse holder clips and work the handle back and forwards two or three times. When removed, the inside of the clips will be found to be bright and clean.

Battery terminals: If you are still using the old-type battery which regularly corrodes its terminals, try glueing a copper coin to the top of the battery, close to but not touching the negative terminal. You will be surprised what a difference it makes.

Aluminium corrosion: to dissolve corrosion between aluminium components, try using vinegar instead of penetrating oil. All that the penetrating oil may do is to seal off the corrosion from other chemicals.

Water hoses and hose clamps: check hoses for unusual softness, cracks, drying out, etc. Any hose that looks less than 100 per cent should be replaced before it leaves you stranded.

When removing old hoses, it is wise to carefully slit them with a knife if they are stuck or bonded to the fittings. Putting too much pressure on the hose while attempting to force it off could cause thin radiator flanges to rupture and rusted steel piping to split. Inspect the pipe stubs for corrosion or rust damage at the ends where the hoses attach. All exposed aluminium or steel pipes should be painted to prevent rust or corrosion damage.

Hoses should be of the best reinforced designs. When cutting off excess length from a hose, exercise caution as they often contain a coiled spring. These springs are a good idea and should be retained if at all possible as they prevent the hose from collapsing due to water pump suction.

If your car will be a concours candidate, use hose clamps of the original design. Otherwise, any good quality stainless steel clamp will suffice. When installing most hoses, the fit should be tight. Again, avoid using undue pressure to force the hose on to the fitting. A silicone spray lubricant like WD40 will help ease the installation and prevent strain on the pipes. On corroded pipe stubs, or with looser fitting hoses, apply small amounts of silicone rubber to the pipe stub surface, then fit the hose and tighten the clamp as soon as possible. Wait a few hours before refilling the system.

Finally, check running clearances between hoses and fan blades, as hoses tend to move slightly when the engine is running. Check tightness of all the hose clamps after the first few hours of operation.

A good, tight water system will ensure proper operation and longer engine life.

Chain lubricant: motorcycle chain lubricant is available in a spray can under various brand names at your local motorcycle shop. The lubricant sprays at about the same viscosity as WD40 to penetrate cracks and crevices, and within minutes thickens to nearly the consistency of grease. Quite remarkable! It can be used with some success to rejuvenate semi-sealed bearings and is great for the rear springs. Unlike WD40, it will not disappear overnight.

Asbestos brake material: when you change your car's brake pads or shoes you probably notice lots of black residue (not the grease) on the backing plates or around the calipers. This black dust contains a lot of asbestos! The inhalation of this asbestos dust must be avoided completely. Do not use compressed air to blow it away or you will stir up an unpleasant cloud. Use water for cleaning it up. The wearing of a face mask is essential.

Brake repair notes: if the primary cup on your car's master cylinder is leaking, you will lose pedal pressure - that is, the pedal will travel all the way to the floor - but there may be little or no loss of brake fluid. If the secondary cup is leaking, you will lose brake fluid. Pinch the boot on the master cylinder and see if you get a drip of brake fluid from it. This is a good sign of a bad secondary cup.

Always check the brake lights when you are checking the master cylinder and if they are not working find out why and rectify the problem first. Another thing about brake systems: try to keep all the wheel and drum parts marked and together, so they go back in the same location on the car. Right front on the right front, and so forth.

Do not leave any twist in the brake hose if a wheel cylinder or hose has to be removed and replaced. Even the slightest twist will cause the hose to unscrew itself from the wheel cylinder as the car is being driven.

Always test fit brake shoes to the drums. The centre of the shoe should contact first while there is still clearance at the ends. The book says five or six thousandths of an inch at each end. A wood rasp works just as well as a brake shoe grinder. Do not breathe the dust - asbestos!

Handbrake: have you greased your handbrake linkage recently? There is a pivot pin on the rear axle that should be checked on a regular basis and greased as necessary.

Tyre valves: a simple tool for removing valve cores is to epoxy a core-removing type valve cap on the end of an old valve stem.

Small oil leaks: stamped valve covers, oil pans, etc, always seem to leak. This is often caused by *over*-tightening of the bolts, causing 'sheet metal pull-down'. Additional tightening may temporarily stop the leak, but results in additional bent metal, causing the leak to return. The proper way to fix leaks is to straighten the sheet metal, install a new gasket (use a sealer) and torque fixings to specification.

Castellated nuts: next time you remove a castellated nut, file a mark across the end of the axle, in line with the cotter pin hole. Lining up the nut will be a lot easier.

Windshield screws: those little screws holding your car's windshield in place must not touch the glass. They must be the exact length to hold the frame of your windshield but, if they touch the side of the windshield, expect the glass to crack.

Water leaks into car: one source of water leaks into the car is where the centre hinge is screwed to the firewall. If the sheet metal cracks, or the screws get loose enough to let water through, it comes down on your feet. Caulk this area with silastic putty. If the wood screws are stripped in the holes, dip a couple of wooden matchsticks in white glue and fit them in the holes before putting the screws back in. Be sure that the screws are flat head and seat flat in the end fitting. Round head, oval head, or oversize screws here are the major source of cracks in the bonnet, at the end of the hinge.

Steering column nuts: periodically check to see if the nut behind the steering wheel is tight! I have seen steering wheels with stripped hubs, resulting from excessive movement on the splines when the nut gets loose.

Emergency repair of threaded parts: since the need for special tools usually crops up at night, on holidays and other times when all suppliers are closed, here are a couple of tips to clean up threaded parts in an emergency.

If a stud or bolt has damaged threads, take a nut of the proper size and thread, saw it in half across the hole, clamp it around the stud or bolt (behind the damaged area if possible) with a pair of vice-grip pliers and unscrew the nut over the damaged section of thread. Cutting the nut in half does two things; it gives two sharp edges to clean up the threads, and it makes the nut a tight fit on the bolt to give a good cleaning action.

For a threaded hole that is damaged, take a bolt of the proper size and thread and file four grooves lengthwise in it with a triangular file. When this bolt is threaded into the hole, it will help clean out the threads.

None of the above is a substitute for taps and dies, but will work when nothing else is available.

Paint removal from plastic/vinyl: if you have ever attempted to remove paint from plastics or vinyl, you know that most paint thinners ruin plastic. Try model aeroplane fuel with about 10 per cent nitro base; it removes the paint with no damage to the plastic.

Gaskets: the standard mechanic's way of making a gasket when at least one of the parts has few if any protrusions, is to lay the gasket material on the part and let it (the part) be the cutting die. Gently tap around the edges of the holes and margins with the round end of a ball-peen hammer.

Oil/hydraulic fittings: use extreme care when replacing any oil or other hydraulic fitting. Threading properly makes a seal. Forcing new threads strips the seal and causes a leak. Always clean the threads and 'start' them by hand.

Carburettor throttle linkage
Lubricate the throttle linkage to the carburettor once every two months. This minimizes wear, maintains smoothness of operation and saves fuel.

Wrinkle-finish paints
One thing which almost all Morgans have in common is wrinkle-finish paint on selected components. The smart appearance of these items is vitally important to a concours-winning car. The refinishing of wrinkle-finished parts is time-consuming, but relatively simple if done in the proper sequence.

1   Strip all of the old wrinkle-finish from the part to be repainted. Use a good quality automotive paint stripper and follow the directions on the container. It may take two or three applications of stripper to completely remove the old finish.

2   Wash the part thoroughly in hot soapy water to remove any residue. Completely dry the component. Finally, clean it lightly with a cloth soaked in lacquer thinner.

3   Carefully mask off any areas you do not want to paint, such as studs or mating surfaces.

4   Prime the part with zinc chromate primer. You can use either a spray can or a brush, as brush marks will not show through the wrinkle-finish. Allow to dry for at least 24 hours. If possible, wait 48 hours.

5   Buy a good quality wrinkle-finish paint. I have found that 'VHT' is a good brand which is available at most accessory shops.

6   In order to achieve results which equal the texture of the original factory finish (which is actually rather fine), you will need to apply three moderately heavy coats.

7   Apply the coats precisely

three minutes apart, spraying each coat from a different direction. For example, spray the first coat in a north-south plane, the second east-west and third diagonally.

8   Be sure to apply moderately heavy coats, but be careful of runs.

9   After the final paint application, let the part sit undisturbed for 20 minutes.

10   Carefully place the part on the rack in the centre of a domestic oven, set the temperature at 200 degrees F and set the timer for 20 minutes. Leave the oven door slightly open so you can observe the progress and so the fumes can escape. Be sure to turn the stove vent fan on as the baking paint emits a very distinctive odour!

11   After about 10 minutes you should observe the paint begin to wrinkle. Be sure to allow the part to bake the full 20 minutes. If the part is too large to completely fit in the oven, let it bake 10 minutes and then turn it end for end for the next 10 minutes of baking.

12   Use gloves to remove the completed part as it will be hot! Do not touch the wrinkle-finish as it will still be soft. Let the paint cure an additional two to three days before installing the part in the car.

13   If you do not have access to an oven, a blow lamp will work, but you must be careful to get even overall heating on large parts.

14   If the paint does not wrinkle and you followed the above directions, you probably did not apply coats that were heavy enough. Go back to step 1 and start all over again.

15   For touching up small areas, you can spray the paint into a small can and use a brush to apply it to the area needing repair. Bake as above and the repair will blend perfectly.

Definition of fit (general)

We've all heard about the type of 'fit' necessary on certain parts of the car, but do we really know what the term means?

The following definitions of the various types of fit are given to assist the restorer in arriving at the correct amount of clearance between moving parts, as well as to enable a better appreciation of why the various tolerances must be adhered to. Generally speaking, all bores are made to a standard size (so standard reamers, plugs, gauges, *etc*, may be used) with a plus tolerance. The maximum size of the male parts is usually a standard size less the minimum clearance required for the fit desired. The minimum size for the male parts is this maximum size minus the tolerance.

1   Running fit. A running fit is one providing enough clearance for there to be a continuous film of oil between the two parts. A running fit usually requires 0.001in for an oil film plus 0.001in for each inch of diameter.

2   Slip fit. A slip fit exists when the male part is slightly smaller than the female part and involves less clearance than a running fit. An example of the minimum allowable clearance for a slip fit would be a piston pin that, from its own weight, would pass slowly through the connecting rod bushing. In most cases (except where a limited movement of the parts is involved) slip fits are specified where, due to anticipated expansion of the female part, enough additional clearance will result to change this type of fit to a running fit and provide adequate clearance for a film of oil.

3   Wring fit. A wring fit is the type of fit required between a bore and a plug gauge to determine the inside diameter of a bore. With a wring fit, it is necessary to turn or wring the plug gauge or part to force it through the bore. This type of fit does not provide for a film of oil.

4   Press fit. A press fit is one that requires force to enter the male part into the bore. Accepted practice for press fit is to have the male part larger by 0.001in for each inch of diameter of the bore into which it is to be pressed. An example of a press fit is the bushing into the spindle on Morgan front suspension.

5   Shrink fit. Generally speaking, a shrink fit is tighter than a press fit. The amount of shrink will range from 0.001-0.002in for each inch of diameter and in some cases even more. Parts having a press fit may be assembled by shrinking rather than force if desired. There are two methods of shrinking two parts together, either or both of which may be used. One method involves expansion of the female member by heating and the other involves contracting the male member by chilling with dry ice.

• EFFECT OF EXPANSION ON FIT

Allowances are made in establishing fit on parts that are exposed to higher temperature to take into account the anticipated expansion of the part during operation and still provide for the type of fit required. Allowances must also be made for unequal expansion of dissimilar materials. Absolute minimum allowance for expansion of parts exposed to flame or exhaust gases (pistons, piston rings and valves) is 0.001in for each inch of diameter of length. In anticipating the expansion of a piston to make allowance for the additional clearance required in the cylinder, 0.001in for each inch of diameter is added. In anticipating the expansion of a piston ring to make allowance for the additional gap required between the ends of the ring, 0.001in for each inch of length (0.003in for each inch of diameter) is added.

The use of a torque wrench (general)

The importance and proper use of a torque wrench are sometimes not appreciated - under-tightening of fasteners (bolts, nuts, *etc*) causes metal fatigue in moving parts and leaks where gaskets are used; over-tightening causes metal fatigue in the fastener itself (stretching), damage to parts (warping, pull-up and stripped threads) and leaks caused by damaged gaskets.

The real reason for tightening threaded fasteners is to create the proper compression between the parts being joined. Because compression cannot easily be measured between the parts, the desired compression force is converted to the measurement of torque. Nobody needs to be told that a rusty or dirty bolt is harder to turn than a clean oiled one, but some people forget that the required torque can be obtained on a rusty bolt long before the proper compression is. Torque requirements are all set for ideal conditions of clean, lubricated male and female threads. Unfortunately, most of us think that cleaning bolts with a high-speed wire brush takes care of this, but actually the resultant distortion of the threads can produce enough jamming to give faulty torque readings. The best way to clean threads is with a tap and die.

It is also very important to use the proper lubricant to attain correct torque; ordinary chassis grease and engine oils are not ideal. If they are used, the torque reading should be increased by 20 per cent. Anti-seize compound is the best lubricant and should be used not only on the threads but also under nuts, washers and bolt heads. The use of anti-seize is doubly important when bolts are threaded into aluminium or magnesium alloys. These light metals tend to 'grow' and when a dry bolt is removed it's inclined to damage threads.

If a bolt has been over-tightened, 'pull-up' often occurs around the bolt holes. This can easily be determined by running a file over the holes which will reveal any high spots. When this condition exists, required torque can be obtained without the proper compression and gaskets may leak. The best way to correct this is to counterbore or chamfer the holes.

The torque wrench is one of the most important tools in your garage, but if it is not used properly you might just as well go back to an open-ended spanner and guess work.

Spark plugs (general)

Spark plugs consist of a threaded metal shell, a piece of porcelain and an electrode and all they do is sit in the combustion chamber and spark at the appropriate time to start the flame that runs your car. That's all. Basically, a plug must fire under very extreme conditions time after time after time. Plus there must be different heat ranges for different types of engines.

For instance, a plug type recommended for a compression ratio of 7:1 would probably burn up rather quickly at 10:1. A plug for 10:1 would probably foul in an engine of 7:1 ratio. The reason being in an engine of 7:1 the cylinder pressures are not too high and the plug can conduct enough heat away to keep from burning and hold just enough heat to keep the electrode end clear of the oil vapour present in the combustion chamber. Now, if we take this plug out and install it in a similar engine with a compression of 10:1 the cylinder pressures are much higher, hence more heat. The plug cannot conduct the additional heat so the electrode starts burning; we would have to install a 'colder' plug or one that will conduct the heat at a higher rate. A cold plug in a low-compression engine would conduct too much heat from itself and not hold enough heat to burn off oil. This causes the spark to earth itself without firing the engine, a condition known as fouling. An over-rich fuel mixture can cause the same condition.

The next question is, how does a plug control its heat conductivity? This is related to how much of the porcelain is in contact with the shell or metal section. If the porcelain is in contact the full length of the shell, much heat is conducted away from the electrode, making it a cold running plug. If the porcelain is in partial contact with the shell, less heat is given up to the head cooling so the plug runs hotter.

The way to tell if a plug is running hot is to install a new set of plugs and run them for a couple of days. Then remove them and arrange them in order. Now see if the centre electrode porcelain insulator is white or has a blistered look. If it is burned, the plug is too hot or is being made to run hot by too lean a mixture or advanced timing. If the plug is sooty or black in colour, the plug is too cold, the mixture too rich or the timing may be retarded. A lot of problems can be identified by reading the plugs.

When the correct plug is used in a correctly tuned engine the centre electrode porcelain insulator will be choco-

late brown or dark grey in colour, depending on the brand of petrol used. If you see a tinge of green on the edges of the plug, do not be alarmed - some petrol additives leave this marking.

Battery selection (general)

Due to recent advances in technology, there are new alternatives to choose from when selecting a battery for your Morgan. Standard automobile batteries have, for years, used antimony as a lead plate bonding agent. An unfortunate result of this, however, is that the reaction of antimony and sulphuric acid in the battery produces bubbles of gas. Therefore, batteries have a vent to atmosphere to allow this gas to escape but this results in having to add water to the battery from time to time. However, the need for access to the cells for topping up creates the possibility of acid spills and damaged paint and metalwork.

There are two new types of batteries on the market:

1 *Low antimony, often advertised as low maintenance.*
2 *Calcium-based, often advertised as no maintenance.*

The low antimony type battery uses a smaller percentage of antimony to bind the lead in the plates together. This results in less gas production and a reduced need for topping up with water. The disadvantages of this battery are the continued possibilites of acid spills and corrosion in the engine compartment.

The calcium-based battery uses calcium instead of antimony as the bonding agent. Calcium produces no gas in its reaction with sulphuric acid. As a result, the battery can be sealed completely from the atmosphere, with only a one-way valve to allow boil-over

in case of over-charging. This completely eliminates the need to add water, and greatly reduces the potential for leaks.

The calcium-based battery is the ideal battery for a Morgan. The lack of potential for leakage protects the engine compartment and paintwork and the no-maintenance feature is especially valuable for owners of two-seaters who would have to remove the luggage floor to check the battery. The calcium-based battery has another big plus for Morgan owners who do not drive their cars for extended periods of time, such as during the winter months. This type of battery will not normally discharge over time, as a regular antimony type will.

Be certain to use the felt washer terminal protectors, which are soaked in anti-corrosion fluid. These prevent any damage from terminal corrosion due to acid migrating up the battery posts, which can occur with any battery.

Finally, be certain to get a battery with at least 400-500 cold cranking amps. This will ensure that the starter on your Morgan will spin the engine over rapidly for quick starting, thereby reducing wear and tear on your starter motor.

• HINTS ON BATTERY MAINTENANCE
Keep your car's battery terminals clean. Dirty terminals prevent current being delivered to the electrical system and can give the impression of a dead battery. Lucas cup-shaped terminals can look perfectly good but be corroded inside sufficiently to reduce current flow and prevent operation of the system.

Purchase a battery charger. Twenty four hours on a 5-amp charger will restore any battery to full strength, if

the battery is still good.

If you have an antimony battery, purchase an inexpensive hydrometer. This will enable you to check the specific gravity of the 'water' in the battery to determine if the battery is charged.

Rewiring your Morgan (all models)

A good, reliable wiring system is absolutely essential to the safe, reliable and pleasurable operation of your Morgan, yet this important aspect of restoration is often given only grudging attention. This fact is surprising since it is well known that wiring and ignition problems are the most common cause of vehicle malfunctions. Consider also that faulty wiring constitutes a definite hazard in that it can lead to disastrous fires. The restorer is well advised, I think, to pay considerable attention to his electrical network early in the restoration project. Not only will the attention pay handsome dividends later in trouble-free operation, but a little extra effort and money will add considerable class when it comes to concours judging.

A number of companies are now offering complete wiring harnesses and most of the products I have seen appear to be very creditable reproductions. A new harness should be a worthwhile investment, in spite of the cost. If not already available from stock, presumably, any one of the firms can duplicate your old wiring harness if you can remove it intact. The wiring harness is the heart of the project but there is still much to do after it is installed, of course.

Remember to use at least 14 gauge for headlamp and horn circuits. 16 gauge is OK for tail lamps, parking lights and turn signals. The connection between the battery and the ammeter carries the entire current for all circuits

Electrical wire size/capacity

CURRENT RATING AMPS	UK SIZE	IMPERIAL SIZE (OBSOLETE)	METRIC SQ MM	AMERICAN WIRE GAUGE
6	14/.25	14/.010	.7	18-19
8.7	14/.30	14/.012	1.0	18
13.5	21/.30	21/.012	1.5	15-16
17.5	28/.30	28/.012	2.0	14
21.75	35/.30	35/.012	2.5	13
27.5	42/.30	42/.012	3.0	12-13
35	65/.30	65/.012	4.5	10-11
42	84/.30	84/.012	6.0	9-10
50	97/.30	97/.012	7.0	8-9
60	120/.30	120/.012	8.5	7-8
99	37/.74	37/.029	16.0	5-6
155	37/.76	37/.030	25.0	3-4
248	61/.90	61/.036	140.0	1-2

Cable produced in the United Kingdom was formerly rated by the number of strands and the diameter (in inches) of each strand, eg 14 strands of 0.012in was shown as 14/.012. Since Britain now uses metric units, this becomes 14/.30 since 0.012in = 0.30mm, which is equivalent to a cross-section 0f 1.0sq mm on the European system and 18 gauge American. Note the European and American systems do not tell you how many strands. The stranding of several small wires (instead of using one big wire) makes it more flexible and less likely to break due to vibration. All automotive cable is formed by using such separate strands of wire in a common insulator.

except starting and maybe the horn, so it should be at least 12 gauge. The wire from the generator carries the entire charging current and should also be 12 gauge. Note that the smaller the gauge number, the larger the wire and hence the current capacity.

Most problems in getting lighting circuits to work properly stem from lack of an adequate earth. Paint or corrosion films may prevent the return currents from the headlights, winglamps or tail lamps from getting back to the battery through the frame. Maybe you did a terrific job of priming on your valances and wings, and then covered every square inch with a heavy coat of paint. Now these parts are perfect insulators. Result? No lights! It may now be necessary to scrape off some of that paint in order to provide a low-resistance electrical path. A pocket ohmmeter is a good piece of equipment to have when looking for high-resistance earths.

• POINTS TO REMEMBER
Make sure that the battery terminal clamps are clean and in first-class condition. If there is any doubt, replace them now!

Check the condition of the engine earthing strap, the wire from the battery to the solenoid and the solenoid to the starter. Replace if worn or if the strands have begun to separate.

Scrape, file or grind the earthing point on the frame and engine earth strap so that a good earth contact is obtained. Check the wiring diagram to determine the proper connection of the battery: is it positive or negative earth?

When working on the wiring, disconnect the earth terminal of the battery to prevent disastrous arcing if you accidentally short or earth wires.

Replace all wires that are frayed, badly worn or oil-soaked. Use stranded wire of the same gauge or larger then the original wires (see chart).

Location of chassis numbers (all models)
Chassis numbers are always stamped on the top of one of the chassis crossmembers on the offside. In the case of two-seaters, it will be found on the member immediately behind the gearbox. On the four-seaters it can be found on the member immediately behind the front seats. Occasionally the number can also be found stamped on certain body panels, such as by the spare wheels and on the wood frame of the door hinge supports. These numbers are occasionally only lightly stamped onto the metal or the wood and are difficult to read.

It is a sound policy to make a note of as many numbers as possible in respect of the major components of your car - chassis, engine, gearbox, rear axle and so on - which will be most useful if ever you need to order or identify replacement parts. This is particularly important if you are not the

first owner as the components may have been changed as a result of wear and tear or even an accident.

Whilst dealing with identification numbers, a brief explanation is necessary as to why the engine numbers on the Morgan do not follow on in sequence. The Morgan company has always purchased engines from outside manufacturers, meaning deliveries are made as stocks run low. When a delivery of 20, 30 or 40 engines is made, their numbers are, more than likely, consecutive, but when unloaded they are placed in front of the remaining stock from the previous delivery, not necessarily in order. When an engine is required, the first in line is invariably taken, and time is not wasted checking the sequence. Eventually all stock is used, but the engine numbers apparently have no logical sequence.

Model terminology (all models)
Over the years it has become apparent there is some confusion as to the correct way to denote the variations of Morgan models, particularly the four-wheelers. I include a short list of these designations as originally used by the

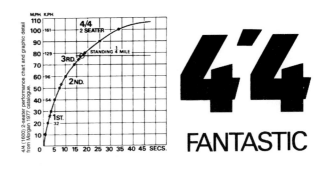

4/4
FANTASTIC

Morgan Motor Company Limited, which are used in all references to the models either in the motoring press or by the motoring public in the UK and most other countries. This will, of course, assist the American reader should he have reason to write to the factory or any other UK Morgan organization.

4-4 or 4/4 - Refers to the model only and is said 'FOUR FOUR'.
Plus 4 - Refers to the model only and is said 'PLUS FOUR'.
Plus 4 Plus - Refers to the model only and is said 'PLUS FOUR PLUS'.
Plus 8 - Refers to the model only and is said 'PLUS EIGHT'.

To indicate which type of body the model has, the name of the model should be used as above, plus the type of body. For example:
PLUS FOUR, two-seater; PLUS FOUR, four-seater; PLUS FOUR, Drop Head Coupé.
In the case of a model which has had a range of engines, the practice is to indicate which model is being referred to by saying the series number or the engine type. For example:
'FOUR FOUR, SERIES TWO' or 'SERIES TWO FOUR FOUR'.
'PLUS FOUR FIAT-ENGINED' or 'FIAT-ENGINED PLUS FOUR'.
It is normally accepted that the above refers to a two-seater and the terms four-seater or Drop Head Coupé are only added if relevant.

Car covers
Since the average Morgan spends much more time in the family garage than it does being driven, it is worthwhile considering which type of cover should be used: even in a closed garage, car covers are essential.

One factor to consider is that of security: it is difficult for prowlers to tell if there's a Morgan in the garage if all they can see is a cover! Also, the amount of dust and dirt that can accumulate on a car in the garage is truly amazing - the car cover will protect your Morgan from this accumulation. The longer the car spends between being used, the more important this factor becomes. Finally, a cover is surprisingly effective in protecting the car from small bumps and, of course, colour fading.

There are many types of car covers on the market. Some are good and some are worse than none at all. This is truly a case where more expensive is not necessarily better. As long as the Morgan is being stored in a garage, there is no need for the expensive canvas or plasticized covers. These covers cannot 'breathe'. True, they will keep rain from the car (if it rains in your garage), but they will also trap moisture under them. This moisture, whether caused by humidity, condensation or precipitation, has no place to go and stays between the cover and the car and slowly attacks the painted surface. Eventually, the paint can become discoloured or even lift from the car.

The best type of cover for a garaged Morgan is a one of plain cotton drill or similar material. These covers can 'breathe' in either direction. Even if the car is rained on and the cover gets wet, the moisture will evaporate out through the cover without damage to the paint. If you are buying a new cover, take the time and spend the money to get one that is made to fit your particular Morgan. Don't let someone talk you into a 'one size fits all' cover.

Laying up your Morgan
For those who need to lay up their cars

for an extended period, there are a number of things that may be done to lessen the problems associated with inactivity of your car.

The best storage area is one that is dry and heated. It's especially important to try and separate your Morgan's storage area from the garage area used every day by the family car; the moisture from outside, exhaust moisture and emissions attack a car rapidly during winter storage.

Run the car for at least 25 miles prior to preparation to thoroughly warm all fluids and soften and lubricate seals.

• FLUIDS
1   **Water:** leave the system full. I recommend using a 50-60 per cent anti-freeze mixture, as it contains rust inhibitors. Drain and refill the system before storing. New anti-freeze should retain its properties for three years in storage.
2   **Petrol:** fill the tank. Drain and refill once a year. I have heard that Mobil detergent petrol precipitates less 'varnish' than other brands.
3   **Oils:** drain and refill the crankcase. Run the engine to distribute the clean oil to all bearings. The old oil will contain acid from combustion by-products which will etch the bearing shells in time. Drain and refill the gearbox differential and steering box.
4   **Brakes:** drain old brake fluid and refill with silicone fluid (this is not necessary if the system already contains silicone fluid). If you refill with Glycol fluid, drain and refill once a year. Glycol fluid absorbs water and water ruins brakes.

• CLEANING
1   Wash the exterior (include under the wings). Dirt absorbs moisture

'The Real Sports Car'

Morgan

and moisture is your enemy.

2   Wax painted surfaces with a non-cleaner wax. Do not buff.

3   Clean chrome and coat with vaseline or grease - particularly wire wheels.

4   Clean and coat leather with Connolly's Hide Food. Not Armoral.

5   Use a fine wood oil on dashboards and on steering wheels, not just a dust spray. The oil will feed the wood and prevent splitting and rotting.

6   Vacuum carpets or mats and check beneath them for any moisture; if damp, dry thoroughly or be ready for mildew (the national plant of England) and rot in the spring.

7   If a moth problem exists in your area, place an open container of moth crystals on the floor.

8   Do not worry too much about the engine compartment. The oil film will protect against rust.

• PREPARE THE ENGINE
(Note: it may be necessary to amend the following tips to suit your particular model).

1   Generally inspect the engine for leaks. Tighten hose clamps, bolts, etc, as needed.

2   Remove the spark plugs and pour about an eggcup-full of oil into each cylinder.

3   Crank the engine over a few times to distribute the oil. Replace the spark plugs loosely.

4   Drain fuel from carburettor(s) float bowl(s). Do not run engine again after this point. This step not applicable to fuel-injected models.

5   Loosen the adjustment on all rocker arms to relieve the tension on the valve springs. Note: only applies to

models with screw-type valve clearances.

6   Use silicone spray on all engine compartment rubber - heater hoses, radiator hoses, belts and weather-stripping.

• PREPARE THE CHASSIS
1   Spray all five tyres with silicone spray. Silicone will stop rubber rot.

2   Place the car on jack stands under the cross-axle and rear axle. Leave the car in neutral with the parking brake off.

3   Lubricate all chassis lubrication points.

4   Prop the clutch pedal in the depressed position to avoid the clutch plate lining sticking to the flywheel. Note: over a period of time this practice may weaken the clutch springs.

5   Remove the battery from the car and wash the exterior with a baking soda solution to remove any spilled acid.

6   Store the battery in a cool (not cold) place. If it is a conventional (antimony system) battery, keep it charged. If it is a sealed (calcium system) battery, it should not discharge in a year.

7   Clean the battery-mounting area with the baking soda solution.

8   Put the tonneau cover on if a roadster.

9   Put a car cover over the entire car.

NOTE: Do not put rat poison or rodent traps in the car; if they should work, the smell will drive you out of the garage. Repellents under the car may keep pests away.

• REVIVAL
1   Remove the car cover and review your check list.

2   Check for any fluid leaks, oil, water, fuel, transmission, brakes, rear end, etc.

3   Remove the car from blocks and check the tyre pressures.

4   Charge (if necessary), clean and install the battery.

5   Check all fluid levels.

6   Check and adjust, if necessary, the belt tensions and hose clamps.

7   Remove spark plugs. Adjust the valve clearances (if applicable). Crank the engine over for 10 or 20 seconds to prime the fuel system, expel any fluid accumulations in the cylinders and distribute oil in the engine.

8   Gap and install the spark plugs.

9   Start the engine and monitor all of the gauges.

• TRIAL
1   Drive slowly for several miles to circulate fluids, soften seals, etc.

2   Use brakes lightly at first. Make several stops while progressively reaching normal brake pedal pressure. This should remove any accumulated rust. If the brakes pull to one side after several stops, examine for fluid leaks, seized pistons, etc.

3   Recheck all fluid levels, belt tensions, hose clamps, etc. Check for leaks. Inspect the exhaust system.

4   Tune the engine.

5   Wash, wax and clean.

VII

MORGAN CLUBS

The Morgan Three-Wheeler Club Ltd

The oldest Morgan club in the world is without doubt the Morgan Three-wheeler Club Limited. The club as it is known today was first formed in 1944.

Before this there was a 'Morgan Club' which existed as far back as the early 1920s. This was a club exclusively for Morgan owners, organized very much on a local basis and predominantly of a social nature but the overall President of the club was HFS Morgan.

However, by the mid 1920s - immediately after EB Ware's crash at Brooklands in September 1924 - more and more pressure was brought to bear by the Junior Car Club and others to get Morgans banned from racing. As the pressure mounted so did the determination of Morgan drivers, particularly those interested in racing and record breaking, to find some way of ensuring they could continue. On what was almost certainly HFS's instigation, it was decided to re-constitute the club to allow membership to any Auto Cycle Union - defined cyclecar, (*ie* under 1100cc and 8cwt in weight - with three or four wheels).

With HFS as President, the new club, named 'The Cyclecar Club' was formed on August 4, 1927, and of course immediately became eligible under BARC rules to organise race meetings at Brooklands. Following objections from the Junior Car Club, which had previously been named the Cyclecar Club, the name was changed to 'The New Cycle Car Club', and by mid-1928 the racing committee organized its first Brooklands race meetings. As from January 1, 1930 the club became the Light Car Club and membership was extended to the owners of all cars up to 1500cc, whereas before it was limited

The first Morgan club was founded in the early 1920s. Although predominantly a social club, a few 'closed to club' competition events were organised.

Arthur Maskell in a Super Sports accelerating hard away from the chicane at Brooklands at the New Cycle Car Club's first race meeting in 1928.

to 1100cc. This change came about mainly because the New Cycle Car Club membership comprised, almost exclusively, Morgan owners. The most notable innovation made by the club was to organise the 90-lap relay races held each year at Brooklands. In its latter years the club began to lose a lot of its impetus, reflecting the decline in the popularity of the cyclecar.

The Second World War curbed all forms of motor sport but the motoring

An early MTWC meeting, believed to be an AGM, at Brandon Hall near Coventry. The unusual Morgan in the foreground is a family model with a fixed head conversion.

4'4

FOUR SEAT
FUN

magazines produced many articles concerning Morgans throughout those dark years; owners could read about their marque even if they could not get the petrol to use their cars. This lack of contact between owners was brought to a head when a letter was sent in 1944 to *Motor Cycling* magazine suggesting the formation of a club for three-wheeler Morgan owners. A regular contributor to the magazine on Morgan matters was WS Seaman who wrote under the pen name of 'Trepenpol'. It was therefore through him that the names of the owners were collected and the first club news sheet was distributed in September 1944. The first meeting was held at Carshalton, Surrey while Flying Bombs fell on London and one of the club's present Vice Presidents, Ernie Woods, attended. In 1945 petrol was made available, albeit in very limited and rationed quantities, for domestic and pleasure uses, and the club organized a few 'runs' for members. The Inaugural General Meeting was held in September that year and over 50 members attended. Slowly, over the next ten years membership increased to about 750 and has remained around that figure ever since.

Over the years the club's function has changed. Originally, most members' cars were in regular everyday use, with spares being readily available from commercial outlets. The club's role then was mostly social and competitive, with a few technical articles being published from time to time in the monthly magazine *The Bulletin*. However, as the value of the cars has increased, traffic conditions have changed and everyday use of the cars diminished, the club has had to fulfill a more technical capacity and, by 1972, found it necessary to organize a comprehensive spare parts

manufacturing service for its members. This built to such a high annual turnover that, in 1980, it was decided to incorporate the club as a limited liability company.

In addition, over the years the club has gathered together a very extensive library, the contents of which are available to members, which helps to ensure that the owners of the surviving three-wheeler Morgans will be catered for well into the future.

The club has affiliated groups in both the USA and Australia, but most other clubs around the world are all willing to accept three-wheeler owners for membership.

Apply for membership in the first instance to the MTWC Membership Secretary, Morris Blease, Arden Cottage, Rocky Lane, Benllech, Anglesey, Gwynedd, Wales.

The Morgan Sports Car Club Ltd (Formerly the Morgan 4-4 Club & Morgan Sports Car Club.)

The publication of this book coincided with the 43rd anniversary of the Morgan Sports Car Club Limited, as it is now known. Any motor club which has been in existence for such a long time will have suffered setbacks and perhaps near-collapse. The Morgan 4-4 Club and Morgan Sports Car Club - both names by which the Morgan Sports Car Club Limited was once known - was no exception. But with the enthusiasm, and even on occasions financial assistance, of a few of the more devoted members, the club staggered its way through early crises to become today one of the largest one-make clubs in the world. It has a membership of almost 3800.

It might have been thought that

A few of the cars that turned up at the inaugural General Meeting of the Morgan 4/4 Club.

the introduction of the four wheeled Morgan would have been followed quickly by the creation of a club specifically for its owners, but this was not the case. At first, the Morgan Three-Wheeler Club decided that the owners of cars fitted with 'the extra wheel' would be allowed to join as associate members, but this idea was never a resounding success. It was not until May 1951 that positive steps were taken to establish a club for 4-4 owners. The turning point came when two Derby men, JS Atkins and DJ Whetton, placed an announcement in the May 18 issue of *The Autocar* inviting any Morgan owner interested in forming a 4-4 Club to contact Mr Whetton. One of those who did so was Lt-Col R (Dick) G Pritchard, TA, of Spondon, and later in the month a meeting of four or five Morgan owners was held at his home.

It was agreed that the number of replies to the invitation had been suffi-cient to warrent the holding of a further meeting, which was arranged to take place at the Flying Horse Hotel in Kegworth. Some 20 people attended and it was agreed that a club should be formed and an inaugural meeting be held at the same venue on the evening of June 30. Interest grew rapidly and

The first road rally organised by the Morgan 4/4 club was held in 1951. The event was won by Bill Allerton in his Le Mans Special. Note the twin upright spare wheels, painted radiator shell and missing 4/4 badge.

the club came into being with an initial membership of 63, including six ladies. Some of those present had travelled over 200 miles to attend.

The Morgan 4-4 Club was chosen as the official title of the club, and club colours of light blue, black and red were adopted. One of the first tasks was the appointment of officers and committee, and the club's first President was Jim Sparrowe, who was well known throughout the motor racing scene for his successes with his rapid 4-4, and who, in fact, had travelled with two other members to this inaugural meeting straight from a day's racing at Silverstone.

Dick Pritchard became the club Chairman, with LA Willsmere Vice-Chairman, J Sutton the Hon. Secretary and Treasurer and DJ Whetton the first Competitions Secretary. They were supported by a six man committee comprising RD Hadley, W Allerton, B Carroll, Flt. Lt. RC Bridges, IA (Tim) Parkes and EP Huxham, although the last-named had to decline office owing to pressures of business.

Although the club's name had been linked with the Morgan 4-4, the Plus 4 model had been in production for several months, so it was decided that owners of the more powerful model should also be eligible for membership, while non-Morgan owners would be admitted as associate members at the same £2.00 annual subscription that applied to full members. It was also agreed the club should apply for affiliation - subsequently granted - to the Royal Automobile Club, which enabled it to run its first officially recognized event the following October.

Meanwhile, the club's first competitive event - a 70 mile road rally from Burton-on-Trent to Banbury - took place on August Bank Holiday, August 5.

This seems to have been a peculiar date to choose which, no doubt, accounted for the somewhat meagre entry. It was very much a case of more Chiefs than Indians, for there were about 15 officials present to attend to a mere five entries! The event ended with a series of driving tests in which most of the officials and marshals tried their hands after the competitors had completed their official runs.

The distinction of winning the club's first event went to Graham Stallard, of Worcester, who drove a TT Replica reputed to have once been the property of HFS, although this was never really established. Second place went to Tim Parkes, of Pershore, and third to Bill Allerton, from Chester, who was driving a Le Mans Replica and also took the award for the best performance on the road sections.

Somewhat to the surprise - and certainly the delight - of the committee, the late Holland Birkett asked the club to enter a team of cars for the first Six-Hours Relay Race which his 750 Motor Club was to organize at Silverstone on August 25, and a team assembled comprising of Sparrowe, Parkes, Allerton and Atkins.

Any number of cars up to six could be nominated as a team and the objective was to carry a coloured sash around the circuit as many times as possible in the six hours, the sash being passed from driver to driver and worn by each in turn as their car did its stint on the circuit. A handicap system was applied by means of credit laps, the Morgan team being credited with 34 laps over the Jaguar XK120 team, which started on scratch. The race was not without incident for the Morgan team, but they held on grimly to average 61.5mph and finish second overall to a team of vin-

tage Bentleys. This was the beginning of a long association with the 'Six-Hours', an event in which the club has by no means disgraced itself.

The club's own first RAC-recognized event was a driving test meeting on October 7, 1951, at Queensford Aerodrome, near Dorchester-on-Thames. It was a well attended competition which was won by Graham Stallard. Then came the club's first night rally, on December 1/2, which attracted 24 entries to starting points in Manchester, Gloucester and Hereford. The route took competitors around Lincoln, Gainsborough and the Derbyshire Dales and back to Leicester, a total of 300 miles.

A few treasure hunts and similar social runs kept the club active for the next few months, culminating in an August Bank Holiday anniversary run over the route of the 1951 inaugural event, but in this instance much better supported. Up to now all the club's events had been restricted to members, but during the winter of 1952 a 200-mile night rally was observed by the RAC, as a result of which they granted the club a permit to organize invitation events of a similar kind. Further progress was made when the 1953 Spring Rally, also over 200 miles, and starting and finishing at Kidlington Aerodrome, Oxfordshire, was again officially observed by the RAC, as a result of which another permit to run invitation events was granted. The RAC observer on this occasion was Holland Birkett, who expressed particular interest in the club's operation of dumb (unmanned) checkpoints along the route and asked if he might copy the idea on events he organized for his own club which, later that year, he did.

One of the features of the club's

Club Driving Tests are always well supported. These three photos show one which was held on the car park of the Metal Box Company in the 1960s.

administration in those early days was that because officials and committee members were so widely dispersed, their regular monthly meetings were arranged by each member in turn. This meant that venues ranged over an area from Chester in the west to Sheffield in the north and Malvern in the south and many hundreds of miles were motored to attend. Some of the people who did so tell that it was great fun, but I believe the high mileage and amount of time involved led indirectly to the setting up of different centres of the club which now operate throughout the country.

The advent of the first cowled-radiator Plus 4s in 1954 caused a certain amount of heart-searching by the committee and quite a few rude remarks by the more committed 'flat-rad' people.

But, of course, the owners of the cowled-radiator models were in due course welcomed to the club, membership of which has grown to 3800, with more than 1000 active overseas members as well. The end of the flat-rad production, however, marked the end of an era, for the club as much as for the company; it was, in a sense, the end of the formative years.

As the club grew, so did its reputation in all forms of motor sport, and in the hey-days of rallies, sprints, driving tests, *etc*, hardly a week passed without the Secretary receiving invitations to enter teams in some event or another.

In order to link the membership, a club magazine was founded which took the form of a monthly newsletter called *The Miscellany*, with a larger quarterly

88

edition under the title *Motoring and Morgans*. Unfortunately, in those early days, production proved to be quite a struggle; the problem was the shortage of printable material. Gradually the membership responded and can now look back on over 30 years of regular publications, while the quality of the production has increased as well; *The Miscellany* now looks a very professionally produced magazine, complete with illustrations.

The membership of the club is divided into full, associate and overseas members, whilst, following an Annual General Meeting of the club on April 30, 1955, family membership became available under which the benefits of membership were extended to a member's immediate family on payment of the appropriate subscription .

As the membership increased so did the complaints about the long distances which some members had to travel in order to attend the noggins 'n' natters held in the Midlands. To overcome this problem Richard Upshall, with the committee's blessing, organized a meeting in the London area late in 1959 with the idea of forming a London Centre. However, the project was shortlived, due to lack of support, and it was not until October 1965 that a committee was formed at an inaugural London Centre meeting held in the garage premises of W Griffiths, in Willesden. This time it was a great success and the London Centre, now one of 30 covering nearly all the UK, has never looked back. Each centre has its own secretary and can organize social and competitive events independently of the main club, while all centre activities are open to any MSCC member, regardless of where they may live - visitors from one centre are always

most welcome at others.

The first attempt to change the name of the clubs was made in August 1962, when a member from Canada proposed that the name be changed to the Morgan Owner's Club, which seemed to echo the thoughts of a number of home-based members, mainly Plus 4 owners. However, when the committee decide to hold a postal vote of members, a large majority opted to keep the original name and the subject was not raised again until 1968. Members were invited to air their views through the pages of *The Miscellany*, but opinion seemed to be evenly divided, so the question was deferred again for 18 months. Then, in November 1969, a postal referendum took place in which 317 of the 451 voting papers sent out were returned completed. To the question whether or not members wished the club's name to be changed, 195 replied 'Yes' and 122 'No'. To the subsequent question, which of three names would members prefer in the event of a change, the scoring was: Morgan Car Club - 121 votes; Morgan 4-Wheeler Club - 39 votes; Morgan Sports Car Club - 136 votes. The remaining 21 papers were either spoilt or unanswered. The club was renamed - from January 1, 1971 - The Morgan Sports Car Club.

The next landmark for the club was the formation of the 4-4 Series I and Plus 4 Registers in mid-1972 to provide, 'a means for owners to contact each other, a source of advice, data and information, help in obtaining spares, *etc*'. John Orton was the first Series I Registrar and Tim Cree the first Plus 4 Registrar. This was the birth of the club's comprehensive spares and advisory service for members which embraces a Series I Registrar and Techni-

cal Adviser, a Plus 4 Registrar and Technical Adviser, a used spares Registrar and a Librarian. In recent years this format has been changed and the club now has a Technical Services section offering a more comprehensive service to members with technical advisers covering the whole four-wheeler production years, and a new and second-hand spares service. The Registers and the Librarian are now entirely separate.

In 1978 David Stretton-Smith put forward the idea of MOGAID, which is an international register of club members who are willing to assist any other member who breaks down in their area. Each member is issued with a list of names, addresses and telephone numbers which he can call upon for assistance if required. It is a splendid idea which other one-make clubs might do well to copy.

As from May 1991 the Club became a Limited Company, its full title now being The Morgan Sports Car Club Limited. Great care is taken with the way the board of directors of the company are elected, and also the length of time they can serve before they must put themselves forward for re-election. The maximum period is three years. All other officers (except for President and Vice President who are elected 'for life') will be elected each year. The only nominated positions are those which pay an honorarium or salary, which are appointed by the board as and when appropriate.

Finally, each officer whose position is elected annually now has a full job description, clearly laying out the responsibilities of each office and the requirements from the company of anyone elected into such office.

I have no doubt that the founder fathers of the original Morgan 4-4 Club

did not envisage its humble beginnings would develop into the present day structure. However, having known at least three of the founders I am sure they would be very proud if they were alive today.

All correspondence should be addressed to Mrs Christine Healey, Registrar, The Morgan Sports Car Club Ltd, 41, Cordwell Close, Castle Donington, Derbyshire, DE74 2JL.

Morgan clubs around the world
To own a Morgan is to own an international calling card. If a Morgan owner visits another country, with or without his car, and spots another Morgan, he will invariably seek out its owner and often the resulting discussion is the start of a lasting friendship.

Morgan ownership is rather like an addiction; once hooked the addict has little chance of being cured. How many times have you heard these familiar words, 'I used to own a Morgan and I wish I'd never sold it'? Through this particular addiction, Morgan owners have helped each other out in many parts of the world and, as the circle's widened, have formed themselves into an exclusive club. Some remain very small, still others have grown into large and very active organizations.

In this chapter the clubs are listed, together with a brief history and rundown of their activities. Also included is a latest known contact name and address of a club official (usually the Secretary). In some cases I have explained the methods adopted by clubs in awarding trophies and staging events in case they may be of interest to other Morgan clubs.

I think the very essence of a Morgan club is epitomized by the wording printed inside the register of members of the Morgan Owners Group - Great Lakes. It reads:

The Morgan Owners Group was established in 1965 to promote the Morgan automobile and to provide technical advice and social companionship for those fortunate enough to have found their very own world's last true sports car.

Morgan Owner's Club of Australia
The club was founded in August 1958 in Sydney, on the instigation of the Ward brothers, Ken and Barry, with 10 members attending the first meeting. Early meetings were informal gatherings at members' homes, but by 1960 increasing membership caused the meeting places to be changed to various halls or club premises in the Sydney area. That year the club joined the Confederation of Australia Motor Sport (CAMS) which is the representative of the FIA in Australia.

By 1963 the membership had grown to 44, by 1968 it was 82 and at the end of 1988 there were 180 fully paid-up members. The club fought and won a five-year battle with CAMS as a result of which all Australian clubs with at least 40 members, and which had been in existence for at least four

The Morgan Owners Club Dawn Dash at Mount Wilson in 1987.

years, were granted full membership with voting rights; hitherto, clubs with less than 100 members had only been granted associate membership with no voting rights.

In 1970 the club joined the Council of Veteran, Vintage and Throughbred Motor Clubs (VCCTMC), an organization which brings together about 30 clubs in the Sydney area and stages a static annual display of between 500 and 700 vehicle and motorcycles at Warwick Farm race course, including a Concours.

Communication between distant members is largely dependent upon the club magazine, which is a 20-page publication named *Morgan Ear* and is published monthly. This is a well-produced informative magazine. Full membership is open to all Morgan owners and associate membership to others who are *simpatico*.

The club organizes about 30 events a year. Competition events include circuit sprints and hill-climbs, there being a vigorous championship in conjunction with the Combined Sports Car Association. Social types are very well catered for, too, with events such as barbecues, dinners, tours to the country and interstate early morning 'dawn dashes', often ending with a picnic somewhere like a distant beach or in the mountains. A useful bridge between social and competition events is the Driver Training Day usually held at Oran Park racing circuit.

There is an extensive array of club regalia available, including T-shirts, windcheaters, caps, car badges, lapel badges and transfers. Club morale is high and members help each other with technical problems and maintenance. The range of cars owned by members is quite extensive and includes several

three-wheelers restored and running, flat-rad 4-4s and Plus 4s - four-seaters and roadsters, modern 4/4s and Plus 8s.

For the name and address of the club contact see the Affiliated Clubs list at the end of the chapter.

The Morgan Sports Car Club of Austria

Upon the initiative of Max Bulla, the importer and dealer of Morgans in Austria, a club was formed on June 26, 1977 with 12 enthusiasts. Statutes were written by Hans Schmolzer, the first president of the officially registered club.

The main purpose of the club is to hold competitive as well as social meetings, and to advise and help other members on technical problems with their Morgans. Membership can be obtained by owning a Morgan car, taking part in club activities at least once a year and the payment of the dues, which have remained the same since the founding date (ASh 500 annually).

At present the club has a membership of some 80 cars/persons, which include three-wheelers, 4/4 four-seaters and Plus 8s, as well as Plus 4s. Most of the members' cars are from the late 1960s, the 1970s and 1980s and are registered in Austria; however, they also have members from Switzerland and Bavaria.

The club is governed by a board which is responsible to the annual general assembly. Present President is Fred Myer, the Vice-President is Max Bulla, Treasurer and Regalia Officer is Peter Taucha, Sporting Events Commissioner Hans Jachim, Club Secretary is Janet Jesch assisted by Sissy Marine and the Editor of the *Morganeer Gazette* is Christine Maschl.

The activities of the MSCC-A include two bi-annual rallies according to the statutes, one at Whitsun and one in early autumn (September or October); the Thanksgiving Goose Eating Festival, with the new wine; the Christmas party with club championships celebration and the presentation of cups; participation at other Morgan rallies in foreign countries or participation at veteran car rallies in Austria due to the acceptance of Morgans as a veteran car in its own class at these events; publishing the *Morganeer Gazette* as well as irregular news bulletins and rally announcements; the Vienna Sections 'Noggin' Round Table, the second Thursday every month.

Production and sale of regalia peculiar to and designed for the MSCC-A such as pins, badges, (cloth or metal) and key chains, can be ordered from the Regalia Officer or the President.

Members welcome visitors from England, France, Switzerland, Germany, Italy and Belgium at club rallies and also participate on an individual

The Belgian Morgan Sports Car Club's stand at the Classic Car Show at Antwerp in 1989.

basis at Morgan meets in foreign countries. Due to having membership of the OMVV they can also participate in FIVA sanctioned rallies in Austria. The Morgan Sports Car Club of Austria has been associated for five years with the Morgan Sports Car Club (GB).

Anybody can join the MSCC-A as long as they own a Morgan, pay the annual dues, participate at one or more functions and adhere to the club's constitution. For name and address of the club contact see the Affiliated Clubs list at the end of the chapter.

Morgan Owner's Club, Belgium

In the summer of 1973 Dr Albert De Mey and Patrice Libiez met at the latter's home along with two other Morgan owners and two Jaguar owners, with the idea of forming a Morgan club in Belgium. From this modest beginning the club had grown to 65 members by 1978 and caters for French-speaking Morgan owners.

Members meet on the second Wednesday of each month at the Café Delta in Brussels, when owners of other sports cars are also welcome, as are any Morgan owners who happen to be in Brussels on that date. The club tries to organize five events each year, comprising of a social run with a visit to a place of historic interest. The main rally of the year must be unique in the Morgan club world, being held in conjunction with an international hot-air balloon meeting. The balloons lift off from the market place in the town of Saint Niklaas, the first one carrying a trophy. The Morgan owners then follow this balloon in their cars and the first one to reach it when it lands claims the trophy. The idea is not as dangerous as it might sound due to the slow progress of the balloons, and the event has the

co-operation of the local police.

Membership is open to all Morgan owners or enthusiasts. For name and address of the club contact see the Affiliated Clubs list at the end of the chapter.

Morgan Sports Car Club, Belgium

This club was started in 1987 when the French-speaking group went its separate way. At this time the club had about 60 members, most of which were French-speaking. However, in just two years the Flemish-speaking club had grown to 60-plus members.

The club organizes at least two events a year with the regular concours and rally tests. The annual dinner is held in January. The main event is the club stand at the Belgium Classic Car Show at Antwerp. Here the club is well known to other clubs for its hospitality - and especially its free champagne! The club also hopes to be able to organize an international event every two years.

There are three board members; President, Secretary and Public Relations Officer, who are all elected by the members. However, most club problems, *etc* are discussed at the monthly 'Noggins'.

The club also produces the well-produced, bi-monthly magazine *Belmognews*.

For name and address of the club contact see the Affiliated Clubs list at the end of the chapter.

Morgan Car Club of Canada (elect) (Toronto Morgan Owner's Club)

The golden era for Morgans in competition in Canada was the 1950s when they competed with great success at the Harewood Airport circuit and on the unpaved hill-climbs at Rattlesnake and Hockley, and dominated the ice races at St. Mary's Lake. On the rallying side they were less successful, perhaps because these events were sometimes 1300 miles long and held in temperatures as low as minus 40°C. However, in November 1961 three Plus 4s won the team prize in the Press-on-Regardless rally.

The first attempt to form a Morgan club occurred in 1962, when 18 Morgan owners met at the Jolly Miller Tavern in Toronto. However, Alan Sands, then 'between Morgans', was concerned that the proliferation of one-make clubs in Canada was undermining the sports car movement and he persuaded the Morgan owners to stay with their existing general purpose sports car clubs. Consequently, the idea of a Morgan Club of Canada faded for five years.

Then, in 1967, Doug Price was driving his Plus 4 when he spotted two Morgans parked at the kerb. A quick U-turn resulted in him meeting Ian Campbell and Ken Miles, as a result of which the first post-1962 meeting was held at Alan Sand's farm, Piper's Hill, where, with the unexpected publicity boost from radio CFRB, 12 Morgans assembled. The next few months were

The Belgian club's annual meet in 1988 was the Vlammog 88 at Lier.

spent locating other Morgan owners, and by 1968 some 25 cars had been traced, including five three-wheelers. Contact was made with the Great Lakes Group in Detriot, and joint meetings arranged and an effort made to form a group in Vancouver.

As with so many clubs, interest waned after the formative years, and whereas some 36 cars were on the register in 1974, two years later, when Reg and Audrey Beer staged a barbeque,

there was only one present apart from their own. Most of the others were rotting in garages under the pretext of undergoing restoration. The club then decided to take action and another meeting was held at Piper's Hill Farm for a 'Spring Tune-up'. A mixture of Plus 4s of older members and 4/4s and Plus 8s of younger and more recent owners turned up, enthusiasm was rekindled and 10 cars were present for the next barbeque. By 1978 club mem-

bership had risen to 89, events had become well supported and at last the club was a viable movement.

The newsletter. published irregularly and called *The Blurb*, covers an area from the Artic Circle to the Great Lakes and carries an illustration of a pig driving a Morgan, This has its origins in the fact that Toronto is sometimes unkindly referred to as Hogtown, and that the MSCC often chooses a name for its centres appropriate to its location, hence Taffmog for South Wales, Hopmog for the hop-growing area of Kent and Hogmog for Canada. Despite the long distances involved, many Canadian members manage to attend the national meeting of the American clubs each year, and some even collect prizes.

At the time of writing the club is in the process of being officially renamed The Morgan Sports Car Club of Canada.

Members of the Canadian club tune-up outside the motel where they stayed when attending the annual American meet.

Co-incidental with the name change will be the production of a new badge.

For name and address of the club contact see the Affiliated Clubs list at the end of the chapter.

Morgan Club of Denmark

The club was founded in October 1973 at a meeting held at the home of an owner, at which six Morgans were present. Since than the membership has grown to over 50, which is thought to represent three-quarters of the total of Morgans in the country. In addition to normal social gatherings and competitive events - including race meetings in Denmark - members of the club (which is now affiliated to the Morgan Sports Car Club and is known as Danmog) also compete in events held by the Swedish Club.

The club is open to all Morgan owners and enthusiasts. For name and address of the club contact see the Affiliated Clubs list at the end of the chapter.

Morgan owner - Finland

Until recently the only Morgan in Finland was the Plus 4 drophead coupé owned by Nick Marchan, so it is not surprising there is no Morgan club in that country. However, Mr Marchan is a member of the MSCC, as well as belonging to the Sports Car Club of Helsinki, which covers all makes and has approximately 100 sports cars within its membership.

The Plus 4 has the chassis number 6851 and engine number CT 80080 and was purchased direct from the factory in 1969. The car is absolutely standard, but was supplied with four extra 72-spoke wire wheels for use with winter tyres. Recently, a 1972 Plus 8 was imported into Finland.

Nick Marschan will always be happy to talk to other Morgan owners should they happen to be in Finland. His address is Bertel Jungs väg 8, 00570 Helsinki 57, Finland.

Morgan Club of France

The club, which is now affiliated to the MSCC, was founded in 1973 by Patrick Boisvieux and another Morgan owner who lived in Paris. From this humble beginning - and an initial lack of interest by other owners - it has grown steadily and now has more than 180 members throughout the country. Because of the large distances involved in attending meetings, the club has been divided into seven regions, each of which runs its own events, including concours and rallies, In addition the club organizes one international event each year, which started in 1981. These events are very popular and attract well over 120 Morgans every year.

The club publishes a quarterly magazine named *News,* which reports on meetings, technical advice and general Morgan news.

The first President of the club, Jaqueline Frot, has been succeeded as President by her son Jean-Christophe.

Four particularly interesting Morgans are owned by club members: Maurice Louche's very rare left-hand drive genuine Plus 4 Super Sports Drophead Coupé, which is fitted with a high grille and twin spare wheels; Marin Frot owns the 1921 speed record-break-

ing Darmont single-seater; Jean-Mare and Francoise Taboutet own an international concours-winning 1957 Plus 4 two-seater and Mme Vian still owns the car brought by her late husband, Boris Vian, who is considered to be one of the most important post-war French authors.

For name and address of the club contact see the Affiliated Clubs list at the end of the chapter.

Morgan Club of Germany

The Morgan Club of Germany, which is now affiliated to the MSCC, was founded in 1970 by six Morgan enthusiasts at a meeting in Frankfurt, where a committee was elected, the first President being Nick Borsch. Slowly, the club grew in numbers and in 1972 Pius Kuhlmann took over as President, who in turn was succeeded by Jurgen Bell in 1976. In 1975 the club adopted a formal constitution and was registered as an association by the city of Essen. Potential members join as guests for a year, then can be granted full membership at a General Meeting after having been proposed by two sponsors, and if elected can display the official club badge on their Morgan. Total membership had risen to 47 by 1976 and to over 300 in 1985.

The club is divided into four regions - North, Central, South and Berlin - each organized by a section leader, who arranges monthly meetings to enable members to meet each other and cultivate friendships. Sharing experiences and technical tips and the restoration and rebuilding of Morgans are recurring popular topics, and the success of the club in helping to forge friendships can be seen in the number of private meetings which take place in members' homes.

As can be seen from this picture, the annual meet of the Morgan Club de France is very well supported. This is Mog Avignon-Ventoux in 1987.

The club has had its own magazine, *The Morgan-Post*, since 1975. Its first editor was Heiner Giersberg, from Berlin, who handed over after one year to Reiner Wandert, originator of the magazine's current illustrated style and presentation. Pressure of work caused him to pass the editorship to Helmet Kuhlemann, who has made the magazine an interesting, informative and colourfully presented source of information to members.

Between 60 and 70 per cent of member's cars are Plus 8s, about 15 per cent are 4/4 four-seaters and the remainder are 4/4 two-seaters. Two flat-radiator Drop Head Coupés are owned by club members, but are in need of rebuilding, and the only registered three-wheeler is a 1934 Super Sports with a water-cooled 998cc Matchless engine, owned by Eberhard Schirdewahn from Delmenhorst.

The club's membership also includes Morgan drivers from Holland, Belgium, Switzerland and Austria, so it can claim to be truly international. For name and address of the club contact see the Affiliated Clubs list at the end of the chapter.

Morgan Sports Car Club - Holland
This club was formed in April 1972 through the enthusiasm of one man, Hans Dee, who, at the time of writing, is Treasurer. The first meeting was attended by 15 Morgan owners, but the club has since gathered momentum and become one of the most active in Europe, with membership of over 130 and affiliation to the MSCC. Of the original 15 members, 14 still have the same car.

The club organizes two big events each year, one in May and the other in October, comprising of driving tests, sprints, concours, social get-togethers and, last but not least, good food. As in nearly all large countries, the club has local centres which organise monthly noggins 'n' natters, local tours and rallies.

Although most Morgans in Holland are stored for the winter to avoid the salt on the roads, the club always holds a New Year's cocktail meeting arranged by the Dutch Morgan agent, who also happens to be the proprietor of the Dutch National Automobile Museum, so the surroundings are ideal.

A quarterly magazine called *Fanta Morgana* and its editor, Dick de Bruyn, excels in obtaining material from all over the world for inclusion. Membership is open to all Morgan owners, as well as 'sympathisers' although the basic rule of the club is No Morgan, No Vote. For name and address of the club contact see the Affiliated Clubs list at the end of the chapter.

Morgan owners - Hong Kong
There is no official Morgan club in Hong Kong , partly because of the strict governmental regulations relating to the formation of clubs, and partly because the majority of Morgan owners travel overseas a great deal and are often transferred to other countries. However, during 1988 and 1989 there was an incredible resurgence of interest in the Morgan in Hong Kong, so much

Celebrating the 15th anniversary of the Morgan Sports Car Club Holland with a scenic tour; the cars are parked in front of the Royal Palace in Amsterdam.

so that the formation of an official club was then being seriously considered. It wass envisaged to be the Morgan Sports Car Club with a constitution and proper legal registration. At the time of writing the 'membership' boasts some 60 enthusiasts with 23 cars in the colony. Among the events being planned is a 'Morgan Drive to China'.

The club functions at the moment through the Classic Car Club of Hong Kong. It may be slightly cheating to include the Classic Car Club of Hong Kong in a list of Morgan clubs because it is not a single marque club. However, it has such important Morgan associations it cannot be passed over!

The CCCHK was born as a result of an abortive attempt in 1970 to found a Morgan club in the Crown Colony. Today the club is almost 100 members strong and it is interesting to note that although there are only four Morgan-owning members, three of these are on the club committee. The four cars are interesting examples in fine condition. The oldest one is known as Betsy and is a 1953 flat-radiator Plus 4 four-seater. This has the most interesting history as it took part in the first Macau Grand Prix in 1954. Its owner, Club Secretary, Dick Worrall, bought the car in late 1967, sold it in April 1970, regretted doing so and bought it back again in July 1973. The President, Tom Surrency, has a 1958 Plus 4 four-seater which he restored to such perfection in the period 1975-8 that it was the overall winner of the 1980 Hong Kong Automobile Association's concours for cars manufactured after 1945. Tom North, the club's Publicity Officer has a 1969 4/4 four-seater and T Gibbs has a 1981 Plus 8.

The bad road conditions of Hong Kong tend to restrict usage of the cars,

and have necessitated the introduction of modifications aimed at curing steering-wheel shake, one such alteration being the fitment of a small shock absorber into the steering. Another hazard for Morgan owners is parking, and it is best to leave your car in a multi-storey car park hidden beneath a specially made nylon cover, otherwise a parked Morgan will immediately attract a crowd which may not be content just to look, but will clamber all over the car to have photographs taken!

Despite the lack of a club, the list of Morgan owners and the literature held by them is maintained, and any Morgan owner moving to, or passing through the colony is assured of a warm welcome from Derek Hinings, Banyan Villas, House B7, 9, Stanley Village Road, Stanley, Hong Kong.

Morgan Club - Italy
The official club was formed on June 10, 1981, and, from its small beginnings, has grown to become a very well organized and well supported club with over 110 members. Membership is strictly confined to active Morgan owners.

The number of events and meetings vary from year to year but include taking part in historical motor events by special arrangements with the promoters. Many other events are open to all Morgans, especially if the cars are 'late built'. The best competition result

achieved by the club was in 1986 when it was placed first, second and third at the Coppa delle Alpi and first overall at the two day meeting at Monza.

Besides issuing newsletters throughout the year, the club also publishes an illustrated year book, which is exceptionally well produced.

For name and address of the club contact see the Affiliated Clubs list at the end of the chapter.

Morgan Sports Car Club of Japan
It is very doubtful whether any Morgans were imported into Japan before World War Two, and after the war the import of foreign-made cars was prohibited until 1958. When this ban was lifted very few Morgans were imported, but the one or two seen in Tokyo in the early 1960s were owned by US serviceman or

British college lecturers.

In 1967 Mr Toshio Takano was appointed Morgan distributor in Japan and took delivery of four new cars. Few people knew about the Morgan car at that time and it took several months to sell them. Now, as nearly everywhere else, orders for new Morgans far outnumber availability.

In late 1972 Masahiro Naito took delivery of a 4/4 two-seater after a two-year wait, and was so impressed with his car that he contacted other Morgan owners and formed the Morgan Sports Car Club of Japan. For the first meeting in December, there were 18 members and, by 1978 (by which time the club had staged 34 events from touring rallies and hill-climbs to gymkhanas, sprints and races), membership had grown to 80. At the time of writing it has risen to 145. National meetings are held each year with the Tokyo Auto Club Sports and the Japan British Automobile Society.

It is believed that about 12 three-wheelers survive in the country, the rarest known being a 1937 barrel-back model with lowered body and an air-cooled Matchless engine, which is owned by Yutak Ando, while the rarest four-wheeler is a 1938 Coventry Climax engined 4-4 owned by Masahiro Naito.

The club now has nine branches throughout Japan, with each branch having its own chairman and organizing its own local events. The branches are located as follows: Central Branch; Tokyo; Chiba; Kanagawa; Kofu; Nagoya; Shizuoka; Kansai; Kyoto; Osaka; Wakayama; Hiroshima; Okayama; Saitama; Tohoku; North Area.

Contact amongst the branches is maintained by the organisation of the annual national meeting and through the club's twice-yearly magazine, *Great Runabout*.

Article 2 of the club constitution says : *The object of the club is to enjoy auto sports through Morgan cars, promote friendship among members, observe traffic rules while trying to improve driving skill and retain the spirit to endure every difficulty experienced with an automobile 'Morgan'*. Anyone agreeing to support these objectives can be admitted to the club, and Morgan enthusiasts visiting Japan are assured of a warm welcome.

Morgan Owners Club Luxembourg

Current membership totals 24 and is open to anyone interested in the marque. The club holds one international event a year, plus some four or five local events, which include the MOCL Tennis Tournament.

The club was started in May 1978 when six Morgan owners held a social meeting, since when membership has increased steadily.

The club produces a quarterly magazine entitled *The Chronicle*. Technical advice is also given. For name and address of the club contact see the Affiliated Clubs list at the end of the chapter.

Morgan Sports Car Club of New Zealand

This club began in 1971 as the result of a chance meeting of Morgan owners on the road, held its first meeting at Easter 1972 and then was run informally for three years until becoming officially established in 1975. On its formation the total membership of 35 represented 80 per cent of Morgans in the country, while at the time of writing the number has risen to around 100. There was a club magazine, *Borrowed Time* (the title

was copied from an article on Morgans by Peter Garnier in *Autocar* in September 1965) which was published monthly, but this since ceased publication and has been replaced by an occasional newsletter.

Marsden Robinson (Club Secretary) and Martin Adams (President) keep the flag flying in the Auckland area - especially in the 'intermarque challenge' (a series of races/sprints/concours culminating in the 'Le Mans Relay' race run by the Porsche Club on the New Zealand Grand Prix circuit.) 'Team Morgan' - always the favourite with the spectators - usually acquits itself quite well at the Le Mans event. It took the chequered flag in 1986, but concours are generally not taken too seriously in New Zealand Morgan circles, so at the time of writing the Challenge Cup has so far eluded them.

Amongst their members' cars are P2038 - the very first Plus 4 ever made in 1950 originally as a DHC, but rebodied by the factory in 1968 with the then current 'cowled roadster' style; P2412 - a one-owner Plus 4 roadster with total mileage of less than 40,000, most of them on racetracks and hillclimbs (and a dislay case of trophies to prove it!); and the 1972 Earls Court Motor Show Plus 8 (R7536) still in the hands of its original owner. And from the 'Old Morgans never die' department - a 1951 example that was 'totalled' by a train some 30 years ago and left to rot in a paddock. It was subsequently uplifted by a keen enthusiast desperate for a Morgan and has recently risen from the dead, with the help of just about everyones' spare parts bins. It proves the basic philosophy of the New Zealand Morgan enthusiast that 'No

The Christchurch area of the New Zealand Morgan Sports Car Club staged a member's run to Hammer Springs in 1987.

Morgan is ever beyond repair!'

Club member, John Rock-Evans, put both the club and the marque on the map in 1978 by appearing in the *Mastermind* competition on New Zealand television and answering questions on the history of the Morgan Motor Company. He reached the semifinals before falling on the question: 'Has the Morgan Motor Company ever produced a model, other than the Plus 4 Plus, which could be classed as an enclosed vehicle?' (They did, but can you name it?)

Another keen owner collected his car, a 1977 4/4 four-seater, in England and drove it to South Africa, all without trouble, before shipping it the remainder of the journey.

Membership of the club is open to all Morgan owners or 'Morgan nuts'.

Morgan owner - Peru

Just before the outbreak of World War Two, three Englishmen each imported a 4-4, but because of the war they had to return to England, leaving their cars behind them. One of these cars has disappeared but the other two were found by A Gardillo, who is now in the

Club member, Lloyd Gleeson, competing in the Thoroughbred & Classic Car Club's sprint meeting in February 1981 on the Pukekoho (New Zealand) Grand Prix circuit.

process of restoring them. The only other known Morgan in the country, a 4/4 two-seater, was imported new in 1963.

Mr Gardillo, who is a member of the MSCC, would be delighted to meet any Morgan owner who visits Peru and can be reached at Luis Felipe Villaran 395, San Isidro, Lima 27, Peru.

Morgan owners - Sicily

Six Morgan have been traced in Sicily, two 4/4 four-seaters, three 4/4 two-seaters and a Plus 8, the owners of which are all known to each other. Although they do not meet on a regular basis or have an official club to link them, they offer each other the usual Morgan mutual assistance whenever necessary.

In 1974 strict exhaust regulations came into effect, and at the same time a 35 per cent VAT was applied to cars over 2000cc, so the owner of the Plus 8 counts himself very lucky to have brought his car just before these rules came into effect.

Anyone visiting Sicily and wanting to talk Morgans should contact R Bonomo, Via Alcide de Gasperi 203, Palermo, Sicily.

Morgan owners - Singapore

Although there is no official Morgan club in Singapore, the five known Morgan owners keep in regular contact with each each other. The earliest of their cars is a pre-war 4-4, which is owned by an English couple who really cherish it. A New Zealander owns a 1954 two-seater, there are two four-seaters dating from 1963 and 1964, and an Indian Singaporian keeps a two-seater in excellent condition.

Several local factors affect the ownership of Morgans and certain other cars in Singapore, one being a rather strange government taxation system which increases tax on all cars over ten years old (regardless of condition) and almost doubles it by the time the car is 15 years old. The weather is also a major influence, for it rains on average once a day and most other times there is very hot sunshine. This has led to hood modifications by Morgan owners, one arrangement being to provide a sedanca hood position, with the top folded back from the screen halfway and fastened to the hood irons. Another way of avoiding being drenched by one of the sudden rainstorms is to drive the car with the hood up, but with a zipped flap for the rear window which can be operated from inside the car.

The five Morgans have proved very popular in Singapore, and their owners are approached almost weekly by people offering to buy their cars. Any visitor wishing to meet a local Morgan owner should first contact WJ Lawrence, PO Box 57, Tanglin Post Office, Singapore 10.

Morgan Owner's Club of South Africa (SAMOG)

Morgan owners in South Africa seem to be independent-minded individuals, so much so that they do not feel the need for a formal Morgan club. Nevertheless, they have formed themselves into an association so that the 30 or so cars spread throughout this large country remain identified and are well looked after.

The group was started by Angela Heinz, an adventurous woman whose hobbies include flying her own aeroplane and selling Morgans and motorcycles, who is a familiar sight to the Police in Johannesburg driving her very potent Plus 8 into town with her plaited

pony tails streaming in the wind. In the days of free import of Morgans into South Africa she acted as the official agent, but now import regulations make it virtually impossible to get a new Morgan into the country.

Her first gathering of Morgan owners was held on July 11, 1971, at her oil executive husband's prestigious house in a select Johannesburg suburb, where seven Morgans gathered together. Since then broadcaster Ronnie Wilson and his wife, Colleen, have organized a number of social events, including drives to gracious old mine managers' homes on the Golden Reef, barbecues, and so on, and recently Ronnie was chosen to be Chairman of SAMOG. As a result of a letter asking him for details for inclusion in this book he arranged a special gathering of Johannesburg-based cars at the Jukskei Motor Museum for a photographic session, which drew approximately a third of all Morgans known in South Africa.

The very first meeting of the South African Club held on July 4th 1971.

In motor sport the Morgan name is upheld in South Africa by former MG owner Steve Spencer, who now races a particularly fast Plus 8, and by John Frewin, from Middleburg, who is a keen rally competitor. South Africans are great travellers, and several owners have made the pilgrimage to Malvern. Likewise, a warm Morgan greeting awaits anyone visiting South Africa. For name and address of the club contact see the Affiliated Clubs list at the end of the chapter.

Morgan Sports Car Club of Spain
The founder and first President of this club in June 1984 was Mrs Maribel Puig. Originally, there were six members of the club (two of whom actually attended the 75th Anniversary celebrations at Malvern that year). Membership has now grown to 25 members from Spain and one from Portugal.

Once a year the club holds a general meeting which is used for planning forthcoming activities for the year. Normally there are six excursions for one,

two or three days and normally no less than eight Morgans take part.

Morgan Owner's Club of Sweden
The formation of this group came about as a result of a chance meeting of two Morgan owners in the car park of a sports car exhibition in Gothenburg in April 1966. When Arne Holmstrom, now Chairman of the group, parked his 1952 Plus 4 Drop Head Coupé, he was approached by another Morgan owner and in the ensuing conversation they discovered that, between them, they knew of 10 Morgan owners in Sweden, and so the idea of forming club was born. The first meeting was held at the Gothenburg home of one of the owners on January 11, 1967.

A provisional name of Morgan Register of Sweden was proposed for the club at a subsequent meeting a few weeks later, but in April that year it was changed to allow the use of the letters MOG.

The first competitive event tackled by the members was a club race at the Dalslandsring, run by the Gothenburg

Sports Car Club, and in July 1967 nine members took part in a two week holiday to England with their cars, the nine Swedish numbered cars attracting a great deal of attention throughout their tour, which included a factory visit at Malvern, where they were warmly greeted by Peter Morgan. The following month, when the first officers and committee of the group were elected at a meeting at Granna, membership had grown to 20. With the help of an active competition programme, including hillclimbs and rallies, and a good social calendar, membership has grown steadily ever since. The most recent count is 61 members, who own 75 Morgans between them.

The club produces its own magazine and has two sub-sections covering the north and south of the country. For name and address of the club contact see the Affiliated Clubs list at the end of the chapter.

Morgan Club of Switzerland
Following a gathering of Morgan owners in July 1976 the Morgan Club of

Members of the Morgan Owners Club committee dressed to contend with the very cold Swedish weather but, in true Morganeering tradition, the hood remains down.

Switzerland came into being the following June, since when the membership has grown from 45 to 135. Each year the club organizes a race, two two-day get-togethers which include a gymkhana, treasure hunt, *etc*, as well as monthly regional gatherings. Nearly all the cars of club members are extremely well kept and original, most with low mileages as very few are used as everyday transport, especially during

winter when salt can remain on the road for anything up to six months. About 80 per cent of the cars within the club were manufactured between 1966 and 1976 and, of these, 60 per cent are Plus 8s, 20 per cent 4/4 two-seaters and 10 per cent 4/4 four-seaters. There are also five three-wheelers (two V-twins and three F models).

Not long ago a Swiss member of the club became the proud owner of a rarity, namely the racing Morgan MMC 4. He also owns the original Morgan 4 built in 1936, chassis no. 037, one of the few vehicles where the doors open backwards. It seems this is the only original 4-4 of this type on the Continent. There are also known to be a Plus 4 Plus, a Plus 4 Super Sports and five other three-wheelers in the country, the owners of which are being encouraged to join the club.

Although the club has very detailed rules (which fill a 12-page book-

let), nobody seems to take them too seriously. The club facilities include technical advice and the supply of cheap parts, while the club magazine, *MCS Organ,* is edited by the Secretary and issued twice a year. A Morgan register is being compiled which, it is hoped, will contain full details and specifications of every Morgan in Switzerland.

Unfortunately, it has not been possible to import new Morgans officially since 1974. Because of this, each owner tries to keep his car in good, if not very good, condition.

The club and its members are always happy to receive visits from Morgan owners from other countries. For name and address of the club contact see the Affiliated Clubs list at the end of the chapter.

Morgan car clubs in the USA
Morgan Plus 4 Club of Southern California

Founded in 1954, this club has the distinction of being the oldest Morgan club in America, and second in the world, after the Morgan Sports Car Club Limited. Without doubt the club is also one of the most active. Regular meetings are held in the rear of Me 'n' Ed's Pizza Parlor in Long Beach, where it is not unusual to find more than 40 enthusiasts present. Two meetings are held every month; one a general business meeting - really a euphemism for a social gathering - and the other a

board meeting. A good balance is maintained between social events, rallies and slaloms, with the occasional wine-tasting tour, baseball game or picnic thrown in. All events are well supported, despite the large distances often involved.

The President and officers adopt parliamentary procedure at their board meetings, business being conducted in a reasonably formal fashion, the size of

the group permitting good delegation of responsibility. Particularly impressive is the roll of Spares Chairman, which is filled by a member who manages a very sizeable inventory of Morgan spares. At the December 1978 meeting I was privileged to be extended Honorary Mem-

The Swiss Club's summer meet.

bership of the club in recognition of my 'extensive contributions to the cause'.

The membership is 250-plus with over 30 events a year. A monthly magazine called *The Format* is issued to all members and contains a great deal of information on club meetings and events, as well as technical articles of a very high standard. Also, in spite of the name, membership is open to all Morgan owners regardless of which model they own.

In the past, an annual social event was held, often at a place called the Sky Ranch, but recently this has given way to something more ambitious, patterned after the 'Luray' event on the east coast of the United States. After having driven her 4/4 across country to Luray in 1981 (and back, with a broken arm and throttle cable), Evelyn (Lynn Bird) Willburn put together a similar west coast event co-hosted by Northern California's Bob Schmidt. The event mush-

roomed from around 80 Moggies the first year to well over 100 at the 75th Anniversary celebration at Laguna Seca Spring vintage races, Monterey, California in 1984. The event was first called Morgans at Morro Bay, but has since been held at Pismo Beach and Cambria; the goal is to find a mid-point between southern and northern California Morgan clubs. Lately, the event is taking over the old MOGWEST name formally associated with the north/south meet at the annual August Laguna Seca historic races.

A significant event occured at the historic races at Laguna Seca in 1978 when three Morgans, one a rare SLR, competed in different events. In the fifth race, Brian Howlett, a past President of the club driving a 1962 Plus 4, utterly humiliated two Porches to win the most exciting race of the series, ensuring the Morgan name would be imprinted in Southern California mo-

tor racing history for some time to come.

A more recent triumph for a Morgan in California happened in August 1993 when Gerry Willburn, a past President of the club, was invited to enter his recently restored one-off 1952 Plus 4 Saloon Morgan in the prestigious Pebble Beach Concours, the first time a Morgan had ever been invited to compete. Although he did not win his class he was placed second, which is a magnificent achievement when one considers that the Pebble Beach concours is the world pinnacle in this type of motoring competition.

The club has a very extensive range of trophies including the Ken Hill 'Close Encounters' award which is awarded by the committee to the member who, in its opinion, has had the closet brush with the law in the previous year. In 1989 it was awarded for the Best Traffic Ticket Evasion.

A fine assortment of Morgans gathered together for the Southern California Club concours.

For name and address of the club contact see the Affiliated Clubs list at the end of the chapter.

Morgan Sports Car Club (formerly Morgan Plus 4 Club) of Northern California

The history of the Morgan Sports Car Club of Northern California is synonymous with the availability of the marque in the San Francisco Bay area. The California club was formed in 1955, shortly after Rene Pellandini established, in Los Angeles, a Morgan distributorship for the Western United States - Worldwide Motors.

Berkeley and Marin County claim the honour of having been residences for the first Morgans in the Bay area, both purchased from Worldwide Motors. Later, a third Morgan was purchased at Malvern Link, which also settled briefly in the East Bay. As en-

A few of the three-wheelers owned by club members lined up at the Morro Bay Show in 1987.

Morgan

thusiasm for Morgan motoring began to take hold in Northen California, Morgans were imported from such far away places as Morocco, Venezuela and the Malay States.

By late 1956 there was sufficient interest among Bay area Morganeers to form a Northern California Club. Minutes of the club record that the inaugural meeting was held on March 24, 1957. Four of the members owned 1953 vintage Morgans and the fifth car is said to have been a TR3-engined model. At about the same time new Morgan dealerships were established: Fergus in New York in 1959 and Triumph Inc., in San Francisco. However, the impact of increasing Morgan imports on the club's membership was felt immediately; nineteen new members had joined the club by the end of 1957. Membership was soon touching the 200 mark and the diversity of models led the club to vote to change its name, which took effect from December 1988.

The club has a very extensive social and competition calendar which caters for all members, no matter what their interests. Originally, the club magazine was named *The Morgan Plus 4 Format*, then in 1973 it was changed to *Morganasm*. This had a very short life and the next title was the *Morgazette*. In more recent years it has become known as *The Flexible Flyer*.

For name and address of the club contact see the Affiliated Clubs list at the end of the chapter.

Morgan Car Club, Washington DC
Founded in March 1959 by a small group of enthusiasts in the area, the club is the third oldest in the USA.

Membership has grown to over 300 and is now run on a national basis. The club holds a monthly social 'noggin'

linked with a brief business meeting. Also there is a monthly driving tour to an event or location of interest. In addition the club organizes and co-ordinates the annual Morgan Owners' Gathering (MOG).

In 1971 the first MOG was held to coincide with the inaugural Ponoco 500 at the Ponoco International Raceway, a venue which the club used for the next four years before moving to Luray, Virginia in 1976. Morgan owners travel hundreds of miles to attend these gatherings, and Mr and Mrs Peter Morgan were guests of honour in 1972 and 1978, and myself and my wife, Janet, in 1980. Since then, due to a fire at the Luray Hotel, the venue has been changed each year.

When the club was formed, club racing was just beginning in the USA and most of the venues were within easy striking distance of Washington DC. A club team of Morgans, called Team Revel, competed at all of these events, but the showcase was the 1.2-mile road circuit at Marlboro, which was to prove an ideal training ground for future stars like Mark Donohue, Peter Revson and Bob Tullus. A highspot of the club's early days was when 50 Morgans attended Patuxent Naval Air Show and associated spring meeting.

When the economic conditions of the mid 1960s caused closure of most of the convenient road circuits, the club turned its attention to rally and autocross events, where its autocross and sprint teams nearly always finished amongst the top three whenever entered.

The policy of the club is to encourage other Morgan clubs to co-sponsor annual MOGs. It is responsible for MANNA (Morgan Aid Network of North America), and is affiliated to the Morgan

Sports Car Club. The club issues a magazine aptly-named *Rough Rider*, which is edited by Edmund (Ed) Zielinski and is of good quality with technical bulletins, a swap-and-sell column and news of club activities, illustrated with photographs by one of the club's past Presidents, John H Sheally II.

Morgan owners the world over are always welcome. For name and address of the club contact see the Affiliated Clubs list at the end of the chapter.

3/4 Morgan Group of America
A group of 15 Morgan owners from New York area who attended the first MOG event at Ponoco, Pennsylvania, decided to form their own club, membership of which has grown to approximately 100. Most live in the north-eastern United States, but the club does have members from as far south as Virginia and as far west as Chicago, while the easternmost member is Peter Morgan, who was presented with honorary membership of the group by the late President Harry J Carter, when he visited the USA in 1977.

As the title infers, the club caters for both three- and four-wheeled Morgans; as a registered corporation it

A general view of the annual meeting of Morgans from all over America and Canada. This is MOG 13 (1983).

has comprehensive articles which extend to 12 typed pages. The clear objectives of the group are:

The purposes for which this corporation has been organized are to promote fellowship and extend acquaintanceships among Morgan car enthusiasts by means of social gatherings and discussions to promote interest in the ownership and enjoyment of the operation of such cars by means of such activities as, but not necessarily limited to, rallies, concours d'elegance, autocross, gymkhanas, races, time trials, technical workshops, meets, noggins and tours; to engage generally in any causes or objects similar to the above-mentioned in order to promote the welfare of the membership and for 'maintaining the breed' (which phrase shall be deemed to mean the promotion or the preservation, and the regular use,

of the three- and four-wheeled Morgan cars which were originally designed by the late HFS Morgan and by his son Peter HG Morgan and which were, and are being, produced by the firm which they built, the Morgan Car Company Limited of Pickersleigh Road, Malvern Link, Worcestershire, England.

The club membership owns a fine assortment of models but the rarest car is the 1938 4-4 TT Replica owned by John Artley. The club magazine, *Morganeer*, is published monthly.

Membership is open to all Morgan enthusiasts. For name and address of the club contact see the Affiliated Clubs list at the end of the chapter.

Ohio Morgan Owners

This is an informal regional group of Morgan owners dedicated to keeping

their cars on the road by sharing technical information, trading spare parts and getting together two or three times a year for various Morgan-related events. It was started in 1973 when three Morgan owners invited all 15 known owners in the area to an initial picnic meeting in Columbus, Ohio, to which 10 of them responded. Mainly by word-of-mouth contact, membership had risen to 72 inidividuals at the last count, owning 82 Morgans between them. All but 20 of the members have become fee-paying since 1978 in order to finance expanded mailings and various club activities.

Ohio developed a good population of Morgans in the early 1970s when Don Simpkins' MM & M Imports of Derby brought many cars into the USA, when they were not as fashionable as they are today. He now runs Morgan

Fab Industries (Morgan restoration shop) in Buford, Georgia, and has probably handled half the cars now owned in Ohio.

The group has always been well represented at national Morgan events sponsored by the Washington DC club, laurels having been won by Walt Squires' 1971 Plus 8, Jerry Boston's 1961 Plus 4 Drop Head Coupé, Jim Bessts' 1958 4/4 Roadster, George Brokaw's 1961 Plus 4 Drop Head Coupé, Charles Miller's 1970 4/4 Roadster and Bob Burrows' 1963 Plus 4 Roadster. The group also participates in local classic and vintage car shows and sports car rallies to promote the marque, and a typical recent season included combined events with Jaguar, MG, Triumph and Austin-Healey clubs involving rallies, sports car shows and swap meets.

Facilities for members include the group's own car badge, lists of all Morgan spare parts available in Ohio, together with lists of recommended parts suppliers and specialist shops for mechanical body and upholstery work.

On the members' roster there are 35 Plus 4 Roadsters, 13 Plus 4 four-seaters, 10 4/4 Roadsters, four 4/4 Competition Roadsters, six Plus 4 Drop Head Coupés, seven Plus 8s, three three-wheelers and two 4/4 Series 1 Drop Head Coupés.

Interesting cars which have been or are being restored include Jim Bessts' 1932 Family Model three-wheeler, Bob Burrows' 1949 4/4 Series 1 Drop Head Coupé, Dutch Junge's 1928 Super Sport three-wheeler, Dick Nelson's 1955 dual spare (long-nose) Plus 4 Drop Head Coupé, Winn Rosch's 1934 three-wheeler and 1964 Plus 4 Plus and Paul Schodorf's 1955 Plus 4 four-seater Drop Head Coupé. An interesting newcomer

is Bruce Edwards' Issis Imports 1978 Plus 8 propane-powered roadster.

It is not necessary to be a Morgan owner to enjoy membership of this group. For name and address of the club contact see the Affiliated Clubs list at the end of the chapter.

Morgans of Philadelphia (MOPS)

Formed on 13 March 1977 when 25 enthusiasts responded to an advertisement in the city newspaper, within two years the club membership had reached almost 40. Monthly gatherings and visits to local auto shows are held, and in the autumn the club hosts a gymkhana which is well supported by other clubs. In a recent event the crowd were treated to the sight of President Gus Spahr's concours-winning 1932 Aero three-wheeler doing very well while competing against a field of 4-4s, Plus 4s and a Plus 8.

There are some interesting cars amongst the membership, and Alex Smith, who used to work for a local Morgan dealer back in the days when the cars could be imported legally, has one of the few Plus 4 Plus models in the USA. Fellow member Bob Lehr, who is also Vice-President of the Washington DC Club, has a right-hand drive Plus 4 Super Sports which was probably the last Super Sports to be imported into the USA and is one-of-a-kind in that it

is not entirely aluminium-bodied. Factory correspondence indicates that in 1967, when the car went into production, the supply of aluminium was low and, rather than wait, the owner elected to have his care built with steel. Bud Bernard's 1967 Plus 4 is a perfect example of a Morgan transition car in that it has the rear treatment of the 1959-66 Plus 4 with other features, including the lockable glovebox, of a 1967, and was one of the first to enter the United States during that last year of legality.

A 1966 Plus 4 Super Sports has been undergoing restoration since 1971 by Dick Larrick, who is so fanatical about detail that some of his restored parts may soon need restoring! Jim Schrader's 1964 Plus 4 has a TR transmission with overdrive to go with its TR engine, this near conversion having been done before he bought the car. In addition to his multi award-winning 1962 Plus 4, member Dick Smith has the last Drop Head Coupé to be imported into the USA, an early 1968 car in concours condition. Alex Knight's 1933 barrel-back three-wheeler Super Sports should be back on the road by now, and Peter Gunshor's 1975 4-4 four-seater is a recent addition to the club strength.

Membership of MOPS is described as 'open to anyone who is tolerant enough to put up with the inexplicable affection they have for Morgans, and the driving pleasure they bring them', and a monthly newsletter, *MOPS Mania*, is supplied to all members.

For name and address of the club contact see the Affiliated Clubs list at the end of the chapter.

Morgan Owner's Group - Great Lakes
This group began informally in 1964 or 1965, its principal founders being Don Frantz and the late Jack Markley, long-time Detroit Morgan enthusiast, who would get together with about 10 other Morgan owners when the mood struck them to socialise a little and discuss their mutual Morgan interests. By chance meetings on the road and word-of-mouth, new members were attracted, but the group remained informal under the unofficial presidencies of Don Frantz and Pat Kobielski until it was decided around 1970 to bring some organisation into the club, with the payment of modest dues, the preparation of a calendar of events and the regular

mailing of notices to members.

This led in 1975 to the official incorporation of the Morgan Owners Group as a Michigan non-profit corporation, and the club had grown to a membership of more than 65 by 1979, most of whom lived in the Detroit, Michigan and surrounding Great Lakes areas of the mid-West, but some were from all over the country and even as far away as Australia. More than 75 Morgans are owned by the membership, including three-wheelers, pre-war 4-4s, a Plus 4 Plus and what is probably the only 1976 4/4 presently in the United States.

A full calendar of events includes monthly meetings at a local restaurant and at least one other monthly function. In the winter events tend to be mainly social as few members are willing to expose their cars to the harsh Michigan weather. The outdoor season begins in the early spring with the annual English day road rally held in conjunction with the Austin-Healey, Jaguar, MG and Triumph clubs, followed by the spring car clinic, a gathering with a technical emphasis to inspect members's cars and prepare them for summer driving, which includes an English day at the Waterford Hills SCCA track and various picnic and cross-country outings.

Highlight of the year is the annual mid-West meet, a weekend affair held at a northern Michigan resort, involving competition events such as a road rally and Concours d'Elegance, as well as a banquet. The first of these was held in 1976, when it was felt that the long journeys to national meets discouraged many local members from participating and that the club had grown large enough to support such an event alone. They have proved a huge suc-

cess, usually with over 30 cars attending. However, in recent years the location of this popular gathering has been extended to include some outstanding resorts in Ohio, and in 1989 the meet was held at Waterloo, Ontario, Canada.

In addition to sponsoring activities, the club also puts out publications of interest to Morgan owners, including event notices and general news in the monthly *Flexible Flyer*. The club is also putting together a technical manual of hints and suggestions on how to maintain the Morgan car, based on the experiences of members and other Morgan owners. This is a very active and enthusiastic group.

For name and address of the club contact see the Affiliated Clubs list at the end of the chapter.

Morgan Owner's Group - Northwest
Morgan Owners Group Northwest was founded in early 1975 in Portland, Oregon, with about a dozen members. As it grew in number it also grew geographically. The club now holds business meetings quarterly in centrally-located Olympia, Washington. They have a monthly gathering for socialising and sharing technical knowledge in Portland, Oregon for the

Sixteen Morgans on the lawn at Deep Bay, the house of George Sterne who, for 15 years, was the Morgan agent on the west coast of Canada. This was just one of the long-distance trips organised by the Morgan Owners Club Group North West.

southern membership and in Seattle, Washington for the northern contingent.

The club has participating members in Washington, Oregon, Idaho and British Columbia. This represents a large territory and most members think nothing of driving one or two hundred miles to arrive at the start of a tour of several hundred miles! Considering that this area of the USA and Canada is blessed with incredible scenery, it is not surprising that the group has evolved into a touring club that enjoys one- or two-day explorations of picturesque coastline, arid desert or snow-capped mountain ranges. Interspersed among the six to eight tours each summer are three or four social gatherings at members' homes.

Additionally, the club supports one long-distance tour each year and, a few years ago, spent 10 days covering the 2500 mile round-trip to Cambria, California for the west coast Morgan Meet, then a further week touring British

The club produces a monthly magazine entitled *Northwest Magazine* which is supplied to all members. For name and address of the club contact see the Affiliated Clubs list at the end of the chapter.

Minnesota Morgan Club
This group had its beginnings in 1978 when Morgan owners, Tom Smisek and David Fellman, ran an ad in a Minneapolis newspaper exhorting fellow Mog-persons to appear with their Morgans at a picnic to be held at Minnehaha Falls. Even though the picnic never took place, the advertisement served to identify enthusiasts. Membership now totals 38 and is open to all Morgan owners and their families.

This is an informal group of Morgan owners dedicated to keeping their cars on the road by sharing technical information, trading spare parts and getting together several times a year for Morgan-

related events.

Club activities include vintage racing at Brainerd International Raceway, British 'Kick-off' tour and picnic, autumn drive to Classic Motorbooks in Osceola, Wisconsin and Freeze-Your-Gizzard Morgan Gathering - a late fall gathering where snow accumulation in the cockpit of attending Morgans is measured and duly recognised!

Member's cars of interest include Dr Bill Nelson's 1953 Plus 4 transition model which recently underwent a lengthy restoration project. Paul Massnick owns the only three-wheeler in the area; it's undergoing a complete rebuild in the kitchen of his historic home, located on Nicollet Island. Fred Nairn owns the only flat-rad in the area, a 1952 Plus 4.

Kathy and George Fink's 1964 Plus 4 Plus Coupé was the 20th car built out of a total production run of 26 cars; only 19 of this model are known to have survived. Ginny and Gordon Spartz

Members inspect Kathy and George Fink's 1962 Plus 4 Super Sports at the Club's 1985 'Freeze Your Gizzard' event. That year there was no snow due to unseasonably warm weather.

draw lots of attention in their 1962 Plus 4 Drop Head Coupé.

While no Plus 8 Morgan is counted among the group, speedy Morgans abound in Minnesota, there's Ken Kauffman's 1967 Weber-carburetted 4/4, Pat Starr's 1958 Plus 4 racing Morgan and George Fink's 1962 Plus 4 Super Sport, which campaigned at Sebring in 1963.

Morgan Motor Car Club - Dallas, Texas

The organisational meeting of the Morgan Motor Car Club was in December 1974, in Dallas, Texas. The primary force behind the organisation was Jim Woodyard, who started making a list of Morgans of which he became aware soon after acquiring his own Plus 4 in 1970; the list included licence numbers of Morgans he saw on the street and checked the ownership of through the State office. The first attempt at a get-together was in June 1974 and resulted in the appearance of nine Morgans of various descriptions, including one three-wheeler. Thereafter,

a meet of some type was held every month prior to the organisational meeting of the club itself. The quartet of Jim Woodyard, Chuck Harris, Bob Moses and Bill Boyless made up a nucleus around which the club was initially formed. Six of the nine owners who joined at the initial meeting remain members today. At the first meeting, Woodyard was elected President, the sole officer.

An interest in the marque is the only criterion for club membership. There are no written rules, nor have any been necessary. The aim of the group is to share the troubles and triumphs of Morgan ownership. The club newsletter, *Mog Log*, is a monthly publication.

An informal 'Flying Mog Squad' has been formed to go to the aid of any

Morgan owner whose car needs attention or assistance. The Mog Squad provides not only camaraderie but also the combined expertise of many members.

Whilst the Morgan Motor Club was the initial club founded in Texas, and all its badges feature the Texas Lone Star, the club was not meant to be a local, provincial organisation. Rather, the organisers hoped to include and serve all Morgan enthusiasts in the southwest portion of the United States that were unrepresented by a formal organisation. Hence, the non-regional official naming of the club as the Morgan Motor Car Club.

Among the more active members there is a lack of appreciation of obstacles to Morgan driving. Four Morgans travelled together on a 3500-mile round trip trek to Washington DC for the 1982 meet, followed the next year by a 4500-mile round trip with five cars to California's initial Morro Bay event. The Plus 4 Plus of Bill and Judi Boyles was shipped to the Zandvoort Holland event in 1987 and logged some 3000 miles while on the continent of Europe.

At one time, three of the known 19 Plus 4 Plus models still existing were owned by MMCC members, including the last one ever built. Also unique is that the Morgan Motor Car Club was the first Western Hemisphere club accepted as an official centre of the home club in England, the Morgan Sports Car Club.

For name and address of the club

Members of the Morgan Owners Group South at the Club's 1989 Spring Meet at Highlands, North Carolina.

contact see the Affiliated Clubs list at the end of the chapter.

Western New York Morgan Owner's Group

This group was started in the winter of 1978 by Alan Isselhard and Dean Meyer. The club has only two 'officers', who have guided it since the beginning: Alan Isselhard is the group organiser, who keeps the club on an informal basis and attempts to keep the treasury from becoming too fat, and Ed Kowalski - who purchased his Plus 4 flat radiator roadster new in 1953 and still owns it - is the treasurer. There are no elections for club officers and, in spite of offers by Alan and Ed to stand down in favour of someone else, no change has taken place as yet. Membership currently stands at 40 and activities include attending Watkins Glen races and social events.

Most of the membership is from the upstate New York area, mainly between Buffalo and Syracuse, with Rochester in the middle. Several of the members own sports/collector cars in addition to their Morgans. As is true with the majority of American Morgan people, most of their member-owned cars are pre-1968 - thanks to the safety-minded bureaucrats in Washington.

A club magazine entitled *Morgandats* is published five times a year. For name and address of the club contact see the Affiliated Clubs list at the end of the chapter.

Morgan Owner's Group South

The club was founded in 1976 at a weekend event held at Myrtle Beach, South Carolina, and has remained active ever since. The current membership totals approximately 60, and membership is open to anyone, without restriction.

MOG South has a broad geographic coverage, with members from the states of Georgia, South Carolina, North Carolina, Tennessee, Alabama, Florida and Virginia. As a result, get-togethers are less frequent but are held in more varied locations.

The club has four events each year.

The first get-together is at the Walter Mitty Challenge at Road Atlanta (in Georgia) the last weekend in April. This is an all-makes vintage racing event. The second event of the year is Spring Meet, which is usually held in May. The site varies from Highlands, North Carolina (which is just across the border from Georgia), to picturesque Charleston, South Carolina. The third get-together is another full weekend affair, traditionally held in the North Carolina Mountains in October when the leaves are in full colour. Fourth and last event of the year is a Christmas Party held in the home of one of the members, usually in the Atlanta, Georgia area. All of the events are informal and generally always include a car show but not a formal concours. The club magazine is called *Southern Fours and Eights*. The current editor is Lance Lipscomb, who lives in Atlanta, Georgia.

For name and address of the club contact see the Affiliated Clubs list at the end of the chapter.

Morgan Three-Wheeler Club, USA Group Organiser

There is no actual club in America catering solely for three-wheelers, but all are welcome as members of the

previously listed clubs. However, the Morgan Three-Wheeler Club of England does have a group in the USA. For name and address of the contact see the Affiliated Clubs list at the end of the chapter.

The World Morgan Regalia Collector's Society

This club is truly international and came about as a direct result of the amount of regalia sold each year at the American MOG meets. A chance conversation between Melvyn Rutter, who was visiting MOG12 in 1982, and Win Sharples, the recently appointed Regalia Chairman of the Washington Club (MCCDC), planted the seed of an idea. After further discussions it was decided that Win Sharples should investigate the possibility of forming such a club. Typical of Win, he was not just content to see if there was any interest in the idea, he spent a year researching Morgan club regalia worldwide, with particular emphasis on badges. Then in June 1983 he sent out invitations to prominent Morgan people all over the world to become charter members of the proposed society.

The inaugural meeting was held at the Abbey Hotel, Malvern, during the 75th Anniversary celebrations, and was attended by 27 of the then 30 members. Today, membership is getting very close to the 100 maximum agreed by the charter members. Membership is not automatically granted to anyone who cares to apply. Before even being considered the applicant must be able to prove that he is a serious collector by producing evidence that he owns at

least ten badges and is also already a member of an established Morgan club.

The Society caters for all collectable Morgan-related items, including toys, models, photographs, brochures, books and handbooks - in fact, anything pertaining to the marque. It produces a quarterly journal and its own regalia which are sold strictly to members only.

For name and address of the club contact see the Affiliated Clubs list at the end of the chapter.

Morgan owner - Latvia

The only known Morgan in the former USSR is the pre-war 4-4 in Riga, which was featured in my first book on the flat-radiator Morgans. Naturally, the owner does not use the car during the winter months, and stores it in a novel way by winching it up and suspending it in the roof space of his garage, above another car.

Modern cars are few in Latvia and collector vehicles are even rarer. So besides being extremely lucky to own this Morgan, he has started what is believed to be the only motor museum in the region and has some very interesting vehicles on display.

He would be most interested to hear from other Morgan owners and his name and address is G Michailow, Lenin Str 121-58, Riga 225012 ind, Latvia.

Morgan clubs affiliated to the Morgan Sports Car Club
AUSTRALIA
Colin Davidson

Part of the badge collection of Win Sharples, founder and chairman of the Morgan Regalia Collectors Society.

The pictures on these two pages are of a Series I 4-4 which was found and restored by its Latvian owner. At the time, he had never seen a Morgan and his initial restoration resulted in the car receiving the wrong back-end treatment.

Over the years the owner made contact with various other Morgan owners, particularly in England, and studied books and photographs. As a result, he was able to rectify the car's rear end. As can be seen, he made a remarkable job of the restoration.

PO Box 44
Sutherland 2232
Australia

AUSTRIA
Peter Taucha
Morgan Sports Car Club of Austria
Weidlinger Hauptstrasse 154
A-3400 Kloster Neuburg
Austria

BELGIUM
Fred de Coster
Morgan Sports Car Club Belgium
Belgium

Leon Giet
Morgan Owners Group Belgium
Rue a la Forge
5170 Arbre
Belgium

CANADA
Mrs Audrey Beer
Morgan Owners Group Toronto
R.R. 3
Bolton
Ontario L7E 5R9
Canada

DENMARK
Alan Hall
Morgan Club Denmark
Mollegaardsvej 16
Gl Hjortkaer
6818 Aarre, Denmark

FRANCE
Mme. Jaqueline Frot
Morgan Club De France

The engine bay complete with Coventry Climax engine, which is readily recognisable even if the layout of the ancillaries is different.

Morgan Club Italia
Via V. Foppa 6
20144 Milano
Italy

20 Rue Daguerre
75014 Paris
France

GERMANY
Klaus Harmut Scholz
Morgan Club Deutchland
Dagoberstrasse 90
5000 Koln
Germany

Rudolf Linke
Morgan Sports Car Club

Deutchland Bonkelaar 15
Burgwedeler Str. 25
D-3002 Bissendorf
Germany

HOLLAND
Machiel Kalf
Morgan Sports Car Club Holland
1633 Gn Avenhorn
Holland

ITALY
Ambbrogio Macchi

Paolo Lazzari
Sun, Sex, Sea & Sound
Via Cuneo 57
16038 S. Margherita Ligure
Genova
Italy

JAPAN
Morgan Sports Car Club of Japan
Satoru Araki
23-8 Narashinodia
2-Chome, Funabash9-Shi
Chiba 274, Japan

LUXEMBOURG
Merens Fred
67 Rue de la Money
498 Reckon/Mess
Luxembourg

NEW ZEALAND
The Morgan Sports Car Club of New
Zealand
PO Box 14-104
Auckland
New Zealand

NORWAY
Fred Ljone
Norsk Sportsvogn Klubb
M. Register Fjordmog
Arnulf Overlands vei 216
0764-Oslo 7
Norway

SOUTH AFRICA
Kevin Bolon
South African Morgan Owners Group
20 Wantage Road
Parkwood
Johannesburg 2193
South Africa

SPAIN
Xavier Romeu
Morgan Sports Car Club Espana
Mas Canyelles
08211 Castellar del Valles
Barcelona
Spain

SWEDEN
Ingvar Fredriksson
Morgan Owners Group of Sweden
P.O. Box 102
S-762 23 Rimbo
Sweden

SWITZERLAND
Daniel Zoller

Morgan Club Schweiz
Via al Chioso
CH-6929 Gravesano
Switzerland

UNITED STATES OF AMERICA
Alan Marsh
Morgan Car Club of
Washington DC
2854 Connecticut Ave. 24
Washington DC 20008
USA

Larry & Patty Moss
Morgan Owners Group Great Lakes
3377 Timber Crest Ct
West Bloomfield
Mi 48324
USA

Bill Boyles
Morgan Motor Car Club
PO Box 50392
DallaS
Texas 75250
USA

Win Sharples
Morgan Regalia Collectors Society
Rrl Box 537a
Round Hill
Va 22141
USA.

Bob Chamberlain
Morgans On The Gulf
Morgan Owners Group
3304 Sunset Blvd.
Houston
Texas 77005
USA

Bob Koupal
Morgan Sports Car Club
of Northern California

919 Mowry Avenue
Fremont
Ca 94536-4141
USA

Chas Wasser
Ohio Morgan Owners Group
7663 Windy Knoll Drive
Cincinnati, Ohio 45241
USA

Craig Seibert
Morgan Owners of Philadelphia
PO Box 242k
Martins Creek
Pa 18063
USA

Lance Lipscomb
Morgan Owners Group South
2932 Melton Court
Lilburn
Georgia 30247
USA
Michael Hattem
Morgan +4 Club
10823 Oregon Avenue
Culver City
CA 90232
USA
Spence Young,
Morgan Three-Wheeler Club, USA GO
Morgan
Three-Wheeler Club
6614 E Corrinne Drive
Scottsdale
AZ 85254
USA

Paul Levitt
3/4 Morgan Group Ltd.
112 Mercer Street
N.Y. 10012
USA

Perry Nuhn

The Gator Mogs Morgans of Florida
9067 S.E. Star Island Way
Hobe Sound
Florida 33455
USA

Wynell Bruce
2721 Acworth Due West Road
Kennesawi
GA 30144
USA

Tony Frederick
Morgan Owners Group
3024 Jarrard Street
Houston
Texas 77005
USA

Nancy Dice
Morgan Owners Group Northwest
13802 S.E. 3rd Place
Bellevue
WA 98005
USA

Bill Warren
Western NY Morgan Owners Group
22 San Rafael Dr.
Rochester
New York 14618
USA

John & Evelyn Willburn
Morgan Plus 4 Club of Southern
California
Mog Cottage
11423 Gradwell
Lakewood
California 90715
USA

Denis Glavis
Morgan Sports Car Club
1322 Redwood Drive
Santa Cruz
California 95060
USA

Ed Zielinski
Morgan Car Club Washington DC
616 Gist Avenue
Silver Spring
Maryland 20910
USA

Dave Bondon
3/4 Morgan Group of America
88-89 24 N. Point Road
Colts Neck
NJ 07722
USA

Robert T Burrows
Ohio Morgan Owners
7080 Westview Drive
Worthington
Ohio 43085
USA

George Fink
Minnesota Morgan Club
2608 West 45th Street
Minneapolis,
Minnesota 55410
USA
Morgan Owners Group -
Great Lakes

Webb Drive
Farmington Hills
Michigan 48018
USA.

Other international Morgan contacts
BRAZIL
Richard J Flynn
Rua Natingui 494
Sao Paulo SP
Brazil

DENMARK
Henning Thyrre
Sommerlyst 26
8500 Grenaa
Denmark

PORTUGAL
Manuel Ramos
Av Das Rosas 152
Francelos
4400 VN GA1A
Portugal

TASMANIA
Rod Macey
20 Taronga Road
Taroona
Tasmania 7053

• *STOP PRESS* •

Since the first volume of this trilogy was published information about a new Morgan club has become available. Called the Covert Model Morgan Club, it is, not surprisingly, for those interested in Morgan models and counts among its members individuals from Canada and Holland. For more information contact C.Baker, 18, Allenby Road, Biggin Hill, Westerham, Kent TN16 3LH, England.

APPENDIX I

ORIGINAL SPECIFICATIONS, PRODUCTION CHANGES, GENERAL DATA

4/4 Series

• 4/4 SERIES FORD 1600 SPECIFICATIONS

Engine:	Ford 2737E.
Type:	Four cylinders, in-line.
Bore & stroke:	81.00mm x 77.7mm
Displacement:	1599cc.
Valve:	Overhead.
Brake horsepower:	70bhp at 4750rpm.
Chassis:	'Z' section steel pressings, underslung crossmembers.
Clutch:	Ford 7.5in diaphragm-spring clutch.
Gearbox:	Ford four-speed all-synchromesh. Ratios 12.19, 8.24, 5.73 and 4.1 to 1. Reverse 13.63 to 1.
Final drive:	Open Hardy Spicer propeller shaft to Salisbury hypoid-bevel axle unit.
Front suspension:	Independent with sliding pillars; coil springs with Armstrong telescopic shock absorbers.
Rear suspension:	Live axle with semi-elliptic springs and Armstrong lever-arm shock absorbers.
Brakes:	Girling, 9in diameter rear drums, hydraulic, 11in disc front brakes.
Wheels:	Pressed steel or spoked.
Tyres:	5.60 x 15in on 4J rims or 4.5J (spoked) rims.
Fuel:	8.5-gallon tank, two-seater; 10-gallon tank, four-seater; rear-mounted.
Steering:	Cam and peg.
Dimensions:	Wheelbase 8ft; length 12ft; lidth 4ft 8in; track 4ft front, 4ft rear.
Weight:	1848lb (two-seater).

• 4/4 SERIES FORD 1600 COMPETITION MODEL
Basically as for the standard model above, but equipped with the Ford 2737GT engine, with Weber carburettor and power output of 95.5bhp at 5500rpm.

• 4/4 SERIES FORD 1600GT
As from May 1971 - chassis no. B2381 - the Ford 2737GT

engine was adopted as standard, all engine numbers for this engine were prefixed by the letter 'A'.

In July 1975, chassis no. B3540, a slightly modified version of the same engine was used, but no significant changes can be listed.

• 4/4 SERIES FORD 1600 MAJOR SPECIFICATION CHANGES (by date and/or chassis number)

February 1968		Engine nos. C1-C36 (B1629) have 1500cc-type engine mounting rubbers and modified brackets. Numbers stamped on manifold side of cylinder block at rear on small flat face.
March 1968		Engine no. C37 (B1635) owards fitted with1600cc rubber mountings and new-type brackets.
July1968	B1683	New-type chassis introduced for all 4/4s except for chassis numbers B1689, B1685 & B1691.
Aug 968	B1713	First de-toxed engine.
Sept 1968	B1732	Four-seater model introduced.
Nov1968	B1766	4.56 rear axles fitted to all GT models.
May 1969	B1916	4.1 rear axles fitted to all standard-engined cars. (Not GT).
Oct 69	B2014	New dashboard based on Plus 8 design, with tachometer to right of steering column, on right-hand-drive cars, and all the other instruments and rocker-type switches in oval panel in centre of the dashboard.
Dec 1969	B2067	4:1 rear axles standard, also Plus 8-type rear springs.
Dec 1969	B2077	Valance tie rods now 0.37in.
Jan 1970	B2084	First 4/4 fitted collapsible steering column. Also Plus 8-type valance tie rods fitted. Alternators now fitted as standard.
April 1970	B2103	Collapsible steering column introduced as standard.
Aug 1970	B2239	4/4s fitted with wire wheels have stub axles with larger spindles type D361A.
Aug 1970	B2243	All 4/4s fitted with collapsible steering columns have Torrington Ltd universal shafts (No. 380 12 0.56in long).
Oct 1970	B2289	Sims nuts and shakeproof washers used on gearbox mountings.
Nov 1970	B2304	Engine No. C712 collapsible steering columns with larger spline ends to take steering wheel boss.
Nov 1970	B2307	Engine No. C705, collapsible steering columns adopted as standard.
Jan 1971	B2375	C782, 72-spoke wire wheels used as ordered.
April 1971	B2380	Last GT model.
May 1971	B2381	Ford 2265E adopted as standard for all cars. Engine number prefixed by
		letter 'A'. Mechanically-operated clutch fitted.
Sept 1971	B2533	Dual braking system introduced. Extra padding provided around dashboard. Protruding instead of flush-mounted rear light assemblies.
Sept 1971	B2546	Handbrake warning lights fitted as standard.
Oct 1971	B2551	Wider front frames fitted to take wider body.
Feb 1972	B2685	All 4/4s for export to Germany fitted with special track rod fastenings. Socket screws in place of bolts.
March 1972	B2691	All 4/4s fitted with wire wheels have stub axles fitted with large spindles type D361A. Also have strengthened steering arms.
March 1972	B2707	From engine number A1116, Ford clutch operating arms used. Also these engines have oil filters fitted at different angle.
Nov 1972	B2876	From engine number A1268, all 4/4s fitted with wire or disc wheels have standard stub axles with strengthened steering arms.
Nov 1972	B2889	Gearboxes now fitted with oil filter plugs on the offside. There are no drain plugs. B2848 (show car) & B2851 fitted with this type gearbox.
June 1973	B3060	Improved fresh-air heater fitted.
Oct 1974	B3367	Windscreen demisting vents introduced.
May 1975	B3506	Engine no. A1906. From this engine number all 4/4s have duplicate engine numbers (1) on cylinder head above No.4 exhaust port and (2) on block below No. 4 exhaust port, in the same position as Ford 'build' numbers.
July 1975	B3539	Works car fitted with new Ford engine as B3540.
July 1975	B3540	New and slightly modified Ford engine fitted, with automatic choke. (Different air filter arrangement, with hot-spot trunking to exhaust manifold. Air filters previously an optional extra).
Sept 1975	B3583	New-type gearbox and cable-operated clutch.
Nov 1975	B3604	All clutch cables now fitted with 6mm bolt to clutch actuating levers.
Nov 1975	B3618	Gearbox brackets braised in.
Nov 1975	B3624	Last of old-type 1600 engine with rod-operated clutch.
Oct 1976 (circa)		Larger side lights fitted.
Dec 1976	B3878	Dual braking system introduced.
Jan 1977	B3905	Aluminium body panels offered as optional extra.
cApril 1978	cB4200	All 4/4s fitted with new braking system. Also new-type master cylinder with fluid level warning light switch.

July 1978	B4259	All 4/4 brake cables now fitted with nylon inserts.
Sept 1978	B4330	New-type handbrake cables made up complete fitted as standard.
July 1978	B4274	All 4/4s fitted with new-type brake linings. (Wire wheels only).
Sept 1978	B4295	All disc wheels now fitted with new-type brake linings.
1979		Final year for Dunlop steel 4in x 15 disc wheels. Introduction of current 5.5in x 15 German-made wheels. (Ex-Volkswagen Beetle).
Jan 1980	B4589	New type of brake pipe system on rear axle introduced.
April 1980	B4659	All 4/4s right & left-hand drive (disc brakes) fitted with new-type wheels.
Sept 1980	B4756	All 4/4s now fitted with pre-engaged starter motors.
April 1981	B4894	New-type chassis, alterations to handbrake and pedal assembly.
April 1981	B4894	All 4/4s fitted new-type chassis including modifications to handbrake and pedal assembly.

• CHASSIS NUMBER SEQUENCE
Numbers   B1600 - B5113
Last number used B5113.

• ENGINE NUMBER SEQUENCE
Engines were not fitted in number sequence.
All cars with engine number prefix 'A' fitted with Ford 2265E engine. First chassis no. B2381.

• OVERALL PRODUCTION DATES
February 1968-March 1982

• PRODUCTION BY BODY & ENGINE
Ford 2737E 1597cc

Production dates	February 1968-May 1971
Two-seaters	142
Four-seaters	3 (chassis nos. B1974, B2068 & B2221).
Total cars produced	145

Ford 2737GT 1597cc

Production dates	February 1968-May 1971
Two-seaters	393
Four-seaters	242
Experimental	1
Total cars produced	636
Total number of cars exported	
Standard & GT-engined:	
Total cars exported to USA	9
Total cars exported	349

Ford 2265GT 1597cc

Production dates	May 1971-March 1982

Two-seaters	1482
Four-seaters	1246
Experimental	3
Chassis nos. not used	1
Total cars	2731
Overall total production	3512
Overall total exports	1540
Overall total USA exports	68

• 4/4 SERIES 1600 FIAT SPECIFICATIONS AT TIME OF INTRODUCTION

Engine:	Fiat twin-cam 1600
Type:	Four cylinders, in-line
Bore and stroke:	84.00mm x 71.50mm
Displacement:	1584cc
Valves:	Overhead
Brake horsepower:	98bhp at 6000rpm
Gearbox:	Fiat five-speed all-syncromesh. Ratios 0.83, 1, 1.36, 2.05 and 3.6 to 1. Reverse 3.24 to 1.

Remainder of specification same as Ford CVH 1600

• 4/4 SERIES FORD CVH 1600 SPECIFICATIONS

Engine:	Ford 1600 CVH
Type:	Four cylinders, in-line
Bore and stroke:	79.96mm x 79.52mm
Displacement:	1597cc
Valve:	Overhead (single cam, hydraulic tappets)
Brake horsepower:	96bhp at 6000rpm
Gearbox:	Ford four-speed all-syncromesh. Ratios 12.19, 8.24, 5.73 and 4.1 to 1. Reverse 13.63 to 1. Changed after a year to Ford five-speed all-syncromesh. Ratios 0.83, 1, 1.37, 1.97 and 3.65 to 1. Reverse 3.66 to 1.
Chassis:	'Z' section steel pressings, five boxed or tubular crossmembers.
Final drive:	Open Hardy Spicer propeller shaft to Salisbury hypoid-bevel axle unit.
Front suspension:	Independent with sliding pillars; coil springs with double-acting telescopic shock absorbers. Rear suspension: Live axle with semi-elliptic springs and Armstrong hydraulic dampers.
Brakes:	Girling hydraulic dual brake system on four wheels, 9in x 1.75in rear drums, hydraulic, 11in disc front brakes.
Wheels:	Pressed steel or spoked.
Tyres:	Radial tyres 165 x 15 or 195/60VR15 on Plus 4 wide-body style 4/4s only, with the Cobra wire wheels.
Fuel:	8.5-gallon tank in two-seater, 10-

gallon in four-seater, rear-mounted. (Later increased to 12.5 gallons).

Steering: Gemmer re-circulating ball with collapsible steering column.

Dimensions: Wheelbase 8ft; length 12ft; width 4ft 8in; track 3ft 11in front, 4ft 1in rear. (Increased later to length 12ft 9in; width 4ft 9in; track 4ft front).

Weight: Two-seater - 1624lb. Four-seater - 1680lb.

• 4/4 SERIES 1600 FIAT & 1600 FORD CVH SPECIFICATION CHANGES

C6107	All 4/4 two-seaters fitted with five leaf rear springs. (September 1982).
C6207	Engine no. 22J27-C4196. First 4/4 two-seater with five-speed gearbox. (January 1983).
C6225	Engine no. 22J27-C4203. All 4/4s now fitted with five-speed gearboxes, except for C6248 which is the last car fitted with old-type four-speed gearbox. (January 1983).
C6279	Engine no. 12F10-C4203. Works car & first four-seater fitted with five-speed gearbox. (March 1983).
C6315	Engine no. 22J27-C4232. All 4/4s now fitted with new-type layout of front brake pipe system. Caliper bracket as on Plus 8s. (May 1983).
C6490	Engine no. 23F19-C4410. All two-seater 4/4s now fitted with new-type five leaf rear springs. ie. longer second spring. (January 1984).
C6603	Engine no. 24A12-C4554. All 4/4's now supplied with SMX oil in gearboxes. (July 1984).
C6654	First 4/4 fitted with Gemmer steering box (September 1984).
C6730	All 4/4s, four & two-seaters, left- & right-hand-drive, fitted with new-type French steering column, except for C6751.(Decemeber 1984).
C7187	CVH 4/4 model now offered with the 'Plus 4 Wide Body' style and Cobra 6in wire wheels as an option. (October 1986). First car so manufactured this chassis number, a four-seater.
C7266	First off new-type steering wheel boss. (February 1987).
C7268	First off new-type fuse box. (February 1987).
C7298	First off new-type heater. (April 1987).
C7306	All 4/4s fitted with engine numbers prefixed 86 or 87 (Ford number) new-type 04 engine. C7306, engine number 86L13AC5078 first off). (April 1987).

C7339	First off Kenlow fan fitted. (May 1987).
C7403	First off new-type petrol pump. (August 1987).
C7422	New-type petrol pump fitted as standard. (September 1987).
C7615	New-style wings introduced. (July 1988).
C7934	First off new-type VDO instruments. (November 1989).
C7955	VDO instruments now fitted as standard. (January 1990).
C8125	Works car.
C8418	First off fitted with front bearings and stub axles which are interchangeable with Plus 4s; now stanard, except for cars fitted with shorter steering arm.
C8452	Works experimental 1600 EFI engine. Registration number J708 BUY.
C8456	Last production two-seater.
C8470	Last production four-seater. (Highest engine no. used: 91E14A-C5950).

• 4/4 SERIES FIAT 1600 4/4 (FACTORY LISTED AS 4/4 T/C)

• CHASSIS NUMBER SEQUENCE
Number F6,001 - F6,956.

• ENGINE NUMBER SEQUENCE
Engines were not fitted in number sequence. Several different sequences in the course of the model's production.

• OVERALL PRODUCTION DATES
November 1981-November 1985.

• PRODUCTION BY BODY

Two-seaters	47
Four-seaters	35
Works cars (2-seater)	1
2-litre cars	10
Total cars produced (including works and 2-litre cars)	93
Total cars exported to West Germany	9 (34.6% of exported cars)
Total cars exported to USA	9 (34.6% of exported cars)
Total cars exported	26 (28.2% of total produced)

Note: Towards the end of the production run Fiat supplied Morgan with ten 2000cc twin cam, carburettored engines. These were fitted in the same body as the other Fiat-engined 4/4s and carried the same designation. The chassis numbers of the cars supplied with these engines are: F6,821 (4-seater); F6,831 (2-seater); F6,865 (2-seater); F6,881 (2-seater); F6,903 (2-seater); F6,915 (2-seater); F6,917 (2-seater); F6,920 (4-seater); F6,947 (4-seater); F6,956 (2-seater).

• 4/4 SERIES FORD 1600 CVH

• CHASSIS NUMBER SEQUENCE
Numbers   C6004 - C8470.
As from chassis number M7606 this sequence also used for Plus 4 model denoted by the prefix 'M'; Prefix 'C' continued for 4/4.

• ENGINE NUMBER SEQUENCE
Engines were not fitted in number sequence and several different sequences in the course of the models' production. Highest number used was 91E14A - C5950.

• OVERALL PRODUCTION DATES
March 1982-November 1991.

• PRODUCTION BY BODY

Two-seaters	1528
Four-seaters	642
Works cars	52
Chassis allocated for France	20
Chassis nos. not used	21
Experimental Rover Plus 4s	4
Total cars produced (including Works & Experimental cars)	2226
Total cars exported to West Germany	41 (4% of exported cars.)
Total cars exported to USA	29 (2.87% of exported cars).
Total cars exported	1010 (45.37% of total produced).

• 4/4 SERIES FORD 1600 EFI

• CHASSIS NUMBER SEQUENCE
Numbers   C8452 - C8781.
As from chassis number C8452 this sequence continued to be used with the prefix 'M' for Plus 4 models up to chassis number M8688, then prefix 'T' was used for the Plus 4 model.

• ENGINE NUMBER SEQUENCE
Engines were not fitted in number sequence and several different sequences in the course of the model's production. Lowest production number used was 91C22B - C5951; highest number used was 91L19 - C6142.

• OVERALL PRODUCTION DATES
November 1991-February 1993.

• PRODUCTION BY BODY

Two-seaters	157
Four-seaters	38
Works cars	1
Chassis nos. not used	1
Total cars produced (including Works & Experimental cars)	196
Total cars exported to West Germany	11 (13.75% of exported cars).
Total cars exported to USA	6 (7.5% of exported cars).
Total cars exported	80 (40.81% of total produced).

• 4/4 SERIES FORD 1800 SPECIFICATIONS AT TIME OF INTRODUCTION

Engine:	Ford 1800 EFI
Type:	Four cylinders, in-line
Bore:	80.6mm x 80.6mm
Displacement:	1796cc
Valves:	Overhead four valves per cylinder, (belt driven ohc, hydraulic tappets)
Brake horsepower:	89bhp at 6000rpm
Carburation:	Bosch indirect multipoint injection.
Gearbox:	Ford MT75 five-speed all-syncromesh. Ratios 0.82, 1, 1.34, 2.08 and 3.89 to 1. Reverse 3.51 to 1.
Chassis:	Plastic coated 'Z' section steel grade HR15. Hot dipped galvanised.
Front suspension:	Independent by vertical coil spring on sliding pillars with telescopic gas-filled shock absorbers.
Rear suspension:	Semi-elliptic springs and gas-filled shock absorbers.
Rear axle:	Three-quarter floating. Hypoid crown wheel and pinion. Ratio 4.1 to 1.
Brakes:	Servo-assisted 9in rear drums and 11in disc and four pot caliper front brakes.
Wheels:	Centre lock wire wheels as standard.
Fuel:	11-gallon tank in two-seater, 10-gallon in four-seater, rear-mounted. 95 or 98 octane unleaded only.
Dimensions:	Wheelbase 8ft; length 12ft 9in; width 4ft 4in, track 4ft 0in front, 4ft 1in rear.

• PLUS 4 FIAT-ENGINED SPECIFICATIONS

Engine:	Fiat 2000 - petrol injection
Type:	Four cylinders, in-line
Bore and stroke:	84.00mm x 90.00mm
Displacement:	1995cc
Valves:	Overhead two valves per cylinder (belt-driven, tohc)
Brake horsepower:	122bhp at 5300rpm.
Carburettor:	Bosch LE Jetronic injection system with Digiplex control.
Chassis:	'Z' section steel pressings, five boxed or tubular crossmembers.
Gearbox:	Fiat five-speed, syncromesh on

forward gears. Ratios 0.83, 1.0,1.36, 2.05 and 3.6 to 1. Reverse 3.24 to 1.

Final drive:	Open Hardy Spicer propeller shaft to Salisbury hypoid-bevel axle unit.
Front suspension:	Independent with sliding pillars; coil springs with double-acting tubular shock absorbers.
Rear suspension:	Live axle with semi-elliptic springs and Armstrong hydraulic-type shock absorbers.
Brakes:	Girling dual system, 9in x 1.75in diameter rear drums, 11in disc front brakes.
Wheels:	Centre-laced 6.00 x 15in wire wheels.
Tyres:	195/60R 15 Avon Turbo Speed radial.
Fuel:	12.5-gallon tank, rear-mounted.
Steering:	Gemmer re-circulating ball; collapsible column.
Dimensions:	Wheelbase 8ft; length 12ft 9in; width 4ft 9in; height 4ft 2in; track 3ft 11in front, 4ft 1in rear.
Weight:	1870lb.

• CHASSIS NUMBER SEQUENCE
Numbers   F6,796 - F7,240

• ENGINE NUMBER SEQUENCE
Engines were not fitted in number sequence. Several different sequences in the course of the model's production.

• OVERALL PRODUCTION DATES
April 1985-January 1987.

• PRODUCTION BY BODY

Two-seaters	90
Four-seaters	32
Total cars produced	122
Total cars exported to West Germany	11 (28.9% of exported cars)
Total cars exported to USA	0
Total cars exported	38 (31.1% of total produced)

• THE NEW PLUS 4 ROVER M16 & T16-ENGINED SPECIFICATIONS AT TIME OF INTRODUCTION.

Engine:	Rover M16 and T16
Type:	Four cylinders, in-line
Bore and stroke:	84.5mm x 89.0mm
Displacement:	1994cc
Valves:	Overhead 4 valves per cylinder (belt-driven. dohc)
Brake horsepower:	138bhp M16; 134bhp T16 at 6000 rpm
Chassis:	'Z' section steel pressings, top hat crossmembers. As 4/4
Clutch:	Single dry-plate 242mm (7.5in). Hydraulic operation
Gearbox:	Rover five-speed all-synchromesh. Ratios 3.32, 2.09, 1.39, 1.0 and 0.79 to 1
Final drive:	Open Hardy Spicer propeller shaft to Salisbury hypoid-bevel axle unit
Front suspension:	Independent with sliding pillars; coil springs with Armstrong telescopic shock absorbers. Front springs uprated from 4/4 specifications
Rear suspension:	Live axle with five leaf springs (seven on four-seater) and Armstrong lever-arm shock absorbers
Brakes:	Girling hydraulic dual-brake system on all four wheels. 9in x 1.75in rear drums, 11in disc front brakes
Wheels:	Spoked wire wheels, locking with rotation
Tyres:	Avon 195/60VR x 15. Low-profile, fitted with tubes
Fuel:	12.5-gallon tank, rear-mounted
Steering:	Worm and peg system with drag link and track rod, universal jointed shaft with collapsible top column
Dimensions:	Wheelbase 8ft 2in; length 13ft; width 5ft 3in; track 4ft 5in front, 4ft 6in rear
Weight:	1900lb

• ROVER M16-ENGINED PLUS 4 SPECIFICATION CHANGES

M7300	Experimental four-seater
M7400	Experimental two-seater
M7606	First production two-seater
M7670	First production four-seater
M7710	First off accelerator cable made by Morgan works, until supply received from Rover. (approximate number 10) (January 1989)
M7798	Works car. (Mrs Heather Morgan)
M7936	First off fitted with VDO instruments (November 1989) NB Blocks of chassis numbers are periodically allocated for cars which are to be exported to France. This means that chassis numbers M7855 & M7856 will be fitted with VDO instruments, but the cars did not leave the works until January & February 1990
M7953	VDO instruments now fitted as standard. All petrol injected Plus 4s from this number fitted with Battery Isolator Switch (December 1989)
M8125	Works car (Derek Day)
C8418	From this chassis number all 4/4s & Plus 4s fitted with heavy duty front bearings and stub axles which are interchangeable with either model, except cars fitted with rack and pinion

	steering with shorter steering arm
M8454	First Plus 4 to be fitted with gas—filled front shock absorbers
M8666	Last production four-seater
M8688	Last production two-seater

• CHASSIS NUMBER SEQUENCE

Various numbers prefixed with the the letter 'M', allocated as required from the 1600 CVH series 4/4 chassis number sequence. First production chassis number M7606. (Experimental four-seater = Chassis M7300, and experimental two-seater = Chassis M7400).

• ENGINE NUMBER SEQUENCE

Engines were not fitted in number sequence, and several different sequences in the course of the model's production.

• OVERALL PRODUCTION DATES

January 1989-November 1992.

• PRODUCTION BY BODY

Two-seaters	259
Four-seaters	96
Works Experimental cars	3
Chassis nos. not used	0
Total cars produced (including Works Experimental cars)	357
Total cars exported to West Germany	11 (3.08% of exported cars)
Total cars exported to USA	5 (1.40% of exported cars)
Total cars exported	115 (30.53% of total produced

• ROVER T16-ENGINED PLUS 4 SPECIFICATION CHANGES UP TO SEPTEMBER 30 1993

T8560	Engine no. 20T4HF82-100111; gearbox no. 28A0129834H; axle no. H90-1582; model T16. Finished in red & black. Works test car
T8681	First production two-seater with new Rover engine. (Sept 1992)
T8729	First off fitted with new-type servo brakes. The complete braking system changed to a system specially designed for Morgan by Lockheed, which includes 'direct acting' servo on the master cylinder with four piston calipers on the front brakes. The front discs and rear drums layouts remain the same. Other changes as a result are; rod operated handbrake replaced by cable attached to the rear shock absorber hoop; rear brakes now self-adjusting
T8763	First production four-seater with new Rover engine. (Dec 1992). The first

	chassis number used for a T16 four-seater was T8723, however this number had been allocated to Savoye, Paris, but was not used until May 1993
T8784	First off fitted with new-type fuel pump and cut-out switch. (January 1993)
T8924	First off fitted with new 1.6 wiring harness. (October 1993)

• CHASSIS NUMBER SEQUENCE

Various numbers prefixed with the the letter 'T' allocated as required from the 1600 CVH series 4/4 chassis number sequence. First production T8681. (T8560 works experimental two-seater). T8549 & T8550 allocated to France but not used until December 1992.

• ENGINE NUMBER SEQUENCE

Engines were not fitted in number sequence, and several different sequences in the course of the model's production.

• OVERALL PRODUCTION DATES

September 1992-to date and continuing.

• PRODUCTION BY BODY

Two-seaters	147
Four-seaters	39
Works Experimental cars	3
Chassis nos. not used	0
Total cars produced (including Works Experimental cars)	189
Total cars exported to West Germany	6 (= 3.22 % of exported cars)
Total cars exported to USA	0
Total cars exported to Canada	2 (= 1.07 % of exported cars)
Total cars exported	78 (= 41.93 % of total produced)

Plus 8

• PLUS 8 SPECIFICATIONS AT TIME OF INTRODUCTION

• MOSS GEARBOX CARS

Produced 1968-May 1972

• CHASSIS NUMBERS

R7000 to R7474, plus R7467, R7477, R7479, R7480, R7481, R7486, R7489, R7492 and R7494.

Engine:	British Leyland/Rover
Type:	Eight cylinders in 90 degree vee formation
Bore and stroke:	88.90mm x 71.12mm

Plus 8 Lightweight Model Chassis Record

Chassis No.	Engine No.	Colour	Date	Destination
R7983*	48114018D	Black	25.10.75	UK
R8035	48114284D	Primer	9.2.76	Sweden
R8044	48114289D	Black	11.2.76	UK
R8050	48114295D	Signal Red	18.3.76	UK
R8052	48114325D	Gold Cream	27.2.76	UK
R8059**	48114328D	Opalescent Silver	17.3.76	UK
R8066	48114352D	Dark Blue	12.3.76	UK
R8069	48114321D	Signal Red	21.4.76	UK
R8094	48114484D	Green	13.5.76	UK
R8102	48114537D	Black	30.6.76	UK
R8103	48114507D	Vauxhall Garnet Starmist	1.7.76	UK
R8104	48114536D	Glacier White	14.7.76	UK
R8111	48114783D	Fiat Turquoise	21.7.76	USA
R8112****	Tranco engine & special gearbox		2.6.76	UK
R8124	48114764D	Black	24.8.76	UK
R8125***	48114760D	Tahiti Blue	1.9.76	UK
R8138	48114784D	Chrysler Carnation	1.10.76	UK
R8140	48114790D	Velvet Green	5.10.76	UK
R8170	48114847D	Silver	22.12.76	UK
R8186*****	48114825D	Opalescent Silver	28.1.77	Guernsey

*	*Motor Show car*
**	*Now in Switzerland and painted Dark Green*
***	*Fitted roll bar, negative camber front frame, special wire wheels and tyres*
****	*Works experimental car. Not officially classed as a production Lightweight*
*****	*Sold to John McLaren, brother of Bruce McLaren*

Displacement:	3528cc
Compression ratio:	10.5 to 1
Brake horsepower:	184bhp (160.5 net) at 5200rpm
Gearbox:	Moss four-speed, synchromesh on second, third and top. Central direct action gearchange. Internal ratios 1.00, 1.205, 1.745 and 2.97 to 1. Reverse 2.97 to 1
Fuel supply:	Twin SU HS6 (1.75in) semi-downdraught carburettors
Chassis:	'Z' section steel pressings, five boxed or tubular crossmembers
Final drive:	Open Hardy Spicer propeller shaft to Salisbury with and ratio Power-Lok limited-slip hypoid-bevel axle unit. 3.58 to 1, 22mph/1000rpm in top gear
Front suspension:	Independent with sliding pillars; coil springs with double-acting Girling telescopic shock absorbers
Rear suspension:	Live axle with semi-elliptic springs and Girling lever arm shock absorbers
Brakes:	Girling servo-assisted with 9in rear drums, 11in discs
Wheels:	Cast magnesium alloy with five-stud fitting. 15in diameter, 5.5in rim width
Tyres:	Dunlop SP Sport 185 VR-15 high-speed on original cars
Fuel:	13.5-gallon tank, rear-mounted
Steering:	Cam gear worm and nut, collapsible steering column. Right- and left-hand drive
Dimensions:	Wheelbase 8ft 2in, length 12ft 8in, width 4ft 9in, track, front 4ft 1in, rear 4ft 3in
Weight:	1820lb

• ROVER 4-SPEED GEARBOX CARS
Produced May 1972-January 1977

• CHASSIS NUMBERS
R7475, R7478, R7482-R7485, R7490, R7491, R7493 and R7495-R8186, except R8151.

Engine compression ratio:	9.355 to 1 from December 1973
Brake horsepower:	143bhp (DIN) at 5000rpm
Gearbox:	Rover four-speed, built by British Leyland, synchromesh on all forward gears. Internal ratios 1.00, 1.391, 2.133 and 3.625 to 1. Reverse 3.43 to 1.
Transmission:	Clutch and gearbox mounted in unit with engine, and a separate shaft from clutch to gearbox no longer fitted. Gearbox therefore considerably further forward in a modified chassis frame.
Fuel supply:	Twin SU HIF6 carburettors
Final drive ratio:	3.58 to 1 at first, then from chassis no. R7659 (October 1973), 3.31 to 1, 23.8mph/1000rpm in top gear.
Dimensions:	Changes from chassis no. R7659 (except R7661). Width 5ft, track, front 4ft 3in, rear 4ft 4in
Weight:	1884lb

• BRITISH/LEYLAND TRIUMPH 5-SPEED GEARBOX CARS
Produced January 1977-September 1984

• CHASSIS NUMBERS
R8151, then R8200-R9414 (except R9300).

Basic layout and specifications remain the same except for the following changes:

Brake horsepower:	155bhp (DIN) at 5250rpm
Gearbox:	Five-speed, built by British Leyland/Triumph, synchromesh on all forward gears. Internal ratios 0.833, 1.000, 1.396, 2.087 and 3.321 to 1. Reverse 3.428 to 1. Centrally- mounted gearlever with remote control change
Transmission:	Clutch and gearbox mounted in unit with engine, and a separate shaft from clutch to gearbox no longer fitted. Gearbox now positioned approximately as in 1972-1977 cars. However, further minor changes were made later
Final drive ratio:	3.31 to 1, 26.2mph/1000rpm in fifth gear
Steering:	Rack & pinion optional from chassis no. R9283
Dimensions:	Track, front 4ft 4in, rear 4ft 5in
Weight:	1826lb

• BRITISH/LEYLAND ROVER VITESSE-ENGINED & VITESSE 5-SPEED GEARBOX CARS
Produced September 1984-to date and continuing

• CHASSIS NUMBERS
R9300, then R9415 onwards.

Basic layout and specifications remain the same except for the following changes:

Engine compression ratio:	9.75 to 1
Brake horsepower:	157bhp (DIN) at 5250rpm
Gearbox:	Five-speed, built by British Leyland/Rover, synchromesh on all forward gears. Internal ratios 0.792, 1.000, 1.396, 2.087 and 3.321 to 1. Reverse 3.428 to 1.
Final drive ratio:	3.31 to 1
Steering:	Rack & pinion fitted to all Vitesse-engined cars
Fuel supply system:	Lucas LE electronic injection system
Dimensions:	Track, front 4ft 5in, rear 4ft 6in, length 12ft, width 5ft 3in, wheelbase 8ft 2in
Weight:	1956lb

• PLUS 8 SPECIFICATION CHANGES
In 21 years of Plus 8 production, there have naturally been numerous specification changes. Many were made as a result of the scarcity of components from outside suppliers, or changes in both national and international motoring law. In addition, many came about as a result of suggestions made by the Morgan owner and from experience gained on the racing circuits.

The more significant changes which have taken place during the production run are listed below, identified by date and/or chassis number. Where necessary, a brief explanation is given.

	R7003	
Oct 1969	R7004	Fitted with 15.5in universal steering shaft.
March 1969	R7038	Left-hand-drive version introduced. Exported France.
March 1969	R7043	Aluminium bodywork available as optional extra. Radiator cowl and scuttle remaining pressed steel. 100lb lighter in this form, therefore increased performance.
July 1969	R7093	Gearboxes now fitted with reversing light switches.
Aug 1969	R7108	Front frames moved forward 0.12in.
Oct 1969	R7115	Dual braking introduced.
Jan 1970	R7178	New-type engine mounting rubbers and brackets.
cJune 1970	cR7233	New gearbox mounting rubbers.
Dec 1970	R7307	All Plus 8s have collapsible steering columns with larger spline ends to take steering wheel boss.

1970/1971		American market effectively closed to Morgan by the introduction of stringent exhaust emission regulations, requiring 50,000-mile test before importation licenses would be granted if the car passed.
1970		Protruding tubular, instead of flush-fitting, rear lights introduced, due to changes in lighting laws. Also changed from metal front floor to wood and gusset plates to chassis.
Jan 1971	R7317	Experimental Drop Head Coupé made.
March 1971	R7338	All Plus 8s now fitted with Torrington Ltd universal propshafts.
April 1971	R7351	First dual exhaust small-bore system. Optional extra.
May 1971	R7370	Dual exhaust large-bore system introduced as standard.
Nov 1971	R7432	Larger water pump pulleys fitted.
Feb 1972	R7449	Strengthened stub axles and steering arms fitted.
March 1972	R7454	Track rods fastened with cap screws instead of bolts on all Plus 8s exported to Germany. Also on all de-toxed cars for USA.
March 1972	R7461	Modified bellhousing for clutch adjustment introduced.
April 1972	R7466	Larger cooling capacity radiator fitted.
April 1972	R7475	First Rover gearbox. Works car BUY 600M.
April 1972	R7478	Moss gearbox replaced by Rover 3500S all-synchromesh gearbox. Propshaft length 40.75in. (Moss gearbox production ceased).
May 1972	R7494	Last Moss gearbox car. Total number of Plus 8s produced with Moss gearboxes: 494.
Aug 1972	R7525	Experimental four-seater. Distance between universal joint centres increased to 14.75in.
April 1973	R7555	Cast-iron pulleys introduced. Also larger water pumps.
March 1973	R7602	New fresh-air heater introduced, due to ceased production by Smiths of old-type heating unit. Also dual braking systems introduced.
Sept 1973	R7655	New-type alternator and bracket fitted.
Oct 1973	R7659	Chassis width increased. Front track 4ft 3in, rear track 4ft 4in. Bodywork and wings altered to suit. R7661 and a few others produced with old-style body.
Dec 1973	R7711	Wider (1.5in) rear springs introduced. This car was used as the test car in USA by Bill Fink.
Jan 1974	R7716	Rover 9.25 to 1 lower compression ratio engine fitted. Except for R7717, R7720, R7721 and R7728 fitted with old-type 10.5 to 1 ratio. Change due to new EEC exhaust emission control regulations.
April 1974	R7733	Longer clutch lever arms.
April 1974	R7748	New-type metric brake calipers fitted. 12mm fixing bolts now used.
May 1974	R7757	0.75in clutch master cylinders introduced.
July 1974	R7780	Old type 1.37in rear springs re-introduced.
Jan 1975	R7871	New-type chassis with straight pedal crossmember, also new rear spring hangers introduced.
Oct 1975	R7983	First of the 'Sports Lightweight' models introduced. Fitted with 14in wheels and light alloy panels. Wider wings to accommodate. Weight 1835lb.
Oct 1976	R8151	First Rover five-speed gearbox. (VOY 194 R). Works car. Motor Show car.
Nov/Dec 1976		Large size sidelights as used on the 4/4 introduced, due to change in UK lighting regulations.
Jan 1977	R8186	Last 'Sports Lightweight' and last four-speed Rover gearbox.
Jan 1977	R8187- R8199	Not used.
Jan 1977	R8200	Rover five-speed gearbox adopted as standard. Handbrake cables now 6in shorter. Introduction of the Rover SD1 engine with a compression ratio of 9.55 to 1, 155bhp. Also new 14in wheels adopted as standard with wider wings to accommodate. Also new dashboard layout. This chassis number and R8201 are works cars.
1977		Alloy bumpers to full width fitted as standard.
Sept 1978	R8455	Servo-assisted brakes fitted. New-type calipers and dual system installed. Master cylinder fitted with fluid level warning light switch. Also new rear brake linings introduced.
Nov 1978	R8478	New-type handbrake cable introduced.
Jan 1979	R8689	New-type brake pipe system on rear axle.
Dec 1980	R8863	New-type tubeless tyres introduced as option.
Jan 1981	R8891	Handbrake cables have nylon inserts.
March 1981	R8913	Automatic transmission fluid now used in gearbox. (Rover directive).
July 1981	R8972	New-type alternator fitted.
Feb 1982	R9067	15in wheels standardized with 6.5in wheel rim widths and low-profile Pirelli P6 tyres of 205/60 section. Wing profile altered to suit. Also Stromberg carburettor with automatic chokes introduced to conform with new emission control regulations.

Oct 1982	R9164	Negative camber front frame introduced. Also new fan belt and alternator pulley.
Sept 1983	R9283	Rack and pinion steering introduced as optional extra.
Oct 1983	R9294	All Plus 8s now fitted with six leaf springs.
Oct 1983	R9300	Engine no. 30A00166. Prototype fuel-injection car.
Aug 1984	R9401	All Plus 8s revert to five leaf springs, but with longer second leaf. Motor Show car fitted with Gemmer steering box. One off.
Sept 1984	R9415	Fuel-injection Rover Vitesse, electronically-injected V8, 190bhp engine and special Rover Vitesse five-speed gearbox introduced. All fuel-injected cars fitted rack and pinion steering.
Nov 1984	R9444	New-type steering columns (French) fitted as standard.
Nov 1986	R9740	New-type accelerator pedal and cable. Also new-type engine harness introduced.
Jan 1987	R9775	Last carburettor car and applicable five-speed gearbox.
Jan 1987	R9784	New-type fuse box.
Apri 1987	R9817	First off dimmer/dip headlamps.
April 1987	R9814	New-type heater.
May 1987	R9830	First off fitted with Kenlowe fan.
June 1987	R9843	First off Avon tyres.
June 1987	R9847	New position of oil valve over clutch pedal.
Jan 1988	R9898	First off Eagle engine.
Oct 1988	R9914	Fan mounted on radiator. Works car.
Nov 1988	R9934	New-type dimmer/dip headlamps, working when ignition on.
July 1988	R10038	New-type wiring harness.
Feb 1989	R10106	First off fitted with UniRoyal tyres.
Aug 1989	R10240	First off fitted with catalytic converter. Now required for all cars exported to West Germany.
Dec 1989	R10277	First off fitted with new VDO instruments.
Dec 1989	R10297	Engine no. 47A00001A, first off Rover 3.9-litre high-compression petrol-injected engine. (Now fitted with catalytic converter). Works car.
March 1990	R10343	Works test car, H91 GWP.
Sept 1990	R10427	Show Chassis. Works car fitted with experimental wire wheels. (Charles Morgan's car).
Oct 1990	R10431	First off new-type exhaust 'L' bracket. (3.9-litre engines with catalytic converter).
1991	R10461	First off twin catalyst single exhaust
Jan 1991	R10483	First production car with flap on back panel over petrol cap. (R10461 also fitted with this but was built after R10483- exported to France.)
March 1991	R10520	First off fitted new-type double acting,

		gas-filled front & rear telescopic shock absorbers.
April 1991	R10531	First off fitted new length and rating front main and rebound coil springs, painted red for easy identification. Only fitted in conjunction with the new shock absorbers (R10520) above. Also first off fitted with modified front shock absorber hanger bracket and wing stay.
Nov 1991	R10640	First off fitted with new wider heater.
Dec 1991	R10666	First off fitted with blue main springs - rebound.
March 1993	R10916	First off production car fitted with wire wheels. Sold to Mr Smith, owner of Motor Wheels Services, makers of the wire wheels. Offered as an option, these wheels are 16 inches in diameter and 7 inches wide, fitted with Avon Turbospeed tubeless tyres. The extra width necessitates increasing the wing width by over one inch. This means that without considerable modification they can not be fitted in retrospect. The cost is just over £1,500. Only three other Plus 8s have left the factory fitted with wire wheels; the original prototype; the 'Traco' specially built in 1976 for possible entry in the Le Mans race, and the prototype R10427.
May 1993	R10942	First off fitted with new-type universal jointed steering column.
July 1993	R10995	First off fitted with new-type thin core radiator.
Aug 1993	R10998	First off fitted with servo assisted brakes. The complete braking system changed to one specially designed for Morgan by Lockheed, which includes 'direct acting' servo on the master cylinder with four piston calipers on the front brakes. The front discs and rear drums layout remains the same. Other changes as a result are; rod operate handbrake replaced by cable attached to the rear shock absorber hoop; rear brakes now self adjusting.
Sept 1993		R11029 First off fitted with new-type heater.

• PLUS 8 PRODUCTION

All figures are calculated up to and including September 30, 1993. Production continues.

• CHASSIS NUMBER SEQUENCE

R7,000 - R11,044 (and continuing)

• ENGINE NUMBER SEQUENCE

Engines were not fitted in number sequence, and several

different sequences in the course of the model's production.

• OVERALL PRODUCTION DATES
27 October 1968-To date and continuing.

• PRODUCTION BY BODY

Two-seaters	4063
Four-seaters	1
Drop Head Coupé (automatic transmission, for the personal use of Mrs J Morgan)	1
Sports Lightweight	19

Works Experimental cars	14
Works show chassis	1
Chassis nos. not used	21
Total cars produced (including Works Experimental cars)	4198
Total cars exported to West Germany and Austria	1131 (50.1% of exported cars)
Total cars exported to USA	272 (12.05% of exported cars)
Total cars exported to Canada	53 (2.35% of exported cars)
Total cars exported produced)	2257 (5% of total

APPENDIX II

WIRING DIAGRAM

Reproduced here is the 1973 wiring diagram, the last published by either the Morgan factory or Lucas. This diagram has been used as the basis for all models produced since, with only minor variations on the theme. Note:1973 generators incorporate the relay and control units internally.

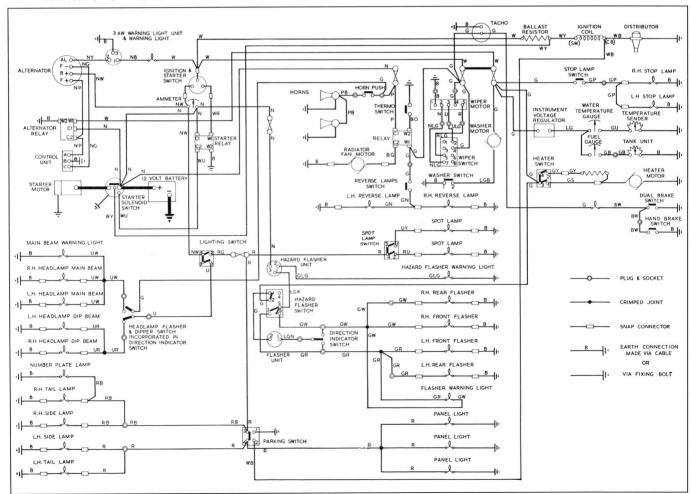

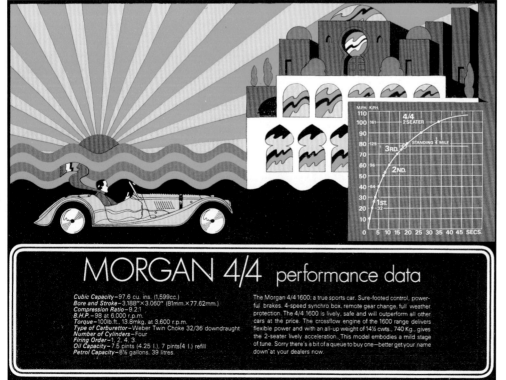

MORGAN 4/4 performance data

Cubic Capacity–97.6 cu. ins. (1,599cc.)
Bore and Stroke–3.188"×3.060" (81mm.×77.62mm.)
Compression Ratio–9.2:1
B.H.P.–98 at 6,000 r.p.m.
Torque–100lb.ft., 13.8mkg, at 3,600 r.p.m.
Type of Carburettor–Weber Twin Choke 32/36 downdraught
Number of Cylinders–Four
Firing Order–1, 2, 4, 3.
Oil Capacity–7.5 pints (4.25 l.), 7 pints(4 l.) refill
Petrol Capacity–8½ gallons, 39 litres.

The Morgan 4/4 1600: a true sports car. Sure-footed control, power-ful brakes. 4-speed synchro box, remote gear change, full weather protection. The 4/4 1600 is lively, safe and will outperform all other cars at the price. The crossflow engine of the 1600 range delivers flexible power and with an all-up weight of 14½ cwts., 740 Kg., gives the 2-seater lively acceleration. This model embodies a mild stage of tune. Sorry there's a bit of a queue to buy one—better get your name down at your dealers now.

This page & overleaf, top: This 1973/74 factory catalogue, with its colourful art deco styling, was designed and drawn by HFS's grandson, Charles Morgan. Charles was also responsible for the per-formance graph featured; the first time such a thing was used in a brochure.

4/4 4 seater

Cubic Capacity–97.6 cu. ins. (1,599cc.)
Bore and Stroke–3.188"×3.060" (81mm×77.62mm)
Compression Ratio–9. 2: 1
B.H.P.–98 at 6,000 rpm.
Torque–100 lb. ft. 13.8 mkg. at 3,600 r.p.m.
Type of Carburettor–Weber Twin Choke 32/36 downdraught
Number of Cylinders–Four
Firing Order–1, 2, 4, 3.
Oil Capacity–7.5 pints (4.25 l.) 7 pints(4 l) refill.
Petrol Capacity–10 gallons, 45.5 litres.

The 4/4 4 seater combines the sporting performance of
the 2 seater with the advantages of a family car. There
is plenty of leg and headroom in the back seat when the
weatherproof hood is raised, a fresh air heater for cold
wintry mornings and opening side windows for all four
passengers.

The Ford 1600 4/4 was in production for just over three years. This Four-seater has all its wet weather equipment in place.

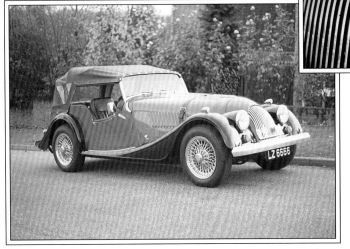

One of the most successful racing Morgans in western America is the early Plus 4 named 'Baby Doll' which, to this day, is still successful even against more modern cars.

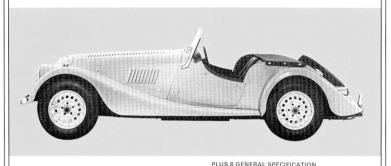

The Big Beefy +8

By the time this 1976 brochure was produced, the Plus 8 had become the company's flagship and was nearly always used on the covers.

Start up your big, beefy Plus 8. Slip into first gear. And tweak the throttle. Wow!
On the road, or in competition, the Morgan Plus 8 sets fantastic performance standards. From start it will take you up to 70 in just 7·5 seconds.
On the autobahn, the Rover V8 aluminium engine growls sweetly at 125 mph. Big safety features too. Powerful servo assisted brakes. Laminated windscreen. Extra wide track for even better road adhesion. Standing at the kerbside, Morgan is pure elegance. Out on the road you soon discover it is all muscle. A gentle giant. And a definitive car for the discerning motorist.

PLUS 8 GENERAL SPECIFICATION

Cubic Capacity	3,528 c
Number of Cylinders	8
Bore and Stroke	89 x 71
Carburettor	Twin SU
Compression Ratio	9·5 : 1
Firing Order	1, 8, 4, 3
B.H.P.	143 DIN
Oil Capacity	5·7 litre
Torque	226 lb.ft
Fuel Tank Capacity	13½ gall
Fuel Consumption	25 m.p.
Valve Gear	O.H.V.
Ignition Timing	Top Dea
Dryweight of Complete Car	— 1

Wherever your want to go, Morgan takes you there in style, and surefooted safety. Very definitely the connoisseur's car, Morgan 4/4 has plenty of gutsy character too.
Big hearted 1600 engine gives you performance plus economy. Big hearted Morgan 4/4, gives you whatever you want to have.

4/4 GENERAL SPECIFICATION

Cubic Capacity	1,599 c.c. (97·6 cu. ins.)
Bore and Stroke	3·188" x 3·060" (81 mm x 77·62 mm)
Compression Ratio	9 : 1
B.H.P.	84 DIN/SAE at 5,500 r.p.m.
Torque	92 lb.ft., 12·7 mkg, at 3,500 r.p.m.
Type of Carburettor	Weber Twin Choke 32/36 downdraught
Number of Cylinders	4
Firing Order	1, 2, 4, 3
Oil Capacity	7·5 pints (4·25 litres), 7 pints (4·1 litres), refill
Petrol Capacity	8½ gallons (39 litres)

The lively 4'4

...d summer joy.
...gan 4/4 Four
... sports car
... or all the family.
...as 4/4 Two Seater
...city — 10 gallons

...comes in a 4 seater too!

First of the Real Sports Cars

Morgan

1911 2-Seater Runabout   *1930 Record Breaking 3-*

Morgan
4/4 1600 4-Seater

1965 Plus 4 Plus

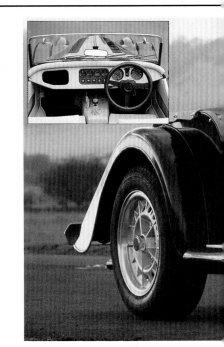

Fiat 1600 T/C Engine   *Ford CVH (XR3) 1600 Engine*

1600 ENGINE (Ford CVH (XR3)
Cubic Capacity	– 1597 cm³ (97.42 cu ins)
Number of Cylinders	– 4
Bore and Stroke	– 79.96 mm x 79.52 mm
Compression Ratio	– 9.5:1
Maximum Torque	– 98 ft/lb @ 4000 rpm (135 nm)
B.H.P.	– 96 DIN @ 6000 rpm
Firing Order	– 1, 3, 4, 2
Valve Gear	– Single central O.H.C. Hydraulic Tappets
Oil Capacity	– 6.6 pints (3.75 litres)
Carburettor	– Single Weber 32/34 DFT twin choke
Petrol Capacity	– 8½ gallons (39 litres)

1600 T/C ENGINE (Fiat)
Cubic Capacity	– 1584 cm³ (96.62 cu ins)
Number of Cylinders	– 4
Bore and Stroke	– 84.00 mm x 71.50mm
Compression Ratio	– 9.0:1
Maximum Torque	– 94 ft/lb @ 3800 rpm (127.5nm)
B.H.P.	– 98 DIN @ 6000 rpm
Firing Order	– 1, 3, 4, 2
Valve Gear	– Twin overhead camshafts
Oil Capacity	– 8.5 pints (4.83 litres)
Carburettor	– Single Weber 32 ADF 53/250 twin choke
Petrol Capacity	– 8½ gallons (39 litres)

The cover of this early 1980s catalogue epitomises all that is Morgan, whilst the inside features Morgans new and old, as well as pictures of the two engines then available, although the Fiat power unit was used for only a very short period. To appeal to the export market the double-page spread is of a left-hand-drive Plus 8.

PLUS 8   GENERAL SPECIFICATION
Cubic Capacity	– 3,528 c.c., (215 cu. ins.)
Number of Cylinders	– 8
Bore and Stroke	– 89 x 71 mm, 3.5 x 2.8 in.
Compression Ratio	– 9.35:1
Maximum Torque	– 198 lb. ft., 27.5 mkg at 2,500 r.p.m.
B.H.P.	– 155 DIN PS at 5,250 r.p.m.
Firing Order	– 1, 8, 4, 3, 6, 5, 7, 2
Valve Gear	– O.H.V. pushrod, hydraulic tappets
Oil Capacity	– 9.5 pints (5.7 litres)
Carburettor	– Twin Stromberg 175 CD
Petrol Capacity	– 13½ gallons (61 litres)
Fuel Consumption	– 20 m.p.g. (9.05 litres/ 100 km.)
Ignition Timing	– 6° BTDC
Dry weight of Complete Car	– 1,826 lbs., 828 kg.

Morgan 4/4 2-seater & 4-seater

1600 ENGINE (Ford CVH)

Cubic Capacity	— 1597 cm³ (97.42 cu ins)	Firing Order	— 1,3,4,2
Number of Cylinders	— 4	Valve Gear	— Single central O.H.C. Hydraulic Tappets
Bore and Stroke	— 79.96 mm x 79.52 mm	Oil Capacity	— 6.2 pints (3.50 litres)
Compression Ratio	— 9.5:1	Carburettor	— Single Weber 32/34 DFT twin choke
Maximum Torque	— 98ft/lb @ 4000 rpm (135 nm)	Petrol Capacity	— 12½ gallons (56 litres)
B.H.P.	— 96 DIN @ 6000 rpm		

Morgan 4/4 & 4/4 4-seater: specification.

- Chassis Frame – Deep Z-shape section with five boxed or tubular cross members. Easily detachable front end.
- Gearbox – Five speed and reverse Ford Gearbox. Synchromesh on all forward gears. Top 5th. 0.83; 4th 1:1; 3rd 1.37:1; 2nd. 1.97:1; 1st 3.65:1; reverse. 3.66:1
- Transmission and Rear Axle – Propshaft with needle roller bearing universal joints transmits power to the tubular Salisbury rear axle fitted with Hypoid gears ratio 4.1 to 1.
- Wheels and Tyres – Pressed steel rims fixed with four studs. Centre lock wire wheels are an optional extra. Radial tyres – 175 x 15.
- Brakes – Girling hydraulic dual brake system on four wheels. 11" dia. discs on front wheels. 9" x 1¼" drum brakes on rear. Cable operated hand brake.
- Steering Gear – Gemmer. Collapsible column. Steering lock ignition switch. Spring alloy wheel, giving 2¼ turns lock to lock. Turning circle 32' (9.7m).
- Suspension – Front wheels – vertically mounted coil springs on sliding axle pin. Double acting tubular shock absorbers. Semi-elliptical rear springs, fitted at both ends with Silentbloc bushes, and controlled by Armstrong hydraulic dampers.
- Electrics – Lucas 12 volt equipment; indicators, hazard warning, instrument panel lighting, two-speed wipers and fresh air heater.
- Instruments – Speedo, rev. counter and warning lights in front of driver, with central steel panel including separate oil, fuel, temp, and volt gauges.
- Bodywork – Sheet steel panels on ash wood frame. Black vinyl upholstery (alternative colours or leather available at extra cost). Detachable tops can be stowed in luggage compartment or behind rear seats in four seater. Laminated windscreen.
- Colours – Deep Brunswick Green, Signal Red, Indigo Blue, Nut Brown or Royal Ivory. Other colours available at extra cost.
- Dimensions (approx.) – Wheelbase 8' (244cm). Track. front 3'11" (119cm), rear 4'1" (124cm). Length 12' (366cm) Width 4'8" (142cm). Ground clearance 7" (18cm). Height. 4/4 two seater 4'3" (129cm). Weight 4/4 two seater 1,624lbs (735 kg). 4/4 four seater – 1,680lbs (760 kg).

In this 1984/85 brochure, the company simply used a picture of the model with its specification. The first illustration has details of the engine specification, whilst the second carries a general specification. The top car is fitted with wire wheels and the bottom with the very attractive standard design wheels.

From the same brochure, this Plus 8 sports a body colour which is now standard. The company has always, with very few exceptions, offered a range of standard colours and is willing to supply the car with its owner's choice of colour - at an extra charge, of course.

'The Real Sports Car'
Morgan Plus 8

- **Chassis Frame**—Deep Z-shape section with five boxed or tubular cross members. Easily detachable front end.
- **Gearbox**—Five speed and reverse Rover gearbox. Synchromesh on all forward gears. Top 5th. 0.83:1; 4th. 1:1; 3rd. 1.39:1; 2nd. 2.08:1; 1st. 3.32:1; Reverse. 3.42:1.
- **Transmission and Rear Axle**—Propshaft with needle roller bearing universal joints transmits power to tubular Salisbury limited-slip axle with Hypoid gears—ratio 3.31 to 1.
- **Wheels and Tyres**—Cast aluminium, 6.5 in wide rims fixed with five studs and fitted with 205/60/15 radial tyres.
- **Brakes**—Girling hydraulic dual brake system 11" dia. discs on front wheels. 9" x 1¾" drum brakes on rear. Cable operated hand brake.
- **Steering Gear**—(Carburettor Model) Gemmer steering box or optional rack and pinion. (Injection Model) Rack and pinion standard. Collapsible column, steering lock ignition switch, leather covered Spring Alloy wheel, giving 2¼ turns lock to lock with steering box and 3¼ turns with rack and pinion. Turning circle 38' (11.5m).
- **Suspension**—Front wheels—independently sprung by vertical coil springs and telescopic hydraulic shock absorbers. Semi-elliptical rear springs with lever type hydraulic dampers.
- **Electrics**—Lucas 12 volt equipment; indicators, hazard warning, instrument panel lighting, two-speed wipers and washer. Twin spotlights and fresh air heater.
- **Instruments**—Speedo, rev. counter and warning lights in front of driver, with central steel panel including separate oil, fuel, temp. and volt gauges.
- **Bodywork**—Sheet steel panels on ash wood frame. Black ambla upholstery (alternative colours or leather available at extra cost). Bucket seats with fore and aft adjustment. Detachable hood can be stowed in the 36" x 20" x 12" (92 x 51 x 30.5cm) luggage compartment. Laminated windscreen.
- **Colours**—Deep Brunswick Green, Signal Red, Indigo Blue, Nut Brown or Royal Ivory. Other colours available at extra cost.
- **Dimensions** (approx)—Wheelbase 8'2" (249cm). Track, front 4'4" (132cm); rear 4'5" (135cm). Overall length 12'3" (373cm). Width 5'2" (158cm). Ground clearance 7" (18cm). Height 4'4" (132 cm). Weight 1,826lbs (828 kg).

GENERAL SPECIFICATION

	Carburettor Engine	Injection Engine
Cubic Capacity	3,528c.c., (215 cu.ins)	3,528c.c., (215 cu.ins)
Number of Cylinders	8	8
Bore and Stroke	89 x 71 mm, 3.5 x 2.8 in.	89 x 71 mm, 3.5 x 2.8 in.
Compression Ratio	9.35:1	9.75:1
Maximum Torque	198lb.ft., 27.5 mkg at 2,500 r.p.m.	220lb.ft., at 4000 r.p.m.
B.H.P.	155 DIN PS at 5,250 r.p.m.	190 BHP at 5280 r.p.m.
Firing Order	1,8,4,3,6,5,7,2	1,8,4,3,6,5,7,2
Valve gear	O.H.V. pushrod, hydraulic tappets	O.H.V. pushrod, hydraulic tappets
Oil Capacity	9.5 pints (5.7 litres)	9.5 pints (5.7 litres)
Carburettor	Twin Stromberg 175 CD	Lucas LE Electronic Injection System
Petrol Capacity	13½ gallons (61 litres)	13½ gallons (61 litres)
Ignition Timing	6° BTDC	8° BTDC
Dryweight of Complete Car	1,826lbs., 828 kg	1,826lbs., 828 kg

Above: With the exception of the prototype (which had wire wheels), this wheel design was used on the Plus 8 model for over ten years before changes were made. It's now possible to have specially developed wire wheels fitted to the Plus 8 as an option. Right: Inside the cockpit of the export Plus 8 fitted with 'extras' such as a bonnet strap and roll-over bar.

Left: This publicity photograph, issued to the motoring press for the launch of the Rover-engined Plus 4 in 1988, was staged in the factory yard with the aid of one or two props. The stained glass window above the door was presented to Peter Morgan by the Plus 4 Club of California to mark the 75th anniversary of the company in 1984.

Below and overleaf: This late 1980s brochure features the Ford 1600 CVH-engined 4/4 - shown as a four-seater complete with luggage rack - and the Plus 8, depicted as a car that both appeals - and is available to - the man in the street. The fabulous painting by Michael English occupies the whole of the centre of this brochure.

Morgan Four/Four two and four seater

Specification

1600 ENGINE (Ford CVH)

Cubic Capacity	1597 cm³ (97.42 cu.ins)
Number of Cylinders	4
Bore and Stroke	79.96 mm x 79.52 mm
Compression Ratio	9.5:1
B.H.P.	96 Din @ 6000 rpm
Maximum Torque	98ft/lb @ 4000 rpm (135 nm)
Valve Gear	Single central O.H.C. Hydraulic Tappets
Carburettor	Single Weber 32/34 DFT twin choke
Petrol Capacity	12½ gallons (56 litres)
Dryweight of Complete Car	2 seater 1624lbs. 735kg. 4 seater 1680lbs. 760kg

Chassis Frame - Deep Z-shape section with five boxed or tubular cross members. Easily detachable front end.

Gearbox - Five speed and reverse Ford Gearbox. Synchromesh on all forward gears. Top 5th 0.83; 4th 1:1; 3rd 1.37:1; 2nd 1.97:1; 1st 3.65:1; reverse 3.66:1

Transmission and Rear Axle - Propshaft with needle roller bearing universal joints transmits power to the tubular Salisbury rear axle fitted with Hypoid gears ratio 4.1 to 1

Wheels and Tyres - Pressed steel rims fixed with four studs. Centre lock wire wheels are an option at extra cost with 5" or 6" wide rims, 175 x 15 or 195/60VR15 tyres.

Brakes - Girling hydraulic dual brake system on four wheels. 11" dia. discs on front wheels. 9" x 1¾" drum brakes on rear. Quick release hand brake.

Steering Gear - Gemmer. Collapsible column. Steering lock ignition switch. Astrali wheel 15" or 14" diameter, giving 2¼ or 2½ turns lock to lock. Turning circle 32' (10m).

Suspension - Front wheels-vertically mounted coil springs on sliding axle pin. Double acting tubular shock absorbers. Semi-elliptical rear springs, fitted at both ends with Silentbloc bushes, and controlled by Armstrong hydraulic dampers.

Electrics - Lucas 12 volt equipment; indicators, hazard warning, instrument panel lighting, two-speed wipers, fresh air heater and demister.

Instruments - Speedo, rev. counter and warning lights in front of driver, with central steel panel including separate oil, fuel, temp., and volt gauges.

Bodywork - Sheet steel or aluminium panels on Cuprinol treated ash wood frame. Zinc plated fixings. Black upholstery (alternative colours and Connolly leather available at extra cost). Detachable tops can be stowed in luggage compartment or behind rear seats in four seater. Rear seatbelts on 4 seater. Laminated windscreen.

Colours - Connaught Green, Corsa Red, Indigo Blue, Black or Royal Ivory. Other colours available at extra cost. Black or Cream wing beading can be specified.

Dimensions(approx) - Wheelbase 8' (244cm). Track, front 4'(122cm), rear 4'1" (124cm). Length 12'9" (389cm). Width 4'9" (150cm). Ground clearance 7" (18cm). Height, 4/4 two seater 4'3" (129cm), four seater 4'6" (135cm).

Morgan Plus Eight

Specification

VITESSE ENGINE (Rover)

Cubic Capacity	3,528c.c., (215cu.ins.)
Number of Cylinders	8
Bore and Stroke	89 x 71mm, 3.5 x 2.8in.
Compression Ratio	9.75:1
B.H.P.	190 DIN @ 5280 rpm
Maximum Torque	220ft.ft. @ 4000 r.p.m.
Valve gear	O.H.V. pushrod, hydraulic tappets
Fuel supply	Lucas LE Electronic Injection System
Petrol Capacity	13½ gallons (61 litres)
Dryweight of Complete Car	1,826lbs., 828kg

Bodywork - Sheet steel or aluminium panels on Cuprinol treated ash wood frame. Zinc plated fixings. Black upholstery (alternative colours and Connolly leather available at extra cost). Bucket seats with fore and aft adjustment. Detachable hood can be stowed in the 36" x 20" x 12" (92 x 51 x 30.5cm) luggage compartment. Laminated windscreen.

Colours - Connaught Green, Corsa Red, Indigo Blue, Black or Royal Ivory. Other colours available at extra cost. Black or Cream wing beading can be specified.

Dimensions(approx) - Wheelbase 8'2" (249cm). Track, front 4'5" (135cm); rear 4'6" (138cm). Overall length 13' (396cm). Width 5'3" (160cm). Ground clearance 6" (15cm). Height 4' (122cm).

Chassis Frame - Deep Z-shape section with five boxed or tubular cross members. Easily detachable front end.

Gearbox - Five speed and reverse Rover gearbox. Synchromesh on all forward gears. Top 5th. 0.83:1; 4th. 1:1; 3rd. 1.39:1; 2nd. 2.08:1; 1st. 3.32:1; Reverse. 3.42:1.

Transmission and Rear Axle - Propshaft with needle roller bearing universal joints transmits power to tubular Salisbury limited-slip axle with Hypoid gears - ratio 3.31 to 1.

Wheels and Tyres - Cast aluminium, 6.5in wide rims fixed with five studs and fitted with 205/60/15 radial tyres.

Brakes - Girling hydraulic dual brake system 11" dia. discs on front wheels. 9" x 1¾" drum brakes on rear. Quick release hand brake.

Steering Gear - Jack Knight rack and pinion, collapsible column, steering lock ignition switch, leather covered Astrali wheel, 15" or 14" dia. giving 3¼ or 3½ turns lock to lock. Turning circle 38' (11.5m).

Suspension - Front wheels-independently sprung by vertical coil springs and telescopic hydraulic shock absorbers. Semi-elliptical rear springs with lever type hydraulic dampers.

Electrics - Lucas 12 volt equipment; indicators, hazard warning, instrument panel lighting, two-speed wipers and washer. Twin spotlights and fresh air heater and demister.

Instruments - Speedo, rev. counter and warning lights in front of driver, with central steel panel including separate oil, fuel, temp. and volt gauges.

Michael English.

Rob Wells leads Peter Garland and Grahame Bryant to a race win at Thruxton in September 1989.

MORGAN
The sports car that goes on

Throughout its history the Morgan Motor Company has always exploited, from an advertising point of view, the marque's competition successes. This 1980 photograph was reproduced on one side of a double-sided sheet, together with a list of Morgan UK main agents. The reverse features the range of three models available at that time.

Willhire Snetterton 24 hour race for Pr...
Winner of the Commanders Cup for the g...
by a single car entry. Plus 8, entered by M...
Motors.

order your Morgan from

Allon White & Son
(Cranfield) Ltd.,
The Garage, High Street, Cranfield,
Beds., MK43 0BT. (0234) 750205

Otley & Ilkley Motors Ltd.,
Cross Green, Otley,
West Yorkshire, LS21 1HE.
(0943) 465222

John Britten Garages Ltd.,
Barnet Road, Arkley, Barnet,
Herts. 01-449 1144

I. & J. MacDonald,
Maiden Law Garage, Lanchester,
Co. Durham. (0207) 520916

Malvern Sports Car Company,
2A Howsell Road, Malvern,
Worcs., WR14 1TH. (06845) 63767

Burlen Services,
Greencroft Garage, The Greencroft,
Salisbury, Wilts., SP1 1JD.
(0722) 21777

John Dangerfield Garages,
115, Staple Hill Road, Fishponds,
Bristol, BS16 5AD. (0272) 566525

F. H. Douglass,
1a, South Ealing Road, Ealing,
London, W5 4QT. 01-567 0570

Mike Duncan,
92 Windmill Hill, Halesowen,
Nr. Birmingham. B63 2BY.
(0384) 67675

Robin Kay,
1a Ceylon Place, Eastbourne,
Sussex, BN21 3JE. (0323) 26462

Lifes Motors Ltd.,
32-36 West Street, Southport,
Lancs., PR8 1QN. (0704) 31375

Parker Bros. (Stepps) Ltd.,
63 Cumbernauld Road, Stepps,
Glasgow, G33 6LS. 041-779 2271

Phoenix Motors,
The Green, Woodbury
Devon, EX5 1LT. (039...

Cliffsea Car Sales,
840-846 London Road,
Leigh-on-Sea, Essex, S...
(0702) 77067

Mike Spence (Reading)
School Green, Shinfiel...
Berks. (0734) 883312

Sports Motors (Manche...
250 Plymouth Grove, N...
M13 0BG. 061-225 343...

Morris Stapleton Moto...
6 Kendrick Place, Reed...
London, SW7. 01-589 6...

Station Garage, Station...
Taplow, Nr. Maidenhe...
SL6 0NT. (06286) 5353...

Morgan

PLUS 8
2 SEATER

It's beautifully fast, tamed by the latest 5-speed gearbox and big Girling disc-brakes up front. The 3528cc V8 delivers 155 b.h.p. at 5,250 r.p.m. yet returns a respectable 24 m.p.g. 0-70 m.p.h. is achieved in less than 9 seconds.

4/4 1600
2 SEATER

All the joys of open-air motoring, with lively acceleration from the 1600cc cross-flow engine up to high speeds with good fuel economy. Dual braking system, on all four wheels of course.

4/4 1600
4 SEATER

The four seats accommodate four people — probably a unique feature where open-top cars are concerned. The specification is otherwise similar to the 4/4 2-seater which allows sufficient power for the larger body.

 MORGAN MOTOR COMPANY LIMITED,
Malvern Link, Worcestershire.
Tel: Malvern 3104/5

The only works-produced Plus 8 Drop Head Coupé, which belongs to Mrs Jane Morgan and carries her personal registration number JM 53.

Ford 1600 CVH engines, as delivered by Ford, await installation in 4/4s.

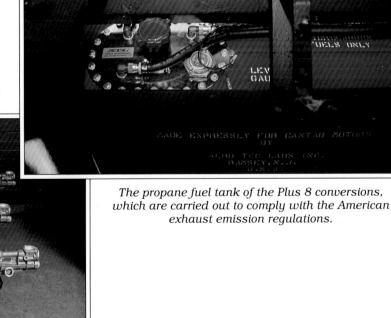

The propane fuel tank of the Plus 8 conversions, which are carried out to comply with the American exhaust emission regulations.

The Prototype Ford 1800 4/4, chassis number D8720, engine number G242, registration number K546 MNP.

New Morgans, lined up in the finishing and despatching bay at the works, await collection by their eager owners.

APPENDIX III

TECHNICAL DATA SHEETS
&
LUCAS ELECTRICAL COMPONENT
DATA SHEETS

Models: Standard 2-seater Tourer and Competition model

ENGINE (Ford)

1. Type ... ... 4-stroke; overhead valves; side camshaft
2. Cooling system ... Water pump, radiator, fan and thermostat
3. Number of cylinders ... 4 (bored direct in block)
4. Firing order and idling 1—2—4—3 (No. 1 at front); 580/620 speed r.p.m. (Comp., 680/720)
5. Bore ... ... 3·1881in. (80·977mm.) mean grade
6. Stroke ... ... 3·056in. (77·62mm.)
7. Cubic capacity ... 1598c.c.
8. Compression ratio and 9:1; 188lb./sq.in. at 300 r.p.m. pressure
9. Brake horse-power (gross) 75 at 5,000 r.p.m. (Comp., 93 at 5,400)
10. Torque (lb.ft.) ... 97 at 2,500 (Comp., 102 at 3,600)
11. Piston oversizes ... ·0025, ·015, ·030in.
12. Piston clearance in bore ... 7/11lb. pull on ·0020in.×¼in. feeler (·0013/·0019in.)
13. Piston rings—number ... 2 compression, 1 oil
14. Piston rings—width ... Comp., ·077 to ·078in.; oil, 0·155 to 0·156in.
15. Piston rings—groove cl'nce Comp., ·0016 to ·0036in.; oil, ·0018 to
16. Piston rings—gap (in bore) ·009 to ·014in. [·0038in.
17. Oil pressure ... ... 35 to 40lb./sq.in.
18. Gudgeon pin diameter ... 0·8119 to 0·8123in.
19. Gudgeon pin fit in piston Interference, selective (heated piston)
20. Gudgeon pin fit in con. rod ·0001 to ·0003in. clearance (selective)
21. Crankpin diameter ... 1·9368 to 1·9376in.
22. Crankpin undersizes ... ·010, ·020, ·030, ·040in.
23. Connecting rod length ... 4·927 to 4·929in. (centres)
24. Big-end bearings ... Steel-backed, copper/lead, lead/bronze or aluminium/tin
25. Big-end bearing clearance ·0004 to ·0024in.
26. Big-end side clearance ... ·004 to ·010in.
27. Main journal diameter ... Blue, 2·1253/57in.; red, 2·1257/61in.
28. Main journal undersizes ... ·010, ·020, ·030in.
29. Main bearings ... 5; steel-backed white metal (Comp., copper/lead, lead/bronze or aluminium/tin.)
31. Main bearing clearance ... ·0005 to ·0020in.
32. Crankshaft end-float ... ·003 to ·011in.
33. Crankshaft end-thrust on Centre main bearing
34. Camshaft journal dia. ... 1·5597 to 1·5605in.
35. Camshaft bearings ... 3; steel-backed white metal
36. Camshaft bearing cl'nce.. ·001 to ·0023in.
37. Camshaft end-float ... ·0025 to ·0075in.
38. Camshaft drive type ... Chain (single); 46×0·375in. pitches
39. Valve head diameter ... Inlet, 1·497/1·507in.; exhaust, 1·240/1·250in.
40. Valve stem diameter ... Inlet, 0·3095/0·3105; exhaust, 0·3086
41. Valve seat angle ... 45° [to 0·3096in.
42. Valve lift ... ... Inlet, 0·315in. (Comp., 0·3420); exhaust, 0·319in. (Comp., 0·3367)
43. Valve guide length ... Inlet, 1·82/1·84in.; exhaust, 2·07/2·09in.
44. Valve stem guide cl'nce... Inlet, ·0008 to ·003in.; exhaust, ·0017 to ·0039in.
45. Valve spring free length... 1·48in.
46. Valve spring rate ... Length (closed), 1·263in. at 44/49lb.
47. Valve work'g cl'nce (hot) Inlet, ·010in. (Comp., ·012); exhaust, ·017in. (Comp., ·022)
48. Valve timing clearance ... Inlet, ·015in. (Comp., ·016); exhaust, ·027in. (Comp., ·026)
49. Valve timing (See 48) ... Inlet opens 17° (*27° B.T.D.C.; closes (*Competition model) 51° (*65°) A.B.D.C. Exhaust opens 51° (*65°) B.B.D.C.; closes 17° (*27°) A.T.D.C.
50. Petrol pump ... ... A.C. mechanical
51. Carburettor ... ... Ford C7BH-B (Comp., Weber dual choke) Ford

	Weber 32DFM	
	Primary	Secondary
52. Choke tube ... ... 28mm.	26mm.	27mm.
53. Main jet ... ... 1·50mm.	150	155
54. Compensating jet ... 1·50mm.	160	140
55. Slow-running jet ... 0·65mm.	50	45
56. Slow-running air bleed ... 1st, 1·05mm.	180 (bush)	70
2nd, 0·6mm.		
57. Emulsion tube	F6	F6
58. Accelerator pump jet ... 0·55mm.	65	
62. Needle valve	1·75mm.	

TRANSMISSION

101. Type ... ... Rear wheel drive
102. Clutch ... ... 7½in. diam., diaphragm type
103. Gearbox ... ... 4 forward speeds, all synchromesh
105. Gearbox ratios ... Top, 1:1; 3rd, 1·397:1; 2nd, 2·010:1; 1st, 2·972:1; reverse, 3·324:1
107. Driving axles ... ... Semi-floating
108. Final drive gear ... Hypoid (Salisbury)
109. Final drive ratio ... 4·56:1 (41/9); Comp., 4·1:1 (41/10)

111. Crown wheel/pinion b'lash ·003 to ·006in.; shim adjustment
112. Pinion bearing pre-load ... 8 to 12lb.in.; shim adjustment
113. Differential brg. pre-load ·003 to ·005in.; shim adjustment

BRAKES

201. Front ... ... Girling hydraulic, 11in. diam. discs
202. Rear ... ... Girling hydraulic, 9in. diam. drums
203. Handbrake ... ... Mechanical, on rear wheels
204. Linings—front ... Ferodo, type 14 calliper pads
205. Linings—rear ... Ferodo, 1¾in. wide

STEERING (see also " Dimensions ")

301. Type ... ... Cam Gear
302. Camber angle ... 2°; non-adjustable
303. Castor angle ... 4°; non-adjustable
304. King-pin inclination ... 2°
305. Toe-in ... ... ⅛ to 3/16 in. at wheel rim
306. Conditions for checking... Unladen

FRONT SUSPENSION

401. Type ... ... Independent, vertical coil springs
402. Number of coils ... 21
403. Coil diameter ... 2¼in. (external)
404. Wire diameter ... 0·31in.
405. Spring length—free ... 14¼in.
406. Spring length—fitted ... 8½in.

REAR SUSPENSION

501. Type ... ... Semi-elliptic leaf springs
504. Spring length (centres) ... 42¾in. (free)
505. Number of leaves ... 5
506. Width of leaves ... 1⅝in.
507. Thickness of leaves ... ¼in.
508. Spring camber—free ... 3⅞in.

ELECTRICAL SYSTEM

601. Ignition timing (static) ... 10° (Comp., 8°B.T.D.C.) (97 oct.); mark on pulley
602. Sparking plugs ... Autolite AG22P
603. Sparking plug gap ... ·023in.
604. Distributor ... Ford, C7BH-A (Comp., –C)
605. Contact breaker gap ... ·025in.; dwell angle 39°/42°

	Standard	Competition
606. Centrif. adv. starts at ...	½°/2½° at 700 r.p.m.	1°/3° at 700
607. Centrif. advance—max....	13°/15° at 2,700	8°/10° at 2,600
608. Vacuum adv. starts at ...	½° to 3½° at 5½in. Hg.	
609. Vacuum advance—max.	5½° to 8½° at 9＋in. Hg.	
	(Distributor degrees and r.p.m.)	

610. Ignition coil ... 12v. oil-filled
611. Battery ... ... Lucas BT7A or C7, 12v. 36a.h.
612. Battery earth ... Negative
613. Dynamo ... ... Lucas C40
614. Control box ... Cut-in, 12·6/13·4v.; drop-off, 9·25/11·25v.; V.R. open circuit setting, 14·4/15·6v. at 68°F
615. Starter motor ... Inertia type

CAPACITIES

701. Engine sump ... 7·2 pints (including filter)
702. Gearbox ... ... 1·97 pints
703. Differential ... 1¾ pints
704. Cooling system ... 12 pints
705. Fuel tank ... 8½ gallons
706. Tyre size ... 5·60×15in.
707. Tyre pressures ... 16/17lb./sq.in., front and rear, normal (add 6lb./sq.in. for sustained high-speed driving on motorways)
708. No. of grease gun points ... 13 (Front sliding axles have 'one-shot' lubrication; press foot plunger every 200 miles approx.)
709. Normal servicing intervals Greasing, 2000/2500 miles; engine oil change, 5000 miles
710. Hydraulic fluid ... Castrol/Girling

DIMENSIONS

801. Length overall ... 12ft.
802. Width overall ... 4ft. 8in.
803. Height overall ... 4ft. 3¾in.
804. Weight (approx.) ... 1,456lb. (13cwt.) dry
805. Ground clearance (min.) 7in.
806. Track ... ... 3ft. 11in. front and rear
807. Wheelbase ... 8ft.
808. Turning circle diameter... 32ft.

TORQUE SPANNER DATA (lb.ft.)

		907. Final drive pinion	
901. Cylinder head nuts ... 65/70		bearing nut	95/100
902. Big-end bearing nuts ... 30/35		908. Crown wheel bolts	50/60
903. Main bearing nuts ... 65/70		909. Diff. bearing nuts	35/40
905. Flywheel bolts ... 50/55		910. Road wheel nuts	65/70
906. Clutch to flywheel bolts ... 12/15			

BODY AND CHASSIS

1001. Type of construction ... Coachbuilt; steel 'Z'-section chassis; ash body frame
1002. Material of body panels... Steel and aluminium
1003. Windscreen glass... ... Toughened (laminated optional extra)

4/4 1600 1969

ENGINE (Rover)

1. Type ... ... 4-stroke V8 (cast-aluminium block); O.H.V.; central camshaft; hydraulic tappets
2. Cooling system ... ... Water pump, radiator, fan and thermo-stat (15lb./sq.in.)
3. Number of cylinders ... 8 (dry liners)
4. Firing order and idling 1L—8R—4R—3L—6R—5L—7L—2R (No. speed   1 at front left); 600/650 r.p.m.
5. Bore ... ... 3·5in. (88·9mm.)
6. Stroke ... ... 2·8in. (71·1mm.)
7. Cubic capacity ... ... 3,525c.c.
8. Compression ratio and 10·5:1; 180/190lb./sq.in. at 185 r.p.m. pressure
9. Brake horse-power (net)... 160·5 at 5,200 r.p.m.
10. Torque (max.) ... ... 210lb.ft. at 2,750 r.p.m.
11. Piston oversizes ... ... ·010, ·020in.
12. Piston clearance in bore ... ·0005/·0011in. (skirt top)
13. Piston rings—number ... 2 compression, 1 oil
14. Piston rings—width ... Compression, ·078/·079in.; oil (ex-pander) 0·1894in. max.
15. Piston rings—groove cl'nce Compression, ·003 to ·005in.
16. Piston rings—gap (in bore) Compression, ·017 to ·022in.
17. Oil pressure (lb./sq.in.) 30 to 40 at 2,400 r.p.m. (55 at 4,000)
18. Gudgeon pin diameter ... 0·8746 to 0·8749in.
19. Gudgeon pin fit in piston ·0001 to ·0003in. clearance
20. Gudgeon pin fit in con. rod Press fit (·00075 to ·00125in. clearance)
21. Crankpin diameter ... 2·0000 to 2·0005in.
22. Crankpin undersizes ... ·010, ·020, ·030, ·040in.
23. Connecting rod length ... 5·662 to 5·658in. (centres)
24. Big-end bearings ... Vandervell, lead-indium
25. Big-end bearing clearance ·0007 to ·0027in.
26. Big-end side clearance ... ·005 to ·015in.
27. Main journal diameter ... 2·2992 to 2·2997in.
28. Main journal undersizes... ·010, ·020, ·030, ·040in.
29. Main bearings ... ... 5; Vandervell, lead-indium
30. Main bearings—length ... (1) (2) (4) (5), 0·797 to 0·807in.; (3), 1·056 to 1·058in.
31. Main bearing clearance ... ·0009 to ·0024in.
32. Crankshaft end-float ... ·004 to ·008in.
33. Crankshaft end-thrust on Centre main bearing
35. Camshaft bearings ... 5; steel-backed babbitt
38. Camshaft drive type ... Chain; 54×0·375in. pitches
39. Valve head diameter ... Inlet, 1·495/1·505in.; exhaust, 1·3075/1·3175in.
40. Valve stem diameter ... Inlet (head) 0·3402/0·3412 to 0·3407/(tapered) 0·3417in.; exhaust, 0·3397/0·3407 to 0·3402/0 3412in.
41. Valve seat angle ... 45°
42. Valve lift ... ... 0·39in.
44. Valve stem/guide cl'nce... Inlet (top), ·001/·003; (bottom), ·0015/·0035. Exhaust (top), ·0015/·0035; (bottom), ·002/·004in.
46. Valve spring rate... ... Inner, 1·63in. at 21·5/26·5lb.; outer, 1·6in. at 39/45lb.
49. Valve timing Inlet opens 30° B.T.D.C. } peak, 112·5°
            Inlet closes 75° A.B.D.C. } A.T.D.C.
            Exhaust opens 68° B.B.D.C. } peak, 105·5°
            Exhaust closes 37° A.T.D.C. } B.T.D.C.
50. Petrol pump ... ... A.C. mechanical
52. Carburettors ... ... 2 S.U. type HS6
52. Diameter ... ... 1·75in.
53. Needle (standard) ... KO
54. Jet diameter ... ... 0·100in.

TRANSMISSION

101. Type ... ... Rear wheel drive
102. Clutch ... ... Borg & Beck, 9in. diam., single dry plate
103. Gearbox ... ... 4 forward speeds; synchromesh on 2nd, 3rd and top gears
105. Gearbox ratios ... ... Top, 1:1; 3rd 1·205:1; 2nd, 1·745:1; 1st and reverse, 2·97:1
106. Overdrive ... ... Not fitted
107. Driving axles ... ... Semi-floating
108. Final drive gear ... ... Hypoid, limited-slip differential
109. Final drive ratio ... 3·58:1
110. Number of gear teeth ... 43/12
111. Crown wheel/pinion b'lash 0·003 to 0·006in.; shim adjustment
112. Pinion bearing pre-load 8 to 12lb.in.
113. Differential brg. pre-load ·003 to ·005in.; shim adjustment

BRAKES

201. Front ... ... Girling hydraulic, 11in. diam. discs
202. Rear ... ... Girling hydraulic, 9in. diam. drums
203. Handbrake ... ... Mechanical, on rear wheels
204. Linings—front ... ... Ferodo, type GX, caliper pads
205. Linings—rear ... ... Ferodo, type LL, 1¾in. wide
206. Power assistance ... Girling servo (twin on L.H. drive cars)

STEERING (see also "Dimensions")

301. Type ... ... Cam Gear
302. Camber angle ... ... 2°, non-adjustable
303. Castor angle ... ... 4°, non-adjustable
304. King-pin inclination ... 2°
305. Toe-in ... ... ⅛ to 3/16 at wheel rims
306. Conditions for checking... Unladen

FRONT SUSPENSION

401. Type ... ... Independent, vertical coil springs
402. Number of coils 18
403. Coil diameter ... ... 2⅜in. (external)
404. Wire diameter ... ... 0·375in.
405. Spring length—free ... 13in.
506. Spring length—fitted ... 9in.

REAR SUSPENSION

501. Type ... ... Semi-elliptic leaf-springs
504. Spring length ... ... 42¾in. (free)
505. Number of leaves ... 6
506. Width of leaves ... 1¾in.
507. Thickness of leaves ... ¼in.
508. Spring camber—free ... 3¼in.

ELECTRICAL SYSTEM

601. Ignition timing—(static) 6° B.T.D.C. (marks on damper)
602. Sparking plugs ... ... Champion L87Y
603. Sparking plug gap ... ·025in.
604. Distributor ... ... Lucas 35D8
605. Contact breaker gap ... ·014 to ·016in.; but set dwell angle, 26°/28° (600 r.p.m.)
606. Centrif. advance starts at 560 to 840 r.p.m.
607. Centrif. advance—max.... 28° at 4,800 r.p.m. (Crankshaft degrees and r.p.m.)
610. Ignition coil ... ... Lucas BA7
611. Battery ... ... 12v. 57a.h., Lucas C9
612. Battery earth ... ... Negative
613. Alternator ... ... Lucas 11AC, 45 amp.
614. Control box ... ... Lucas 4TR
615. Starter motor ... ... Lucas M45G, pre-engaged

CAPACITIES

701. Engine sump ... ... 8 pints (plus 1 pint for new filter)
702. Gearbox ... ... 2¼ pints
703. Differential ... ... 1¾ pints
704. Cooling system ... ... 15 pints
705. Fuel tank ... ... 14 gallons
706. Tyre size ... ... 185×15in.
707. Tyre pressures ... Front 22 (fast driving, 24-26)
    (lb./sq.in.) ... Rear 22 (fast driving, 24-26)
708. No. of grease gun points 7
709. Servicing intervals ... Greasing, 3000 miles; engine oil change, 5000
710. Hydraulic fluid ... ... Castrol-Girling

DIMENSIONS

801. Length overall ... ... 12ft. 8in.
802. Width overall ... ... 57in.
803. Height overall ... ... 50in.
804. Weight (approx.) 1900lb. (17cwt.)
805. Ground clearance (min.) 6in. (engine sump)
806. Track ... ... Front, 49in.; rear, 51in.
807. Wheelbase ... ... 98in.
808. Turning circle diameter... 38ft.

TORQUE SPANNER DATA (lb.ft.)

901. Cylinder head bolts ... 65/70
902. Big-end bearing bolts ... 30/35
903. Main bearing bolts ... 50/55
           —Rear ... 65/70
905. Flywheel bolts 120
906. Clutch to flywheel bolts... 20
907. Drive pinion bearing nut 95/100
908. Crown wheel bolts ... 50/60
909. Differential bearing nuts 35/40
910. Road wheel nuts... ... 65/70
911. Steering wheel nut ... 40

BODY AND CHASSIS

1001. Type of construction ... Steel 'Z'-section chassis
1002. Material of body panels... Steel and aluminium
1003. Type of glass ... ... Windscreen laminated

Plus 8 1969

147

Models: Standard 2-seater Tourer and Competition model

ENGINE (Ford)

1.	Type	4-stroke; overhead valves; side camshaft
2.	Cooling system ...	Water pump, radiator, fan and thermostat
3.	Number of cylinders ...	4 (bored direct in block)
4.	Firing order and idling speed	1—2—4—3 (No. 1 at front); 580/620 r.p.m. (Comp., 680/720)
5.	Bore	3·1881in. (80·977mm.) mean grade
6.	Stroke	3·056in. (77·62mm.)
7.	Cubic capacity	1598c.c.
8.	Compression ratio and pressure	9:1; 188lb./sq.in. at 300 r.p.m.
9.	Brake horse-power (gross)	75 at 5,000 r.p.m. (Comp., 93 at 5,400)
10.	Torque (lb.ft.)	97 at 2,500 (Comp., 102 at 3,600)
11.	Piston oversizes ...	·0025, ·015, ·030in.
12.	Piston clearance in bore ...	7/11lb. pull on ·0020in. × ½in. feeler (·0013/·0019in.)
13.	Piston rings—number ...	2 compression, 1 oil
14.	Piston rings—width ...	Comp., ·077 to ·078in.; oil, 0·155 to 0·156in.
15.	Piston rings—groove cl'nce	Comp., ·0016 to ·0036in.; oil, ·0018 to ·0038in.
16.	Piston rings—gap (in bore)	·009 to ·014in.
17.	Oil pressure	35 to 40lb./sq.in.
18.	Gudgeon pin diameter ...	0·8119 to 0·8123in.
19.	Gudgeon pin fit in piston	Interference, selective (heated piston)
20.	Gudgeon pin fit in con. rod	·0001 to ·0003in. clearance (selective)
21.	Crankpin diameter ...	1·9368 to 1·9376in.
22.	Crankpin undersizes ...	·010, ·020, ·030, ·040in.
23.	Connecting rod length ...	4·927 to 4·929in. (centres)
24.	Big-end bearings ...	Steel-backed, copper/lead, lead/bronze or aluminium/tin
25.	Big-end bearing clearance	·0004 to ·0024in.
26.	Big-end side clearance ...	·004 to ·010in.
27.	Main journal diameter ...	Blue, 2·1253/57in.; red, 2·1257/61in.
28.	Main journal undersizes ...	·010, ·020, ·030in.
29.	Main bearings ...	5; steel-backed white metal (Comp., copper/lead, lead/bronze or aluminium/tin.)
31.	Main bearing clearance ...	·0005 to ·0020in.
32.	Crankshaft end-float ...	·003 to ·011in.
33.	Crankshaft end-thrust on	Centre main bearing
34.	Camshaft journal dia. ...	1·5597 to 1·5605in.
35.	Camshaft bearings ...	3; steel-backed white metal
36.	Camshaft bearing cl'nce.	·001 to ·0023in.
37.	Camshaft end-float ...	·0025 to ·0075in.
38.	Camshaft drive type ...	Chain (single); 46 × 0·375in. pitches
39.	Valve head diameter ...	Inlet, 1·497/1·507in.; exhaust, 1·240/1·250in.
40.	Valve stem diameter ...	Inlet, 0·3095/0·3105; exhaust, 0·3086 [to 0·3096in.
41.	Valve seat angle ...	45°
42.	Valve lift	Inlet, 0·315in. (Comp., 0·3420); exhaust, 0·319in. (Comp., 0·3367)
43.	Valve guide length ...	Inlet, 1·82/1·84in.; exhaust, 2·07/2·09in.
44.	Valve stem/guide cl'nce.	Inlet, ·0008 to ·003in.; exhaust, ·0017 to ·0039in.
45.	Valve spring free length..	1·48in.
46.	Valve spring rate ...	Length (closed), 1·263in. at 44/49lb.
47.	Valve work'g cl'nce (hot)	Inlet, ·010in. (Comp., ·012); exhaust, ·017in. (Comp., ·022)
48.	Valve timing clearance ...	Inlet, ·015in. (Comp., ·016); exhaust, ·027in. (Comp., ·026)
49.	Valve timing (See 48) (*Competition model)	Inlet opens 17° (*27°) B.T.D.C.; closes 51° (*65°) A.B.D.C. Exhaust opens 51° (*65°) B.B.D.C.; closes 17° (*27°) A.T.D.C.
50.	Petrol pump	A.C. mechanical
51.	Carburettor	Ford C7BH-B (Comp., Weber dual choke)

		Ford	Weber 32DFM	
			Primary	Secondary
52.	Choke tube	28mm.	26mm.	27mm.
53.	Main jet	1·50mm.	150	155
54.	Compensating jet ...	1·50mm.	160	140
55.	Slow-running jet ...	0·65mm.	50	45
56.	Slow-running air bleed ...	1st, 1·05mm. 2nd, 0·6mm.	180 (bush)	70
57.	Emulsion tube		F6	F6
58.	Accelerator pump jet ...	0·55mm.	65	
62.	Needle valve		1·75mm.	

TRANSMISSION

101.	Type	Rear wheel drive
102.	Clutch	7½in. diam., diaphragm type
103.	Gearbox	4 forward speeds, all synchromesh
105.	Gearbox ratios ...	Top, 1:1; 3rd, 1·397:1; 2nd, 2·010:1; 1st, 2·972:1; reverse, 3·324:1
107.	Driving axles ...	Semi-floating
108.	Final drive gear ...	Hypoid (Salisbury)

109.	Final drive ratio ...	4·56:1 (41/9); Comp., 4·1:1 (41/10)
111.	Crownwheel/pinion b'lash	·003 to ·006in.; shim adjustment
112.	Pinion bearing pre-load ...	8 to 12lb.in.; shim adjustment
113.	Differential brg. pre-load	·003 to ·005in.; shim adjustment

BRAKES

201.	Front	Girling hydraulic, 11in. diam. discs
202.	Rear	Girling hydraulic, 9in. diam. drums
203.	Handbrake	Mechanical, on rear wheels
204.	Linings—front ...	Ferodo, type 14 calliper pads
205.	Linings—rear ...	Ferodo, 1¾in. wide

STEERING (see also " Dimensions ")

301.	Type	Cam Gear
302.	Camber angle ...	2°; non-adjustable
303.	Castor angle ...	4°; non-adjustable
304.	King-pin inclination ...	2°
305.	Toe-in	⅛ to 3/16in. at wheel rim
306.	Conditions for checking...	Unladen

FRONT SUSPENSION

401.	Type	Independent, vertical coil springs
402.	Number of coils ...	21
403.	Coil diameter ...	2¼in. (external)
404.	Wire diameter ...	0·31in.
405.	Spring length—free ...	14½in.
406.	Spring length—fitted ...	8½in.

REAR SUSPENSION

501.	Type	Semi-elliptic leaf springs
504.	Spring length (centres) ...	42¼in. (free)
505.	Number of leaves ...	5
506.	Width of leaves ...	1¾in.
507.	Thickness of leaves ...	¼in.
508.	Spring camber—free ...	3⅜in.

ELECTRICAL SYSTEM

601.	Ignition timing (static) ...	10° (Comp., 8°B.T.D.C.) (97 oct.); mark on pulley
602.	Sparking plugs ...	Autolite AG22P
603.	Sparking plug gap ...	·023in.
604.	Distributor ...	Ford, C7BH-A (Comp., -C)
605.	Contact breaker gap ...	·025in.; dwell angle 39°/42°

		Standard	Competition
606.	Centrif. adv. starts at ...	½°/2½° at 700 r.p.m.	1°/3° at 700
607.	Centrif. advance—max. ...	13°/15° at 2,700	8°/10° at 2,600
608.	Vacuum adv. starts at ...	....	½° to 3½° at 5½in. Hg. ....
609.	Vacuum advance—max. ...	....	5½° to 8½° at 9+in. Hg. .... (Distributor degrees and r.p.m.)

610.	Ignition coil ...	12v. oil-filled
611.	Battery	Lucas BT7A or C7, 12v. 36a.h.
612.	Battery earth ...	Negative
613.	Alternator ...	Lucas 15ACR, 336 watts
614.	Control box ...	Incorporated in alternator
615.	Starter motor ...	Inertia type

CAPACITIES

701.	Engine sump ...	7·2 pints (including filter)
702.	Gearbox	1·97 pints
703.	Differential ...	1¾ pints
704.	Cooling system ...	12 pints
705.	Fuel tank ...	8½ gallons
706.	Tyre size	155 × 15 or 165 × 15
707.	Tyre pressures (lb./sq.in.)	Front, 18; rear, 19
708.	No. of grease gun points ...	12 (Front sliding axles have 'one-shot' lubrication; press foot plunger every 200 miles approx.)
709.	Normal servicing intervals	Greasing, 2000/2500 miles; engine oil change, 5000 miles
710.	Hydraulic fluid ...	Castrol/Girling

DIMENSIONS

801.	Length overall ...	12ft.
802.	Width overall ...	4ft. 8in.
803.	Height overall ...	4ft. 3¼in.
804.	Weight (approx.) ...	1,456lb. (13cwt.) dry
805.	Ground clearance (min.)	7in.
806.	Track	3ft. 11in. front and rear
807.	Wheelbase ...	8ft.
808.	Turning circle diameter...	32ft.

TORQUE SPANNER DATA (lb.ft.)

901.	Cylinder head nuts ...	65/70	907.	Final drive pinion	
902.	Big-end bearing nuts ...	30/35		bearing nut	95/100
903.	Main bearing nuts ...	65/70	908.	Crown wheel bolts	50/60
905.	Flywheel bolts ...	50/55	909.	Diff. bearing nuts	35/40
906.	Clutch to flywheel bolts ...	12/15	910.	Road wheel nuts	65/70

BODY AND CHASSIS

1001.	Type of construction ...	Coachbuilt; steel 'Z'-section chassis; ash body frame
1002.	Material of body panels...	Steel and aluminium
1003.	Windscreen glass... ...	Toughened (laminated optional extra)

4/4 1600 1970

Model: 2-seater Tourer

ENGINE (Rover)

1.	Type	4-stroke V8 (cast-aluminium block); O.H.V.; central camshaft; hydraulic tappets
2.	Cooling system	Water pump, radiator, fan and thermo-stat (15lb./sq.in.)
3.	Number of cylinders ...	8 (dry liners)
4.	Firing order and idling speed	1L—8R—4R—3L—6R—5L—7L—2R (No. 1 at front left); 600/650 r.p.m.
5.	Bore	3·5in. (88·9mm.)
6.	Stroke	2·8in. (71·1mm.)
7.	Cubic capacity	3,525c.c.
8.	Compression ratio and pressure	10·5:1; 180/190lb./sq.in. at 185 r.p.m.
9.	Brake horse-power (net) ...	160·5 at 5,200 r.p.m.
10.	Torque (max.)	210lb.ft. at 2,750 r.p.m.
11.	Piston oversizes	·010, ·020in.
12.	Piston clearance in bore ...	·0005/·0011in. (skirt top)
13.	Piston rings—number ...	2 compression, 1 oil
14.	Piston rings—width ...	Compression, ·078/·079in.; oil (expander) 0·1894in. max.
15.	Piston rings—groove cl'nce	Compression, ·003 to ·005in.
16.	Piston rings—gap (in bore)	Compression, ·017 to ·022in.
17.	Oil pressure (lb./sq.in.) ...	30 to 40 at 2,400 r.p.m. (55 at 4,000)
18.	Gudgeon pin diameter ...	0·8746 to 0·8749in.
19.	Gudgeon pin fit in piston	·0001 to ·0003in. clearance
20.	Gudgeon pin fit in con. rod	Press fit (·00075 to ·00125in. clearance)
21.	Crankpin diameter ...	2·0000 to 2·0005in.
22.	Crankpin undersizes ...	·010, ·020, ·030, ·040in.
23.	Connecting rod length ...	5·662 to 5·658in. (centres)
24.	Big-end bearings ...	Vandervell, lead-indium
25.	Big-end bearing clearance	·0007 to ·0027in.
26.	Big-end side clearance ...	·005 to ·015in.
27.	Main journal diameter ...	2·2992 to 2·2997in.
28.	Main journal undersizes...	·010, ·020, ·030, ·040in.
29.	Main bearings	5; Vandervell, lead-indium
30.	Main bearings—length ...	(1) (2) (4) (5), 0·797 to 0·807in.; (3), 1·056 to 1·058in.
31.	Main bearing clearance ...	·0009 to ·0024in.
32.	Crankshaft end-float ...	·004 to ·008in.
33.	Crankshaft end-thrust on	Centre main bearing
35.	Camshaft bearings ...	5; steel-backed babbitt
38.	Camshaft drive type ...	Chain; 54×0·375in. pitches
39.	Valve head diameter ...	Inlet, 1·495/1·505in.; exhaust, 1·3075/1·3175in.
40.	Valve stem diameter (tapered)	Inlet (head) 0·3402/0·3412 to 0·3407/0·3417in.; exhaust, 0·3397/0·3407 to 0·3402/0·3412in.
42.	Valve lift	0·39in.
44.	Valve stem/guide cl'nce...	Inlet (top), ·001/·003; (bottom), ·0015/·0035. Exhaust (top), ·0015/·0035; (bottom), ·002/·004in.
46.	Valve spring rate... ...	Inner, 1·63in. at 21·5/26·5lb.; outer, 1·6in. at 39/45lb.

49.	Valve timing	Inlet opens 30° B.T.D.C. } peak, 112·5° A.T.D.C.
		Inlet closes 75° A.B.D.C.
		Exhaust opens 68° B.B.D.C. } peak, 105·5° B.T.D.C.
		Exhaust closes 37° A.T.D.C.
50.	Petrol pump	A.C. mechanical
52.	Carburettors	2 S.U. type HS6
52.	Diameter	1·75in.
53.	Needle (standard) ...	KO
54.	Jet diameter	0·100in.

TRANSMISSION

101.	Type	Rear wheel drive
102.	Clutch	Borg & Beck, 9in. diam., single dry plate
103.	Gearbox	4 forward speeds; synchromesh on 2nd, 3rd and top gears
105.	Gearbox ratios	Top, 1:1; 3rd 1·205:1; 2nd, 1·745:1; 1st and reverse, 2·97:1
106.	Overdrive	Not fitted
107.	Driving axles	Semi-floating
108.	Final drive gear ...	Hypoid, limited-slip differential
109.	Final drive ratio ...	3·58:1
110.	Number of gear teeth ...	43/12
111.	Crown wheel/pinion b'lash	0·003 to 0·006in.; shim adjustment
112.	Pinion bearing pre-load	8 to 12lb.in.
113.	Differential brg. pre-load	·003 to ·005in.; shim adjustment

BRAKES

201.	Front	Girling hydraulic, 11in. diam. discs
202.	Rear	Girling hydraulic, 9in. diam. drums
203.	Handbrake	Mechanical, on rear wheels
204.	Linings—front	Ferodo, type GX, caliper pads
205.	Linings—rear	Ferodo, type LL, 1¾in. wide
206.	Power assistance ...	Girling servo (twin on L.H. drive cars)

STEERING (see also "Dimensions")

301.	Type	Cam Gear
302.	Camber angle ...	2°, non-adjustable
303.	Castor angle ...	4°, non-adjustable
304.	King-pin inclination ...	2°
305.	Toe-in	⅛ to 1/16 at wheel rims
306.	Conditions for checking...	Unladen

FRONT SUSPENSION

401.	Type	Independent, vertical coil springs
402.	Number of coils ...	18
403.	Coil diameter ...	2⅜in. (external)
404.	Wire diameter ...	0·375in.
405.	Spring length—free ...	13in.
506.	Spring length—fitted ...	9in.

REAR SUSPENSION

501.	Type	Semi-elliptic leaf-springs
504.	Spring length ...	42¾in. (free)
505.	Number of leaves ...	6
506.	Width of leaves ...	1¾in.
507.	Thickness of leaves ...	¼in.
508.	Spring camber—free ...	3½in.

ELECTRICAL SYSTEM

601.	Ignition timing—(static)	6° B.T.D.C. (marks on damper)
602.	Sparking plugs	Champion L87Y
603.	Sparking plug gap ...	·025in.
604.	Distributor	Lucas 35D8
605.	Contact breaker gap ...	·014 to ·016in.; but set dwell angle, 26°/28° (600 r.p.m.)
606.	Centrif. advance starts at	560 to 840 r.p.m.
607.	Centrif. advance—max....	28° at 4,800 r.p.m. (Crankshaft degrees and r.p.m.)
610.	Ignition coil	Lucas BA7
611.	Battery	12v. 57a.h., Lucas C9
612.	Battery earth	Negative
613.	Alternator	Lucas 11AC, 45 amp.
614.	Control box	Lucas 4TR
615.	Starter motor	Lucas M45G, pre-engaged

CAPACITIES

701.	Engine sump	8 pints (plus 1 pint for new filter)
702.	Gearbox	2½ pints
703.	Differential	1¾ pints
704.	Cooling system	15 pints
705.	Fuel tank	14 gallons
706.	Tyre size	185 × 15in.
707.	Tyre pressures ... Front (lb./sq.in.) ... Rear	22 (fast driving, 24-26) 22 (fast driving, 24-26)
708.	No. of grease gun points	12
709.	Servicing intervals ...	Greasing, 3000 miles; engine oil change, 5000
710.	Hydraulic fluid ...	Castrol-Girling

DIMENSIONS

801.	Length overall	12ft. 8in.
802.	Width overall	57in.
803.	Height overall	50in.
804.	Weight (approx.) ...	1900lb. (17cwt.)
805.	Ground clearance (min.)	6in. (engine sump)
806.	Track	Front, 49in.; rear, 51in.
807.	Wheelbase	98in.
808.	Turning circle diameter...	38ft.

TORQUE SPANNER DATA (lb.ft.)

901.	Cylinder head bolts ...	65/70
902.	Big-end bearing bolts ...	30/35
903.	Main bearing bolts ...	50/55
	—Rear ...	65/70
905.	Flywheel bolts	120
906.	Clutch to flywheel bolts...	20
907.	Drive pinion bearing nut	95/100
908.	Crown wheel bolts ...	50/60
909.	Differential bearing nuts	35/40
910.	Road wheel nuts... ...	65/70
911.	Steering wheel nut ...	40

BODY AND CHASSIS

1001.	Type of construction ...	Steel 'Z'-section chassis
1002.	Material of body panels...	Steel and aluminium
1003.	Type of glass	Windscreen laminated

Plus 8 1970

Models: 4-seat Tourer and 2-seat Competition model

ENGINE (Ford 1600GT)

1. Type ... ... 4-stroke; overhead valves; side camshaft
2. Cooling system ... Water pump, radiator, fan and thermostat
3. Number of cylinders ... 4 (bored direct in block)
4. Firing order and idling 1—2—4—3 (No. 1 at front); 680/720
   speed r.p.m.
5. Bore ... ... 3·1881in. (80·977mm.) mean grade
6. Stroke ... ... 3·056in. (77·62mm.)
7. Cubic capacity ... 1598c.c.
8. Compression ratio and 9:1; 188lb./sq.in. at 300 r.p.m.
   pressure
9. Brake horse-power (DIN) 86 at 5,500 r.p.m.
10. Torque (DIN) ... 92lb.ft. at 4,000 r.p.m.
11. Piston oversizes ... ·0025, ·015, ·030in.
12. Piston clearance in bore ... 7/11lb. pull on ·0020in. × ½in. feeler
    (·0013/·0019in.)
13. Piston rings—number ... 2 compression, 1 oil
14. Piston rings—width ... Comp., ·007 to ·078in.; oil, 0·155 to
    0·156in.
15. Piston rings—groove cl'nce Comp., ·0016 to ·0036in.; oil, ·0018 to
16. Piston rings—gap (in bore) ·009 to ·014in. [·0038in.
17. Oil pressure ... ... 35 to 40lb. sq.in.
18. Gudgeon pin diameter ... 0·8119 to 0·8123in. (in 4 grades)
19. Gudgeon pin fit in piston Interference, selective (heated piston)
20. Gudgeon pin fit in con. rod ·0001 to ·0003in. clearance (selective)
21. Crankpin diameter ... 1·9368 to 1·9376in.
22. Crankpin undersizes ... (·002, bearing) ·010, ·020, ·030, ·040in.
23. Connecting rod length ... 4·927 to 4·929in. (centres)
24. Big-end bearings ... Steel-backed, copper/lead, lead/bronze
    or aluminium/tin
25. Big-end bearing clearance ·0005 to ·0020in.
26. Big-end side clearance ... ·004 to ·010in.
27. Main journal diameter ... Blue, 2·1253/57in.; red, 2·1257/61in.
28. Main journal undersizes... (·002, bearing) ·010, ·020, ·030in.
29. Main bearings ... ... 5; steel-backed copper-lead or lead-
31. Main bearing clearance ... ·0005 to ·0020in. [bronze
32. Crankshaft end-float ... ·003 to ·011in.
33. Crankshaft end-thrust on Centre main bearing
34. Camshaft journal diameter 1·5597 to 1·5605in.
35. Camshaft bearings ... 3; steel-backed white metal
36. Camshaft bearing cl'ance ·001 to ·0023in.
37. Camshaft end-float ... ·0025 to ·0075in.
38. Camshaft drive type ... Chain (single); 46 × 0·375in. pitches
39. Valve head diameter ... Inlet, 1·580/1·550in; exhaust, 1·340/
    1·330in.
40. Valve stem diameter ... In., 0·3098/0·3105in.; exh., 0·3089/
    0·3096in.
41. Valve seat angle ... 44° 30′ to 45° (in head)
42. Valve lift ... ... Inlet, 0·3556in.; exhaust, 0·3574in.
44. Valve stem/guide cl'ance In., ·0008/·0027in.; exh., ·0017/·0036in.
45. Valve spring free length ... 1·48in.
46. Valve spring rate... ... Length (closed), 1·263in. at 44/49lb.
47. Valve working clearance Inlet, ·012in.; exhaust, ·022in. (hot)
49. Valve timing ... ... Inlet opens 27° B.T.D.C.; closes 65°
    A.B.D.C. Exhaust opens 65° B.B.D.C.;
    closes 27° A.T.D.C.
50. Petrol pump ... ... A.C. mechanical
51. Carburettor ... ... Weber 32DFM-2 dual choke

	Primary	Secondary
52. Choke tube (Venturi) ...	26/4·5	27/4·5
53. Main jet ...	140	135
54. Compensating jet ...	165	160
55. Slow-running jet ...	50	45
56. Slow-running air bleed ...	180	70
57. Emulsion tube ...	F50	F6
58. Accelerator pump jet ...		50
62. Needle valve		1·75mm.

TRANSMISSION

101. Type ... ... Rear wheel drive
102. Clutch ... ... 7½in. diam., diaphragm type
103. Gearbox ... ... 4 forward speeds, all synchromesh
105. Gearbox ratios ... Top, 1:1; 3rd, 1·397:1; 2nd, 2·010:1;
     1st, 2·972:1; reverse, 3·324:1
107. Driving axles ... ... Semi-floating
108. Final drive gear ... Hypoid (Salisbury)
109. Final drive ratio ... 4·1:1 (41/10)
111. Crown wheel/pinion b'lash ·003 to ·006in.; shim adjustment
112. Pinion bearing pre-load ... 8 to 12lb.ft.: shim adjustment
113. Differential brg. pre-load ·003 to ·005in.; shim adjustment

BRAKES

201. Front ... ... Girling hydraulic, 11in. diam. discs
202. Rear ... ... Girling hydraulic, 9in. diam. drums
203. Handbrake ... ... Mechanical, on rear wheels
204. Linings—front ... Ferodo, type 14 calliper pads
205. Linings—rear ... ... Ferodo, 1¾in. wide

STEERING (see also "Dimensions

301. Type ... ... Cam Gear
302. Camber angle ... ... 2°; non-adjustable
303. Castor angle ... ... 4°; non-adjustable
304. King-pin inclination ... 2°
305. Toe-in ... ... ⅛ to 3/16in. at wheel rim
306. Conditions for checking ... Unladen

FRONT SUSPENSION

401. Type ... ... Independent, vertical coil springs
402. Number of coils 21
403. Coil diameter ... ... 2¼in. (external)
404. Wire diameter ... ... 0·31in.
405. Spring length—free ... 14¼in.
406. Spring length—fitted ... 8½in.

REAR SUSPENSION

501. Type ... ... Semi-elliptic leaf springs
504. Spring length (centres) ... 42¾in. (free)
505. Number of leaves ... 5
506. Width of leaves ... 1¾in.
507. Thickness of leaves ... ¼in.
508. Spring camber—free ... 3⅝in.

ELECTRICAL SYSTEM

601. Ignition timing (static) ... 8° B.T.D.C. (97 oct.); mark on pulley
602. Sparking plugs ... ... Autolite AG22
603. Sparking plug gap ... ·023in.
604. Distributor ... ... Ford C7BH-C
605. Contact breaker gap ... ·025in.; dwell angle 38°/40°
606. Centrif. advance starts at 1°/3° at 700 r.p.m.
607. Centrif. advance—max.... 8°/10° at 2,600 r.p.m.
608. Vacuum adv. starts at ... ½° to 3½° at 5¼in. Hg.
609. Vacuum adv.—max. ... 5½° to 8½° at 9=in. Hg.
     (Distributor degrees and r.p.m.)
610. Ignition coil ... ... 12v. oil-filled
611. Battery ... ... 12v. 36a.h.
612. Battery earth ... ... Negative
613. Dynamo/Alternator ... Lucas C40 or 15ACR
615. Starter motor ... ... Inertia type

CAPACITIES

701. Engine sump ... ... Total 6·74 pints; refill 6 pints (incl. filter)
702. Gearbox ... ... 1·97 pints (refill, 1·7 pints)
703. Differential ... ... 1¾ pints
704. Cooling system ... ... 12 pints
705. Fuel tank ... ... 8½ gallons
706. Tyre size ... ... 165 × 15
707. Tyre pressures (lb./sq.in.) Front, 18; rear, 19
708. No. of grease gun points ... 12 (Front sliding axles have 'one-shot'
     lubrication; press foot plunger every
     200 miles approx.)
709. Normal servicing intervals Greasing, 2000/2500 miles; engine oil
     change, 5000 miles
710. Hydraulic fluid ... ... Castrol Girling

DIMENSIONS

801. Length overall 12ft. (3658mm.)
802. Width overall 56in. (1422mm.)
803. Height overall ... ... 51·75in. (1314mm.)
804. Weight—2-seat Comp. ... 1460lb. (13cwt.) (662kg.)
     (dry) —4-seat 1516lb. (13·5cwt.) (688kg.)
805. Ground cl'ance (min.) ... 7in. (178mm.)
806. Track ... ... 47in. (1194mm.) front and rear
807. Wheelbase 96in. (2438mm.)
808. Turning circle diameter... 32ft. (9·75m.)

TORQUE SPANNER DATA (lb.ft.)

901. Cylinder head nuts ...	65/70	907. Final drive pinion		
902. Big-end bearing nuts ...	30/35	bearing nut		95/100
903. Main bearing nuts ...	65/70	908. Crown wheel bolts		50/60
905. Flywheel bolts ...	50/54	909. Diff. bearing nuts		35/40
906. Clutch to flywheel bolts	12/15	910. Road wheel nuts		65/70

BODY AND CHASSIS

1001. Type of construction ... Coachbuilt; steel 'Z'-section chassis; ash
      body frame
1002. Material of body panels ... Steel and aluminium
1003. Windscreen glass ... Toughened (laminated optional extra)

4/4 1600 1971

Model: 2-seater Tourer

ENGINE (Rover)

1. Type ... ... 4-stroke V8 (cast-aluminium block); O.H.V.; central camshaft; hydraulic tappets
2. Cooling system ... Water pump, radiator, fan and thermostat (15lb./sq.in.)
3. Number of cylinders ... 8 (dry liners)
4. Firing order and idling 1L—8R—4R—3L—6R—5L—7L—2R (No. speed 1 at front left); 600/650 r.p.m.
5. Bore ... ... 3·5in. (88·9mm.)
6. Stroke ... ... 2·8in. (71·1mm.)
7. Cubic capacity ... ... 3,525c.c.
8. Compression ratio and 10·5:1; 180/190lb./sq.in. at 185 r.p.m. pressure
9. Brake horse-power (net)... 160·5 at 5,200 r.p.m.
10. Torque (max.) ... ... 210lb.ft. at 2,750 r.p.m.
11. Piston oversizes ... ·010, ·020in.
12. Piston clearance in bore ·0005/·0011in. (skirt top)
13. Piston rings—number ... 2 compression, 1 oil
14. Piston rings—width ... Compression, ·078/·079in.; oil (expander) 0·1894in. max.
15. Piston rings—groove cl'nce Compression, ·003 to ·005in.
16. Piston rings—gap (in bore) Compression, ·017 to ·022in.
17. Oil pressure (lb./sq.in.) 30 to 40 at 2,400 r.p.m. (55 at 4,000)
18. Gudgeon pin diameter ... 0·8746 to 0·8749in.
19. Gudgeon pin fit in piston ·0001 to ·0003in. clearance
20. Gudgeon pin fit in con. rod Press fit (·00075 to ·00125in. clearance)
21. Crankpin diameter ... 2·0000 to 2·0005in.
22. Crankpin undersizes ... ·010, ·020, ·030, ·040in.
23. Connecting rod length ... 5·662 to 5·658in. (centres)
24. Big-end bearings ... Vandervell, lead-indium
25. Big-end bearing clearance ·0007 to ·0027in.
26. Big-end side clearance ... ·005 to ·015in.
27. Main journal diameter ... 2·2992 to 2·2997in.
28. Main journal undersizes ... ·010, ·020, ·030, ·040in.
29. Main bearings ... ... 5; Vandervell, lead-indium
30. Main bearings—length ... (1) (2) (4) (5), 0·797 to 0·807in.; (3), 1·056 to 1·058in.
31. Main bearing clearance ... ·0009 to ·0024in.
32. Crankshaft end-float ... ·004 to ·008in.
33. Crankshaft end-thrust on Centre main bearing
35. Camshaft bearings ... 5; steel-backed babbitt
38. Camshaft drive type ... Chain; 54×0·375in. pitches
39. Valve head diameter ... Inlet, 1·495/1·505in.; exhaust, 1·3075/1·3175in.
40. Valve stem diameter ... Inlet (head) 0·3402/0·3412 to 0·3407/ (tapered) 0·3417in.; exhaust, 0·3397/0·3407 to 0·3402/0·3412in.
42. Valve lift ... ... 0·39in.
44. Valve stem/guide cl'nce ... Inlet (top), ·001/·003; (bottom), ·0015/·0035. Exhaust (top), ·0015/·0035; (bottom), ·002/·004in.
46. Valve spring rate... ... Inner, 1·63in. at 21·5/26·5lb.; outer, 1·6in. at 39/45lb.
49. Valve timing Inlet opens 30° B.T.D.C. } peak, 112·5°
   Inlet closes 75° A.B.D.C. } A.T.D.C.
   Exhaust opens 68° B.B.D.C. } peak, 105·5°
   Exhaust closes 37° A.T.D.C. } B.T.D.C.
50. Petrol pump ... ... A.C. mechanical
52. Carburettors ... ... 2 S.U. type HS6
52. Diameter ... ... 1·75in.
53. Needle (standard) ... BAK
54. Jet diameter ... ... 0·100in.
   [Float level 1/8 to 9/16in.]

TRANSMISSION

101. Type ... ... Rear wheel drive
102. Clutch ... ... Borg & Beck, 9in. diam., single dry plate
103. Gearbox ... ... 4 forward speeds; synchromesh on 2nd, 3rd and top gears
105. Gearbox ratios ... ... Top, 1:1; 3rd 1·205:1; 2nd, 1·745:1; 1st and reverse, 2·97:1
106. Overdrive ... ... Not fitted
107. Driving axles ... ... Semi-floating
108. Final drive gear ... Hypoid, limited-slip differential
109. Final drive ratio ... 3·58:1
110. Number of gear teeth ... 43/12
111. Crown wheel/pinion b'lash 0·003 to 0·006in.; shim adjustment
112. Pinion bearing pre-load 8 to 12lb.in.
113. Differential brg. pre-load ·003 to ·005in.; shim adjustment

BRAKES

201. Front ... ... Girling hydraulic, 11in. diam. discs
202. Rear ... ... Girling hydraulic, 9in. diam. drums
203. Handbrake ... ... Mechanical, on rear wheels
204. Linings—front ... ... Ferodo, type GX
205. Linings—rear ... ... Ferodo, type LL, 1¾in. wide
206. Power assistance ... Girling servo (twin on L.H. drive cars)

STEERING (see also "Dimensions")

301. Type ... ... Cam Gear
302. Camber angle ... ... 2°, non-adjustable
303. Castor angle ... ... 4°, non-adjustable
304. King-pin inclination ... 2°
305. Toe-in ... ... ⅛ to 3/16 at wheel rims
306. Conditions for checking... Unladen

FRONT SUSPENSION

401. Type ... ... Independent, vertical coil springs
402. Number of coils ... 18
403. Coil diameter ... ... 2⅜in. (external)
404. Wire diameter ... ... 0·375in.
405. Spring length—free ... 13in.
506. Spring length—fitted ... 9in.

REAR SUSPENSION

501. Type ... ... Semi-elliptic leaf-springs
504. Spring length ... ... 42¾in. (free)
505. Number of leaves ... 6
506. Width of leaves ... 1⅜in.
507. Thickness of leaves ... ¼in.
508. Spring camber—free ... 3½in.

ELECTRICAL SYSTEM

601. Ignition timing—100 oct. 6° B.T.D.C. } Static or 600 r.p.m.
   —96 oct. T.D.C. } (mark on damper)
602. Sparking plugs ... ... Champion L87Y
603. Sparking plug gap ... ·025in.
604. Distributor ... ... Lucas 35D8
605. Contact breaker gap ... ·014 to ·016in.; but set dwell angle 26°/28° (600 r.p.m.)
606. Centrif. advance starts at 560 to 840 r.p.m.
607. Centrif. advance—max.... 28° at 4,800 r.p.m. (Crankshaft degrees and r.p.m.)
610. Ignition coil ... ... Lucas BA7
611. Battery ... ... 12v. 57a.h.
612. Battery earth ... ... Negative
613. Alternator ... ... Lucas 11AC, 45 amp.
614. Control box ... ... Lucas 4TR
615. Starter motor ... ... Lucas M45G, pre-engaged

CAPACITIES

701. Engine sump ... ... 8 pints (plus 1 pint for new filter)
702. Gearbox ... ... 2¼ pints
703. Differential ... ... 1½ pints
704. Cooling system ... ... 15 pints
705. Fuel tank ... ... 14 gallons
706. Tyre size ... ... 185×15in.
707. Tyre pressures —Front 22 (fast driving, 24-26)
   (lb./sq.in.) ... Rear 22 (fast driving, 24-26)
708. No. of grease gun points 12
709. Servicing intervals ... Greasing. 3000 miles; engine oil change, 5000
710. Hydraulic fluid ... ... Castrol-Girling

DIMENSIONS

801. Length overall 12ft. 8in. (3861mm.)
802. Width overall 57in. (1448mm.)
803. Height overall 50in. (1270mm.)
804. Weight (dry) ... ... 1884lb. (16·8cwt.) (855kg.) approx.
805. Ground clearance (min.) 6in. (152mm.) (engine sump)
806. Track —Front 49in. (1245mm.)
   —Rear 51in. (1295mm.)
807. Wheelbase 98in. (2489mm.)
808. Turning circle diameter... 38ft (11·6mm.)

TORQUE SPANNER DATA (lb.ft.)

901. Cylinder head bolts ... 65/70
902. Big-end bearing bolts ... 30/35
903. Main bearing bolts ... 50/55
   —Rear 65/70
905. Flywheel bolts 120
906. Clutch to flywheel bolts... 20
907. Drive pinion bearing nut 95/100
908. Crown wheel bolts ... 50/60
909. Differential bearing nuts 35/40
910. Road wheel nuts... ... 65/70
911. Steering wheel nut ... 40

BODY AND CHASSIS

1001. Type of construction ... Steel 'Z'-section chassis
1002. Material of body panels... Steel and aluminium
1003. Type of glass ... ... Windscreen laminated

Plus 8 1971

Models: 4-seat Tourer and 2-seat Competition model

ENGINE (Ford 1600GT)

1.	Type	4-stroke; overhead valves; side camshaft
2.	Cooling system ...	Water pump, radiator, fan and thermostat
3.	Number of cylinders ...	4 (bored direct in block)
4.	Firing order and idling speed	1—2—4—3 (No. 1 at front); 680/720 r.p.m.
5.	Bore	3·1881in. (80·977mm.) mean grade
6.	Stroke	3·056in. (77·62mm.)
7.	Cubic capacity	1598c.c.
8.	Compression ratio and pressure	9:1; 188lb./sq.in. at 300 r.p.m.
9.	Brake horse-power (DIN)	86 at 5,500 r.p.m.
10.	Torque (DIN)	92lb.ft. at 4,000 r.p.m.
11.	Piston oversizes	·0025, ·015, ·030in.
12.	Piston clearance in bore ...	7/11lb. pull on ·0020in. × ½in. feeler (·0013/·0019in.)
13.	Piston rings—number ...	2 compression, 1 oil
14.	Piston rings—width ...	Comp., ·077 to ·078in.; oil, 0·155 to 0·156in.
15.	Piston rings—groove cl'nce	Comp., ·0016 to ·0036in.; oil, ·0018 to ·0038in.
16.	Piston rings—gap (in bore)	·009 to ·014in.
17.	Oil pressure	35 to 40lb./sq.in.
18.	Gudgeon pin diameter ...	0·8119 to 0·8123in. (in 4 grades)
19.	Gudgeon pin fit in piston	Interference, selective (heated piston)
20.	Gudgeon pin fit in con. rod	·0001 to ·0003in. clearance (selective)
21.	Crankpin diameter ...	1·9368 to 1·9376in.
22.	Crankpin undersizes ...	(·002, bearing) ·010, ·020, ·030, ·040in.
23.	Connecting rod length ...	4·927 to 4·929in. (centres)
24.	Big-end bearings ...	Steel-backed, copper/lead, lead/bronze or aluminium/tin
25.	Big-end bearing clearance	·0005 to ·0020in.
26.	Big-end side clearance ...	·004 to ·010in.
27.	Main journal diameter ...	Blue, 2·1253/57in.; red, 2·1257/61in.
28.	Main journal undersizes...	(·002, bearing) ·010, ·020, ·030in.
29.	Main bearings	5; steel-backed copper-lead or lead-bronze
31.	Main bearing clearance ...	·0005 to ·0020in.
32.	Crankshaft end-float ...	·003 to ·011in.
33.	Crankshaft end-thrust on	Centre main bearing
34.	Camshaft journal diameter	1·5597 to 1·5605in.
35.	Camshaft bearings ...	3; steel-backed white metal
36.	Camshaft bearing cl'ance	·001 to ·0023in.
37.	Camshaft end-float ...	·0025 to ·0075in.
38.	Camshaft drive type ...	Chain (single); 46×0·375in. pitches
39.	Valve head diameter ...	Inlet, 1·580/1·550in; exhaust, 1·340/1·330in.
40.	Valve stem diameter ...	In., 0·3098/0·3105in.; exh., 0·3089/0·3096in.
41.	Valve seat angle ...	44° 30′ to 45° (in head)
42.	Valve lift	Inlet, 0·3556in.; exhaust, 0·3574in.
44.	Valve stem/guide cl'ance	In., ·0008/·0027in.; exh., ·0017/·0036in.
45.	Valve spring free length ...	1·48in.
46.	Valve spring rate... ...	Length (closed), 1·263in. at 44/49lb.
47.	Valve working clearance	Inlet, ·012in.; exhaust, ·022in. (hot)
49.	Valve timing	Inlet opens 27° B.T.D.C.; closes 65° A.B.D.C. Exhaust opens 65° B.B.D.C.; closes 27° A.T.D.C.
50.	Petrol pump	A.C. mechanical
51.	Carburettor	Ford ref. 32/36 DGV-FA, dual choke

	Primary	Secondary
52. Choke tube (Venturi) ...	26/4·5	27/4·5
53. Main jet	140	135
54. Compensating jet ...	165	160
55. Slow-running jet ...	50	45
56. Slow-running air bleed ...	180	70
57. Emulsion tube ...	F50	F6
58. Accelerator pump jet ...		50
62. Needle valve		1·75mm.

TRANSMISSION

101.	Type	Rear wheel drive
102.	Clutch	7¼in. diam., diaphragm type
103.	Gearbox	4 forward speeds, all synchromesh
105.	Gearbox ratios ...	Top, 1:1; 3rd, 1·397:1; 2nd, 2·010:1; 1st, 2·972:1; reverse, 3·324:1
107.	Driving axles ...	Semi-floating
108.	Final drive gear ...	Hypoid (Salisbury)
109.	Final drive ratio ...	4·1:1 (41/10)
111.	Crown wheel/pinion b'lash	·003 to ·006in.; shim adjustment
112.	Pinion bearing pre-load ...	8 to 12lb.in.; shim adjustment
113.	Differential brg. pre-load	·003 to ·005in.; shim adjustment

BRAKES

201.	Front	Girling hydraulic, 11in. diam. discs
202.	Rear	Girling hydraulic, 9in. diam. drums
203.	Handbrake	Mechanical, on rear wheels
204.	Linings—front ...	Ferodo, type 14 calliper pads
205.	Linings—rear ...	Ferodo, 1¾in. wide

STEERING (see also "Dimensions

301.	Type	Cam Gear
302.	Camber angle ...	2°; non-adjustable
303.	Castor angle ...	4°; non-adjustable
304.	King-pin inclination ...	2°
305.	Toe-in	⅛ to 3/16in. at wheel rim
306.	Conditions for checking ...	Unladen

FRONT SUSPENSION

401.	Type	Independent, vertical coil springs
402.	Number of coils ...	21
403.	Coil diameter ...	2¼in. (external)
404.	Wire diameter ...	0·31in.
405.	Spring length—free ...	14½in.
406.	Spring length—fitted ...	8½in.

REAR SUSPENSION

501.	Type	Semi-elliptic leaf springs
504.	Spring length (centres)	42¾in. (free)
505.	Number of leaves ...	5
506.	Width of leaves ...	1¾in.
507.	Thickness of leaves ...	¼in.
508.	Spring camber—free ...	3⅝in.

ELECTRICAL SYSTEM

601.	Ignition timing (static) ...	8° B.T.D.C. (97 oct.); mark on pulley
602.	Sparking plugs ...	Motorcraft AG22
603.	Sparking plug gap ...	·023in.
604.	Distributor ...	Ford C7BH-C
605.	Contact breaker gap ...	·025in; dwell angle 38°/40°
606.	Centrif. advance starts at	1° 3° at 700 r.p.m.
607.	Centrif. advance—max. ...	8° 10° at 2,600 r.p.m.
608.	Vacuum adv. starts at ...	½° to 3½° at 5½in. Hg.
609.	Vacuum adv.—max. ...	5½° to 8½° at 9+in. Hg. (Distributor degrees and r.p.m.)
610.	Ignition coil ...	Oil-filled, low voltage; use with 1·5ohm ballast resistor
611.	Battery	12v. 36a.h.
612.	Battery earth ...	Negative
613.	Dynamo/Alternator ...	Lucas C40 or 15ACR
615.	Starter motor ...	Inertia type

CAPACITIES

701.	Engine sump	Total 6·74 pints; refill 6 pints (incl. filter)
702.	Gearbox	1·97 pints (refill, 1·7 pints)
703.	Differential ...	1¼ pints
704.	Cooling system ...	12 pints
705.	Fuel tank ...	8½ gallons
706.	Tyre size ...	165×15
707.	Tyre pressures (lb./sq.in.)	Front, 18; rear, 19
708.	No. of grease gun points...	12 (Front sliding axles have 'one-shot' lubrication; press foot plunger every 200 miles approx.)
709.	Normal servicing intervals	Greasing, 2000/2500 miles; engine oil change, 5000 miles
710.	Hydraulic fluid ...	Castrol/Girling

DIMENSIONS

801.	Length overall ...	12ft. (3658mm.)
802.	Width overall ...	56in. (1422mm.)
803.	Height overall ...	51·75in. (1314mm.)
804.	Weight—2-seat Comp.	1460lb. (13cwt.) (662kg.)
	(dry) —4-seat	1516lb. (13·5cwt.) (688kg.)
805.	Ground cl'ance (min.) ...	7in. (178mm.)
806.	Track ...	47in. (1194mm.) front and rear
807.	Wheelbase ...	96in. (2438mm.)
808.	Turning circle diameter...	32ft. (9·75m.)

TORQUE SPANNER DATA (lb.ft.)

901.	Cylinder head nuts ...	65/70	907.	Final drive pinion	
902.	Big-end bearing nuts ...	30/35		bearing nut	95/100
903.	Main bearing nuts ...	65/70	908.	Crown wheel bolts	50/60
905.	Flywheel bolts ...	50/54	909.	Diff. bearing nuts	35/40
906.	Clutch to flywheel bolts	12/15	910.	Road wheel nuts	65/70

BODY AND CHASSIS

1001.	Type of construction ...	Coachbuilt; steel 'Z'-section chassis; ash body frame
1002.	Material of body panels ...	Steel and aluminium
1003.	Windscreen glass ...	Toughened (laminated optional extra)

4/4 1600 1972

Model: 2-seater Tourer

ENGINE (Rover)

1. Type ... ... 4-stroke V8 (cast-aluminium block); O.H.V.; central camshaft; hydraulic tappets
2. Cooling system ... ... Water pump, radiator, fan and thermostat (15lb./sq.in.)
3. Number of cylinders ... 8 (dry liners)
4. Firing order and idling speed 1L—8R—4R—3L—6R—5L—7L—2R (No. 1 at front left); 600/650 r.p.m.
5. Bore ... ... 3·5in. (88·9mm.)
6. Stroke ... ... 2·8in. (71·1mm.)
7. Cubic capacity ... ... 3,525c.c.
8. Compression ratio and pressure 10·5:1; 180/190lb./sq.in. at 185 r.p.m.
9. Brake horse-power (net)... 160·5 at 5,200 r.p.m.
10. Torque (max.) ... ... 210lb.ft. at 2,750 r.p.m.
11. Piston oversizes ... ... ·010, ·020in.
12. Piston clearance in bore ... ·0007/·0013in. (skirt bottom)
13. Piston rings—number ... 2 compression, 1 oil
14. Piston rings—width ... Compression, ·078/·079in.; oil (expander) 0·1894in. max.
15. Piston rings—groove cl'nce Compression, ·003 to ·005in.
16. Piston rings—gap (in bore) Compression, ·017 to ·022in.
17. Oil pressure (lb./sq.in.) 30 to 40 at 2,400 r.p.m. (55 at 4,000)
18. Gudgeon pin diameter ... 0·8746 to 0·8749in.
19. Gudgeon pin fit in piston ·0001 to ·0003in. clearance
20. Gudgeon pin fit in con. rod Press fit (·00075 to ·00125in. clearance)
21. Crankpin diameter ... 2·0000 to 2·0005in.
22. Crankpin undersizes ... ·010, ·020, ·030, ·040in.
23. Connecting rod length ... 5·662 to 5·658in. (centres)
24. Big-end bearings ... Vandervell, lead-indium
25. Big-end bearing clearance ·0007 to ·0027in.
26. Big-end side clearance ... ·005 to ·015in.
27. Main journal diameter ... 2·2992 to 2·2997in.
28. Main journal undersizes... ·010, ·020, ·030, ·040in.
29. Main bearings ... ... 5; Vandervell, lead-indium
30. Main bearings—length ... (1) (2) (4) (5), 0·797 to 0·807in.; (3), 1·056 to 1·058in.
31. Main bearing clearance ... ·0009 to ·0024in.
32. Crankshaft end-float ... ·004 to ·008in.
33. Crankshaft end-thrust on Centre main bearing
35. Camshaft bearings ... 5; steel-backed babbitt
38. Camshaft drive type ... Chain; 54 × 0·375in. pitches
39. Valve head diameter ... Inlet, 1·495/1·505in.; exhaust, 1·3075/1·3175in.
40. Valve stem diameter (tapered) ... Inlet (head) 0·3402/0·3412 to 0·3407/0·3417in.; exhaust, 0·3397/0·3407 to 0·3402/0·3412in.
42. Valve lift ... ... 0·39in.
44. Valve stem/guide cl'nce... Inlet (top), ·001/·003; (bottom), ·0015/·0035. Exhaust (top), ·0015/·0035; (bottom), ·002/·004in.
46. Valve spring rate .. ... Inner, 1·63in. at 21·5/26·5lb.; outer, 1·6in. at 39/45lb.
49. Valve timing Inlet opens 30° B.T.D.C. } peak, 112·5° A.T.D.C.; Inlet closes 75° A.B.D.C.; Exhaust opens 68° B.B.D.C. } peak, 105·5° B.T.D.C.; Exhaust closes 37° A.T.D.C.
50. Petrol pump ... ... A.C. mechanical
52. Carburettors ... ... 2 S.U. type HS6 (or HIF6)
52. Diameter ... ... 1·75in.
53. Needle (standard) ... BAK (BBG for HIF6)
54. Jet diameter ... ... 0·100in.

[Float level $\frac{1}{8}$ to $\frac{3}{16}$in.]

TRANSMISSION

101. Type ... ... Rear wheel drive
102. Clutch ... ... Borg & Beck, 9in. diam., single dry plate
103. Gearbox ... ... 4 forward speeds; synchromesh on 2nd, 3rd and top gears
105. Gearbox ratios ... ... Top, 1:1; 3rd 1·205:1; 2nd, 1·745:1; 1st and reverse, 2·97:1
106. Overdrive ... ... Not fitted
107. Driving axles ... ... Semi-floating
108. Final drive gear ... ... Hypoid, limited-slip differential
109. Final drive ratio ... 3·58:1
110. Number of gear teeth ... 43/12
111. Crown wheel/pinion b'lash 0·003 to 0·006in.; shim adjustment
112. Pinion bearing pre-load 8 to 12lb.in.
113. Differential brg. pre-load ·003 to ·005in.; shim adjustment

BRAKES

201. Front ... ... Girling hydraulic, 11in. diam. discs
202. Rear ... ... Girling hydraulic, 9in. diam. drums
203. Handbrake ... ... Mechanical, on rear wheels
204. Linings—front ... ... Ferodo, type GX
205. Linings—rear ... ... Ferodo, type LL, 1$\frac{3}{4}$in. wide
206. Power assistance ... Girling servo (twin on L.H. drive cars)

STEERING (see also "Dimensions")

301. Type ... ... Cam Gear
302. Camber angle ... ... 2°, non-adjustable
303. Castor angle ... ... 4°, non-adjustable
304. King-pin inclination ... 2°
305. Toe-in ... ... $\frac{1}{8}$ to $\frac{3}{16}$ at wheel rims
306. Conditions for checking... Unladen

FRONT SUSPENSION

401. Type ... ... Independent, vertical coil springs
402. Number of coils 18
403. Coil diameter ... ... 2$\frac{3}{8}$in. (external)
404. Wire diameter ... ... 0·375in.
405. Spring length—free ... 13in.
506. Spring length—fitted ... 9in.

REAR SUSPENSION

501. Type ... ... Semi-elliptic leaf-springs
504. Spring length ... ... 42$\frac{3}{4}$in. (free)
505. Number of leaves ... 6
506. Width of leaves ... ... 1$\frac{3}{8}$in.
507. Thickness of leaves ... $\frac{1}{4}$in.
508. Spring camber—free ... 3$\frac{1}{2}$in.

ELECTRICAL SYSTEM

601. Ignition timing—100 oct. 6° B.T.D.C.; —96 oct. T.D.C. } Static or 600 r.p.m. (mark on damper)
602. Sparking plugs ... ... Champion L87Y
603. Sparking plug gap ... ·025in.
604. Distributor ... ... Lucas 35D8
605. Contact breaker gap ... ·014 to ·016in.; but set dwell angle 26°/28° (600 r.p.m.)
606. Centrif. advance starts at 560 to 840 r.p.m.
607. Centrif. advance—max.... 28° at 4,800 r.p.m. (Crankshaft degrees and r.p.m.)
610. Ignition coil ... ... Lucas BA7
611. Battery ... ... 12v. 57a.h.
612. Battery earth ... ... Negative
613. Alternator ... ... Lucas 11AC, 45 amp.
614. Control box ... ... Lucas 4TR
615. Starter motor ... ... Lucas M45G, pre-engaged

CAPACITIES

701. Engine sump ... ... 8 pints (plus 1 pint for new filter)
702. Gearbox ... ... 2$\frac{1}{2}$ pints
703. Differential ... ... 1$\frac{3}{4}$ pints
704. Cooling system ... ... 15 pints
705. Fuel tank ... ... 14 gallons
706. Tyre size ... ... 185 × 15in.
707. Tyre pressures (lb./sq.in.) —Front 22 (fast driving, 24-26); —Rear 22 (fast driving, 24-26)
708. No. of grease gun points 12
709. Servicing intervals ... Greasing, 3000 miles; engine oil change, 5000
710. Hydraulic fluid ... ... Castrol-Girling

DIMENSIONS

801. Length overall 12ft. 8in. (3861mm.)
802. Width overall 57in. (1448mm.)
803. Height overall 50in. (1270mm.)
804. Weight (dry) ... ... 1884lb. (16·8cwt.) (855kg.) approx.
805. Ground clearance (min.) 6in. (152mm.) (engine sump)
806. Track ... —Front 49in. (1245mm.); —Rear 51in. (1295mm.)
807. Wheelbase 98in. (2489mm.)
808. Turning circle diameter... 38ft (11·6mm.)

TORQUE SPANNER DATA (lb.ft.)

901. Cylinder head bolts ... 65/70
902. Big-end bearing bolts ... 30/35
903. Main bearing bolts ... 50/55; —Rear ... 65/70
905. Flywheel bolts 120
906. Clutch to flywheel bolts... 20
907. Drive pinion bearing nut 95/100
908. Crown wheel bolts ... 50/60
909. Differential bearing nuts 35/40
910. Road wheel nuts... ... 65/70
911. Steering wheel nut ... 40

BODY AND CHASSIS

1001. Type of construction ... Steel 'Z'-section chassis
1002. Material of body panels... Steel and aluminium
1003. Type of glass ... ... Windscreen laminated

Plus 8 1972

Models: 4-seat Tourer and 2-seat Competition model

ENGINE (Ford 1600GT)

1.	Type	4-stroke; overhead valves; side camshaft
2.	Cooling system	Water pump, radiator, fan and thermostat
3.	Number of cylinders	4 (bored direct in block)
4.	Firing order and idling speed	1—2—4—3 (No. 1 at front); 680/720 r.p.m.
5.	Bore	3·1881in. (80·977mm.) mean grade
6.	Stroke	3·056in. (77·62mm.)
7.	Cubic capacity	1598c.c.
8.	Compression ratio and pressure	9:1; 188lb./sq.in. at 300 r.p.m.
9.	Brake horse-power (DIN)	86 at 5,500 r.p.m.
10.	Torque (DIN)	92lb.ft. at 4,000 r.p.m.
11.	Piston oversizes	·0025, ·015, ·030in.
12.	Piston clearance in bore	7/11lb. pull on ·0020in. × $\frac{1}{2}$in. feeler (·0013/·0019in.)
13.	Piston rings—number	2 compression, 1 oil
14.	Piston rings—width	Comp., ·077 to ·078in.; oil, 0·155 to 0·156in.
15.	Piston rings—groove cl'nce	Comp., ·0016 to ·0036in.; oil, ·0018 to ·0038in.
16.	Piston rings—gap (in bore)	·009 to ·014in.
17.	Oil pressure	35 to 40lb./sq.in.
18.	Gudgeon pin diameter	0·8119 to 0·8123in. (in 4 grades)
19.	Gudgeon pin fit in piston	Interference, selective (heated piston)
20.	Gudgeon pin fit in con. rod	·0001 to ·0003in. clearance (selective)
21.	Crankpin diameter	1·9368 to 1·9376in.
22.	Crankpin undersizes	(·002, bearing) ·010, ·020, ·030, ·040in.
23.	Connecting rod length	4·927 to 4·929in. (centres)
24.	Big-end bearings	Steel-backed, copper/lead, lead/bronze or aluminium/tin
25.	Big-end bearing clearance	·0005 to ·0020in.
26.	Big-end side clearance	·004 to ·010in.
27.	Main journal diameter	Blue, 2·1253/57in.; red, 2·1257/61in.
28.	Main journal undersizes	(·002, bearing) ·010, ·020, ·030in.
29.	Main bearings	5; steel-backed copper-lead or lead-bronze
31.	Main bearing clearance	·0005 to ·0020in.
32.	Crankshaft end-float	·003 to ·011in.
33.	Crankshaft end-thrust on	Centre main bearing
34.	Camshaft journal diameter	1·5597 to 1·5605in.
35.	Camshaft bearings	3; steel-backed white metal
36.	Camshaft bearing cl'ance	·001 to ·0023in.
37.	Camshaft end-float	·0025 to ·0075in.
38.	Camshaft drive type	Chain (single); 46 × 0·375in. pitches
39.	Valve head diameter	Inlet, 1·580/1·550in; exhaust, 1·340/1·330in.
40.	Valve stem diameter	In., 0·3098/0·3105in.; exh., 0·3089/0·3096in.
41.	Valve seat angle	44° 30′ to 45° (in head)
42.	Valve lift	Inlet, 0·3556in.; exhaust, 0·3574in.
44.	Valve stem/guide cl'ance	In., ·0008/·0027in.; exh., ·0017/·0036in.
45.	Valve spring free length	1·48in.
46.	Valve spring rate	Length (closed), 1·263in. at 44/49lb.
47.	Valve working clearance	Inlet, ·012in.; exhaust, ·022in. (hot)
49.	Valve timing	Inlet opens 27° B.T.D.C.; closes 65° A.B.D.C. Exhaust opens 65° B.B.D.C.; closes 27° A.T.D.C.
50.	Petrol pump	A.C. mechanical
51.	Carburettor	Weber 32DFM-2

		Primary	Secondary
52.	Choke tube (Venturi)	26/4·5	27/4·5
53.	Main jet	140	135
54.	Compensating jet	165	160
55.	Slow-running jet	50	45
56.	Slow-running air bleed	180	70
57.	Emulsion tube	F50	F6
58.	Accelerator pump jet	50	
62.	Needle valve	1·75mm.	

TRANSMISSION

101.	Type	Rear wheel drive
102.	Clutch	7$\frac{1}{2}$in. diam., diaphragm type
103.	Gearbox	4 forward speeds, all synchromesh
105.	Gearbox ratios	Top, 1:1; 3rd, 1·397:1; 2nd, 2·010:1; 1st, 2·972:1; reverse, 3·324:1
107.	Driving axles	Semi-floating
108.	Final drive gear	Hypoid (Salisbury)
109.	Final drive ratio	4·1:1 (41/10)
111.	Crown wheel/pinion b'lash	·003 to ·006in.; shim adjustment
112.	Pinion bearing pre-load	8 to 12lb.in.; shim adjustment
113.	Differential brg. pre-load	·003 to·005in.; shim adjustment

BRAKES

201.	Front	Girling hydraulic, 11in. diam. discs
202.	Rear	Girling hydraulic, 9in. diam. drums
203.	Handbrake	Mechanical, on rear wheels
204.	Linings—front	Ferodo, type 14 calliper pads
205.	Linings—rear	Ferodo, 1$\frac{3}{4}$in. wide

STEERING (see also "Dimensions)

301.	Type	Cam Gear
302.	Camber angle	2°; non-adjustable
303.	Castor angle	4°; non-adjustable
304.	King-pin inclination	2°
305.	Toe-in	$\frac{1}{8}$ to $\frac{3}{16}$in. at wheel rim
306.	Conditions for checking	Unladen

FRONT SUSPENSION

401.	Type	Independent, vertical coil springs
402.	Number of coils	21
403.	Coil diameter	2$\frac{1}{4}$in. (external)
404.	Wire diameter	0·31in.
405.	Spring length—free	14$\frac{1}{4}$in.
406.	Spring length—fitted	8$\frac{1}{2}$in.

REAR SUSPENSION

501.	Type	Semi-elliptic leaf springs
504.	Spring length (centres)	42$\frac{3}{4}$in. (free)
505.	Number of leaves	5
506.	Width of leaves	1$\frac{3}{8}$in.
507.	Thickness of leaves	$\frac{1}{4}$in.
508.	Spring camber—free	3$\frac{5}{8}$in.

ELECTRICAL SYSTEM

601.	Ignition timing (static)	8° B.T.D.C. (97 oct.); mark on pulley
602.	Sparking plugs	Motorcraft AG22
603.	Sparking plug gap	·023in.
604.	Distributor	Ford C7BH-C
605.	Contact breaker gap	·025in; dwell angle 38°/40°
606.	Centrif. advance starts at	1°/3° at 700 r.p.m.
607.	Centrif. advance—max.	8°/10° at 2,600 r.p.m.
608.	Vacuum adv. starts at	$\frac{1}{2}$° to 3$\frac{1}{4}$° at 5$\frac{1}{2}$in. Hg.
609.	Vacuum adv.—max.	5$\frac{1}{2}$° to 8$\frac{1}{2}$° at 9+in. Hg. (Distributor degrees and r.p.m.)
610.	Ignition coil	Oil-filled, low voltage; use with 1·5ohm ballast resistor
611.	Battery	12v. 36a.h.
612.	Battery earth	Negative
613.	Dynamo/Alternator	Lucas C40 or 15ACR
615.	Starter motor	Inertia type

CAPACITIES

701.	Engine sump	Total 6·74 pints; refill 6 pints (incl. filter)
702.	Gearbox	1·97 pints (refill, 1·7 pints)
703.	Differential	1$\frac{3}{4}$ pints
704.	Cooling system	12 pints
705.	Fuel tank	8$\frac{1}{2}$ gallons
706.	Tyre size	165 × 15
707.	Tyre pressures (lb./sq.in.)	Front, 18; rear, 19
708.	No. of grease gun points	12 (Front sliding axles have 'one-shot' lubrication; press foot plunger every 200 miles approx.)
709.	Normal servicing intervals	Greasing, 2000/2500 miles; engine oil change, 5000 miles
710.	Hydraulic fluid	Castrol/Girling

DIMENSIONS

801.	Length overall	12ft. (3658mm.)
802.	Width overall	56in. (1422mm.)
803.	Height overall	51·75in. (1314mm.)
804.	Weight—2-seat Comp. (dry) —4-seat	1460lb. (13cwt.) (662kg.) 1516lb. (13·5cwt.) (688kg.)
805.	Ground cl'ance (min.)	7in. (178mm.)
806.	Track	47in. (1194mm.) front and rear
807.	Wheelbase	96in. (2438mm.)
808.	Turning circle diameter	32ft. (9·75m.)

TORQUE SPANNER DATA (lb.ft.)

901.	Cylinder head nuts	65/70	907.	Final drive pinion bearing nut	95/100
902.	Big-end bearing nuts	30/35			
903.	Main bearing nuts	65/70	908.	Crown wheel bolts	50/60
905.	Flywheel bolts	50/54	909.	Diff. bearing nuts	35/40
906.	Clutch to flywheel bolts	12/15	910.	Road wheel nuts	65/70

BODY AND CHASSIS

1001.	Type of construction	Coachbuilt; steel 'Z'-section chassis; ash body frame
1002.	Material of body panels	Steel and aluminium
1003.	Windscreen glass	Toughened (laminated optional extra)

4/4 1600 1973

Model: 2-seat Tourer

ENGINE (Rover)

1. Type	... ...	4-stroke V8 (cast-aluminium block); O.H.V.; central camshaft; hydraulic tappets
2. Cooling system	...	Water pump, radiator, fan and thermo-stat (15lb./sq.in.)
3. Number of cylinders	...	8 (dry liners)
4. Firing order and idling speed		1ʟ—8ʀ—4ʀ—3ʟ—6ʀ—5ʟ—7ʟ—2ʀ (No. 1 at front left); 600/650 r.p.m.
5. Bore	... ...	3·5in. (88·9mm.)
6. Stroke	... ...	2·8in. (71·12mm.)
7. Cubic capacity	...	3532c.c.
8. Compression ratio and pressure		10·5:1; 180/190lb./sq.in. at 185 r.p.m.
9. Brake horse-power (net)	...	160·5 at 5,200 r.p.m.
10. Torque (max.)	...	210lb.ft. at 2,750 r.p.m.
11. Piston oversizes	...	·010, ·020in.
12. Piston clearance in bore	...	·0007/·0013in. (skirt bottom)
13. Piston rings—number	...	2 compression, 1 oil
14. Piston rings—width	...	Compression, ·078/·079in.; oil (expander) 0·1894in. max.
15. Piston rings—groove cl'nce		Compression, ·003 to ·005in.
16. Piston rings—gap (in bore)		Compression, ·017 to ·022in.
17. Oil pressure (lb./sq.in.)	...	30 to 40 at 2,400 r.p.m. (55 at 4,000)
18. Gudgeon pin diameter	...	0·8746 to 0·8749in.
19. Gudgeon pin fit in piston		·0001 to ·0003in. clearance
20. Gudgeon pin fit in con. rod		Press fit ·00075 to ·00125in. clearance
21. Crankpin diameter	...	2·0000 to 2·0005in.
22. Crankpin undersizes	...	·010, ·020, ·030, ·040in.
23. Connecting rod length	...	5·662 to 5·658in. (centres)
24. Big-end bearings	...	Vandervell, lead-indium
25. Big-end bearing clearance	...	·0007 to ·0027in.
26. Big-end side clearance	...	·005 to ·015in.
27. Main journal diameter	...	2·2992 to 2·2997in.
28. Main journal undersizes	...	·010, ·020, ·030, ·040in.
29. Main bearings	...	5; Vandervell, lead-indium
30. Main bearings—length	...	(1) (2) (4) (5), 0·797 to 0·807in.; (3), 1·056 to 1·058in.
31. Main bearing clearance	...	·0009 to ·0024in.
32. Crankshaft end-float	...	·004 to ·008in.
33. Crankshaft end-thrust on		Centre main bearing
35. Camshaft bearings	...	5; steel-backed babbit
38. Camshaft drive type	...	Chain; 54 × 0·375in. pitches
39. Valve head diameter	...	Inlet, 1·495/1·505in.; exhaust, 1·3075/1·3175in.
40. Valve stem diameter (tapered)	...	Inlet (head) 0·3402/0·3412 to 0·3407/0·3417in.; exhaust, 0·3397/0·3407 to 0·3402/0·3412in.
42. Valve lift	...	0·39in.
44. Valve stem/guide cl'nce	...	Inlet (top), ·001/·003; (bottom), ·0015/·0035. Exhaust (top), ·0015/·0035; (bottom), ·002/·004in.
46. Valve spring rate	...	Inner, 1·63in. at 21·5/26·5lb.; outer, 1·6in. at 39/45lb.
49. Valve timing	Inlet opens 30° B.T.D.C. } peak, 112·5°	
	Inlet closes 75° A.B.D.C. } A.T.D.C.	
	Exhaust opens 68° B.B.D.C. } peak, 105·5°	
	Exhaust closes 37° A.T.D.C. } B.T.D.C.	
50. Petrol pump	...	A.C. mechanical
52. Carburettors	...	2 S.U., type HIF6; needle BBG. (Mixture ratio preset and sealed; only the engine idling speed may be adjusted)

TRANSMISSION

101. Type	... ...	Rear wheel drive
102. Clutch	... ...	Borg & Beck, 9·5in.diam., single dry plate, diaphragm spring
103. Gearbox	... ...	4 forward speeds, all synchromesh
105. Gearbox ratios	...	1; 1·391; 2·133; 3·625; R., 3·43:1
106. Overdrive	...	Not fitted
107. Driving axles	...	Semi-floating
108. Final drive gear	...	Hypoid, limited-slip differential
109. Final drive ratio	...	3·31:1
111. Crown wheel/pinion b'lash	0·003 to 0·006in.; shim adjustment	
112. Pinion bearing pre-load	8 to 12lb.in.	
113. Differential brg. pre-load	·003 to ·005in.; shim adjustment	

BRAKES

201. Front	... ...	Girling hydraulic, 11in. diam. discs
202. Rear	... ...	Girling hydraulic, 9in. diam. drums
203. Handbrake	...	Mechanical, on rear wheels
204. Linings—front	...	Ferodo, type GX
205. Linings—rear	...	Ferodo, type LL, 1¾in. wide
206. Power assistance	...	Girling servo (twin on L.H. drive cars)

STEERING (see also "Dimensions")

301. Type	... ...	Cam Gear
302. Camber angle	...	2°, non-adjustable
303. Castor angle	...	4°, non-adjustable
304. King-pin inclination	...	2°
305. Toe-in	...	⅛ to ³/₁₆ at wheel rims
306. Conditions for checking	...	Unladen

FRONT SUSPENSION

401. Type	...	Independent, vertical coil springs
402. Number of coils	...	18
403. Coil diameter	...	2⅜in. (external)
404. Wire diameter	...	0·375in.
405. Spring length—free	...	13in.
506. Spring length—fitted	...	9in.

REAR SUSPENSION

501. Type	...	Semi-elliptic leaf-springs
504. Spring length	...	42¾in. (free)
505. Number of leaves	...	6
506. Width of leaves	...	1¾in.
507. Thickness of leaves	...	¼in.
508. Spring camber—free	...	3¼in.

ELECTRICAL SYSTEM

601. Ignition timing	—100 oct. 6° B.T.D.C. } Static or 600 r.p.m.	
	—96 oct. T.D.C. } (mark on damper)	
602. Sparking plugs	...	Champion L87Y
603. Sparking plug gap	...	·025in.
604. Distributor	...	Lucas 35D8
605. Contact breaker gap	...	·014 to ·016in.; but set dwell angle 26°/28° (600 r.p.m.)
606. Centrif. advance starts at		560 to 840 r.p.m.
607. Centrif. advance—max.	...	28° at 4,800 r.p.m. (Crankshaft degrees and r.p.m.)
610. Ignition coil	...	Lucas BA7
611. Battery	...	12v. 57a.h.
612. Battery earth	...	Negative
613. Alternator	...	Lucas 11AC, 45 amp.
614. Control box	...	Lucas 4TR
615. Starter motor	...	Lucas M45G, pre-engaged

CAPACITIES

701. Engine sump	...	8 pints (plus 1 pint for new filter)
702. Gearbox	...	3¼ pints
703. Differential	...	1¾ pints
704. Cooling system	...	15 pints
705. Fuel tank	...	14 gallons
706. Tyre size	...	185 × 15in.
707. Tyre pressures (lb./sq.in.)	—Front	22 (fast driving, 24-26)
	—Rear	22 (fast driving, 24-26)
708. No. of grease gun points		12
709. Servicing intervals	...	Greasing, 3000 miles; engine oil change, 5000 miles
710. Hydraulic fluid	...	Castrol-Girling

DIMENSIONS

801. Length overall	...	12ft. 8in. (3861mm.)
802. Width overall	...	57in. (1448mm.)
803. Height overall	...	50in. (1270mm.)
804. Weight (dry)	...	1884lb. (16·8cwt.) (855kg.) approx.
805. Ground clearance (min.)		6in. (152mm.) (engine sump)
806. Track	—Front	49in. (1245mm.)
	—Rear	52·5in. (1333mm.)
807. Wheelbase	...	98in. (2489mm.)
808. Turning circle diameter	...	38ft (11·6mm.)

TORQUE SPANNER DATA (lb.ft.)

901. Cylinder head bolts	...	65/70
902. Big-end bearing bolts	...	30/35
903. Main bearing bolts	...	50/55
	—Rear	65/70
905. Flywheel bolts	...	50/60
906. Clutch to flywheel bolts	...	20
907. Drive pinion bearing nut		95/100
908. Crown wheel bolts	...	50/60
909. Differential bearing nuts		35/40
910. Road wheel nuts	...	65/70
911. Steering wheel nut	...	40

BODY AND CHASSIS

1001. Type of construction	...	Steel 'Z'-section chassis
1002. Material of body panels	...	Steel and aluminium
1003. Type of glass	...	Windscreen laminated

Plus 8 1973

Models: 4-seat Tourer and 2-seat Competition model

ENGINE (Ford 1600GT)

1. Type ... ... 4-stroke; overhead valves; side camshaft
2. Cooling system ... ... Water pump, radiator, fan and thermostat
3. Number of cylinders ... 4 (bored direct in block)
4. Firing order and idling 1—2—4—3 (No. 1 at front); 680/720
   speed r.p.m.
5. Bore ... ... 3·1881in. (80·977mm.) mean grade
6. Stroke ... ... 3·056in. (77·62mm.)
7. Cubic capacity ... ... 1598c.c.
8. Compression ratio and 9:1; 188lb./sq.in. at 300 r.p.m.
   pressure
9. Brake horse-power (DIN) 86 at 5,500 r.p.m.
10. Torque (DIN) ... ... 92lb.ft. at 4,000 r.p.m.
11. Piston oversizes ... ... ·0025, ·015, ·030in.
12. Piston clearance in bore ... 7/11lb. pull on ·0020in. × ⅛in. feeler
    (·0013/·0019in.)
13. Piston rings—number ... 2 compression, 1 oil
14. Piston rings—width ... Comp., ·077 to ·078in.; oil, 0·155 to
    0·156in.
15. Piston rings—groove cl'nce Comp., ·0016 to ·0036in.; oil, ·0018 to
16. Piston rings—gap (in bore) ·009 to ·014in.   [·0038in.
17. Oil pressure ... ... 35 to 40lb./sq.in.
18. Gudgeon pin diameter ... 0·8119 to 0·8123in. (in 4 grades)
19. Gudgeon pin fit in piston Interference, selective (heated piston)
20. Gudgeon pin fit in con. rod ·0001 to ·0003in. clearance (selective)
21. Crankpin diameter ... 1·9368 to 1·9376in.
22. Crankpin undersizes ... (·002, bearing) ·010, ·020, ·030, ·040in.
23. Connecting rod length ... 4·927 to 4·929in. (centres)
24. Big-end bearings ... Steel-backed, copper/lead, lead/bronze
    or aluminium/tin
25. Big-end bearing clearance ·0005 to ·0020in.
26. Big-end side clearance ... ·004 to ·010in.
27. Main journal diameter ... Blue, 2·1253/57in.; red, 2·1257/61in.
28. Main journal undersizes... (·002, bearing) ·010, ·020, ·030in.
29. Main bearings ... ... 5; steel-backed copper-lead or lead-
31. Main bearing clearance ... ·0005 to ·0020in.   [bronze
32. Crankshaft end-float ... ·003 to ·011in.
33. Crankshaft end-thrust on Centre main bearing
34. Camshaft journal diameter 1·5597 to 1·5605in.
35. Camshaft bearings ... 3; steel-backed white metal
36. Camshaft bearing cl'ance ·001 to ·0023in.
37. Camshaft end-float ... ·0025 to ·0075in.
38. Camshaft drive type ... Chain (single); 46 × 0·375in. pitches
39. Valve head diameter ... Inlet, 1·580/1·550in.; exhaust, 1·340/
    1·330in.
40. Valve stem diameter ... In., 0·3098/0·3105in.; exh., 0·3089/
    0·3096in.
41. Valve seat angle ... ... 44° 30' to 45° (in head)
42. Valve lift ... ... Inlet, 0·3556in.; exhaust, 0·3574in.
44. Valve stem/guide cl'ance In., ·0008/·0027in.; exh., ·0017/·0036in.
45. Valve spring free length ... 1·48in.
46. Valve spring rate... ... Length (closed), 1·263in. at 44/49lb.
47. Valve working clearance ·012in.; exhaust ·022in. (hot)
49. Valve timing ... ... Inlet opens 27° B.T.D.C.; closes 65°
    A.B.D.C. Exhaust opens 65° B.B.D.C.;
    closes 27° A.T.D.C.
50. Petrol pump ... ... A.C. mechanical
51. Carburettor ... ... Weber 32/36DGV-O5A

	Primary	Secondary
52. Choke tube (Venturi) ...	26/4·5	27/4·5
53. Main jet	140	135
54. Compensating jet ...	165	160
55. Slow-running jet ...	50	45
56. Slow-running air bleed ...	180	70
57. Emulsion tube ...	F50	F6
58. Accelerator pump jet ...	50	
62. Needle valve	1·75mm.	

TRANSMISSION

101. Type ... ... Rear wheel drive
102. Clutch ... ... 7½in. diam., diaphragm type
103. Gearbox ... ... 4 forward speeds, all synchromesh
105. Gearbox ratios ... ... Top, 1:1; 3rd, 1·397:1; 2nd, 2·010:1;
     1st, 2·972:1; reverse, 3·324:1
107. Driving axles ... ... Semi-floating
108. Final drive gear ... Hypoid (Salisbury)
109. Final drive ratio ... 4·1:1 (41/10)
111. Crown wheel/pinion b'lash ·003 to ·006in.; shim adjustment
112. Pinion bearing pre-load ... 8 to 12lb.in.; shim adjustment
113. Differential brg. pre-load ·003 to·005in.; shim adjustment

BRAKES

201. Front ... ... Girling hydraulic, 11in. diam. discs
202. Rear ... ... Girling hydraulic, 9in. diam. drums
203. Handbrake ... ... Mechanical, on rear wheels
204. Linings—front ... Ferodo, type 14 calliper pads
205. Linings—rear ... ... Ferodo, 1⅜in. wide

STEERING (see also "Dimensions)

301. Type ... ... Cam Gear
302. Camber angle ... ... 2°; non-adjustable
303. Castor angle ... ... 4°; non-adjustable
304. King-pin inclination ... 2°
305. Toe-in ... ... ⅛ to ³⁄₁₆in. at wheel rim
306. Conditions for checking ... Unladen

FRONT SUSPENSION

401. Type ... ... Independent, vertical coil springs
402. Number of coils 21
403. Coil diameter ... ... 2¼in. (external)
404. Wire diameter ... ... 0·31in.
405. Spring length—free ... 14½in.
406. Spring length—fitted ... 8½in.

REAR SUSPENSION

501. Type ... ... Semi-elliptic leaf springs
504. Spring length (centres) ... 42¾in. (free)
505. Number of leaves ... 5
506. Width of leaves ... 1¾in.
507. Thickness of leaves ... ¼in.
508. Spring camber—free ... 3⅞in.

ELECTRICAL SYSTEM

601. Ignition timing ... ... 8° B.T.D.C. at 800 r.p.m. (vac. pipe off);
     mark on pulley
602. Sparking plugs ... Motorcraft AG22
603. Sparking plug gap ... ·023in.
604. Distributor ... ... Ford C7BH-G
605. Contact breaker gap ... ·025in; dwell angle 38°/40°
606. Centrif. advance starts at 1°/3° at 700 r.p.m.
607. Centrif. advance—max.... 8°/10° at 2,600 r.p.m.
608. Vacuum adv. starts at ... ½° to 3½° at 5⅛ in. Hg.
609. Vacuum adv.—max. ... 5½° to 8½° at 9+in. Hg.
     (Distributor degrees and r.p.m.)
610. Ignition coil ... ... Oil-filled, low voltage; use with 1·5ohm
     ballast resistor
611. Battery ... ... 12v. 36a.h.
612. Battery earth ... ... Negative
613. Dynamo/Alternator ... Lucas C40 or 15ACR
615. Starter motor ... ... Inertia type

CAPACITIES

701. Engine sump ... ... Total 6·74 pints; refill 6 pints (incl. filter)
702. Gearbox ... ... 1·97 pints (refill, 1·7 pints)
703. Differential ... ... 1½ pints
704. Cooling system ... ... 12 pints
705. Fuel tank ... ... 8½ gallons
706. Tyre size ... ... 165 × 15
707. Tyre pressures (lb./sq.in.) Front, 18; rear, 19
708. No. of grease gun points ... 12 (Front sliding axles have 'one-shot'
     lubrication; press foot plunger every
     200 miles approx.)
709. Normal servicing intervals Greasing, 2000/2500 miles; engine oil
     change, 5000 miles
710. Hydraulic fluid ... ... Castrol/Girling

DIMENSIONS

801. Length overall 12ft. (3658mm.)
802. Width overall 56in. (1422mm.)
803. Height overall ... ... 51·75in. (1314mm.)
804. Weight—2-seat Comp. ... 1460lb. (13cwt.) (662kg.)
     (dry) 4-seat ... 1516lb. (13·5cwt.) (688kg.)
805. Ground cl'ance (min.) ... 7in. (178mm.)
806. Track ... ... 47in. (1194mm.) front and rear
807. Wheelbase 96in. (2438mm.)
808. Turning circle diameter... 32ft. (9·75m.)

TORQUE SPANNER DATA (lb.ft.)

901. Cylinder head nuts ...	65/70	907. Final drive pinion	
902. Big-end bearing nuts ...	30/35	bearing nut	95/100
903. Main bearing nuts ...	65/70	908. Crown wheel bolts	50/60
905. Flywheel bolts ...	50/54	909. Diff. bearing nuts	35/40
906. Clutch to flywheel bolts	12/15	910. Road wheel nuts	65/70

BODY AND CHASSIS

1001. Type of construction ... Coachbuilt; steel 'Z'-section chassis; ash
      body frame
1002. Material of body panels ... Steel and aluminium
1003. Windscreen glass ... Toughened (laminated optional extra)

4/4 1600 1974

Model: 2-seat Tourer

ENGINE (Rover)

1. Type ... ... 4-stroke V8 (cast-aluminium block); O.H.V.; central camshaft; hydraulic tappets
2. Cooling system ... Water pump, radiator, fan and thermo-stat (15lb./sq.in.)
3. Number of cylinders ... 8 (dry liners)
4. Firing order and idling 1L—8R—4R—3L—6R—5L—7L—2R (No. 1 at front left); 600/650 r.p.m.
   speed
5. Bore ... ... 3·5in. (88·9mm.)
6. Stroke ... ... 2·8in. (71·12mm.)
7. Cubic capacity ... ... 3532c.c.
8. Compression ratio and 9·25:1; 165lb./in.² min. at 185 r.p.m.
   pressure
9. Brake horse-power (DIN) 143 at 5,000 r.p.m.
10. Torque (DIN) ... ... 202lb.ft. at 2,700 r.p.m.
11. Piston oversizes ... ·010, ·020in.
12. Piston clearance in bore ... ·0007/·0013in. (skirt bottom)
13. Piston rings—number ... 2 compression, 1 oil
14. Piston rings—width ... Compression, ·078/·079in.; oil (ex-pander) 0·1894in. max.
15. Piston rings—groove cl'nce Compression, ·003 to ·005in.
16. Piston rings—gap (in bore) Compression, ·017 to ·022in.
17. Oil pressure (lb./sq.in.) 30 to 40 at 2,400 r.p.m. (55 at 4,000)
18. Gudgeon pin diameter ... 0·8746 to 0·8749in.
19. Gudgeon pin fit in piston ·0001 to ·0003in. clearance
20. Gudgeon pin fit in con. rod Press fit (·00075 to ·00125in. clearance)
21. Crankpin diameter ... 2·0000 to 2·0005in.
22. Crankpin undersizes ... ·010, ·020, ·030, ·040in.
23. Connecting rod length ... 5·662 to 5·658in. (centres)
24. Big-end bearings ... Vandervell, lead-indium
25. Big-end bearing clearance ·0007 to ·0027in.
26. Big-end side clearance ... ·005 to ·015in.
27. Main journal diameter ... 2·2992 to 2·2997in.
28. Main journal undersizes ... ·010, ·020, ·030, ·040in.
29. Main bearings ... 5; Vandervell, lead-indium
30. Main bearings—length ... (1) (2) (4) (5), 0·797 to 0·807in.; (3), 1·056 to 1·058in.
31. Main bearing clearance ... ·0009 to ·0024in.
32. Crankshaft end-float ... ·004 to ·008in.
33. Crankshaft end-thrust on Centre main bearing
35. Camshaft bearings ... 5; steel-backed babbitt
38. Camshaft drive type ... Chain; 54 × 0·375in. pitches
39. Valve head diameter ... Inlet, 1·495/1·505in.; exhaust, 1·3075/1·3175in.
40. Valve stem diameter ... Inlet (head) 0·3402/0·3412 to 0·3407/
    (tapered)   0·3417in.; exhaust, 0·3397/0·3407 to 0·3402/0·3412in.
42. Valve lift ... ... 0·39in.
44. Valve stem/guide cl'nce ... Inlet (top), ·001/·003; (bottom), ·0015/·0035. Exhaust (top), ·0015/·0035; (bottom), ·002/·004in.
46. Valve spring rate... ... Inner, 1·63in. at 21·5/26·5lb.; outer, 1·6in. at 39/45lb.
49. Valve timing Inlet opens 30° B.T.D.C. } peak, 112·5°
               Inlet closes 75° A.B.D.C. } A.T.D.C.
               Exhaust opens 68° B.B.D.C. } peak, 105·5°
               Exhaust closes 37° A.T.D.C. } B.T.D.C.
50. Petrol pump ... ... A.C. mechanical
52. Carburettors ... ... 2 S.U., type HIF6; needle BBG. (Mixture ratio preset and sealed; only the engine idling speed may be adjusted)

TRANSMISSION

101. Type ... ... Rear wheel drive
102. Clutch ... ... Borg & Beck, 9·5in.diam., single dry plate, diaphragm spring
103. Gearbox ... ... 4 forward speeds, all synchromesh
105. Gearbox ratios ... ... 1; 1·391; 2·133; 3·625; R., 3·43:1
106. Overdrive ... ... Not fitted
107. Driving axles ... ... Semi-floating
108. Final drive gear ... Hypoid, limited-slip differential
109. Final drive ratio ... 3·31:1
111. Crown wheel/pinion b'lash 0·003 to 0·006in.; shim adjustment
112. Pinion bearing pre-load 8 to 12lb.in.
113. Differential brg. pre-load ·003 to ·005in.; shim adjustment

BRAKES

201. Front ... ... Girling hydraulic, 11in. diam. discs
202. Rear ... ... Girling hydraulic, 9in. diam. drums
203. Handbrake ... ... Mechanical, on rear wheels
204. Linings—front ... Ferodo, type GX
205. Linings—rear ... Ferodo, type LL, 1¾in. wide
206. Power assistance ... Girling servo (twin on L.H. drive cars)

STEERING (see also "Dimensions")

301. Type ... ... Cam Gear
302. Camber angle ... ... 2°, non-adjustable
303. Castor angle ... ... 4°, non-adjustable
304. King-pin inclination ... 2°
305. Toe-in ... ... ⅛ to ⅟₁₆ at wheel rims
306. Conditions for checking... Unladen

FRONT SUSPENSION

401. Type ... ... Independent, vertical coil springs
402. Number of coils ... 18
403. Coil diameter ... ... 2⅜in. (external)
404. Wire diameter ... ... 0·375in.
405. Spring length—free ... 13in.
506. Spring length—fitted ... 9in.

REAR SUSPENSION

501. Type ... ... Semi-elliptic leaf-springs
504. Spring length ... ... 42⅜in. (free)
505. Number of leaves ... 6
506. Width of leaves ... 1⅜in.
507. Thickness of leaves ... ¼in.
508. Spring camber—free ... 3½in.

ELECTRICAL SYSTEM

601. Ignition timing—100 oct. 6° B.T.D.C. } Static or 600 r.p.m.
                  —96 oct. T.D.C. } (mark on damper)
602. Sparking plugs ... Champion L87Y
603. Sparking plug gap ... ·025in.
604. Distributor ... ... Lucas 35D8
605. Contact breaker gap ... ·014 to ·016in.; but set dwell angle 26°/28° (600 r.p.m.)
606. Centrif. advance starts at 560 to 840 r.p.m.
607. Centrif. advance—max.... 28° at 4,800 r.p.m. (Crankshaft degrees and r.p.m.)
610. Ignition coil ... Lucas 16C6
611. Battery ... ... 12v. 57a.h.
612. Battery earth ... ... Negative
613. Alternator ... ... Lucas 18ACR, 43 amp.
614. Control box ... ... Integral with alternator
615. Starter motor ... ... Lucas 3M100, pre-engaged

CAPACITIES

701. Engine sump ... ... 8 pints (plus 1 pint for new filter)
702. Gearbox ... ... 3¼ pints
703. Differential ... ... 1½ pints
704. Cooling system ... 15 pints
705. Fuel tank ... ... 14 gallons
706. Tyre size ... ... 185 × 15in.
707. Tyre pressures —Front 22 (fast driving, 24-26)
    (lb./sq.in.) —Rear 22 (fast driving, 24-26)
708. No. of grease gun points 12
709. Servicing intervals ... Greasing, 3000 miles; engine oil change, 5000 miles
710. Hydraulic fluid ... ... Castrol-Girling

DIMENSIONS

801. Length overall 12ft. 8in. (3861mm.)
802. Width overall 60in. (1524mm.)
803. Height overall 50in. (1270mm.)
804. Weight (dry) ... ... 1884lb. (16·8cwt.) (855kg.) approx.
805. Ground clearance (min.) 6in. (152mm.) (engine sump)
806. Track —Front 51in. (1295mm.)
         —Rear 52in. (1321mm.)
807. Wheelbase 98in. (2489mm.)
808. Turning circle diameter... 38ft (11·6mm.)

TORQUE SPANNER DATA (lb.ft.)

901. Cylinder head bolts ... 65/70
902. Big-end bearing bolts ... 30/35
903. Main bearing bolts ... 50/55
         —Rear ... 65/70
905. Flywheel bolts 50/60
906. Clutch to flywheel bolts... 20
907. Drive pinion bearing nut 95/100
908. Crown wheel bolts ... 50/60
909. Differential bearing nuts 35/40
910. Road wheel nuts... ... 65/70
911. Steering wheel nut ... 40

BODY AND CHASSIS

1001. Type of construction ... Steel 'Z'-section chassis
1002. Material of body panels... Steel and aluminium
1003. Type of glass ... ... Windscreen laminated

Plus 8 1974

Models: 4-seat Tourer and 2-seat Competition model

ENGINE (Ford 1600GT)

1.	Type	...	4-stroke; overhead valves; side camshaft
2.	Cooling system	...	Water pump, radiator, fan and thermostat
3.	Number of cylinders	...	4 (bored direct in block)
4.	Firing order and idling speed	...	1—2—4—3 (No. 1 at front); 680/720 r.p.m.
5.	Bore	...	3·1881in. (80·977mm.) mean grade
6.	Stroke	...	3·056in. (77·62mm.)
7.	Cubic capacity	...	1598cm.³
8.	Compression ratio and pressure		9:1; 188lb./in.² at 300 r.p.m.
9.	Brake horse-power (DIN)		86 at 5500 r.p.m.
10.	Torque (DIN)	...	92lb.ft. at 4000 r.p.m.
11.	Piston oversizes	...	·0025, ·015, ·030in.
12.	Piston clearance in bore	...	7/11lb. pull on ·0020in. × ½in. feeler (·0013/·0019in.)
13.	Piston rings—number	...	2 compression, 1 oil
14.	Piston rings—width	...	Comp., ·077 to ·078in.; oil, 0·155 to 0·156in.
15.	Piston rings—groove cl'nce		Comp., ·0016 to ·0036in.; oil, ·0018 to
16.	Piston rings—gap (in bore)	...	·009 to ·014in. [·0038in.
17.	Oil pressure	...	35 to 40lb./in.²
18.	Gudgeon pin diameter	...	0·8119 to 0·8123in. (in 4 grades)
19.	Gudgeon pin fit in piston		Interference, selective (heated piston)
20.	Gudgeon pin fit in con. rod		·0001 to ·0003in. clearance (selective)
21.	Crankpin diameter	...	1·9368 to 1·9376in.
22.	Crankpin undersizes	...	(·002, bearing) ·010, ·020, ·030, ·040in.
23.	Connecting rod length	...	4·927 to 4·929in. (centres)
24.	Big-end bearings	...	Steel-backed, copper/lead, lead/bronze or aluminium/tin
25.	Big-end bearing clearance		·0005 to ·0020in.
26.	Big-end side clearance	...	·004 to ·010in.
27.	Main journal diameter	...	Blue, 2·1253/57in.; red, 2·1257/61in.
28.	Main journal undersizes	...	(·002, bearing) ·010, ·020, ·030in.
29.	Main bearings	...	5; steel-backed copper-lead or lead-
31.	Main bearing clearance	...	·0005 to ·0020in. [bronze
32.	Crankshaft end-float	...	·003 to ·011in.
33.	Crankshaft end-thrust on		Centre main bearing
34.	Camshaft journal diameter		1·5597 to 1·5605in.
35.	Camshaft bearings	...	3; steel-backed white metal
36.	Camshaft bearing cl'ance		·001 to ·0023in.
37.	Camshaft end-float	...	·0025 to ·0075in.
38.	Camshaft drive type	...	Chain (single); 46 × 0·375in. pitches
39.	Valve head diameter	...	Inlet, 1·580/1·550in; exhaust, 1·340/1·330in.
40.	Valve stem diameter	...	In., 0·3098/0·3105in.; exh., 0·3089/0·3096in.
41.	Valve seat angle	...	44° 30' to 45° (in head)
42.	Valve lift	...	Inlet, 0·3556in.; exhaust, 0·3574in.
44.	Valve stem/guide cl'ance		In., ·0008/·0027in.; exh., ·0017/·0036in.
45.	Valve spring free length	...	1·48in.
46.	Valve spring rate	...	Length (closed), 1·263in. at 44/49lb.
47.	Valve working clearance		Inlet, ·012in.; exhaust, ·022in. (hot)
49.	Valve timing	...	Inlet opens 27° B.T.D.C.; closes 65° A.B.D.C. Exhaust opens 65° B.B.D.C.; closes 27° A.T.D.C.
50.	Petrol pump	...	A.C. mechanical
51.	Carburettor	...	Weber 32/36DGV-O5A

		Primary	Secondary
52.	Choke tube (Venturi)	26/4·5	27/4·5
53.	Main jet	140	135
54.	Compensating jet	165	160
55.	Slow-running jet	50	45
56.	Slow-running air bleed	180	70
57.	Emulsion tube	F50	F6
58.	Accelerator pump jet	50	
62.	Needle valve	1·75mm.	

TRANSMISSION

101.	Type	...	Rear wheel drive
102.	Clutch (mechanical)	...	7½in. diam., diaphragm type; free travel at lever, ⁱ⁄₁₆in. (1·6mm.)
103.	Gearbox	...	4 forward speeds, all synchromesh
105.	Gearbox ratios	...	Top, 1:1; 3rd, 1·397:1; 2nd, 2·010:1; 1st, 2·972:1; reverse, 3·324:1
107.	Driving axles	...	Semi-floating
108.	Final drive gear	...	Hypoid (Salisbury)
109.	Final drive ratio	...	4·1:1 (41/10)
111.	Crown wheel/pinion b'lash		·003 to ·006in.; shim adjustment
112.	Pinion bearing pre-load		8 to 12lb.in.; shim adjustment
113.	Differential brg. pre-load		·003 to ·005in.; shim adjustment

BRAKES

201.	Front	...	Girling hydraulic, 11in. diam. discs
202.	Rear	...	Girling hydraulic, 9in. diam. drums
203.	Handbrake	...	Mechanical, on rear wheels
204.	Linings—front	...	Ferodo, type 14 calliper pads
205.	Linings—rear	...	Ferodo, 1¾in. wide

STEERING (see also "Dimensions")

301.	Type	...	Cam Gear
302.	Camber angle	...	2°; non-adjustable
303.	Castor angle	...	4°; non-adjustable
304.	King-pin inclination	...	2°
305.	Toe-in	...	⅛ to ³⁄₁₆in. (3 to 5mm.) at wheel rim
306.	Conditions for checking	...	Unladen

FRONT SUSPENSION

401.	Type	...	Independent, vertical coil springs
402.	Number of coils	...	21
403.	Coil diameter	...	2¼in. (external)
404.	Wire diameter	...	0·31in.
405.	Spring length—free	...	14½in.
406.	Spring length—fitted	...	8½in.

REAR SUSPENSION

501.	Type	...	Semi-elliptic leaf springs
504.	Spring length (centres)	...	42¾in. (free)
505.	Number of leaves	...	5
506.	Width of leaves	...	1¾in.
507.	Thickness of leaves	...	¼in.
508.	Spring camber—free	...	3⅝in.

ELECTRICAL SYSTEM

601.	Ignition timing	...	8° B.T.D.C. at 800 r.p.m. (vac. pipe off); mark on pulley
602.	Sparking plugs	...	Motorcraft AG22
603.	Sparking plug gap	...	·023in.
604.	Contact breaker	...	Ford C7BH-C
605.	Contact breaker gap	...	·025in; dwell angle 38°/40°
606.	Centrif. advance starts at		1°/3° at 700 r.p.m.
607.	Centrif. advance—max.	...	8°/10° at 2600 r.p.m.
608.	Vacuum adv. starts at	...	1° to 3½° at 5½in. Hg.
609.	Vacuum adv.—max.	...	5½° to 8½° at 9+in. Hg. (Distributor degrees and r.p.m.)
610.	Ignition coil	...	Oil-filled, low voltage; use with 1·5Ohm ballast resistor
611.	Battery	...	12V. 36A.h.
612.	Battery earth	...	Negative
613.	Dynamo/Alternator	...	Lucas C40 or 15ACR
615.	Starter motor	...	Inertia type

CAPACITIES

701.	Engine sump	...	Total 6·74 pints; refill 6 pints (incl. filter)
702.	Gearbox	...	1·97 pints (refill, 1·7 pints)
703.	Differential	...	1¼ pints
704.	Cooling system	...	12 pints
705.	Fuel tank	...	8½ gallons
706.	Tyre size	...	165 × 15
707.	Tyre pressures (lb./in.²)	...	Front, 18; rear, 19
708.	No. of grease gun points	...	12 (Front sliding axles have 'one-shot' lubrication; press foot plunger every 200 miles approx.)
709.	Normal servicing intervals		Greasing, 2000/2500 miles; engine oil change, 5000 miles
710.	Hydraulic fluid	...	Castrol/Girling

DIMENSIONS

801.	Length overall	...	12ft. (3658mm.)
802.	Width overall	...	56in. (1422mm.)
803.	Height overall	...	51·75in. (1314mm.)
804.	Weight—2-seat Comp.	...	1460lb. (13cwt.) (662kg.)
	(dry) —4-seat	...	1516lb. (13·5cwt.) (688kg.)
805.	Ground cl'ance (min.)	...	7in. (178mm.)
806.	Track	...	47in. (1194mm.) front and rear
807.	Wheelbase	...	96in. (2438mm.)
808.	Turning circle diameter	...	32ft. (9·75m.)

TORQUE SPANNER DATA (lb.ft.)

901.	Cylinder head nuts	65/70	907.	Final drive pinion		
902.	Big-end bearing nuts	30/35		bearing nut	95/100	
903.	Main bearing nuts	65/70	908.	Crown wheel bolts	50/60	
905.	Flywheel bolts	50/54	909.	Diff. bearing nuts	35/40	
906.	Clutch to flyweel bolts	12/15	910.	Road wheel nuts	65/70	

BODY AND CHASSIS

1001.	Type of construction	...	Coachbuilt; steel 'Z'-section chassis; ash body frame
1002.	Material of body panels	...	Steel and aluminium
1003.	Windscreen glass	...	Toughened (laminated optional extra)

4/4 1600 1975

Model: 2-seat Tourer

ENGINE (Rover)

1.	Type	4-stroke V8 (cast-aluminium block); O.H.V.; central camshaft; hydraulic tappets
2.	Cooling system ...	Water pump, radiator (15lb./in.²), fan and thermostat
3.	Number of cylinders ...	8 (dry liners)
4.	Firing order and idling speed	1L—8R—4R—3L—6R—5L—7L—2R (No. 1 at front left); 600/650 r.p.m.
5.	Bore	3·5in. (88·9mm.)
6.	Stroke	2·8in. (71·12mm.)
7.	Cubic capacity ...	3532cm.³
8.	Compression ratio and pressure	9·25:1; 165lb./in.² min. at 185 r.p.m.
9.	Brake horse-power (DIN)	143 at 5,000 r.p.m.
10.	Torque (DIN) ...	202lb.ft. at 2,700 r.p.m.
11.	Piston oversizes ...	·010, ·020in.
12.	Piston clearance in bore ...	·0007/·0013in. (skirt bottom)
13.	Piston rings—number ...	2 compression, 1 oil
14.	Piston rings—width ...	Compression, ·078/·079in.; oil (expander) 0·1894in. max.
15.	Piston rings—groove cl'nce	Compression, ·003 to ·005in.
16.	Piston rings—gap (in bore)	Compression, ·017 to ·022in.
17.	Oil pressure (lb./in.²) ...	30 to 40 at 2,400 r.p.m. (55 at 4,000)
18.	Gudgeon pin diameter ...	0·8746 to 0·8749in.
19.	Gudgeon pin fit in piston	·0001 to ·0003in. clearance
20.	Gudgeon pin fit in con. rod	Press fit (·00075 to ·00125in. clearance)
21.	Crankpin diameter ...	2·0000 to 2·0005in.
22.	Crankpin undersizes ...	·010, ·020, ·030, ·040in.
23.	Connecting rod length ...	5·662 to 5·658in. (centres)
24.	Big-end bearings ...	Vandervell, lead-indium
25.	Big-end bearing clearance	·0007 to ·0027in.
26.	Big-end side clearance ...	·005 to ·015in.
27.	Main journal diameter ...	2·2992 to 2·2997in.
28.	Main journal undersizes...	·010, ·020, ·030, ·040in.
29.	Main bearings	5; Vandervell, lead-indium
30.	Main bearings—length ...	(1) (2) (4) (5), 0·797 to 0 807in.; (3), 1·056 to 1·058in.
31.	Main bearing clearance ...	·0009 to ·0024in.
32.	Crankshaft end-float ...	·004 to ·008in.
33.	Crankshaft end-thrust on	Centre main bearing
35.	Camshaft bearings ...	5; steel-backed Babbitt
38.	Camshaft drive type ...	Chain; 54 × 0·375in. pitches
39.	Valve head diameter ...	Inlet, 1·495/1·505in.; exhaust, 1·3075/1·3175in.
40.	Valve stem diameter (tapered)	Inlet (head) 0·3402/0·3412 to 0·3407/0·3417in.; exhaust, 0·3397/0·3407 to 0·3402/0 3412in.
42.	Valve lift ...	0·39in.
44.	Valve stem/guide cl'nce	Inlet (top), ·001/·003; (bottom), ·0015/·0035. Exhaust (top), ·0015/·0035; (bottom), ·002/·004in.
46.	Valve spring rate...	Inner, 1·63in. at 21·5/26·5lb.; outer, 1·6in. at 39/45lb.
49.	Valve timing Inlet opens	30° B.T.D.C. } peak, 112·5° A.T.D.C.
	Inlet closes	75° A.B.D.C.
	Exhaust opens	68° B.B.D.C. } peak, 105·5° B.T.D.C
	Exhaust closes	37° A.T.D.C.
50.	Petrol pump ...	A.C. mechanical
52.	Carburettors	2 S.U., type HIF6; needle BBG. (Mixture ratio preset and sealed; only the engine idling speed may be adjusted)

TRANSMISSION

101.	Type	Rear wheel drive
102.	Clutch (hydraulic) ...	Borg & Beck, 9·5in.diam., single dry plate, diaphragm spring, free travel at lever, 1/16in. (1·6mm.)
103.	Gearbox	4 forward speeds, all synchromesh
105.	Gearbox ratios ...	1; 1·391; 2·133; 3·625; R., 3·43:1
106.	Overdrive	Not fitted
107.	Driving axles ...	Semi-floating
108.	Final drive gear ...	Hypoid, limited-slip differential
109.	Final drive ratio ...	3·31:1
111.	Crown wheel/pinion b'lash	·003 to 0·006in.; shim adjustment
112.	Pinion bearing pre-load	8 to 12lb.in.
113.	Differential brg. pre-load	·003 to ·005in.; shim adjustment

BRAKES

201.	Front	Girling hydraulic, 11in. diam. discs
202.	Rear	Girling hydraulic, 9in. diam. drums
203.	Handbrake ...	Mechanical, on rear wheels
204.	Linings—front ...	Ferodo, type GX
205.	Linings—rear ...	Ferodo, type LL, 1¾in. wide
206.	Power assistance ...	Girling servo (twin on L.H. drive cars)

STEERING (see also "Dimensions")

301.	Type	Cam Gear
302.	Camber angle ...	2°, non-adjustable
303.	Castor angle ...	4°, non-adjustable
304.	King-pin inclination ...	2°
305.	Toe-in	⅛ to 3/16in. (3 to 5mm.) at wheel rims
306.	Conditions for checking...	Unladen

FRONT SUSPENSION

401.	Type	Independent, vertical coil springs
402.	Number of coils ...	18
403.	Coil diameter ...	2⅜in. (external)
404.	Wire diameter ...	0·375in.
405.	Spring length—free ...	13in.
506.	Spring length—fitted ...	9in.

REAR SUSPENSION

501.	Type	Semi-elliptic leaf-springs
504.	Spring length ...	42¾in. (free)
505.	Number of leaves ...	6
506.	Width of leaves ...	1⅞in.
507.	Thickness of leaves ...	¼in.
508.	Spring camber—free ...	3¼in.

ELECTRICAL SYSTEM

601.	Ignition timing —98 oct.	4° B.T.D.C. } Static or 600 r.p.m.
	—96 oct.	T.D.C. } (mark on damper)
602.	Sparking plugs ...	Champion L92Y
603.	Sparking plug gap ...	·025in.
604.	Distributor ...	Lucas 35D8
605.	Contact breaker gap ...	·014 to ·016in.; but set dwell angle 26°/28° (600 r.p.m.)
606.	Centrif. advance starts at	560 to 840 r.p.m.
607.	Centrif. advance—max.	28° at 4,800 r.p.m. (Crankshaft degrees and r.p.m.)
610.	Ignition coil ...	Lucas 16C6
611.	Battery	12V. 57A.h.
612.	Battery earth ...	Negative
613.	Alternator ...	Lucas 18ACR, 43 amp.
614.	Control box ...	Integral with alternator
615.	Starter motor ...	Lucas 3M100, pre-engaged

CAPACITIES

701.	Engine sump ...	8 pints (plus 1 pint for new filter)
702.	Gearbox	3¼ pints
703.	Differential ...	2½ pints
704.	Cooling system ...	15 pints
705.	Fuel tank ...	14 gallons
706.	Tyre size	185 × 15in.
707.	Tyre pressures —Front	22 (fast driving, 24/26)
	(lb./in.²) —Rear	22 (fast driving, 24/26)
708.	No. of grease gun points	12
709.	Servicing intervals ...	Greasing, 3000 miles; engine oil change, 5000 miles
710.	Hydraulic fluid ...	Castrol-Girling

DIMENSIONS

801.	Length overall ...	12ft. 8in. (3861mm.)
802.	Width overall ...	60in. (1524mm.)
803.	Height overall ...	50in. (1270mm.)
804.	Weight (dry) ...	1884lb. (16·8cwt.) (855kg.) approx.
805.	Ground clearance (min.)	6in. (152mm.) (engine sump)
806.	Track —Front	51in. (1295mm.)
	—Rear	52in. (1321mm.)
807.	Wheelbase ...	98in. (2489mm.)
808.	Turning circle diameter...	38ft (11·6mm.)

TORQUE SPANNER DATA (lb.ft.)

901.	Cylinder head bolts ...	65/70
902.	Big-end bearing bolts ...	30/35
903.	Main bearing bolts ...	50/55
	—Rear ...	65/70
905.	Flywheel bolts ...	50/60
906.	Clutch to flywheel bolts...	20
907.	Drive pinion bearing nut	95/100
908.	Crown wheel bolts ...	50/60
909.	Differential bearing nuts	35/40
910.	Road wheel nuts... ...	65/70
911.	Steering wheel nut ...	40

BODY AND CHASSIS

1001.	Type of construction ...	Steel 'Z'-section chassis
1002.	Material of body panels...	Steel and aluminium
1003.	Type of glass ...	Windscreen laminated

Plus 8 1975

Models: 4-seat Tourer and 2-seat Competition model

ENGINE (Ford 1600GT)

1. Type	4-stroke; overhead valves; side camshaft
2. Cooling system	Water pump, radiator, fan and thermostat
3. Number of cylinders	4 (bored direct in block)
4. Firing order	1—2—4—3 (No. 1 at front)
4a. Idling speed	800±20 r.p.m.; fast idle, 1900±100 r.p.m.
5. Bore	3·1881in. (80·977mm.) mean grade
6. Stroke	3·056in. (77·62mm.)
7. Cubic capacity	1598cm.³
8. Compression ratio and pressure	9:1; 188lb./in.² at 300 r.p.m.
9. Brake horse-power (DIN)	84 at 5500 r.p.m.
10. Torque (DIN)	92lb.ft. at 4000 r.p.m.
11. Piston oversizes	·0025, ·015, ·030in.
12. Piston clearance in bore	·0009/·0016in.
13. Piston rings—number	2 compression, 1 oil
14. Piston rings—width	Comp., ·077/·078in.; oil, 0·155/0·156in.
15. Piston rings—groove cl'nce	Comp., ·0016/·0036in.; oil, ·0018/·0038
16. Piston rings—gap (in bore)	·009/·014in.
17. Oil pressure (minimum)	8·5lb./in.² at 700 r.p.m.; 21lb./in.² at 2000 r.p.m.
18. Gudgeon pin diameter	0·8119/0·8123in. (in 4 grades)
19. Gudgeon pin fit in piston	Interference, selective (heated piston)
20. Gudgeon pin fit in con. rod	·0002/·0004in. clearance (selective)
21. Crankpin diameter	1·9368/1·9376in.
22. Crankpin undersizes	(·002, bearing) ·010, ·020, ·030, ·040in.
23. Connecting rod length	4·927/4·929in. (centres)
24. Big-end bearings	Steel-backed, copper/lead, lead/bronze or aluminium/tin
25. Big-end bearing clearance	·0002/·003in.
26. Big-end side clearance	·004/·010in.
27. Main journal diameter	Blue, 2·1253/57in.; red, 2·1257/61in.
28. Main journal undersizes	(·002, bearing) ·010, ·020, ·030in.
29. Main bearings	5; steel-backed copper-lead or lead-bronze
31. Main bearing clearance	·0004/·0024in.
32. Crankshaft end-float	·003/·011in.
33. Crankshaft end-thrust on	Centre main bearing
34. Camshaft journal diameter	1·5597/1·5605in.
35. Camshaft bearings	3; steel-backed white metal
36. Camshaft bearing cl'ance	·001/·0023in.
37. Camshaft end-float	·0025/·0075in.
38. Camshaft drive type	Chain (single); 46×0·375in. pitches
39. Valve head diameter	Inlet, 1·543/1·560in.; exhaust, 1·330/1·340in.
40. Valve stem diameter	In., 0·3098/0·3105in.; exh., 0·3089/0·3096in.
41. Valve seat angle	44° 30' to 45° (in head)
42. Valve lift	Inlet, 0·3556in.; exhaust, 0·3574in.
44. Valve stem/guide cl'ance	In., ·0008/·0027in.; exh., ·0017/·0036in.
45. Valve spring free length	1·48in.
46. Valve spring rate	Length (closed), 1·263in. at 44/49lb.
47. Valve working clearance	Inlet, ·012in.; exhaust, ·022in. (hot)
49. Valve timing	Inlet opens 27° B.T.D.C.; closes 65° A.B.D.C. Exhaust opens 65° B.B.D.C.; closes 27° A.T.D.C.
50. Petrol pump	A.C. mechanical
51. Carburettor	Weber twin choke; ref. 761F-9510-BA
	1st
52. Choke tube (Venturi)	23mm.
52a. Choke plate pull down	6·5mm. max.
53. Main jet	120
63. Float level	41·0±0·3mm. (1·61±0·01in.)
64. Exhaust gas analysis	1·5%±0·25 CO

	2nd
52.	24mm.
53.	115

TRANSMISSION

101. Type	Rear wheel drive
102. Clutch (mechanical)	7½in. diam., diaphragm type; free travel at lever, ⅟₁₆in. (1·6mm.)
103. Gearbox	4 forward speeds, all synchromesh
105. Gearbox ratios	1; 1·397; 2·010; 2·972; R., 3·324:1
107. Driving axles	Semi-floating
108. Final drive gear	Hypoid (Salisbury)
109. Final drive ratio	4·1:1 (41/10)
111. Crown wheel/pinion b'lash	·003 to ·006in.; shim adjustment
112. Pinion bearing pre-load	8 to 12lb.in.; shim adjustment
113. Differential brg. pre-load	·003 to·005in.; shim adjustment

BRAKES

201. Front	Girling hydraulic, 11in. diam. discs
202. Rear	Girling hydraulic, 9in. diam. drums
203. Handbrake	Mechanical, on rear wheels
204. Linings—front	Ferodo, type 14 calliper pads
205. Linings—rear	Ferodo, 1·75in. wide

STEERING (see also "Dimensions)

301. Type	Cam Gear
302. Camber angle	2°; non-adjustable
303. Castor angle	4°; non-adjustable
304. King-pin inclination	2°
305. Toe-in	⅛ to ⁵⁄₁₆in. (3 to 5mm.) at wheel rim
306. Conditions for checking	Unladen

FRONT SUSPENSION

401. Type	Independent, vertical coil springs
402. Number of coils	21
403. Coil diameter	2¼in. (external)
404. Wire diameter	0·31in.
405. Spring length—free	14½in.
406. Spring length—fitted	8½in.

REAR SUSPENSION

501. Type	Semi-elliptic leaf springs
504. Spring length (centres)	42¾in. (free)
505. Number of leaves	5
506. Width of leaves	1⅜in.
507. Thickness of leaves	¼in.
508. Spring camber—free	3⅜in.

ELECTRICAL SYSTEM

601. Ignition timing	10° B.T.D.C. at 800 r.p.m. (vac. pipe off); mark on pulley
602. Sparking plugs	Motorcraft AGR12
603. Sparking plug gap	·030in.
604. Distributor	Motorcraft
605. Contact breaker gap	·025in.; dwell angle 48°/52°
606. Centrif. advance starts at	-½°/+½° at 500 r.p.m.
607. Centrif. advance—max.	10·75°/12·75° at 2000 r.p.m.
608. Vacuum adv. starts at	1°/4° at 5in. Hg.
609. Vacuum adv.—max.	5°/8° at 9in. Hg. (Distributor degrees and r.p.m.)
610. Ignition coil	Oil-filled, low voltage; use with 1·5Ohm ballast resistor
611. Battery	12V. 36A.h.
612. Battery earth	Negative
613. Alternator	Lucas 15ACR
615. Starter motor	Lucas M35J or 5M90

CAPACITIES

701. Engine sump	Total 6·74 pints; refill 6 pints (incl. filter)
702. Gearbox	1·97 pints (refill, 1·7 pints)
703. Differential	1·75
704. Cooling system	12 pints
705. Fuel tank	8·5 gallons
706. Tyre size	165×15
707. Tyre pressures (lb./in.²)	Front, 18; rear, 19
708. No. of grease gun points	12 (Front sliding axles have 'one-shot' lubrication; press foot plunger every 200 miles approx.)
709. Normal servicing intervals	Greasing, 2000/2500 miles; engine oil change, 5000 miles
710. Hydraulic fluid	Castrol/Girling

DIMENSIONS

801. Length overall	12ft. (3658mm.)
802. Width overall	56in. (1422mm.)
803. Height overall	51·75in. (1314mm.)
804. Weight—2-seat Comp.	1460lb. (13cwt.) (662kg.)
(dry) —4-seat	1516lb. (13·5cwt.) (688kg.)
805. Ground cl'ance (min.)	7in. (178mm.)
806. Track	47in. (1194mm.) front and rear
807. Wheelbase	96in. (2438mm.)
808. Turning circle diameter	32ft. (9·75m.)

TORQUE SPANNER DATA (lb.ft.)

901. Cylinder head nuts	65/70	907. Final drive pinion bearing nut	95/100
902. Big-end bearing nuts	30/35		
903. Main bearing nuts	55/60	908. Crown wheel bolts	50/60
905. Flywheel bolts	50/54	909. Diff. bearing nuts	35/40
906. Clutch to flywheel bolts	12/15	910. Road wheel nuts	65/70

BODY AND CHASSIS

1001. Type of construction	Coachbuilt; steel 'Z'-section chassis; ash body frame
1002. Material of body panels	Steel and aluminium
1003. Windscreen glass	Toughened (laminated optional extra)

4/4 1600 1976

Model: 2-seat Tourer

ENGINE (Rover)

1.	Type	4-stroke V8 (cast-aluminium block); O.H.V.; central camshaft; hydraulic tappets
2.	Cooling system	Water pump, radiator (15lb./in.²), fan and thermostat
3.	Number of cylinders ...	8 (dry liners)
4.	Firing order and idling speed	1L—8R—4R—3L—6R—5L—7L—2R (No. 1 at front left); 600/650 r.p.m.
5.	Bore	3·5in. (88·9mm.)
6.	Stroke	2·8in. (71·12mm.)
7.	Cubic capacity	3532cm.³
8.	Compression ratio and pressure	9·25:1; 165lb./in.² min. at 135 r.p.m.
9.	Brake horse-power (DIN)	143 at 5,000 r.p.m.
10.	Torque (DIN)	202lb.ft. at 2,700 r.p.m.
11.	Piston oversizes	·010, ·020in.
12.	Piston clearance in bore ...	·0007/·0013in. (skirt bottom)
13.	Piston rings—number ...	2 compression, 1 oil
14.	Piston rings—width ...	Compression, ·078/·079in.; oil (expander) 0·1894in. max.
15.	Piston rings—groove cl'nce	Compression, ·003 to ·005in.
16.	Piston rings—gap (in bore)	Compression, ·017 to ·022in.
17.	Oil pressure (lb./in.²) ...	30 to 40 at 2,400 r.p.m. (55 at 4,000)
18.	Gudgeon pin diameter ...	0·8746 to 0·8749in.
19.	Gudgeon pin fit in piston ...	·0001 to ·0003in. clearance
20.	Gudgeon pin fit in con. rod	Press fit (·00075 to ·00125in. clearance)
21.	Crankpin diameter ...	2·0000 to 2·0005in.
22.	Crankpin undersizes ...	·010, ·020, ·030, ·040in.
23.	Connecting rod length ...	5·662 to 5·658in. (centres)
24.	Big-end bearings ...	Vandervell, lead-indium
25.	Big-end bearing clearance	·0007 to ·0027in.
26.	Big-end side clearance ...	·005 to ·015in.
27.	Main journal diameter ...	2·2992 to 2·2997in.
28.	Main journal undersizes ...	·010, ·020, ·030, ·040in.
29.	Main bearings	5; Vandervell, lead-indium
30.	Main bearings—length ...	(1) (2) (4) (5), 0·797 to 0·807in.; (3), 1·056 to 1·058in.
31.	Main bearing clearance ...	·0009 to ·0024in.
32.	Crankshaft end-float ...	·004 to ·008in.
33.	Crankshaft end-thrust on	Centre main bearing
35.	Camshaft bearings ...	5; steel-backed Babbitt
38.	Camshaft drive type ...	Chain; 54 × 0·375in. pitches
39.	Valve head diameter ...	Inlet, 1·495/1·505in.; exhaust, 1·3075/1·3175in.
40.	Valve stem diameter (tapered)	Inlet (head) 0·3402/0·3412 to 0·3407/0·3417in.; exhaust, 0·3397/0·3407 to 0·3402/0·3412in.
42.	Valve lift	0·39in.
44.	Valve stem/guide cl'nce...	Inlet (top), ·001/·003; (bottom), ·0015/·0035. Exhaust (top), ·0015/·0035; (bottom), ·002/·004in.
46.	Valve spring rate... ...	Inner, 1·63in. at 21·5/26·5lb.; outer, 1·6in. at 39/45lb.
49.	Valve timing	Inlet opens 30° B.T.D.C. peak, 112·5° A.T.D.C. Inlet closes 75° A.B.D.C. Exhaust opens 68° B.B.D.C. peak, 105·5° B.T.D.C. Exhaust closes 37° A.T.D.C.
50.	Petrol pump	A.C. mechanical
52.	Carburettors	2 S.U., type HIF6; needle BBG. (Mixture ratio preset and sealed; only the engine idling speed may be adjusted)

TRANSMISSION

101.	Type	Rear wheel drive
102.	Clutch (hydraulic) ...	Borg & Beck, 9·5in.diam., single dry plate, diaphragm spring, free travel at lever, 1/16in. (1·6mm.)
103.	Gearbox	4 forward speeds, all synchromesh
105.	Gearbox ratios ...	1; 1·391; 2·133; 3·625; R., 3·43:1
106.	Overdrive	Not fitted
107.	Driving axles ...	Semi-floating
108.	Final drive gear ...	Hypoid, limited-slip differential
109.	Final drive ratio ...	3·31:1
111.	Crown wheel/pinion b'lash	0·003 to 0·006in.; shim adjustment
112.	Pinion bearing pre-load	8 to 12lb.in.
113.	Differential brg. pre-load	·003 to ·005in.; shim adjustment

BRAKES

201.	Front	Girling hydraulic, 11in. diam. discs
202.	Rear	Girling hydraulic, 9in. diam. drums
203.	Handbrake ...	Mechanical, on rear wheels
204.	Linings—front ...	Ferodo, type GX
205.	Linings—rear ...	Ferodo, type LL, 1¾in. wide
206.	Power assistance ...	Girling servo (twin on L.H. drive cars)

STEERING (see also "Dimensions")

301.	Type	Cam Gear
302.	Camber angle ...	2°, non-adjustable
303.	Castor angle ...	4°, non-adjustable
304.	King-pin inclination	2°
305.	Toe-in	⅛ to 3/16in. (3 to 5mm.) at wheel rims
306.	Conditions for checking...	Unladen

FRONT SUSPENSION

401.	Type	Independent, vertical coil springs
402.	Number of coils ...	18
403.	Coil diameter ...	2⅜in. (external)
404.	Wire diameter ...	0·375in.
405.	Spring length—free ...	13in.
506.	Spring length—fitted ...	9in.

REAR SUSPENSION

501.	Type	Semi-elliptic leaf-springs
504.	Spring length ...	42¾in. (free)
505.	Number of leaves ...	6
506.	Width of leaves ...	1¾in.
507.	Thickness of leaves ...	¼in.
508.	Spring camber—free ...	3¼in.

ELECTRICAL SYSTEM

601.	Ignition timing ...	6° B.T.D.C. with 96 octane minimum (mark on pulley)
602.	Sparking plugs ...	Champion L92Y
603.	Sparking plug gap ...	·025in.
604.	Distributor ...	Lucas 35D8
605.	Contact breaker gap ...	·014 to ·016in.; but set dwell angle 26°/28° (600 r.p.m.)
606.	Centrif. advance starts at	560 to 840 r.p.m.
607.	Centrif. advance—max....	28° at 4,800 r.p.m. (Crankshaft degrees and r.p.m.)
610.	Ignition coil ...	Lucas 16C6
611.	Battery	12V. 57A.h.
612.	Battery earth ...	Negative
613.	Alternator ...	Lucas 18ACR, 43 amp.
614.	Control box ...	Integral with alternator
615.	Starter motor ...	Lucas 3M100, pre-engaged

CAPACITIES

701.	Engine sump ...	8 pints (plus 1 pint for new filter)
702.	Gearbox	3¼ pints
703.	Differential ...	2¼ pints
704.	Cooling system ...	15 pints
705.	Fuel tank ...	14 gallons
706.	Tyre size	185 × 15in.
707.	Tyre pressures —Front (lb./in.²) —Rear	22 (fast driving, 24/26) 22 (fast driving, 24/26)
708.	No. of grease gun points	12
709.	Servicing intervals ...	Greasing, 3000 miles; engine oil change, 5000 miles
710.	Hydraulic fluid ...	Castrol-Girling

DIMENSIONS

801.	Length overall ...	12ft. 8in. (3861mm.)
802.	Width overall ...	60in. (1524mm.)
803.	Height overall ...	50in. (1270mm.)
804.	Weight (dry) ...	1884lb. (16·8cwt.) (855kg.) approx.
805.	Ground clearance (min.)	6in. (152mm.) (engine sump)
806.	Track —Front —Rear	51in. (1295mm.) 52in. (1321mm.)
807.	Wheelbase ...	98in. (2489mm.)
808.	Turning circle diameter...	38ft (11·6mm.)

TORQUE SPANNER DATA (lb.ft.)

901.	Cylinder head bolts ...	65/70
902.	Big-end bearing bolts ...	30/35
903.	Main bearing bolts ...	50/55
	—Rear ...	65/70
905.	Flywheel bolts ...	50/60
906.	Clutch to flywheel bolts....	20
907.	Drive pinion bearing nut	95/100
908.	Crown wheel bolts ...	50/60
909.	Differential bearing nuts	35/40
910.	Road wheel nuts... ...	65/70
911.	Steering wheel nut ...	40

BODY AND CHASSIS

1001.	Type of construction ...	Steel 'Z'-section chassis
1002.	Material of body panels...	Steel and aluminium
1003.	Type of glass ...	Windscreen laminated

PLus 8 1976

Models: 4-seat Tourer and 2-seat Competition model

ENGINE (Ford 1600GT)

1. Type ... ... 4-stroke; overhead valves; side camshaft
2. Cooling system ... Water pump, radiator, fan and thermostat
3. Number of cylinders ... 4 (bored direct in block)
4. Firing order ... 1—2—4—3 (No. 1 at front)
4a. Idling speed ... ... 800±20 r.p.m.; fast idle, 1900±100 r.p.m.
5. Bore ... ... 3·1881in. (80·977mm.) mean grade
6. Stroke ... ... 3·056in. (77·62mm.)
7. Cubic capacity ... 1598cm.³
8. Compression ratio and 9:1; 188lb./in.² at 300 r.p.m.
   pressure
9. Brake horse-power (DIN) 84 at 5500 r.p.m.
10. Torque (DIN) ... ... 92lb.ft. at 4000 r.p.m.
11. Piston oversizes ... ·0025, ·015, ·030in.
12. Piston clearance in bore ... ·0009/·0016in.
13. Piston rings—number ... 2 compression, 1 oil
14. Piston rings—width ... Comp., ·077/·078in.; oil, 0·155/0·156in.
15. Piston rings—groove cl'nce Comp., ·0016/·0036in.; oil, ·0018/·0038
16. Piston rings—gap (in bore) ·009/·014in. [in.
17. Oil pressure (minimum) 8·5lb./in.² at 700 r.p.m.; 21lb./in.² at
    2000 r.p.m.
18. Gudgeon pin diameter ... 0·8119/0·8123in. (in 4 grades)
19. Gudgeon pin fit in piston Interference, selective (heated piston)
20. Gudgeon pin fit in con. rod ·0002/·0004in. clearance (selective)
21. Crankpin diameter ... 1·9368/1·9376in.
22. Crankpin undersizes ... (·002, bearing) ·010, ·020, ·030, ·040in.
23. Connecting rod length ... 4·927/4·929in. (centres)
24. Big-end bearings ... Steel-backed, copper/lead, lead/bronze
    or aluminium/tin
25. Big-end bearing clearance ·0002/·003in.
26. Big-end side clearance ... ·004/·010in.
27. Main journal diameter ... Blue, 2·1253/57in.; red, 2·1257/61in.
28. Main journal undersizes ... (·002, bearing) ·010, ·020, ·030in.
29. Main bearings ... ... 5; steel-backed copper-lead or lead-
31. Main bearing clearance ... ·0004/·0024in. [bronze
32. Crankshaft end-float ... ·003/·011in.
33. Crankshaft end-thrust on Centre main bearing
34. Camshaft journal diameter 1·5597/1·5605in.
35. Camshaft bearings ... 3; steel-backed white metal
36. Camshaft bearing cl'ance ·001/·0023in.
37. Camshaft end-float ... ·0025/·0075in.
38. Camshaft drive type ... Chain (single); 46×0·375in. pitches
39. Valve head diameter ... Inlet, 1·543/1·560in.; exhaust, 1·330/
    1·340in.
40. Valve stem diameter ... In., 0·3098/0·3105in.; exh., 0·3089/
    0·3096in.
41. Valve seat angle ... 44° 30′ to 45° (in head)
42. Valve lift ... ... Inlet, 0·3556in.; exhaust, 0·3574in.
44. Valve stem/guide cl'ance In., ·0008/·0027in.; exh., ·0017/·0036in.
45. Valve spring free length ... 1·48in.
46. Valve spring rate... ... Length (closed), 1·263in. at 44/49lb.
47. Valve working clearance Inlet, ·012in.; exhaust, ·022in. (hot)
49. Valve timing ... ... Inlet opens 27° B.T.D.C.; closes 65°
    A.B.D.C. Exhaust opens 65° B.B.D.C.;
    closes 27° A.T.D.C.
50. Petrol pump ... ... A.C. mechanical
51. Carburettor ... ... Weber twin choke; ref. 761F-9510-BA

	1st	2nd
52. Choke tube (Venturi)	23mm.	24mm.
52a. Choke plate pull down	6·5mm. max.	
53. Main jet	120	115

63. Float level ... ... 41·0±0·3mm. (1·61±0·01in.)
64. Exhaust gas analysis ... 1·5%±0·25 CO

TRANSMISSION

101. Type ... ... Rear wheel drive
102. Clutch (mechanical) ... 7½in. diam., diaphragm type; free travel
     at lever, 1/16in. (1·6mm.)
103. Gearbox ... ... 4 forward speeds, all synchromesh
105. Gearbox ratios ... 1; 1·397; 2·010; 2·972; R., 3·324:1
107. Driving axles ... ... Semi-floating
108. Final drive gear ... Hypoid (Salisbury)
109. Final drive ratio ... 4·1:1 (41/10)
111. Crown wheel/pinion b'lash ·003 to ·006in.; shim adjustment
112. Pinion bearing pre-load ... 8 to 12lb.in.; shim adjustment
113. Differential brg. pre-load ·003 to ·005in.; shim adjustment

BRAKES

201. Front ... ... Girling hydraulic, 11in. diam. discs
202. Rear ... ... Girling hydraulic, 9in. diam. drums
203. Handbrake ... ... Mechanical, on rear wheels
204. Linings—front ... Ferodo, type 14 calliper pads
205. Linings—rear ... .. Ferodo, 1·75in. wide

STEERING (see also "Dimensions")

301. Type ... ... Cam Gear
302. Camber angle ... 2°; non-adjustable
303. Castor angle ... 4°; non-adjustable
304. King-pin inclination ... 2°
305. Toe-in ... ... ⅛ to 3/16in. (3 to 5mm.) at wheel rim
306. Conditions for checking Unladen

FRONT SUSPENSION

401. Type ... ... Independent, vertical coil springs
402. Number of coils ... 21
403. Coil diameter ... 2¼in. (external)
404. Wire diameter ... 0·31in.
405. Spring length—free ... 14½in.
406. Spring length—fitted ... 8½in.

REAR SUSPENSION

501. Type ... ... Semi-elliptic leaf springs
504. Spring length (centres) ... 42¾in. (free)
505. Number of leaves ... 5
506. Width of leaves ... 1¾in.
507. Thickness of leaves ... ¼in.
508. Spring camber—free ... 3⅞in.

ELECTRICAL SYSTEM

601. Ignition timing ... 10° B.T.D.C. at 800 r.p.m. (vac. pipe
     off); mark on pulley
602. Sparking plugs ... Motorcraft AGR12
603. Sparking plug gap ... ·030in.
604. Distributor ... Motorcraft
605. Contact breaker gap ... ·025in.; dwell angle 48°/52°
606. Centrif. advance starts at −½°/+½° at 500 r.p.m.
607. Centrif. advance—max... 10·75°/12·75° at 2000 r.p.m.
608. Vacuum adv. starts at ... 1°/4° at 5in. Hg.
609. Vacuum adv.—max. ... 5°/8° at 9in. Hg.
     (Distributor degrees and r.p.m.)
610. Ignition coil ... ... Oil-filled, low voltage; use with 1·5Ohm
     ballast resistor
611. Battery ... ... 12V. 36A.h.
612. Battery earth ... Negative
613. Alternator ... Lucas 15ACR
615. Starter motor ... Lucas M35J or 5M90

CAPACITIES

701. Engine sump ... ... Total 6·74 pints; refill 6 pints (incl. filter)
702. Gearbox ... ... 1·97 pints (refill, 1·7 pints)
703. Differential ... 1·75 pints
704. Cooling system ... 12 pints
705. Fuel tank ... ... 8·5 gallons
706. Tyre size ... ... 165×15
707. Tyre pressures (lb./in.²) Front, 18; rear, 19
708. No. of grease gun points ... 12 (Front sliding axles have 'one-shot'
     lubrication; press foot plunger every
     200 miles approx.)
709. Normal servicing intervals Greasing, 2000/2500 miles; engine oil
     change, 5000 miles
710. Hydraulic fluid ... ... Castrol/Girling

DIMENSIONS

801. Length overall ... 12ft. (3658mm.)
802. Width overall ... 56in. (1422mm.)
803. Height overall ... 51·75in. (1314mm.)
804. Weight—2-seat Comp. 1460lb. (13cwt.) (662kg.)
     (dry) —4-seat 1516lb. (13·5cwt.) (688kg.)
805. Ground cl'ance (min.) ... 7in. (178mm.)
806. Track ... ... 47in. (1194mm.) front and rear
807. Wheelbase ... 96in. (2438mm.)
808. Turning circle diameter... 32ft. (9·75m.)

TORQUE SPANNER DATA (lb.ft.)

901. Cylinder head nuts	65/70	907. Final drive pinion		
902. Big-end bearing nuts	30/35	bearing nut	95/100
903. Main bearing nuts	55/60	908. Crown wheel bolts	50/60
905. Flywheel bolts	50/54	909. Diff. bearing nuts	35/40
906. Clutch to flyweel bolts	12/15	910. Road wheel nuts	65/70

BODY AND CHASSIS

1001. Type of construction ... Coachbuilt; steel 'Z'-section chassis; ash
      body frame
1002. Material of body panels ... Steel and aluminium
1003. Windscreen glass ... Toughened (laminated optional extra)

4/4 1600 1977

Model: 2-seat Tourer

ENGINE (Rover)

1.	Type	4-stroke V8 (cast-aluminium block); O.H.V.; central camshaft; hydraulic tappets
2.	Cooling system ...	Water pump, radiator (15lb./in.²), fan (viscous coupling) and thermostat
3.	Number of cylinders ...	8 (dry liners)
4.	Firing order and idling speed	1L—8R—4R—3L—6R—5L—7L—2R (No. 1 at front left); 725/775 r.p.m.
5.	Bore	3·5in. (88·9mm.)
6.	Stroke	2·8in. (71·12mm.)
7.	Cubic capacity ...	3532cm.³
8.	Compression ratio and pressure	9·35:1; 165lb./in.² min. at 150/200 r.p.m.
9.	Brake horse-power (DIN)	155 at 5250 r.p.m.
10.	Torque (DIN) ...	198lb.ft. at 2500 r.p.m.
11.	Piston oversizes ...	·010, ·020in.
12.	Piston clearance in bore	·0007/·0013in. (skirt bottom)
13.	Piston rings—number ...	2 compression, 1 oil
14.	Piston rings—width ...	Compression, ·0615/·0625in.; oil (expander) 0·1894in. max.
15.	Piston rings—groove cl'nce	Compression, ·003/·005in.
16.	Piston rings—gap (in bore)	Compression, ·017/·022in.
17.	Oil pressure (lb./in.²) ...	30/40 at 2400 r.p.m. (55 at 4000)
18.	Gudgeon pin diameter ...	0·8746/0·8749in.
19.	Gudgeon pin fit in piston	·0001/·0003in. clearance
20.	Gudgeon pin fit in con. rod	Press fit
21.	Crankpin diameter ...	2·0000/2·0005in.
22.	Crankpin undersizes ...	·010, ·020, ·030, ·040in.
23.	Connecting rod length ...	5·662/5·658in. (centres)
24.	Big-end bearings ...	Vandervell, lead-indium
25.	Big-end bearing clearance	·0007/·0027in.
26.	Big-end side clearance ...	·005/·015in.
27.	Main journal diameter ...	2·2992/2·2997in.
28.	Main journal undersizes...	·010, ·020, ·030, ·040in.
29.	Main bearings ...	5; Vandervell, lead-indium
30.	Main bearings—length ...	(1) (2) (4) (5), 0·797/0·807in.; (3), 0·909/0·911in. clearance [1·056/1·058in.
31.	Main bearing clearance ...	·0009/·0024in.
32.	Crankshaft end-float ...	·004/·008in.
33.	Crankshaft end-thrust on	Centre main bearing
35.	Camshaft bearings ...	5; steel-backed Babbitt
38.	Camshaft drive type ...	Chain; 54×0·375in. pitches
39.	Valve head diameter ...	Inlet, 1·565/1·575in.; exhaust, 1·3475/1·3575
40.	Valve stem diameter (tapered)	Inlet (head) 0·3402/0·3412 to 0·3407/0·3417in.; exhaust, 0·3397/0·3407 to 0·3402/0·3412in.
42.	Valve lift	0·39in.
43.	Valve guide length ...	Fitted height, 19mm. above step surrounding valve guide boss
44.	Valve stem/guide cl'nce...	Inlet (top), ·001/·003; (bottom), ·0015/·0035. Exhaust (top), ·0015/·0035; (bottom), ·002/·004in.
46.	Valve spring loaded length	1·577in. at 70±3·5lb.; 1·350in. at 130±6·5lb.; 1·187in. at 176±7·5lb.
49.	Valve timing	Inlet opens 30° B.T.D.C. } peak, 112·5° A.T.D.C. Inlet closes 75° A.B.D.C. Exhaust opens 68° B.B.D.C. } peak, 105·5° B.T.D.C. Exhaust closes 37° A.T.D.C.
50.	Petrol pump	Electric
52.	Carburettors ...	2 S.U. type HIF6
53.	Needle	BAK
56.	Piston spring ...	Yellow
63.	Float level ...	·020/·060in. (0·5/1·5mm.)
64.	Exhaust gas analysis ...	2%/4·5% CO

TRANSMISSION

101.	Type	Rear wheel drive
102.	Clutch (hydraulic) ...	Borg & Beck, 9·5in.diam., single dry plate, diaphragm spring, free travel at lever, 1/16in. (1·6mm.)
103.	Gearbox ...	5 forward speeds, all synchromesh
105.	Gearbox ratios ...	0·833; 1; 1·396; 2·087; 3·321; R., [3·428:1
106.	Overdrive ...	Not fitted
107.	Driving axles ...	Semi-floating
108.	Final drive gear ...	Hypoid, limited-slip differential
109.	Final drive ratio ...	3·31:1
111.	Crown wheel/pinion b'lash	0·003/0·006in.; shim adjustment
112.	Pinion bearing pre-load	8/12lb.in.
113.	Differential brg. pre-load	·003/·005in.; shim adjustment

BRAKES

201.	Front	Girling hydraulic, 11in. diam. discs
202.	Rear	Girling hydraulic, 9in. diam. drums
203.	Handbrake	Mechanical, on rear wheels
204.	Linings—front ...	Ferodo, type GX
205.	Linings—rear ...	Ferodo, type LL, 1¾in. wide
206.	Power assistance ...	Girling servo (twin on L.H. drive cars)

STEERING (see also "Dimensions")

301.	Type	Cam Gear
302.	Camber angle ...	2°, non-adjustable
303.	Castor angle ...	4°, non-adjustable
304.	King-pin inclination ...	2°
305.	Toe-in	1/8/1/16in. (3/5mm.) at wheel rims
306.	Conditions for checking...	Unladen

FRONT SUSPENSION

401.	Type	Independent, vertical coil springs
402.	Number of coils ...	18
403.	Coil diameter ...	2¾in. (external)
404.	Wire diameter ...	0·375in.
405.	Spring length—free ...	13in.
506.	Spring length—fitted ...	9in.

REAR SUSPENSION

501.	Type	Semi-elliptic leaf-springs
504.	Spring length ...	42½in. (free)
505.	Number of leaves ...	6
506.	Width of leaves ...	1¾in.
507.	Thickness of leaves ...	¼in.
508.	Spring camber—free ...	3¼in.

ELECTRICAL SYSTEM

601.	Ignition timing	—static 6° BTDC (pulley) —stroboscope 10° at 1200 r.p.m.; 17° at 1800; 22° at 2600; vac. hose off
602.	Sparking plugs ...	Champion N12Y
603.	Sparking plug gap ...	·030in.
604.	Distributor ...	Lucas 35DE8 (electronic)
605.	Pick-up air gap ...	·014/·016in. (0·36/0·40mm.)
606.	Centrifugal advance ...	0° at 300 r.p.m.; 1°/3° at 600; 4·5°/7° at 900; 7°/9° at 1300; 9·5°/11·5° at 2200; 10°/12° at 2800
608.	Vacuum advance ...	0°/0·5° at 0in.Hg., 0°/3° at 4·3in.; 6°/9° at 10in.; 7°/9° at 20in. Distributor degrees and r.p.m.
610.	Ignition coil ...	Lucas 22C12; 9BR ballast resistor
611.	Battery	12V. 57A.h.
612.	Battery earth ...	Negative
613.	Alternator ...	Lucas 18ACR, 43 amp.
614.	Control box ...	Integral with alternator
615.	Starter motor ...	Lucas 3M100, pre-engaged; lock, 16·5 lb.ft. at 545A.

CAPACITIES

701.	Engine oil—Total ...	9·5 pints (incl. filter)
	—Drain/Refill	8·25 pints
702.	Gearbox (dry) ...	2·7 pints
703.	Differential ...	2·5 pints
704.	Cooling system ...	15 pints
705.	Fuel tank ...	14 gallons
706.	Tyre size ...	195VR14
707.	Tyre pressures —Front (lb./in.²) —Rear	18 (fast driving, 22) 18 (fast driving, 22)
708.	No. of grease gun points	12
709.	Servicing intervals ...	Greasing, 3000 miles; engine oil change, 5000 miles
710.	Hydraulic fluid ...	Castrol/Girling Universal

DIMENSIONS

801.	Length overall ...	12ft. 8in. (3861mm.)
802.	Width overall ...	60in. (1524mm.)
803.	Height overall ...	50in. (1270mm.)
804.	Weight (dry) ...	1884lb. (16·8cwt.) (855kg.) approx.
805.	Ground clearance (min.)	6in. (152mm.) (engine sump)
806.	Track —Front —Rear	52in. (1321mm.) 53in. (1346mm.)
807.	Wheelbase ...	98in. (2489mm.)
808.	Turning circle diameter...	38ft (11·6mm.)

TORQUE SPANNER DATA (lb.ft.)

901.	Cylinder head bolts ...	65/70 (3·8in. and 2·6in. bolts) 40/50 (2·16in. bolts)
902.	Big-end bearing bolts ...	30/35
903.	Main bearing bolts ...	50/55 —Rear ... 65/70
905.	Flywheel bolts ...	50/60
906.	Clutch to flywheel bolts...	20
907.	Drive pinion bearing nut	95/100
908.	Crown wheel bolts ...	50/60
909.	Differential bearing nuts	35/40
910.	Road wheel nuts...	65/70
911.	Steering wheel nut ...	40

BODY AND CHASSIS

1001.	Type of construction ...	Steel 'Z'-section chassis
1002.	Material of body panels...	Steel and aluminium
1003.	Type of glass ...	Windscreen laminated

Plus 8 1977

Models: 4-seat Tourer and 2-seat Competition model

ENGINE (Ford 1600GT)

#			
1.	Type	...	4-stroke; overhead valves; side camshaft
2.	Cooling system	...	Water pump, radiator, fan and thermostat
3.	Number of cylinders	...	4 (bored direct in block)
4.	Firing order	...	1—2—4—3 (No. 1 at front)
4a.	Idling speed		800±20 r.p.m.; fast idle, 1900±100 r.p.m.
5.	Bore	...	3·1881in. (80·977mm.) mean grade
6.	Stroke	...	3·056in. (77·62mm.)
7.	Cubic capacity	...	1598cm.³
8.	Compression ratio and pressure		9:1; 188lb./in.² at 300 r.p.m.
9.	Brake horse-power (DIN)		84 at 5500 r.p.m.
10.	Torque (DIN)	...	92lb.ft. at 4000 r.p.m.
11.	Piston oversizes	...	·0025, ·015, ·030in.
12.	Piston clearance in bore	...	·0009/·0016in.
13.	Piston rings—number	...	2 compression, 1 oil
14.	Piston rings—width	...	Comp., ·077/·078in.; oil, 0·155/0·156in.
15.	Piston rings—groove cl'nce	Comp., ·0016/·0036in.; oil, ·0018/·0038
16.	Piston rings—gap (in bore)	·009/·014in. [in.
17.	Oil pressure (minimum)	3·5lb./in.² at 700 r.p.m.; 21lb./in.² at 2000 r.p.m.
18.	Gudgeon pin diameter	0·8119/0·8123in. (in 4 grades)
19.	Gudgeon pin fit in piston	Interference, selective (heated piston)
20.	Gudgeon pin fit in con. rod	Clearance (selective) ·0002/·0004in.
21.	Crankpin diameter	1·9368/1·9376in.
22.	Crankpin undersizes	(·002, bearing) ·010, ·020, ·030, ·040in.
23.	Connecting rod length	4·927/4·929in. (centres)
24.	Big-end bearings	Steel-backed, copper/lead, lead/bronze or aluminium/tin
25.	Big-end bearing clearance	·0002/·003in.
26.	Big-end side clearance	·004/·010in.
27.	Main journal diameter	Blue, 2·1253/57in.; red, 2·1257/61in.
28.	Main journal undersizes	(·002, bearing) ·010, ·020, ·030in.
29.	Main bearings	5; steel-backed copper-lead or lead-bronze
31.	Main bearing clearance	·0004/·0024in. [bronze
32.	Crankshaft end-float	·003/·011in.
33.	Crankshaft end-thrust on	Centre main bearing
34.	Camshaft journal diameter	1·5597/1·5605in.
35.	Camshaft bearings	3; steel-backed white metal
36.	Camshaft bearing cl'ance	·001/·0023in.
37.	Camshaft end-float	·0025/·0075in.
38.	Camshaft drive type	Chain (single); 46×0·375in. pitches
39.	Valve head diameter	In., 1·543/1·560in.; exhaust, 1·330/1·340in.
40.	Valve stem diameter	In., 0·3098/0·3105in.; exh., 0·3089/0·3096in.
41.	Valve seat angle	44° 30′ to 45° (in head)
42.	Valve lift	Inlet, 0·3556in.; exhaust, 0·3574in.
44.	Valve stem/guide cl'ance	In., ·0008/·0027in.; exh., ·0017/·0036in.
45.	Valve spring free length	1·48in.
46.	Valve spring rate	Length (closed), 1·263in. at 44/49lb.
47.	Valve working clearance	Inlet, ·012in.; exhaust, ·022in. (hot)
49.	Valve timing	Inlet opens 27° B.T.D.C.; closes 65° A.B.D.C. Exhaust opens 65° B.B.D.C.; closes 27° A.T.D.C.
50.	Petrol pump	A.C. mechanical
51.	Carburettor	Weber twin choke; ref. 761F-9510-BA
		1st 2nd
52.	Choke tube (Venturi)	23mm. 24mm.
52a.	Choke plate pull down	6·5mm. max.
53.	Main jet	120 115
63.	Float level	41·0±0·3mm. (1·61±0·01in.)
64.	Exhaust gas analysis	1·5%±0·25 CO

TRANSMISSION

#			
101.	Type	...	Rear wheel drive
102.	Clutch (mechanical)	7½in. diam., diaphragm type; free travel at lever, ⁱ⁄₁₆in. (1·6mm.)
103.	Gearbox	4 forward speeds, all synchromesh
105.	Gearbox ratios	1; 1·397; 2·010; 2·972; R., 3·324:1
107.	Driving axles	Semi-floating
108.	Final drive gear	Hypoid (Salisbury)
109.	Final drive ratio	4·1:1 (41/10)
111.	Crown wheel/pinion b'lash	·003 to ·006in.; shim adjustment
112.	Pinion bearing pre-load	8 to 12lb.in.; shim adjustment
113.	Differential brg. pre-load	·003 to ·005in.; shim adjustment

BRAKES

#			
201.	Front	...	Girling hydraulic, 11in. diam. discs
202.	Rear	...	Girling hydraulic, 9in. diam. drums
203.	Handbrake	...	Mechanical, on rear wheels
204.	Linings—front	...	Ferodo, type 14 calliper pads
205.	Linings—rear	...	Ferodo, 1·75in. wide

STEERING (see also "Dimensions")

#			
301.	Type	...	Worm and nut
302.	Camber angle	...	2°; non-adjustable
303.	Castor angle	...	4°; non-adjustable
304.	King-pin inclination	...	2°
305.	Toe-in	...	⅛ to ³⁄₁₆in. (3 to 5mm.) at wheel rim
306.	Conditions for checking	...	Unladen

FRONT SUSPENSION

#			
401.	Type	...	Independent, vertical coil springs
402.	Number of coils	...	21
403.	Coil diameter	...	2¼in. (external)
404.	Wire diameter	...	0·31in.
405.	Spring length—free	...	14¼in.
406.	Spring length—fitted	...	8½in.

REAR SUSPENSION

#			
501.	Type	...	Semi-elliptic leaf springs
504.	Spring length (centres)	...	42¾in. (free)
505.	Number of leaves	...	5
506.	Width of leaves	...	1¾in.
507.	Thickness of leaves	...	¼in.
508.	Spring camber—free	...	3⅝in.

ELECTRICAL SYSTEM

#			
601.	Ignition timing	...	10° B.T.D.C. at 800 r.p.m. (vac. pipe off); mark on pulley
602.	Sparking plugs	...	Motorcraft AGR12
603.	Sparking plug gap	...	·030in. (0·8mm.)
604.	Distributor	...	Motorcraft
605.	Contact breaker gap	...	·025in. (0·6mm.)
605a.	Dwell angle	...	48°·52°
606.	Centrif. advance starts at	−½°/−⅓° at 500 r.p.m.
607.	Centrif. advance—max.	10·75°/12·75° at 2000 r.p.m.
608.	Vacuum adv. starts at	1°/4° at 5in. Hg.
609.	Vacuum adv.—max.	5°/8° at 9in. Hg. (Distributor degrees and r.p.m.)
610.	Ignition coil	Oil-filled, low voltage; use with 1·5Ohm ballast resistor
611.	Battery	12V. 36A.h.
612.	Battery earth	Negative
613.	Alternator	Lucas 15ACR
615.	Starter motor	Lucas M35J or 5M90

CAPACITIES

#			
701.	Engine sump	—Total 6·74 pints (3·3 litres)
		—Refill 6 pints (3·4 litres) incl. filter
702.	Gearbox	1·97 pints (1·1 litres); refill, 1·7 (0·97)
703.	Differential	1·75 pints (1·0 litres)
704.	Cooling system	12 pints (6·8 litres)
705.	Fuel tank	8·5 gallons (38·6 litres)
706.	Tyre size	165×15
707.	Tyre pressures (lb./in.²)	Front, 18; rear, 19
708.	No. of grease gun points	12 (Front sliding axles have 'one-shot' lubrication; press foot plunger every 200 miles approx.)
709.	Normal servicing intervals	Greasing, 2000/2500 miles; engine oil change. 5000 miles
710.	Hydraulic fluid	Castrol Girling Universal

DIMENSIONS

#			
801.	Length overall	...	12ft. (3658mm.)
802.	Width overall	...	56in. (1422mm.)
803.	Height overall	...	51·75in. (1314mm.)
804.	Weight—2-seat Comp.	1460lb. (13cwt.) (662kg.)
	(dry) —4-seat	1516lb. (13·5cwt.) (688kg.)
805.	Ground cl'ance (min.)	7in. (178mm.)
806.	Track	47in. (1194mm.) front and rear
807.	Wheelbase	96in. (2438mm.)
808.	Turning circle diameter	32ft. (9·75m.)

TORQUE SPANNER DATA (lb.ft.)

#			#		
901.	Cylinder head nuts	65/70	907.	Final drive pinion bearing nut	95/100
902.	Big-end bearing nuts	30/35	908.	Crown wheel bolts	50/60
903.	Main bearing nuts	55/60	909.	Diff. bearing nuts	35/40
905.	Flywheel bolts	50/54	910.	Road wheel nuts	65/70
906.	Clutch to flyweel bolts	12/15			

BODY AND CHASSIS

#			
1001.	Type of construction	...	Coachbuilt; steel 'Z'-section chassis: ash body frame
1002.	Material of body panels	...	Steel and aluminium
1003.	Windscreen glass	...	Toughened (laminated optional extra)

4/4 1600 1978

Model: 2-seat Tourer

ENGINE (Rover)

1. Type ... ... 4-stroke V8 (cast-aluminium block); O.H.V.; central camshaft; hydraulic tappets
2. Cooling system ... Water pump, radiator (15lb./in.²), fan (electric) and thermostat
3. Number of cylinders ... 8 (dry liners)
4. Firing order and idling 1ʟ—8ʀ—4ʀ—3ʟ—6ʀ—5ʟ—7ʟ—2ʀ (No. speed 1 at front left); 725/775 r.p.m.
5. Bore ... ... 3·5in. (88·9mm.)
6. Stroke ... ... 2·8in. (71·12mm.)
7. Cubic capacity ... 3532cm.³
8. Compression ratio and 9·35:1; 135lb./in.² min. at 150/200 r.p.m. pressure
9. Brake horse-power (DIN) 155 at 5250 r.p.m.
10. Torque (DIN) ... ... 198lb.ft. at 2500 r.p.m.
11. Piston oversizes ... ·010, ·020in.
12. Piston clearance in bore ·0007/·0013in. (skirt bottom)
13. Piston rings—number ... 2 compression, 1 oil
14. Piston rings—width ... Compression, ·0615/·0625in.; oil (expander) 0·1894in. max.
15. Piston rings—groove cl'nce Compression, ·003/·005in.
16. Piston rings—gap (in bore) Compression, ·017/·022in.
17. Oil pressure (lb./in.²) ... 30/40 at 2400 r.p.m. (55 at 4000)
18. Gudgeon pin diameter ... 0·8746/0·8749in.
19. Gudgeon pin fit in piston ·0001/·0003in. clearance
20. Gudgeon pin fit in con. rod Press fit
21. Crankpin diameter ... 2·0000/2·0005in.
22. Crankpin undersizes ... ·010, ·020, ·030, ·040in.
23. Connecting rod length ... 5·662/5·658in. (centres)
24. Big-end bearings ... Vandervell, lead-indium
25. Big-end bearing clearance ·0007/·0027in.
26. Big-end side clearance ... ·005/·015in.
27. Main journal diameter ... 2·2992/2·2997in.
28. Main journal undersizes... ·010, ·020, ·030, ·040in.
29. Main bearings ... ... 5; Vandervell, lead-indium
30. Main bearings—length ... (1) (2) (4) (5), 0·797/0·807in.; (3), 1·056/1·058in.
31. Main bearing clearance ... ·0009/·0024in.
32. Crankshaft end-float ... ·004/·008in.
33. Crankshaft end-thrust on Centre main bearing
35. Camshaft bearings ... 5; steel-backed Babbitt
38. Camshaft drive type ... Chain; 54×0·375in. pitches
39. Valve head diameter ... Inlet, 1·565/1·575in.; exhaust, 1·3475/1·3575
40. Valve stem diameter ... Inlet (head) 0·3402/0·3412 to 0·3407/ (tapered) 0·3417in.; exhaust 0·3397/0·3407 to 0·3402/0·3412in.
42. Valve lift ... ... 0·39in. [0·3402/0·3412in.]
43. Valve guide length ... Fitted height, 19mm. above step surrounding valve guide boss
44. Valve stem/guide cl'nce... Inlet (top), ·001/·003; (bottom), ·0015/·0035. Exhaust (top), ·0015/·0035; (bottom), ·002/·004in.
46. Valve spring loaded length 1·577in. at 70±3·5lb.; 1·350in. at 130 ±6·5lb.; 1·187in. at 176±7·5lb.
49. Valve timing Inlet opens 30° B.T.D.C. } peak, 112·5° Inlet closes 75° A.B.D.C. } A.T.D.C. Exhaust opens 63° B.B.D.C. } peak, 105·5° Exhaust closes 37° A.T.D.C. } B.T.D.C.
50. Petrol pump ... ... Electric
52. Carburettors ... ... 2 S.U. type HIF6
53. Needle ... ... BAK
56. Piston spring ... ... Yellow
63. Float level ... ... ·020/·060in. (0·5/1·5mm.)
64. Exhaust gas analysis ... 2%/4·5% CO

TRANSMISSION

101. Type ... ... Rear wheel drive
102. Clutch (hydraulic) ... Borg & Beck, 9·5in.diam., single dry plate, diaphragm spring, free travel at lever, ₁/₁₆in. (1·6mm.)
103. Gearbox ... ... 5 forward speeds, all synchromesh
105. Gearbox ratios ... ... 0·833; 1; 1·396; 2·087; 3·321; R., 3·428:1
106. Overdrive ... ... Not fitted
107. Driving axles ... ... Semi-floating
108. Final drive gear ... Hypoid, limited-slip differential
109. Final drive ratio ... 3·31:1
111. Crown wheel/pinion b'lash 0·003/0·006in.; shim adjustment
112. Pinion bearing pre-load 8/12lb.in.
113. Differential brg. pre-load ·003/·005in.; shim adjustment

BRAKES

201. Front ... ... Girling hydraulic, 11in. diam. discs
202. Rear ... ... Girling hydraulic, 9in. diam. drums
203. Handbrake ... ... Mechanical, on rear wheels
204. Linings—front ... ... Ferodo, type GX
205. Linings—rear ... ... Ferodo, type LL, 1¾in. wide
206. Power assistance ... Girling servo (twin on L.H. drive cars)

STEERING (see also "Dimensions")

301. Type ... ... Worm and nut
302. Camber angle ... ... 2°, non-adjustable
303. Castor angle ... ... 4°, non-adjustable
304. King-pin inclination ... 2°
305. Toe-in ... ... ₁/₈/₃/₁₆in. (3/5mm.) at wheel rims
306. Conditions for checking... Unladen

FRONT SUSPENSION

401. Type ... ... Independent, vertical coil springs
402. Number of coils 18
403. Coil diameter ... ... 2¾in. (external)
404. Wire diameter ... ... 0·375in.
405. Spring length—free ... 13in.
506. Spring length—fitted ... 9in.

REAR SUSPENSION

501. Type ... ... Semi-elliptic leaf-springs
504. Spring length ... ... 42¾in. (free)
505. Number of leaves ... 6
506. Width of leaves ... ... 1¾in.
507. Thickness of leaves ... ¼in.
508. Spring camber—free ... 3½in.

ELECTRICAL SYSTEM

601. Ignition timing —static 6° BTDC (pulley) —stroboscope 10° at 1200 r.p.m.; 17° at 1800; 22° at 2600; vac. hose off
602. Sparking plugs ... ... Champion N12Y
603. Sparking plug gap ... ·030in.
604. Distributor ... ... Lucas 35DE8 (electronic)
605. Pick-up air gap ... ... ·014/·016in. (0·36/0·40mm.)
606. Centrifugal advance ... 0° at 300 r.p.m.; 1°/3° at 600; 4·5°/7° at 900; 7°/9° at 1300; 9·5°/11·5° at 2200; 10°/12° at 2800
608. Vacuum advance 0°/0·5° at 0in.Hg.; 0°/3° at 4·3in.; 6°/9° at 10in.; 7°/9° at 20in. Distributor degrees and r.p.m.
610. Ignition coil ... ... Lucas 22C12; 9BR ballast resistor
611. Battery ... ... 12V. 57A.h.
612. Battery earth ... ... Negative
613. Alternator ... ... Lucas 18ACR, 43 amp.
614. Regulator ... ... Integral with alternator
615. Starter motor ... ... Lucas 3M100, pre-engaged; lock, 16·5 lb.ft. at 545A.

CAPACITIES

701. Engine oil—Total ... 9·5 pints (5·4 litres) incl. filter —Drain/Refill 8·25 pints (4·7 litres)
702. Gearbox (dry) ... ... 2·7 pints (1·5 litres)
703. Differential ... ... 2·5 pints (1·4 litres)
704. Cooling system ... ... 15 pints (8·5 litres)
705. Fuel tank ... ... 14 gallons (64 litres)
706. Tyre size 195VR14
707. Tyre pressures —Front 18 (fast driving, 22) (lb./in.²) —Rear 18 (fast driving, 22)
708. No. of grease gun points 12
709. Servicing intervals ... Greasing, 3000 miles; engine oil change 5000 miles
710. Hydraulic fluid ... ... Castrol/Girling Universal

DIMENSIONS

801. Length overall 12ft. 8in. (3861mm.)
802. Width overall 60in. (1524mm.)
803. Height overall 50in. (1270mm.)
804. Weight (dry) ... ... 1884lb. (16·8cwt.) (855kg.) approx.
805. Ground clearance ... 6in. (152mm.) unladen (sump)
806. Track —Front 52in. (1321mm.) —Rear 53in. (1346mm.)
807. Wheelbase 98in. (2489mm.)
808. Turning circle diameter... 38ft (11·6mm.)

TORQUE SPANNER DATA (lb.ft.)

901. Cylinder head bolts ... 65/70 (3·8in. and 2·6in. bolts) — 40/50 (2·16in. bolts)
902. Big-end bearing bolts ... 30/35
903. Main bearing bolts ... 50/55 —Rear 65/70
905. Flywheel bolts 50/60
906. Clutch to flywheel bolts... 20
907. Drive pinion bearing nut 95/100
908. Crown wheel bolts ... 50/60
909. Differential bearing nuts 35/40
910. Road wheel nuts... ... 65/70
911. Steering wheel nut ... 40

BODY AND CHASSIS

1001. Type of construction ... Steel 'Z'-section chassis
1002. Material of body panels... Steel and aluminium
1003. Type of glass ... ... Windscreen laminated

Plus 8 1978

165

Models: 4-seat Tourer and 2-seat Competition model

ENGINE (Ford 1600GT)

1.	Type	4-stroke; overhead valves; side camshaft
2.	Cooling system ...	Water pump, radiator, fan and thermostat
3.	Number of cylinders ...	4 (bored direct in block)
4.	Firing order ...	1—2—4—3 (No. 1 at front)
4a.	Idling speed ...	800±20 r.p.m.; fast idle, 1900±100 r.p.m.
5.	Bore	3·1881in. (80·977mm.) mean grade
6.	Stroke	3·056in. (77·62mm.)
7.	Cubic capacity ...	1598cm.³
8.	Compression ratio and pressure	9:1; 188lb./in.² at 300 r.p.m.
9.	Brake horse-power (DIN)	84 at 5500 r.p.m.
10.	Torque (DIN) ...	92lb.ft. at 4000 r.p.m.
11.	Piston oversizes ...	·0025, ·015, ·030in.
12.	Piston clearance in bore ...	·0009/·0016in.
13.	Piston rings—number ...	2 compression, 1 oil
14.	Piston rings—width ...	Comp., ·077/·078in.; oil, 0·155/0·156in.
15.	Piston rings—groove cl'nce	Comp., ·0016/·0036in.; oil, ·0018/·0038 [in.
16.	Piston rings—gap (in bore)	·009/·014in.
17.	Oil pressure (minimum)	8·5lb./in.² at 700 r.p.m.; 21lb./in.² at 2000 r.p.m.
18.	Gudgeon pin diameter ...	0·8119/0·8123in. (in 4 grades)
19.	Gudgeon pin fit in piston	Interference, selective (heated piston)
20.	Gudgeon pin fit in con. rod	·0002/·0004in. clearance (selective)
21.	Crankpin diameter ...	1·9368/1·9376in.
22.	Crankpin undersizes ...	(·002, bearing) ·010, ·020, ·030, ·040in.
23.	Connecting rod length ...	4·927/4·929in. (centres)
24.	Big-end bearings	Steel-backed, copper/lead, lead/bronze or aluminium/tin
25.	Big-end bearing clearance	·0002/·003in.
26.	Big-end side clearance ...	·004/·010in.
27.	Main journal diameter ...	Blue, 2·1253/57in.; red, 2·1257/61in.
28.	Main journal undersizes ...	(·002, bearing) ·010, ·020, ·030in.
29.	Main bearings ...	5; steel-backed copper-lead or lead- [bronze
31.	Main bearing clearance ...	·0004/·0024in.
32.	Crankshaft end-float ...	·003/·011in.
33.	Crankshaft end-thrust on	Centre main bearing
34.	Camshaft journal diameter	1·5597/1·5605in.
35.	Camshaft bearings ...	3; steel-backed white metal
36.	Camshaft bearing cl'ance	·001/·0023in.
37.	Camshaft end-float ...	·0025/·0075in.
38.	Camshaft drive type ...	Chain (single); 46×0·375in. pitches
39.	Valve head diameter ...	Inlet, 1·543/1·560in.; exhaust, 1·330/1·340in.
40.	Valve stem diameter ...	In., 0·3098/0·3105in.; exh., 0·3089/0·3096in.
41.	Valve seat angle ...	44° 30′ to 45° (in head)
42.	Valve lift	Inlet, 0·3556in.; exhaust, 0·3574in.
44.	Valve stem/guide cl'ance	In., ·0008/·0027in.; exh., ·0017/·0036in.
45.	Valve spring free length ...	1·48in.
46.	Valve spring rate...	Length (closed), 1·263in. at 44/49lb.
47.	Valve working clearance	Inlet, ·012in.; exhaust, ·022in. (hot)
49.	Valve timing ...	27°BT—65°AB—65°BB—27°AT
50.	Petrol pump ...	A.C. mechanical
51.	Carburettor ...	Weber twin choke; ref. 761F-9510-BA

	1st	2nd
52. Choke tube (Venturi) ...	23mm.	24mm.
52a. Choke plate pull down ...	6·5mm. max.	
53. Main jet	120	115
63. Float level ...	41·0±0·3mm. (1·61±0·01in.)	
64. Exhaust gas analysis ...	1·5%±0·25 CO	

TRANSMISSION

101.	Type	Rear wheel drive
102.	Clutch (mechanical) ...	7½in. diam., diaphragm type; free travel at lever, 1/16in. (1·6mm.)
103.	Gearbox ...	4 forward speeds, all synchromesh
105.	Gearbox ratios ...	1; 1·397; 2·010; 2·972; R., 3·324:1
107.	Driving axles ...	Semi-floating
108.	Final drive gear ...	Hypoid (Salisbury)
109.	Final drive ratio ...	4·1:1 (41/10)
111.	Crown wheel/pinion b'lash	·003 to ·006in.; shim adjustment
112.	Pinion bearing pre-load ...	8/12lb.in.; shim adjustment
113.	Differential brg. pre-load ...	·003/·005in.; shim adjustment

BRAKES

201.	Front	Girling hydraulic, 11in. diam. discs
202.	Rear	Girling hydraulic, 9in. diam. drums
203.	Handbrake ...	Mechanical, on rear wheels
204.	Linings—front ...	Ferodo, type 14 calliper pads
205.	Linings—rear ...	Ferodo, 1·75in. wide

STEERING (see also "Dimensions)

301.	Type	Worm and nut
302.	Camber angle ...	2°; non-adjustable
303.	Castor angle ...	4°; non-adjustable
304.	King-pin inclination ...	2°
305.	Toe-in ...	⅛ to 3/16in. (3 to 5mm.) at wheel rim
306.	Conditions for checking ...	Unladen

FRONT SUSPENSION

401.	Type	Independent, vertical coil springs
402.	Number of coils ...	21
403.	Coil diameter ...	2¼in. (external)
404.	Wire diameter ...	0·31in.
405.	Spring length—free ...	14¼in.
406.	Spring length—fitted ...	8½in.

REAR SUSPENSION

501.	Type	Semi-elliptic leaf springs
504.	Spring length (centres) ...	42¾in. (free)
505.	Number of leaves ...	5
506.	Width of leaves ...	1¾in.
507.	Thickness of leaves ...	¼in.
508.	Spring camber—free ...	3⅜in.

ELECTRICAL SYSTEM

601.	Ignition timing ...	10° B.T.D.C. at 800 r.p.m. (vac. pipe off); mark on pulley
602.	Sparking plugs ...	Motorcraft AGR12
603.	Sparking plug gap ...	·030in. (0·8mm.)
604.	Distributor ...	Motorcraft
605.	Contact breaker gap ...	·025in. (0·6mm.)
605a.	Dwell angle ...	48°/52°
606.	Centrif. advance starts at ...	−½°/+½° at 500 r.p.m.
607.	Centrif. advance—max. ...	10·75°/12·75° at 2000 r.p.m.
608.	Vacuum adv. starts at ...	1°/4° at 5in. Hg.
609.	Vacuum adv.—max. ...	5°/8° at 9in. Hg. (Distributor degrees and r.p.m.)
610.	Ignition coil ...	Oil-filled, low voltage; use with 1·50hm ballast resistor
611.	Battery	12V. 36A.h.
612.	Battery earth ...	Negative
613.	Alternator ...	Lucas 15ACR
615.	Starter motor ...	Lucas M35J or 5M90

CAPACITIES

701.	Engine sump	—Total 6·74 pints (3·8 litres) —Refill 6 pints (3·4 litres) incl. filter
702.	Gearbox ...	1·97 pints (1·1 litres); refill, 1·7 (0·97)
703.	Differential ...	1·75 pints (1·0 litres)
704.	Cooling system ...	12 pints (6·8 litres)
705.	Fuel tank ...	8·5 gallons (38·6 litres)
706.	Tyre size ...	165×15
707.	Tyre pressures (lb./in.²) ...	Front, 18; rear, 19
708.	No. of grease gun points ...	12 (Front sliding axles have 'one-shot' lubrication; press foot plunger every 200 miles approx.)
709.	Normal servicing intervals	Greasing, 2000/2500 miles; engine oil change, 5000 miles
710.	Hydraulic fluid ...	Castrol/Girling Universal

DIMENSIONS

801.	Length overall ...	12ft. (3658mm.)
802.	Width overall ...	56in. (1422mm.)
803.	Height overall ...	51·75in. (1314mm.)
804.	Weight—2-seat Comp. ...	1460lb. (13cwt.) (662kg.) —4-seat 1516lb. (13·5cwt.) (688kg.)
805.	Ground cl'ance (min.) ...	7in. (178mm.)
806.	Track ...	47in. (1194mm.) front and rear
807.	Wheelbase ...	96in. (2438mm.)
808.	Turning circle diameter...	32ft. (9·75m.)

TORQUE SPANNER DATA (lb.ft.)

901.	Cylinder head nuts ...	65/70	907.	Final drive pinion	
902.	Big-end bearing nuts ...	30/35		bearing nut	95/100
903.	Main bearing nuts ...	55/60	908.	Crown wheel bolts	50/60
905.	Flywheel bolts ...	50/54	909.	Diff. bearing nuts	35/40
906.	Clutch to flywheel bolts ...	12/15	910.	Road wheel nuts	65/70

BODY AND CHASSIS

1001.	Type of construction ...	Coachbuilt; steel 'Z'-section chassis; ash body frame
1002.	Material of body panels ...	Steel and aluminium
1003.	Windscreen glass ...	Toughened (laminated optional extra)

4/4 1600 1979

Model: 2-seat Tourer

ENGINE (Rover)

1.	Type	4-stroke V8 (cast-aluminium block); O.H.V.; central camshaft; hydraulic tappets
2.	Cooling system	Water pump, radiator (15lb./in.²), fan (electric) and thermostat
3.	Number of cylinders ...	8 (dry liners)
4.	Firing order and idling speed	1L—8R—4R—3L—6R—5L—7L—2R (No. 1 at front left); 725/775 r.p.m.
5.	Bore	3·5in. (88·9mm.)
6.	Stroke	2·8in. (71·12mm.)
7.	Cubic capacity	3532cm.³
8.	Compression ratio and pressure	9·35:1; 135lb./in.² min. at 150/200 r.p.m.
9.	Brake horse-power (DIN)	155 at 5250 r.p.m.
10.	Torque (DIN)	198lb.ft. at 2500 r.p.m.
11.	Piston oversizes	·010, ·020in.
12.	Piston clearance in bore ...	·0007/·0013in. (skirt bottom)
13.	Piston rings—number ...	2 compression, 1 oil
14.	Piston rings—width ...	Compression, ·0615/·0625in.; oil (expander) 0·1894in. max.
15.	Piston rings—groove cl'nce	Compression, ·003/·005in.
16.	Piston rings—gap (in bore)	Compression, ·017/·022in.
17.	Oil pressure (lb./in.²) ...	30/40 at 2400 r.p.m. (55 at 4000)
18.	Gudgeon pin diameter ...	0·8746/0·8749in.
19.	Gudgeon pin fit in piston	·0001/·0003in. clearance
20.	Gudgeon pin fit in con. rod	Press fit
21.	Crankpin diameter ...	2·0000/2·0005in.
22.	Crankpin undersizes ...	·010, ·020, ·030, ·040in.
23.	Connecting rod length ...	5·662/5·658in. (centres)
24.	Big-end bearings ...	Vandervell, lead-indium
25.	Big-end bearing clearance	·0007/·0027in.
26.	Big-end side clearance ...	·005/·015in.
27.	Main journal diameter ...	2·2992/2·2997in.
28.	Main journal undersizes...	·010, ·020, ·030, ·040in.
29.	Main bearings	5; Vandervell, lead-indium
30.	Main bearings—length ...	(1) (2) (4) (5), 0·797/0·807in.; (3), [1·056/1·058in.
31.	Main bearing clearance ...	·0009/·0024in.
32.	Crankshaft end-float ...	·004/·008in.
33.	Crankshaft end-thrust on	Centre main bearing
35.	Camshaft bearings ...	5; steel-backed Babbitt
38.	Camshaft drive type ...	Chain; 54×0·375in. pitches
39.	Valve head diameter ...	Inlet, 1·565/1·575in.; exhaust, 1·3475/1·3575
40.	Valve stem diameter (tapered)	Inlet (head) 0·3402/0·3412 to 0·3407/0·3417in.; exhaust, 0·3397/0·3407 to [C·3402/0·3412in.
42.	Valve lift	0·39in.
43.	Valve guide length ...	Fitted height, 19mm. above step surrounding valve guide boss
44.	Valve stem/guide cl'nce...	Inlet (top), ·001/·003; (bottom), ·0015/·0035. Exhaust (top), ·0015/·0035; (bottom), ·002/·004in.
46.	Valve spring loaded length	1·577in. at 70±3·5lb.; 1·350in. at 130±6·5lb.; 1·187in. at 176±7·5lb.
49.	Valve timing Inlet opens	30° B.T.D.C. } peak, 112·5°
	Inlet closes	75° A.B.D.C. } A.T.D.C.
	Exhaust opens	68° B.B.D.C. } peak, 105·5°
	Exhaust closes	37° A.T.D.C. } B.T.D.C
50.	Petrol pump	Electric
52.	Carburettors	2 S.U. type HIF6
53.	Needle	BAK
56.	Piston spring	Yellow
63.	Float level	·020/·060in. (0·5/1·5mm.)
64.	Exhaust gas analysis ...	2%/4·5% CO

TRANSMISSION

101.	Type	Rear wheel drive
102.	Clutch (hydraulic) ...	Borg & Beck, 9·5in.diam., single dry plate, diaphragm spring, free travel at lever, 1/16in. (1·6mm.)
103.	Gearbox	5 forward speeds, all synchromesh
105.	Gearbox ratios	0·833; 1; 1·396; 2·087; 3·321; R., [3·428:1
106.	Overdrive	Not fitted
107.	Driving axles	Semi-floating
108.	Final drive gear	Hypoid, limited-slip differential
109.	Final drive ratio ...	3·31:1
111.	Crown wheel/pinion b'lash	0·003/0·006in.; shim adjustment
112.	Pinion bearing pre-load	8/12lb.in.
113.	Differential brg. pre-load	·003/·005in.; shim adjustment

BRAKES

201.	Front	Girling hydraulic, 11in. diam discs
202.	Rear	Girling hydraulic, 9in. diam drums
203.	Handbrake	Mechanical, on rear wheels
204.	Linings—front	Ferodo, type GX
205.	Linings—rear	Ferodo, type LL, 1¾in. wide
206.	Power assistance ...	Girling servo (twin on L.H. drive cars)

STEERING (see also "Dimensions")

301.	Type	Worm and nut
302.	Camber angle	2°, non-adjustable
303.	Castor angle	4°, non-adjustable
304.	King-pin inclination ...	2°
305.	Toe-in	1/8/3/16in. (3/5mm.) at wheel rims
306.	Conditions for checking...	Unladen

FRONT SUSPENSION

401.	Type	Independent, vertical coil springs
402.	Number of coils	18
403.	Coil diameter	2⅜in. (external)
404.	Wire diameter	0·375in.
405.	Spring length—free ...	13in.
506.	Spring length—fitted ...	9in.

REAR SUSPENSION

501.	Type	Semi-elliptic leaf-springs
504.	Spring length	42⅞in. (free)
505.	Number of leaves ...	6
506.	Width of leaves	1⅜in.
507.	Thickness of leaves ...	¼in.
508.	Spring camber—free ...	3½in.

ELECTRICAL SYSTEM

601.	Ignition timing —static	6° BTDC (pulley)
	—stroboscope	10° at 1200 r.p.m.; 17° at 1800; 22° at 2600; vac. hose off
602.	Sparking plugs	Champion N12Y
603.	Sparking plug gap ...	·030in.
604.	Distributor	Lucas 35DE8 (electronic)
605.	Pick-up air gap	·014/·016in. (0·36/0·40mm.)
606.	Centrifugal advance ...	0° at 300 r.p.m.; 1°/3° at 600; 4·5°/7° at 900; 7°/9° at 1300; 9·5°/11·5° at 2200; 10°/12° at 2800
608.	Vacuum advance ...	0°/0·5° at 0in.Hg., 0°/3° at 4·3in.; 6°/9° at 10in.; 7°/9° at 20in. Distributor degrees and r.p.m.
610.	Ignition coil	Lucas 22C12; 9BR ballast resistor
611.	Battery	12V. 57A.h.
612.	Battery earth	Negative
613.	Alternator	Lucas 18ACR, 43 amp.
614.	Regulator	Integral with alternator
615.	Starter motor	Lucas 3M100, pre-engaged; lock, 16·5 lb.ft. at 545A.

CAPACITIES

701.	Engine oil—Total ...	9·5 pints (5·4 litres) incl. filter
	—Drain/Refill	8·25 pints (4·7 litres)
702.	Gearbox (dry)	2·7 pints (1·5 litres)
703.	Differential	2·5 pints (1·4 litres)
704.	Cooling system	15 pints (8·5 litres)
705.	Fuel tank	14 gallons (64 litres)
706.	Tyre size	195VR14
707.	Tyre pressures —Front	18 (fast driving, 22)
	(lb./in.²) —Rear	18 (fast driving, 22)
708.	No. of grease gun points	12
709.	Servicing intervals ...	Greasing, 3000 miles; engine oil change, 5000 miles
710.	Hydraulic fluid	Castrol/Girling Universal

DIMENSIONS

801.	Length overall	12ft. 8in. (3861mm.)
802.	Width overall	60in. (1524mm.)
803.	Height overall	50in. (1270mm.)
804.	Weight (dry)	1884lb. (16·8cwt.) (855kg.) approx.
805.	Ground clearance ...	6in. (152mm.) unladen (sump)
806.	Track ... —Front	52in. (1321mm.)
	—Rear	53in. (1346mm.)
807.	Wheelbase	98in. (2489mm.)
808.	Turning circle diameter...	38ft (11·6mm.)

TORQUE SPANNER DATA (lb.ft.)

901.	Cylinder head bolts —	65/70 (3·8in. and 2·6in. bolts)
	—	40/50 (2·16in. bolts)
902.	Big-end bearing bolts ...	30/35
903.	Main bearing bolts ...	50/55
	—Rear ...	65/70
905.	Flywheel bolts	50/60
906.	Clutch to flywheel bolts...	20
907.	Drive pinion bearing nut	95/100
908.	Crown wheel bolts ...	50/60
909.	Differential bearing nuts	35/40
910.	Road wheel nuts... ..	65/70
911.	Steering wheel nut ..	40

BODY AND CHASSIS

1001.	Type of construction ...	Steel 'Z'-section chassis
1002.	Material of body panels..	Steel and aluminium
1003.	Type of glass . ..	Windscreen laminated

Plus 8 1979

Models: 4-seat Tourer and 2-seat Competition model

ENGINE (Ford 1600GT)

1.	Type	4-stroke; overhead valves; side camshaft
2.	Cooling system ...	Water pump, radiator, fan and thermostat
3.	Number of cylinders	4 (bored direct in block)
4.	Firing order	1—2—4—3 (No. 1 at front)
4a.	Idling speed	800±20 r.p.m.; fast idle, 1900±100 r.p.m
5.	Bore	3·188 lin. (80·977mm.) mean grade
6.	Stroke	3·056in. (77·62mm.)
7.	Cubic capacity ...	1598cm.³
8.	Compression ratio and pressure	9:1; 188lb./in.² at 300 r.p.m.
9.	Brake horse-power (DIN)	84 at 5500 r.p.m.
10.	Torque (DIN)	92lb.ft. at 4000 r.p.m.
11.	Piston oversizes ...	·0025, ·015, ·030in.
12.	Piston clearance in bore ...	·0009/·0016in.
13.	Piston rings—number ...	2 compression, 1 oil
14.	Piston rings—width ...	Comp., ·077/·078in.; oil, 0·155/0·156in.
15.	Piston rings—groove cl'nce	Comp., ·0016/·0036in.; oil, ·0018/·0038
16.	Piston rings—gap (in bore)	·009/·014in. [in.
17.	Oil pressure (minimum)...	8·5lb./in.² at 700 r.p.m.; 21lb./in.² at 2000 r.p.m.
18.	Gudgeon pin diameter ...	0·8119/0·8123in. (in 4 grades)
19.	Gudgeon pin fit in piston...	Interference, selective (heated piston)
20.	Gudgeon pin fit in con.rod	·0002/·0004in. clearance (selective)
21.	Crankpin diameter ...	1·9368/1·9376in.
22.	Crankpin undersizes ...	(·002, bearing) ·010, ·020, ·030, ·040in.
23.	Connecting rod length ...	4·927/4·929in. (centres)
24.	Big-end bearings ...	Steel-backed, copper/lead, lead/bronze or aluminium/tin
25.	Big-end bearing clearance	·0002/·003in.
26.	Big-end side clearance ...	·004/·010in.
27.	Main journal diameter ...	Blue, 2·1253/57in.; red, 2·1257/61in.
28.	Main journal undersizes...	(·002, bearing) ·010, ·020, ·030in.
29.	Main bearings	5; steel-backed copper-lead or lead-bronze [bronze
31.	Main bearing clearance ...	·0004/·0024in.
32.	Crankshaft end-float ...	·003/·011in.
33.	Crankshaft end-thrust on	Centre main bearing
34.	Camshaft journal diameter	1·5597/1·5605in.
35.	Camshaft bearings ...	3; steel-backed white metal
36.	Camshaft bearing cl'nce ...	·001/·0023in.
37.	Camshaft end-float ...	·0025/·0075in.
38.	Camshaft drive type ...	Chain (single); 46×0·375in. pitches
39.	Valve head diameter ...	Inlet, 1·543/1·560in.; exhaust, 1·330/ 1·340in.
40.	Valve stem diameter ...	In., 0·3098/0·3105in.; exh., 0·3089/ 0·3096in.
41.	Valve seat angle	44° 30' to 45° (in head)
42.	Valve lift	Inlet, 0·3556in.; exhaust, 0·3574in.
44.	Valve stem/guide c'lance	In., ·0008/·0027in.; exh., ·0017/·0036in.
45.	Valve spring free length ...	1·48in.
46.	Valve spring rate... ...	Length (closed), 1·263in. at 44/49lb.
47.	Valve working clearance	Inlet, ·012in.; exhaust, ·022in. (hot)
49.	Valve timing	27°BT—65°AB—65°BB—27°AT
50.	Petrol pump	A.C. mechanical
51.	Carburettor	Weber twin choke; ref. 761F-9510-BA

		1st	2nd
52.	Choke tube (Venturi) ...	23mm.	24mm.
52a.	Choke plate pull down ...	6·5mm. max.	
53.	Main jet	120	115
63.	Float level	41·0±0·3mm. (1·61±0·01in.)	
64.	Exhaust gas analysis ...	1·5%±0·25 CO	

TRANSMISSION

101.	Type	Rear wheel drive
102.	Clutch (cable op.) ...	7½in. diam., diaphragm type; free travel at lever, 1/16in. (1·6mm.)
103.	Gearbox	4 forward speeds, all synchromesh
105.	Gearbox ratios ...	1; 1·397; 2·010; 2·972; R., 3·324:1
107.	Driving axles	Semi-floating
108.	Final drive gear ...	Hypoid (Salisbury)
109.	Final drive ratio ...	4·1:1 (41/10)
111.	Crown wheel/pinion b'lash	·003/·006in.; shim adjustment
112.	Pinion bearing pre-load ...	8/12lb.in.; shim adjustment
113.	Differential brg. pre-load	·003/·005in.; shim adjustment

BRAKES

201.	Front	Girling hydraulic, 11in. diam. discs
202.	Rear	Girling hydraulic, 9in. diam. drums
203.	Handbrake	Mechanical, on rear wheels
204.	Linings—front ...	Ferodo, type 14 calliper pads
205.	Linings—rear ...	Ferodo, 1·75in. wide

STEERING (see also "Dimensions")

301.	Type	Worm and nut
302.	Camber angle	2°; non-adjustable
303.	Castor angle	4°; non-adjustable
304.	King-pin inclination ...	2°
305.	Toe-in	1/8 to 3/16in. (3 to 5mm.) at wheel rim
306.	Condition for checking ...	Unladen

FRONT SUSPENSION

401.	Type	Independent, vertical coil springs
402.	Number of coils ...	21
403.	Coil diameter	2⅛in. (external)
404.	Wire diameter	0·31in.
405.	Spring length—free ...	14½in.
406.	Spring length—fitted ...	8¾in.

REAR SUSPENSION

501.	Type	Semi-elliptic leaf springs
504.	Spring length (centres) ...	42¾in. (free)
505.	Number of leaves ...	5
506.	Width of leaves ...	1¾in.
507.	Thickness of leaves ...	¼in.
508.	Spring camber—free ...	3⅝in.

ELECTRICAL SYSTEM

601.	Ignition timing	10° B.T.D.C. at 800 r.p.m. (vac. pipe off); mark on pulley
602.	Sparking plugs ...	Motorcraft AGR12
603.	Sparking plug gap ...	·030in. (0·8mm.)
604.	Distributor	Motorcraft
605.	Contact breaker gap ...	·025in. (0·6mm.)
605a.	Dwell angle	48°/52°
606.	Centrif. advance starts at	−⅓+⅓° at 500 r.p.m.
607.	Centrif. advance—max. ...	10·75°/12·75° at 2000 r.p.m.
608.	Vacuum adv. starts at ...	1°/4° at 5in.Hg.
609.	Vacuum adv.—max. ...	5°/8° at 9in.Hg. (Distributor degrees and r.p.m.)
610.	Ignition coil	Oil-filled, low voltage; use with 1·5Ohm ballast resistor
611.	Battery	12V. 36A.h.
612.	Battery earth	Negative
613.	Alternator	Lucas 15ACR
615.	Starter motor	Lucas M35J or 5M90

CAPACITIES

701.	Engine sump —Total	6·74 pints (3·8 litres)
	—Refill	6 pints (3·4 litres) incl. filter
702.	Gearbox	1·97 pints (1·1 litres); refill, 1·7 (0·97)
703.	Differential	1·75 pints (1·0 litres)
704.	Cooling system ...	12 pints (6·8 litres)
705.	Fuel tank	8·5 gallons (38·6 litres)
706.	Tyre size	165×15
707.	Tyre pressures —Front	18 (1·24)
	lb./in.² (bars) —Rear	19 (1·31)
708.	No. of grease gun points ...	12 (Front sliding axles have 'one-shot' lubrication; press foot plunger every 200 miles approx.)
709.	Normal servicing intervals	Greasing, 2000/2500 miles; engine oil change, 5000 miles
710.	Hydraulic fluid	Castrol/Girling Universal

DIMENSIONS

801.	Length overall ...	12ft. (3658mm.)
802.	Width overall ...	56in. (1422mm.)
803.	Height overall ...	51·75in. (1314mm.)
804.	Weight (dry) —2-seat	1460lb. or 13cwt. (662kg.)
	—4-seat	1516lb. or 13·5cwt. (688kg.)
805.	Ground cl'nce (unladen)	7in. (178mm.)
806.	Track	47in. (1194mm.) front and rear
807.	Wheelbase	96in. (2438mm.)
808.	Turning circle diameter ...	32ft. (9·75m.)

TORQUE SPANNER DATA (lb.ft.)

901.	Cylinder head nuts ...	65/70	907. Drive pinion bearing nut	95/100
902.	Big-end bearing nuts ...	30/35	908. Crown wheel bolts	50/60
903.	Main bearing nuts ...	55/60	909. Diff. bearing nuts	35/40
905.	Flywheel bolts ...	50/54	910. Road wheel nuts	65/70
906.	Clutch to flywheel bolts ...	12/15		

BODY AND CHASSIS

1001.	Type of construction ...	Coachbuilt; steel 'Z'-section chassis; ash body frame
1002.	Material of body panels ...	Steel and aluminium
1003.	Windscreen glass... ...	Toughened (laminated optional extra)

4/4 1600 1980

Model: "2-seat Tourer"

ENGINE (Rover)

1.	Type	4-stroke V8 (cast-aluminium block); O.H.V.; central camshaft; hydraulic tappets
2.	Cooling system ...	Water pump, radiator (15lb./in.²), fan (electric) and thermostat
3.	Number of cylinders ...	8 (dry liners)
4.	Firing order and idling speed	1L—8R—4R—3L—6R—5L—7L—2R (No. 1 at front left); 725/775 r.p.m.
5.	Bore	3·5in. (88·9mm.)
6.	Stroke	2·8in. (71·12mm.)
7.	Cubic capacity ...	3532cm.³
8.	Compression ratio and pressure	9·35:1; 135lb./in.² min. at 150/200 r.p.m.
9.	Brake horse-power (DIN)	155 at 5250 r.p.m.
10.	Torque (DIN) ...	198lb.ft. at 2500 r.p.m.
11.	Piston oversizes ...	·010, ·020in.
12.	Piston clearance in bore ...	·0007/·0013in. (skirt bottom)
13.	Piston rings—number ...	2 compression, 1 oil
14.	Piston rings—width ...	Compression, ·0615/·0625in.; oil (expander) 0·1894in. max.
15.	Piston rings—groove cl'nce	Compression, ·003/·005in.
16.	Piston rings—gap (in bore)	Compression, ·017/·022in.
17.	Oil pressure (lb./in.²) ...	30/40 at 2400 r.p.m. (55 at 4000)
18.	Gudgeon pin diameter ...	0·8746/0·8749in.
19.	Gudgeon pin fit in piston	·0001/·0003in. clearance
20.	Gudgeon pin fit in con. rod	Press fit
21.	Crankpin diameter ...	2·0000/2·0005in.
22.	Crankpin undersizes ...	·010, ·020, ·030, ·040in.
23.	Connecting rod length ...	5·662/5·658in. (centres)
24.	Big-end bearings ...	Vandervell, lead-indium
25.	Big-end bearing clearance	·0007/·0027in.
26.	Big-end side clearance ...	·005/·015in.
27.	Main journal diameter ...	2·2992/2·2997in.
28.	Main journal undersizes ...	·010, ·020, ·030, ·040in.
29.	Main bearings	5; Vandervell, lead-indium
30.	Main bearings—length ...	(1) (2) (4) (5), 0·797/0·807in.; (3)
31.	Main bearing clearance ...	·0009/·0024in. [1·056/1·058in.
32.	Crankshaft end-float ...	·004/·008in.
33.	Crankshaft end-thrust on	Centre main bearing
35.	Camshaft bearings ...	5; steel-backed Babbitt
38.	Camshaft drive type ...	Chain; 54×0·375in. pitches
39.	Valve head diameter ...	Inlet, 1·565/1·575in.; exhaust, 1·3475/ 1·3575
40.	Valve stem diameter (tapered)	Inlet (head) 0·3402/0·3412 to 0·3407/ 0·3417in.; exhaust, 0·3397/0·3407 to
42.	Valve lift	0·39in. [0·3402/0·3412in.
43.	Valve guide length ...	Fitted height, 19mm. above step surrounding valve guide boss
44.	Valve stem/guide cl'nce ...	Inlet (top), ·001/·003; (bottom), ·0015/ ·0035. Exhaust (top), ·0015/·0035; (bottom), ·002/·004in.
46.	Valve spring loaded length	1·577in. at 70±3·5lb.; 1·350in. at 130 ±6·5lb.; 1·187in. at 176±7·5lb.
49.	Valve timing	Inlet opens 30° B.T.D.C. } peak, 112·5° Inlet closes 75° A.B.D.C. } A.T.D.C. Exhaust opens 68° B.B.D.C. } peak, 105·5° Exhaust closes 37° A.T.D.C. } B.T.D.C.
50.	Petrol pump	Electric
52.	Carburettors	2 S.U. type HIF6
53.	Needle	BAK
56.	Piston spring	Yellow
63.	Float level	·020/·060in. (0·5/1·5mm.)
64.	Exhaust gas analysis ...	2%/4·5% CO

TRANSMISSION

101.	Type	Rear wheel drive
102.	Clutch (hydraulic) ...	Borg & Beck, 9·5in. diam., single dry plate, diaphragm spring, free travel at lever, ¹⁄₁₆in. (1·6mm.)
103.	Gearbox	5 forward speeds, all synchromesh
105.	Gearbox ratios ...	0·833; 1; 1·396; 2·087; 3·321; R., [3·428:1
106.	Overdrive	Not fitted
107.	Driving axles ...	Semi-floating
108.	Final drive gear ...	Hypoid, limited-slip differential
109.	Final drive ratio ...	3·31:1
111.	Crown wheel/pinion b'lash	0·003/0·006in.; shim adjustment
112.	Pinion bearing pre-load ...	8/12lb.in.
113.	Differential brg. pre-load	·003/·005in.; shim adjustment

BRAKES

201.	Front	Girling hydraulic, 11in. diam. discs
202.	Rear	Girling hydraulic, 9in. diam. drums
203.	Handbrake	Mechanical, on rear wheels
204.	Linings—front ...	Ferodo, type GX
205.	Linings—rear ...	Ferodo, type LL, 1¾in. wide
206.	Power assistance ...	Girling servo (twin on L.H. drive cars)

STEERING (see also "Dimensions")

301.	Type	Worm and nut
302.	Camber angle ...	2°, non-adjustable
303.	Castor angle ...	4°, non-adjustable
304.	King-pin inclination ...	2°
305.	Toe-in	¹⁄₈/¹⁄₁₆in. (3/5mm.) at wheel rims
306.	Condition for checking ...	Unladen

FRONT SUSPENSION

401.	Type	Independent, vertical coil springs
402.	Number of coils ...	18
403.	Coil diameter ...	2⅜in. (external)
404.	Wire diameter ...	0·375in.
405.	Spring length—free ...	13in.
506.	Spring length—fitted ...	9in.

REAR SUSPENSION

501.	Type	Semi-elliptic leaf-springs
504.	Spring length ...	42⅞in. (free)
505.	Number of leaves ...	6
506.	Width of leaves ...	1⅞in.
507.	Thickness of leaves ...	¼in.
508.	Spring camber—free ...	3¼in.

ELECTRICAL SYSTEM

601.	Ignition timing —static	6° BTDC (pulley)
	—stroboscope	10° at 1200 r.p.m.; 17° at 1800; 22° at 2600; vac. hose off
602.	Sparking plugs ...	Champion N12Y
603.	Sparking plug gap ...	·030in.
604.	Distributor ...	Lucas 35DE8 (electronic)
605.	Pick-up air gap ...	·014/·016in. (0·36/·40mm.)
606.	Centrifugal advance ...	0° at 300 r.p.m.; 1°/3° at 600; 4·5°/7° at 900; 7°/9° at 1300; 9·5°/11·5° at 2200; 10°/12° at 2800
608.	Vacuum advance ...	0°/0·5° at 0in.Hg., 0°/3° at 4·3in.; 6°/9° at 10in.; 7°/9° at 20in. (Distributor degrees and r.p.m.)
610.	Ignition coil ...	Lucas 22C12; 9BR ballast resistor
611.	Battery	12V. 57A.h.
612.	Battery earth ...	Negative
613.	Alternator ...	Lucas 18ACR, 43 amp.
614.	Regulator ...	Integral with alternator
615.	Starter motor ...	Lucas 3M100, pre-engaged; lock, 16·5 lb.ft. at 545A.

CAPACITIES

701.	Engine oil —Total	9·5 pints (5·4 litres) incl. filter
	—Drain/Refill	8·25 pints (4·7 litres) plus filter
702.	Gearbox (dry) ...	2·7 pints (1·5 litres)
703.	Differential ...	2·5 pints (1·4 litres)
704.	Cooling system ...	15 pints (8·5 litres)
705.	Fuel tank ...	14 gallons (64 litres)
706.	Tyre size ...	195VR14
707.	Tyre pressures —Front	18 (1·24); fast driving, 22 (1·5)
	lb./in.² (bars) —Rear	18 (1·24); fast driving, 22 (1·5)
708.	No. of grease gun points ...	12
709.	Servicing intervals ...	Greasing, 3000 miles; engine oil change, 5000 miles
710.	Hydraulic fluid ...	Castrol/Girling Universal

DIMENSIONS

801.	Length overall ...	12ft. 8in. (3861mm.)
802.	Width overall ...	60in. (1524mm.)
803.	Height overall ...	50in. (1270mm.)
804.	Weight (dry) ...	1884lb. (16·8cwt.) (855kg.) approx.
805.	Ground clearance ...	6in. (152mm.) unladen (sump)
806.	Track —Front	52in. (1321mm.)
	—Rear	53in. (1346mm.)
807.	Wheelbase ...	98in. (2489mm.)
808.	Turning circle diameter ...	38ft. (11·6m.)

TORQUE SPANNER DATA (lb.ft.)

901.	Cylinder head bolts	65/70 (3·8in. and 2·6in. bolts)
		40/50 (2·16in. bolts)
902.	Big-end bearing bolts ...	30/35
903.	Main bearing bolts ...	50/55
	—Rear ...	65/70
905.	Flywheel bolts ...	50/60
906.	Clutch to flywheel bolts ...	20
907.	Drive pinion bearing nut	95/100
908.	Crown wheel bolts ...	50/60
909.	Differential bearing nuts	35/40
910.	Road wheel nuts ...	65/70
911.	Steering wheel nut ...	40

BODY AND CHASSIS

1001.	Type of construction ...	Steel 'Z'-section chassis
1002.	Material of body panels ...	Steel and aluminium
1003.	Type of glass	Windscreen laminated

Plus 8 1980

Models: 4-seat Tourer and 2-seat Competition model

ENGINE (Ford 1600GT)

1.	Type	4-stroke; overhead valves; side camshaft
2.	Cooling system	Water pump, radiator, fan and thermostat
3.	Number of cylinders	4 (bored direct in block)
4.	Firing order	1—2—4—3 (No. 1 at front)
4a.	Idling speed	800±20 r.p.m.; fast idle, 1900±100 r.p.m
5.	Bore	3·1881in. (80·977mm.) mean grade
6.	Stroke	3·056in. (77·62mm.)
7.	Cubic capacity	1598cm.^{3}
8.	Compression ratio and pressure	9:1; 188lb./in.^{2} at 300 r.p.m.
9.	Brake horse-power (DIN)	84 at 5500 r.p.m.
10.	Torque (DIN)	92lb.ft. at 4000 r.p.m.
11.	Piston oversizes	·0025, ·015, ·030in.
12.	Piston clearance in bore	·0009/·0016in.
13.	Piston rings—number	2 compression, 1 oil
14.	Piston rings—width	Comp., ·077/·078in.; oil, 0·155/0·156in.
15.	Piston rings—groove cl'nce	Comp., ·0016/·0036in.; oil, ·0018/·0038 [in.
16.	Piston rings—gap (in bore)	·009/·014in.
17.	Oil pressure (minimum)	8·5lb./in.^{2} at 700 r.p.m.; 21lb./in.^{2} at 2000 r.p.m.
18.	Gudgeon pin diameter	0·8119/0·8123in. (in 4 grades)
19.	Gudgeon pin fit in piston	Interference, selective (heated piston)
20.	Gudgeon pin fit in con.rod	·0002/·0004in. clearance (selective)
21.	Crankpin diameter	1·9368/1·9376in.
22.	Crankpin undersizes	(·002, bearing) ·010, ·020, ·030, ·040in.
23.	Connecting rod length	4·927/4·929in. (centres)
24.	Big-end bearings	Steel-backed, copper/lead, lead/bronze or aluminium/tin
25.	Big-end bearing clearance	·0002/·003in.
26.	Big-end side clearance	·004/·010in.
27.	Main journal diameter	Blue, 2·1253/57in.; red, 2·1257/61in.
28.	Main journal undersizes	(·002, bearing) ·010, ·020, ·030in.
29.	Main bearings	5; steel-backed copper-lead or lead-[bronze
31.	Main bearing clearance	·0004/·0024in.
32.	Crankshaft end-float	·003/·011in.
33.	Crankshaft end-thrust on	Centre main bearing
34.	Camshaft journal diameter	1·5597/1·5605in.
35.	Camshaft bearings	3; steel-backed white metal
36.	Camshaft bearing cl'nce	·001/·0023in.
37.	Camshaft end-float	·0025/·0075in.
38.	Camshaft drive type	Chain (single); 46×0·375in. pitches
39.	Valve head diameter	Inlet, 1·543/1·560in.; exhaust, 1·330/1·340in.
40.	Valve stem diameter	In., 0·3098/0·3105in.; exh., 0·3089/0·3096in.
41.	Valve seat angle	44° 30′ to 45° (in head)
42.	Valve lift	Inlet, 0·3556in.; exhaust, 0·3574in.
44.	Valve stem/guide c'lance	In., ·0008/·0027in.; exh., ·0017/·0036in.
45.	Valve spring free length	1·48in.
46.	Valve spring rate	Length (closed), 1·263in. at 44/49lb.
47.	Valve working clearance	Inlet, ·012in.; exhaust, ·022in. (hot)
49.	Valve timing	27°BT—65°AB—65°BB—27°AT
50.	Petrol pump	A.C. mechanical
51.	Carburettor	Weber twin choke; ref. 761F-9510-BA

		1st	2nd
52.	Choke tube (Venturi)	23mm.	24mm.
52a.	Choke plate pull down	6·5mm. max.	
53.	Main jet	120	115
63.	Float level	41·0±0·3mm. (1·61±0·01in.)	
64.	Exhaust gas analysis	1·5%±0·25 CO	

TRANSMISSION

101.	Type	Rear wheel drive
102.	Clutch (cable op.)	7½in. diam., diaphragm type; free travel at lever, 1/16in. (1·6mm.)
103.	Gearbox	4 forward speeds, all synchromesh
105.	Gearbox ratios	1; 1·397; 2·010; 2·972; R., 3·324:1
107.	Driving axles	Semi-floating
108.	Final drive gear	Hypoid (Salisbury)
109.	Final drive ratio	4·1:1 (41/10)
111.	Crown wheel/pinion b'lash	·003/·006in.; shim adjustment
112.	Pinion bearing pre-load	8/12lb.in.; shim adjustment
113.	Differential brg. pre-load	·003/·005in.; shim adjustment

BRAKES

201.	Front	Girling hydraulic, 11in. diam. discs
202.	Rear	Girling hydraulic, 9in. diam. drums
203.	Handbrake	Mechanical, on rear wheels
204.	Linings—front	Ferodo, type 14 calliper pads
205.	Linings—rear	Ferodo, 1·75in. wide

STEERING (see also "Dimensions")

301.	Type	Worm and nut
302.	Camber angle	2°; non-adjustable
303.	Castor angle	4°; non-adjustable
304.	King-pin inclination	2°
305.	Toe-in	⅛ to 3/16in. (3 to 5mm.) at wheel rim
306.	Condition for checking	Unladen

FRONT SUSPENSION

401.	Type	Independent, vertical coil springs
402.	Number of coils	21
403.	Coil diameter	2¼in. (external)
404.	Wire diameter	0·31in.
405.	Spring length—free	14¼in.
406.	Spring length—fitted	8½in.

REAR SUSPENSION

501.	Type	Semi-elliptic leaf springs
504.	Spring length (centres)	42¾in. (free)
505.	Number of leaves	5
506.	Width of leaves	1⅜in.
507.	Thickness of leaves	¼in.
508.	Spring camber—free	3⅝in.

ELECTRICAL SYSTEM

601.	Ignition timing	10° B.T.D.C. at 800 r.p.m. (vac. pipe off); mark on pulley
602.	Sparking plugs	Motorcraft AGR12
603.	Sparking plug gap	·030in. (0·8mm.)
604.	Distributor	Motorcraft
605.	Contact breaker gap	·025in. (0·6mm.)
605a.	Dwell angle	48°/52°
606.	Centrif. advance starts at	−½° to +½° at 500 r.p.m.
607.	Centrif. advance—max.	10·75°/12·75° at 2000 r.p.m.
608.	Vacuum adv. starts at	1°/4° at 5in.Hg.
609.	Vacuum adv.—max.	5°/8° at 9in.Hg. (Distributor degrees and r.p.m.)
610.	Ignition coil	Oil-filled, low voltage; use with 1·5Ohm ballast resistor
611.	Battery	12V. 36A.h.
612.	Battery earth	Negative
613.	Alternator	Lucas 15ACR
615.	Starter motor	Lucas M35J or 5M90

CAPACITIES

701.	Engine sump —Total	6·74 pints (3·8 litres)
	—Refill	6 pints (3·4 litres) incl. filter
702.	Gearbox	1·97 pints (1·1 litres); refill, 1·7 (0·97)
703.	Differential	1·75 pints (1·0 litres)
704.	Cooling system	12 pints (6·8 litres)
705.	Fuel tank	8·5 gallons (38·6 litres)
706.	Tyre size	165×15
707.	Tyre pressures lb./in.^{2} (bars) —Front	18 (1·24)
	—Rear	19 (1·31)
708.	No. of grease gun points	12 (Front sliding axles have 'one-shot' lubrication; press foot plunger every 200 miles approx.)
709.	Normal servicing intervals	Greasing, 2000/2500 miles; engine oil change, 5000 miles
710.	Hydraulic fluid	Castrol/Girling Universal

DIMENSIONS

801.	Length overall	12ft. (3658mm.)
802.	Width overall	56in. (1422mm.)
803.	Height overall	51·75in. (1314mm.)
804.	Weight (dry) —2-seat	1460lb. or 13cwt. (662kg.)
	—4-seat	1516lb. or 13·5cwt. (688kg.)
805.	Ground cl'nce (unladen)	7in. (178mm.)
806.	Track	47in. (1194mm.) front and rear
807.	Wheelbase	96in. (2438mm.)
808.	Turning circle diameter	32ft. (9·75m.)

TORQUE SPANNER DATA (lb.ft.)

901.	Cylinder head nuts	65/70	907.	Drive pinion bearing nut	95/100
902.	Big-end bearing nuts	30/35	908.	Crown wheel bolts	50/60
903.	Main bearing nuts	55/60	909.	Diff. bearing nuts	35/40
905.	Flywheel bolts	50/54	910.	Road wheel nuts	65/70
906.	Clutch to flywheel bolts	12/15			

BODY AND CHASSIS

1001.	Type of construction	Coachbuilt; steel 'Z'-section chassis; ash body frame
1002.	Material of body panels	Steel and aluminium
1003.	Windscreen glass	Toughened (laminated optional extra)

4/4 1600 1981

Model: 2-seat Tourer

ENGINE (Rover)

1.	Type	4-stroke V8 (cast-aluminium block); O.H.V.; central camshaft; hydraulic tappets
2.	Cooling system	Water pump, radiator (15lb./in.²), fan (electric) and thermostat
3.	Number of cylinders ...	8 (dry liners)
4.	Firing order and idling speed	1L—8R—4R—3L—6R—5L—7L—2R (No. 1 at front left); 725/775 r.p.m.
5.	Bore	3·5in. (88·9mm.)
6.	Stroke	2·8in. (71·12mm.)
7.	Cubic capacity	3532cm.³
8.	Compression ratio and pressure	9·35:1; 135lb./in.² min. at 150/200 r.p.m.
9.	Brake horse-power (DIN)	155 at 5250 r.p.m.
10.	Torque (DIN)	198lb.ft. at 2500 r.p.m.
11.	Piston oversizes	·010, ·020in.
12.	Piston clearance in bore ...	·0007/·0013in. (skirt bottom)
13.	Piston rings—number ...	2 compression, 1 oil
14.	Piston rings—width ...	Compression, ·0615/·0625in.; oil (expander) 0·1894in. max.
15.	Piston rings—groove cl'nce	Compression, ·003/·005in.
16.	Piston rings—gap (in bore)	Compression, ·017/·022in.
17.	Oil pressure (lb./in.²) ...	30/40 at 2400 r.p.m. (55 at 4000)
18.	Gudgeon pin diameter ...	0·8746/0·8749in.
19.	Gudgeon pin fit in piston	·0001/·0003in. clearance
20.	Gudgeon pin fit in con. rod	Press fit
21.	Crankpin diameter ...	2·0000/2·0005in.
22.	Crankpin undersizes ...	·010, ·020, ·030, ·040in.
23.	Connecting rod length ...	5·662/5·658in. (centres)
24.	Big-end bearings	Vandervell, lead-indium
25.	Big-end bearing clearance	·0007/·0027in.
26.	Big-end side clearance ...	·005/·015in.
27.	Main journal diameter ...	2·2992/2·2997in.
28.	Main journal undersizes...	·010, ·020, ·030, ·040in.
29.	Main bearings	5; Vandervell, lead-indium
30.	Main bearings—length ...	(1) (2) (4) (5), 0·797/0·807in.; (3)
31.	Main bearing clearance ...	·0009/·0024in. [1·056/1·058in.
32.	Crankshaft end-float ...	·004/·008in.
33.	Crankshaft end-thrust on	Centre main bearing
35.	Camshaft bearings ...	5; steel-backed Babbitt
38.	Camshaft drive type ...	Chain; 54×0·375in. pitches
39.	Valve head diameter ...	Inlet, 1·565/1·575in.; exhaust, 1·3475/1·3575
40.	Valve stem diameter (tapered)	Inlet (head) 0·3402/0·3412 to 0·3407/0·3417in.; exhaust, 0·3397/0·3407 to
42.	Valve lift	0·39in. [0·3402/0·3412in.
43.	Valve guide length ...	Fitted height, 19mm. above step surrounding valve guide boss
44.	Valve stem/guide cl'nce ...	Inlet (top), ·001/·003; (bottom), ·0015/·0035. Exhaust (top), ·0015/·0035; (bottom), ·002/·004in.
46.	Valve spring loaded length	1·577in. at 70±3·5lb.; 1·350in. at 130±6·5lb.; 1·187in. at 176±7·5lb.
49.	Valve timing Inlet opens	30° B.T.D.C. } peak, 112·5°
	Inlet closes	75° A.B.D.C. } A.T.D.C.
	Exhaust opens	68° B.B.D.C. } peak, 105·5°
	Exhaust closes	37° A.T.D.C. } B.T.D.C.
50.	Petrol pump	Electric
52.	Carburettors	2 S.U. type HIF6
53.	Needle	BAK
56.	Piston spring	Yellow
63.	Float level	·020/·060in. (0·5/1·5mm.)
64.	Exhaust gas analysis ...	2%/4·5% CO

TRANSMISSION

101.	Type	Rear wheel drive
102.	Clutch (hydraulic) ...	Borg & Beck, 9·5in. diam., single dry plate, diaphragm spring, free travel at lever, 1/16in. (1·6mm.)
103.	Gearbox	5 forward speeds, all synchromesh
105.	Gearbox ratios	0·833; 1; 1·396; 2·087; 3·321; R.,
106.	Overdrive	Not fitted [3·428:1
107.	Driving axles	Semi-floating
108.	Final drive gear	Hypoid, limited-slip differential
109.	Final drive ratio	3·31:1
111.	Crown wheel/pinion b'lash	0·003/0·006in.; shim adjustment
112.	Pinion bearing pre-load ...	8/12lb.in.
113.	Differential brg. pre-load	·003/·005in.; shim adjustment

BRAKES

201.	Front	Girling hydraulic, 11in. diam. discs
202.	Rear	Girling hydraulic, 9in. diam. drums
203.	Handbrake	Mechanical, on rear wheels
204.	Linings—front	Ferodo, type GX
205.	Linings—rear	Ferodo, type LL, 1¾in. wide
206.	Power assistance	Girling servo (twin on L.H. drive cars)

STEERING (see also "Dimensions")

301.	Type	Worm and nut
302.	Camber angle	2°, non-adjustable
303.	Castor angle	4°, non-adjustable
304.	King-pin inclination ...	2°
305.	Toe-in	1/8 / 3/16in. (3/5mm.) at wheel rims
306.	Condition for checking ...	Unladen

FRONT SUSPENSION

401.	Type	Independent, vertical coil springs
402.	Number of coils	18
403.	Coil diameter	2⅜in. (external)
404.	Wire diameter	0·375in.
405.	Spring length—free ...	13in.
506.	Spring length—fitted ...	9in.

REAR SUSPENSION

501.	Type	Semi-elliptic leaf-springs
504.	Spring length	42¾in. (free)
505.	Number of leaves ...	6
506.	Width of leaves	1⅜in.
507.	Thickness of leaves ...	¼in.
508.	Spring camber—free ...	3½in.

ELECTRICAL SYSTEM

601.	Ignition timing —static	6° BTDC (pulley)
	—stroboscope	10° at 1200 r.p.m.; 17° at 1800; 22° at 2600; vac. hose off
602.	Sparking plugs	Champion N12Y
603.	Sparking plug gap ...	·030in.
604.	Distributor	Lucas 35DE8 (electronic)
605.	Pick-up air gap	·014/·016in. (0·36/·40mm.)
606.	Centrifugal advance ...	0° at 300 r.p.m.; 1°/3° at 600; 4·5°/7° at 900; 7°/9° at 1300; 9·5°/11·5° at 2200; 10°/12° at 2800
608.	Vacuum advance ...	0°/0·5° at 0in.Hg., 0°/3° at 4·3in.; 6°/9° at 10in.; 7°/9° at 20in. (Distributor degrees and r.p.m.)
610.	Ignition coil	Lucas 22C12; 9BR ballast resistor
611.	Battery	12V. 57A.h.
612.	Battery earth	Negative
613.	Alternator	Lucas 18ACR, 43 amp.
614.	Regulator	Integral with alternator
615.	Starter motor	Lucas 3M100, pre-engaged; lock, 16·5 lb.ft. at 545A.

CAPACITIES

701.	Engine oil —Total ...	9·5 pints (5·4 litres) incl. filter
	—Drain/Refill	8·25 pints (4·7 litres) plus filter
702.	Gearbox (dry)	2·7 pints (1·5 litres)
703.	Differential	2·5 pints (1·4 litres)
704.	Cooling system	15 pints (8·5 litres)
705.	Fuel tank	14 gallons (64 litres)
706.	Tyre size	195VR14
707.	Tyre pressures —Front	18 (1·24); fast driving, 22 (1·5)
	lb./in.² (bars) —Rear	18 (1·24); fast driving, 22 (1·5)
708.	No. of grease gun points ...	12
709.	Servicing intervals ...	Greasing, 3000 miles; engine oil change, 5000 miles
710.	Hydraulic fluid	Castrol/Girling Universal

DIMENSIONS

801.	Length overall	12ft. 8in. (3861mm.)
802.	Width overall	60in. (1524mm.)
803.	Height overall	50in. (1270mm.)
804.	Weight (dry)	1884lb. (16·8cwt.) (855kg.) approx.
805.	Ground clearance ...	6in. (152mm.) unladen (sump)
806.	Track —Front	52in. (1321mm.)
	—Rear	53in. (1346mm.)
807.	Wheelbase	98in. (2489mm.)
808.	Turning circle diameter ...	38ft. (11·6m.)

TORQUE SPANNER DATA (lb.ft.)

901.	Cylinder head bolts —	65/70 (3·8in. and 2·6in. bolts)
	—	40/50 (2·16in. bolts)
902.	Big-end bearing bolts ...	30/35
903.	Main bearing bolts ...	50/55
	—Rear ...	65/70
905.	Flywheel bolts	50/60
906.	Clutch to flywheel bolts ...	20
907.	Drive pinion bearing nut	95/100
908.	Crown wheel bolts ...	50/60
909.	Differential bearing nuts	35/40
910.	Road wheel nuts	65/70
911.	Steering wheel nut ...	40

BODY AND CHASSIS

1001.	Type of construction ...	Steel 'Z'-section chassis
1002.	Material of body panels ...	Steel and aluminium
1003.	Type of glass	Windscreen laminated

Plus 8 1981

Models: 4-seat Tourer and 2-seat Competition model

ENGINE (Ford CVH)

1. Type	4-stroke; central O.H.C.; V-formation valves; hydraulic tappets
2. Cooling system ...	Water pump, radiator (0·85/1·1 bar), electric fan, thermostat (85°/89°C)
3. Number of cylinders ...	4 (direct in block)
4. Firing order	1—3—4—2 (No. 1 front)
4a. Idling speed	800 ± 25 r.p.m. (fan on)
5. Bore	79·96mm.
6. Stroke	79·52mm.
7. Cubic capacity	1597cm.³
8. Compression ratio ...	9·5:1
8a. Compression pressure ...	11·2/14·8kg./cm.² (159/210lb./in.²) warm; L.T. detached from coil
9. Brake horse-power (DIN)	96 (71 kW) at 6000 r.p.m.
10. Torque (DIN)	13·5kg.m. (98lb.ft.) at 4000 r.p.m.
10a. Piston diameter (standard)	79·930/79·955mm. (service)
11. Piston oversizes ...	80·210/80·235, 80·430/80·455mm.
12. Piston clearance in bore	Prod., 0·020/0·040mm.; serv., 0·010/0·045mm.
16. Piston rings—gap (in bore)	(1) (2) 0·30/0·50mm.; (3) 0·4/1·4mm.
17. Oil pressure (minimum)...	2·8 bar (40·6lb./in.²) at 2000 r.p.m. (10W 30)
18. Gudgeon pin diameter ...	20·622/20·634mm., in 4 grades
19. Gudgeon pin fit in piston	0·013/0·045mm. clearance
20. Gudgeon pin fit in con. rod	Interference; heat small end to 260°/ 400°C.
21. Crankpin diameter ...	47·89/47·91mm.
22. Crankpin undersizes ...	0·25, 0·50, 0·75, 1·00mm.
25. Big-end bearing clearance	0·006/0·060mm. (·0002/·0023in.)
27. Main journal diameter ...	57·98/58·00mm.
28. Main journal undersizes ...	0·25, 0·50, 0·75, 1·00mm.
29. Main bearings	5
31. Main bearing clearance...	0·011/0·058mm. (·0004/·0023in.)
32. Crankshaft end-float ...	0·09/0·30mm. (·004/·012in.)
33. Crankshaft end-thrust on	Centre bearing (width, 28·825/28·875 mm.)
34. Camshaft journal diameter	(1) 44·75; (2) 45·00; (3) 45·25; (4) 45·50; (5) 45·75mm.
35. Camshaft bearings ...	5; steel-backed
37. Camshaft end-float ...	0·05/0·15mm. (·002/·006in.)
38. Camshaft drive type ...	Toothed belt
38a. Cam lift	6·09mm. (0·240in.)
39. Valve head diameter ...	I., 41·9/42·1mm.; E., 36·9/37·1mm.
40. Valve stem diameter ...	I., 8·025/8·043mm.; E., 7·999/8·017. (O.S. 0·2 & 0·4mm.)
40a. Valve length	I., 134·54/135·00mm.; E., 131·57/132·03
41. Valve seat angle	45°
42. Valve lift	I., 10·19mm.; E., 10·16mm.
44. Valve stem/guide c'lance	I., 0·020/0·063mm.; E., 0·046/0·089
45. Valve spring free length	47·2mm.
46. Valve spring loaded length	37·08±mm. at 402·4/441·6N (90·5/ 99·3lb.)
47. Valve working clearance	Hydraulic tappets
48. Valve timing clearance ...	N.A. Timing below at 1mm. cam lift
49. Valve timing	8°BT—36°AB—34°BB—6°AT
50. Petrol pump	Mech.; 0·22/0·35 bar (3·2/5·1lb./in.²)
51. Carburettor	Weber twin-choke
52. Choke tube (Venturi) ...	24mm. 25mm.
52a. Choke pull-down ...	5·5mm. ± 0·3
52b. Choke phasing ...	2·0mm. ± 0·5mm.
53. Main jet	112 125
54. Compensating jet ...	160 150
55. Slow-running jet... ...	50 60
57. Emulsion tube	F30 F30
64. Exhaust gas analysis ...	CO, 1·25% ± 0·25

TRANSMISSION

101. Type	Rear wheel drive
102. Clutch (cable op.) ...	Ford/L.U.K. 8·5in.
	—pedal free-travel 23/31mm. (0·9/1·2in.)
103. Gearbox	4 forward speeds, all synchromesh
105. Gearbox ratios ...	1; 1·37; 1·97; 3·65; R., 3·66:1
107. Driving axles	Semi-floating
108. Final drive gear ...	Hypoid (Salisbury)
109. Final drive ratio ...	4·1:1 (41/10)
111. Crown wheel/pinion b'lash	·003/·006in.; shim adjustment
112. Pinion bearing pre-load	8/12lb.in.; shim adjustment
113. Differential brg. pre-load	·003/·005in.; shim adjustment

BRAKES (Single circuit, dual master cyl.)

201. Front	Girling hydraulic, 11in. diam. discs
202. Rear	Girling hydraulic, 9in. diam. drums
203. Handbrake	Mechanical, on rear wheels
204. Linings—front ...	Ferodo, type 14 calliper pads
205. Linings—rear ...	Ferodo, 1·75in. wide

STEERING (see also "Dimensions")

301. Type	Worm and nut
302. Camber angle	2° (alt., 0°); non-adjustable
303. Castor angle	4°; non-adjustable
304. King-pin inclination ...	2°
305. Toe-in	$\frac{1}{8}/\frac{3}{16}$ in. (3 to 5mm.) at wheel rim
306. Condition for checking ...	Unladen

FRONT SUSPENSION

401. Type	Independent, vertical coil springs
402. Number of coils ...	21
403. Coil diameter	2$\frac{1}{4}$in. (external)
404. Wire diameter	0·31in.
405. Spring length—free ...	14$\frac{1}{2}$in.
406. Spring length—fitted ...	8$\frac{1}{2}$in.

REAR SUSPENSION

501. Type	Semi-elliptic leaf springs
504. Spring length (centres) ...	42$\frac{3}{4}$in. (free)
505. Number of leaves ...	5
506. Width of leaves ...	1$\frac{3}{4}$in.
507. Thickness of leaves ...	$\frac{1}{4}$in.
508. Spring camber—free ...	3$\frac{5}{8}$in.

ELECTRICAL SYSTEM

601. Ignition timing (inital) ...	12°BTDC (pulley)
602. Sparking plugs ...	Motorcraft AGP12C or AGPR12C
603. Sparking plug gap ...	·025in. (0·6mm.)
604. Distributor	Lucas or Bosch, electronic
606. Centrif. advance starts at	0°/2° at 200 r.p.m.
607. Centrif. advance—max....	21°/29° at 5500 r.p.m.
608. Vacuum advance starts ...	−1°/+3° at 75mm. Hg.
609. Vacuum advance—max.	8°/14° at 225mm. Hg.
609a. Vacuum retard starts ...	−3°/+1° at 38mm. Hg.
609b. Vacuum retard—max.	−16°/−10° at 270mm.Hg. (Crankshaft degrees and r.p.m.)
610. Ignition coil	Prim. res., 0·72/0·88Ω; sec. res., 4·5/7kΩ
611. Battery	12V. 40A.h., Lucas QOA9
612. Battery earth	Negative
613. Alternator	35A.
614. Regulated voltage ...	13·7/14·6V. at 3/7A., 4000 r.p.m.
615. Starter motor	0·9kW.

CAPACITIES

701. Engine oil (refill) ...	6·6 pints (3·75 litres) with filter
702. Gearbox	2·6 pints (1·5 litres)
703. Differential	1·75 pints (1·0 litres)
704. Cooling system ...	13 pints (7·4 litres)
705. Fuel tank	8·5 gallons (38·6 litres)
706. Tyre size	165 × 15
707. Tyre pressures —Front	18 (1·24)
lb./in.² (bars) —Rear	19 (1·31)
708. No. of grease gun points ...	12 (Front sliding axles have 'one-shot' lubrication; press foot plunger every 200 miles approx.)
709. Normal servicing intervals	5000 miles
710. Hydraulic fluid	Castrol/Girling Universal

DIMENSIONS

801. Length overall	12ft. (3658mm.)
802. Width overall	56in. (1422mm.)
803. Height overall	51·75in. (1314mm.)
804. Weight (dry) —2-seat	1460lb. or 13cwt. (662kg.)
—4-seat	1516lb. or 13·5cwt. (688kg.)
805. Ground cl'nce (unladen)	7in. (178mm.)
806. Track	47in. (1194mm.) front and rear
807. Wheelbase	96in. (2438mm.)
808. Turning circle diameter ...	32ft. (9·75m.)

TORQUE SPANNER DATA (lb.ft.)

901. Cylinder head nuts (in stages) ...	(1) 18; (2) 41; (3) +90°; (4) +90°		
902. Big-end bearing nuts	19/24	908. Crown wheel bolts	50/60
903. Main bearing bolts	66/74	909. Diff. bearing nuts	35/40
905. Flywheel bolts ...	61/69	910. Road wheel nuts	65/70
906. Clutch to flywheel bolts	13/15	911. Steering wheel nut	25/35
907. Drive pinion nut...	95/100		

BODY AND CHASSIS

1001. Type of construction ...	Coachbuilt; steel 'Z'-section chassis; timber (ash) body frame
1002. Material of body panels ...	Steel and aluminium
1003. Windscreen glass ...	Laminated

Commencing Chassis No. C6000, 1st January 1982

4/4 1600 1982

Model: 2-seat Tourer

ENGINE (Rover)

1.	Type	4-stroke V8 (cast-aluminium block); O.H.V.; central camshaft; hydraulic tappets
2.	Cooling system ...	Water pump, radiator (15lb./in.²), fan (electric) and thermostat
3.	Number of cylinders	8 (dry liners)
4.	Firing order and idling speed	1L—8R—4R—3L—6R—5L—7L—2R (No. 1 at front left); 725/775 r.p.m.
5.	Bore	3·5in. (88·9mm.)
6.	Stroke	2·8in. (71·12mm.)
7.	Cubic capacity ...	3532cm.³
8.	Compression ratio and pressure	9·35:1; 135lb./in.² min. at 150/200 r.p.m.
9.	Brake horse-power (DIN)	157 at 5250 r.p.m.
10.	Torque (DIN) ...	198lb.ft. at 2500 r.p.m.
11.	Piston oversizes ...	·010, ·020in.
12.	Piston clearance in bore	·0007/·0013in. (skirt bottom)
13.	Piston rings—number	2 compression, 1 oil
14.	Piston rings—width	Compression, ·0615/·0625in.; oil (expander) 0·1894in. max.
15.	Piston rings—groove cl'nce	Compression, ·003/·005in.
16.	Piston rings—gap (in bore)	Compression, ·017/·022in.
17.	Oil pressure (lb./in.²)	30/40 at 2400 r.p.m. (55 at 4000)
18.	Gudgeon pin diameter	0·8746/0·8749in.
19.	Gudgeon pin fit in piston	·0001/·0003in. clearance
20.	Gudgeon pin fit in con. rod	Press fit
21.	Crankpin diameter ...	2·0000/2·0005in.
22.	Crankpin undersizes ...	·010, ·020, ·030, ·040in.
23.	Connecting rod length ...	5·662/5·658in. (centres)
24.	Big-end bearings ...	Vandervell, lead-indium
25.	Big-end bearing clearance	·0007/·0027in.
26.	Big-end side clearance ...	·005/·015in.
27.	Main journal diameter ...	2·2992/2·2997in.
28.	Main journal undersizes ...	·010, ·020, ·030, ·040in.
29.	Main bearings ...	5; Vandervell, lead-indium
30.	Main bearings—length ...	(1) (2) (4) (5), 0·797/0·807in.; (3)
31.	Main bearing clearance ...	·0009/·0024in. [1·056/1·058in.
32.	Crankshaft end-float ...	·004/·008in.
33.	Crankshaft end-thrust on	Centre main bearing
35.	Camshaft bearings ...	5; steel-backed Babbitt
38.	Camshaft drive type ...	Chain; 54×0·375in. pitches
39.	Valve head diameter ...	Inlet, 1·565/1·575in.; exhaust, 1·3475/1·3575
40.	Valve stem diameter (tapered)	Inlet (head) 0·3402/0·3412 to 0·3407/0·3417in.; exhaust, 0·3397/0·3407 to 0·3402/0·3412in.
42.	Valve lift	0·39in. [0·3402/0·3412in.
43.	Valve guide length ...	Fitted height, 19mm. above step surrounding valve guide boss
44.	Valve stem/guide cl'nce	Inlet (top), ·001/·003; (bottom), ·0015/·0035. Exhaust (top), ·0015/·0035; (bottom), ·002/·004in.
46.	Valve spring loaded length	1·577in. at 70±3·5lb.; 1·350in. at 130 ±6·5lb.; 1·187in. at 176±7·5lb.
49.	Valve timing Inlet opens	30° B.T.D.C. ⎫ peak, 112·5°
	Inlet closes	75° A.B.D.C. ⎬ A.T.D.C.
	Exhaust opens	68° B.B.D.C. ⎫ peak, 105·5°
	Exhaust closes	37° A.T.D.C. ⎬ B.T.D.C.
50.	Petrol pump	Electric
52.	Carburettors ...	2 Zenith Stromberg 175CDEF
53.	Needle	B1FB
64.	Exhaust gas analysis	3·0/3·5% CO

TRANSMISSION

101.	Type	Rear wheel drive
102.	Clutch (hydraulic) ...	Borg & Beck, 9·5in. diam., single dry plate, diaphragm spring, free travel at lever, 1/16in. (1·6mm.)
103.	Gearbox	5 forward speeds, all synchromesh
105.	Gearbox ratios ...	0·792; 1; 1·396; 2·087; 3·321; R., [3·428:1
106.	Overdrive	Not fitted
107.	Driving axles ...	Semi-floating
108.	Final drive gear ...	Hypoid, limited-slip differential
109.	Final drive ratio ...	3·31:1
111.	Crown wheel/pinion b'lash	0·003/0·006in.; shim adjustment
112.	Pinion bearing pre-load ...	8/12lb.in.
113.	Differential brg. pre-load	·003/·005in.; shim adjustment

BRAKES

201.	Front	Girling hydraulic, 11in. diam. discs
202.	Rear	Girling hydraulic, 9in. diam. drums
203.	Handbrake ...	Mechanical, on rear wheels
204.	Linings—front ...	Ferodo, type GX
205.	Linings—rear ...	Ferodo, type LL, 1¾in. wide
206.	Power assistance ...	Girling servo (twin on L.H. drive cars)

STEERING (see also "Dimensions")

301.	Type	Worm and nut
302.	Camber angle ...	2°, non-adjustable
303.	Castor angle ...	4°, non-adjustable
304.	King-pin inclination ...	2°
305.	Toe-in	⅛/3/16in. (3/5mm.) at wheel rims
306.	Condition for checking ...	Unladen

FRONT SUSPENSION

401.	Type	Independent, vertical coil springs
402.	Number of coils ...	18
403.	Coil diameter ...	2¾in. (external)
404.	Wire diameter ...	0·375in.
405.	Spring length—free ...	13in.
506.	Spring length—fitted ...	9in.

REAR SUSPENSION

501.	Type	Semi-elliptic leaf-springs
504.	Spring length ...	42¾in. (free)
505.	Number of leaves ...	6
506.	Width of leaves ...	1¾in.
507.	Thickness of leaves ...	¼in.
508.	Spring camber—free ...	3½in.

ELECTRICAL SYSTEM

601.	Ignition timing	—static 6° BTDC (pulley) —stroboscope 10° at 1200 r.p.m.; 17° at 1800; 22° at 2600; vac. hose off
602.	Sparking plugs ...	Champion N12Y
603.	Sparking plug gap ...	·030in.
604.	Distributor ...	Lucas 35DE8 (electronic)
605.	Pick-up air gap ...	·014/·016in. (0·36/·40mm.)
606.	Centrifugal advance ...	0° at 300 r.p.m.; 1°/3° at 600; 4·5°/7° at 900; 7°/9° at 1300; 9·5°/11·5° at 2200; 10°/12° at 2800
608.	Vacuum advance ...	0°/0·5° at 0in.Hg., 0°/3° at 4·3in.; 6°/9° at 10in.; 7°/9° at 20in. (Distributor degrees and r.p.m.)
610.	Ignition coil ...	Lucas 22C12; 9BR ballast resistor
611.	Battery	12V. 60A.h., Lucas QOA13
612.	Battery earth ...	Negative
613.	Alternator ...	Lucas 18ACR, 43 amp.
614.	Regulator ...	Integral with alternator
615.	Starter motor ...	Lucas 3M100, pre-engaged; lock, 16·5 lb.ft. at 545A.

CAPACITIES

701.	Engine oil —Total	9·5 pints (5·4 litres) incl. filter
	—Drain/Refill	8·25 pints (4·7 litres) plus filter
702.	Gearbox (dry) ...	2·7 pints (1·5 litres)
703.	Differential ...	2·5 pints (1·4 litres)
704.	Cooling system ...	15 pints (8·5 litres)
705.	Fuel tank	14 gallons (64 litres)
706.	Tyre size ...	205VR15, 60 Series
707.	Tyre pressures —Front	18 (1·24); fast driving, 22 (1·5)
	lb./in.² (bars) —Rear	18 (1·24); fast driving, 22 (1·5)
708.	No. of grease gun points ...	10
709.	Servicing intervals ...	Greasing, 3000 miles; engine oil change, 5000 miles
710.	Hydraulic fluid ...	Castrol/Girling Universal

DIMENSIONS

801.	Length overall ...	12ft. 8in. (3861mm.)
802.	Width overall ...	60in. (1524mm.)
803.	Height overall ...	50in. (1270mm.)
804.	Weight (dry) ...	1884lb. (16·8cwt.) (855kg.) approx.
805.	Ground clearance ...	6in. (152mm.) unladen (sump)
806.	Track —Front	52in. (1321mm.)
	—Rear	53in. (1346mm.)
807.	Wheelbase ...	98in. (2489mm.)
808.	Turning circle diameter ...	38ft. (11·6m.)

TORQUE SPANNER DATA (lb.ft.)

901.	Cylinder head bolts	— 65/70 (3·8in. and 2·6in. bolts) — 40/50 (2·16in. bolts)
902.	Big-end bearing bolts	30/35
903.	Main bearing bolts	50/55
	—Rear	65/70
905.	Flywheel bolts ...	50/60
906.	Clutch to flywheel bolts ...	20
907.	Drive pinion bearing nut	95/100
908.	Crown wheel bolts ...	50/60
909.	Differential bearing nuts	35/40
910.	Road wheel nuts ...	65/70
911.	Steering wheel nut ...	25/35

BODY AND CHASSIS

1001.	Type of construction ...	Steel 'Z'-section chassis
1002.	Material of body panels ...	Steel and aluminium
1003.	Type of glass ...	Windscreen laminated

Plus 8 1982

Models: 4-seat Tourer and 2-seat Competition model

ENGINE (Ford CVH)—see footnote

1.	Type	4-stroke; central O.H.C.; V-formation valves; hydraulic tappets
2.	Cooling system	Water pump, radiator (0·85/1·1 bar), electric fan, thermostat (85°/89°C)
3.	Number of cylinders ...	4 (direct in block)
4.	Firing order	1—3—4—2 (No. 1 front)
4a.	Idling speed	800±25 r.p.m. (fan on)
5.	Bore	79·96mm.
6.	Stroke	79·52mm.
7.	Cubic capacity	1597cm.^{3}
8.	Compression ratio ...	9·5:1
8a.	Compression pressure ...	11·2/14·8kg./cm.^{2} (159/210lb./in.^{2}) warm; L.T. detached from coil
9.	Brake horse-power (DIN)	96 (71 kW) at 6000 r.p.m.
10.	Torque (DIN)	13·5kg.m. (98lb.ft.) at 4000 r.p.m.
10a.	Piston diameter (standard)	79·930/79·955mm. (service)
11.	Piston oversizes	80·210/80·235, 80·430/80·455mm.
12.	Piston clearance in bore	Prod., 0·020/0·040mm.; serv., 0·010/0·045mm.
16.	Piston rings—gap (in bore)	(1) (2) 0·30/0·50mm.; (3) 0·4/1·4mm.
17.	Oil pressure (minimum)...	2·8 bar (40·6lb./in.^{2}) at 2000 r.p.m. (10W 30)
18.	Gudgeon pin diameter ...	20·622/20·634mm., in 4 grades
19.	Gudgeon pin fit in piston	0·013/0·045mm. clearance
20.	Gudgeon pin fit in con. rod	Interference; heat small end to 260°/400°C.
21.	Crankpin diameter ...	47·89/47·91mm.
22.	Crankpin undersizes ...	0·25, 0·50, 0·75, 1·00mm.
25.	Big-end bearing clearance	0·006/0·060mm. (·0002/·0023in.)
27.	Main journal diameter ...	57·98/58·00mm.
28.	Main journal undersizes	0·25, 0·50, 0·75, 1·00mm.
29.	Main bearings	5
31.	Main bearing clearance...	0·011/0·058mm. (·0004/·0023in.)
32.	Crankshaft end-float ...	0·09/0·30mm. (·004/·012in.)
33.	Crankshaft end-thrust on	Centre bearing (width, 28·825/28·875 mm.)
34.	Camshaft journal diameter	(1) 44·75; (2) 45·00; (3) 45·25; (4) 45·50; (5) 45·75mm.
35.	Camshaft bearings ...	5; steel-backed
37.	Camshaft end-float ...	0·05/0·15mm. (·002/·006in.)
38.	Camshaft drive type ...	Toothed belt
38a.	Cam lift	6·09mm. (0·240in.)
39.	Valve head diameter ...	I., 41·9/42·1mm.; E., 36·9/37·1mm.
40.	Valve stem diameter ...	I., 8·025/8·043mm.; E., 7·999/8·017. (O/S, 0·2 & 0·4mm.)
40a.	Valve length	I., 134·54/135·00mm.; E., 131·57/132·03
41.	Valve seat angle	45°
42.	Valve lift	I., 10·19mm.; E., 10·16mm.
44.	Valve stem/guide c'lance	I., 0·020/0·063mm.; E., 0·046/0·089
45.	Valve spring free length	47·2mm.
46.	Valve spring loaded length	37·084mm. at 402·4/441·6N (90·5/99·3lb.)
47.	Valve working clearance	Hydraulic tappets
48.	Valve timing clearance ...	N.A. Timing below at 1mm. cam lift
49.	Valve timing	8°BT—36°AB—34°BB—6°AT
50.	Petrol pump	Mech.; 0·22/0·35 bar (3·2/5·1lb./in.^{2})
51.	Carburettor	Weber twin-choke

52.	Choke tube (Venturi) ...	24mm.	25mm.
52a.	Choke pull-down ...	5·5mm. ±0·3	
52b.	Choke phasing	2·0mm. ±0·5mm.	
53.	Main jet	112	125
54.	Compensating jet ...	160	150
55.	Slow-running jet... ...	50	60
57.	Emulsion tube	F30	F30
64.	Exhaust gas analysis ...	CO, 1·25% ±0·25	

TRANSMISSION

101.	Type	Rear wheel drive
102.	Clutch (cable op.) ...	Ford/L.U.K. 8·5in.
	—pedal free-travel	23/31mm. (0·9/1·2in.)
103.	Gearbox	4 forward speeds, all synchromesh
105.	Gearbox ratios	1; 1·37; 1·97; 3·65; R., 3·66:1
107.	Driving axles ...	Semi-floating
108.	Final drive gear	Hypoid (Salisbury)
109.	Final drive ratio	4·1:1 (41/10)
111.	Crown wheel/pinion b'lash	·003/·006in.; shim adjustment
112.	Pinion bearing pre-load ...	8/12lb.in.; shim adjustment
113.	Differential brg. pre-load	·003/·005in.; shim adjustment

BRAKES (Single circuit, dual master cyl.)

201.	Front	Girling hydraulic, 11in. diam. discs
202.	Rear	Girling hydraulic, 9in. diam. drums
203.	Handbrake	Mechanical, on rear wheels
204.	Linings—front	Ferodo, type 14 calliper pads
205.	Linings—rear	Ferodo, 1·75in. wide

STEERING (see also "Dimensions")

301.	Type	Worm and nut
302.	Camber angle	2° (alt., 0°); non-adjustable
303.	Castor angle	4°; non-adjustable
304.	King-pin inclination ...	2°
305.	Toe-in	⅛ to 3/16in. (3 to 5mm.) at wheel rim
306.	Condition for checking ...	Unladen

FRONT SUSPENSION

401.	Type	Independent, vertical coil springs
402.	Number of coils	21
403.	Coil diameter	2¼in. (external)
404.	Wire diameter	0·31in.
405.	Spring length—free ...	14¼in.
406.	Spring length—fitted ...	8½in.

REAR SUSPENSION

501.	Type	Semi-elliptic leaf springs
504.	Spring length (centres) ...	42¾in. (free)
505.	Number of leaves ...	5
506.	Width of leaves	1⅜in.
507.	Thickness of leaves ...	¼in.
508.	Spring camber—free ...	3⅝in.

ELECTRICAL SYSTEM—see footnote

601.	Ignition timing (inital) ...	12°BTDC (pulley)
602.	Sparking plugs	Motorcraft AGP12C or AGPR12C
603.	Sparking plug gap ...	·025in. (0·6mm.)
604.	Distributor	Lucas or Bosch, electronic
606.	Centrif. advance starts at	0°/4° at 200 r.p.m.
607.	Centrif. advance—max....	14·8°/22·8° at 6000 r.p.m.
608.	Vacuum advance starts ...	−1°/+3° at 90mm. Hg.
609.	Vacuum advance—max.	14°/22° at 218mm. Hg. (Crankshaft degrees and r.p.m.)

N.B. Advance data above replace the values in the 1982 edition

610.	Ignition coil	Prim. res., 0·72/0·88Ω; sec. res., 4·5/7kΩ
611.	Battery	12V. 40A.h., Lucas QOA9
612.	Battery earth	Negative
613.	Alternator	35A.
614.	Regulated voltage ...	13·7/14·6V. at 3/7A., 4000 r.p.m.
615.	Starter motor	0·9kW.

CAPACITIES

701.	Engine oil (refill) ...	6·6 pints (3·75 litres) with filter
702.	Gearbox	2·6 pints (1·5 litres)
703.	Differential	1·75 pints (1·0 litres)
704.	Cooling system	13 pints (7·4 litres)
705.	Fuel tank	8·5 gallons (38·6 litres)
706.	Tyre size	165×15
707.	Tyre pressures —Front	18 (1·24)
	lb./in.^{2} (bars) —Rear	19 (1·31)
708.	No. of grease gun points ...	12 (Front sliding axles have 'one-shot' lubrication; press foot plunger every 200 miles approx.)
709.	Normal servicing intervals	5000 miles
710.	Hydraulic fluid	Castrol/Girling Universal

DIMENSIONS

801.	Length overall	12ft. (3658mm.)
802.	Width overall	56in. (1422mm.)
803.	Height overall	51·75in. (1314mm.)
804.	Weight (dry) —2-seat	1460lb. or 13cwt. (662kg.)
	—4-seat	1516lb. or 13·5cwt. (688kg.)
805.	Ground cl'nce (unladen)	7in. (178mm.)
806.	Track	47in. (1194mm.) front and rear
807.	Wheelbase	96in. (2438mm.)
808.	Turning circle diameter ...	32ft. (9·75m.)

TORQUE SPANNER DATA (lb.ft.)—see footnote

901. Cylinder head nuts (in stages) ... (1) 18; (2) 41; (3) +90°; (4) +90°

902.	Big-end bearing nuts ...	19/24	908.	Crown wheel bolts	50/60
903.	Main bearing bolts ...	66/74	909.	Diff. bearing nuts	35/40
905.	Flywheel bolts	61/66	910.	Road wheel nuts	65/70
906.	Clutch to flywheel bolts ...	13/15	911.	Steering wheel nut	25/35
907.	Drive pinion nut... ...	95/100			

BODY AND CHASSIS

1001.	Type of construction ...	Coachbuilt; steel 'Z'-section chassis; timber (ash) body frame
1002.	Material of body panels ...	Steel and aluminium
1003.	Windscreen glass ...	Laminated

Note. See p. 100, 1982 edition, Fiat Supermirafiori for details of the alternative twin-overhead-camshaft engine

4/4 1600 1983

Model: 2-seat Tourer

ENGINE (Rover)

1. Type	... ...	4-stroke V8 (cast-aluminium block); O.H.V.; central camshaft; hydraulic tappets
2. Cooling system	...	Water pump, radiator (15lb./in.^{2}), fan (electric) and thermostat
3. Number of cylinders	...	8 (dry liners)
4. Firing order and idling speed		1L—8R—4R—3L—6R—5L—7L—2R (No. 1 at front left); 725/775 r.p.m.
5. Bore	... ...	3·5in. (88·9mm.)
6. Stroke	... ...	2·8in. (71·12mm.)
7. Cubic capacity	...	3532cm.^{3}
8. Compression ratio and pressure		9·35:1; 135lb./in.^{2} min. at 150/200 r.p.m.
9. Brake horse-power (DIN)		157 at 5250 r.p.m.
10. Torque (DIN)	...	198lb.ft. at 2500 r.p.m.
11. Piston oversizes	...	·010, ·020in.
12. Piston clearance in bore	...	·0007/·0013in. (skirt bottom)
13. Piston rings—number	...	2 compression, 1 oil
14. Piston rings—width		Compression, ·0615/·0625in.; oil (expander) 0·1894in. max.
15. Piston rings—groove cl'nce		Compression, ·003/·005in.
16. Piston rings—gap (in bore)		Compression, ·017/·022in.
17. Oil pressure (lb./in.^{2})	...	30/40 at 2400 r.p.m. (55 at 4000)
18. Gudgeon pin diameter	...	0·8746/0·8749in.
19. Gudgeon pin fit in piston		·0001/·0003in. clearance
20. Gudgeon pin fit in con. rod		Press fit
21. Crankpin diameter	...	2·0000/2·0005in.
22. Crankpin undersizes	...	·010, ·020, ·030, ·040in.
23. Connecting rod length	...	5·662/5·658in. (centres)
24. Big-end bearings	...	Vandervell, lead-indium
25. Big-end bearing clearance		·0007/·0027in.
26. Big-end side clearance	...	·005/·015in.
27. Main journal diameter	...	2·2992/2·2997in.
28. Main journal undersizes	...	·010, ·020, ·030, ·040in.
29. Main bearings	...	5; Vandervell, lead-indium
30. Main bearings—length	...	(1) (2) (4) (5), 0·797/0·807in.; (3)
31. Main bearing clearance	...	·0009/·0024in. [1·056/1·058in.]
32. Crankshaft end-float	...	·004/·008in.
33. Crankshaft end-thrust on		Centre main bearing
35. Camshaft bearings	...	5; steel-backed Babbitt
38. Camshaft drive type	...	Chain; 54 × 0·375in. pitches
39. Valve head diameter		Inlet, 1·565/1·575in.; exhaust, 1·3475/1·3575
40. Valve stem diameter (tapered)		Inlet (head) 0·3402/0·3412 to 0·3407/0·3417in.; exhaust, 0·3397/0·3407 to 0·3402/0·3412in.
42. Valve lift	...	0·39in. [0·3402/0·3412in.
43. Valve guide length		Fitted height, 19mm. above step surrounding valve guide boss
44. Valve stem/guide cl'nce		Inlet (top), ·001/·003; (bottom), ·0015/·0035. Exhaust (top), ·0015/·0035; (bottom), ·002/·004in.
46. Valve spring loaded length		1·577in. at 70±3·5lb.; 1·350in. at 130 ±6·5lb.; 1·187in. at 176±7·5lb.
49. Valve timing Inlet opens		30° B.T.D.C. } peak, 112·5°
	Inlet closes	75° A.B.D.C. } A.T.D.C.
	Exhaust opens	68° B.B.D.C. } peak, 105·5°
	Exhaust closes	37° A.T.D.C. } B.T.D.C.
50. Petrol pump	...	Electric
52. Carburettors	...	2 Zenith Stromberg 175CDEF
53. Needle	...	B1FB
64. Exhaust gas analysis	...	3·0/3·5% CO

TRANSMISSION

101. Type	... ...	Rear wheel drive
102. Clutch (hydraulic)		Borg & Beck, 9·5in. diam., single dry plate, diaphragm spring, free travel at lever, $\frac{1}{16}$in. (1·6mm.)
103. Gearbox	...	5 forward speeds, all synchromesh
105. Gearbox ratios	...	0·792; 1; 1·396; 2·087; 3·321; R., [3·428:1
106. Overdrive	...	Not fitted
107. Driving axles	...	Semi-floating
108. Final drive gear	...	Hypoid, limited-slip differential
109. Final drive ratio	...	3·31:1
111. Crown wheel/pinion b'lash		0·003/0·006in.; shim adjustment
112. Pinion bearing pre-load	...	8/12lb.in.
113. Differential brg. pre-load		·003/·005in.; shim adjustment

BRAKES

201. Front	... ...	Girling hydraulic, 11in. diam. discs
202. Rear	... ...	Girling hydraulic, 9in. diam. drums
203. Handbrake	...	Mechanical, on rear wheels
204. Linings—front	...	Ferodo, type GX
205. Linings—rear	...	Ferodo, type LL, 1$\frac{3}{4}$in. wide
206. Power assistance	...	Girling servo (twin on L.H. drive cars)

STEERING (see also "Dimensions")

301. Type	... ...	Worm and nut
302. Camber angle	...	2°, non-adjustable
303. Castor angle	...	4°, non-adjustable
304. King-pin inclination	...	2°
305. Toe-in	...	$\frac{1}{8}$/$\frac{3}{16}$in. (3/5mm.) at wheel rims
306. Condition for checking	...	Unladen

FRONT SUSPENSION

401. Type	...	Independent, vertical coil springs
402. Number of coils	...	18
403. Coil diameter	...	2$\frac{5}{8}$in. (external)
404. Wire diameter	...	0·375in.
405. Spring length—free	...	13in.
506. Spring length—fitted	...	9in.

REAR SUSPENSION

501. Type	... ...	Semi-elliptic leaf-springs
504. Spring length	...	42$\frac{3}{4}$in. (free)
505. Number of leaves	...	6
506. Width of leaves	...	1$\frac{3}{4}$in.
507. Thickness of leaves	...	$\frac{1}{4}$in.
508. Spring camber—free	...	3$\frac{1}{4}$in.

ELECTRICAL SYSTEM

601. Ignition timing	—static	6° BTDC (pulley)
	—stroboscope	10° at 1200 r.p.m.; 17° at 1800; 22° at 2600; vac. hose off
602. Sparking plugs	...	Champion N12Y
603. Sparking plug gap	...	·030in.
604. Distributor	...	Lucas 35DE8 (electronic)
605. Pick-up air gap	...	·014/·016in. (0·36/·40mm.)
606. Centrifugal advance		0° at 300 r.p.m.; 1°/3° at 600; 4·5°/7° at 900; 7°/9° at 1300; 9·5°/11·5° at 2200; 10°/12° at 2800
608. Vacuum advance		0°/0·5° at 0in.Hg., 0°/3° at 4·3in.; 6°/9° at 10in.; 7°/9° at 20in. (Distributor degrees and r.p.m.)
610. Ignition coil	...	Lucas 22C12; 9BR ballast resistor
611. Battery	...	12V. 60A.h., Lucas QOA13
612. Battery earth	...	Negative
613. Alternator	...	Lucas 18ACR, 43 amp.
614. Regulator	...	Integral with alternator
615. Starter motor	...	Lucas 3M100, pre-engaged; lock, 16·5 lb.ft. at 545A.

CAPACITIES

701. Engine oil —Total		9·5 pints (5·4 litres) incl. filter
—Drain/Refill		8·25 pints (4·7 litres) plus filter
702. Gearbox (dry)	...	2·7 pints (1·5 litres)
703. Differential	...	2·5 pints (1·4 litres)
704. Cooling system	...	15 pints (8·5 litres)
705. Fuel tank	...	14 gallons (64 litres)
706. Tyre size	...	205VR15, 60 Series
707. Tyre pressures —Front		18 (1·24); fast driving, 22 (1·5)
lb./in.^{2} (bars) —Rear		18 (1·24); fast driving, 22 (1·5)
708. No. of grease gun points	...	10
709. Servicing intervals		Greasing, 3000 miles; engine oil change, 5000 miles
710. Hydraulic fluid	...	Castrol/Girling Universal

DIMENSIONS

801. Length overall	...	12ft. 8in. (3861mm.)
802. Width overall	...	60in. (1524mm.)
803. Height overall	...	50in. (1270mm.)
804. Weight (dry)	...	1884lb. (16·8cwt.) (855kg.) approx.
805. Ground clearance	...	6in. (152mm.) unladen (sump)
806. Track —Front		52in. (1321mm.)
—Rear		53in. (1346mm.)
807. Wheelbase	...	98in. (2489mm.)
808. Turning circle diameter	...	38ft. (11·6m.)

TORQUE SPANNER DATA (lb.ft.)

901. Cylinder head bolts		— 65/70 (3·8in. and 2·6in. bolts) — 40/50 (2·16in. bolts)
902. Big-end bearing bolts	...	30/35
903. Main bearing bolts	...	50/55
—Rear		65/70
905. Flywheel bolts	...	50/60
906. Clutch to flywheel bolts	...	20
907. Drive pinion bearing nut		95/100
908. Crown wheel bolts	...	50/60
909. Differential bearing nuts		35/40
910. Road wheel nuts	...	65/70
911. Steering wheel nut	...	25/35

BODY AND CHASSIS

1001. Type of construction	...	Steel 'Z'-section chassis
1002. Material of body panels	...	Steel and aluminium
1003. Type of glass	...	Windscreen laminated

Plus 8 1983

Models: 4-seat Tourer and 2-seat Competition model

ENGINE (Ford CVH)

1.	Type	4-stroke; central O.H.C.; V-formation valves; hydraulic tappets
2.	Cooling system	Water pump, radiator (0·85/1·1 bar), electric fan, thermostat (85°/89°C)
3.	Number of cylinders ...	4 (direct in block)
4.	Firing order	1—3—4—2 (No. 1 front)
4a.	Idling speed	800±25 r.p.m. (fan on)
5.	Bore	79·96mm.
6.	Stroke	79·52mm.
7.	Cubic capacity	1597cm.³
8.	Compression ratio ...	9·5:1
8a.	Compression pressure ...	11·2/14·8kg./cm.² (159/210lb./in.²) warm; L.T. detached from coil
9.	Brake horse-power (DIN)	96 (71 kW) at 6000 r.p.m.
10.	Torque (DIN)	13·5kg.m. (98lb.ft.) at 4000 r.p.m.
10a.	Piston diameter (standard)	79·930/79·955mm. (service)
11.	Piston oversizes	80·210/80·235, 80·430/80·455mm.
12.	Piston clearance in bore	Prod., 0·020/0·040mm.; serv., 0·010/0·045mm.
16.	Piston rings—gap (in bore)	(1) (2) 0·30/0·50mm.; (3) 0·4/1·4mm.
17.	Oil pressure (minimum)...	2·8 bar (40·6lb./in.²) at 2000 r.p.m. (10W 30)
18.	Gudgeon pin diameter ...	20·622/20·634mm., in 4 grades
19.	Gudgeon pin fit in piston	0·013/0·045mm. clearance
20.	Gudgeon pin fit in con. rod	Interference; heat small end to 260°/[400°C.
21.	Crankpin diameter ...	47·89/47·91mm.
22.	Crankpin undersizes ...	0·25, 0·50, 0·75, 1·00mm.
25.	Big-end bearing clearance	0·006/0·060mm. (·0002/·0023in.)
27.	Main journal diameter ...	57·98/58·00mm.
28.	Main journal undersizes	0·25, 0·50, 0·75, 1·00mm.
29.	Main bearings	5
31.	Main bearing clearance...	0·011/0·058mm. (·0004/·0023in.)
32.	Crankshaft end-float ...	0·09/0·30mm. (·004/·012in.)
33.	Crankshaft end-thrust on	Centre bearing (width, 28·825/28·875 mm.)
34.	Camshaft journal diameter	(1) 44·75; (2) 45·00; (3) 45·25; (4) 45·50; (5) 45·75mm.
35.	Camshaft bearings ...	5; steel-backed
37.	Camshaft end-float ...	0·05/0·15mm. (·002/·006in.)
38.	Camshaft drive type ...	Toothed belt
38a.	Cam lift	6·09mm. (0·240in.)
39.	Valve head diameter ...	I., 41·9/42·1mm.; E., 36·9/37·1mm.
40.	Valve stem diameter ...	I., 8·025/8·043mm.; E., 7·999/8·017. (O/S, 0·2 & 0·4mm.)
40a.	Valve length	I., 134·54/135·00mm.; E., 131·57/132·03
41.	Valve seat angle	45°
42.	Valve lift	I., 10·19mm.; E., 10·16mm.
44.	Valve stem/guide c'lance	I., 0·020/0·063mm.; E., 0·046/0·089
45.	Valve spring free length	47·2mm.
46.	Valve spring loaded length	37·084mm. at 402·4/441·6N (90·5/99·3lb.)
47.	Valve working clearance	Hydraulic tappets
48.	Valve timing clearance ...	N.A. Timing below at 1mm. cam lift
49.	Valve timing	8°BT—36°AB—34°BB—6°AT
50.	Petrol pump	Mech.; 0·22/0·35 bar (3·2/5·1lb./in.²)
51.	Carburettor	Weber twin-choke

52.	Choke tube (Venturi) ...	24mm.	25mm.
52a.	Choke pull-down ...	5·5mm.±0·3	
52b.	Choke phasing ...	2·0mm.±0·5mm.	
53.	Main jet	112	125
54.	Compensating jet ...	160	150
55.	Slow-running jet... ...	50	60
57.	Emulsion tube	F30	F30
64.	Exhaust gas analysis ...	CO, 1·25%±0·25	

TRANSMISSION

101.	Type	Rear wheel drive
102.	Clutch (cable op.) ...	Ford/L.U.K. 8·5in.
	—pedal free-travel	23/31mm. (0·9/1·2in.)
103.	Gearbox	5 forward speeds, all synchromesh
105.	Gearbox ratios	0·85; 1; 1·37; 1·97; 3·65; R., 3·66:1
107.	Driving axles	Semi-floating
108.	Final drive gear	Hypoid (Salisbury)
109.	Final drive ratio	4·1:1 (41/10)
111.	Crown wheel/pinion b'lash	·003/·006in.; shim adjustment
112.	Pinion bearing pre-load ...	8/12lb.in.; shim adjustment
113.	Differential brg. pre-load	·003/·005in.; shim adjustment

BRAKES (Single circuit, dual master cyl.)

201.	Front	Girling hydraulic, 11in. diam. discs
202.	Rear	Girling hydraulic, 9in. diam. drums
203.	Handbrake	Mechanical, on rear wheels
204.	Linings—front	Ferodo, type 14 calliper pads
205.	Linings—rear	Ferodo, 1·75in. wide

STEERING (see also "Dimensions")

301.	Type	Worm and nut
302.	Camber angle	2° (alt., 0°); non-adjustable
303.	Castor angle	4°; non-adjustable
304.	King-pin inclination ...	2°
305.	Toe-in	⅛ to 3/16in. (3 to 5mm.) at wheel rim
306.	Condition for checking ...	Unladen

FRONT SUSPENSION

401.	Type	Independent, vertical coil springs
402.	Number of coils	21
403.	Coil diameter	2¼in. (external)
404.	Wire diameter	0·31in.
405.	Spring length—free ...	14¼in.
406.	Spring length—fitted ...	8½in.

REAR SUSPENSION

501.	Type	Semi-elliptic leaf springs
504.	Spring length (centres) ...	42¾in. (free)
505.	Number of leaves ...	5
506.	Width of leaves	1⅜in.
507.	Thickness of leaves ...	¼in.
508.	Spring camber—free ...	3⅝in.

ELECTRICAL SYSTEM—see footnote

601.	Ignition timing (inital) ...	12°BTDC (pulley)
602.	Sparking plugs	Motorcraft AGP12C or AGPR12C
603.	Sparking plug gap ...	·025in. (0·6mm.)
604.	Distributor	Lucas or Bosch, electronic
606.	Centrif. advance starts at	0°/4° at 200 r.p.m.
607.	Centrif. advance—max....	14·8°/22·8° at 6000 r.p.m.
608.	Vacuum advance starts ...	−1°/+3° at 90mm. Hg.
609.	Vacuum advance—max.	14°/22° at 218mm. Hg. (Crankshaft degrees and r.p.m.)
610.	Ignition coil	Prim. res., 0·72/0·88Ω; sec. res., 4·5/7kΩ
611.	Battery	12V. 40A.h.
612.	Battery earth	Negative
613.	Alternator	35A.
614.	Regulated voltage ...	13·7/14·6V. at 3/7A., 4000 r.p.m.
615.	Starter motor	0·9kW.

CAPACITIES

701.	Engine oil (refill) ...	6·6 pints (3·75 litres) with filter
702.	Gearbox	2·6 pints (1·5 litres)
703.	Differential	1·75 pints (1·0 litres)
704.	Cooling system	13 pints (7·4 litres)
705.	Fuel tank	8·5 gallons (38·6 litres)
706.	Tyre size	165×15
707.	Tyre pressures —Front	18 (1·24)
	lb./in.² (bars) —Rear	19 (1·31)
708.	No. of grease gun points ...	12 (Front sliding axles have 'one-shot' lubrication; press foot plunger every 200 miles approx.)
709.	Normal servicing intervals	Greasing, 3000 miles; engine oil change, 5000 miles
710.	Hydraulic fluid	Castrol/Girling Universal

DIMENSIONS

801.	Length overall	12ft. (3658mm.)
802.	Width overall	56in. (1422mm.)
803.	Height overall	51·75in. (1314mm.)
804.	Weight (dry) —2-seat	1460lb. or 13cwt. (662kg.)
	—4-seat	1516lb. or 13·5cwt. (688kg.)
805.	Ground cl'nce (unladen)	7in. (178mm.)
806.	Track	47in. (1194mm.) front and rear
807.	Wheelbase	96in. (2438mm.)
808.	Turning circle diameter ...	32ft. (9·75m.)

TORQUE SPANNER DATA (lb.ft.)

901. Cylinder head nuts (in stages) ... (1) 18; (2) 41; (3) +90°; (4) +90°

902.	Big-end bearing nuts ...	19/24	908.	Crown wheel bolts	50/60
903.	Main bearing bolts ...	66/74	909.	Diff. bearing nuts	35/40
905.	Flywheel bolts	61/66	910.	Road wheel nuts	65/70
906.	Clutch to flywheel bolts ...	13/15	911.	Steering wheel nut	25/35
907.	Drive pinion nut... ...	95/100			

BODY AND CHASSIS

1001.	Type of construction ...	Coachbuilt; steel 'Z'-section chassis; timber (ash) body frame
1002.	Material of body panels ...	Steel and aluminium
1003.	Windscreen glass ...	Laminated

4/4 1600 (Ford engine) 1984

Models: 4-seat Tourer and 2-seat Competition model

ENGINE

1.	Type (131B1)	4-stroke; twin O.H.C.; light alloy head
2.	Cooling system	Water pump, radiator, electric fan (in 90°/94°, out 85°/89°C), thermostat (78°/82°C)
3.	Number of cylinders ...	4 (direct in block)
4.	Firing order	1—3—4—2 (No. 1 front)
4a.	Idling speed	900 r.p.m.
5.	Bore	84 mm.
6.	Stroke	71·5mm.
7.	Cubic capacity	1585cm.³
8.	Compression ratio ...	9:1
9.	Brake horse-power (DIN)	96 at 6000 r.p.m.
10.	Torque (DIN) kg.m.(lb.ft.)	13·0 (94) at 3800 r.p.m.
10a.	Piston diameter (standard)	83·920/83·970 mm. (in 3 grades)
11.	Piston oversizes	0·2, 0·4, 0·6mm. [crown
12.	Piston clearance in bore...	0·070/0·090mm., 52·4±0·254mm. from
13.	Piston rings—number ...	1 compression, 2 oil
14.	Piston rings—width ...	(1) 1·478/1·490mm.; (2) 1·980/2·000 mm.; (3) 3·925/3·937mm.
15.	Piston rings—groove cl'nce	(1) 0·045/0·077mm.; (2) 0·030/0·070 mm.; (3) 0·030/0·062mm.
16.	Piston rings—gap (in bore)	(1) (2) 0·30/0·45mm.; (3) 0·25/0·40
17.	Oil pressure (normal) ...	3·5/5kg./cm.²
18.	Gudgeon pin diameter ...	21·991/21·997mm. in 2 grades
19.	Gudgeon pin fit in piston	0·002/0·008mm. clearance
20.	Gudgeon pin fit in con. rod	0·010/0·016 mm. clearance
21.	Crankpin diameter (A)	48·234/48·244mm.
	(B)	48·224/48·234mm.
22.	Crankpin undersizes... ...	·010, ·020, ·030, ·040in.
25.	Big-end bearing clearance	0·030/0·074mm.
27.	Main journal diameter	52·985/53·005mm.
28.	Main journal undersizes	·010, ·020, ·030, ·040in.
29.	Main bearings	5
31.	Main bearing clearance ...	0·032/0·077mm.
32.	Crankshaft end-float ...	0·055/0·305mm. (·002/·012in.)
33.	Crankshaft end-thrust on	Rear main bearing
34.	Camshaft journal diameter	(1) 29·944/29·960mm.; (2) 45·755/45·771mm.; (3) 46·155/46·171mm.
34a.	Aux. shaft journal diam.	(1) 48·013/48·038mm.; (2) 38·929/38·954mm.
36.	Camshaft bearing cl'nce...	(1) 0·049/0·090mm.; (2) (3) 0·029/0·070mm.
36a.	Aux. shaft bearing cl'nce	0·046/0·091mm., both bearings
38.	Camshaft drive type ...	Toothed belt
38a.	Cam lift	9·714mm.
39.	Valve head diameter ...	I., 42·20/42·60mm.; E., 35·85/36·45
40.	Valve stem diameter ...	7·974/7·992mm.
41.	Valve seat angle ...	45°±5' (face angle, 45° 30'±5')
44.	Valve stem/guide clance	0·030/0·066mm. (·001/·0026in.)
46.	Valve spring rate—Inner	31mm. at 14·9kg. (32·8lb.); limit, 13·5kg
	—Outer	36mm. at 38·9kg. (85·8lb.); limit, 36kg.
47.	Valve clearance (cold) ...	I., 0·45mm. (·018in.); E., 0·50 (·020)
48.	Valve timing clearance ...	0·8mm. (·031in.)
49.	Valve timing	12°BT—53°AB—54°BB—11°AT
50.	Petrol pump	Mechanical; 0·18kg./cm.² (2·6lb./in.²)
51.	Carburettor	Weber 32ADF
52.	Venturi—mm.	22 24
53.	Main jet	115 115
54.	Compensating jet ...	165 170
55.	Slow-running jet ...	50 80
56.	Slow-running air bleed ...	130 70
57.	Emulsion tube	F20 F5
58.	Accelerator pump jet ...	40
62.	Needle valve	1·75mm.
63.	Float level—mm. ...	6±0·25

TRANSMISSION

101.	Type	Rear-wheel drive
102.	Clutch	215mm.; pedal free-travel, 25mm.; diaphragm spring travel, 8·5mm.
103.	Gearbox	5 forward speeds, all synchromesh
105.	Gearbox ratios	0·870; 1; 1·357; 2·045; 3·612; R., 3·244:1
107.	Driving axles	Semi-floating
108.	Final drive gear	Hypoid (Salisbury)
109.	Final drive ratio ...	4·1:1 (41/10)
111.	Crown wheel/pinion b'lash	·003/·006in.; shim adjustment
112.	Pinion bearing pre-load ...	8/12lb.in.; shim adjustment
113.	Differential brg. pre-load	·003/·005in.; shim adjustment

BRAKES (Single circuit, dual master cyl.)

201.	Front	Girling hydraulic, 11in. diam. discs
202.	Rear	Girling hydraulic, 9in. diam. drums
203.	Handbrake	Mechanical, on rear wheels
204.	Linings—front	Ferodo, type 14 calliper pads
205.	Linings—rear	Ferodo, 1·75 in. wide

STEERING (see also "Dimensions")

301.	Type	Worm and nut
302.	Camber angle	2° (alt., 0°); non-adjustable
303.	Castor angle	4°; non-adjustable
304.	King-pin inclination ...	2°
305.	Toe-in	$\frac{1}{8}$ to $\frac{3}{16}$in. (3 to 5mm.) at wheel rim
306.	Condition for checking ...	Unladen

FRONT SUSPENSION

401.	Type	Independent, vertical coil springs
402.	Number of coils ...	21
403.	Coil diameter	$2\frac{1}{4}$in. (external)
404.	Wire diameter	0·31in.
405.	Spring length—free ...	$14\frac{1}{4}$in.
406.	Spring length—fitted ...	$8\frac{1}{2}$in.

REAR SUSPENSION

501.	Type	Semi-elliptic leaf springs
504.	Spring length (centres) ...	$42\frac{3}{4}$in. (free)
505.	Number of leaves ...	5
506.	Width of leaves	$1\frac{3}{8}$in.
507.	Thickness of leaves ...	$\frac{1}{4}$in.
508.	Spring camber—free ...	$3\frac{5}{8}$in.

ELECTRICAL SYSTEM

601.	Ignition timing	10°BTDC (pulley)
602.	Sparking plugs	Champion N7Y; Marelli CW78LP
603.	Sparking plug gap ...	0·6/0·7mm (·024/·027in.)
604.	Distributor	Marelli
605.	Contact breaker gap ...	0·37/0·43mm. (·015/·017in.)
605a.	Dwell angle	55°±3°
607.	Centrif. advance max. ...	28°±2° (crankshaft)
610.	Ignition coil	Marelli BES200A or Martinetti G37SU
611.	Battery	12V. 40 A.h., negative earth
613.	Alternator	Marelli AA125-14V-45A or Bosch K1-14V-45A24
614.	Regulator	Electronic (integral)
615.	Starter motor	Fiat E100-1·3/12 or Bosch GF12V1·1PS

CAPACITIES

701.	Engine oil—Total (dry)	4·83 litres (8·5 pints)
	—Oil change ...	4·125 litres (7·3 pints) with filter
702.	Gearbox	1·8 litres (3·2 pints)
703.	Differential	1·75 pints (1·0 litres)
704.	Cooling system	13 pints (7·4 litres)
705.	Fuel tank	8·5 gallons (38·6 litres)
706.	Tyre size	165×15
707.	Tyre pressures —Front	18 (1·24)
	lb./in.² (bars) —Rear	19 (1·31)
708.	No. of grease gun points...	12 (Front sliding axles have 'one-shot' lubrication; press foot plunger every 200 miles approx.)
709.	Normal servicing intervals	Greasing, 3000 miles; engine oil change, 5000 miles
710.	Hydraulic fluid	Castrol/Girling Universal

DIMENSIONS

801.	Length overall	12ft. (3658mm.)
802.	Width overall	56in. (1422mm.)
803.	Height overall	51·75in. (1314mm.)
804.	Weight (dry) —2-seat	1460lb. or 13cwt. (662kg.)
	—4-seat	1516lb. or 13·5cwt. (688kg.)
805.	Ground cl'nce (unladen)	7in. (178mm.)
806.	Track	47in. (1194mm.) front and rear
807.	Wheelbase	96in. (2438mm.)
808.	Turning circle diameter...	32ft. (9·75m.)

TORQUE SPANNER DATA (lb.ft.)

		lb.ft.	kg.m.
901.	Cylinder head bolts ...	61	8·5
902.	Big-end bearing nuts ...	36	5·0
903.	Main b'ring screws—Front	58	8·0
	—Self-locking	83	11·5
905.	Flywheel bolts	61	8·5
906.	Clutch to flywheel bolts ...	22	3·0
907.	Drive pinion bearing nut	95/100	13·1/13·8
908.	Crown wheel bolts ...	50/60	6·9/8·3
909.	Differential bearing nuts...	35/40	4·8/5·5
910.	Road wheel nuts... ...	65/70	9·0/9·6
911.	Steering wheel nut ...	25/35	3·5/4·8

BODY AND CHASSIS

1001.	Type of construction ...	Coachbuilt; steel 'Z' section chassis; timber (ash) body frame
1002.	Material of body panels ...	Steel and aluminium
1003.	Windscreen glass ...	Laminated

4/4 1600 (Fiat engine) 1984

Model: 2-seat Tourer

ENGINE (Rover)

1.	Type	4-stroke V8 (cast-aluminium block); O.H.V.; central camshaft; hydraulic tappets
2.	Cooling system	Water pump, radiator (15lb./in.²), fan (electric) and thermostat
3.	Number of cylinders	8 (dry liners)
4.	Firing order and idling speed	1L—8R—4R—3L—6R—5L—7L—2R (No. 1 at front left); 725/775 r.p.m.
5.	Bore	3·5in. (88·9mm.)
6.	Stroke	2·8in. (71·12mm.)
7.	Cubic capacity	3532cm.³
8.	Compression ratio and pressure	9·35:1; 135lb./in.² min. at 150/200 r.p.m.
9.	Brake horse-power (DIN)	157 at 5250 r.p.m.
10.	Torque (DIN)	198lb.ft. at 2500 r.p.m.
11.	Piston oversizes	·010, ·020in.
12.	Piston clearance in bore	·0007/·0013in. (skirt bottom)
13.	Piston rings—number	2 compression, 1 oil
14.	Piston rings—width	Compression, ·0615/·0625in.; oil (expander) 0·1894in. max.
15.	Piston rings—groove cl'nce	Compression, ·003/·005in.
16.	Piston rings—gap (in bore)	Compression, ·017/·022in.
17.	Oil pressure (lb./in.²)	30/40 at 2400 r.p.m. (55 at 4000)
18.	Gudgeon pin diameter	0·8746/0·8749in.
19.	Gudgeon pin fit in piston	·0001/·0003in. clearance
20.	Gudgeon pin fit in con. rod	Press fit
21.	Crankpin diameter	2·0000/2·0005in.
22.	Crankpin undersizes	·010, ·020, ·030, ·040in.
23.	Connecting rod length	5·662/5·658in. (centres)
24.	Big-end bearings	Vandervell, lead-indium
25.	Big-end bearing clearance	·0007/·0027in.
26.	Big-end side clearance	·005/·015in.
27.	Main journal diameter	2·2992/2·2997in.
28.	Main journal undersizes	·010, ·020, ·030, ·040in.
29.	Main bearings	5; Vandervell, lead-indium
30.	Main bearings—length	(1) (2) (4) (5), 0·797/0·807in.; (3)
31.	Main bearing clearance	·0009/·0024in. [1·056/1·058in.
32.	Crankshaft end-float	·004/·008in.
33.	Crankshaft end-thrust on	Centre main bearing
35.	Camshaft bearings	5; steel-backed Babbitt
38.	Camshaft drive type	Chain; 54×0·375in. pitches
39.	Valve head diameter	Inlet, 1·565/1·575in.; exhaust, 1·3475/1·3575
40.	Valve stem diameter (tapered)	Inlet (head) 0·3402/0·3412 to 0·3407/0·3417in.; exhaust, 0·3397/0·3407 to
42.	Valve lift	0·39in. [0·3402/0·3412in.
43.	Valve guide length	Fitted height, 19mm. above step surrounding valve guide boss
44.	Valve stem/guide cl'nce	Inlet (top), ·001/·003; (bottom), ·0015/·0035. Exhaust (top), ·0015/·0035; (bottom), ·002/·004in.
46.	Valve spring loaded length	1·577in. at 70±3·5lb.; 1·350in. at 130±6·5lb.; 1·187in. at 176±7·5lb.
49.	Valve timing Inlet opens	30° B.T.D.C. } peak, 112·5°
	Inlet closes	75° A.B.D.C. } A.T.D.C.
	Exhaust opens	68° B.B.D.C. } peak, 105·5°
	Exhaust closes	37° A.T.D.C. } B.T.D.C.
50.	Petrol pump	Electric
52.	Carburettors	2 Zenith Stromberg 175CDEF
53.	Needle	B1FB
64.	Exhaust gas analysis	3·0/3·5% CO

TRANSMISSION

101.	Type	Rear wheel drive
102.	Clutch (hydraulic)	Borg & Beck, 9·5in. diam., single dry plate, diaphragm spring, free travel at lever, 1/16in. (1·6mm.)
103.	Gearbox	5 forward speeds, all synchromesh
105.	Gearbox ratios	0·792; 1; 1·396; 2·087; 3·321; R.,
106.	Overdrive	Not fitted [3·428:1
107.	Driving axles	Semi-floating
108.	Final drive gear	Hypoid, limited-slip differential
109.	Final drive ratio	3·31:1
111.	Crown wheel/pinion b'lash	0·003/0·006in.; shim adjustment
112.	Pinion bearing pre-load	8/12lb.in.
113.	Differential brg. pre-load	·003/·005in.; shim adjustment

BRAKES

201.	Front	Girling hydraulic, 11in. diam. discs
202.	Rear	Girling hydraulic, 9in. diam. drums
203.	Handbrake	Mechanical, on rear wheels
204.	Linings—front	Ferodo, type GX
205.	Linings—rear	Ferodo, type LL, 1¾in. wide
206.	Power assistance	Girling servo (twin on L.H. drive cars)

STEERING (see also "Dimensions")

301.	Type	Worm and nut
302.	Camber angle	2°, non-adjustable
303.	Castor angle	4°, non-adjustable
304.	King-pin inclination	2°
305.	Toe-in	1/8/3/16in. (3/5mm.) at wheel rims
306.	Condition for checking	Unladen

FRONT SUSPENSION

401.	Type	Independent, vertical coil springs
402.	Number of coils	18
403.	Coil diameter	2⅜in. (external)
404.	Wire diameter	0·375in.
405.	Spring length—free	13in.
406.	Spring length—fitted	9in.

REAR SUSPENSION

501.	Type	Semi-elliptic leaf-springs
504.	Spring length	42¾in. (free)
505.	Number of leaves	6
506.	Width of leaves	1⅜in.
507.	Thickness of leaves	¼in.
508.	Spring camber—free	3½in.

ELECTRICAL SYSTEM

601.	Ignition timing —static	6° BTDC (pulley)
	—stroboscope	10° at 1200 r.p.m.; 17° at 1800; 22° at 2600; vac. hose off
602.	Sparking plugs	Champion N12Y
603.	Sparking plug gap	·030in.
604.	Distributor	Lucas 35DE8 (electronic)
605.	Pick-up air gap	·014/·016in. (0·36/;·40mm.)
606.	Centrifugal advance	0° at 300 r.p.m.; 1°/3° at 600; 4·5°/7° at 900; 7°/9° at 1300; 9·5°/11·5° at 2200; 10°/12° at 2800
608.	Vacuum advance	0°/0·5° at 0in.Hg., 0°/3° at 4·3in.; 6°/9° at 10in.; 7°/9° at 20in. (Distributor degrees and r.p.m.)
610.	Ignition coil	Lucas 22C12; 9BR ballast resistor
611.	Battery	12V. 60A.h., Lucas QOA13
612.	Battery earth	Negative
613.	Alternator	Lucas 18ACR, 43 amp.
614.	Regulator	Integral with alternator
615.	Starter motor	Lucas 3M100, pre-engaged; lock, 16·5 lb.ft. at 545A.

CAPACITIES

701.	Engine oil —Total	9·5 pints (5·4 litres) incl. filter
	—Drain/Refill	8·25 pints (4·7 litres) plus filter
702.	Gearbox (dry)	2·7 pints (1·5 litres)
703.	Differential	2·5 pints (1·4 litres)
704.	Cooling system	15 pints (8·5 litres)
705.	Fuel tank	14 gallons (64 litres)
706.	Tyre size	205VR15, 60 Series
707.	Tyre pressures —Front	18 (1·24); fast driving, 22 (1·5)
	lb./in.² (bars) —Rear	18 (1·24); fast driving, 22 (1·5)
708.	No. of grease gun points	10
709.	Servicing intervals	Greasing, 3000 miles; engine oil change, 5000 miles
710.	Hydraulic fluid	Castrol/Girling Universal

DIMENSIONS

801.	Length overall	12ft. 8in. (3861mm.)
802.	Width overall	60in. (1524mm.)
803.	Height overall	50in. (1270mm.)
804.	Weight (dry)	1884lb. (16·8cwt.) (855kg.) approx.
805.	Ground clearance	6in. (152mm.) unladen (sump)
806.	Track —Front	52in. (1321mm.)
	—Rear	53in. (1346mm.)
807.	Wheelbase	98in. (2489mm.)
808.	Turning circle diameter	38ft. (11·6m.)

TORQUE SPANNER DATA (lb.ft.)

901.	Cylinder head bolts	— 65/70 (3·8in. and 2·6in. bolts)
		— 40/50 (2·16in. bolts)
902.	Big-end bearing bolts	30/35
903.	Main bearing bolts	50/55
	—Rear	65/70
905.	Flywheel bolts	50/60
906.	Clutch to flywheel bolts	20
907.	Drive pinion bearing nut	95/100
908.	Crown wheel bolts	50/60
909.	Differential bearing nuts	35/40
910.	Road wheel nuts	65/70
911.	Steering wheel nut	25/35

BODY AND CHASSIS

1001.	Type of construction	Steel 'Z'-section chassis
1002.	Material of body panels	Steel and aluminium
1003.	Type of glass	Windscreen laminated

Plus 8 1984

Models: 4-seat Tourer and 2-seat Competition model

ENGINE (Ford CVH)

1. Type	...	4-stroke; central O.H.C.; V-formation valves; hydraulic tappets
2. Cooling system ...	...	Water pump, radiator (0·85/1·1 bar), electric fan, thermostat (85°/89°C)
3. Number of cylinders	...	4 (direct in block)
4. Firing order	...	1—3—4—2 (No. 1 front)
4a. Idling speed	...	800 ± 25 r.p.m. (fan on)
5. Bore	...	79·96mm.
6. Stroke	...	79·52mm.
7. Cubic capacity ...	...	1597cm.³
8. Compression ratio	...	9·5:1
8a. Compression pressure	...	11·2/14·8kg./cm.² (159/210lb./in.²) warm; L.T. detached from coil
9. Brake horse-power (DIN)		96 (71 kW) at 6000 r.p.m.
10. Torque (DIN) ...	...	13·5kg.m. (98lb.ft.) at 4000 r.p.m.
10a. Piston diameter (standard)		79·930/79·955mm. (service)
11. Piston oversizes ...	...	80·210/80·235, 80·430/80·455mm.
12. Piston clearance in bore		Prod., 0·020/0·040mm.; serv., 0·010/0·045mm.
16. Piston rings—gap (in bore)		(1) (2) 0·30/0·50mm.; (3) 0·4/1·4mm.
17. Oil pressure (minimum)	...	2·8 bar (40·6lb./in.²) at 2000 r.p.m. (10W 30)
18. Gudgeon pin diameter	...	20·622/20·634mm., in 4 grades
19. Gudgeon pin fit in piston		0·013/0·045mm. clearance
20. Gudgeon pin fit in con. rod		Interference; heat small end to 260°/[400°C.
21. Crankpin diameter	...	47·89/47·91mm.
22. Crankpin undersizes	...	0·25, 0·50, 0·75, 1·00mm.
25. Big-end bearing clearance		0·006/0·060mm. (·0002/·0023in.)
27. Main journal diameter	...	57·98/58·00mm.
28. Main journal undersizes	...	0·25, 0·50, 0·75, 1·00mm.
29. Main bearings	...	5
31. Main bearing clearance...		0·011/0·058mm. (·0004/·0023in.)
32. Crankshaft end-float	...	0·09/0·30mm. (·004/·012in.)
33. Crankshaft end-thrust on		Centre bearing (width, 28·825/28·875 mm.)
34. Camshaft journal diameter		(1) 44·75; (2) 45·00; (3) 45·25; (4) 45·50; (5) 45·75mm.
35. Camshaft bearings	...	5; steel-backed
37. Camshaft end-float	...	0·05/0·15mm. (·002/·006in.)
38. Camshaft drive type	...	Toothed belt
38a. Cam lift ...	...	6·09mm. (0·240in.)
39. Valve head diameter	...	I., 41·9/42·1mm.; E., 36·9/37·1mm.
40. Valve stem diameter	...	I., 8·025/8·043mm.; E., 7·999/8·017. (O/S, 0·2 & 0·4mm.)
40a. Valve length ...	...	I., 134·54/135·00mm.; E., 131·57/132·03
41. Valve seat angle ...	...	45°
42. Valve lift	...	I., 10·19mm.; E., 10·16mm.
44. Valve stem/guide c'lance		I., 0·020/0·063mm.; E., 0·046/0·089
45. Valve spring free length		47·2mm.
46. Valve spring loaded length		37·084mm. at 402·4/441·6N (90·5/99·3lb.)
47. Valve working clearance		Hydraulic tappets
48. Valve timing clearance	...	N.A. Timing below at 1mm. cam lift
49. Valve timing ...	...	8°BT—36°AB—34°BB—6°AT
50. Petrol pump ...	...	Mech.; 0·22/0·35 bar (3·2/5·1lb./in.²)
51. Carburettor ...	...	Weber twin-choke
52. Choke tube (Venturi)	...	24mm. 25mm.
52a. Choke pull-down	...	$5 \cdot 5mm. \pm 0 \cdot 3$
52b. Choke phasing ...	...	$2 \cdot 0mm. \pm 0 \cdot 5mm.$
53. Main jet	...	112 125
54. Compensating jet ...		160 150
55. Slow-running jet...	...	50 60
57. Emulsion tube ...	...	F30 F30
64. Exhaust gas analysis	...	CO, $1 \cdot 25\% \pm 0 \cdot 25$

TRANSMISSION

101. Type	...	Rear wheel drive
102. Clutch (cable op.)	...	Ford/L.U.K. 8·5in. —pedal free-travel 23/31mm. (0·9/1·2in.)
103. Gearbox ...	...	5 forward speeds, all synchromesh
105. Gearbox ratios	...	0·85; 1; 1·37; 1·97; 3·65; R., 3·66:1
107. Driving axles	...	Semi-floating
108. Final drive gear	...	Hypoid (Salisbury)
109. Final drive ratio	...	4·1:1 (41/10)
111. Crown wheel/pinion b'lash		·003/·006in.; shim adjustment
112. Pinion bearing pre-load	...	8/12lb.in.; shim adjustment
113. Differential brg. pre-load		·003/·005in.; shim adjustment

BRAKES (Single circuit, dual master cyl.)

201. Front	...	Girling hydraulic, 11in. diam. discs
202. Rear	...	Girling hydraulic, 9in. diam. drums
203. Handbrake ...	...	Mechanical, on rear wheels
204. Linings—front ...		Ferodo, type 14 calliper pads
205. Linings—rear ...		Ferodo, 1·75in. wide

STEERING (see also "Dimensions")

301. Type	...	Recirculating ball
302. Camber angle ...	...	2° (alt., 0°); non-adjustable
303. Castor angle ...	...	4°; non-adjustable
304. King-pin inclination	...	2°
305. Toe-in	...	⅛ to ³⁄₁₆in. (3 to 5mm.) at wheel rim
306. Condition for checking	...	Unladen

FRONT SUSPENSION

401. Type	...	Independent, vertical coil springs
402. Number of coils ...		21
403. Coil diameter ...		2¼in. (external)
404. Wire diameter ...		0·31in.
405. Spring length—free		14¼in.
406. Spring length—fitted		8¼in.

REAR SUSPENSION

501. Type	...	Semi-elliptic leaf springs
504. Spring length (centres)		42¾in. (free)
505. Number of leaves	...	5
506. Width of leaves ...		1¾in.
507. Thickness of leaves	...	¼in.
508. Spring camber—free		3⅜in.

ELECTRICAL SYSTEM

601. Ignition timing (inital)	...	12°BTDC (pulley)
602. Sparking plugs ...		Motorcraft AGP12C or AGPR12C
603. Sparking plug gap	...	·025in. (0·6mm.)
604. Distributor ...	...	Lucas or Bosch, electronic
606. Centrif. advance starts at		0°/4° at 200 r.p.m.
607. Centrif. advance—max.		14·8°/22·8° at 6000 r.p.m.
608. Vacuum advance starts	...	-1°/+3° at 90mm. Hg.
609. Vacuum advance—max.		14°/22° at 218mm. Hg. (Crankshaft degrees and r.p.m.)
610. Ignition coil ...	...	Prim. res., 0·72/0·88Ω; sec. res., 4·5/7kΩ
611. Battery		12V. 40A.h.
612. Battery earth ...		Negative
613. Alternator ...	...	35A.
614. Regulated voltage	...	13·7/14·6V. at 3/7A., 4000 r.p.m.
615. Starter motor ...		0·9kW.

CAPACITIES

701. Engine oil (refill)	...	6·6 pints (3·75 litres) with filter
702. Gearbox ...	...	2·6 pints (1·5 litres)
703. Differential ...	...	1·75 pints (1·0 litres)
704. Cooling system ...		13 pints (7·4 litres)
705. Fuel tank ...	...	12·5 gallons (56 litres)
706. Tyre size ...	...	175/70HR15
707. Tyre pressures —Front		18 (1·24)
lb./in.² (bars) —Rear		18 (1·24)
708. No. of grease gun points	...	12 (Front sliding axles have 'one-shot' lubrication; press foot plunger every 200 miles approx.)
709. Normal servicing intervals		Greasing, 3000 miles; engine oil change, 5000 miles
710. Hydraulic fluid ...	...	Castrol/Girling Universal

DIMENSIONS

801. Length overall ...	...	12ft. (3658mm.)
802. Width overall ...	...	56in. (1422mm.)
803. Height overall ...		51·75in. (1314mm.)
804. Weight (dry) —2-seat		1460lb. or 13cwt. (662kg.)
—4-seat		1516lb. or 13·5cwt. (688kg.)
805. Ground cl'nce (unladen)	...	7in. (178mm.)
806. Track		47in. (1194mm.) front and rear
807. Wheelbase ...	...	96in. (2438mm.)
808. Turning circle diameter	...	32ft. (9·75m.)

TORQUE SPANNER DATA (lb.ft.)

901. Cylinder head nuts (in stages)	...	(1) 18; (2) 41; (3) +90°; (4) +90°	
902. Big-end bearing nuts ...	19/24	908. Crown wheel bolts	50/60
903. Main bearing bolts ...	66/74	909. Diff. bearing nuts	35/40
905. Flywheel bolts ...	61/66	910. Road wheel nuts	65/70
906. Clutch to flywheel bolts ...	13/15	911. Steering wheel nut	25/35
907. Drive pinion nut...	... 95/100		

BODY AND CHASSIS

1001. Type of construction	...	Coachbuilt; steel 'Z'-section chassis; timber (ash) body frame
1002. Material of body panels	...	Steel and aluminium
1003. Windscreen glass	...	Laminated

4/4 1600 1985

Models: 2- or 4-seater. Introduced Jan. 1985

ENGINE (Fiat)

1.	Type	4-stroke; twin O.H.C.; light alloy head
2.	Cooling system ...	Water pump, radiator, electric fan (on 95°, off 89°C), thermostat (87°C)
3.	Number of cylinders ...	4 (direct in block)
4.	Firing order ...	1—3—4—2 (No. 1 front)
4a.	Idling speed ...	900 r.p.m.
5.	Bore	84 mm.
6.	Stroke	90mm.
7.	Cubic capacity ...	1995cm.³
8.	Compression ratio ...	8·9:1
9.	Brake horse-power (DIN)	122 at 5500 r.p.m.
10.	Torque (DIN) kg.m.(lb.ft.)	17·9 (129) at 3500 r.p.m.
10a.	Piston diameter (standard)	83·940/83·990mm. (in 3 grades)
11.	Piston oversizes ...	0·2, 0·4, 0·6mm.
12.	Piston clearance in bore	0·050/0·070mm., 25mm., from base of [skirt
13.	Piston rings—number ...	1 compression, 2 oil
14.	Piston rings—width ...	(1) 1·478/1·490mm.; (2) 1·980/2·000 mm.; (3) 3·925/3·937mm.
15.	Piston rings—groove cl'nce	(1) 0·045/0·077mm.; (2) 0·030/0·070 mm.; (3) 0·030/0·062mm.
16.	Piston rings—gap (in bore)	(1) (2) 0·30/0·45mm.; (3) 0·25/0·40
17.	Oil pressure (normal) ...	3·5/5kg./cm.² at 100°C
18.	Gudgeon pin diameter ...	21·991/21·997mm. in 2 grades
19.	Gudgeon pin fit in piston	0·002/0·008mm. clearance
20.	Gudgeon pin fit in con. rod	0·010/0·016 mm. clearance
21.	Crankpin diameter ...	50·782/50·802mm.
22.	Crankpin undersizes... ...	·010, ·020, ·030, ·040in.
25.	Big-end bearing clearance	0·021/0·065mm.
26.	Main journal diameter	52·985/53·005mm.
28.	Main journal undersizes	·010, ·020, ·030, ·040in.
29.	Main bearings	5
31.	Main bearing clearance	0·032/0·077mm.
32.	Crankshaft end-float ...	0·055/0·305mm. (·002/·012in.)
33.	Crankshaft end-thrust on	Rear main bearing
34.	Camshaft journal diam.	(1) 29·944/29·960mm.; (2) 45·755/ 45·771mm.; (3) 46·155/46·171mm.
34a.	Aux. shaft journal diam.	(1) 48·013/48·038mm.; (2) 38·929/ 38·954mm.
36.	Camshaft bearing cl'nce	(1) 0·049/0·090mm.; (2) (3) 0·029/ 0·070mm.
36a.	Aux. shaft bearing cl'nce	0·046/0·091mm., both bearings
38.	Camshaft drive type ...	Toothed belt
38a.	Cam lift	9·564mm.
39.	Valve head diameter ...	I., 42·20/42·60mm.; E., 35·85/36·45
40.	Valve stem diameter ...	7·974/7·992mm.
41.	Valve seat angle ...	45°±5' (face angle, 45° 30′±5')
44.	Valve stem/guide cl'ance	0·030/0·066mm. (·001/·0026in.)
46.	Valve spring rate—Inner	31mm. at 14·9kg. (32·8lb.); limit, 13·5kg —Outer 36mm. at 38·9kg. (85·8lb.); limit, 36kg.
47.	Valve clearance (cold) ...	I., 0·45mm. (·018in.); E., 0·50 (·020)
48.	Valve timing clearance ...	0·8mm. (·031in.)
49.	Valve timing	5°BT—53°AB—53°BB—5°AT

FUEL SYSTEM (Petrol injection)

50.	Petrol pump	Mechanical. 0·26/0·32 bar (3·8/4·6lb./ in.²) at 6000 shaft r.p.m.
51.	Injection system ...	Bosch L-Jetronic

TRANSMISSION

101.	Type	Rear-wheel drive
102.	Clutch	Valeo 215mm.; pedal free-travel, 25mm.
103.	Gearbox	5 forward speeds, all synchromesh
105.	Gearbox ratios ...	0·834; 1; 1·357; 2·045; 3·612; R., [3·244:1
107.	Driving axles ...	Semi-floating
108.	Final drive gear ...	Hypoid (Salisbury)
109.	Final drive ratio ...	4·1:1 (41/10)
111.	Crown wheel/pinion b'lash	·003/·006in.; shim adjustment
112.	Pinion bearing pre-load ...	8/12lb.in.; shim adjustment
113.	Differential brg. pre-load	·003/·005in.; shim adjustment

BRAKES (Single circuit, dual master cyl.)

201.	Front	Girling hydraulic, 11in. diam. discs
202.	Rear	Girling hydraulic, 9in. diam. drums
203.	Handbrake	Mechanical, on rear wheels
204.	Linings—front ...	Girling 535 pads
205.	Linings—rear ...	Girling 784

STEERING (see also "Dimensions")

301.	Type	Recirculating ball
302.	Camber angle ...	2°; non-adjustable
303.	Castor angle ...	4°; non-adjustable
304.	King-pin inclination ...	2°
305.	Toe-in	3/5mm. at wheel rim (0°30′ nom.)
306.	Condition for checking ...	Unladen

FRONT SUSPENSION

401.	Type	Independent, vertical coil springs
402.	Number of coils ...	21
403.	Coil diameter ...	2½in. (external)
404.	Wire diameter ...	0·31in.
405.	Spring length—free ...	13½in.
406.	Spring length—fitted ...	8½in.

REAR SUSPENSION

501.	Type	Semi-elliptic leaf springs
504.	Spring length (centres) ...	43in. (free)
505.	Number of leaves ...	5
506.	Width of leaves ...	1¾in.
507.	Thickness of leaves ...	¼in.
508.	Spring camber—free ...	3½in.

ELECTRICAL SYSTEM

601.	Ignition timing—static ...	10°BTDC (pulley/cover)
	—stroboscope	28° at 3200 r.p.m.
602.	Sparking plugs ...	Champion N9Y
603.	Sparking plug gap ...	0·6/0·7mm (·024/·027in.)
604.	Distributor ...	Digiplex computerized ignition system
610.	Ignition coil ...	Marelli BAE500B
611.	Battery	12V. 40 A.h., negative earth
613.	Alternator ...	Marelli or Bosch 55A
614.	Regulated voltage ...	14·2V
615.	Starter motor ...	Marelli 0·9kW. Lock torque, 13Nm. (9·6lb. ft.)

CAPACITIES

701.	Engine oil—Total (dry) ...	5 litres (8·8 pints)
	—Oil change ...	4·4 litres (7·7 pints) with filter
702.	Gearbox	1·8 litres (3·2 pints)
703.	Differential ...	1·75 pints (1·0 litre)
704.	Cooling system ...	18 pints (10·2 litres)
705.	Fuel tank ...	12·5 gallons (56 litres)
706.	Tyre size ...	175/70 HR15
707.	Tyre pressures —Front	18 (1·24)
	lb/in.² (bars) —Rear	18 (1·24)
708.	No. of grease gun points ...	10
709.	Normal servicing intervals	5000 miles or 6 months
710.	Hydraulic fluid ...	Castrol/Girling Universal

DIMENSIONS

801.	Length overall ...	12ft. (3658mm.)
802.	Width overall ...	58in. (1473mm.)
803.	Height overall ...	51·75in. (1314mm.)
804.	Weight (dry) —2-seat	1460lb. or 13cwt. (662kg.)
	—4-seat	1516lb. or 13·5cwt. (688kg.)
805.	Ground cl'nce (unladen)	7in. (178mm.)
806.	Track ...	47in. (1194mm.) front and rear
807.	Wheelbase	96in. (2438mm.)
808.	Turning circle diameter...	32ft. (9·75m.)

TORQUE SPANNER DATA

		lb.ft.	kg.m.
901.	Cyl. head bolts (4 stages)	14; 29; 90°; 90°	2; 4; 90°; 90°
902.	Big-end bearing nuts ...	55	7·6
903.	Main b'ring screws—Front	60	8·3
	—Self-locking	85	11·7
905.	Flywheel bolts	107	14·8
906.	Clutch to flywheel bolts ...	15	2·0
907.	Drive pinion bearing nut	95/100	13·1/13·8
908.	Crown wheel bolts ...	50/60	6·9/8·3
909.	Differential bearing nuts...	35/40	4·8/5·5
910.	Road wheel nuts ...	65/70	9·0/9·6
911.	Steering wheel nut ...	25/35	3·5/4·8

BODY AND CHASSIS

1001.	Type of construction ...	Coachbuilt; steel 'Z' section chassis; timber (ash) body frame
1002.	Material of body panels ...	Steel and aluminium
1003.	Windscreen glass ...	Laminated

Plus 4 (Fiat engine) 1985

Model: 2-seat Tourer; standard (carburettor) or fuel injection engine

ENGINE (Rover)

		Standard	Injection
1.	Type	4-stroke V8 (cast-aluminium block); O.H.V.; central camshaft; hydraulic tappets	
2.	Cooling system ...	Water pump, radiator (15lb./in.²), fan (electric) and thermostat	
3.	Number of cylinders ...	8 (dry liners)	
4.	Firing order (No. 1 front)	1ʟ—8ʀ—4ʀ—3ʟ—6ʀ—5ʟ—7ʟ—2ʀ	
4a.	Idling speed	750 ± 25 r.p.m.	775 ± 25 r.p.m.
5.	Bore	3·5in. (88·9mm.)	
6.	Stroke	2·8in. (71·12mm.)	
7.	Cubic capacity ...	3532cm.³	
8.	Compression ratio ...	9·35:1	9·75:1
8a.	Compression pressure ...	130lb./in.²	130lb./in.²
9.	Brake horse-power (DIN)	157 at 5250 r.p.m.	190 at 5280 r.p.m.
10.	Torque (DIN)—lb.ft. ...	198 at 2500 r.p.m.	200 at 4000 r.p.m.
11.	Piston oversizes ...	·010, ·020in.	
12.	Piston clearance in bore ...	·0007/·0013in. (skirt bottom)	
13.	Piston rings—number ...	2 compression, 1 oil	
14.	Piston rings—width ...	Compression, ·0615/·0625in.; oil (expander) 0·1894in. max.	
15.	Piston rings—groove cl'nce	Compression, ·003/·005in.	
16.	Piston rings—gap (in bore)	Compression, ·017/·022in.	
17.	Oil pressure (lb./in.²) ...	30/40 at 2400 r.p.m. (55 at 4000)	
18.	Gudgeon pin diameter ...	0·8746/0·8749in.	
19.	Gudgeon pin fit in piston	·0001/·0003in. clearance	
20.	Gudgeon pin fit in con. rod	Press fit	
21.	Crankpin diameter ...	2·0000/2·0005in.	
22.	Crankpin undersizes ...	·010, ·020, ·030, ·040in.	
23.	Connecting rod length ...	5·662/5·658in. (centres)	
24.	Big-end bearings ...	Vandervell, lead-indium	
25.	Big-end bearing clearance	·0007/·0027in.	
26.	Big-end side clearance ...	·005/·015in.	
27.	Main journal diameter ...	2·2992/2·2997in.	
28.	Main journal undersizes ...	·010, ·020, ·030, ·040in.	
29.	Main bearings	5; Vandervell, lead-indium	
30.	Main bearings—length ...	(1) (2) (4) (5), 0·797/0·807in.; (3)	
31.	Main bearing clearance ...	·0009/·0024in.	[1·056/1·058in.
32.	Crankshaft end-float ...	·004/·008in.	
33.	Crankshaft end-thrust on	Centre main bearing	
35.	Camshaft bearings ...	5; steel-backed Babbitt	
38.	Camshaft drive type ...	Chain; 54×0·375in. pitches	
39.	Valve head diameter ...	I., 1·565/1·575in.; E., 1·3475/1·3575	
40.	Valve stem diameter	Inlet (head) 0·3402/0·3412 to 0·3407/ 0·3417in.; exhaust 0·3397/0·3407 to	
	(tapered)	0·3402/0·3412in.	
42.	Valve lift	0·39in.	
43.	Valve guide length ...	Fitted height, 19mm. above step surrounding valve guide boss	
44.	Valve stem/guide cl'nce ...	Inlet (top), ·001/·003; (bottom), ·0015/ ·0035. Exhaust (top), ·0015/·0035; (bottom), ·002/·004in.	
46.	Valve spring loaded length	1·577in. at 70±3·5lb.; 1·350in. at 130 ±6·5lb.; 1·187in. at 176±7·5lb.	
49.	Valve timing Inlet opens	30° B.T.D.C. } peak, 112·5°	
	Inlet closes	75° A.B.D.C. } A.T.D.C.	
	Exhaust opens	68° B.B.D.C. } peak, 105·5°	
	Exhaust closes	37° A.T.D.C. } B.T.D.C.	
50.	Petrol pump ...	AC Delco electric (in tank); 6lb./in.²	Lucas 4FP elect.
51.	Carburettors/Inj. ...	2 Zenith 175CDEF	Lucas 'L' system, electronic fuel injection. Pump delivery pressure, 26/36lb./in.²
53.	Needle	B1FB*	
54.	Jet diameter ...	0·100in.	
56.	Piston spring ...	Blue	
64.	Exhaust gas analysis ...	CO, 1·5/2·5%	CO, 1·5% ± 0·5
		*Initial setting, shoulder flush with piston	

TRANSMISSION

101.	Type	Rear wheel drive
102.	Clutch (hydraulic) ...	Borg & Beck, 9·5in. diam., single dry plate, diaphragm spring, free travel at lever, 1/16in. (1·6mm.)
103.	Gearbox	5 forward speeds, all synchromesh
105.	Gearbox ratios ...	0·792; 1; 1·396; 2·087; 3·321; R., 3·428:1
106.	Overdrive	Not fitted
107.	Driving axles ...	Semi-floating
108.	Final drive gear ...	Hypoid, limited-slip differential
109.	Final drive ratio ...	3·31:1
111.	Crown wheel/pinion b'lash	0·003/0·006in.; shim adjustment
112.	Pinion bearing pre-load ...	8/12lb.in.
113.	Differential brg. pre-load	·003/·005in.; shim adjustment

BRAKES

201.	Front	Girling hydraulic, 11in. diam. discs
202.	Rear	Girling hydraulic, 9in. diam. drums
203.	Handbrake	Mechanical, on rear wheels
204.	Linings—front ...	Ferodo, type GX
205.	Linings—rear ...	Ferodo, type LL, 1¾in. wide
206.	Power assistance ...	Girling servo (twin on L.H. drive cars)

STEERING (see also "Dimensions")

301.	Type	Recirc. ball (Inj., rack and pinion)
302.	Camber angle ...	2°, non-adjustable
303.	Castor angle ...	4°, non-adjustable
304.	King-pin inclination ...	2°
305.	Toe-in	3/5mm. at rims (0°30′ nom.)
306.	Condition for checking ...	Unladen

FRONT SUSPENSION

401.	Type	Independent, vertical coil springs
402.	Number of coils ...	18
403.	Coil diameter ...	2⅜in. (external)
404.	Wire diameter ...	0·375in.
405.	Spring length—free ...	13in.
406.	Spring length—fitted ...	9in.

REAR SUSPENSION

501.	Type	Semi-elliptic leaf-springs
504.	Spring length ...	42¼in. (free)
505.	Number of leaves ...	6
506.	Width of leaves ...	1¾in.
507.	Thickness of leaves ...	¼in.
508.	Spring camber—free ...	3½in.

ELECTRICAL SYSTEM

		Standard	Injection
601.	Ignition timing (pulley)	6°BT at 600r.p.m.	8°BT at 600r.p.m.
602.	Sparking plugs ...	Unipart GSP131	Unipart GSP151
603.	Sparking plug gap ...	0·035in. (0·9mm.)	
604.	Distributor (Lucas 35DM8)	41893	41935A
605.	Pick-up air gap ...	·014/·016in. (0·36/0·40mm.)	
606.	Centrifugal advance ...	6·75/9° at 2600	7/7·5° at 2500
	⌈Centrif. & vac. advance	3·5/5·5° at 900	5·5/6° at 1000
	⎹ in distributor degrees/	2·5/4·5° at 700	2/2·5° at 500
	⌊ r.p.m.	0·75/2·75° at 550	None <400
608.	Vacuum advance starts at	5·5/10in.Hg.	4in.Hg.
609.	Vacuum advance—max.	4°/6° at 22in.Hg.	3·5/4·5° at 20·1in.
610.	Ignition module ...	Lucas 22C12	Lucas 32C5
611.	Battery	12V. 60A.h.	
612.	Battery earth ...	Negative	
613.	Alternator ...	Lucas A133, 65A.	
614.	Regulated voltage ...	13·6/14·4V.	
615.	Starter motor ...	Lucas 9M90PE; copper field	
	—Lock torque	12·5lb.ft. (16·9N.m.) at 505/550A.	

CAPACITIES

701.	Engine oil—Total ...	9·7 pints (5·5 litres) incl. filter
	—Drain/Refill	8·25 pints (4·7 litres) plus filter
702.	Gearbox (dry) ...	2·7 pints (1·5 litres)
703.	Differential ...	2·5 pints (1·4 litres)
704.	Cooling system ...	15 pints (8·5 litres); Inj., 24 (13·6)
705.	Fuel tank	14 gallons (64 litres)
706.	Tyre size	205VR15, 60 Series
707.	Tyre pressures —Front	18 (1·24); fast driving, 22 (1·5)
	lb./in.² (bars) —Rear	18 (1·24); fast driving, 22 (1·5)
708.	No. of grease gun points ...	10
709.	Servicing intervals ...	5000 miles or 6 months
710.	Hydraulic fluid ...	Castrol/Girling Universal

DIMENSIONS

801.	Length overall ...	12ft. 8in. (3861mm.)
802.	Width overall ...	60in. (1524mm.)
803.	Height overall ...	50in. (1270mm.)
804.	Weight (dry) ...	1884lb. (16·8cwt.) (855kg.) approx.
805.	Ground clearance ...	6in. (152mm.) unladen (sump)
806.	Track —Front	52in. (1321mm.)
	—Rear	53in. (1346mm.)
807.	Wheelbase ...	98in. (2489mm.)
808.	Turning circle diameter ...	38ft. (11·6m.)

TORQUE SPANNER DATA (lb.ft.)

901.	Cylinder head bolts	— 65/70 (3·8in. and 2·6in. bolts)
		— 40/50 (2·16in. bolts)
902.	Big-end bearing bolts ...	30/35
903.	Main bearing bolts ...	50/55
	—Rear	65/70
905.	Flywheel bolts ...	50/60
906.	Clutch to flywheel bolts ...	20
907.	Drive pinion bearing nut	95/100
908.	Crown wheel bolts ...	50/60
909.	Differential bearing nuts	35/40
910.	Road wheel nuts ...	65/70
911.	Steering wheel nut ...	25/35

BODY AND CHASSIS

1001.	Type of construction ...	Steel 'Z'-section chassis
1002.	Material of body panels ...	Steel and aluminium
1003.	Type of glass ...	Windscreen laminated

Plus 8 1985

ENGINE—TUNING DATA

1	Type	Ford CVH; 4 cyl in line mounted
2	Number of cylinders	4; No 1 pulley end
3	Cubic capacity	1597cm³
4	Bore/Stroke	79.96/79.52mm
5	Compression ratio/pressure	9.5:1/11 bar (159lb/in²) minimum
6	Octane rating (RON)	98
7	Brake horsepower (DIN)	96 at 6000rpm
8	Torque (DIN) Nm (lb ft)	133 (98) at 4000rpm
9	Valve operation	OHC V formation valves, hydraulic tappets
10	Valve timing	8°BT—36°AB—34°BB—6°AT
11	Valve clearances mm (in)	Not Applicable
12	Spark plugs make/type	Motocraft AGP12C or AGPR12C
13	Gap	0.6mm (.25in)
14	Distributor make/type	Lucas or Bosch, electronic
15	Firing order/rotation	1—3—4—2/anticlock
16	Dwell angle	
17	Contact breaker gap	} Electronic
18	Pick up air gap	
19	Ignition timing—stroboscopic	12° BTDC idling
20	Ignition timing—static	12° BTDC
21	Timing marks	Pulley
22	Centrifugal advance commences	−1.5°/3° at 1000rpm
23	Centrifugal advance—max	18°/34.5° at 5000rpm
24	Vacuum advance commences	−1°/2° at 90mm Hg
25	Vacuum advance—max	8°/15.2° at 187.5mm Hg
26	Ignition coil make	†
27	Prim res—sec res	0.72/0.88 ohms—4.5/7.0 kohms
28	Fuel pump	Mech; 0.22/0.35 bar (3.2/5.1lb/in²)
29	Carburettor make/type	Weber twin-choke
30	Specification no	†
31	Idle speed (Fast idle)	800±25rpm
32	Exhaust gas analysis	CO, 1.25%±0.25
33	Cold start operation	Auto
34	Choke tube (Venturi)	24mm — 25mm
35	Main jet	112 — 125
36	Compensating jet	160 — 150
37	Slow-running jet	50 — 60
38	Slow-running air bleed	†
39	Accelerator pump jet	†
40	Float level	†
41	Needle valve	†

ADDITIONAL INFORMATION

A	Emulsion tube	F30 — F30

ENGINE—GENERAL DATA

50	Piston diameter (standard)	79.930/79.955mm (service)
51	Piston oversizes	0.28, 0.50mm
52	Piston clearance in bore	0.023/0.043mm
53	Piston rings—number	2 compression 1 oil
54	Piston rings—width	†
55	Piston rings—groove clearance	(1)(2) 0.041/0.091mm (3) 0.046/0.096
56	Piston rings—gap in bore	(1) (2) 0.30/0.50mm; (3) 0.4/1.4
57	Oil pressure bar (lb/in²)	2.8 (40.6) at 2000rpm
58	Gudgeon pin diameter	20.622/20.632mm, in 4 grades
59	Gudgeon pin fit in piston	Clearance 0.013/0.045mm
60	Gudgeon pin fit in con rod	Interference; heat small end to 260°/400°C
61	Connecting rod length	109.83/109.88mm
62	Crankpin diameter	47.89/47.91mm
63	Crankpin undersizes	0.25, 0.50, 0.75, 1.00mm
64	Big end bearing clearance	0.006/0.060mm
65	Big end side clearance	0.10/0.25mm
66	Main bearings	5
67	Main journal diameter	57.98/58.00mm
68	Main journal undersizes	0.25, 0.50, 0.75, 1.00mm
69	Main bearing clearance	0.011/0.058mm
70	Crankshaft end-float	0.09/0.30mm
71	Crankshaft end-thrust on	Centre Bearing
72	Camshaft bearings	5
73	Camshaft journal diameter	(1) 44.75mm; (2) 45.00; (3) 45.25; (4) 45.50; (5) 45.75
74	Camshaft bearing clearance	0.025/0.059mm
75	Camshaft end-float	0.05/0.15mm
76	Camshaft drive type	Toothed belt
77	Cam lift	6.09mm
78	Valve head diameter	In 41.9/42.1mm; Ex 36.9/37.1
79	Valve stem diameter	In 8.025/8.043mm; Ex 7.999/8.017
80	Valve length	In 134.54/135.00mm; Ex 131.57/132.03
81	Valve seat/face angle	45°
82	Valve lift	In 10.19mm; Ex 10.16
83	Valve guide length	†
84	Valve stem/guide clearance	In 0.020/0.068mm Ex 0.043/0.091
85	Valve spring free length	47.2mm
86	Valve spring loaded length	37.084mm at 402.4/441.6N (90.5/99.3lb)

COOLING SYSTEM

95	Type	Water pump, radiator
96	Radiator pressure cap	0.9 bar (13lb/in²)
97	Fan	Electric
98	Thermostat	85°/89°C

TRANSMISSION

100	Type	Rear wheel drive
101	Clutch	216mm cable operation
102	Manual gearbox type	5 speed
103	Manual gearbox ratios	0.82; 1; 1.37; 1.97; 3.65; R, 3.66:1
104	Automatic gearbox type	}
105	Automatic gearbox ratios	} Not
106	Stall speed	} Applicable
107	Change speeds	}
108	Drive shafts	Semi-floating
109	Final drive ratio	4.1:1
110	Differential bearing pre-load	0.076/0.152mm; shim adjustment
111	Pinion bearing pre-load	8/12lb in; shim adjustment

BRAKES

200	Type	Dual circuit
201	Power assistance	Not Applicable
202	Front	Discs 279mm
203	Rear	Drums 229mm
204	Handbrake	Mechanical, on rear wheels
205	Linings—front	Min thickness 1.5mm
206	Linings—rear	Width 45mm

STEERING

300	Type	Recirculating ball
301	Condition for checking	Unladen
302	Camber	2° non-adjustable
303	Castor	4° non-adjustable
304	King pin inclination	2°
305	Wheel alignment—front	Toe in 0/3mm
306	Toe out on turns	†
307	Turning circle diameter	9.75m
308	Front hub end-float	†

FRONT SUSPENSION

330	Type	Independent, vertical coil springs
331	Number of coils	21
332	Spring length	362mm
333	Spring rate	†
334	Coil diameter	58mm
335	Wire diameter	7.8mm

REAR SUSPENSION

360	Type	Semi-elliptic leaf springs
361	Wheel camber	} Not
362	Wheel alignment—rear	} Applicable
363	Number of leaves	5 or 7
364	Spring length	1086mm
365	Spring rate	†
366	Width of leaves	36mm
367	Thickness of leaves	6.4mm

ELECTRICAL

400	Battery	12V 45Ah neg earth
401	Alternator	45A
402	Regulated voltage	13.7/14.6V at 3/7A, 4000rpm
403	Starter motor	0.8kW

CAPACITIES

500	Engine oil	3.5 litres inc filter
501	Gearbox oil	1.9 litres
502	Differential oil	1.0 litres
503	Cooling system	10.2 litres
504	Fuel tank	56 litres
505	Tyre size	175/70HR15
506	Pressures bar (lb/in²)	F 1.2 (18) R 1.2 (18)
507	Max towing weight	508kg
508	Hydraulic fluid type	DOT 3 spec
509	Service intervals	Greasing, 3000 miles; engine oil change, 5000 miles

ADDITIONAL INFORMATION

A	Grease points	12

DIMENSIONS

600	Length overall	3890mm (153in)
601	Width overall	1500mm (57in)
602	Height overall	1314mm (51.75in)
603	Weight—kerb	2-seat 869kg (1912lb) 4-seat 920kg (2024lb)
604	Ground clearance	165mm (6.5in)
605	Wheelbase	2438mm (96in)
606	Track—front/rear	1220/1245mm (48/49in)

TORQUE WRENCH SETTINGS

		Nm	lb ft		
700	Cylinder head nuts/bolts	24; 56	18; 41	+90°	+90°
701	Big end bearing bolts	26/33	19/24		
702	Main bearing bolts	89/100	66/74		
703	Flywheel bolts	83/89	61/66		
704	Clutch to flywheel bolts	18/20	13/15		
705	Drive plate to torque converter	Not Applicable			
706	Crown wheel bolts	68/81	50/60		
707	Drive pinion nut	129/136	95/100		
708	Differential bearing bolts	47/54	35/40		
709	Road wheel nuts	88/95	65/70		
710	Steering wheel nut	34/47	25/35		

4/4 1600 1986

ENGINE—TUNING DATA

1	Type	Fiat; 4 cyl in line mounted
2	Number of cylinders	4; No 1 pulley end
3	Cubic capacity	1995cm³
4	Bore/Stroke	84/90mm
5	Compression ratio/pressure	8.9:1
6	Octane rating (RON)	97
7	Brake horsepower (DIN)	122 at 5300rpm
8	Torque (DIN) Nm (lb ft)	175 (129) at 3500rpm
9	Valve operation	DOHC V formation valves
10	Valve timing	5°BT—53°AB—53°BB—5°AT
11	Valve clearances mm (in)	In, 0.45mm (.018in); Ex, 0.65 (.025)
12	Spark plugs make/type	Champion N9Y
13	Gap	0.6/0.7mm (.024/.027in)
14	Distributor make/type	Digiplex computerised ignition system
15	Firing order/rotation	1—3—4—2/clockwise
16	Dwell angle	
17	Contact breaker gap	} Electronic
18	Pick up air gap	
19	Ignition timing—stroboscopic	28° at 3200rpm
20	Ignition timing—static	10° BTDC
21	Timing marks	Pulley
22	Centrifugal advance commences	
23	Centrifugal advance—max	} Computer controlled
24	Vacuum advance commences	electronic advance
25	Vacuum advance—max	
26	Ignition coil make	Marelli BAE 500B
27	Prim res—sec res	0.344 ± 10% ohms/3.7 kohms
28	Fuel lift pump	Electric
29	Injection system make	Bosch L-Jetronic
30	Type	†
31	Idle speed	900rpm
32	Exhaust gas analysis	†
33	Injection pressure	†

ENGINE—GENERAL DATA

50	Piston diameter (standard)	83.940/83.990mm (in 3 grades)
51	Piston oversizes	0.2, 0.4, 0.6mm
52	Piston clearance in bore	0.050/0.070mm, 25mm, from base of skirt
53	Piston rings—number	1 compression, 2 oil
54	Piston rings—width	(1) 1.478/1.490mm; (2) 1.980/2.000; (3) 3.925/3.937
55	Piston rings—groove clearance	(1) 0.045/0.077mm; (2) 0.030/0.070; (3) 0.030/0.062
56	Piston rings—gap in bore	(1) (2) 0.30/0.45mm; (3) 0.25/0.40
57	Oil pressure bar (lb/in²)	3.4/4.9 (50/71)
58	Gudgeon pin diameter	21.991/21.997mm in 2 grades
59	Gudgeon pin fit in piston	Clearance 0.002/0.008mm
60	Gudgeon pin fit in con rod	Clearance 0.010/0.016mm
61	Connecting rod length	†
62	Crankpin diameter	50.782/50.802mm
63	Crankpin undersizes	0.254, 0.508, 0.762, 1.016mm
64	Big end bearing clearance	0.021/0.065mm
65	Big end side clearance	†
66	Main bearings	5
67	Main journal diameter	52.985/53.005mm
68	Main journal undersizes	0.254, 0.508, 0.762, 1.016mm
69	Main bearing clearance	0.027/0.072mm
70	Crankshaft end-float	0.055/0.305mm
71	Crankshaft end-thrust on	Rear bearing
72	Camshaft bearings	3
73	Camshaft journal diameter	(1) 29.944/29.960mm; (2) 45.755/45.771; (3) 46.155/46.171
74	Camshaft bearing clearance	(1) 0.049/0.090mm; (2) (3) 0.029/0.070mm
75	Camshaft end-float	†
76	Camshaft drive type	Toothed belt
7	Cam lift	9.564mm
78	Valve head diameter	In, 42.20/42.60mm; Ex, 35.85/36.45
79	Valve stem diameter	7.974/7.992mm
80	Valve length	†
81	Valve seat/face angle	45° ± 5'/45° 30' ± 5'
82	Valve lift	†
83	Valve guide length	†
84	Valve stem/guide clearance	0.030/0.066mm
85	Valve spring free length	†
86	Valve spring loaded length	31mm at 14.9kg (32.8lb); limit, 13.5kg
	Valve spring loaded length	36mm at 38.9kg (85.8lb); limit, 36kg

COOLING SYSTEM

95	Type	Water pump, radiator
96	Radiator pressure cap	0.9 bar (14lb in²)
97	Fan	Electric, on 94°C off 87°C
98	Thermostat	87°C

TRANSMISSION

100	Type	Rear-wheel drive
101	Clutch	215mm; cable operation
102	Manual gearbox type	5 speed
103	Manual gearbox ratios	0.834; 1; 1.357; 2.045; 3.612; R, 3.244:1
04	Automatic gearbox type	
105	Automatic gearbox ratios	} Not
106	Stall speed	} Applicable
107	Change speeds	
108	Drive shafts	Semi-floating
109	Final drive ratio	4.1:1
110	Differential bearing pre-load	0.076/0.152mm shim adjustment
111	Pinion bearing pre-load	8/12lb in; shim adjustment

BRAKES

200	Type	Dual circuit
201	Power assistance	Not Applicable
202	Front	Discs 279mm
203	Rear	Drums 229mm
204	Handbrake	Mechanical, on rear wheels
205	Linings—front	Min thickness 1.5mm
206	Linings—rear	Width 45mm

STEERING

300	Type	Recirculating ball
301	Condition for checking	Unladen
302	Camber	−1° ± 30' non-adjustable
303	Castor	4°; non-adjustable
304	King pin inclination	2°
305	Wheel alignment—front	Toe in 0/3.2mm
306	Toe out on turns	†
307	Turning circle diameter	9.75m
308	Front hub end-float	†

FRONT SUSPENSION

330	Type	Independent, vertical coil springs
331	Number of coils	21
332	Spring length	362mm
333	Spring rate	†
334	Coil diameter	58mm
335	Wire diameter	7.8mm

REAR SUSPENSION

360	Type	Semi-elliptic leaf springs
361	Wheel camber	} Not
362	Wheel alignment—rear	} Applicable
363	Number of leaves	5 or 7
364	Spring length	1086mm
365	Spring rate	†
366	Width of leaves	36m
367	Thickness of leaves	6.4mm

ELECTRICAL

400	Battery	12V 45Ah, neg earth
401	Alternator	Marelli 55A
402	Regulated voltage	14.2V
403	Starter motor	Marelli 0.9kW Lock torque, 13Nm (9.6lb ft)

CAPACITIES

500	Engine oil	4.4 litres inc filter
501	Gearbox oil	1.8 litres
502	Differential oil	1.0 litre
503	Cooling system	10.2 litres
504	Fuel tank	56 litres
505	Tyre size	195/60HR15
506	Pressures bar (lb/in²)	F/R 1.52 (22)
507	Max towing weight	508kg (1120lb)
508	Hydraulic fluid type	DOT 3 spec
509	Service intervals	5000 miles or 6 months

ADDITIONAL INFORMATION

A	Grease points	10

DIMENSIONS

600	Length overall	3890mm (153in)
601	Width overall	1500mm (57in)
602	Height overall	1290mm (51in)
603	Weight—kerb	2 seater 840kg
	Weight—kerb	4 seater 892kg
604	Ground clearance	150mm (6in)
605	Wheelbase	2438mm (96in)
606	Track—front/rear	1270/1295mm (50/51in)

TORQUE WRENCH SETTINGS

		Nm	lb ft	
700	Cylinder head nuts/bolts	19; 26	14; 19;	+90° +90°
701	Big end bearing bolts	75	55	
702	Main bearing bolts	81	60	
		115	85	Front
703	Flywheel bolts	145	107	self locking
704	Clutch to flywheel bolts	20	15	
705	Drive plate to torque converter	Not Applicable		
706	Crown wheel bolts	68/81	50/60	
707	Drive pinion nut	129/136	95/100	
708	Differential bearing bolts	47/54	35/40	
709	Road wheel nuts	88/95	65/70	
710	Steering wheel nut	34/47	25/35	

Plus 4 1986

ENGINE—TUNING DATA

1	Type	Rover; V8 cyl in line mounted
2	Number of cylinders	8; No 1 front left
3	Cubic capacity	3532cm³
4	Bore/Stroke	88.9/71.12mm
5	Compression ratio/pressure	9.75:1/8.97 bar
6	Octane rating (RON)	98
7	Brake horsepower (DIN)	190 at 5280rpm
8	Torque (DIN) Nm (lb ft)	298 (220) at 4000rpm
9	Valve operation	OHV in line valves, hydraulic tappets
10	Valve timing	30°BT—75°AB—68°BB—37°AT
11	Valve clearances mm (in)	Not applicable
12	Spark plugs make/type	Unipart GSP151
13	Gap	0.9mm (.035in)
14	Distributor make/type	Lucas 35DM8 41935A
15	Firing order/rotation	1—8—4—3—6—5—7—2/clockwise
16	Dwell angle	Not
17	Contact breaker gap	Applicable
18	Pick up air gap	0.36/0.40mm (.014/.016in)
19	Ignition timing—stroboscopic	8° BTDC at 600rpm
20	Ignition timing—static	†
21	Timing marks	Pulley
22	Centrifugal advance commences	400rpm
23	Centrifugal advance—max	7°/7.5° at 2500rpm
24	Vacuum advance commences	76.2mm Hg
25	Vacuum advance—max	7°/9° 304.8mm Hg
26	Ignition coil—make	Lucas or Bosch
27	Prim res—sec res	0.71/0.81 ohms
28	Fuel lift pump	Electric
29	Injection system make	Lucas 'L'
30	Type	Electronic
31	Idle speed (Fast idle)	775±25rpm
32	Exhaust gas analysis	CO 1.5%±0.5
33	Injection pressure	1.8/2.49 bar

ENGINE—GENERAL DATA

50	Piston diameter (standard)	88.88mm
51	Piston oversizes	0.26, 0.51mm
52	Piston clearance in bore	0.018/0.033mm
53	Piston rings—number	2 compression, 1 oil
54	Piston rings—width	(1)(2) 1.56/1.58mm (3) 4.81
55	Piston rings—groove clearance	(1)(2) 0.038/0.89mm
56	Piston rings—gap in bore	(1)(2) 0.43/0.56mm (3) 0.38/1.40
57	Oil pressure bar (lb/in²)	2.1/2.8 (30/40) at 2400rpm
58	Gudgeon pin diameter	22.21/22.22mm
59	Gudgeon pin fit in piston	Clearance 0.002/0.007mm
60	Gudgeon pin fit in con rod	Press fit
61	Connecting rod length	143.71/143.81mm (centres)
62	Crankpin diameter	50.80/50.81mm
63	Crankpin undersizes	0.26, 0.51mm
64	Big end bearing clearance	0.015/0.055mm
65	Big end side clearance	0.15/0.356mm
66	Main bearings	5
67	Main journal diameter	58.41/58.42mm
68	Main journal undersizes	0.26, 0.51mm
69	Main bearing clearance	0.013/0.056mm
70	Crankshaft end-float	0.10/0.20mm
71	Crankshaft end-thrust on	Centre bearing
72	Camshaft bearings	5
73	Camshaft journal diameter	(1) 45.34/45.36mm (2) 44.45/44.58 (3) 43.82/43.84 (4) 43.05/43.08 (5) 42.29/42.36
74	Camshaft bearing clearance	†
75	Camshaft end-float	†
76	Camshaft drive type	Chain
77	Cam lift	†
78	Valve head diameter	In 40.00/41.30mm Ex 34.48/35.60
79	Valve stem diameter	In 8.63/8.65mm Ex 8.64/8.66
80	Valve length	116.59/117.35mm
81	Valve seat/face angle	46°±15'/45°±15'
82	Valve lift	9.91mm
83	Valve guide length	†
84	Valve stem/guide clearance	In 0.03/0.07mm Ex 0.04/0.08
85	Valve spring free length	48.30mm
86	Valve spring loaded length	40.40mm at 66.50mm

COOLING SYSTEM

95	Type	Water pump, radiator
96	Radiator pressure cap	1.03 bar
97	Fan	Electric
98	Thermostat	88°C

TRANSMISSION

100	Type	Rear wheel drive
101	Clutch	241.3mm hydraulic operation
102	Manual gearbox type	5 speed
103	Manual gearbox ratios	0.792; 1; 1.396; 2.087; 3.321; R 3.428:1
104	Automatic gearbox type	
105	Automatic gearbox ratios	Not
106	Stall speed	Applicable
107	Change speeds	
108	Drive shafts	Semi-floating
109	Final drive ratio	3.31:1
110	Differential bearing pre-load	0.076/0.152mm
111	Pinion bearing pre-load	0.9/1.4Nm

BRAKES

200	Type	Dual circuit
201	Power assistance	Vacuum servo
202	Front	Discs 279.4mm
203	Rear	Drums 229mm
204	Handbrake	Mechanical on rear wheels
205	Linings—front	Min thickness 1.5mm
206	Linings—rear	Width 45mm

STEERING

300	Type	Rack and pinion
301	Condition for checking	Unladen
302	Camber	−1° no adjustment
303	Castor	4° no adjustment
304	King pin inclination	2°
305	Wheel alignment—front	Toe in 0/3.2mm
306	Toe out on turns	†
307	Turning circle diameter	11.6m
308	Front hub end-float	†

FRONT SUSPENSION

330	Type	Independent vertical coil springs
331	Number of coils	18
332	Spring length	330mm
333	Spring rate	†
334	Coil diameter	60mm
335	Wire diameter	9.52mm

REAR SUSPENSION

360	Type	Semi elliptic leaf springs
361	Wheel camber	Not
362	Wheel alignment—rear	Applicable
363	Number of leaves	6
364	Spring length	1086mm
365	Spring rate	†
366	Width of leaves	36mm
367	Thickness of leaves	6.4mm

ELECTRICAL

400	Battery	12V58Ah neg earth
401	Alternator	Lucas A133, 65A
402	Regulated voltage	13.6/14.4V
403	Starter motor	Lucas

CAPACITIES

500	Engine oil	5.5 litres inc filter
501	Gearbox oil	1.6 litres
502	Differential oil	1.4 litres
503	Cooling system	13.6 litres
504	Fuel tank	64 litres
505	Tyre size	205 VR15
506	Pressures bar (lb/in²)	F/R 1.52 (22)
507	Max towing weight	575kg
508	Hydraulic fluid type	DOT 3 spec
509	Service intervals	5000 miles or 6 months

DIMENSIONS

600	Length overall	3960mm (156in)
601	Width overall	1600mm (63in)
602	Height overall	1220mm (48in)
603	Weight—kerb	889kg (1956lb)
604	Ground clearance	140mm (5.5in)
605	Wheelbase	2489mm (98in)
606	Track—front/rear	1345/1375mm (53/54in)

TORQUE WRENCH SETTINGS

		Nm	lb ft
700	Cylinder head nuts/bolts	95	70 (long)
		68	50 (short)
701	Big end bearing bolts	47	35
702	Main bearing bolts	75 (Rear 95)	55 (Rear 70)
703	Flywheel bolts	81	60
704	Clutch to flywheel bolts	27	20
705	Drive plate to torque converter	Not Applicable	
706	Crown wheel bolts	68/81	50/60
707	Drive pinion nut	129/136	95/100
708	Differential bearing bolts	47/54	35/40
709	Road wheel nuts	88/95	65/70
710	Steering wheel nut	34/47	25/35

Plus 8 F1 1986

ENGINE—TUNING DATA

1	Type	Ford CVH; 4 cyl in line mounted
2	Number of cylinders	4; No 1 pulley end
3	Cubic capacity	1597cm³
4	Bore/Stroke	79.96/79.52mm
5	Compression ratio/pressure	9.5:1/12-14 bar
6	Octane rating (RON)	98
7	Brake horsepower (DIN)	95 at 5750rpm
8	Torque (DIN) Nm (lb ft)	132 (97) at 4000rpm
9	Valve operation	OHC V formation valves, hydraulic tappets
10	Valve timing	8°BT—36°AB—34°BB—6°AT
11	Valve clearances mm (in)	Not Applicable
12	Spark plugs make/type	Motorcraft AGPR22C
13	Gap	0.75mm (.030in)
14	Distributor make/type	Lucas or Bosch, electronic
15	Firing order/rotation	1—3—4—2/anticlock
16	Dwell angle	
17	Contact breaker gap	} Electronic
18	Pick up air gap	
19	Ignition timing—stroboscopic	12° BTDC at idle
20	Ignition timing—static	†
21	Timing marks	Pulley
22	Centrifugal advance commences	−1.5°/3° at 1000rpm
23	Centrifugal advance—max	17°/23° at 6000rpm
24	Vacuum advance commences	−1°/+3° at 81mm Hg
25	Vacuum advance—max	9°/17° at 231mm Hg
26	Ignition coil make	Bosch or Lucas
27	Prim res—sec res	0.72/0.88 ohms—4.5/7.0 kohms
28	Fuel pump	Mech; 0.22/0.35 bar (3.2/5.1lb/in²)
29	Carburettor make/type	Weber twin-choke
30	Specification no	28/32 TLDM 10/A
31	Idle speed (Fast idle)	800 ±25rpm
32	Exhaust gas analysis	CO 1.25% ± 0.25
33	Cold start operation	Auto
34	Choke tube (Venturi)	21mm / 23mm
35	Main jet	117 / 127
36	Compensating jet	185 / 125
37	Slow-running jet	47 / 60
38	Slow-running air bleed	140 / 100
39	Accelerator pump jet	40
40	Float level	31.0mm
41	Needle valve	2.0

ADDITIONAL INFORMATION

	Unleaded fuel suitability	Suitable only with modifications: (95 RON) set ignition timing to 8°BTDC
A	Emulsion tube	F30 / F30

ENGINE—GENERAL DATA

50	Piston diameter (standard)	79.910/79.920mm (in 4 production grades)
51	Piston oversizes	0.29, 0.50mm (See A)
52	Piston clearance in bore	0.020/0.040mm (See B)
53	Piston rings—number	2 compression 1 oil
54	Piston rings—width	†
55	Piston rings—groove clearance	(1)(2) 0.041/0.091mm (3) 0.046/0.096
56	Piston rings—gap in bore	(1) (2) 0.30/0.50mm (3) 0.4/1.4
57	Oil pressure bar (lb/in²)	2.8 (40.6) at 2000rpm
58	Gudgeon pin diameter	20.622/20.632mm (in 4 grades)
59	Gudgeon pin fit in piston	Clearance 0.013/0.045mm
60	Gudgeon pin fit in con rod	Interference 0.013/0.045mm
61	Connecting rod length	109.83/109.88mm
62	Crankpin diameter	47.89/47.91mm
63	Crankpin undersizes	0.25, 0.50, 0.75, 1.00mm
64	Big end bearing clearance	0.006/0.060mm
65	Big end side clearance	0.10/0.25mm
66	Main bearings	5
67	Main journal diameter	57.98/58.00mm
68	Main journal undersizes	0.25, 0.50, 0.75, 1.00mm
69	Main bearing clearance	0.011/0.058mm
70	Crankshaft end-float	0.09/0.30mm
71	Crankshaft end-thrust on	Centre Bearing
72	Camshaft bearings	5
73	Camshaft journal diameter	(1) 44.75mm (2) 45.00 (3) 45.25 (4) 45.50 (5) 45.75
74	Camshaft bearing clearance	0.025/0.059mm
75	Camshaft end-float	0.05/0.15mm
76	Camshaft drive type	Toothed belt
77	Cam lift	6.09mm
78	Valve head diameter	In 41.9/42.1mm Ex 36.9/37.1
79	Valve stem diameter	In 8.025/8.043mm Ex 7.999/8.017
80	Valve length	In 134.54/135.00mm Ex 131.57/132.03
81	Valve seat/face angle	45°
82	Valve lift	In 10.19mm Ex 10.16mm
83	Valve guide length	†
84	Valve stem/guide clearance	In 0.020/0.068mm Ex 0.043/0.091
85	Valve spring free length	47.2mm
86	Valve spring loaded length	37.084mm at 402.4/441.6N (90.5/99.3lb)

ADDITIONAL INFORMATION

A	Piston oversizes	Standard service size 79.930/79.955mm
B	Piston clearance in bore	Service 0.010/0.045mm

COOLING SYSTEM

95	Type	Water pump, radiator
96	Radiator pressure cap	0.9 bar (13lb/in²)
97	Fan	Electric
98	Thermostat	85°/89°C

TRANSMISSION

100	Type	Rear wheel drive
101	Clutch	216mm cable operation
102	Manual gearbox type	5 speed
103	Manual gearbox ratios	0.83; 1; 1.37; 1.97; 3.65; R, 3.66:1
104	Automatic gearbox type	
105	Automatic gearbox ratios	} Not
106	Stall speed	Applicable
107	Change speeds	
108	Drive shafts	Semi-floating
109	Final drive ratio	4.1:1
110	Differential bearing pre-load	0.076/0.152mm
111	Pinion bearing pre-load	0.9/1.4Nm

BRAKES

200	Type	Dual circuit
201	Power assistance	None
202	Front	Discs 279mm
203	Rear	Drums 229mm
204	Handbrake	Mechanical, on rear wheels
205	Linings—front	Min thickness 1.5mm
206	Linings—rear	Width 45mm

STEERING

300	Type	Recirculating ball
301	Condition for checking	Unladen
302	Camber	2°, Plus 4 style —1° (non-adjustable)
303	Castor	4° (non-adjustable)
304	King pin inclination	2°
305	Wheel alignment—front	Parallel to toe in 3mm
306	Toe out on turns	†
307	Turning circle diameter	10m
308	Front hub end-float	†

FRONT SUSPENSION

330	Type	Independent, vertical coil springs
331	Number of coils	21
332	Spring length	362mm
333	Spring rate	†
334	Coil diameter	58mm
335	Wire diameter	7.8mm

REAR SUSPENSION

360	Type	Semi-elliptic leaf springs
361	Wheel camber	} Not
362	Wheel alignment—rear	Applicable
363	Number of leaves	5 or 7
364	Spring length	1086mm
365	Spring rate	†
366	Width of leaves	36mm
367	Thickness of leaves	6.4mm

ELECTRICAL

400	Battery	12V 45Ah neg earth
401	Alternator	45A
402	Regulated voltage	13.7/14.6V
403	Starter motor	0.8kW

CAPACITIES

500	Engine oil	3.5 litres inc filter
501	Gearbox oil	1.9 litres
502	Differential oil	1.0 litres
503	Cooling system	10.2 litres
504	Fuel tank	56 litres
505	Tyre size	165SR15, Plus 4 style 195/60HR15
506	Pressures bar (lb/in²)	F/R 1.2 (18), Plus 4 style F/R 1.5 (22)
507	Max towing weight	508kg
508	Hydraulic fluid type	DOT 3 spec
509	Service intervals	5000 miles or 6 months

DIMENSIONS

		4/4 style	Plus 4 style
600	Length overall	3890mm (153in)	3890 (153)
601	Width overall	1500mm (57in)	1500 (57)
602	Height overall	1314mm (51.75in)	1290 (51)
603	Weight—kerb 2-seat	869kg (1912lb)	875 (1925)
	4-seat	920kg (2024lb)	926 (2037)
604	Ground clearance	165mm (6.5in)	150 (6.0)
605	Wheelbase	2438mm (96in)	2438 (96)
606	Track—front/rear	1220/1245mm (48/49in)	1270/1295 (50/51)

TORQUE WRENCH SETTINGS

		Nm	lb ft		
700	Cylinder head nuts/bolts	24, 56	18, 41	+90°	+90°
701	Big end bearing bolts	30/36	22/27		
702	Main bearing bolts	89/100	66/74		
703	Flywheel bolts	82/92	60/68		
704	Clutch to flywheel bolts	18/20	13/15		
705	Drive plate to torque converter	Not Applicable			
706	Crown wheel bolts	68/81	50/60		
707	Drive pinion nut	129/136	95/100		
708	Differential bearing bolts	47/54	35/40		
709	Road wheel nuts	88/95	65/70		
710	Steering wheel nut	34/47	25/35		

4/4 1600 & 4/4 1600 (Plus 4 body style) 1987

ENGINE—TUNING DATA

1	Type	Rover; V8 cyl in line mounted
2	Number of cylinders	8; No 1 front left
3	Cubic capacity	3532cm³
4	Bore/Stroke	88.9/71.12mm
5	Compression ratio/pressure	9.75:1/8.97 bar
6	Octane rating (RON)	98
7	Brake horsepower (DIN)	190 at 5280rpm
8	Torque (DIN) Nm (lb ft)	298 (220) at 4000rpm
9	Valve operation	OHV in line valves, hydraulic tappets
10	Valve timing	30°BT—75°AB—68°BB—37°AT
11	Valve clearances mm (in)	Not Applicable
12	Spark plugs make/type	Unipart GSP151
13	Gap	0.9mm (.035in)
14	Distributor make/type	Lucas 35DM8 41935A
15	Firing order/rotation	1—8—4—3—6—5—7—2/clockwise
16	Dwell angle	⎫ Not
17	Contact breaker gap	⎬ Applicable
18	Pick up air gap	0.36/0.40mm (.014/.016in)
19	Ignition timing—stroboscopic	8° BTDC at 600rpm
20	Ignition timing—static	†
21	Timing marks	Pulley
22	Centrifugal advance commences	400rpm
23	Centrifugal advance—max	7°/7.5° at 2500rpm
24	Vacuum advance commences	76.2mm Hg
25	Vacuum advance—max	7°/9° 304.8mm Hg
26	Ignition coil—make	Lucas or Bosch
27	Prim res—sec res	0.71/0.81 ohms
28	Fuel lift pump	Electric
29	Injection system make	Lucas 'L'
30	Type	Electronic
31	Idle speed (Fast idle)	775 ± 25rpm
32	Exhaust gas analysis	CO 1.5% ± 0.5
33	Injection pressure	1.8/2.49 bar

ADDITIONAL INFORMATION

Unleaded fuel suitability	Suitable only with modifications: 'Correction to ignition timing'

ENGINE—GENERAL DATA

50	Piston diameter (standard)	88.88mm
51	Piston oversizes	0.26, 0.51mm
52	Piston clearance in bore	0.018/0.033mm
53	Piston rings—number	2 compression, 1 oil
54	Piston rings—width	(1)(2) 1.56/1.58mm (3) 4.81
55	Piston rings—groove clearance	(1)(2) 0.038/0.89mm
56	Piston rings—gap in bore	(1)(2) 0.43/0.56mm (3) 0.38/1.40
57	Oil pressure bar (lb/in²)	2.1/2.8 (30/40) at 2400rpm
58	Gudgeon pin diameter	22.21/22.22mm
59	Gudgeon pin fit in piston	Clearance 0.002/0.007mm
60	Gudgeon pin fit in con rod	Press fit
61	Connecting rod length	143.71/143.81mm (centres)
62	Crankpin diameter	50.80/50.81mm
63	Crankpin undersizes	0.26, 0.51mm
64	Big end bearing clearance	0.015/0.055mm
65	Big end side clearance	0.15/0.356mm
66	Main bearings	5
67	Main journal diameter	58.41/58.42mm
68	Main journal undersizes	0.26, 0.51mm
69	Main bearing clearance	0.013/0.056mm
70	Crankshaft end-float	0.10/0.20mm
71	Crankshaft end-thrust on	Centre bearing
72	Camshaft bearings	5
73	Camshaft journal diameter	(1) 45.34/45.36mm (2) 44.45/44.58 (3) 43.82/43.84 (4) 43.05/43.08 (5) 42.29/42.36
74	Camshaft bearing clearance	†
75	Camshaft end-float	†
76	Camshaft drive type	Chain
77	Cam lift	†
78	Valve head diameter	In 40.00/41.30mm Ex 34.48/35.60
79	Valve stem diameter	In 8.63/8.65mm Ex 8.64/8.66
80	Valve length	116.59/117.35mm
81	Valve seat/face angle	46° ± 15'/45° ± 15'
82	Valve lift	9.91mm
83	Valve guide length	Fitted height, 19mm above step in boss
84	Valve stem/guide clearance	In 0.03/0.07mm Ex 0.04/0.08
85	Valve spring free length	48.30mm
86	Valve spring loaded length	40.40mm at 66.50Nm

COOLING SYSTEM

95	Type	Water pump, radiator
96	Radiator pressure cap	1.03 bar (15lb/in²)
97	Fan	Electric
98	Thermostat	88°C

TRANSMISSION

100	Type	Rear wheel drive (L.S.D.)
101	Clutch	241.3mm hydraulic operation
102	Manual gearbox type	5 speed
103	Manual gearbox ratios	0.79; 1; 1.39; 2.08; 3.32; R 3.42:1
104	Automatic gearbox type	⎫
105	Automatic gearbox ratios	⎪ Not
106	Stall speed	⎬ Applicable
107	Change speeds	⎭
108	Drive shafts	Semi-floating
109	Final drive ratio	3.31:1
110	Differential bearing pre-load	0.076/0.152mm
111	Pinion bearing pre-load	0.9/1.4Nm

BRAKES

200	Type	Dual circuit
201	Power assistance	None
202	Front	Discs 279.4mm
203	Rear	Drums 229mm
204	Handbrake	Mechanical, on rear wheels
205	Linings—front	Min thickness 1.5mm
206	Linings—rear	Width 45mm

STEERING

300	Type	Rack and pinion
301	Condition for checking	Unladen
302	Camber	−1° (non-adjustable)
303	Castor	4° (non-adjustable)
304	King pin inclination	2°
305	Wheel alignment—front	Parallel to toe in 3.2mm
306	Toe out on turns	†
307	Turning circle diameter	11.6m
308	Front hub end-float	†

FRONT SUSPENSION

330	Type	Independent vertical coil springs
331	Number of coils	18
332	Spring length	330mm
333	Spring rate	†
334	Coil diameter	60mm
335	Wire diameter	9.52mm

REAR SUSPENSION

360	Type	Semi elliptic leaf springs
361	Wheel camber	⎫ Not
362	Wheel alignment—rear	⎬ Applicable
363	Number of leaves	6
364	Spring length	1086mm
365	Spring rate	†
366	Width of leaves	36mm
367	Thickness of leaves	6.4mm

ELECTRICAL

400	Battery	12V 58Ah neg earth
401	Alternator	65A
402	Regulated voltage	13.6/14.4V
403	Starter motor	Lucas

CAPACITIES

500	Engine oil	5.5 litres inc filter
501	Gearbox oil	1.6 litres
502	Differential oil	1.4 litres
503	Cooling system	13.6 litres
504	Fuel tank	64 litres
505	Tyre size	205/60 VR15
506	Pressures bar (lb/in²)	F/R 1.52 (22)
507	Max towing weight	575kg
508	Hydraulic fluid type	DOT 3 spec
509	Service intervals	5000 miles or 6 months

DIMENSIONS

600	Length overall	3960mm (156in)
601	Width overall	1600mm (63in)
602	Height overall	1220mm (48in)
603	Weight—kerb	889kg (1956lb)
604	Ground clearance	140mm (5.5in)
605	Wheelbase	2489mm (98in)
606	Track—front/rear	1345/1375mm (53/54in)

TORQUE WRENCH SETTINGS

		Nm	lb ft	
700	Cylinder head nuts/bolts	95	70	(long)
		68	50	(short)
701	Big end bearing bolts	47	35	
702	Main bearing bolts	75 (95)	55 (70)	(Rear)
703	Flywheel bolts	81	60	
704	Clutch to flywheel bolts	27	20	
705	Drive plate to torque converter	Not Applicable		
706	Crown wheel bolts	68/81	50/60	
707	Drive pinion nut	129/136	95/100	
708	Differential bolts	47/54	35/40	
709	Road wheel nuts	88/95	65/70	
710	Steering wheel nut	34/47	25/35	

Plus 8 1987

ENGINE—TUNING DATA

1	Type	Ford CVH; 4 cyl in line mounted	
2	Number of cylinders	4; No 1 pulley end	
3	Cubic capacity	1597cm³	
4	Bore/Stroke	79.96/79.52mm	
5	Compression ratio/pressure	9.5:1/12-14 bar	
6	Octane rating (RON)	98	
7	Brake horsepower (DIN)	95 at 5750rpm	
8	Torque (DIN) Nm (lb ft)	132 (97) at 4000rpm	
9	Valve operation	OHC V formation valves, hydraulic tappets	
10	Valve timing	8°BT—36°AB—34°BB—6°AT	
11	Valve clearances mm (in)	Not Applicable	
12	Spark plugs make/type	Motorcraft AGPR22C or Champion RE7YC	
13	Gap	0.75mm (.030in)	
14	Distributor make/type	Lucas or Bosch, electronic	
15	Firing order/rotation	1—3—4—2/anticlock	
16	Dwell angle		
17	Contact breaker gap	} Electronic	
18	Pick up air gap		
19	Ignition timing—stroboscopic	12° BTDC at idle	
20	Ignition timing—static	†	
21	Timing marks	Pulley	
22	Centrifugal advance commences	−1.5°/3° at 1000rpm	
23	Centrifugal advance—max	17°/23° at 6000rpm	
24	Vacuum advance commences	−1°/+3° at 81mm Hg	
25	Vacuum advance—max	9°/17° at 231mm Hg	
26	Ignition coil make	Bosch or Lucas	
27	Prim res — sec res	0.72/0.88 ohms—4.5/7.0 kohms	
28	Fuel pump	Mech; 0.22/0.35 bar (3.2/5.1lb/in²)	
29	Carburettor make/type	Weber twin-choke	
30	Specification no	28/32 TLDM 10/A	
31	Idle speed (Fast idle)	800 ±25rpm	
32	Exhaust gas analysis	CO 1.25% ± 0.25	
33	Cold start operation	Auto	
34	Choke tube (Venturi)	21mm	23mm
35	Main jet	117	127
36	Compensating jet	185	125
37	Slow-running jet	47	60
38	Slow-running air bleed	140	100
39	Accelerator pump jet	40	
40	Float level	31.0mm	
41	Needle valve	2.0	

ADDITIONAL INFORMATION

A	Emulsion tube	F30	F30

ENGINE—GENERAL DATA

50	Piston diameter (standard)	79.910/79.920mm (in 4 production grades)
51	Piston oversizes	0.29, 0.50mm (See A)
52	Piston clearance in bore	0.020/0.040mm (See B)
53	Piston rings—number	2 compression 1 oil
54	Piston rings—width	†
55	Piston rings—groove clearance	(1)(2) 0.041/0.091mm (3) 0.046/0.096
56	Piston rings—gap in bore	(1) (2) 0.30/0.50mm (3) 0.4/1.4
57	Oil pressure bar (lb/in²)	2.8 (40.6) at 2000rpm
58	Gudgeon pin diameter	20.622/20.632mm (in 4 grades)
59	Gudgeon pin fit in piston	Clearance 0.013/0.045mm
60	Gudgeon pin fit in con rod	Interference 0.013/0.045mm
61	Connecting rod length	109.83/109.88mm
62	Crankpin diameter	47.89/47.91mm
63	Crankpin undersizes	0.25, 0.50, 0.75, 1.00mm
64	Big end bearing clearance	0.006/0.060mm
65	Big end side clearance	0.10/0.25mm
66	Main bearings	5
67	Main journal diameter	57.98/58.00mm
68	Main journal undersizes	0.25, 0.50, 0.75, 1.00mm
69	Main bearing clearance	0.011/0.058mm
70	Crankshaft end-float	0.09/0.30mm
71	Crankshaft end-thrust on	Centre Bearing
72	Camshaft bearings	5
73	Camshaft journal diameter	(1) 44.75mm (2) 45.00 (3) 45.25 (4) 45.50 (5) 45.75
74	Camshaft bearing clearance	0.025/0.059mm
75	Camshaft end-float	0.05/0.15mm
76	Camshaft drive type	Toothed belt
77	Cam lift	6.09mm
78	Valve head diameter	In 41.9/42.1mm Ex 36.9/37.1
79	Valve stem diameter	In 8.025/8.043mm Ex 7.999/8.017
80	Valve length	In 134.54/135.00mm Ex 131.57/132.03
81	Valve seat/face angle	45°
82	Valve lift	In 10.19mm Ex 10.16mm
83	Valve guide length	†
84	Valve stem/guide clearance	In 0.020/0.068mm Ex 0.043/0.091
85	Valve spring free length	47.2mm
86	Valve spring loaded length	37.084mm at 402.4/441.6N (90.5/99.3lb)

ADDITIONAL INFORMATION

A	Piston oversizes	Standard service size 79.930/79.955mm
B	Piston clearance in bore	Service 0.010/0.045mm

COOLING SYSTEM

95	Type	Water pump, radiator
96	Radiator pressure cap	0.9 bar (13lb/in²)
97	Fan	Electric
98	Thermostat	85°/89°C

TRANSMISSION

100	Type	Rear wheel drive
101	Clutch	216mm cable operation
102	Manual gearbox type	5 speed
103	Manual gearbox ratios	0.83; 1; 1.37; 1.97; 3.65; R, 3.66:1
104	Automatic gearbox type	
105	Automatic gearbox ratios	Not
106	Stall speed	} Applicable
107	Change speeds	
108	Drive shafts	Semi-floating
109	Final drive ratio	4.1:1
110	Differential bearing pre-load	0.076/0.152mm
111	Pinion bearing pre-load	0.9/1.4Nm

BRAKES

200	Type	Dual circuit
201	Power assistance	None
202	Front	Discs 279mm
203	Rear	Drums 229mm
204	Handbrake	Mechanical, on rear wheels
205	Linings—front	Min thickness 1.5mm
206	Linings—rear	Width 45mm

STEERING

300	Type	Worm and roller
301	Condition for checking	Unladen
302	Camber	2°, Plus 4 style —1° (non-adjustable)
303	Castor	4° (non-adjustable)
304	King pin inclination	2°
305	Wheel alignment—front	Parallel to toe in 3mm
306	Toe out on turns	†
307	Turning circle diameter	10m
308	Front hub end-float	†

FRONT SUSPENSION

330	Type	Independent, vertical coil springs
331	Number of coils	21
332	Spring length	362mm
333	Spring rate	93.3 lb/in
334	Coil diameter	58mm
335	Wire diameter	7.8mm

REAR SUSPENSION

360	Type	Semi-elliptic leaf springs
361	Wheel camber	0°
362	Wheel alignment—rear	Parallel
363	Number of leaves	5 or 7
364	Spring length	1086mm
365	Spring rate	2 str. 133.26 lb/in, 4 str. 184.6
366	Width of leaves	36mm
367	Thickness of leaves	6.4mm

ELECTRICAL

400	Battery	12V 45Ah neg earth
401	Alternator	45A
402	Regulated voltage	13.7/14.6V
403	Starter motor	0.8kW

CAPACITIES

500	Engine oil	3.5 litres inc filter
501	Gearbox oil	1.9 litres
502	Differential oil	1.0 litres
503	Cooling system	10.2 litres
504	Fuel tank	56 litres
505	Tyre size	165SR15, Plus 4 style 195/60HR15
506	Pressures bar (lb/in²)	F/R 1.2 (18), Plus 4 style F/R 1.5 (22)
507	Max towing weight	500kg (1102.5lb)
508	Hydraulic fluid type	DOT 3 spec
509	Service intervals	5000 miles or 6 months

DIMENSIONS

		4/4 style	Plus 4 style
600	Length overall	3890mm (153in)	3890 (153)
601	Width overall	1500mm (57in)	1500 (57)
602	Height overall	1314mm (51.75in)	1290 (51)
603	Weight—kerb 2 str.	869kg (1912lb)	875 (1925)
	4 str.	920kg (2024lb)	926 (2037)
604	Ground clearance	165mm (6.5in)	150 (6.0)
605	Wheelbase	2438mm (96in)	2438 (96)
606	Track—front/rear	1220/1245mm (48/49in)	1270/1295 (50/51)

TORQUE WRENCH SETTINGS

		Nm	lb ft		
700	Cylinder head nuts/bolts	24, 56	18, 41	+90°	+90°
701	Big end bearing bolts	30/36	22/27		
702	Main bearing bolts	89/100	66/74		
703	Flywheel bolts	82/92	60/68		
704	Clutch to flywheel bolts	18/20	13/15		
705	Drive plate to torque converter	Not Applicable			
706	Crown wheel bolts	68/81	50/60		
707	Drive pinion nut	129/136	95/100		
708	Differential bearing bolts	47/54	35/40		
709	Road wheel nuts	88/95	65/70		
710	Steering wheel nut	34/47	25/35		

4/4 1600 & 4/4 1600 (Plus 4 body style) 1988

ENGINE—TUNING DATA

1	Type	20 HD (M16i); 4 cyl in line mounted
2	Number of cylinders	4; No 1 front
3	Cubic capacity	1994 cm³
4	Bore/Stroke	84.45/89mm
5	Compression ratio/pressure	10:1/10.3 bar min
6	Octane rating (RON)	95 (min)
7	Brake horsepower (DIN)	138 at 6000rpm
8	Torque (DIN) Nm (lb ft)	178 (131) at 4500rpm
9	Valve operation	DOHC, 4 valves per cyl
10	Valve timing	18°BT−46°AB−52°BB−12°AT
11	Valve clearances mm (in)	Not Applicable
12	Spark plugs make/type	Unipart GSP4662 or GSP3662
13	Gap	1.0/1.1mm (.039/.043in)
14	Distributor make/type	Lucas
15	Firing order/rotation	1−3−4−2/anticlock
16	Dwell angle	
17	Contact breaker gap	} Electronic
18	Pick up air gap	
19	Ignition timing—stroboscopic	15° BTDC at 900rpm
20	Ignition timing—static	†
21	Timing marks	Electronic sensor on flywheel
22	Centrifugal advance commences	
23	Centrifugal advance—max	} Electronic
24	Vacuum advance commences	Computer controlled
25	Vacuum advance—max	
26	Ignition coil—make	GCL 141
27	Prim res—sec res	0.71/0.81 ohms
28	Fuel lift pump	Lucas, 4.1 bar max
29	Injection system make	Lucas L-Hot wire
30	Type	4FP multi point, computer controlled
31	Idle speed	900rpm ± 50 controlled by E.C.U. (See A)
32	Exhaust gas analysis	CO 1% ± 0.5
33	Injection pressure	Fuel pressure: 3.0 bar above manifold depression

ADDITIONAL INFORMATION

A Idle speed .... Base idle speed setting with air valve closed: 750rpm ± 25

ENGINE—GENERAL DATA

50	Piston diameter (standard)	†
51	Piston oversizes	†
52	Piston clearance in bore	0.04/0.05mm
53	Piston rings—number	2 compression, 1 oil
54	Piston rings—width	†
55	Piston rings—groove clearance	†
56	Piston rings—gap in bore	(1) 0.3/0.5mm (2) 0.25/0.50
57	Oil pressure bar (psi)	3.8 (55) at 3000rpm
58	Gudgeon pin diameter	23.810/23.815mm
59	Gudgeon pin fit in piston	Push fit
60	Gudgeon pin fit in con rod	Clearance 0.003/0.025mm
61	Connecting rod length	†
62	Crankpin diameter	47.635/47.647mm
63	Crankpin undersizes	†
64	Big end bearing clearance	0.038/0.081mm
65	Big end side clearance	†
66	Main bearings	5
67	Main journal diameter	54.005/54.026mm
68	Main journal undersizes	†
69	Main bearing clearance	0.03/0.38mm
70	Crankshaft end-float	0.03/0.14mm
71	Crankshaft end-thrust on	Centre bearing
72	Camshaft bearings	5 per shaft
73	Camshaft journal diameter	†
74	Camshaft bearing clearance	0.04/0.09mm
75	Camshaft end-float	0.06/0.19mm
76	Camshaft drive type	Toothed belt
77	Cam lift	†
78	Valve head diameter	In 31.7/32.0mm Ex 29.2/29.4
79	Valve stem diameter	In 7.09/7.10mm Ex 7.07/7.09
80	Valve length	†
81	Valve seat/face angle	45°/45°30′
82	Valve lift	8.83mm (nominal)
83	Valve guide length	Protrusion: 12mm above head
84	Valve stem/guide clearance	In 0.03/0.05mm Ex 0.04/0.07
85	Valve spring free length	41mm
86	Valve spring loaded length	27.5mm at 560/570N

COOLING SYSTEM

95	Type	Water pump, radiator
96	Radiator pressure cap	1.03 bar (15 lb/in²)
97	Fan	Electric
98	Thermostat	88°C

TRANSMISSION

100	Type	Rear wheel drive
101	Clutch	267mm hydraulic operation
102	Manual gearbox type	5 speed
103	Manual gearbox ratios	0.79; 1; 1.39; 2.08; 3.32; R 3.42:1
104	Automatic gearbox type	
105	Automatic gearbox ratios	} Not
106	Stall speed	} Applicable
107	Change speeds	
108	Drive shafts	Semi-floating
109	Final drive ratio	3.73:1
110	Differential bearing pre-load	0.076/0.152mm
111	Pinion bearing pre-load	0.9/1.4Nm

BRAKES

200	Type	Dual circuit
201	Power assistance	None
202	Front	Discs 279mm
203	Rear	Drums 229mm
204	Handbrake	Mechanical, on rear wheels
205	Linings—front	Min thickness 1.5mm
206	Linings—rear	Min thickness 1.5mm

STEERING

300	Type	Worm and roller
301	Condition for checking	Unladen
302	Camber	−1° (non-adjustable)
303	Castor	4° (non-adjustable)
304	King pin inclination	2°
305	Wheel alignment—front	Parallel to toe in 3mm
306	Toe out on turns	†
307	Turning circle diameter	10m
308	Front hub end-float	†

FRONT SUSPENSION

330	Type	Independant, vertical coil springs
331	Number of coils	21
332	Spring length	362mm
333	Spring rate	39.3 lb/in
334	Coil diameter	58mm
335	Wire diameter	7.8mm

REAR SUSPENSION

360	Type	Semi-elliptic leaf springs
361	Wheel camber	0°
362	Wheel alignment—rear	Parallel
363	Number of coils	(See A)
364	Spring length	1086mm
365	Spring rate	2 str. 133.26 lb/in, 4 str. 184.6
366	Coil diameter	(See B)
367	Wire diameter	(See C)

ADDITIONAL INFORMATION

A Number of leaves ...... 2 str. 5, 4 str. 7
B Width of leaves 36mm
C Thickness of leaves ... 6.4mm

ELECTRICAL

400	Battery	12V 45Ah neg earth
401	Alternator	64A
402	Regulated voltage	13.6/14.4V
403	Starter motor	1.0kW

CAPACITIES

500	Engine oil	4.5 litres inc filter
501	Gearbox oil	1.6 litres
502	Differential oil	1.0 litre
503	Cooling system	10.2 litres
504	Fuel tank	56 litres
505	Tyre size	195/60 HR 15
506	Pressures bar (psi)	F/R 1.5 (22)
507	Max towing weight	500kg (1102.5 lb)
508	Hydraulic fluid type	DOT 3 spec
509	Service intervals	5000 miles or 6 months

DIMENSIONS

600	Length overall	3890mm (153in)
601	Width overall	1500mm (57in)
602	Height overall	1290mm (51in)
603	Weight—kerb	2 str. 885kg (1951lb) 4 str. 936 (2064)
604	Ground clearance	150mm (6.07in)
605	Wheelbase	2438mm (96in)
606	Track—front/rear	1270/1295mm (50/51in)

TORQUE WRENCH SETTINGS

		Nm	lb ft	
700	Cylinder head nuts/bolts	40,80	30,59	(See A)
701	Big end bearing bolts	45	33	
702	Main bearing bolts	105	75	
703	Flywheel bolts	85	63	
704	Clutch to flywheel bolts	26	19	
705	Drive plate to torque converter	Not Applicable		
706	Crown wheel bolts	68/81	50/60	
707	Drive pinion unit	129/136	95/100	
708	Differential bearing bolts	47/54	35/40	
709	Road wheel nuts	88/95	65/70	
710	Steering wheel nut	34/47	25/35	

ADDITIONAL INFORMATION

A Final tighten .... +90° or 107Nm (79lbft) which ever comes first

Plus 4 (Rover engine) 1988

ENGINE—TUNING DATA

1	Type	Rover; V8 cyl in line mounted
2	Number of cylinders	8; No 1 front left
3	Cubic capacity	3532cm³
4	Bore/Stroke	88.9/71.12mm
5	Compression ratio/pressure	9.75:1/8.97 bar
6	Octane rating (RON)	98
7	Brake horsepower (DIN)	190 at 5280rpm
8	Torque (DIN) Nm (lb ft)	298 (220) at 4000rpm
9	Valve operation	OHV in line valves, hydraulic tappets
10	Valve timing	30°BT—75°AB—68°BB—37°AT
11	Valve clearances mm (in)	Not Applicable
12	Spark plugs make/type	Unipart GSP151
13	Gap	0.9mm (.035in)
14	Distributor make/type	Lucas 35DM8 41935A
15	Firing order/rotation	1—8—4—3—6—5—7—2/clockwise
16	Dwell angle	⎱ Not
17	Contact breaker gap	⎰ Applicable
18	Pick up air gap	0.36/0.40mm (.014/.016in)
19	Ignition timing—stroboscopic	8° BTDC at 600rpm
20	Ignition timing—static	†
21	Timing marks	Pulley
22	Centrifugal advance commences	400rpm
23	Centrifugal advance—max	7°/7.5° at 2500rpm
24	Vacuum advance commences	76.2mm Hg
25	Vacuum advance—max	7°/9° 304.8mm Hg
26	Ignition coil—make	Lucas or Bosch
27	Prim res—sec res	0.71/0.81 ohms
28	Fuel lift pump	Electric
29	Injection system make	Lucas 'L'
30	Type	Electronic
31	Idle speed (Fast idle)	775 ± 25rpm
32	Exhaust gas analysis	CO 1.5% ± 0.5
33	Injection pressure	1.8/2.49 bar

ENGINE—GENERAL DATA

50	Piston diameter (standard)	88.88mm
51	Piston oversizes	0.26, 0.51mm
52	Piston clearance in bore	0.018/0.033mm
53	Piston rings—number	2 compression, 1 oil
54	Piston rings—width	(1)(2) 1.56/1.58mm (3) 4.81
55	Piston rings—groove clearance	(1)(2) 0.038/0.89mm
56	Piston rings—gap in bore	(1)(2) 0.43/0.56mm (3) 0.38/1.40
57	Oil pressure bar (lb/in²)	2.1/2.8 (30/40) at 2400rpm
58	Gudgeon pin diameter	22.21/22.22mm
59	Gudgeon pin fit in piston	Clearance 0.002/0.007mm
60	Gudgeon pin fit in con rod	Press fit
61	Connecting rod length	143.71/143.81mm (centres)
62	Crankpin diameter	50.80/50.81mm
63	Crankpin undersizes	0.26, 0.51mm
64	Big end bearing clearance	0.015/0.055mm
65	Big end side clearance	0.15/0.356mm
66	Main bearings	5
67	Main journal diameter	58.41/58.42mm
68	Main journal undersizes	0.26, 0.51mm
69	Main bearing clearance	0.013/0.056mm
70	Crankshaft end-float	0.10/0.20mm
71	Crankshaft end-thrust on	Centre bearing
72	Camshaft bearings	5
73	Camshaft journal diameter	(1) 45.34/45.36mm (2) 44.45/44.58 (3) 43.82/43.84 (4) 43.05/43.08 (5) 42.29/42.36
74	Camshaft bearing clearance	†
75	Camshaft end-float	†
76	Camshaft drive type	Chain
77	Cam lift	†
78	Valve head diameter	In 40.00/41.30mm Ex 34.48/35.60
79	Valve stem diameter	In 8.63/8.65mm Ex 8.64/8.66
80	Valve length	116.59/117.35mm
81	Valve seat/face angle	46° ± 15'/45° ± 15'
82	Valve lift	9.91mm
83	Valve guide length	Fitted height, 19mm above step in boss
84	Valve stem/guide clearance	In 0.03/0.07mm Ex 0.04/0.08
85	Valve spring free length	48.30mm
86	Valve spring loaded length	40.40mm at 66.50Nm

COOLING SYSTEM

95	Type	Water pump, radiator
96	Radiator pressure cap	1.03 bar (15lb/in²)
97	Fan	Electric
98	Thermostat	88°C

TRANSMISSION

100	Type	Rear wheel drive (L.S.D.)
101	Clutch	241.3mm hydraulic operation
102	Manual gearbox type	5 speed
103	Manual gearbox ratios	0.79; 1; 1.39; 2.08; 3.32; R 3.42:1
104	Automatic gearbox type	⎫
105	Automatic gearbox ratios	⎪ Not
106	Stall speed	⎬ Applicable
107	Change speeds	⎭
108	Drive shafts	Semi-floating
109	Final drive ratio	3.31:1
110	Differential bearing pre-load	0.076/0.152mm
111	Pinion bearing pre-load	0.9/1.4Nm

BRAKES

200	Type	Dual circuit
201	Power assistance	None
202	Front	Discs 279.4mm
203	Rear	Drums 229mm
204	Handbrake	Mechanical, on rear wheels
205	Linings—front	Min thickness 1.5mm
206	Linings—rear	Width 45mm

STEERING

300	Type	Rack and pinion
301	Condition for checking	Unladen
302	Camber	−1° (non-adjustable)
303	Castor	4° (non-adjustable)
304	King pin inclination	2°
305	Wheel alignment—front	Parallel to toe in 3.2mm
306	Toe out on turns	†
307	Turning circle diameter	11.6m
308	Front hub end-float	†

FRONT SUSPENSION

330	Type	Independent vertical coil springs
331	Number of coils	18
332	Spring length	330mm
333	Spring rate	140 lb/in
334	Coil diameter	60mm
335	Wire diameter	9.52mm

REAR SUSPENSION

360	Type	Semi elliptic leaf springs
361	Wheel camber	0°
362	Wheel alignment—rear	Parallel
363	Number of leaves	6
364	Spring length	1086mm
365	Spring rate	133.26 lb/in
366	Width of leaves	36mm
367	Thickness of leaves	6.4mm

ELECTRICAL

400	Battery	12V 58Ah neg earth
401	Alternator	65A
402	Regulated voltage	13.6/14.4V
403	Starter motor	Lucas

CAPACITIES

500	Engine oil	5.5 litres inc filter
501	Gearbox oil	1.6 litres
502	Differential oil	1.4 litres
503	Cooling system	13.6 litres
504	Fuel tank	64 litres
505	Tyre size	205/60 VR15
506	Pressures bar (lb/in²)	F/R 1.52 (22)
507	Max towing weight	575kg (1268lb)
508	Hydraulic fluid type	DOT 3 spec
509	Service intervals	5000 miles or 6 months

DIMENSIONS

600	Length overall	3960mm (156in)
601	Width overall	1600mm (63in)
602	Height overall	1220mm (48in)
603	Weight—kerb	889kg (1956lb)
604	Ground clearance	140mm (5.5in)
605	Wheelbase	2489mm (98in)
606	Track—front/rear	1345/1375mm (53/54in)

TORQUE WRENCH SETTINGS

		Nm	lb ft	
700	Cylinder head nuts/bolts	95	70	(long)
		68	50	(short)
701	Big end bearing bolts	47	35	
702	Main bearing bolts	75 (95)	55 (70)	(Rear)
703	Flywheel bolts	81	60	
704	Clutch to flywheel bolts	27	20	
705	Drive plate to torque converter	Not Applicable		
706	Crown wheel bolts	68/81	50/60	
707	Drive pinion nut	129/136	95/100	
708	Differential bearing bolts	47/54	35/40	
709	Road wheel nuts	88/95	65/70	
710	Steering wheel nut	34/47	25/35	

Plus 8 1988

ENGINE—TUNING DATA

1	Type	Ford CVH; 4 cyl in line mounted
	Number of cylinders	4; No 1 pulley end
	Cubic capacity	1597cm³
4	Bore/Stroke	79,96/79,52mm
5	Compression ratio/pressure	9,5:1/12—14 bar
6	Octane rating (RON)	98
7	Brake horsepower (DIN)	95 at 5750rpm
8	Torque (DIN) Nm (lb ft)	132 (97) at 4000rpm
9	Valve operation	OHC V formation valves, hydraulic tappets
10	Valve timing	8°BT—36°AB—34°BB—6°AT
11	Valve clearances mm (in)	Not Applicable
12	Spark plugs make/type	Motocraft AGPR22C or Champion RE7YC
13	Gap	0,75mm (,030in)
14	Distributor make/type	Lucas or Bosch electronic
15	Firing order/rotation	1—3—4—2/anticlock
16	Dwell angle	
17	Contact breaker gap	} Electronic
18	Pick up air gap	
19	Ignition timing—stroboscopic	12° BTDC at idle
20	Ignition timing—static	†
21	Timing marks	Pulley
22	Centrifugal advance commences	−1,5°/3° at 1000rpm
23	Centrifugal advance—max	17°/23° at 6000rpm
24	Vacuum advance commences	−1°/+3° at 81mm Hg
25	Vacuum advance—max	9°/17° at 231mm Hg
26	Ignition coil—make	Bosch or Lucas
27	Prim res—sec res	0,72/0,88 ohms—4,5/7,0 kohms
28	Fuel pump	Mech 0,22/0,35 bar (3,2/5,1lb/in²)
29	Carburettor make/type	Weber twin choke
30	Specification number	28/32 TLDM 10/A
31	Idle speed (fast idle)	800rpm±25
32	Exhaust gas analysis	CO 1,25%±0,25
33	Cold start operation	Auto
34	Choke tube (venturi)	21mm — 23mm
35	Main jet	117 — 127
36	Compensating jet	185 — 125
37	Slow-running jet	47 — 60
38	Slow-running air bleed	140 — 100
39	Accelerator pump jet	40
40	Float level	31,0mm
41	Needle valve	2,0
ADDITIONAL INFORMATION		
A	Emulsion tube	F30 — F30

ENGINE—GENERAL DATA

50	Piston diameter (standard)	79,910/79,920mm (in 4 production grades)
51	Piston oversizes	0,26; 0,50mm (See A)
52	Piston clearance in bore	0,020/0,040mm (See B)
53	Piston rings—number	2 compression 1 oil
54	Piston rings—width	†
55	Piston rings—groove clearance	(1)(2) 0,041/0,091mm (3) 0,046/0,096
56	Piston rings—gap in bore	(1) (2) 0,30/0,50mm (3) 0,4/1,4
57	Oil pressure bar (psi)	2,8 (40) at 2000rpm
58	Gudgeon pin diameter	20,622/20,632mm (in 4 grades)
59	Gudgeon pin fit in piston	Clearance 0,013/0,045mm
60	Gudgeon pin fit in con rod	Interference 0,013/0,045mm
61	Connecting rod length	109,83/109,88mm
62	Crankpin diameter	47,89/47,91mm
63	Crankpin undersizes	0,25; 0,50; 0,75; 1,00mm
64	Big end bearing clearance	0,006/0,060mm
65	Big end side clearance	0,10/0,25mm
66	Main bearings	5
67	Main journal diameter	57,98/58,00mm
68	Main journal undersizes	0,25; 0,50; 0,75; 1,00mm
69	Main bearing clearance	0,011/0,058mm
70	Crankshaft end-float	0,09/0,30mm
71	Crankshaft end-thrust on	Centre Bearing
72	Camshaft bearings	5
73	Camshaft journal diameter	(1) 44,75mm (2) 45,00 (3) 45,25 (4) 45,50 (5) 45,75
74	Camshaft bearing clearance	0,025/0,059mm
75	Camshaft end-float	0,05/0,15mm
76	Camshaft drive type	Toothed belt
77	Cam lift	In/Ex 6,09mm
78	Valve head diameter	In 41,9/42,1mm Ex 36,9/37,1
79	Valve stem diameter	In 8,025/8,043mm Ex 7,999/8,017
80	Valve length	In 134,54/135,00mm Ex 131,57/132,03
81	Valve seat/face angle	45°
82	Valve lift	In 10,19mm Ex 10,16mm
83	Valve guide length	†
84	Valve stem/guide clearance	In 0,020/0,068mm Ex 0,043/0,091
85	Valve spring free length	47,2mm
86	Valve spring loaded length	37,084mm at 402,4/441,6N (90,5/99,3lb)
ADDITIONAL INFORMATION		
A	Piston oversizes	Service 79,930/79,955mm
B	Piston clearance in bore	Service 0,010/0,045mm

COOLING SYSTEM

95	Type	Water pump radiator
96	Radiator pressure cap	0,9 bar (13lb/in²)
97	Fan	Electric
98	Thermostat	85°/89°C

TRANSMISSION

100	Type	Rear wheel drive
101	Clutch	216mm cable operation
102	Manual gearbox type	5 speed; Ford
103	Manual gearbox ratios	0,83; 1; 1,37; 1,97; 3,65; R 3,66:1
104	Automatic gearbox type	
105	Automatic gearbox ratios	} Not
106	Stall speed	} Applicable
107	Change speeds	
108	Drive shafts	Semi-floating
109	Final drive ratio	4,1:1
110	Differential bearing pre-load	0,076/0,152mm
111	Pinion bearing pre-load	0,9/1,4Nm

BRAKES

200	Type	Dual circuit
201	Power assistance	None
202	Front	Discs 279mm
203	Rear	Drums 229mm
204	Handbrake	Mechanical on rear wheels
205	Linings—front	Min thickness 1,5mm
206	Linings—rear	Width 45mm

STEERING

300	Type	Worm and roller
301	Condition for checking	Unladen
302	Camber	2°; Plus 4 style −1° (non-adjustable)
303	Castor	4° (non-adjustable)
304	King pin inclination	2°
305	Wheel alignment—front	Parallel to toe in 3mm
306	Toe out on turns	†
307	Turning circle diameter	10m
308	Front hub end-float	†

FRONT SUSPENSION

330	Type	Independent, vertical coil springs
331	Number of coils	21
332	Spring length	362mm
333	Spring rate	93,3 lb/in
334	Coil diameter	58mm
335	Wire diameter	7,8mm

REAR SUSPENSION

360	Type	Semi-elliptic leaf springs
361	Wheel camber	Zero
362	Wheel alignment—rear	Parallel
363	Number of coils	Not Applicable (See A)
364	Spring length	1086mm
365	Spring rate	2str 133,26lb/in; 4str 184,6
366	Coil diameter	Not Applicable (See B)
367	Wire diameter	Not Applicable (See C)
ADDITIONAL INFORMATION		
A	Number of leaves	5 or 7
B	Width of leaves	36mm
C	Thickness of leaves	6,4mm

ELECTRICAL

400	Battery	12V 45Ah neg earth
401	Alternator	45A
402	Regulated voltage	13,7/14,6V
403	Starter motor	0,8kW

CAPACITIES

500	Engine oil	3,5 litres inc filter
501	Gearbox oil	1,9 litres
502	Differential oil	1,0 litres
503	Cooling system	10,2 litres
504	Fuel tank	56 litres
505	Tyre size	165 SR 15; Plus 4 style 195/60 HR 15
506	Pressures bar (psi)	F/R 1,2 (18); Plus 4 style F/R 1,5 (22)
507	Max towing weight	500kg (1102,5lb)
508	Hydraulic fluid type	DOT 3 spec
509	Service intervals	5000 miles or 6 months

DIMENSIONS

		4/4	Plus 4 style
600	Length overall	3890mm (153in)	3890 (153)
601	Width overall	1500mm (57in)	1500 (57)
602	Height overall	1314mm (51,75in)	1290 (51)
603	Weight—kerb	2 Str, 869kg (1912lb)	875 (1925)
		4 Str, 920kg (2024lb)	926 (2037)
604	Ground clearance	165mm (6,5in)	150 (6,0)
605	Wheelbase	2438mm (96in)	2438 (96)
606	Track—front/rear	1220/1245mm (48/49in)	1270/1295 (50/51)

TORQUE WRENCH SETTINGS

		Nm	lb ft
700	Cylinder head nuts/bolts	24; 56; +90°+90°	18; 41; +90°+90°
701	Big end bearing bolts	30/36	22/27
702	Main bearing bolts	89/100	66/74
703	Flywheel bolts	82/92	60/68
704	Clutch to flywheel bolts	18/20	13/15
705	Drive plate to torque converter	Not Applicable	
706	Crown wheel bolts	68/81	50/60
707	Drive pinion unit	129/136	95/100
708	Differential bearing bolts	47/54	35/40
709	Road wheel nuts	95	70
710	Steering wheel nut	34/47	25/35

4/4 1600 & 4/4 1600 (Plus 4 body style) 1989

ENGINE–TUNING DATA

1	Type....................................	20 HD (M16i); 4 cyl in line mounted
2	Number of cylinders......................	4; No 1 front
3	Cubic capacity...........................	1994 cm³
4	Bore/Stroke..............................	84,45/89mm
5	Compression ratio/pressure	10:1/10,3 bar min
6	Octane rating (RON).....................	95 (min)
7	Brake horsepower (DIN)................	138 at 6000rpm
8	Torque (DIN) Nm (lb ft)................	178 (131) at 4500rpm
9	Valve operation..........................	DOHC 4 valves per cyl
10	Valve timing..............................	18°BT–46°AB–52°BB–12°AT
11	Valve clearances mm (in)	Not Applicable
12	Spark plugs make/type	Unipart GSP4662 or GSP3662
13	Gap..	1,0/1,1mm (,039/,043in)
14	Distributor make/type	Lucas
15	Firing order/rotation...................	1–3–4–2/anticlock
16	Dwell angle...............................	}Electronic
17	Contact breaker gap....................	
18	Pick up air gap..........................	
19	Ignition timing–stroboscopic	15° BTDC at 900rpm
20	Ignition timing–static...................	†
21	Timing marks.............................	Electronic sensor on flywheel
22	Centrifugal advance commences	}Electronic
23	Centrifugal advance–max............	
24	Vacuum advance commences	}Computer controlled
25	Vacuum advance–max	
26	Ignition coil–make.......................	GCL 141
27	Prim res–sec res	0,71/0,81 ohms
28	Fuel lift pump.............................	Lucas 4,1 bar max
29	Injection system make	Lucas L Hot wire
30	Type.......................................	4FP multi point computer controlled
31	Idle speed................................	900rpm±50 controlled by ECU (See A)
32	Exhaust gas analysis	CO 1%±0,5
33	Injection pressure	Fuel pressure 3,0 bar above manifold depression

ADDITIONAL INFORMATION
A	Idle speed	Base idle speed setting with air valve closed; 750rpm±25

ENGINE–GENERAL DATA

50	Piston diameter (standard)	†
51	Piston oversizes........................	†
52	Piston clearance in bore	0,04/0,05mm
53	Piston rings–number...................	2 compression 1 oil
54	Piston rings–width......................	†
55	Piston rings–groove clearance	†
56	Piston rings–gap in bore	(1) 0,3/0,5mm (2) 0,25/0,50
57	Oil pressure bar (psi)...................	3,8 (55) at 3000rpm
58	Gudgeon pin diameter	23,810/23,815mm
59	Gudgeon pin fit in piston.............	Push fit
60	Gudgeon pin fit in con rod	Clearance 0,003/0,025mm
61	Connecting rod length	†
62	Crankpin diameter	47,635/47,647mm
63	Crankpin undersizes...................	†
64	Big end bearing clearance	0,038/0,081mm
65	Big end side clearance................	†
66	Main bearings	5
67	Main journal diameter	54,005/54,026mm
68	Main journal undersizes...............	†
69	Main bearing clearance	0,03/0,38mm
70	Crankshaft end-float...................	0,03/0,14mm
71	Crankshaft end-thrust on	Centre bearing
72	Camshaft bearings	5 per shaft
73	Camshaft journal diameter	†
74	Camshaft bearing clearance	0,04/0,09mm
75	Camshaft end-float...................	0,06/0,19mm
76	Camshaft drive type	Toothed belt
77	Cam lift..................................	†
78	Valve head diameter	In 31,7/32,0mm Ex 29,2/29,4
79	Valve stem diameter	In 7,09/7,10mm Ex 7,07/7,09
80	Valve length	†
81	Valve seat/face angle	45°/45° 30′
82	Valve lift.................................	8,83mm (nominal)
83	Valve guide length	Protrusion 12mm above head
84	Valve stem/guide clearance	In 0,03/0,05mm Ex 0,04/0,07
85	Valve spring free length	41mm
86	Valve spring loaded length...........	27,5mm at 560/570N

COOLING SYSTEM

95	Type..	Water pump radiator
96	Radiator pressure cap..................	1,03 bar (15 lb/in²)
97	Fan..	Electric
98	Thermostat...............................	88°C

TRANSMISSION

100	Type..	Rear wheel drive
101	Clutch.....................................	267mm hydraulic operation
102	Manual gearbox type	5 speed; LT77
103	Manual gearbox ratios..................	0,79; 1; 1,39; 2,08; 3,32; R 3,42:1
104	Automatic gearbox type................	
105	Automatic gearbox ratios............	}Not
106	Stall speed...............................	}Applicable
107	Change speeds...........................	
108	Drive shafts..............................	Semi-floating
109	Final drive ratio..........................	3,73:1
110	Differential bearing pre-load	0,076/0,152mm
111	Pinion bearing pre-load	0,9/1,4Nm

BRAKES

200	Type..	Dual circuit
201	Power assistance	None
202	Front......................................	Discs 279mm
203	Rear.......................................	Drums 229mm
204	Handbrake................................	Mechanical on rear wheels
205	Linings–front.............................	Min thickness 1,5mm
206	Linings–rear..............................	Min thickness 1,5mm

STEERING

300	Type..	Worm and roller
301	Condition for checking..................	Unladen
302	Camber....................................	–1° (non-adjustable)
303	Castor.....................................	4° (non-adjustable)
304	King pin inclination	2°
305	Wheel alignment–front..................	Parallel to toe in 3mm
306	Toe out on turns	†
307	Turning circle diameter	10m
308	Front hub end-float	†

FRONT SUSPENSION

330	Type..	Independent, vertical coil springs
331	Number of coils	21
332	Spring length	362mm
333	Spring rate	39,3 lb/in
334	Coil diameter.............................	58mm
335	Wire diameter	7,8mm

REAR SUSPENSION

360	Type..	Semi-elliptic leaf springs
361	Wheel camber............................	Zero
362	Wheel alignment–rear	Parallel
363	Number of coils	(See A)
364	Spring length	1086mm
365	Spring rate	2 str 133,26 lb/in; 4 str 184,6
366	Coil diameter.............................	(See B)
367	Wire diameter	(See C)

ADDITIONAL INFORMATION
A	Number of leaves	2 str 5; 4 str 7
B	Width of leaves	36mm
C	Thickness of leaves.....................	6,4mm

ELECTRICAL

400	Battery....................................	12V 45Ah neg earth
401	Alternator.................................	55A
402	Regulated voltage	13,6/14,4V
403	Starter motor.............................	1,0kW

CAPACITIES

500	Engine oil.................................	4,5 litres inc filter
501	Gearbox oil...............................	1,6 litres
502	Differential oil............................	1,0 litres
503	Cooling system	10,2 litres
504	Fuel tank..................................	56 litres
505	Tyre size..................................	195/60 HR 15
506	Pressures bar (psi).....................	F/R 1,5 (22)
507	Max towing weight.......................	500kg (1102,5 lb)
508	Hydraulic fluid type	DOT 3 spec
509	Service intervals	5000 miles or 6 months

DIMENSIONS

600	Length overall	3890mm (153in)
601	Width overall	1500mm (57in)
602	Height overall	1290mm (51in)
603	Weight–kerb..............................	2 str 885kg (1951lb); 4 str 936 (2064)
604	Ground clearance	150mm (6,07in)
605	Wheelbase	2438mm (96in)
606	Track–front/rear	1270/1295mm (50/51in)

TORQUE WRENCH SETTINGS

		Nm	lb ft	
700	Cylinder head nuts/bolts	40, 80	30, 59	(See A)
701	Big end bearing bolts...................	45	33	
702	Main bearing bolts.......................	105	75	
703	Flywheel bolts............................	85	63	
704	Clutch to flywheel bolts................	26	19	
705	Drive plate to torque converter	Not Applicable		
706	Crown wheel bolts.......................	68/82	50/60	
707	Drive pinion unit.........................	129/136	95/100	
708	Differential bearing bolts...............	47/54	35/40	
709	Road wheel nuts.........................	95	70	
710	Steering wheel nut......................	34/47	25/35	

ADDITIONAL INFORMATION
A	Final tighten	+90° or 107Nm (79lbft) which ever comes first

Plus 4 1989

ENGINE–TUNING DATA

1	Type	Rover; V8 cyl in line mounted
2	Number of cylinders	8; No 1 front left
3	Cubic capacity	3532cm³
4	Bore/Stroke	88,9/71,12mm
5	Compression ratio/pressure	9,75:1/8,97 bar
6	Octane rating (RON)	98
7	Brake horsepower (DIN)	190 at 5280rpm
8	Torque (DIN) Nm (lb ft)	298 (220) at 4000rpm
9	Valve operation	OHV in line valves hydraulic tappets
10	Valve timing	30°BT–75°AB–68°BB–37°AT
11	Valve clearances mm (in)	Not Applicable
12	Spark plugs make/type	Unipart GSP151 or Champion N9YC
13	Gap	0,9mm (,035in)
14	Distributor make/type	Lucas 35DM8 41935A
15	Firing order/rotation	1–8–4–3–6–5–7–2/clockwise
16	Dwell angle	Not
17	Contact breaker gap	Applicable
18	Pick up air gap	0,36/0,40mm (,014/,016in)
19	Ignition timing–stroboscopic	8° BTDC at 600rpm
20	Ignition timing–static	†
21	Timing marks	Pulley
22	Centrifugal advance commences	400rpm
23	Centrifugal advance–max	7°/7,5° at 2500rpm
24	Vacuum advance commences	76,2mm Hg
25	Vacuum advance–max	7°/9° 304,8mm Hg
26	Ignition coil–make	Lucas or Bosch
27	Prim res–sec res	0,71/0,81 ohms
28	Fuel lift pump	Electric
29	Injection system make	Lucas 'L'
30	Type	Electronic
31	Idle speed	775rpm±25
32	Exhaust gas analysis	CO 1,5%±0,5
33	Injection pressure	1,8/2,49 bar

ENGINE–GENERAL DATA

50	Piston diameter (standard)	88,88mm
51	Piston oversizes	0,26; 0,51mm
52	Piston clearance in bore	0,018/0,033mm
53	Piston rings–number	2 compression 1 oil
54	Piston rings–width	(1)(2) 1,56/1,58mm (3) 4,81
55	Piston rings–groove clearance	(1)(2) 0,038/0,89mm
56	Piston rings–gap in bore	(1)(2) 0,43/0,56mm (3) 0,38/1,40
57	Oil pressure bar (psi)	2,1/2,8 (30/40) at 2400rpm
58	Gudgeon pin diameter	22,21/22,22mm
59	Gudgeon pin fit in piston	Clearance 0,002/0,007mm
60	Gudgeon pin fit in con rod	Press fit
61	Connecting rod length	143,71/143,81mm (centres)
62	Crankpin diameter	50,80/50,81mm
63	Crankpin undersizes	0,26; 0,51mm
64	Big end bearing clearance	0,015/0,055mm
65	Big end side clearance	0,15/0,356mm
66	Main bearings	5
67	Main journal diameter	58,41/58,42mm
68	Main journal undersizes	0,26; 0,51mm
69	Main bearing clearance	0,013/0,056mm
70	Crankshaft end-float	0,10/0,20mm
71	Crankshaft end-thrust on	Centre bearing
72	Camshaft bearings	5
73	Camshaft journal diameter	(1) 45,34/45,36mm (2) 44,45/44,58 (3) 43,82/43,84 (4) 43,05/43,08 (5) 42,29/42,36
74	Camshaft bearing clearance	†
	Camshaft end-float	†
	Camshaft drive type	Chain
77	Cam lift	†
78	Valve head diameter	In 40,00/41,0mm Ex 34,48/35,60
79	Valve stem diameter	In 8,63/8,65mm Ex 8,64/8,66
80	Valve length	116,59/117,35mm
81	Valve seat/face angle	46°±15'/45°±15'
82	Valve lift	In/Ex 9,91mm
83	Valve guide length	Fitted height 19mm above step in boss
84	Valve stem/guide clearance	In 0,03/0,07mm Ex 0,04/0,08
85	Valve spring free length	48,30mm
86	Valve spring loaded length	40,40mm at 66,50N

COOLING SYSTEM

95	Type	Water pump radiator
96	Radiator pressure cap	1,03 bar (15lb/in²)
97	Fan	Electric
98	Thermostat	88°C

TRANSMISSION

100	Type	Rear wheel drive; LSD
101	Clutch	241,3mm hydraulic operation
102	Manual gearbox type	5 speed; LT77
103	Manual gearbox ratios	0,79; 1; 1,39; 2,08; 3,32; R 3,42:1
	Automatic gearbox type	Not
	Automatic gearbox ratios	Applicable
106	Stall speed	
107	Change speeds	
108	Drive shafts	Semi-floating
109	Final drive ratio	3,31:1
110	Differential bearing pre-load	0,076/0,152mm
111	Pinion bearing pre-load	0,9/1,4Nm

BRAKES

200	Type	Dual circuit
201	Power assistance	None
202	Front	Discs 279,4mm
203	Rear	Drums 229mm
204	Handbrake	Mechanical on rear wheels
205	Linings–front	Min thickness 1,5mm
206	Linings–rear	Width 45mm

STEERING

300	Type	Rack and pinion
301	Condition for checking	Unladen
302	Camber	–1° (non-adjustable)
303	Castor	4° (non-adjustable)
304	King pin inclination	2°
305	Wheel alignment–front	Parallel to toe in 3,2mm
306	Toe out on turns	†
307	Turning circle diameter	11,6m
308	Front hub end-float	†

FRONT SUSPENSION

330	Type	Independent vertical coil springs
331	Number of coils	18
332	Spring length	330mm
333	Spring rate	140 lb/in
334	Coil diameter	60mm
335	Wire diameter	9,52mm

REAR SUSPENSION

360	Type	Semi elliptic leaf springs
361	Wheel camber	Zero
362	Wheel alignment–rear	Parallel
363	Number of coils	Not Applicable (See A)
364	Spring length	1086mm
365	Spring rate	133,26 lb/in
366	Coil diameter	Not Applicable (See B)
367	Wire diameter	Not Applicable (See C)

ADDITIONAL INFORMATION

A	Number of leaves	6
B	Width of leaves	36mm
C	Thickness of leaves	6,4mm

ELECTRICAL

400	Battery	12V 58Ah neg earth
401	Alternator	65A
402	Regulated voltage	13,6/14,4V
403	Starter motor	Lucas

CAPACITIES

500	Engine oil	5,5 litres inc filter
501	Gearbox oil	1,6 litres
502	Differential oil	1,4 litres
503	Cooling system	13,6 litres
504	Fuel tank	64 litres
505	Tyre size	205/60 VR 15
506	Pressures bar (psi)	F/R 1,5 (22)
507	Max towing weight	575kg (1268lb)
508	Hydraulic fluid type	DOT 3 spec
509	Service intervals	5000 miles or 6 months

DIMENSIONS

600	Length overall	3960mm (156in)
601	Width overall	1600mm (63in)
602	Height overall	1220mm (48in)
603	Weight–kerb	889kg (1956lb)
604	Ground clearance	140mm (5,5in)
605	Wheelbase	2489mm (98in)
606	Track–front/rear	1345/1375mm (53/54in)

TORQUE WRENCH SETTINGS

		Nm	lb ft	
700	Cylinder head nuts/bolts	95	70	(long)
		68	50	(short)
701	Big end bearing bolts	47	35	
702	Main bearing bolts	75 (95)	55 (70)	(Rear)
703	Flywheel bolts	81	60	
704	Clutch to flywheel bolts	27	20	
705	Drive plate to torque converter	Not Applicable		
706	Crown wheel bolts	68/81	50/60	
707	Drive pinion unit	129/136	95/100	
708	Differential bearing bolts	47/54	35/40	
709	Road wheel nuts	95	70	
710	Steering wheel nut	34/47	25/35	

Plus 8 1989

ENGINE–TUNING DATA

1	Type	Ford CVH; 4 cyl in line mounted
2	Number of cylinders	4; No 1 pulley end
3	Cubic capacity	1597cm³
4	Bore/Stroke	79,96/79,52mm
5	Compression ratio/pressure	9,5:1/12–14 bar
6	Octane rating (RON)	98
7	Brake horsepower (DIN)	95 at 5750rpm
8	Torque (DIN) Nm (lb ft)	132 (97) at 4000rpm
9	Valve operation	OHC V formation valves, hydraulic tappets
10	Valve timing	8°BT–36°AB–34°BB–6°AT
11	Valve clearances mm (in)	Not Applicable
12	Spark plugs make/type	Motorcraft AGPR22C or Champion RE7YC
13	Gap	0,75mm (,030in)
14	Distributor make/type	Lucas or Bosch electronic
15	Firing order/rotation	1–3–4–2/anticlock
16	Dwell angle	} Electronic
17	Contact breaker gap	
18	Pick up air gap	
19	Ignition timing–stroboscopic	12° BTDC at idle
20	Ignition timing–static	†
21	Timing marks	Pulley
22	Centrifugal advance commences	−1,5°/3° at 1000rpm
23	Centrifugal advance–max	17°/23° at 6000rpm
24	Vacuum advance commences	−1°/+3° at 81mm Hg
25	Vacuum advance–max	9°/17° at 231mm Hg
26	Ignition coil–make	Bosch or Lucas
27	Prim res–sec res	0,72/0,88 ohms–4,5/7,0 kohms
28	Fuel pump	Mech 0,22/0,35 bar (3,2/5,1lb/in²)
29	Carburettor make/type	Weber twin choke
30	Specification number	28/32 TLDM 10/A
31	Idle speed (fast idle)	800rpm±25
32	Exhaust gas analysis	CO 1,25%±0,25
33	Cold start operation	Auto

34	Choke tube (venturi)	21mm	23mm
35	Main jet	117	127
36	Compensating jet	185	125
37	Slow-running jet	47	60
38	Slow-running air bleed	140	100
39	Accelerator pump jet	40	
40	Float level	31,0mm	
41	Needle valve	2,0	

ADDITIONAL INFORMATION

A	Emulsion tube	F30	F30

ENGINE–GENERAL DATA

50	Piston diameter (standard)	79,910/79,920mm (in 4 production grades)
51	Piston oversizes	0,26; 0,50mm (See A)
52	Piston clearance in bore	0,020/0,040mm (See B)
53	Piston rings–number	2 compression 1 oil
54	Piston rings–width	†
55	Piston rings–groove clearance	(1)(2) 0,041/0,091mm (3) 0,046/0,096
56	Piston rings–gap in bore	(1) 0,30/0,50mm (3) 0,4/1,4
57	Oil pressure bar (psi)	2.8 (40) at 2000rpm
58	Gudgeon pin diameter	20,622/20,632mm (in 4 grades)
59	Gudgeon pin fit in piston	Clearance 0,013/0,045mm
60	Gudgeon pin fit in con rod	Interference 0,013/0,045mm
61	Connecting rod length	109,83/109,88mm
62	Crankpin diameter	47,89/47,91mm
63	Crankpin undersizes	0,25; 0,50; 0,75; 1,00mm
64	Big end bearing clearance	0,006/0,060mm
65	Big end side clearance	0,10/0,25mm
66	Main bearings	5
67	Main journal diameter	57,98/58,00mm
68	Main journal undersizes	0,25; 0,50; 0,75; 1,00mm
69	Main bearing clearance	0,011/0,058mm
70	Crankshaft end-float	0,09/0,30mm
71	Crankshaft end-thrust on	Centre Bearing
72	Camshaft bearings	5
73	Camshaft journal diameter	(1) 44,75mm (2) 45,00 (3) 45,25 (4) 45,50 (5) 45,75
74	Camshaft bearing clearance	0,025/0,059mm
75	Camshaft end-float	0,05/0,15mm
76	Camshaft drive type	Toothed belt
77	Cam lift	In/Ex 6,09mm
78	Valve head diameter	In 41,9/42,1mm Ex 36,9/37,1
79	Valve stem diameter	In 8,025/8,043mm Ex 7,999/8,017
80	Valve length	In 134,54/135,00mm Ex 131,57/132,03
81	Valve seat/face angle	45°
82	Valve lift	In 10,19mm Ex 10,16mm
83	Valve guide length	†
84	Valve stem/guide clearance	In 0,020/0,068mm Ex 0,043/0,091
85	Valve spring free length	47,2mm
86	Valve spring loaded length	37,084mm at 402,4/441,6N (90,5/99,3lb)

ADDITIONAL INFORMATION

A	Piston oversizes	Service 79,930/79,955mm
B	Piston clearance in bore	Service 0,010/0,045mm

COOLING SYSTEM

95	Type	Water pump radiator
96	Radiator pressure cap	0,9 bar (13lb/in²)
97	Fan	Electric
98	Thermostat	85°/89°C

TRANSMISSION

100	Type	Rear wheel drive
101	Clutch	216mm cable operation
102	Manual gearbox type	5 speed; Ford
103	Manual gearbox ratios	0,83; 1; 1,37; 1,97; 3,65; R 3,66:1
104	Automatic gearbox type	} Not Applicable
105	Automatic gearbox ratios	
106	Stall speed	
107	Change speeds	
108	Drive shafts	Semi-floating
109	Final drive ratio	4,1:1
110	Differential bearing pre-load	0,076/0,152mm
111	Pinion bearing pre-load	0,9/1,4Nm

BRAKES

200	Type	Dual circuit
201	Power assistance	None
202	Front	Discs 279mm
203	Rear	Drums 229mm
204	Handbrake	Mechanical on rear wheels
205	Linings–front	Min thickness 1,5mm
206	Linings–rear	Width 45mm

STEERING

300	Type	Worm and roller
301	Condition for checking	Unladen
302	Camber	2°; Plus 4 style −1° (non-adjustable)
303	Castor	4° (non-adjustable)
304	King pin inclination	2°
305	Wheel alignment–front	Parallel to toe in 3mm
306	Toe out on turns	†
307	Turning circle diameter	10m
308	Front hub end-float	†

FRONT SUSPENSION

330	Type	Independent, vertical coil springs
331	Number of coils	21
332	Spring length	362mm
333	Spring rate	93,3 lb/in
334	Coil diameter	58mm
335	Wire diameter	7,8mm

REAR SUSPENSION

360	Type	Semi-elliptic leaf springs
361	Wheel camber	Zero
362	Wheel alignment–rear	Parallel
363	Number of coils	Not Applicable (See A)
364	Spring length	1086mm
365	Spring rate	2str 133,26lb/in; 4str 184,6
366	Coil diameter	Not Applicable (See B)
367	Wire diameter	Not Applicable (See C)

ADDITIONAL INFORMATION

A	Number of leaves	5 or 7
B	Width of leaves	36mm
C	Thickness of leaves	6,4mm

ELECTRICAL

400	Battery	12V 45Ah neg earth
401	Alternator	45A
402	Regulated voltage	13,7/14,6V
403	Starter motor	0,8kW

CAPACITIES

500	Engine oil	3,5 litres inc filter
501	Gearbox oil	1,9 litres
502	Differential oil	1,0 litres
503	Cooling system	10,2 litres
504	Fuel tank	56 litres
505	Tyre size	165 SR 15; Plus 4 style 195/60 HR 15
506	Pressures bar (psi)	F/R 1,2 (18); Plus 4 style F/R 1,5 (22)
507	Max towing weight	500kg (1102,5lb)
508	Hydraulic fluid type	DOT 3 spec
509	Service intervals	5000 miles or 6 months

DIMENSIONS

		4/4	Plus 4 style
600	Length overall	3890mm (153in)	3890 (153)
601	Width overall	1500mm (57in)	1500 (57)
602	Height overall	1314mm (51,75in)	1290 (51)
603	Weight–kerb	2 Str, 869kg (1912lb)	875 (1925)
		4 Str, 920kg (2024lb)	926 (2037)
604	Ground clearance	165mm (6,5in)	150 (6,0)
605	Wheelbase	2438mm (96in)	2438 (96)
606	Track–front/rear	1220/1245mm (48/49in)	1270/1295 (50/51)

TORQUE WRENCH SETTINGS

		Nm	lb ft
700	Cylinder head nuts/bolts	24; 56; +90°+90°	18; 41; +90°+90°
701	Big end bearing bolts	30/36	22/27
702	Main bearing bolts	89/100	66/74
703	Flywheel bolts	82/92	60/68
704	Clutch to flywheel bolts	18/20	13/15
705	Drive plate to torque converter	Not Applicable	
706	Crown wheel bolts	68/81	50/60
707	Drive pinion unit	129/136	95/100
708	Differential bearing bolts	47/54	35/40
709	Road wheel nuts	95	70
710	Steering wheel nut	34/47	25/35

4/4 1600 & 4/4 1600 (Plus 4 body style) 1990

ENGINE–TUNING DATA

1	Type..	20 HD (M16i); 4 cyl in line mounted
2	Number of cylinders.......................	4; No 1 front
3	Cubic capacity.............................	1994 cm³
4	Bore/Stroke...............................	84,45/89mm
5	Compression ratio/pressure	10:1/10,3 bar min
6	Octane rating (RON)	95 (min)
7	Brake horsepower (DIN)................	138 at 6000rpm
8	Torque (DIN) Nm (lb ft)	178 (131) at 4500rpm
9	Valve operation...........................	DOHC 4 valves per cyl
10	Valve timing...............................	18°BT–46°AB–52°BB–12°AT
11	Valve clearances mm (in)	Not Applicable
12	Spark plugs make/type	Unipart GSP4662 or GSP3662
13	Gap.......................................	1,0/1,1mm (,039/,043in)
14	Distributor make/type	Lucas
15	Firing order/rotation	1–3–4–2/anticlock
16	Dwell angle...............................	
17	Contact breaker gap.....................	} Electronic
18	Pick up air gap...........................	
19	Ignition timing–stroboscopic	12° BTDC at 900rpm
20	Ignition timing–static....................	†
21	Timing marks.............................	Electronic sensor on flywheel
22	Centrifugal advance commences	
23	Centrifugal advance–max............	} Electronic
24	Vacuum advance commences	} Computer controlled
25	Vacuum advance–max	
26	Ignition coil–make	GCL 141
27	Prim res–sec res	0,71/0,81 ohms
28	Fuel lift pump.............................	Lucas 4,1 bar max
29	Injection system make	Lucas L Hot wire
30	Type.......................................	4FP multi point computer controlled
31	Idle speed.................................	900rpm±50 controlled by ECU (See A)
32	Exhaust gas analysis	CO 1%±0,5
33	Injection pressure	Fuel pressure 3,0 bar above manifold depression

ADDITIONAL INFORMATION

A	Idle speed	Base idle speed setting with air valve closed; 750rpm±25

ENGINE–GENERAL DATA

50	Piston diameter (standard)	†
51	Piston oversizes..........................	†
52	Piston clearance in bore	0,04/0,05mm
53	Piston rings–number.....................	2 compression 1 oil
54	Piston rings–width	†
55	Piston rings–groove clearance	†
56	Piston rings–gap in bore	(1) 0,3/0,5mm (2) 0,25/0,50
57	Oil pressure bar (psi)...................	3,8 (55) at 3000rpm
58	Gudgeon pin diameter	23,810/23,815mm
59	Gudgeon pin fit in piston..............	Push fit
60	Gudgeon pin fit in con rod...........	Clearance 0,003/0,025mm
61	Connecting rod length	†
62	Crankpin diameter	47,635/47,647mm
63	Crankpin undersizes	†
64	Big end bearing clearance	0,038/0,081mm
65	Big end side clearance.................	†
66	Main bearings	5
67	Main journal diameter	54,005/54,026mm
68	Main journal undersizes	†
69	Main bearing clearance	0,03/0,38mm
70	Crankshaft end-float....................	0,03/0,14mm
71	Crankshaft end-thrust on	Centre bearing
72	Camshaft bearings	5 per shaft
73	Camshaft journal diameter	†
74	Camshaft bearing clearance	0,04/0,09mm
75	Camshaft end-float.....................	0,06/0,19mm
76	Camshaft drive type	Toothed belt
77	Cam lift	†
78	Valve head diameter	In 31,7/32,0mm Ex 29,2/29,4
79	Valve stem diameter	In 7,09/7,10mm Ex 7,07/7,09
80	Valve length	†
81	Valve seat/face angle	45°/45° 30'
82	Valve lift	8,83mm (nominal)
83	Valve guide length	Protrusion 12mm above head
84	Valve stem/guide clearance	In 0,03/0,05mm Ex 0,04/0,07
85	Valve spring free length	41mm
86	Valve spring loaded length..........	27,5mm at 560/570N

COOLING SYSTEM

95	Type.......................................	Water pump radiator
96	Radiator pressure cap..................	1,03 bar (15 lb/in²)
97	Fan...	Electric
98	Thermostat................................	88°C

TRANSMISSION

100	Type.......................................	Rear wheel drive
101	Clutch.....................................	267mm hydraulic operation
102	Manual gearbox type	5 speed; LT77
103	Manual gearbox ratios..................	0,79; 1; 1,39; 2,08; 3,32; R 3,42:1
104	Automatic gearbox type................	
105	Automatic gearbox ratios............	} Not
106	Stall speed	} Applicable
107	Change speeds	
108	Drive shafts...............................	Semi-floating
109	Final drive ratio	3,73:1
110	Differential bearing pre-load	0,076/0,152mm
111	Pinion bearing pre-load	0,9/1,4Nm

BRAKES

200	Type.......................................	Dual circuit
201	Power assistance	None
202	Front......................................	Discs 279mm
203	Rear.......................................	Drums 229mm
204	Handbrake................................	Mechanical on rear wheels
205	Linings–front	Min thickness 1,5mm
206	Linings–rear	Min thickness 1,5mm

STEERING

300	Type.......................................	Worm and roller
301	Condition for checking.................	Unladen
302	Camber....................................	−1° (non-adjustable)
303	Castor.....................................	4° (non-adjustable)
304	King pin inclination	2°
305	Wheel alignment–front.................	Parallel to toe in 3mm
306	Toe out on turns	†
307	Turning circle diameter	10m
308	Front hub end-float.....................	†

FRONT SUSPENSION

330	Type.......................................	Independent, vertical coil springs
331	Number of coils	21
332	Spring length	362mm
333	Spring rate	39,3 lb/in
334	Coil diameter	58mm
335	Wire diameter	7,8mm

REAR SUSPENSION

360	Type.......................................	Semi-elliptic leaf springs
361	Wheel camber............................	Zero
362	Wheel alignment–rear	Parallel
363	Number of coils	(See A)
364	Spring length	1086mm
365	Spring rate	2 str 133,26 lb/in; 4 str 184,6
366	Coil diameter.............................	(See B)
367	Wire diameter	(See C)

ADDITIONAL INFORMATION

A	Number of leaves	2 str 5; 4 str 7
B	Width of leaves	36mm
C	Thickness of leaves	6,4mm

ELECTRICAL

400	Battery.....................................	12V 45Ah neg earth
401	Alternator	55A
402	Regulated voltage	13,6/14,4V
403	Starter motor.............................	1,0kW

CAPACITIES

500	Engine oil..................................	4,5 litres inc filter
501	Gearbox oil................................	1,6 litres
502	Differential oil............................	1,0 litres
503	Cooling system	10,2 litres
504	Fuel tank..................................	56 litres
505	Tyre size..................................	195/60 HR 15
506	Pressures bar (psi)......................	F/R 1,5 (22)
507	Max towing weight.......................	500kg (1102,5 lb)
508	Hydraulic fluid type	DOT 3 spec
509	Service intervals	5000 miles or 6 months

DIMENSIONS

600	Length overall	3890mm (153in)
601	Width overall..............................	1500mm (57in)
602	Height overall.............................	1290mm (51in)
603	Weight–kerb...............................	2 str 885kg (1951lb); 4 str 936 (2064)
604	Ground clearance........................	150mm (6,07in)
605	Wheelbase.................................	2438mm (96in)
606	Track–front/rear	1270/1295mm (50/51in)

TORQUE WRENCH SETTINGS

		Nm	lb ft	
700	Cylinder head nuts/bolts	40, 80	30, 59	(See A)
701	Big end bearing bolts....................	45	33	
702	Main bearing bolts........................	105	75	
703	Flywheel bolts.............................	85	63	
704	Clutch to flywheel bolts.................	26	19	
705	Drive plate to torque converter	Not Applicable		
706	Crown wheel bolts........................	68/81	50/60	
707	Drive pinion unit	129/136	95/100	
708	Differential bearing bolts................	47/54	35/40	
709	Road wheel nuts..........................	95	70	
710	Steering wheel nut........................	34/47	25/35	

ADDITIONAL INFORMATION

A	Final tighten	+90° or 107Nm (79lbft) which ever comes first

Plus 4 1990

194

ENGINE–TUNING DATA

1	Type	Rover; V8 cyl in line mounted
2	Number of cylinders	8; No 1 front left
3	Cubic capacity	3532cm³
4	Bore/Stroke	88,9/71,12mm
5	Compression ratio/pressure	9,75:1/8,97 bar
6	Octane rating (RON)	98
7	Brake horsepower (DIN)	190 at 5280rpm
8	Torque (DIN) Nm (lb ft)	298 (220) at 4000rpm
9	Valve operation	OHV in line valves hydraulic tappets
10	Valve timing	30°BT–75°AB–68°BB–37°AT
11	Valve clearances mm (in)	Not Applicable
12	Spark plugs make/type	Unipart GSP151 or Champion N9YC
13	Gap	0,9mm (,035in)
14	Distributor make/type	Lucas 35DM8 41935A
15	Firing order/rotation	1–8–4–3–6–5–7–2/clockwise
16	Dwell angle	Not
17	Contact breaker gap	Applicable
18	Pick up air gap	0,36/0,40mm (,014/,016in)
19	Ignition timing–stroboscopic	8° BTDC at 600rpm
20	Ignition timing–static	†
21	Timing marks	Pulley
22	Centrifugal advance commences	400rpm
23	Centrifugal advance–max	7°/7,5° at 2500rpm
24	Vacuum advance commences	76,2mm Hg
25	Vacuum advance–max	7°/9° 304,8mm Hg
26	Ignition coil–make	Lucas or Bosch
27	Prim res–sec res	0,71/0,81 ohms
28	Fuel lift pump	Electric
29	Injection system make	Lucas 'L'
30	Type	Electronic
31	Idle speed	775rpm±25
32	Exhaust gas analysis	CO 1,5%±0,5
33	Injection pressure	1,8/2,49 bar

ENGINE–GENERAL DATA

50	Piston diameter (standard)	88,88mm
51	Piston oversizes	0,26; 0,51mm
52	Piston clearance in bore	0,018/0,033mm
53	Piston rings–number	2 compression 1 oil
54	Piston rings–width	(1)(2) 1,56/1,58mm (3) 4,81
55	Piston rings–groove clearance	(1)(2) 0,038/0,89mm
56	Piston rings–gap in bore	(1)(2) 0,43/0,56mm (3) 0,38/1,40
57	Oil pressure bar (psi)	2,1/2,8 (30/40) at 2400rpm
58	Gudgeon pin diameter	22,21/22,22mm
59	Gudgeon pin fit in piston	Clearance 0,002/0,007mm
60	Gudgeon pin fit in con rod	Press fit
61	Connecting rod length	143,71/143,81mm (centres)
62	Crankpin diameter	50,80/50,81mm
63	Crankpin undersizes	0,26; 0,51mm
64	Big end bearing clearance	0,015/0,055mm
65	Big end side clearance	0,15/0,356mm
66	Main bearings	5
67	Main journal diameter	58,41/58,42mm
68	Main journal undersizes	0,26; 0,51mm
69	Main bearing clearance	0,013/0,056mm
70	Crankshaft end-float	0,10/0,20mm
71	Crankshaft end-thrust on	Centre bearing
72	Camshaft bearings	5
73	Camshaft journal diameter	(1) 45,34/45,36mm (2) 44,45/44,58 (3) 43,82/43,84 (4) 43,05/43,08 (5) 42,29/42,36
74	Camshaft bearing clearance	†
75	Camshaft end-float	†
76	Camshaft drive type	Chain
77	Cam lift	†
78	Valve head diameter	In 40,00/41,0mm Ex 34,48/35,60
79	Valve stem diameter	In 8,63/8,65mm Ex 8,64/8,66
80	Valve length	116,59/117,35mm
81	Valve seat/face angle	46°±15'/45°±15'
82	Valve lift	In/Ex 9,91mm
83	Valve guide length	Fitted height 19mm above step in boss
84	Valve stem/guide clearance	In 0,03/0,07mm Ex 0,04/0,08
85	Valve spring free length	48,30mm
86	Valve spring loaded length	40,40mm at 66,50N

COOLING SYSTEM

95	Type	Water pump radiator
96	Radiator pressure cap	1,03 bar (15lb/in²)
97	Fan	Electric
98	Thermostat	88°C

TRANSMISSION

100	Type	Rear wheel drive; LSD
101	Clutch	241,3mm hydraulic operation
102	Manual gearbox type	5 speed; LT77
103	Manual gearbox ratios	0,79; 1; 1,39; 2,08; 3,32; R 3,42:1
104	Automatic gearbox type	
105	Automatic gearbox ratios	Not
106	Stall speed	Applicable
107	Change speeds	
108	Drive shafts	Semi-floating
109	Final drive ratio	3,31:1
110	Differential bearing pre-load	0,076/0,152mm
111	Pinion bearing pre-load	0,9/1,4Nm

BRAKES

200	Type	Dual circuit
201	Power assistance	None
202	Front	Discs 279,4mm
203	Rear	Drums 229mm
204	Handbrake	Mechanical on rear wheels
205	Linings–front	Min thickness 1,5mm
206	Linings–rear	Width 45mm

STEERING

300	Type	Rack and pinion
301	Condition for checking	Unladen
302	Camber	–1° (non-adjustable)
303	Castor	4° (non-adjustable)
304	King pin inclination	2°
305	Wheel alignment–front	Parallel to toe in 3,2mm
306	Toe out on turns	†
307	Turning circle diameter	11,6m
308	Front hub end-float	†

FRONT SUSPENSION

330	Type	Independent vertical coil springs
331	Number of coils	18
332	Spring length	330mm
333	Spring rate	140 lb/in
334	Coil diameter	60mm
335	Wire diameter	9,52mm

REAR SUSPENSION

360	Type	Semi elliptic leaf springs
361	Wheel camber	Zero
362	Wheel alignment–rear	Parallel
363	Number of coils	Not Applicable (See A)
364	Spring length	1086mm
365	Spring rate	133,26 lb/in
366	Coil diameter	Not Applicable (See B)
367	Wire diameter	Not Applicable (See C)

ADDITIONAL INFORMATION

A	Number of leaves	6
B	Width of leaves	36mm
C	Thickness of leaves	6,4mm

ELECTRICAL

400	Battery	12V 58Ah neg earth
401	Alternator	65A
402	Regulated voltage	13,6/14,4V
403	Starter motor	Mag Marelli

CAPACITIES

500	Engine oil	5,5 litres inc filter
501	Gearbox oil	1,6 litres
502	Differential oil	1,4 litres
503	Cooling system	13,6 litres
504	Fuel tank	64 litres
505	Tyre size	205/60 VR 15
506	Pressures bar (psi)	F/R 1,5 (22)
507	Max towing weight	575kg (1268lb)
508	Hydraulic fluid type	DOT 3 spec
509	Service intervals	5000 miles or 6 months

DIMENSIONS

600	Length overall	3960mm (156in)
601	Width overall	1600mm (63in)
602	Height overall	1220mm (48in)
603	Weight–kerb	889kg (1956lb)
604	Ground clearance	140mm (5,5in)
605	Wheelbase	2489mm (98in)
606	Track–front/rear	1345/1375mm (53/54in)

TORQUE WRENCH SETTINGS

		Nm	lb ft	
700	Cylinder head nuts/bolts	95	70	(long)
		68	50	(short)
701	Big end bearing bolts	47	35	
702	Main bearing bolts	75 (95)	55 (70)	(Rear)
703	Flywheel bolts	81	60	
704	Clutch to flywheel bolts	27	20	
705	Drive plate to torque converter	Not Applicable		
706	Crown wheel bolts	68/81	50/60	
707	Drive pinion unit	129/136	95/100	
708	Differential bearing bolts	47/54	35/40	
709	Road wheel nuts	95	70	
710	Steering wheel nut	34/47	25/35	

Plus 8 1990

195

ENGINE–TUNING DATA

1	Type	Ford CVH; 4 cyl in line mounted	
2	Number of cylinders	4; No 1 pulley end	
3	Cubic capacity	1597cm^3	
4	Bore/Stroke	79,96/79,52mm	
5	Compression ratio/pressure	9,5:1/12–14 bar	
6	Octane rating (RON)	98	
7	Brake horsepower (DIN)	95 at 5750rpm	
8	Torque (DIN) Nm (lb ft)	132 (97) at 4000rpm	
9	Valve operation	OHC V formation valves, hydraulic tappets	
10	Valve timing	8°BT–36°AB–34°BB–6°AT	
11	Valve clearances mm (in)	Not Applicable	
12	Spark plugs make/type	Motocraft AGPR22C or Champion RE7YC	
13	Gap	0,75mm (,030in)	
14	Distributor make/type	Lucas or Bosch electronic	
15	Firing order/rotation	1–3–4–2/anticlock	
16	Dwell angle		
17	Contact breaker gap	Electronic	
18	Pick up air gap		
19	Ignition timing–stroboscopic	12° BTDC at idle	
20	Ignition timing–static	†	
21	Timing marks	Pulley	
22	Centrifugal advance commences	–1,5°/3° at 1000rpm	
23	Centrifugal advance–max	17°/23° at 6000rpm	
24	Vacuum advance commences	–1°/+3° at 81mm Hg	
25	Vacuum advance–max	9°/17° at 231mm Hg	
26	Ignition coil–make	Bosch or Lucas	
27	Prim res–sec res	0,72/0,88 ohms–4,5/7,0 kohms	
28	Fuel pump	Mech 0,22/0,35 bar (3,2/5,1lb/in²)	
29	Carburettor make/type	Weber twin choke	
30	Specification number	28/32 TLDM 10/A	
31	Idle speed (fast idle)	800rpm ±25	
32	Exhaust gas analysis	CO 1,25% ±0,25	
33	Cold start operation	Auto	
34	Choke tube (venturi)	21mm	23mm
35	Main jet	117	127
36	Compensating jet	185	125
37	Slow-running jet	47	60
38	Slow-running air bleed	140	100
39	Accelerator pump jet	40	
40	Float level	31,0mm	
41	Needle valve	2,0	

ADDITIONAL INFORMATION

A	Emulsion tube	F30	F30

ENGINE–GENERAL DATA

50	Piston diameter (standard)	79,910/79,920mm (in 4 production grades)
51	Piston oversizes	0,26; 0,50mm (See A)
52	Piston clearance in bore	0,020/0,040mm (See B)
53	Piston rings–number	2 compression 1 oil
54	Piston rings–width	†
55	Piston rings–groove clearance	(1)(2) 0,041/0,091mm (3) 0,046/0,096
56	Piston rings–gap in bore	(1) (2) 0,30/0,50mm (3) 0,4/1,4
57	Oil pressure bar (psi)	2,8 (40) at 2000rpm
58	Gudgeon pin diameter	20,622/20,632mm (in 4 grades)
59	Gudgeon pin fit in piston	Clearance 0,013/0,045mm
60	Gudgeon pin fit in con rod	Interference 0,013/0,045mm
61	Connecting rod length	109,83/109,88mm
62	Crankpin diameter	47,89/47,91mm
63	Crankpin undersizes	0,25; 0,50, 0,75; 1,00mm
64	Big end bearing clearance	0,006/0,060mm
65	Big end side clearance	0,10/0,25mm
66	Main bearings	5
67	Main journal diameter	57,98/58,00mm
68	Main journal undersizes	0,25; 0,50, 0,75; 1,00mm
69	Main bearing clearance	0,011/0,058mm
70	Crankshaft end-float	0,09/0,30mm
71	Crankshaft end-thrust on	Centre Bearing
72	Camshaft bearings	5
73	Camshaft journal diameter	(1) 44,75mm (2) 45,00 (3) 45,25 (4) 45,50 (5) 45,75
74	Camshaft bearing clearance	0,025/0,059mm
75	Camshaft end-float	0,05/0,15mm
76	Camshaft drive type	Toothed belt
77	Cam lift	In/Ex 6,09mm
78	Valve head diameter	In 41,9/42,1mm Ex 36,9/37,1
79	Valve stem diameter	In 8,025/8,043mm Ex 7,999/8,017
80	Valve length	In 134,54/135,00mm Ex 131,57/132,03
81	Valve seat/face angle	45°
82	Valve lift	In 10,19mm Ex 10,16mm
83	Valve guide length	†
84	Valve stem/guide clearance	In 0,020/0,068mm Ex 0,043/0,091
85	Valve spring free length	47,2mm
86	Valve spring loaded length	37,084mm at 402,4/441,6N (90,5/99,3lb)

ADDITIONAL INFORMATION

A	Piston oversizes	Service 79,930/79,955mm
B	Piston clearance in bore	Service 0,010/0,045mm

COOLING SYSTEM

95	Type	Water pump radiator
96	Radiator pressure cap	0,9 bar (13lb/in²)
97	Fan	Electric
98	Thermostat	85°/89°C

TRANSMISSION

100	Type	Rear wheel drive
101	Clutch	216mm cable operation
102	Manual gearbox type	5 speed; Ford
103	Manual gearbox ratios	0,83; 1; 1,37; 1,97; 3,65; R 3,66:1
104	Automatic gearbox type	
105	Automatic gearbox ratios	Not
106	Stall speed	Applicable
107	Change speeds	
108	Drive shafts	Semi-floating
109	Final drive ratio	4,1:1
110	Differential bearing pre-load	0,076/0,152mm
111	Pinion bearing pre-load	0,9/1,4Nm

BRAKES

200	Type	Dual circuit
201	Power assistance	None
202	Front	Discs 279mm
203	Rear	Drums 229mm
204	Handbrake	Mechanical on rear wheels
205	Linings–front	Min thickness 1,5mm
206	Linings–rear	Width 45mm

STEERING

300	Type	Worm and roller
301	Condition for checking	Unladen
302	Camber	2°; Plus 4 style –1° (non-adjustable)
303	Castor	4° (non-adjustable)
304	King pin inclination	2°
305	Wheel alignment–front	Parallel to toe in 3mm
306	Toe out on turns	†
307	Turning circle diameter	10m
308	Front hub end-float	†

FRONT SUSPENSION

330	Type	Independent, vertical coil springs
331	Number of coils	21
332	Spring length	362mm
333	Spring rate	93,3 lb/in
334	Coil diameter	58mm
335	Wire diameter	7,8mm

REAR SUSPENSION

360	Type	Semi-elliptic leaf springs
361	Wheel camber	Zero
362	Wheel alignment–rear	Parallel
363	Number of coils	Not Applicable (See A)
364	Spring length	1086mm
365	Spring rate	2str 133,26lb/in; 4str 184,6
366	Coil diameter	Not Applicable (See B)
367	Wire diameter	Not Applicable (See C)

ADDITIONAL INFORMATION

A	Number of leaves	5 or 7
B	Width of leaves	36mm
C	Thickness of leaves	6,4mm

ELECTRICAL

400	Battery	12V 45Ah neg earth
401	Alternator	45A
402	Regulated voltage	13,7/14,6V
403	Starter motor	0,8kW

CAPACITIES

500	Engine oil	3,5 litres inc filter
501	Gearbox oil	1,9 litres
502	Differential oil	1,0 litres
503	Cooling system	10,2 litres
504	Fuel tank	56 litres
505	Tyre size	165 SR 15; Plus 4 style 195/60 HR 15
506	Pressures bar (psi)	F/R 1,2 (18); Plus 4 style F/R 1,5 (22)
507	Max towing weight	500kg (1102,5lb)
508	Hydraulic fluid type	DOT 3 spec
509	Service intervals	5000 miles or 6 months

DIMENSIONS

		4/4	Plus 4 style
600	Length overall	3890mm (153in)	3890 (153)
601	Width overall	1500mm (57in)	1500 (57)
602	Height overall	1314mm (51,75in)	1290 (51)
603	Weight–kerb	2 Str, 869kg (1912lb)	875 (1925)
		4 Str, 920kg (2024lb)	926 (2037)
604	Ground clearance	165mm (6,5in)	150 (6,0)
605	Wheelbase	2438mm (96in)	2438 (96)
606	Track–front/rear	1220/1245mm (48/49in)	1270/1295 (50/51)

TORQUE WRENCH SETTINGS

		Nm	lb ft
700	Cylinder head nuts/bolts	24; 56; +90°+90°	18; 41; +90°+90°
701	Big end bearing bolts	30/36	22/27
702	Main bearing bolts	89/100	66/74
703	Flywheel bolts	82/92	60/68
704	Clutch to flywheel bolts	18/20	13/15
705	Drive plate to torque converter	Not Applicable	
706	Crown wheel bolts	68/81	50/60
707	Drive pinion nut	129/136	95/100
708	Differential bearing bolts	47/54	35/40
709	Road wheel nuts	95	70
710	Steering wheel nut	34/47	25/35
711	Spark plugs	17/33	12/24
712	Drive shaft nut	†	

4/4 1600 & 4/4 1600 (Plus 4 body style 1991

ENGINE—TUNING DATA

1	Type	20 HD (M16i); 4 cyl in line mounted
2	Number of cylinders	4; No 1 front
3	Cubic capacity	1994 cm^3
4	Bore/Stroke	84,45/89mm
5	Compression ratio/pressure	10:1/10,3 bar min
6	Octane rating (RON)	95 (min)
7	Brake horsepower (DIN)	138 at 6000rpm
8	Torque (DIN) Nm (lb ft)	178 (131) at 4500rpm
9	Valve operation	DOHC 4 valves per cyl
10	Valve timing	18°BT—46°AB—52°BB—12°AT
11	Valve clearances mm (in)	Not Applicable
12	Spark plugs make/type	Unipart GSP4662 or GSP3662
13	Gap	1,0/1,1mm (,039/,043in)
14	Distributor make/type	Lucas
15	Firing order/rotation	1—3—4—2/anticlock
16	Dwell angle	⎫
17	Contact breaker gap	⎬ Electronic
18	Pick up air gap	⎭
19	Ignition timing—stroboscopic	12° BTDC at 900rpm
20	Ignition timing—static	†
21	Timing marks	Electronic sensor on flywheel
22	Centrifugal advance commences	⎫
23	Centrifugal advance—max	⎬ Electronic
24	Vacuum advance commences	⎬ Computer controlled
25	Vacuum advance—max	⎭
26	Ignition coil—make	GCL 141
27	Prim res—sec res	0,71/0,81 ohms
28	Fuel lift pump	Lucas 4,1 bar max
29	Injection system make	Lucas L Hot wire
30	Type	4FP multi point computer controlled
31	Idle speed	900rpm ±50 controlled by ECU (See A)
32	Exhaust gas analysis	CO 1% ±0,5
33	Injection pressure	Fuel pressure 3,0 bar above manifold depression

ADDITIONAL INFORMATION

A	Idle speed	Base idle speed setting with air valve closed; 750rpm ±25

ENGINE—GENERAL DATA

50	Piston diameter (standard)	†
51	Piston oversizes	†
52	Piston clearance in bore	0,04/0,05mm
53	Piston rings—number	2 compression 1 oil
54	Piston rings—width	†
55	Piston rings—groove clearance	(1) 0,3/0,5mm (2) 0,25/0,50
56	Piston rings—gap in bore	(1) 0,3/0,5mm (2) 0,25/0,50
57	Oil pressure bar (psi)	3,8 (55) at 3000rpm
58	Gudgeon pin diameter	23,810/23,815mm
59	Gudgeon pin fit in piston	Push fit
60	Gudgeon pin fit in con rod	Clearance 0,003/0,025mm
61	Connecting rod length	†
62	Crankpin diameter	47,635/47,647mm
63	Crankpin undersizes	†
64	Big end bearing clearance	0,038/0,081mm
65	Big end side clearance	†
66	Main bearings	5
67	Main journal diameter	54,005/54,026mm
68	Main journal undersizes	†
69	Main bearing clearance	0,03/0,38mm
70	Crankshaft end-float	0,03/0,14mm
71	Crankshaft end-thrust on	Centre bearing
72	Camshaft bearings	5 per shaft
73	Camshaft journal diameter	†
74	Camshaft bearing clearance	0,04/0,09mm
75	Camshaft end-float	0,06/0,19mm
76	Camshaft drive type	Toothed belt
77	Cam lift	†
78	Valve head diameter	In 31,7/32,0mm Ex 29,2/29,4
79	Valve stem diameter	In 7,09/7,10mm Ex 7,07/7,09
80	Valve length	†
81	Valve seat/face angle	45°/45° 30'
82	Valve lift	8,83mm (nominal)
83	Valve guide length	Protrusion 12mm above head
84	Valve stem/guide clearance	In 0,03/0,05mm Ex 0,04/0,07
85	Valve spring free length	41mm
86	Valve spring loaded length	27,5mm at 560/570N

COOLING SYSTEM

95	Type	Water pump radiator
96	Radiator pressure cap	1,03 bar (15 lb/in^2)
97	Fan	Electric
98	Thermostat	88°C

TRANSMISSION

100	Type	Rear wheel drive
101	Clutch	267mm hydraulic operation
102	Manual gearbox type	5 speed; LT77
103	Manual gearbox ratios	0,79; 1; 1,39; 2,08; 3,32; R 3,42:1
104	Automatic gearbox type	⎫
105	Automatic gearbox ratios	⎬ Not
106	Stall speed	⎬ Applicable
107	Change speeds	⎭
108	Drive shafts	Semi-floating
109	Final drive ratio	3,73:1
110	Differential bearing pre-load	0,076/0,152mm
111	Pinion bearing pre-load	0,9/1,4Nm

BRAKES

200	Type	Dual circuit
201	Power assistance	None
202	Front	Discs 279mm
203	Rear	Drums 229mm
204	Handbrake	Mechanical on rear wheels
205	Linings—front	Min thickness 1,5mm
206	Linings—rear	Min thickness 1,5mm

STEERING

300	Type	Worm and roller
301	Condition for checking	Unladen
302	Camber	−1° (non-adjustable)
303	Castor	4° (non-adjustable)
304	King pin inclination	2°
305	Wheel alignment—front	Parallel to toe in 3mm
306	Toe out on turns	†
307	Turning circle diameter	10m
308	Front hub end-float	†

FRONT SUSPENSION

330	Type	Independent, vertical coil springs
331	Number of coils	18
332	Spring length	330mm
333	Spring rate	140 lb/in
334	Coil diameter	60mm
335	Wire diameter	9,52mm

REAR SUSPENSION

360	Type	Semi-elliptic leaf springs
361	Wheel camber	Zero
362	Wheel alignment—rear	Parallel
363	Number of coils	(See A)
364	Spring length	1086mm
365	Spring rate	2 str 133,26 lb/in; 4 str 184,6
366	Coil diameter	(See B)
367	Wire diameter	(See C)

ADDITIONAL INFORMATION

A	Number of leaves	2 str 5; 4 str 7
B	Width of leaves	36mm
C	Thickness of leaves	6,4mm

ELECTRICAL

400	Battery	12V 45Ah neg earth
401	Alternator	55A
402	Regulated voltage	13,6/14,4V
403	Starter motor	1,0kW

CAPACITIES

500	Engine oil	4,5 litres inc filter
501	Gearbox oil	1,6 litres
502	Differential oil	1,0 litres
503	Cooling system	10,2 litres
504	Fuel tank	56 litres
505	Tyre size	195/60 HR 15
506	Pressures bar (psi)	F/R 1,5 (22)
507	Max towing weight	500kg (1102,5 lb)
508	Hydraulic fluid type	DOT 3 spec
509	Service intervals	5000 miles or 6 months

DIMENSIONS

600	Length overall	3890mm (153in)
601	Width overall	1500mm (57in)
602	Height overall	1290mm (51in)
603	Weight—kerb	2 str 885kg (1951lb); 4 str 936 (2064)
604	Ground clearance	150mm (6,07in)
605	Wheelbase	2438mm (96in)
606	Track—front/rear	1270/1295mm (50/51in)

TORQUE WRENCH SETTINGS

		Nm	lb ft	
700	Cylinder head nuts/bolts	40; 80	30; 59	(See A)
701	Big end bearing bolts	45	33	
702	Main bearing bolts	105	75	
703	Flywheel bolts	85	63	
704	Clutch to flywheel bolts	26	19	
705	Drive plate to torque converter	Not Applicable		
706	Crown wheel bolts	68/81	50/60	
707	Drive pinion nut	129/136	95/100	
708	Differential bearing bolts	47/54	35/40	
709	Road wheel nuts	95	70	
710	Steering wheel nut	34/47	25/35	
711	Spark plugs	18	13	
712	Drive shaft nut	†		

ADDITIONAL INFORMATION

A	Final tighten	+90° or 107Nm (79lbft) which ever comes first

Plus 4 1991

ENGINE—TUNING DATA

1	Type	Rover; V8 cyl in line mounted
2	Number of cylinders	8; No 1 front left
3	Cubic capacity	3946cm³
4	Bore/Stroke	94,0/71,12mm
5	Compression ratio/pressure	9,35:1
6	Octane rating (RON)	Unleaded only
7	Brake horsepower (DIN)	185 at 4750rpm
8	Torque Nm (lb ft)	312 (230) at 2600rpm
9	Valve operation	OHV in line valves hydraulic tappets
10	Valve timing	32°BT–73°AB–70°BB–35°AT
11	Valve clearances mm (in)	Not Applicable
12	Spark plugs make/type	Champion RN9YC
13	Gap	0,9mm (,035in)
14	Distributor make/type	Lucas 35DM8
15	Firing order/rotation	1–8–4–3–6–5–7–2/clockwise
16	Dwell angle	⎫ Not
17	Contact breaker gap	⎬ Applicable
18	Pick up air gap	0,20/0,35mm
19	Ignition timing–stroboscopic	4° BTDC at 600rpm
20	Ignition timing–static	†
21	Timing marks	Pulley
22	Centrifugal advance commences	600rpm
23	Centrifugal advance–max	8°/10° at 2300rpm Decelerating, vac hose off (Distributor degrees and rpm)
24	Vacuum advance commences	†
25	Vacuum advance–max	†
26	Ignition coil–make	Bosch 0221 122 392
27	Prim res–sec res	†
28	Fuel lift pump	Electric
29	Injection system make	Lucas 'L'
30	Type	Electronic
31	Idle speed	650/750rpm
32	Exhaust gas analysis	†
33	Injection pressure	1,8/2,49 bar

ENGINE—GENERAL DATA

50	Piston diameter (standard)	†
51	Piston oversizes	0,26; 0,51mm
52	Piston clearance in bore	0,018/0,033mm
53	Piston rings–number	2 compression 1 oil
54	Piston rings–width	(1)(2) 1,478/1,490mm (3) 3,00 max
55	Piston rings–groove clearance	(1)(2) 0,038/0,89mm
56	Piston rings–gap in bore	(1)(2) 0,44/0,57mm (3) 0,38/1,40
57	Oil pressure bar (psi)	2,1/2,8 (30/40) at 2400rpm
58	Gudgeon pin diameter	22,21/22,22mm
59	Gudgeon pin fit in piston	Clearance 0,002/0,007mm
60	Gudgeon pin fit in con rod	Press fit
61	Connecting rod length	143,71/143,81mm (centres)
62	Crankpin diameter	50,80/50,81mm
63	Crankpin undersizes	0,26; 0,51mm
64	Big end bearing clearance	0,015/0,055mm
65	Big end side clearance	0,15/0,356mm
66	Main bearings	5
67	Main journal diameter	58,41/58,42mm
68	Main journal undersizes	0,26. 0,51mm
69	Main bearing clearance	0,010/0,048mm
70	Crankshaft end-float	0,10/0,20mm
71	Crankshaft end-thrust on	Centre bearing
72	Camshaft bearings	5
73	Camshaft journal diameter	(1) 45,34/45,36mm (2) 44,45/44,58 (3) 43,82/43,84 (4) 43,05/43,08 (5) 42,29/42,36
74	Camshaft bearing clearance	†
75	Camshaft end-float	†
76	Camshaft drive type	Chain
77	Cam lift	†
78	Valve head diameter	In 40,00/41,0mm Ex 34,48/35,60
79	Valve stem diameter	In 8,664/8,679mm Ex 8,651/8,666
80	Valve length	116,59/117,35mm
81	Valve seat/face angle	46° ± 15'/45° ± 15'
82	Valve lift	In/Ex 9,91mm
83	Valve guide length	†
84	Valve stem/guide clearance	In 0,025/0,066mm Ex 0,038/0,078
85	Valve spring free length	48,30mm
86	Valve spring loaded length	40,40mm at 66,50N

COOLING SYSTEM

95	Type	Water pump radiator
96	Radiator pressure cap	1,03 bar (15 lb/in²)
97	Fan	Electric
98	Thermostat	88°C

TRANSMISSION

100	Type	Rear wheel drive; LSD
101	Clutch	241,3mm hydraulic operation
102	Manual gearbox type	5 speed; LT77
103	Manual gearbox ratios	0,79; 1; 1,39; 2,08; 3,32; R 3.42:1
104	Automatic gearbox type	⎫
105	Automatic gearbox ratios	⎬ Not
106	Stall speed	⎬ Applicable
107	Change speeds	⎭
108	Drive shafts	Semi-floating
109	Final drive ratio	3,31:1
110	Differential bearing pre-load	0,076/0,152mm
111	Pinion bearing pre-load	0,9/1,4Nm

BRAKES

200	Type	Dual circuit
201	Power assistance	None
202	Front	Discs 279,4mm
203	Rear	Drums 229mm
204	Handbrake	Mechanical on rear wheels
205	Linings–front	Min thickness 1,5mm
206	Linings–rear	Width 45mm

STEERING

300	Type	Rack and pinion
301	Condition for checking	Unladen
302	Camber	Zero to –0° 30'
303	Castor	4° (non-adjustable)
304	King pin inclination	2°
305	Wheel alignment–front	Toe in 0,25° ±0,15°
306	Toe out on turns	†
307	Turning circle diameter	11,6m
308	Front hub end-float	†

FRONT SUSPENSION

330	Type	Independent vertical coil springs
331	Number of coils	18
332	Spring length	347mm
333	Spring rate	85 lb/in
334	Coil diameter	60mm
335	Wire diameter	7,5mm

REAR SUSPENSION

360	Type	Semi elliptic leaf springs
361	Wheel camber	Zero
362	Wheel alignment–rear	Parallel
363	Number of coils	Not Applicable (See A)
364	Spring length	1086mm
365	Spring rate	133,26 lb/in
366	Coil diameter	Not Applicable (See B)
367	Wire diameter	Not Applicable (See C)

ADDITIONAL INFORMATION

A	Number of leaves	6
B	Width of leaves	36mm
C	Thickness of leaves	6,4mm

ELECTRICAL

400	Battery	12V 58Ah neg earth
401	Alternator	65A
402	Regulated voltage	13,6/14,4V
403	Starter motor	Mag Marelli

CAPACITIES

500	Engine oil	5,5 litres inc filter
501	Gearbox oil	1,6 litres
502	Differential oil	1,4 litres
503	Cooling system	13,6 litres
504	Fuel tank	55 litres
505	Tyre size	205/60 VR 15
506	Pressures bar (psi)	F/R 1,5 (22)
507	Max towing weight	575kg (1268lb)
508	Hydraulic fluid type	DOT 4 spec
509	Service intervals	5000 miles or 6 months

DIMENSIONS

600	Length overall	3960mm (156in)
601	Width overall	1600mm (63in)
602	Height overall	1220mm (48in)
603	Weight–kerb	940kg (2072lb)
604	Ground clearance	140mm (5,5in)
605	Wheelbase	2489mm (98in)
606	Track–front/rear	1345/1375mm (53/54in)

TORQUE WRENCH SETTINGS

		Nm	lb ft	
700	Cylinder head nuts/bolts	95	70	(long)
		68	50	(short)
701	Big end bearing bolts	47/54	35/40	
702	Main bearing bolts	75 (95)	55 (70)	(Rear)
703	Flywheel bolts	81	60	
704	Clutch to flywheel bolts	27	20	
705	Drive plate to torque converter	Not Applicable		
706	Crown wheel bolts	68/81	50/60	
707	Drive pinion nut	129/136	95/100	
708	Differential bearing bolts	47/54	35/40	
709	Road wheel nuts	95	70	
710	Steering wheel nut	34/47	25/35	
711	Spark plugs	14/16	10/12	
712	Front hub nut	†		
713	Rear hub nut	†		

Plus 8 1991

ENGINE–TUNING DATA

#		
1	Type	Ford CVH; 4 cyl in line mounted
2	Number of cylinders	4; No 1 pulley end
3	Cubic capacity	1597cm³
4	Bore/Stroke	79,96/79,52mm
5	Compression ratio/pressure	9,75:1/12–14 bar
6	Octane rating (RON)	Unleaded only
7	Brake horsepower (DIN)	100 at 6000rpm
8	Torque (DIN) Nm (lb ft)	138 (102) at 2800rpm
9	Valve operation	OHC V formation valves, hydraulic tappets
10	Valve timing	4°BT–30°AB–44°BB–10°AT
11	Valve clearances mm (in)	Not Applicable
12	Spark plugs make/type	Motocraft AGPR22CDI
13	Gap	1,00mm (,040in)
14	Distributor make/type	Lucas or Bosch electronic
15	Firing order/rotation	1–3–4–2/anticlock
16	Dwell angle	⎫
17	Contact breaker gap	⎬ Electronic
18	Pick up air gap	⎭
19	Ignition timing–stroboscopic	10° BTDC at idle (pre set)
20	Ignition timing–static	†
21	Timing marks	Pulley
22	Centrifugal advance commences.	⎫
23	Centrifugal advance–max	⎬ Computer Controlled
24	Vacuum advance commences	⎬ Electronic Advance
25	Vacuum advance–max	⎭
26	Ignition coil–make	Various
27	Prim res–sec res	4,5/5,0 ohms
28	Fuel lift pump	Electric
29	Injection system make	Weber
30	Type	Multipoint
31	Idle speed	900rpm ±50
32	Exhaust gas analysis	CO 0,5%
33	Injection pressure	3,0 bar

ADDITIONAL INFORMATION

A	Emulsion tube	F30	F30

ENGINE–GENERAL DATA

#		
50	Piston diameter (standard)	79,915/79,955mm (in 4 production grades)
51	Piston oversizes	0,25, 0,50mm
52	Piston clearance in bore	0,010/0,040mm
53	Piston rings–number	2 compression 1 oil
54	Piston rings–width	†
55	Piston rings–groove clearance	†
56	Piston rings–gap in bore	(1)(2) 0,30/0,50mm (3) 0,25/0,40
57	Oil pressure bar (psi)	2,8 (40) at 2000rpm
58	Gudgeon pin diameter	20,622/20,632mm (in 4 grades)
59	Gudgeon pin fit in piston	Clearance 0,005/0,011mm
60	Gudgeon pin fit in con rod	Interference 0,013/0,045mm
61	Connecting rod length	109,83/109,88mm
62	Crankpin diameter	47,89/47,91mm
63	Crankpin undersizes	0,25, 0,50; 0,75; 1,00mm
64	Big end bearing clearance	0,006/0,060mm
65	Big end side clearance	0,10/0,25mm
66	Main bearings	5
67	Main journal diameter	57,98/58,00mm
68	Main journal undersizes	0,25; 0,50; 0,75; 1,00mm
69	Main bearing clearance	0,011/0,058mm
70	Crankshaft end-float	0,09/0,30mm
71	Crankshaft end-thrust on	Centre Bearing
72	Camshaft bearings	5
73	Camshaft journal diameter	(1) 44,75mm (2) 45,00 (3) 45,25 (4) 45,50 (5) 45,75
74	Camshaft bearing clearance	0,025/0,059mm
75	Camshaft end-float	0,05/0,15mm
76	Camshaft drive type	Toothed belt
77	Cam lift	In/Ex 6,09mm
78	Valve head diameter	In 41,9/42,1mm Ex 36,9/37,1
79	Valve stem diameter	In 8,025/8,043mm Ex 7,999/8,017
80	Valve length	In 134,54/135,00mm Ex 131,57/132,03
81	Valve seat/face angle	45°
82	Valve lift	In/Ex 10,5 ±0,2mm
83	Valve guide length	†
84	Valve stem/guide clearance	In 0,020/0,063mm Ex 0,046/0,089
85	Valve spring free length	46,9/48,3mm
86	Valve spring loaded length	†

ADDITIONAL INFORMATION

A	Piston oversizes	Service 79,930/79,955mm
B	Piston clearance in bore	Service 0,010/0,045mm

COOLING SYSTEM

#		
95	Type	Water pump radiator
96	Radiator pressure cap	0,9 bar (13lb/in²)
97	Fan	Electric
98	Thermostat	85°/89°C

TRANSMISSION

#		
100	Type	Rear wheel drive
101	Clutch	216mm cable operation
102	Manual gearbox type	5 speed; Ford
103	Manual gearbox ratios	0,83; 1; 1,37; 1,97; 3,65; R 3,66:1
104	Automatic gearbox type	⎫
105	Automatic gearbox ratios	⎬ Not
106	Stall speed	⎬ Applicable
107	Change speeds	⎭
108	Drive shafts	Semi-floating
109	Final drive ratio	4,1:1
110	Differential bearing pre-load	0,076/0,152mm
111	Pinion bearing pre-load	0,9/1,4Nm

BRAKES

#		
200	Type	Dual circuit
201	Power assistance	None
202	Front	Discs 279mm
203	Rear	Drums 229mm
204	Handbrake	Mechanical on rear wheels
205	Linings–front	Min thickness 1,5mm
206	Linings–rear	Width 45mm

STEERING

#		
300	Type	Worm and roller
301	Condition for checking	Unladen
302	Camber	Zero to –0° 30'
303	Castor	4° (non-adjustable)
304	King pin inclination	2°
305	Wheel alignment–front	Parallel to toe in 3mm
306	Toe out on turns	†
307	Turning circle diameter	10m
308	Front hub end-float	†

FRONT SUSPENSION

#		
330	Type	Independent, vertical coil springs
331	Number of coils	21
332	Spring length	362mm
333	Spring rate	93,3 lb/in
334	Coil diameter	58mm
335	Wire diameter	7,8mm

REAR SUSPENSION

#		
360	Type	Semi-elliptic leaf springs
361	Wheel camber	Zero
362	Wheel alignment–rear	Parallel
363	Number of coils	Not Applicable (See A)
364	Spring length	1086mm
365	Spring rate	2str 133,26lb/in; 4str 184,6
366	Coil diameter	Not Applicable (See B)
367	Wire diameter	Not Applicable (See C)

ADDITIONAL INFORMATION

A	Number of leaves	5 or 7
B	Width of leaves	36mm
C	Thickness of leaves	6,4mm

ELECTRICAL

#		
400	Battery	12V 45Ah neg earth
401	Alternator	45A
402	Regulated voltage	13,7/14,6V
403	Starter motor	0,8kW

CAPACITIES

#		
500	Engine oil	3,5 litres inc filter
501	Gearbox oil	1,9 litres
502	Differential oil	1,0 litres
503	Cooling system	10,2 litres
504	Fuel tank	56 litres
505	Tyre size	165 SR 15; Plus 4 style 195/60 HR 15
506	Pressures bar (psi)	F/R 1,2 (18); Plus 4 style F/R 1,5 (22)
507	Max towing weight	500kg (1102,5lb)
508	Hydraulic fluid type	DOT 3 spec
509	Service intervals	5000 miles or 6 months

DIMENSIONS

#		4/4	Plus 4 style
600	Length overall	3890mm (153in)	3890 (153)
601	Width overall	1500mm (57in)	1500 (57)
602	Height overall	1314mm (51,75in)	1290 (51)
603	Weight–kerb	2 Str, 869kg (1912lb)	875 (1925)
		4 Str, 920kg (2024lb)	926 (2037)
604	Ground clearance	165mm (6,5in)	150 (6,0)
605	Wheelbase	2438mm (96in)	2438 (96)
606	Track–front/rear	1220/1245mm (48/49in)	1270/1295 (50/51)

TORQUE WRENCH SETTINGS

#		Nm	lb ft
700	Cylinder head nuts/bolts	24; 56; +90°+90°	18; 41; +90°+90°
701	Big end bearing bolts	30/36	22/27
702	Main bearing bolts	89/100	66/74
703	Flywheel bolts	82/92	60/68
704	Clutch to flywheel bolts	18/20	13/15
705	Drive plate to torque converter	Not Applicable	
706	Crown wheel bolts	68/81	50/60
707	Drive pinion nut	129/136	95/100
708	Differential bearing bolts	47/54	35/40
709	Road wheel nuts	95	70
710	Steering wheel nut	34/47	25/35
711	Spark plugs	17/33	12/24
712	Front hub nut	†	
713	Rear hub nut	†	

4/4 1600 & 4/4 1600 (Plus 4 body style) 1992

ENGINE–TUNING DATA

1	Type	20 HD (M16i); 4 cyl in line mounted
	Number of cylinders	4; No 1 front
	Cubic capacity	1994 cm^3
4	Bore/Stroke	84,45/89mm
5	Compression ratio/pressure	10:1/10,3 bar min
6	Octane rating (RON)	95 (min)
7	Brake horsepower (DIN)	138 at 6000rpm
8	Torque (DIN) Nm (lb ft)	178 (131) at 4500rpm
9	Valve operation	DOHC 4 valves per cyl
10	Valve timing	18°BT–46°AB–52°BB–12°AT
11	Valve clearances mm (in)	Not Applicable
12	Spark plugs make/type	Unipart GSP4662 or GSP3662
13	Gap	1,0/1,1mm (,039/,043in)
14	Distributor make/type	Lucas
15	Firing order/rotation	1–3–4–2/anticlock
16	Dwell angle	} Electronic
17	Contact breaker gap	
18	Pick up air gap	
19	Ignition timing–stroboscopic	12° BTDC at 900rpm
20	Ignition timing–static	†
21	Timing marks	Electronic sensor on flywheel
22	Centrifugal advance commences	} Electronic
23	Centrifugal advance–max	
24	Vacuum advance commences	} Computer controlled
25	Vacuum advance–max	
26	Ignition coil–make	GCL 141
27	Prim res–sec res	0,71/0,81 ohms
28	Fuel lift pump	Lucas 4,1 bar max
29	Injection system make	Lucas L Hot wire
30	Type	4FP multi point computer controlled
31	Idle speed	900rpm ±50 controlled by ECU (See A)
32	Exhaust gas analysis	CO 1% ±0,5
33	Injection pressure	Fuel pressure 3,0 bar above manifold depression

DITIONAL INFORMATION

Idle speed	Base idle speed setting with air valve closed; 750rpm ±25

ENGINE–GENERAL DATA

50	Piston diameter (standard)	†
51	Piston oversizes	†
52	Piston clearance in bore	0,04/0,05mm
53	Piston rings–number	2 compression 1 oil
54	Piston rings–width	†
55	Piston rings–groove clearance	†
56	Piston rings–gap in bore	(1) 0,3/0,5mm (2) 0,25/0,50
57	Oil pressure bar (psi)	3,8 (55) at 3000rpm
58	Gudgeon pin diameter	23,810/23,815mm
59	Gudgeon pin fit in piston	Push fit
60	Gudgeon pin fit in con rod	Clearance 0,003/0,025mm
61	Connecting rod length	†
62	Crankpin diameter	47,635/47,647mm
63	Crankpin undersizes	†
64	Big end bearing clearance	0,038/0,081mm
65	Big end side clearance	†
66	Main bearings	5
67	Main journal diameter	54,005/54,026mm
68	Main journal undersizes	†
69	Main bearing clearance	0,03/0,38mm
70	Crankshaft end-float	0,03/0,14mm
71	Crankshaft end-thrust on	Centre bearing
72	Camshaft bearings	5 per shaft
	Camshaft journal diameter	†
	Camshaft bearing clearance	0,04/0,09mm
	Camshaft end-float	0,06/0,19mm
76	Camshaft drive type	Toothed belt
77	Cam lift	†
78	Valve head diameter	In 31,7/32,0mm Ex 29,2/29,4
79	Valve stem diameter	In 7,09/7,10mm Ex 7,07/7,09
80	Valve length	†
81	Valve seat/face angle	45°/45° 30'
82	Valve lift	8,83mm (nominal)
83	Valve guide length	Protrusion 12mm above head
84	Valve stem/guide clearance	In 0,03/0,05mm Ex 0,04/0,07
85	Valve spring free length	41mm
86	Valve spring loaded length	27,5mm at 560/570N

COOLING SYSTEM

95	Type	Water pump radiator
96	Radiator pressure cap	1,03 bar (15 lb/in^2)
97	Fan	Electric
98	Thermostat	88°C

TRANSMISSION

100	Type	Rear wheel drive
101	Clutch	267mm hydraulic operation
102	Manual gearbox type	5 speed; LT77
	Manual gearbox ratios	0,79; 1; 1,39; 2,08; 3,32; R 3,42:1
	Automatic gearbox type	} Not Applicable
105	Automatic gearbox ratios	
106	Stall speed	
107	Change speeds	
108	Drive shafts	Semi-floating
109	Final drive ratio	3,73:1
110	Differential bearing pre-load	0,076/0,152mm
111	Pinion bearing pre-load	0,9/1,4Nm

BRAKES

200	Type	Dual circuit
201	Power assistance	None
202	Front	Discs 279mm
203	Rear	Drums 229mm
204	Handbrake	Mechanical on rear wheels
205	Linings–front	Min thickness 1,5mm
206	Linings–rear	Min thickness 1,5mm

STEERING

300	Type	Worm and roller
301	Condition for checking	Unladen
302	Camber	Zero to –0° 30'
303	Castor	4° (non-adjustable)
304	King pin inclination	2°
305	Wheel alignment–front	Toe in 0,25° ±0,15°
306	Toe out on turns	†
307	Turning circle diameter	10m
308	Front hub end-float	†

FRONT SUSPENSION

330	Type	Independent, vertical coil springs
331	Number of coils	18
332	Spring length	330mm
333	Spring rate	140 lb/in
334	Coil diameter	60mm
335	Wire diameter	9,52mm

REAR SUSPENSION

360	Type	Semi-elliptic leaf springs
361	Wheel camber	Zero
362	Wheel alignment–rear	Parallel
363	Number of coils	(See A)
364	Spring length	1086mm
365	Spring rate	2 str 133,26 lb/in; 4 str 184,6
366	Coil diameter	(See B)
367	Wire diameter	(See C)

ADDITIONAL INFORMATION

A	Number of leaves	2 str 5; 4 str 7
B	Width of leaves	36mm
C	Thickness of leaves	6,4mm

ELECTRICAL

400	Battery	12V 45Ah neg earth
401	Alternator	55A
402	Regulated voltage	13,6/14,4V
403	Starter motor	1,0kW

CAPACITIES

500	Engine oil	4,5 litres inc filter
501	Gearbox oil	1,6 litres
502	Differential oil	1,0 litres
503	Cooling system	10,2 litres
504	Fuel tank	56 litres
505	Tyre size	195/60 HR 15
506	Pressures bar (psi)	F/R 1,5 (22)
507	Max towing weight	500kg (1102,5 lb)
508	Hydraulic fluid type	DOT 3 spec
509	Service intervals	5000 miles or 6 months

DIMENSIONS

600	Length overall	3890mm (153in)
601	Width overall	1500mm (57in)
602	Height overall	1290mm (51in)
603	Weight–kerb	2 str 885kg (1951lb); 4 str 936 (2064)
604	Ground clearance	150mm (6,07in)
605	Wheelbase	2438mm (96in)
606	Track–front/rear	1270/1295mm (50/51in)

TORQUE WRENCH SETTINGS

		Nm	lb ft	
700	Cylinder head nuts/bolts	40; 80	30; 59	(See A)
701	Big end bearing bolts	45	33	
702	Main bearing bolts	105	75	
703	Flywheel bolts	85	63	
704	Clutch to flywheel bolts	26	19	
705	Drive plate to torque converter	Not Applicable		
706	Crown wheel bolts	68/81	50/60	
707	Drive pinion nut	129/136	95/100	
708	Differential bearing bolts	47/54	35/40	
709	Road wheel nuts	95	70	
710	Steering wheel nut	34/47	25/35	
711	Spark plugs	18	13	
712	Front hub nut	†		
713	Rear hub nut	†		

ADDITIONAL INFORMATION

A	Final tighten	+90° or 107Nm (79lbft) which ever comes first

Plus 4 1992

ENGINE—TUNING DATA

1	Type	Rover; V8 cyl in line mounted
2	Number of cylinders	8; No 1 front left
3	Cubic capacity	3946cm³
4	Bore/Stroke	94,0/71,12mm
5	Compression ratio/pressure	9,35:1
6	Octane rating (RON)	Unleaded only
7	Brake horsepower (DIN)	185 at 4750rpm
8	Torque (DIN) Nm (lb ft)	312 (230) at 2600rpm
9	Valve operation	OHV in line valves hydraulic tappets
10	Valve timing	32°BT–73°AB–70°BB–35°AT
11	Valve clearances mm (in)	Not Applicable
12	Spark plugs make/type	Champion RN9YC
13	Gap	0,9mm (,035in)
14	Distributor make/type	Lucas 35DM8
15	Firing order/rotation	1–8–4–3–6–5–7–2/clockwise
16	Dwell angle	⎫ Not
17	Contact breaker gap	⎬ Applicable
18	Pick up air gap	0,20/0,35mm
19	Ignition timing—stroboscopic	4° BTDC at 600rpm
20	Ignition timing—static	†
21	Timing marks	Pulley
22	Centrifugal advance commences	600rpm
23	Centrifugal advance—max	8°/10° at 2300rpm Decelerating, vac hose off (Distributor degrees and rpm)
24	Vacuum advance commences	†
25	Vacuum advance—max	†
26	Ignition coil—make	Bosch 0221 122 392
27	Prim res–sec res	†
28	Fuel lift pump	Electric
29	Injection system make	Lucas 'L'
30	Type	Electronic
31	Idle speed	650/750rpm
32	Exhaust gas analysis	†
33	Injection pressure	1,8/2,49 bar

ENGINE—GENERAL DATA

50	Piston diameter (standard)	†
51	Piston oversizes	0,26; 0,51mm
52	Piston clearance in bore	0,018/0,033mm
53	Piston rings—number	2 compression 1 oil
54	Piston rings—width	(1)(2) 1,478/1,490mm (3) 3,00 max
55	Piston rings—groove clearance	(1)(2) 0,038/0,089mm
56	Piston rings—gap in bore	(1)(2) 0,44/0,57mm (3) 0,38/1,40
57	Oil pressure bar (psi)	2,1/2,8 (30/40) at 2400rpm
58	Gudgeon pin diameter	22,21/22,22mm
59	Gudgeon pin fit in piston	Clearance 0,002/0,007mm
60	Gudgeon pin fit in con rod	Press fit
61	Connecting rod length	143,71/143,81mm (centres)
62	Crankpin diameter	50,80/50,81mm
63	Crankpin undersizes	0,26; 0,51mm
64	Big end bearing clearance	0,015/0,055mm
65	Big end side clearance	0,15/0,356mm
66	Main bearings	5
67	Main journal diameter	58,41/58,42mm
68	Main journal undersizes	0,26; 0,51mm
69	Main bearing clearance	0,010/0,048mm
70	Crankshaft end-float	0,10/0,20mm
71	Crankshaft end-thrust on	Centre bearing
72	Camshaft bearings	5
73	Camshaft journal diameter	(1) 45,34/45,36mm (2) 44,45/44,58 (3) 43,82/43,84 (4) 43,05/43,08 (5) 42,29/42,36
74	Camshaft bearing clearance	†
75	Camshaft end-float	†
76	Camshaft drive type	Chain
77	Cam lift	†
78	Valve head diameter	In 40,00/41,0mm Ex 34,48/35,60
79	Valve stem diameter	In 8,664/8,679mm Ex 8,651/8,666
80	Valve length	116,59/117,35mm
81	Valve seat/face angle	46° ± 15'/45° ± 15'
82	Valve lift	In/Ex 9,91mm
83	Valve guide length	†
84	Valve stem/guide clearance	In 0,025/0,066mm Ex 0,038/0,078
85	Valve spring free length	48,30mm
86	Valve spring loaded length	40,40mm at 66,50N

COOLING SYSTEM

95	Type	Water pump radiator
96	Radiator pressure cap	1,03 bar (15 lb/in²)
97	Fan	Electric
98	Thermostat	88°C

TRANSMISSION

100	Type	Rear wheel drive; LSD
101	Clutch	241,3mm hydraulic operation
102	Manual gearbox type	5 speed; LT77
103	Manual gearbox ratios	0,79; 1; 1,39; 2,08; 3,32; R 3,42:1
104	Automatic gearbox type	⎫
105	Automatic gearbox ratios	⎪ Not
106	Stall speed	⎬ Applicable
107	Change speeds	⎭
108	Drive shafts	Semi-floating
109	Final drive ratio	3,31:1
110	Differential bearing pre-load	0,076/0,152mm
111	Pinion bearing pre-load	0,9/1,4Nm

BRAKES

200	Type	Dual circuit
201	Power assistance	None
202	Front	Discs 279,4mm
203	Rear	Drums 229mm
204	Handbrake	Mechanical on rear wheels
205	Linings—front	Min thickness 1,5mm
206	Linings—rear	Width 45mm

STEERING

300	Type	Rack and pinion
301	Condition for checking	Unladen
302	Camber	Zero to –0° 30'
303	Castor	4° (non-adjustable)
304	King pin inclination	2°
305	Wheel alignment—front	Toe in 0,25° ±0,15°
306	Toe out on turns	†
307	Turning circle diameter	11,6m
308	Front hub end-float	†

FRONT SUSPENSION

330	Type	Independent vertical coil springs
331	Number of coils	18
332	Spring length	347mm
333	Spring rate	85 lb/in
334	Coil diameter	60mm
335	Wire diameter	7,5mm

REAR SUSPENSION

360	Type	Semi elliptic leaf springs
361	Wheel camber	Zero
362	Wheel alignment—rear	Parallel
363	Number of coils	Not Applicable (See A)
364	Spring length	1086mm
365	Spring rate	133,26 lb/in
366	Coil diameter	Not Applicable (See B)
367	Wire diameter	Not Applicable (See C)

ADDITIONAL INFORMATION

A	Number of leaves	6
B	Width of leaves	36mm
C	Thickness of leaves	6,4mm

ELECTRICAL

400	Battery	12V 58Ah neg earth
401	Alternator	65A
402	Regulated voltage	13,6/14,4V
403	Starter motor	Mag Marelli

CAPACITIES

500	Engine oil	5.5 litres inc filter
501	Gearbox oil	1,6 litres
502	Differential oil	1,4 litres
503	Cooling system	13,6 litres
504	Fuel tank	55 litres
505	Tyre size	205/60 VR 15
506	Pressures bar (psi)	F/R 1,5 (22)
507	Max towing weight	575kg (1268lb)
508	Hydraulic fluid type	DOT 4 spec
509	Service intervals	5000 miles or 6 months

DIMENSIONS

600	Length overall	3960mm (156in)
601	Width overall	1600mm (63in)
602	Height overall	1220mm (48in)
603	Weight—kerb	940kg (2072lb)
604	Ground clearance	140mm (5,5in)
605	Wheelbase	2489mm (98in)
606	Track—front/rear	1345/1375mm (53/54in)

TORQUE WRENCH SETTINGS

		Nm	lb ft	
700	Cylinder head nuts/bolts	95	70	(long)
		68	50	(short)
701	Big end bearing bolts	47/54	35/40	
702	Main bearing bolts	75 (95)	55 (70)	(Rear)
703	Flywheel bolts	81	60	
704	Clutch to flywheel bolts	27	20	
705	Drive plate to torque converter	Not Applicable		
706	Crown wheel bolts	68/81	50/60	
707	Drive pinion nut	129/136	95/100	
708	Differential bearing bolts	47/54	35/40	
709	Road wheel nuts	95	70	
710	Steering wheel nut	34/47	25/35	
711	Spark plugs	14/16	10/12	
712	Front hub nut	†		
713	Rear hub nut	†		

Plus 8 1992

Description	Year	Part No	Description	Year	Part No
Alternator	1970	23581A	Lamps (continued)		
	Use	23799		1972–74	54930A
	Later 1970–72	23590A		Use	54990
	Use	23799		1975 on	54782A
	1973 on	23728D		Use	52731
	Use	23799	Plinth (U.S.A.)	1970 on	54574177
Fan	1970	54217652		Use	NA
Ammeter	1969	36191B	Fog (optional)	1969–70	55187D
	1970–76	36429B	Fog rearguard	1977 on	56540D
Battery (2 seater)				Use	LFB300
U.K.	1969–72	54027787	Head, R.H.D.	1969–74	58811A/B
Export	1969–72	54027787		1975 on	58903D
U.K.	1973 on	54027445		Use	58811
Export	1973 on	54027445	Head, L.H.D. (except countries stated)	1971 on	60208A
Battery (4 seater)				Use	60066
U.K.	1969–72	54027322	Head, France	1969–74	58815A/F
Export	1969–72	54027322		Use	61148
U.K.	1973 on	54027445		1975 on	59450B
Export	1973 on	54027445		Use	61148
Ballast resistor	1969 on	47170A	Head, U.S.A.	1969 on	59191A/B
	Use	47222	Head, Germany	1972 on	59408A/B
Bulbholder, panel	1969	39010A		Use	61149
	Later 1969–72	554734	Number plate	1969–70	53093H/K
	Use	54364382		Use	56790
Bulb	1969–72	987		Later 1970 on	53836J
	Use	LLB987		Use	56790
Coil, ignition (ballasted)	1969–74	45206B	Reversing (optional)	1976 on	54552E
	Use	45290	Side	1969–75	52182F
	1975 on	45262D		Use	52436
	Use	54041287	Side marker (U.S.A.)		
Control box (dynamo)	1969–74	37543D	Front	1972–74	54714A
	Use	37568	Rear	1972–74	54716A
Dynamo	1969–74	22763A/D	Spot (optional)	1969–70	55195B
Flasher unit	1969	35020A	Stop tail	1969	53330D
	Use	SFB105		1970	54605A
	Later 1969 on	35048A		Use	54884
	Use	SFB114		Later 1970–71	54138A
Hazard warning	1970	54362147		Use	54884
	Use	54006501		1972 on	54708A
	Later 1970 on	35053A	Radiator pressure cap	1969–74	LC6
	Use	SFB130	Radiator thermostat		
Fuse box	1969	54038034	Normal	1969–74	LT1
	Use	54038068	Winter	1969–74	LT 2
	1970–76	37521A	Reflex reflector	1971 on	57098A
	1977 on	54038066		Use	LAB741
	Use	37521	Spark plug	1969–74	N9Y
Cover	1969 on	54382845	Starter	1969–70	25142A/B
Hazard warning device	1969 on	54006277		Use	25148
	Use	54006501		Later 1970 on	25148H
Horn	1969	69219A	Switches		
Bracket	1969	54680686	Auxiliary	1969–74	35947A
Horn	1970–74	70200A	Direction indicator	1969	31743A
	Use	70256	Direction indicator, flash h/push and dip		
Horn (Low note)	1975 on	70256A		1970	39399A
Horn push	1969–74	76205D		Use	NA
Inspection lamp socket	1969–74	39507E		1971–76	39540F
	Use	CAB189		Use	30390
LAMPS				1977 on	39897D
Flasher	1969	52337B	Fan motor	1977 on	30993A
Flasher, front	1970	52584A	Fog lamp	1977 on	30995A
	1971 on	54480D	Handbrake	1972 on	34933D
	Use	54990	Hazard warning	1970–71	35888A
Flasher, rear	1970	53956D		Use	39846
	Use	52731		1972–76	39687A
	1971	52778D		Use	39846
	Use	52731			

Lucas electrical component data: 4/4 1600 1969 on

Description	Year		Part No
Switches (continued)			
Hazard warning	1977 on		30996A
Nacelle	1972–76		54326327
		Use	54340377
Heater	1970 on		39119A
Ignition/start	1969–70		34680A
Lighting	1969		34340B/D
		Use	34317
Knob	1969		316154
		Use	316102
Lighting	1970–76		35870
	1977 on		30992A
Nacelle	1970–76		54326327
		Use	54350377
Panel light dimmer	1978 on		78526A
Knob	1978 on		54323272
Plain	1975–76		35947A
Screenjet	1970		39116A
		Use	NA
Solenoid starter	1969		76766H
Solenoid, starter (with ballast resistor	1969		76795A/B
Stop light	1969–74		34542B
		Use	SPB400
	1975 on		34619B
		Use	SPB401
Washer (headlamp) Sweden	1975–76		30708A
	1977		30994A
Windshield wiper	1969		31836F
		Use	31780
	1970 on		35889A
Warning light			
Brake	1975–77		38189A
		Use	54363522
Direction indicator	1975–77		54361251
Flasher	1969–74		38191A
Hazard warning	1970–77		38726A
		Use	38723
Bulbholder			54945043
		Use	54364380
Bulb			281
		Use	LLB281
Warning light cluster	1978 on		38804A
		Use	NA
Bezel	1978 on		54364317
Bulb	1978 on		280
		Use	LLB280
Wash/wipe headlamp (Sweden)			
Motor	1975–77		75840A
		Use	75665

Description	Year		Part No
Wash/wipe headlamp (Sweden)	(continued)		
Rim and bridge L.H.	1975–77		54720077
R.H.	1975–77		54720078
Pump	1975–77		54071781
		Use	WSB100
Windshield washer	1969–74		54071451
		Use	54071821
	1975 on		54071821
		Use	WSB101
Nozzle (twin)	1975 on		295110
		Use	NA
Tubing	1975 on		842100
Windshield wiper			
Motor	1969		75414B
		Use	75801
Motor, R.H.D.	1970 on		75710H
		Use	75664
Motor, L.H.D.	1970 on		75687H
		Use	75664
Wheelbox	1969		72674B
		Use	72850
	1970–74		72775A
		Use	72841
	1975 on		72889A
Rack (cut to 44.2 ins)	1969		743235
Rack (cut to 44⅞ ins)	1970 on		743235
Outer casing			
Motor to wheelbox	1969 on		54717032
		Use	60600539
Wheelbox to wheelbox			
R.H.D.	1970 on		54703836
		Use	60600539
L.H.D.	1970 on		745043
		Use	60600539
Short, wheelbox	1969 on		54702605
Ferrule, casing retaining	1969		740715
	1970–74		54704623
	1975 on		54701385
		Use	54704623
Arm	1969		54712085
		Use	54707271
R.H.D.	1970 on		54712064
		Use	NA
L.H.D.	1970 on		54712065
		Use	NA
Blade	1969		737680
		Use	WBB401
	1970 on		54703832
		Use	54725124

Lucas electrical component data: 4/4 1600 1969 on

203

Left

Description	Year	Part No
Alternator	1969–74	23545D
	1975–76	23758A
	1977 on	23702A/E
	Use	23758
Fan	1969–74	54216148
	1975 on	54219773
Ammeter	1966–77	36429B
Battery		
U.K.	1969 on	54027456
Export	1969 on	54027456
Ballast resistor	1969–75	47170A
	Use	47222
	1976 on	47246A
Coil, ignition	1969–70	45226A
	Use	45290
	later 1970–71	45227A
	1972–75	45232A/E
	Use	45290
	1976 on	45270A
	Use	DLB193
Control unit	1969–74	37423E
	Use	37585
Distributor	1969	41176F
	Use	41393
	1970–72	41278A
	Use	41393
	1973–74	41393A
	1975	41573F
	Use	41633
	1976–79	41673A
	1980 on	41799A
	1982 on	41893A
Ignition module	1982 on	54041354
Filter		
Oil	1969–72	CF537
Fuel	1969–72	CF700
Air	1969–72	CF806
Flasher unit	1969 on	35048A
	Use	SFB114
Hazard warning	1969–70	54362147
	Use	54006501
	1971 on	35053A
	Use	SFB130
Fuse box	1975 on	54038066
	Use	37521
Horn		
High note	1969–74	70199A
	Use	70255
	1975 on	70255A
Low note	1969–74	70200A
	Use	70256
	1975 on	70256A
Lamps		
Flasher, front	1969–70	52584B
	1971 on	54480D
	Use	54990
Flasher, rear	1969–70	53956D
	Use	52731
	1971	52778D
	Use	52731
	1972–74	54930A
	Use	54990
	1975 on	54782A
	Use	52731
Plinth (U.S.A.)	1970 on	54574177
	Use	NA
Fog (optional)	1969–70	55187D

Right

Description	Year	Part No
Lamps (continued)		
Fog rearguard	1977 on	56540D
	Use	LFB300
Head, R.H.D.	1969–74	58811A/B
	1975 on	58903D
	Use	58811
Head, L.H.D. (except countries stated)	1971 on	60208A
	Use	60066
Head, U.S.A.	1969 on	59191A/B
Head, France	1969–74	58815A/E
	Use	61148
	1975 on	59450B
	Use	61148
Head, Germany	1972 on	59408A/B
	Use	61149
Number plate	1969–71	53093H/K
	Use	56790
	1972 on	53836F/J
	Use	56790
Reversing	1972 on	54552E
Side	1969–75	52182D/F
	Use	52436
	1976 on	56879A
	1971	52999B
Side flasher (N. America)		
Side flasher (N. America)		
Front	1971–74	54714A
Rear	1971–74	54716A
Spot (optional)	1969–70	55195B
Stop tail	1969–72	54605A
	Use	54884
	1973 on	54708A
N. America	1971	54769A
Reflex reflector	1971 on	57098A
	Use	LAB741
Relay		
Alternator	1969–74	33293D
	Use	SRB108
Heater and starter	1969 on	33213F/J
	Use	SRB101
Screenjet	1969–74	54071451
	Use	54071821
	1975 on	54071821
	Use	WSB101
Nozzle		295110
	Use	NA
Tubing		842100
Spark plug	1969 on	L-87Y
Starter	1969–74	26266D
	Use	25745
	1975 on	25701A
	Use	25745
Switches		
Direction indicator flash and dip	1969–70	35920A
	Use	30390
	1971–76	39540B/F
	Use	30390
	1977 on	39897D
Fan motor	1977 on	30993A
Fog or spot	1969–76	35916A
	Use	35870
	1977 on	30995A
Handbrake	1969 on	34933D
Hazard warning	1969–71	35888A
	Use	39846
	1972–76	39687A
	Use	39846
	1977 on	30996A

Lucas electrical component data: Plus 8 1969 on

Description	Year	Part No	Description	Year	Part No
Switches (continued)			Warning light control (11AC)	1969–74	38706A
Nacelle		54326327	Wash/wipe, headlamp (Sweden)		
	Use	54340377	Motor	1975–77	75840A
Heater	1969 on	39119A		Use	75665
Lighting	1969–76	35870A	Rim and bridge, left hand	1975–77	54720077
	1977 on	30992A	Rim and bridge, right hand	1975–77	54700278
Nacelle	1969–76	54326327	Pump	1975–77	54071781
	Use	54340377		Use	WSB100
Panel light dimmer	1978 on	78526A	Windshield wiper		
Knob	1978 on	54323272	Motor, R.H.D.	1969 on	75710A/H
Parking light	1969–76	39117A		Use	75664
	Use	39857	Motor, L.H.D.	1969 on	75687A/H
Screenjet	1969 on	39116A		Use	75664
	Use	NA	Wheelbox	1969–74	72775A
Stop light	1969–74	34542B		Use	72841
	Use	SPB400		1975 on	72889A
	1975 on	34619B	Rack (cut to 44.9 ins)	1969 on	743235
	Use	SPB401	Outer casing		
Washer, headlamp (Sweden)	1975–76	30708A	Motor to wheelbox	1969 on	54703836
	1977	30994A		Use	60600539
Windshield wiper	1969 on	35889A	Wheelbox to wheelbox		
Warning light			R.H.D.	1969 on	54703836
Brake	1969–77	38189A		Use	60600539
	Use	54363522	L.H.D.	1969 on	745043
Direction indicator	1969–77	54361251		Use	60600539
Hazard warning	1969–77	38726A	Short, wheelbox	1969 on	54702605
	Use	38723	Ferrule, retaining	1969 on	54701385
Bulbholder		54045043		Use	54704623
Bulb		281	Arm, R.H.D.	1969 on	54712064
	Use	LLB281		Use	NA
Warning light cluster	1978 on	38804A	Arm, L.H.D.	1969 on	54712065
	Use	NA		Use	NA
Bezel	1978 on	54364317	Blade	1969 on	54703832
Bulb	1978 on	280		Use	54725124
	Use	LLB280			

Lucas electrical component data: Plus 8 1969 on

APPENDIX IV

SPECIALISTS, MANUFACTURERS AND DISTRIBUTORS

Below are details of Morgan specialist companies from around the world. The vast majority of them only offer services in connection with four-wheeler Morgans but, where they include three-wheelers, or are only operating a service for three-wheelers, this is indicated.

All of the Morgan main distributors worldwide carry some spares and many have extensive stocks. All are willing to give advice. Companies are therefore only listed in this section if they offer any special service other than normal spares. By listing these companies neither the author or the publisher is endorsing or recommending them.

UK
Angel Fabrications
Castle Bank Cottage
Ewloe
Deeside
Clwyd
England
Telephone 0244 532714
Three-wheeler chassis and exhaust systems.

Black Phey Ltd
Raleigh Cottage
The Street
Takeley
Nr. Bishops Stortford
Hertfordshire
England
Telephone 0279-870698
Wooden body frames and restoration.

Brands Hatch Morgans
Brands Hatch Circuit
Dartford
Kent DA3 8NG
England
Telephone 0474-874147
Competition tuning repairs. Spares, sales

transporting.

Hamilton Brooks
Ullingswick
Herefordshire
England
Telephone 0432-820320
Morgan pedal cars for ages 2-4.

David Browne
'Woodview'
Jenkins Lane
Tring
Hertfordshire HP23 6NW
England
Telephone 0240-29644
Three-wheeler bearings.

Burlen Services
Spitfire House
Castle Road
Salisbury
Wilts SP1 3SA
Telephone 0722 412500
Carburettor specialists.

Busby Engineering
1, Desford Lane
Ratby
Leicestershire LE6 0LE
England
Telephone 0533-393564
Three-wheeler castings & machining.

F.H. Douglass
1A, South Ealing Road
London W5 4QT
England
Telephone 081-567-0570
Spares, service, repairs, sales for three- and four-wheelers including Series I 4-4s.

Packer Duncan Ltd
Waterloo Garage
Hagley Road

Oldswinford
Stourbridge
West Midlands DY8 2JB
England
Telephone 0384-395186
Spares and used car sales.

Ivan Dutton
Unit 12
The Metropolitan Centre
Derby Road
Greenford
Middlesex
England
Telephone 081-578-3810
Reproduction castings for three-wheelers.

Fred Gudgeon
'Cassis'
Avon Castle Drive
Avon Castle
Ringwood
Hampshire
England
Telephone 04254-77368
Repairs & restoration, particularly flat radiator models.

Roy Halford
11, Larksfield Close
Caterton
Oxford
England
Telephone 0993-841993
All electrical components.

Harpers
The Bothy
Essex Lane
Hunton Bridge
Kings Langley
Herfordshire WD4 8PN
England
Telephone 09277-60299/60290
Coachwork & trim specialists. Restoration, spares.

Janet Hill Ventures
Woodfidley
Brockenhurst
Hampshire SO42 7QL
England
Telephone 0590-22091
Scale Morgan models & toys. Morgan jewellery, books, goodies, etc. (list available).

W.H.Hunter (Motors) Ltd
Braid Road
Edinburg EH10 6AP
Scotland

Telephone 0314-471707
Spares, servicing, tuning.

Libra Motive Ltd
2 Rosemont Road
Hampstead
London NW3 6NE
Telephone 071 435 8159/794 7009
Race tuning, repairs, spares.

Light Car & Cyclecar Restoration Co
Unit 226
Artic Trading Estate
Droitwich Road
Hartlebury
Worcestershire
England
Telephone 0564-826891 (evenings)
Three-wheeler restoration badges, spares, some four-wheeler work.

I & J Macdonald Ltd
Maiden Law Garage
Lanchester DH7 0QR
Telephone 0207 520916
Competition, tuning, spares.

Morgan Motor Company Limited
Pickersleigh Road
Malvern
Worcestershire WR14 2LL
England
Telephone 0689-3104/5
All parts including body frame & panels. Three- and four-wheelers.

Morgan Sports Car Club
Spares Registrar Secretary
Bob Cragg
1, Manor Farm
Culham
Abingdon
Oxon
England
Members only

Morgan Three-Wheeler Club
Spares Manager
Nev Lear
1, Hollies Close
Middlezoy
Bridgewater
Somerset
England
Telephone 0823-69591
Members only

Colin Musgrove & Associates
Lanes End Garage
Kenilworth Road
Meer End
Nr Kenilworth

Warwickshire CV8 1PT
England
Telephone 0676-33120/33014
Competition, tuning, restoration. Used car sales

Phaeton Engineering
Palmers Road
Emsworth
Hampshire
England
Telephone 0243-372040.
Servicing, repairs.

George Proudfoot
49 King George Road
Porchester
Hampshire
England
Telephone 0705-327184
Repairs and restoration

Rutherford Engineering
Crackling Farm
Agden Lane
High Leigh
Cheshire WA16 6NY
England
Telephone 0565-830224
Restoration, spares, service.

Melvyn Rutter Ltd
The Morgan Garage
Little Hallingbury
Nr Bishops Stortford
Hertfordshire CM22 7RA
England
Telephone 0279-725725
Three- and four-wheeler spares. Used car sales (catalogue available).

S G T
Station Road
Taplow
Maidenhead
Berkshire SL6 0NT
England
Telephone 0628-65353/64044
Repairs, spares

John Smith
Inworth
Nr Colchester
Essex
England
Telephone 0376-70438
Gearbox and axle rebuilds.

Colin Wilson
Mount Works
Mill Lane
Horndon-on-the-Hill

Essex
England
Telephone 0375-672313
Three-wheeler spares manufacturer.

USA
Dave Bean Engineering Inc
925 Punta Gorda Street
Santa Barbara
California 93103
USA
Telephone 805-962-8125.
Tuning.

Bonnets Up
5736 Spring Street
Clinton
MD 20735
USA
Telephone 301-297-4759.
Restoration and tuning

British Frame & Engine Co
4831 Ryland Avenue
Temple City
California
USA
Telephone 818-443-0939
Morgan spares

British Racing Green
P O Box 581
Pittston
Pennsylvania 18640
USA
Telephone717-654-2082
Sales, restoration, parts, service.

Cantab Motors Ltd.
RR1, PO Box 537A
Roundhill
Virginia 22141
USA
Sales & parts

Design With Wood
Brad Davis
P O Box 189A Salisbury Road
Sheffield
Mass 01257
USA
Telephone 413-229-3574.
Wood fabrication.

Engine Room
Greg Solow
318A River Street
Santa Cruz
California 95060
USA
Telephone 408-429-1800,
Mechanical and electrical service.

Ferrari of Los Gatos
Dennis Glavis
66 East Main Street
Los Gatos
California 95030
USA
Telephone 408-354-4000
Sales, spares Plus 4 specialist.

Isis Imports
PO Box 2290
US Custom House
San Francisco
California 94126
USA
Sales and parts.

Lederman Rupp
P O Box 21412
Columbus
Ohio 43221
USA
Accoutrements

Lindskog Balancing Corporation
6 Alfred Circle
Bedford
Mass 01730
USA
Balancing all types of engines, including JAP and Matchless.

Malvern Lane Trading
P O Box 7758
Station G
Colubus
Ohio 43207
USA
Spares

Morgan Fab
P O Box 589
Buford
Georgia 30518
USA
Spares

Morgan Spares Ltd
PO Box 1761
Lakeville
CT 06039
USA
Telephone 518-789-3877
Restoration parts & services

Moss Motors
P O Box M G
Goleta
California 93116
USA
Telephone 805-968-1041.
Wire wheel specialists and TR parts.

Mostly Morgan
23 Baker Street
Brockton
Mass 02402
USA
Restoration parts and services.

Steve Miller
Imported Car Service
1375 Park Avenue
Emeryville
California 94608
USA
Restoration and parts.

Nisonger Corporation,
Smiths Instruments
35 Bartels Place
New Rochelle
New York 10801
USA
Instrument rebuilding.

Olde World Restorations
90 Sunset Lane
Hatborough
Pennsylvania 19040
USA
Telephone 215-441-4151.
Restoration and spares.

Racing International
RD1
Millerton
New York 12546
USA
Restoration tuning information.

Sports & Classics
512 Boston Post Road
Darien
Connecticut 06820
USA
Telephone 203-655-8731
Upholstery and car covers.

TEK Bearing Co Inc
Westwood
MA 02090
USA
Bearing and transmission specialists.

Bill Tracy
3179 Woodland Lane
Alexandria
Virginia 22309
USA
Telephone 703-360-6652.
Electrical spares.

Very British
Locust Avenue Extension

Amsterdam
New York 12010
USA
English spares.

CANADA
CMC Enterprises (1990) Inc
RR3 Bolton
Ontario L7E 5R9
Canada
Parts, sales

Main distributors
UK
Andreas Adamou
Autorapide
Unit 1 Whitehouse Farm
Cocklake
Wedmore
N. Somerset BS28 4HE
England
Telephone 0934 713224

*Brands Hatch Morgans
Brands Hatch Circuit
Fawkham
Kent DA3 8NG
England
Telephone 0474 874147

*Burlen Services
Spitfire House, Castle Road
Salisbury
Wilts SP1 3SA
England
Telephone 0722 412500

Mike Spence
Classic Cars Ltd
Unit 1 Bloomfield Hatch
Mortimer
Reading
Berks RG7 3AD
England
Telephone 0734 333633

Cliffsea Car Sales
Bridge Garage
Ness Road
Shoeburyness SS3 9PG
England
Telephone 0702 295323

Donaldson & Evans
The Wolf Garage
Ashley Road
Hale
Cheshire WA15 9NQ
England
Telephone 061 9291208 (sales)
061 9411916 (service & admin)

*John Dangerfield Garages Ltd
Staplehill Road
Fishponds
Bristol BS16 5AD
England
Telephone 0272 566525/566373

F.H. Douglass
1a South Ealing Road
Ealing
London W5 4QT
England
Telephone 081 567 0570

*Mike Duncan
250 Ikon Estate,
Droitwich Road
Hartlebury
Worcs DY10 4EU
England
Telephone 0299 250025

Robin Kay & Sons
Marine Road
Eastbourne
BN22 7AU
England
Telephone 0323 26462/25563

*Libra Motive Ltd
2, Rosemont Road
Hampstead
London NW3 6NE
England
Telephone 071 435 8159/794 7009

*Lifes Motors Ltd
West Street
Southport PR8 1QN
England
Telephone 0704 531375

*I & J Macdonald Ltd
Maiden Law Garage
Lanchester DH7 0QR
England
Telephone 0207 520916

Otley Motors
Cross Green
Otley
West Yorks LS21 1HE
England
Telephone 0943 465222

Parker of Stepps
Hayston Garage
38 Glasgow Road
Kirkintilloch
Glasgow G66 1BJ
Scotland
Telephone 041 776 1708

*Phoenix Motors
The Green
Woodbury
Exeter
Devon EX5 1LT
England
Telephone 0395 32255

*Station Garage
Station Road
Taplow
Nr Maidenhead SL6 0NT
England
Telephone 06286 605353

Thomson & Potter Ltd
High Street
Burrelton
Blairgowrie
Perthshire PH13 9NX
Scotland
Telephone 08287 247
*Allon White & Son Ltd

The Morgan Garage
High Street
Cranfield
Beds MK43 0BT
England
Telephone 0234 750205

*Wykehams Ltd
6, Kendrick Place
Reece Mews
South Kensington
London SW7 3HF
England
Telephone 071 589 6894/8309

* *May have secondhand Morgans in stock*

AUSTRALIA
Calder Sports Cars
Distributors Australia Pty Ltd
Box 140 PO
Gisborne 3437
Australia

AUSTRIA
Max Bulla
Liebenstr. 40/60/5
A1120 Vienna
Austria

BELGIUM
Garage Albert
Anc Ets Stammet Et Fils
S.P.R.L.

84/86 Rue Osseghemstraat
1080 Brussels
Belgium

CANADA
CMC Enterprises (1990) Inc
RR3 Bolton
Ontario L7E 5R9

CYPRUS
Reliable Sports Cars Ltd
Grivas Digenis Ave
PO Box 5428
Nicosia
Cyprus

DENMARK
Alan Hall
Mollegardsvej 16
GL Hjortkaer
DK-6818 ARRE
Denmark

FRANCE
Jacques Savoye S.A.
237 Boulevard Pereire
75017 Paris
France

GERMANY
Merz & Pabst
Alexanderstr. 46
7000 Stuttgart 1
Germany

K.W. Flaving
4750 Unna
Hochstr. 4
Germany

HOLLAND
BV Nimag
Reedijk 9 3274 Ke
Heinenoord
Holland

IRELAND
Scott Macmillan
Holybrooke Hall
Kilmacanogue
Co. Wicklow
Ireland

ITALY
Ditta
Armando Anselmo
Via Vincenzo Tiberio 64
00191 Rome
Italy

JAPAN
Morgan Auto Takano Ltd
9-25 2 Chome Tsumada-Minami
Atsugi Shi
Kanagawa Ken 243
Japan

LUXEMBOURG
Yesteryear Luxembourg
Import Ltd SA
19 Rue Du Parc
L-8083 Bertrange
Luxembourg

NORWAY
Hallan AS
Malmogt 7
0566 Oslo 5
Norway

PORTUGAL
Manuel F Monteiro & FIlho
Representacoes e Comércio LDA
Rua Dos Correeiros 71
1100 Lisbon
Portugal

SOUTH AFRICA
Angela Heinz (Pty) Ltd
6, The Munro Drive
Houghton 2198
PO Box 2687
Johannesburg 2000
South Africa

SPAIN
Tayre S.A.
Principe de Vergara 253
28016 Madrid
Spain

SWEDEN
A.B. Wendels Bil & Motor
Box 74 Testvagen 10A
S-23200 Arlov
Sweden

SWITZERLAND
Garage De L'Autoroute
Signy S/Nyon
Switzerland

Rolf Wehrlin
Haupstr. 132
Aesch BL
Switzerland

USA
Isis Imports Ltd
PO Box 2290
US Custom House
San Francisco
California 94126
USA

Cantab Motors Ltd
RR1 Box 537A Round Hill
Virginia 22141
USA

FOUR SEAT
FUN

APPENDIX V

BIBLIOGRAPHY

• THREE-WHEELERS

The Best of The Bulletin
by Barry Davidson, editor of the Morgan Three-wheeler Club's *Bulletin*. Published by The Morgan Three-Wheeler Club,1973.
Long out-of-print but the Club may be producing a reprint. Useful source for finding out how to adapt parts to fit your Three-wheeler.

Morgan Sweeps The Board
by Dr J D Alderson & D M Rushton. Published by Gentry Books, London, 1978. 250 pages.
The most comprehensive book on Morgan Three-wheeler competition history ever. Contains a lot of detail for those interested in racing, some general history and information regarding various models.

The Vintage Years of the Morgan Three-Wheeler
by Bill Boddy. Published by Grenville Publishing, London, 1970. 28 pages.
Book form of a series of articles from *Motor Sport* magazine, Historical gem covering production of the various models and racing.

The Book of the Morgan Three-Wheeler
by R.M. Clarke. Published by Pitman & Sons Ltd, London.
An absolute necessity for any Three-wheeler owner who intends to carry out their own maintenance and running repairs.

Morgan Three-Wheelers 1930-1952
by R.M. Clarke. Published By Brooklands Books, Surrey. 100 pages.
Copies of road test reports and much more useful information for Three-wheeler owners. A good companion to

The Book of the Three-Wheeler. Morgan Three-Wheeler Gold Portfolio. 1910-1952
by R.M. Clarke. Distributed by Brooklands Book Distribution Ltd, 1989.
Compilation of road and comparison tests, technical data, etc., compiled from various motoring magazines.

J.A.P. The Vintage Years
by Jeff Clew. Published by Haynes Publishing Group, England, 1985.
A detailed history of this famous engine manufacturer with many references to Morgans & H.F.S. Morgan..

J.A.P. The End of an Era
by Jeff Clew. Published by Haynes Publishing Group, England, 1988.
The continuing history of the J.A.P. Company with many references to Morgans.

No More Twins
by Clarrie Coombes. Published by the Morgan Three-wheeler Club, circa 1965. History of the Morgan Three-wheeler Club.

Morgan 75 Years on the Road
by Ken Hill. Published by Blandford Press Ltd, Dorset. 1984. 160 pages.
Traces the history of Morgans -Three- and Four-wheelers - through the Morgan Motor Company's advertising. Reproduction of advertisements with linking text.

Three-Wheelers
by Ken Hill. Published by Shire Publications Ltd. 1986. 32 pages.
Traces the history of Three-wheelers from 1885 to date, with a complete chapter on the Morgan. Compares the marque with others.

Illustrated Morgan Buyers Guide
by Ken Hill. Published by Motorbooks International, Wisconsin, USA, 1989, (second edition 1990).
Detailed study of each model and its investment potential.

The Book of the Morgan
by G.T. Walton. Published by Pitman & Sons Ltd. 1932. 109 pages.
Contemporary book containing a lot of good general information, especially relating to pre-1932 Three-wheelers. Much of the content is reproduced in either of R.M. Clarke's books. (See also under author Harold Jelly).

ABC Of the Morgan
Compiled and published by the Morgan Three-wheeler Club.
Practical tips on owning and running a Three-wheeler - a must for all Three-wheeler owners.

Morgan, History of a Famous Car
Written and published by the Morgan Motor Company Ltd. Three editions, first with hard cover, second soft (two editions).
Also contains information on the history of Four-wheelers.

The Book of the Morgan
by Harold Jelly. Published by Pitman & Sons Ltd, 1933 (first edition); 1934 (second edition); 1935 (third edition. Each edition is a yearly update.
Contemporary book containing a lot of good general information, especially for pre-1936 Three-wheeler owners. Much of the content is reproduced in either of R.M. Clarke's books. (See also under author G.T. Walton).

The Three-Wheeler
By Brian Watts. Published by The Morgan Three-Wheeler Club. 1970. 68 pages.
Another historical gem which details all Three-wheeler models.

• FOUR-WHEELERS

Morgan Sports: From Three Wheels to Four
Published by I P C Transport Press, Ltd. 1977. 80 pages.
Reproduced articles from *Autocar & Motor Cycle* magazines from 1910-1977, including road test reports on various models. Interesting.

Morgan 1910-1980
Published by the combined Morgan Clubs (MSCC & MMTWC). 57 pages. Produced as part of the celebration of the 70th anniversary of Morgan. Contains a general history including competition events and personal reminiscences from prominent Morgan personalities over the years.

The Great Cars/Morgan: 'On Four Wheels'
by Bill Boddy. Part of issue No.71, pages 1409-1419 of a motoring encyclopaedia published in monthly parts. Collectable by the enthusiast but not of too much interest to the prospective buyer.

Morgan - First and Last of the Real Sports Cars
by Gregory Houston Bowden. Published by Gentry Books, London. 1972. 192 pages. Reprinted 1973. New and revised second edition 1986.
General development of the marque, including business and competition history. Contains a lot of useful information.

More Morgan
by Gregory Houston Bowden. Published by Gentry Books, London. 1976. 224 pages. Described as 'A Pictorial History of the Morgan Sports Car'.

Morgan Autobook One
by R. Clarke. Published by Auto Press Ltd, Brighton, England. 1968. 168 pages.
Workshop manual for four-wheeler Morgans up to 1967.

Brooklands Books Series
Morgan Cars 1936-1960.
Morgan Cars 1960-1970.
Morgan Cars 1969-1970.
Edited by R.M. Clarke. Published by Brooklands Books, Surrey, England. All these books are an absolute must for any Morgan owner who intends to carry out their own maintenance and running repairs. An invaluable source of technical information, equivalent to workshop manuals.

Morgan Cars Gold Portfolio 1968-1989
by R.M. Clarke. Distributed by Brooklands Book Distribution Ltd. 1989.
Compilation of road and comparison tests, technical data, etc., compiled from

various motoring magazines.
Morgan Plus 4 & 4/4 Gold Portfolio 1936-1967
by R.M. Clarke. Distributed by Brooklands Book Distribution Ltd. 1993.
Compilation of road and comparison tests, technical data, etc., compiled from various motoring magazines.

Morgan Four Owners Workshop Manual
by R.M. Clarke. Distributed by Brooklands Book Distribution Ltd. 1989.
Updated version of *The Four-wheeler Workshop Manual*. Contains useful information on all models up to and including 1981, except for the Plus 8.

The Morgan Four-Wheeler Workshop Manual
by John Dowdeswell, Distributed by Brooklands Book Distribution Ltd.
Contains very useful information up to and including Series V 4/4s.

The Plus Four Morgan
by Eric Dymock. Published By Profile Publications, Surrey, England. 1967.
A brief but surprisingly detailed history of the model.

Morgan: The Last Survivor
by Chris Harvey. Published by Oxford Illustrated Press. 1987. 273 pages.
An extensive technical history of four-wheelers which is interesting and informative even though many of the 'facts' and photograph captions are either incorrect or misleading.

The Four-Wheeled Morgan
Volume No.1: The Flat Radiator Models
by Ken Hill. Published by Motor Racing Publications. 1977. 136 pages.
Comprehensive history of early Four-wheelers, including competition history, production figures, model specifications and servicing and restoration details.

The Four-Wheeled Morgan
Volume No.2: The Cowled Radiator Models
by Ken Hill. Published by Motor Racing Publications. 1980. 144 pages.
Comprehensive history of later Four-wheelers, including competition history, production figures, model specifications and Morgan clubs worldwide.

Morgan 75 Years on the Road
by Ken Hill. Published by Blandford

Press, Dorset, England. 1984.
(See under Three-wheeler books).

Illustrated Morgan Buyers Guide
by Ken Hill. Published by Motorbooks International, Wisconsin, USA. 1989. (Second edition 1990).
Detailed study of each model and its investment potential. *(See also under Three-wheeler books).*

Morgan (Famous Car Factory Series)
by Bengt Ason Holm. Published by Motorbooks International, Wisconsin, USA 1992.
A brief outline of the history of the Morgan factory from 1909 to date, followed by an in-depth study of the present day manufacturing process, stage-by-stage through the factory.

Morgan. Auto Histoire No. 38.
by F. Wilson McComb. Published by EPA, Paris, France. 1985. 69 pages.
Printed in French, this small format book contains a surprising amount of information.

Moggie: The Purchase, Maintenance and Enjoyment of Morgan Sports Cars
by Colin Musgrove. Published by Quills Publishing, Herts, England. 1980. 112 pages.
A must for any serious Morgan buyer, coverage includes before you buy, what to look for, where to look for it and what to do if you find it.

The Morgan Year Book 1980-81
by Colin Musgrove. Published by The Magpie Publishing Co, Hong Kong. 1981.
The first of what was intended to be a yearly publication. Contains details of Morgan events worldwide for the year in question.

Morgan: Buying & Restoration Book
Published by *Practical Classics & Car Restorer* magazine, 1992.
Reproduction of various articles previously printed in *Practical Classics & Car Restorer* magazine. A useful addition to any practical Morgan owner's bookshelf.

The Morgan Cartoon Book
by Terry Quirk. Published by Quills Publishing, Herts, England. 1980.
Cartoons and poems about Morgans. Pure 'coffee table' book with little to recommend it other than the artistic skill of the author.

Postwar MGs & Morgans
by Henry Rasmussen and John Blakemore. Published by Picturama Publishing, California, USA. 1979.
An interesting comparison of the two marques.

Morgan Plus 8
by Graham Robson. Published by Osprey, London, 1984. 135 pages.
Comprehensive book on the model

Morgan Sport-Und-Tourenwagen 1935-1981
by Halwart Schrader. Published by Schrader Verlag, Germany. 1991. 96 pages.

Attempts to trace the history of the Four-wheeler Morgan through the company's sales brochures. Captions tend to be inaccurate and should not be used as a reliable guide by collectors of Morgan sales literature. German text.

Morgans in the Colonies
by John H. Sheally. Published by Jordan & Co. Virginia Beach, USA. 1978.
A photographic study - with text - of Morgans in America.

Morgans, Pride of the British
by John H. Sheally. Published by TAB Books Inc. Pennsylvania, USA. 1982.
Another photographic study of Morgans in America but with far more useful text and information.

Original Morgan
by John Worrall & Liz Turner. Published by Bay View Books Ltd, Devon, England. 1992.
A detailed examination of each of the Morgan Four-Wheeler models produced by the Morgan Motor Company. Excellent colour photographs of various components, with fairly detailed technical information. By one of the leading Morgan authorities, this is a must for the restorer looking for complete authenticity.

Plus 4 Super Profile
by John Teague. Published by G.T. Foulis, England. 1987.
Detailed study of the model including specifications and production details.

APPENDIX VI

MORGAN MINIATURE MODELS

Three-wheelers

For some strange reason three-wheelers have never seemed particularly attractive to model companies as subjects, especially those which mass-produced models. Back in the 1960s a number of Bubble Car models came on the market, but there were no Morgans. Inevitably, a few private model hobbyists who happened to be Morgan owners or enthusiasts have produced scratch models of their favourite cars, one famous example of which is a Grand Prix which was made in silver by a professional silversmith and carried as mascot on his car. Unfortunately, the whereabouts of this model is now unknown.

The following is a list of manufacturers of known Three-wheelers models, complete with comments where applicable.

• THE MECCANO THREE-WHEEL SPORTS CAR
Produced in the 1930s to a scale of approximately 1/16. It is illustrated on page 82 of Gregory Houston Bowden's book *More Morgan*.
Although very rarely found at model swap meets, examples, when they do appear, tend to fetch £40-£60, depending on condition.

• GAIETY TOYS (A CASTLE ART PRODUCTION UK)
This rather crude metal representation of an air-cooled, Beetle-back Super Sports was produced in the mid-to-late '50s in the UK to an approximate scale of 1/24. The models were made in both clockwork and push-along versions, both types being sold in blue, green, red and all chrome plate. Again, a very collectable model and one in mint boxed condition would easily fetch £120 at a model swap meet, other examples being valued pro-rata dependent on condition.

• GAKKEN OR RIKO
Both Japanese companies produced the same model in the late 1960s/early 1970s, a 1/16 scale plastic kit of a 1935 Matchless-engined Super Sports.

• ENTEX
'A lot of fun from Entex'; this Japanese model, carrying registration number MOG 750 and featuring vinyl seat covers, appears to be similar to the previous Matchless-engined model. Marketed as "The MOG".

• MINICRAFT
Produced in the late 1980s in the USA under licence, this appears to be based on the Gakken/Riko model already described. It was produced for a very limited period only and is unlikely to be available new in the UK.

• ACORN MODELS
Around 1969-70 a cast metal model of a 1933-34 Super Sports with top mounted spare wheel was produced in the UK to a scale of 1/57th in a very limited quantity. Two versions were made: one with hood up and low exhaust and the other a racing version with high exhausts, wire mesh aero-screens and complete with a driver and riding mechanic, racing overalls, helmet and goggles. It is believed only two or three examples of each model were produced and that they were originally intended as prototypes for a possible Matchbox model. The same company also produced a very poor vacuum-cast plastic model of a Three-wheeler.

• BRUMM
In the late 1970s and early 1980s this

A selection of various Three-wheeler models. Back row: Brumm models of Morgan and Sandford Three-wheelers. Front row, l-r: South Eastern Finecast 1932 Super Sports, scratch-built 1930's Super Sports, Acorn racing with driver and riding mechanic and Acorn Super Sports. The last two were prototypes for possible Matchbox production.

Italian company produced three versions of a 1/43 scale die-cast metal model of a 1923 Morgan Cycle Car, all of which, for some inexplicable reason, were finished with gold-coloured brightwork. One version had a white body with black hood erected and red interior; the second was similar but fitted with aero-screens and single racing number 3 on its tail and the third finished in British Racing Green, with brown interior, had the racing number 3 on both sides of the tail. These models were used as the basis for the 7500 Limited Edition series produced in July 1990.

Brumm also made three models of the 1929 Darmont Morgan, all with chromed brightwork. One was finished in red with the hood erected and brown interior and two more in blue with brown interiors and aero-screens and with a choice of racing numbers 9 or 13 on both sides of the tail.

The white metal die-cast range
• SOUTH EASTERN FINECAST (FORMERLY WILLS FINECAST)

A selection of 1/43 and 1/57 scale Morgan models produced by various companies in the past twenty years. Back row, l-r: Acorn Plus 4, Mikansue 1938 Le Mans Majorette, Grand Prix 1962 Le Mans Plus 4 Majorette and BKL 1949 4/4 Drop Head Coupé Czechoslovakia magnetic drive 4/4. Front row: a selection of 1/57 scale toys produced by various manufacturers worldwide.

Two models - a 1/24 scale 1934 Super Sports and a 1/43 scale 1932 Super Sports - are offered in kit form only. Both models are very good on detail in relation to scale.

• SCALELINK
1/76 scale 1928 Aero Super Sports, either as a kit or made up.

• BKL AUTOREPLICA
1/72 scale 1939 'F4'. 1/48 scale 'F2' and 'F4' either as a kit or made up.

• ABS
1/76 scale 1933 Super Sports, offered as a kit or made up.

Of the last three models listed, Scalelink's has the most detail which, inevitably, tends to mean it is also more fragile.

Four-wheeler models
Models of Four-wheeler Morgans have been in much more plentiful supply from the mass-produced model manufacturers. This is especially true of the 1/57 scale models manufactured in Japan and Hong Kong for the toy market, while there has also been a far larger choice available in the die-cast white metal models, in particular from UK manufactures.

White metal die-cast range
1/43 scale
• WESTERN MODELS
Produced an excellent model of a Flat Radiator Plus 4 from 1980 to 1987.

In 1994 this company produced a limited edition of a 1993 Plus 8, 100 each of red or British Racing Green with side screws. The models were made exclusively for the Dutch company Automobile Collection.

• MOTORKITS
Offered a model of a Plus 4 Plus which is no longer produced. (see *B.K.L. Autoreplica*).

• GRAND PRIX
A model of the 1962 Le Mans Plus 4 - again, out of production.
• MIKANSUE
A model of the 1938 Le Mans 4/4, now no longer produced.

• ANDRE-MARIS RUF (AMR)
A model of a 4/4 Four-seater, no longer produced.
• METAL 43
A 4/4 Four-seater, as AMR above and no longer produced.

• BKL AUTOREPLICA
1970s Plus 8 (no longer produced).
1980s PLUS 8.
1960s/80s 4/4 Four-seater, Cowled Radiator.
1963 Plus 4 Plus Fixed Head Coupé.
1950 4/4 Drop Head Coupé, Flat Radiator.
1946 4/4 Two-seater, Standard Special engine.
1938 4/4 Two-seater, Coventry Climax engine.

1938 4/4 Four-seater, Coventry Climax engine.

• AUTO FANTASY
1971 4/4 four-seater and 1971 Plus - made up only.

Resin range 1/43 scale
• PROVENCE MOULAGE
Resin kit of 1962 Plus 4 Le Mans car number 29. Also will be producing a Plus 8 in autumn 1994.

1/24 scale
• BKL AUTOREPLICA
A 1979 4/4 Ford Kent-engined Two-or Four-seater with lift-off bonnet revealing full engine detail (approximately 160mm long).

• METAL 24
A Plus 8 (no longer produced).

• SOUTH EASTERN FINECAST
A 1983 Plus 8 in kit form only.

1/86 scale
• BKL AUTOREPLICA
A 1960s/80s Cowled Radiator Two-seater (approximately 50mm long).

Plastic die-cast range
1/16 scale
• POLISTIL
Die-cast plastic ready-made models, approximately 250mm long, of a Plus 8 Roadster and a Plus 8 Competition were produced in a choice of colours from 1980 to 1992 but are no longer in production.

• L/S MOTORISED
An electric-powered model, offered as a kit only, of a Plus 8 Roadster or Competition, but no longer produced.

1/20 scale (approx)
• MASUDAYA
Representation, with friction drive, of a Two-seater Morgan with a nodding figure of Mickey Mouse, Donald Duck or Goofy as driver.

• AREMONTOIR
Hong Kong-produced copy of the Masudaya models, but with a figure of a helmeted driver.

1/43 scale
• ACORN MODELS
In production in the UK for about two years from early 1969 were very thin, plastic die-cast models of a Plus 4 and a 4/4 with removable hood.

• MAKER UNKNOWN
Believed to date from the late 1960s, a model of a Plus 4 in grey plastic with a large raised figure 8 moulded on top of the bonnet has been found in Norway.

Die-cast metal toys

1/57 scale (approx)
• MAJORETTE
A 75mm long toy model of a cowled-

The contrast of 1/43 and 1/86 scale diecast white metal models ... 1/43 scale, l-r: BKL Plus 8, BKL 4/4 Series I four-seater, Western Models Flat Radiator Plus 4, Grand Prix 1962 Le Mans Plus 4 Super Sports, BKL 4/4 Series I two-seater and BKL Cowled Radiator four-seater. 1/86, l-r: BKL 'F4' and BKL Plus 8. All were or are still available in fully finished or kit form.

radiator 4/4 was produced in a variety of colours and packaging from about 1980 but is no longer in production.

• SIKU
A Plus 8 produced in blue or British Racing Green.

• TOMICA
A Plus 8 with Miss Piggy as driver (not to be confused with the Corgi Miss Piggy, which is not a Morgan.) Tomica also produced a toy Plus 8 in a variety of colours, but none of these described are still produced.

• TOMY
A Plus 8 in various colours no longer produced.

• OLD TIMER MODELS
A Plus 8, no longer produced.

• ZEE
A Plus 8 in various colours, no longer produced.

• DYNAWHEELS
Same model as Zee, above, no longer produced.

• CORGI ROCKETS
A Plus 8, no longer produced.

• WIZZWHEELS
Plus 8, no longer produced.

• L/B MODELS
Plus 8, no longer produced.

• PLASTIC MAGNETIC DRIVE
Very basic 4/4 made in Czechoslovakia in the late 1960s which is no longer produced.

• MANUFACTURER UNKNOWN
A tin-plate 1/24 model of a Plus 8.

• FUNRISE
Vaguely Morgan shaped, very poor representation, about 25mm long, made in China.

Other Morgan model-based memorabilia
Silver or gold jewellery
Cowled Radiator Two-seater, 42mm long.
Cowled Radiator Two-seater, 20mm long *(These models are supplied as keyrings, earrings, necklaces, brooches, etc).*

Silver-plated pewter
1/57 scale miniatures of a 1932 Super Sports and a 1980s Plus 8, each mounted on a wooden plinth.

Crystal glass
Replica of a Plus 8, mounted on a wooden plinth. No longer produced.

Wooden models
Representations in wood of a Three-wheeler Tourer and Racer and Flat Radiator Four-wheeler.

Toiletries
Bath soap-on-a-string moulded in the shape of a Plus 8. Originally produced for Marks & Spencer but now only for the Morgan Motor Company.

Pedal car
A Morgan 4/4 suitable for children aged 3-7 years.

Famosa electric car
A Morgan 4/4 suitable for children aged 3-7 years, powered by battery and approximately 1.09m long.

The tables on the following four pages contain a complete listing of all known Morgan models ever produced and is reproduced here courtesy of Mr Cliff Baker.

Key to countries

CHI	-	China
CZ	-	Czechoslovakia
F	-	France
GB	-	Great Britain
HK	-	Hong Kong
I	-	Italy
JAP	-	Japan
KOR	-	Korea
N	-	Norway
NL	-	Holland
THAI	-	Thailand

MODEL MAKER	No.	SCALE	YEAR	MODEL	DESCRIPTION	Made
A.B.S.	R715	72nd	1933	S S	3 Wheeler	GB
Acorn		43rd			3 Wheeler	GB
		43rd		4/4	2 Seater	GB
Automobile		43rd	1994	+ 8	2 Seater hood down red	NL
Collections		43rd	1994	+ 8	2 Seater sidescreen up B.R.green	NL
B.K.L.		72nd	1939	F4	3 Wheeler	GB
Autoreplica		72nd	1968	+ 8	2 Seater	GB
	8	86th	1960	4/4	2 Seater Cowled Rad. can be +8	GB
	AR44	43rd	1938	4/4	2 Seater Coventry Climax	GB
	AR38		1938	4/4	4 Seater Coventry Climax	GB
modified	AR44		1946	4/4	2 Seater Standard Special	GB
	AR25		1950	+ 4	2 Seater D.H.C.	GB
modified	AR 7		1960	4/4	2 Seater (adaption of + 8)	GB
	AR11		1960	+ 4	4 Seater	GB
	AR10		1963	+4+	2 Seater Coupé	GB
	AR 7		1968	+ 8	2 Seater	GB
	AR47	43rd	1940	F 2	3 Wheeler	GB
	AR48	43rd	1940	F 4	3 Wheeler	GB
	AR1007	24th	1979	4/4	2 Seater	GB
	AR1005		1979	4/4	4 Seater	GB
Brumm	1	43rd	1923		Morgan 3 Wheeler green open	I
(can have	2		1923		3 Wheeler white hood up	I
a variety	3		1929		Darmont 3 Wheeler blue open	I
of racing	4		1929		3 Wheeler red hood up	I
numbers)						
SS			1933		Morgan 3 Wheeler red/black open	I
LIM.EDIT.			1933		3 Wheeler yell/black open	I
MODELTIME			1933		3 Wheeler black open	I
Corgi Rocket	921	55th	1968	+ 8	✿ Met.Red white rad chrome wheels	GB
	921		1968	+ 8	✿ Met.Red silver rad black wheels	GB
Corgi Junior	64		1968	+ 8	✿ Red ✿(all with	GB
	64		1968	+ 8	✿ Yellow black interior)	GB
	64			+ 8	✿ Red with label 6 roundal	GB
					seen with number 20 on all of door	GB
Czechoslo.					Blue Plastic magnet powered	CZ
					Green (Made in the 1970's)	CZ
					Red	CZ
					Yellow	CZ
Dynawheels/	D69	57th	1968	+ 8	Metallic Green {also marketed	CHI
DynaClassics	D69		1968	+ 8	Metallic Red by Zee models}	CHI
French		43rd		4/4	4 Seater made by Andre Marie Ruf	F
Gaiety Toy	850429				3 Wheeler Red	GB
(Castle Art					3 Wheeler light Blue	GB
Products)					3 Wheeler Chrome	GB
					3 Wheeler light Green	GB

MODEL MAKER	No.	SCALE	YEAR	MODEL	DESCRIPTION	Made
Gakken					3 Wheeler	
Glass Cryst.		24th	1969	+ 8	2 Seater	GB
Grand Prix		43rd	1962	+ 4	Le Mans 2 litre Class Winner	GB
Hong Kong	201	57th	1968	+ 8	Yellow tan inter. manu.unknown	HK
			1968	+ 8	Yellow black inter.	HK
L/B Models		57th	1968	+ 8	2 Seater	HK
L/S	02002	16th	1979	+ 8	Roadster	JAP
Motorised	2,400		1979	+ 8	Competition	JAP
Majorette						
250 series⌐	261	50th	1969	+ 8	Blue chrome	F
	261		1969	+ 8	Green chrome	F
200 series	261		1968	+ 8	Pink	F
	261		1968	+ 8	Colour changes with temperature	F
	261		1968	+ 8	with case bubble pack (Girls)	F
	261		1969	+ 8	Red /black roof/black interior	F
	261		1969	+ 8	Red /black roof/grey interior	F
	261		1969	+ 8	Red /cream roof/cream interior	F
	261		1969	+ 8	Red /cream roof /cream interior	F
	261		1969	+ 8	Red metallic	F
	261		1969	+ 8	Green / brown roof/brown interior	F
	261		1969	+ 8	Green / cream roof/cream interior	F
	261		1969	+ 8	Green bright " "	F
	261		1969	+ 8	Green mint " "	F
	261		1969	+ 8	Green metallic " "	F
	261		1969	+ 8	Blue metallic	F
	261		1969	+ 8	Mauve metallic (purple)	F
"Crazy						
Roadsters"	455		1969	+ 8	Mauve/black with Big Bebert	THAI
450 series	456		1969	+ 8	Yellow/black with Elliot the Cat	THAI
Masudaya				4/4	Yellow with Mickey Mouse	JAP
Corp.1986				4/4	Pink with Mickey Mouse	JAP
				4/4	Red with Mickey Mouse	JAP
				4/4	with Goofy	JAP
				4/4	Pink with Donald Duck	JAP
				4/4	Red with Donald Duck	JAP
				4/4	Yellow with Donald Duck	JAP
Model World	3301	???		4/4	Light Green multicoloured parts	CHI
wind up	3301			4/4	Yellow multicoloured parts	CHI
(also	3301			4/4	Light Blue multicoloured parts	CHI
marketed	3301			4/4	Pink multicoloured parts	CHI
by	3301			4/4	Blue gold bumper	CHI
Aremmontoir)	3301			4/4	Light Blue gold bumper	H K
{Copies of	3301			4/4	Red gold bumper	H K
Disney	3301			4/4	Yellow gold bumper	H K
originals}	3301			4/4	Green gold bumper	H K
	3301			4/4	White gold bumper	H K
	3301			4/4	Brown gold bumper	H K
	3301			4/4	Purple gold bumper	H K
	3301			4/4	Purple light gold bumper	H K
Meccano					3 Wheeler	GB

MODEL MAKER	No.	SCALE	YEAR	MODEL	DESCRIPTION	Made
Mikansue		43rd	1939		Le Mans	GB
Minicraft	1513	16th	1935	S S	3 Wheeler ACADEMY {American firm}	KOR
Motorkits		43rd		+4+	Coupé	
Norway				+ 4	8 embossed on bonnet	
Old Timer		57th		+ 8	2 Seater	
Piccolino		76th	1920		3 Wheeler	I
Polistil (Tonka)	TG2	16th	1968	+ 8	Racer Light Blue	I
	TG2		1968	+ 8	Racer Blue + Black	I
	TG2		1968	+ 8	Road Yellow + Black Wings	I
	TG2		1968	+ 8	Racer Yellow + Silver Wings	I
	TG2		1968	+ 8	Road British Racing Green	I
Provence Moulage	K715	43rd	1962	+ 4	Le Mans 2 Seater	F
Riko					3 Wheeler	
Scalelink	SLC122	72nd	1928	S S	Aero Super Sports	GB
Siku	1062	55th	1968	+ 8	Metallic Blue	D
	1062		1968	+ 8	British Racing Green	D
	0836		1968	+ 8	Metallic Green	D
	0836		1968	+ 8	Metallic Blue (differ.wheels)	D
South East Finecast (Wills fine)	AO 36	43rd	1934	S S	3 Wheeler	GB
	AO 20	24th	1934	S S	3 Wheeler	GB
	A2 16	24th	1984	+ 8	2 Seater	GB
Standard Soap Co.				+ 8	wire wheel brown(Marks & Sparks)	GB
				+ 8	wire wheel cream(Morgan Factory)	GB
Tomica (Tomy)	26	57th	1980	+ 8	Red Black interior	JAP
	26		1980	+ 8	Met.Blue Tan interior	JAP
	16		1980	+ 8	Red Black interior	CHI
			1980	+ 8	with Miss Piggy	CHI
Western		43rd	1951	+ 4	2 Seater Flat Rad.	GB
		24th	1968	+ 8	2 Seater (made for Danhausen out of production since 1982)	GB

MODEL MAKER	No.	SCALE	YEAR	MODEL	DESCRIPTION	Made
BRUMM	7		1922		Sandford 3 Wheeler silver open	I
	8		1922		3 Wheeler gold hood up	I
Japanese				4/4	yellow badged as MG	JAP
Tin plate				4/4	red with roof badged as MG	JAP

Other models of interest (not actual Morgans)

APPENDIX VII

MORGAN FACTORY
SALES LITERATURE
(FOUR-WHEELER CARS)

Definitions

Catalogue - *Booklet of three or more pages which are secured on one edge, stapled, or sewn with thread and/or glued.*

Folder - *Consists of a single sheet of paper folded in various ways and sizes to form a booklet.*

Sheet - *A single sheet of paper not folded. Various sizes but normally 8.25in by 11.75in. Printed on one or both sides.*

Post Card - *Printed on a single piece of card with an illustration on the front and specifications on the back.*

Variation - *Any variation to the original, either in printing, prices, number of sheets, colour, changes, etc, is regarded as a variation.*

Road Test Reports - *Factory reprint of magazine articles, which were used as sales material.*

Colour Charts - *Colour charts of standard colours used on the Morgan cars at the time of issue.*

1936 **4-4** Folder. White with green lettering and highlights, "Advanced Specifications of the Morgan 4/4" lists mechanical and size specifications, including the price of 185 Guineas *(note: Guinea = £1.1s. 0d)*. Printed on the back is "A. & S. H. 36620". Also has an illustration of the factory with "Morgan Motors" on the roof.

1936 **4-4** Road Test Sheet. Black/white. Reprinted from *The Motor*, January 7 1936. 2 photos and 4 line drawings. Hand stamped with a price of 185 Guineas. Printed by Temple Press Ltd., 5-17 Rosebery Avenue, EC1. Issued by the factory.

1937 **4-4** Folder. 2 folds, printed black/white with orange-red highlights throughout. Cover illustrates a man and women in a 4/4 two seater, with another man leaning on the off side of the car. Titled "The Morgan 4/4". When opened illustrates two seater (registration number MM 44) at speed. Price is 185 Guineas complete, plus tax of seven pounds 10 shillings. Inside illustrated with pictures of the dashboard, engine, and two seater. Back illustrated with two seater which has hood erected. Adams and Sons, printers, Hereford. Number 37798.

1937 **4-4** Road Test Sheet. Printed one side only. "News for Motorists" is headline of newspaper article by Mercurius. Reprinted from *Sunday Referee*, April 18 1937. Issued by the Morgan Factory.

1937 **4-4** Road Test. Printed both sides. Reprinted from *The Motor*, August 24 1937. Introduces the 4/4 4-seater.

1938 **4-4** Folder. 2 folds, black/white with red highlights. Cover printed with a man and women in a 4/4 two seater, with another man leaning on the off side of the car. Titled "The Morgan 4/4". When opened, illustrates two seater (registration number MM 44) at speed. Price as follows: two seater is £210; four seater is £225. Tax is £7 10. Inside illustrated with the dashboard, engine, and two seater. Back illustrates a two seater which has hood erected. Adams and Sons, printers, Hereford. Number 39762.

1939 **4-4** Folder. 2 folds. Black/cream, with green highlights. Morgan 4/4 "wings" on cover, and titled "In a Class of its Own". Opens to show three models and prices as follows: two seater - 190 Guineas; four seater - 205 Guineas and the Drop Head Coupé- 225 Guineas. Rear cover: Adams and Sons (Printers) Ltd., Hereford.

1939 **4-4** Road Test. Black/white. Reprinted from *The Autocar*, September 9 1938, by the Morgan Motor Company. The front cover printed "Read what the Autocar says of the Famous Morgan 4/4". Has photographs of the two seater and the four seater, also introduces the new Drop Head Coupé. Lists a price reduction from those of 1938. Prices listed the same as 1939F. Back page shows Morgan Motor Co. Ltd., Malvern Link, Worcs, in big letters in side of a boxed outline. Printed by The Cornwall Press Ltd., Paris Garden, SE1.

1939 **4-4** Four Seater Road Test. Black/white. Reprinted by the Morgan Motor Company from *The Light Car*, December 30 1938. Three pages, with photographs of car with registration number CNP 507. Back page has advertisement for The Light Car and print number 4073-39.

1939 Road Test of the **4-4**. Black/white. Reprinted from *The Light Car*, May 26 1939. Entitled "The New Morgan Engine", it refers to the fitting of the new Standard Motor Company engine in the Drop Head Coupé as standard equipment also as a £5 extra option on the 4/4s. Has several illustrations of the engine and gearbox mounts. Number 5477-39.

1946 **4/4** Folder. 2 folds. Black/cream, with green highlights. Cover has the Morgan 4/4 "wings, and "Class of its Own". When opened it has illustrations of all three models with prices: two seater - 190 Guineas; four seater - 205 Guineas and the Drop Head Coupé - 225 Guineas. Similar to 1939 Folder, but with as small prices, glued to the front update sheet. White paper with red ink, listing the following prices: Drop Head Coupé, £435; 4/4 four seater, £408 and 4/4 two seater, £390. Dated August, 1946. Back cover printed: Adams and Sons (Printers) Ltd., Hereford.

1946 **4/4** Road Test Folder. One fold. Black/white. Reprinted from *The Motor*, December 26 1945. The first page is titled "The Morgan 4/4", "1946 Version has New Engine". Article shows Drop Head Coupé registration number CWP 823, and details the Standard

Special Engine. Prices listed: two seater, £355 (plus £99 15s.1d. purchase tax) and DHC - £395 (plus £110 18s. 3d. purchase tax). Number 357-46.

1947 **4/4** Post Card. Black/white. Picture of 4/4 two seater on one side and specifications on the other. Prices: two seater is £390 plus tax; four seater is £408 plus tax.

1947 **4/4** Post Card with Model Variation. Black/white. Picture of 4/4 Drop Head Coupé on one side and specifications on the other. Price listed: £435 plus tax.

1948 **4/4** Folder. Two folds. Green cover and highlighted with black/white pictures and text. Cover printed has 4/4 "Wings" and reads "In a Class of its Own". Prices listed inside: two seater - £409 10s.; four seater - £428 8s and Drop Head Coupé £478 10s. All prices plus purchase tax. Back cover, "Read what others say about this famous car", and Adam and Sons (Printers) Ltd., Hereford.

1949 **4/4** Folder. Two folds. Blue cover and highlighted with black/white pictures and text. Cover printed has 4/4, "Wings" and reads "In a Class of its Own". Prices listed inside: two seater - £435; four seater - £450 and Drop Head Coupé £495; all prices plus purchase tax. Back cover, "Form of Guarantee", and Adam and Sons (Printers) Ltd., Hereford.

1949 **4/4** Folder with Price Variation. Two folds. As for previous entry, but with revised prices.

1950 **4/4** Folder. Two folds. Red cover and highlighted with black/white pictures and text. Cover has 4/4 "Wings" and reads "In a Class of its Own". Prices listed inside: two seater - £435 (plus £121 11s. purchase tax); four seater - £450 (plus £125 15s. purchase tax) and Drop Head Coupé £495 (plus £138 5s. purchase tax). Back cover, "Form of Guarantee", and Adam and Sons (Printers) Ltd., Hereford.

1950 **Plus 4** Sheet. Two sides. Black/white. Entitled "Advance Details of Plus Four Model". Text gives specifications of the new Plus 4 model and improvements over the 4/4 model.

1951 **Plus 4** Folder. One fold. Black/white with Dark Blue highlights. Front cover depicts a Plus 4 two seater, and the back cover depicts a Drop Head Coupé, registration number JNP 239 with hood up. Prices listed: two seater - £510 plus purchase tax (£142 8s. 4d.); Drop Head Coupé £ £565 plus purchase tax (£157 13s. 10d.).

1951 **Plus 4** Folder with Price Variation. As previous folder but with price variation.

1951 **Plus 4** Folder (Print Variation). One fold. Black/white with dark blue highlights. Front cover shows a Plus 4 two seater, back cover illustrates a Drop Head Coupé, registration number JNP 239 with hood up. Prices listed: two seater - £510 plus purchase tax (£142 8s. 4d.); Drop Head Coupé - £565 plus purchase tax (£157 13s. 10d.). Purchase tax amounts crossed out by two broad horizontal dark blue ink lines in the printing process, therefore this is a variation.

1951 **Plus 4** Road Test Folder. Black/white. Entitled "Morgan Plus Four Coupé", reprinted from *Autocar*, April 27 1951. Nine photos of Drop Head Coupé number JNP 239, and three line drawings. *Autocar* Road Test number 1428, reprint number RP9735-K6703.

1951 **Plus 4** Road Test Folder. Black and white. Entitled "The Morgan 'Plus Four' Two Seater". Reprinted from *The Motor*, 19th September 1951. Front page printed Morgan Motor Co., Limited, with address and telephone number. Text shows four photos of HUY 982. Reprint number 8980-51.

1951 **Plus 4** Sheet. Black and white. Two sided. Entitled "The Morgan Plus Four". Reprinted from *Autocar*, 29th September 1950. Three photos, and a "cut away" line drawing of the chassis on reverse. Printed in England by The Cornwall Press Ltd., Paris Gardens, London, SE1.

1951-2 **Plus 4** Folder. Black and white, one fold. Front has photograph of the winning team in the R.A.C. International Rally in 1951 and 1952. Registration numbers JNP 239, JWP 537, and HUY 982 from left to right. Prices list the two seater - £565 plus tax; the four seater - £580 plus tax and the Drop Head Coupé - £620 plus tax. Rear cover lists rally results from 1951 and 1952. Printed by Adams and Sons (Printers) Ltd., Hereford.

1952 **Plus 4** Folder. Two folds. Black/white with red and aquamarine blue highlight. Two seater on the front, with a four seater on the back. Drop Head Coupé (number JNP 239) the inside with specifications and prices listed as: two seater - £535 plus purchase tax (£298 14s. 6d.); four seater £550 plus purchase tax (£307 1s. 2d.) and Drop Head Coupé - £590 plus purchase tax (£329 5s. 6d.). Adams and Sons (Printers) Ltd. Hereford.

1952 **Plus 4** Folder Variation. As previous entry but without prices.

1952 **Plus 4** Folder with Price Variation. As previous two entries, but with price variation listed as two seater - £535 plus purchase tax (£298 14s. 6d.); four seater £550 plus purchase tax (£307 1s. 2d.) and Drop Head Coupé - £590 plus purchase tax (£329 5s. 6d.). Price increases are printed on a sticker glued over the old prices. Sticker white printed in red ink. New prices listed: two seater - £565 plus tax (£315 7s. 9d.); four seater - £580 plus tax (£323 14s. 6d.) and Drop Head Coupé - £620 plus tax (£345 18s. 10d.). Price increase

sheet is dated June 1, 1952.

1952 **Plus 4** Road Test Folder. Black and white. One fold. Entitled "John Bolster Tests the Morgan 'Plus Four'. Reprinted from *Autosport*, 11th July 1952. Illustrated with a two seater on front and "The Morgan Motor Company Limited". Different from magazine article. Back page has a Drop Head Coupé supplement to magazine article with a price of £620 plus tax of £345 18s. 10d. Printed by Keliher, Hudson and Kearns, Ltd., Hatfields, London, SE1.

1952 **Plus 4** Post Card. Black/white. Photograph of Drop Head Coupé registration number JNP 239 one side and specifications on the other with a price of £565 plus tax. Circulated to main agents to be issued by them, therefore often found with agents sticker or stamp on back.

1952-53 **Plus 4** Catalogue. 12 pages including oversize blue imitation leather grained cover. Black and white with blue cover and blue/green highlights inside. Two seater pictured is registration number HUY 982 (priced at £565 plus tax of £315 7s. 9d.); four seater pictured is number CWP 81? (priced at £580 plus tax of £323 14s. 6d.) and the Drop Head Coupé is registration number JNP 239 (priced at £620 plus tax of £345 18s. 10d.). Printed by Adams and Sons (Printers) Ltd., Dalok Works, Hereford.

1952-53 **Plus 4** Catalogue with Price Variation. As previous entry but with no price list.

1953-54 **Plus 4** Catalogue. 12 pages including oversize tan imitation leather grained cover. Black and white with tan cover and light orange highlights inside. Two seater pictured is interim grille model; four seater pictured is registration number CWP 81?, with the number plate overprinted to read "Morgan"; Drop Head Coupé registration number JNP 239, with the number plate overprinted to read "Morgan". No prices listed. Printed by Adams and Sons (Printers) Ltd., Dalok Works, Hereford.

1953-54 **Plus 4** Catalogue with Price Variation. As previous entry but with prices listed as; two seater - £565 plus tax of £236 10s. 10d. (old tax of £315 7s. 9d. is overprinted with horizontal line); four seater is £580 plus tax of £242 15s. 10d. (old tax of £323 14s. 6d. overprinted with horizontal line) and Drop Head Coupé is £620 with tax of £259 9s. 2d. (old tax of £345 18s. 10d. overprinted with horizontal line). Printed by Adams and Sons (Printers) Ltd., Dalok Works, Hereford.

1953-54 **Plus 4** Catalogue with Price Variation. As previous entries but with prices listed as; two seater - £565 plus tax of £236 10s. 10d.; four seater is £580 plus tax of £242 15s. 10d and Drop Head Coupé is £620 with tax of £259 9s. 2d. Purchase taxes are printed on a separate piece of paper and glued over the old tax at the bottom of page 7. Printed by Adams and Sons (Printers) Ltd., Dalok Works, Hereford.

1954 **Plus 4** Folder. Black and white, one fold. Front cover illustrated with a right hand drive white two seater with dark coloured disc wheels and twin spares. Prices listed as: two seater - £565 plus tax; four seater is £580 plus tax and the Drop Head Coupé - £620 plus tax. The back page lists rally results from 1951, 1952 and 1953. Printed by Adams and Sons (Printers) Ltd., Hereford. Number 68152.

1954 **Plus 4** Folder Variation. Black and white, one fold. Front cover depicts a left hand drive dark coloured two seater with disc wheels and twin spares, fitted with badge bar and spot light. Prices listed as: two seater - £565 plus tax; four seater is £580 plus tax and the Drop Head Coupé - £620 plus tax. Back page lists rally results from 1951, 1952 and 1953. Printed by Adams and Sons (Printers) Ltd., Hereford. Number 68152.

1954 **Plus 4** Folder Variation. Black and white, one fold. Front has illustration of a right hand drive light coloured two seater with disc wheels and twin spares, the same photograph was used on page three of 1953-54C. Prices listed as: two seater - £565 plus tax; four seater is £580 plus tax and the Drop Head Coupé - £620 plus tax. Back page lists rally results from 1951, 1952 and 1953. Printed by Adams and Sons (Printers) Ltd., Hereford. Number 68152.

1954 **Plus 4** Road Test Folder. One fold. Black and white. Reprinted from *The Autocar*, May 7 1952. Two seater with twin spare wheels is tested (number KUY 387). Printed in England by Cornwall Press Ltd., Paris Garden, London, SE1, number RP5888 - L5163.

1954 **Plus 4** Road Test Folder. One fold. Black and white. Entitled "Road Test of the Morgan 'Plus-Four'". Reprinted from *Autosport*, August 6 1954. John Bolster tests registration number HUY 982, now fitted to a Plus 4 two seater with twin spare wheels, fitted with TR2 engine. Printed in England by Keliher, Hudson and Kerns Ltd., Hatfields, London, SE1.

1955 **Plus 4** Catalogue. Black and white, green highlights. 12 pages including cover. Cover has illustration of a green right hand drive Plus 4 at speed amongst hills by a stone wall. Photographs illustrate two seater with price of £555 (plus tax of £232 5s. 10d.); four seater tourer with a price of £580 (plus tax of £242 15s. 10d.); two seater Drop Head Coupé with a price of £610 (plus tax of £255 5s. 10d.) and the four seater Drop Head Coupé with a price of £620 (plus tax of £259 9s. 2d.). Specifications for Vanguard and TR2 engine. Printed by Adams and Sons (Printers) Ltd., Dalok Works, Hereford.

1955 **Plus 4** Catalogue with Price Variation. As previous entry but with no prices listed.

1955 **Plus 4** Folder. One fold. Black and white. Cover shows dark coloured two seater with twin spare wheels with badge bar and spot light, and printed "Winner of Many International Awards". Inside lists specifications and prices: two seater (Vanguard engine) - £555 plus tax; two seater (TR2 engine) - £595; 2-seater Drop Head Coupé £610; four seater Drop Head Coupé - £620 and four seater for £580 all with the Vanguard engine. Back page lists results from 1951, 1952 and 1953 rallies. Printed by Adams and Sons (Printers) Ltd., Hereford. Number 69492 similar to 1954 Folder Variation.

1956 Plus 4 and 4/4 Series II Catalogue. Black and white, with light blue highlights. 12 pages. Cover, Light Blue with "Morgan Catalogue 1956" printed top left. Illustrates the two seater, four seater, two seater Drop Head Coupé, and the two seater 4/4 tourer Series II. No prices. Specifications for the Vanguard engine and TR2 engine. Printed by Adams and Sons (Printers) Ltd, Dalok Works, Hereford.

1956 **Plus 4** and **4/4 Series II** Catalogue with Price Variation Details. 12 pages. As above with prices as: photographs illustrate two seater at £595 (plus tax of £232 5s. 10d.) TR2 engine; four seater at £580 (plus tax of £242 15s. 10d.) for Vanguard engine and £610 (plus tax of £255 5s. 10d.) for TR-2 engine; two seater Drop Head Coupé at £610 (plus tax of £255 5s. 10d.) for Vanguard engine and £640 (plus tax of £267 15s. 10d.) for TR2 engine; the two seater Series II at £450 (plus tax of £188 12s. 6d.). Specifications for Vanguard and TR2 engines. Printed by Adams and Sons (Printers) Ltd., Dalok Works, Hereford.

1956 **Plus 4** and **4/4 Series II** Catalogue with Price Variation. Details as previous two entries but with 12 pages, increased Purchase Tax, shows two seater (plus tax of £298 17s. 0d.); four seater (plus tax of £291 7s. 0d.) Vanguard engine (plus tax of £306 7s. 0d.) TR2 engine; two seater Drop Head Coupé (plus tax of £306 7s. 0d.) Vanguard engine and (plus tax of £321 7s. 0d.) TR-2 engine; and the two seater tourer Series II (plus tax of £226 7s.0d.). New purchase tax is printed on a small sheet) glued at the top of page three. Printed by Adams and Sons (Printers) Ltd., Dalok Works, Hereford.

1956 **Plus 4** and **4/4 Series II** Folder. One fold. Black and white. Front cover illustrates 4/4 Series II tourer, models and specifications listed are the same as previous three entries. No prices listed. No printer shown.

1956 **Plus 4** and **4/4 Series II** Folder. As above. Black and white with blue lettering to Morgan wings on cover, title and inside headings.

1957 **Plus 4** and **4/4 Series II** Catalogue. Black and white, with red highlights. 12 pages. Front cover has a red illustration of a right

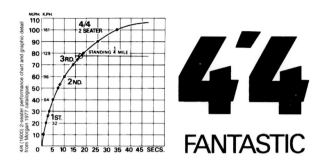

4'4
FANTASTIC

hand drive Plus 4 at speed amongst hills by a stone wall. Photographs illustrate two seater Plus 4, four seater, two seater Drop Head Coupé, and the 4/4 Series II tourer. Prices on a small sheet bound between pages 2 and 3. Prices listed as: two seater Plus 4 - Vanguard engine - £848 17s. 0d. - TR engine - £923 17s. 0d.; four seater Plus 4 - Vanguard engine - £871 7s. 0d TR engine £946 7s. 0d.; two seater Drop Head Coupé - Vanguard engine - £916 7s. 0d. - TR engine £991 7s. 0d.; and 4/4 Series II two seater £713 17s. 0d. Price list captioned "1956-7 Prices". Printed by Adams and Sons (Printers) Ltd., Dalok Works, Hereford. Number 1956/7.

1957 **Plus 4** and **4/4 Series II** Catalogue with Price Variation. Details as previous entry. 12 pages. Prices on a small sheet bound between pages 2 and 3. Prices listed as: two seater Plus 4 - Vanguard engine - £848 17s. 0d. - TR engine - £923 17s. 0d.; four seater Plus 4 - Vanguard engine - £871 7s. 0d. - TR engine £946 7s. 0d.; two seater Drop Head Coupé - Vanguard engine - £916 7s. 0d. - TR engine - £991 7s. 0d.; and 4/4 Series II two seater £713 17s. 0d. Price list captioned "1956-7 Prices". Printed by Adams and Sons (Printers) Ltd., Dalok Works, Hereford. Number 1956/7. Also has a Morgan Motor Co. Ltd., letterhead which lists the directors, glued to top of page 3. The letter states prices have been increased due to the increase in wages and the cost of steel, and is dated 19th August 1957. Signed by George H Goodall, Managing Director, 1957-8, prices are the same as listed in next entry.

1958 **Plus 4** and **4/4 Series II** Catalogue. Black and white, with green highlights. 12 pages. Front cover is pale yellow with green highlights, depicts two Morgans taking the chequered flag as seen through a pair of binoculars. 1958 on bottom right of cover. 4/4 Series II two seater. Plus 4 two seater, Plus 4 four seater, and Plus 4 Drop Head Coupé are illustrated. Prices on a small sheet bound between pages 2 and 3. Prices listed: two seater Plus 4 - Vanguard engine £892 7s. 0d. - TR engine - £968 17s. 0d.; four seater Plus 4 - Vanguard engine - £914 17s. 0d. - TR engine £991 7s. 0d.; two seater Drop Head Coupé - Vanguard engine - £962 17s. 0d. - TR engine - £1040 17s. 0d.; and 4/4 Series II two seater - £748 7s. 0d.; 4/4 Series II Competition Model - £826 7d. 0s. Price list entitled "1957-8 Prices". Printed by Adams and Sons (Printers) Ltd., Dalok Works, Hereford. Number 1957/8.

1958 **Plus 4** and **4/4 Series II** Folder. One fold. Black and white with green highlights. Cover shows Plus 4 two seater with disc wheels. Prices listed on page 2: two seater Plus 4 - £645 plus tax; four seater Plus 4 - £660 plus tax; two seater Drop Head Coupé - £693 plus tax and 4/4 Series II two seater - £498 (competition model £550) all plus tax. Specifications page 3, and engine specifications page 4. Printed by Adams and Sons (Printers) Ltd., East Street, Hereford.

1958 **Plus 4** and **4/4 Series II** Folder. As above but with blue highlights.

1958 **Plus 4** Road Test Folder. 6 pages. Reprinted from *The Motor*, 1st January 1958, featuring TUY 875 fitted with the Triumph TR3 engine. Printed by Temple Press, London, number 1773-502.

1958 **Plus 4** Road Test Sheet. Black and white. Entitled "John Bolster Tests the Morgan Plus Four". Reprinted from *Autosport*, 8th August 1958. Four photographs of Plus 4. Printed on the back page is: "A fully illustrated catalogue may be obtained on request from The Morgan Motor Co. Ltd., address and telephone number. Printed in England by Keliher, Hudson and Kearns Ltd., Hatfields, London, SE1.

1959 **Plus 4** and **4/4 Series II** Catalogue. Black and white, Red highlights. 12 pages. Front black with red highlights. Cover has a caricature illustration of a Morgan top right. 1959 printed top left. 4/4 Series II two seater, Plus 4 two seater, Plus 4 four seater, and Plus 4 Drop Head Coupé are pictured in catalogue. Prices on a small sheet bound between pages 2 and 3. Prices listed: two seater Plus 4 - TR engine - £968 17s. 0d.; four seater Plus 4 - TR engine £991 7s. 0d.; two seater Drop Head Coupé - TR engine - £1040 17s. 0d.; and 4/4 Series II two seater £748 7s. 0d.; 4/4 Series II Competition Model - £826 7d. 0s. Price list headed "1958-9 Prices". Printed by Adams and Sons (Printers) Ltd., Dalok Works, Hereford. Number 1958/9.

1959 **Plus 4** and **4/4 Series II** Folder. One fold. Black and white, with red highlights. Cover illustrates a Plus 4 two seater with wire wheels. Prices listed on page 2: two seater Plus 4 - £645 plus tax; four seater Plus 4 - £660 plus tax; two seater Drop Head Coupé £693 plus tax, and 4/4 Series II two seater - £498 (competition model £550) all plus tax. Specifications page 3, and engine specifications page 4. Printed by Adams and Sons (Printers) Ltd., East Street, Hereford.

1959 **Plus 4** and **4/4 Series II** Folder. As above but without "(Competition Model £550)".

1960 **Plus 4** and **4/4 Series II** Catalogue. Black and white, with red highlights. 12 pages. Front black with red highlights. Cover has a caricature illustration of a Morgan with Number 4 racing number in front of grandstand. Also 1960 printed top left. Inside are illustrated 4/4 Series II two seater, Plus 4 two seater, Plus 4 four seater, and Plus 4 Drop Head Coupé (with wide whitewall tyres for the first time). Prices on a small sheet bound between pages 2 and 3. Prices listed as: two seater Plus 4 - TR engine - £914 17s. 6d.; four seater Plus 4 - TR engine - £936 2s. 6d.; two seater Drop Head Coupé - TR engine - £982 17s. 6d.; and 4/4 Series II two seater £706 12s. 6d.; 4/4 Series II Competition Model - £780 5d. 10s. Price list headed "1959-60 Prices". This is the first catalogue to list UK agents

and overseas distributors which are printed on the back cover. Printed by Adams and Sons (Printers) Ltd., Dalok Works, Hereford. Number 1959/60.

1960 **Plus 4** Road Test Folder. One fold. Black and white. Entitled "John Bolster Tests the Morgan Plus Four", reprinted from *Autosport*, 1st July 1960" under title. Contains three photographs, one with John Bolster driving. Back cover "Printed in England by Keliher, Hudson and Kearns, Ltd., London, SE1".

1961 **Plus 4** and **4/4 Series III** Catalogue. Black and white, with light blue highlights. 12 pages. Cover light blue with black and white highlights, Printed "Morgan 1910-1961" "Fifty Years of Experience". 4/4 Series III two seater, Plus 4 two seater, Plus 4 four seater, and Plus 4 Drop Head Coupé are illustrated in catalogue. Prices on a small sheet bound between pages 2 and 3. Prices listed as: two seater Plus 4 - TR engine - £929 0s. 10d.; four seater Plus 4 - TR engine - £950 5s. 10d.; two seater Drop Head Coupé - TR engine - £1006 19s. 2d.; and 4/4 Series III two seater £737 15s. 10d. Price list headed "1960-61 Prices". UK agents and overseas distributors are listed on rear cover. Printed by Adams and Sons (Printers) Ltd., Dalok Works, Hereford. Number 1960/61.

1961 **Plus 4** and **4/4 Series III** Folder. One fold. Black and white with light blue highlights. Cover illustrates Plus 4 two seater with wire wheels. Page 2 lists the prices as: two seater Plus 4 - £655 plus tax; four seater Plus 4 - £670 plus tax; two seater Drop Head Coupé £710 plus tax; and 4/4 Series III two seater - £520 plus tax. Specifications page 3, engine specifications page 4. Printed by Adams and Sons (Printers) Ltd., East Street, Hereford.

1961 Morgan Paint Colour Chart. 6 colour cards plus front and back covers secured by a chrome rivet in top left corner. Cover is ivory coloured heavy paper, and reads: "Morgan Motor Co. Ltd., colour range in Dulux 98 Coach Finish. Manufactured by Imperial Chemical Industries Limited, Paints Division". Colours shown are from front to back: Westminster Green (P339-69), Kingfisher Blue (P339-39), Light Grey (P339-6673), Crimson (P339-5), Avion Blue (P339-189), and Broken White (P339-51). Back cover has ICI symbol.

1962 **Plus 4** and **4/4 Series IV** Catalogue. Black and white, with dark green highlights. 12 pages. Cover is dark green with black and white highlights. Printed "Morgan 1910- 1962" "Over Fifty Years of Experience". 4/4 Series IV two seater, Plus 4 two seater, Plus 4 four seater, and Plus 4 Drop Head Coupé illustrated. Prices listed on a small sheet bound between pages 1 and 2 or 2 and 3. Prices: two seater Plus 4 - TR engine - £956 3s. 11d.; two seater Super Sports - £1313 14s. 9d.; four seater Plus 4 - TR engine £978 6s. 5d.; Drop Head Coupé - TR engine - £1036 13s. 1d.; and 4/4 Series IV two seater £774 3s. 1d. Price list is headed "1961-62 Prices". Bottom

of page 9 lists specifications for the "Super Sport" model. UK agents and overseas distributors listed on the back cover. Printed by Adams and Sons (Printers) Ltd., Dalok Works, Hereford. Number 1961/62.

1962 **Plus 4** and **4/4 Series IV** Folder. One fold. Black and white. Cover depicts 4/4 Series IV two seater with disc wheels. Prices listed on page 2: two seater Plus 4 - £655 plus tax (£301 8s. 11d.); four seater Plus 4 - £670 plus tax (£308 6s. 5d.); Drop Head Coupé £710 plus tax (326 13s. 1d.); and 4/4 Series IV two seater - £530 plus tax (£244 3s. 1d.). Photograph of Plus 4 four seater page 3, specifications on page 4. At bottom of page 4 under Morgan Motors, main London distributor is listed as Basil Roy Ltd. with address and telephone number. Printed by Adams and Sons (Printers) Ltd., Hereford.

1963 **Plus 4** and **4/4 Series IV** Catalogue. Black and white, with olive green highlights. 12 pages. Cover, white with black and olive green highlights, printed "Morgan for 1962-3", "Over Fifty Years of Experience", and "The Car for the Sports Enthusiast". 4/4 Series IV two seater, Plus 4 two seater, Plus 4 four seater, and Plus 4 Drop Head Coupé illustrated in catalogue. Prices listed on small sheet bound between pages 10 and 11. Basic prices are listed as: 4/4 Series IV two seater £545; two seater Plus 4 - TR engine - £675; four seater Plus 4 - TR engine - £690; Drop Head Coupé - TR engine - £730; and two seater Super Sports - £925. Price list headed "1962-63 Prices". At the top of page 9 specifications for the "Super Sport" model are listed. UK agents and overseas distributors are listed on the back cover. "Printed in England" on the bottom right of back page.

1963 **Plus 4** and **4/4 Series IV** Catalogue with Price Variation. As previous but without price list supplement bound between pages 10 and 11.

1963 **Plus 4** and **4/4 Series IV** Sheet. Black and white. One side only. Photograph of TOK 258 taking the chequered flag at Le Mans in 1962. Under that are the prices, and below those is a list of UK agents. Basic prices only: 4/4 Series IV - £545 (plus tax); Plus 4 two seater £675 (plus tax); Plus 4 four seater - £690 (plus tax); Plus 4 Drop Head Coupé - £730 (plus tax); and Plus 4 Super Sports - £925 (plus tax). Morgan Motor Co. Ltd., with address and telephone number listed is at bottom of sheet. No printer listed.

1963 Road Test Sheet of **4/4 Series IV**. Printed two sides. Black and white. Reprinted from Autosport, 18th January 1963. Patrick McNally road tests number 296 FNP. Top speed achieved, 92 mph. Four photographs. Printed in England by Keliher, Hudson and Kearns Ltd., London, SE1.

1964 **Plus 4** and **4/4 Series V** Catalogue. Black and white, with red highlights. 12 pages. Cover white with black and red highlights, printed "Morgan for 1964", "Over Fifty Years of Experience", and

"The Car for the Sports Enthusiast". 4/4 Series V two seater, Plus 4 two seater, Plus 4 four seater, and Plus 4 Drop Head Coupé illustrated. Basic prices listed on small sheet bound between pages 10 and 11. 4/4 Series V 1498cc Ford Engine - £565: 4/4 Series V Competition Model - £625; Plus 4 two seater - £675; Plus 4 four seater - £690; and Plus 4 Super Sports - £925. Price list headed "1963/64 Prices for full range of cars". At the top of page 9 lists specifications for the "Super Sport" model. UK agents and overseas distributors are listed on the back cover. "Printed in England" on bottom right of back page.

1964 **Plus 4** and **4/4 Series V** Catalogue with Price Variation. Same as previous entry but with no small price list included.

1964 **Plus 4 Plus** Folder. One fold. Black and white with red highlights. Cover has photographs of Plus 4 Plus, "The New Car for the Sports Enthusiast", and "Morgan Plus Four Plus". Inside has two views of 869 KAB. Price printed below car on page 3: £1055 plus purchase tax of £220 7s. 1d. for a total of £1275 7s. 1d. Page 4 lists specifications and UK distributors. Designed and produced by Granville, Lang and Partners Ltd.

1964 **Plus 4 Plus** Folder with Price Variation. As previous entry but with no prices printed on page 3.

1965 **Plus 4 and 4/4 Series V** Catalogue. Black and white, with blue highlights. 16 pages. Cover is white with black and blue highlights, printed "The Car for the SPORTS Enthusiast". Includes photograph of a Plus 4 Plus with a three wheeler drawing superimposed on the Plus 4 Plus. 4/4 Series V two seater, Plus 4 two seater, Plus 4 four seater, Plus 4 Drop Head Coupé and the Plus 4 Plus illustrated in catalogue. Prices on a small sheet between pages 14 and 15, (not fixed). Basic prices only listed: 4/4 Series V 1498cc Ford engine - £565; 4/4 Series V Competition Model - £625; Plus 4 two seater - £675; Plus 4 four seater - £690; Plus 4 Drop Head Coupé - £730; Plus 4 Super Sports - £925; Plus 4 Plus - £1055, all plus tax. Price list headed "Prices for full range of cars 1964/5". UK agents and overseas distributors listed on page 15. Specifications given for both the Super Sports model and the 4/4 Series V Competition Model. Pages numbered for the first time. No printer is listed, but price sheet "Made in England".

1965 **Plus 4** and **4/4 Series V** Sheet. Black and white with blue highlights, same design as previous entry. Two sides. The front illustrates a Plus 4 Plus priced as £1276 7s. 1d. including tax and the 4/4 two seater Series V priced at £684 5s. 5d. including tax for the Ford 1498 engine, and the Competition Model is priced at £756 15s. 5d. including tax. Back depicts the Plus 4 two seater (TR4 engine) at £817 3s. 9d. including tax, and the Plus 4 four seater (TR4 engine) at £835 6s. 3d. including tax. UK agents also listed. No printer listed.

1966 **Plus 4** and **4/4 Series V** Catalogue. Black and white, with gold highlights. 16 pages. Cover has illustration of two seater 4/4 in woods surrounded by trees tinted in gold colour with the words "MORGAN First of the Real Sports Cars" in white letters. Cars illustrated are: 4/4 Series V two seater; Plus 4 Drop Head Coupé; Plus 4 two seater; Plus 4 four seater; Plus 4 Plus two seater sports; and the Plus 4 Competition model. Prices on a small sheet between pages 14 and 15, not glued. Basic prices listed as: 4/4 Series V 1498cc Ford engine - £590; 4/4 Series V Competition Model - £650; Plus 4 two seater - £695; Plus 4 four seater - £725; Plus 4 Drop Head Coupé - £780; Plus 4 Competition two seater - £775; Plus 4 Super Sports - £950; Plus 4 Plus - £1055, all plus tax. Price list headed "Prices for full range of cars 1965/6". UK agents and overseas distributors listed on page 15. Specifications for the Super Sports model and the 4/4 Series V Competition Model included. No printer listed, but price sheet "Printed in England".

1966 **Plus 4** and **4/4 Series V** Sheet. Black and white with gold highlights (sheet has same design as previous entry). Two sides. Front shows a 4/4 in the woods. The back illustrates the Plus 4 Drop Head Coupé (with 2138cc TR4A engine) at £944 1s. 3d. including tax; 4/4 two seater Series V (with Ford 1498cc engine) at £714 9s. 7d. including tax and 4/4 Competition Model at £786 19s. 7d. including tax; Plus 4 Competition two seater (with 2138cc TR4A engine) at £938 0s. 5d. including tax; and the Plus 4 four seater (with 2138cc TR4A engine) at £877 12s. 1d. including tax. UK agents are listed on the back page. Photograph of worker adjusting door on wood framework. No printer listed.

1966 **Plus 4** and **4/4 Series V** Catalogue with Colour Variation. As entry for Plus 4 and 4/4 Series V Catalogue (two entries previous) but with the front cover tinted in dull green except the words "MORGAN First of the real sports cars" in white letters.

1966 **Plus 4** and **4/4 Series V** Sheet with Colour Variation. As for previous entry (two entries previous) except it has dull green highlights on front.

1967 **Plus 4** and **4/4 Series V** Catalogue. Black and white, with blue highlights. 16 pages. Cover has illustration of a Morgan two seater (number 3) preparing to race. Cover blue with "Morgan Competitive" in white. Cars illustrated are: 4/4 Series V two seater; Plus 4 Drop Head Coupé; Plus 4 two seater; and the Plus 4 four seater; also has a "cutaway" drawing of a Super Sports. Prices listed on small sheet between pages 14 and 15, not glued. Basic prices only listed: 4/4 Series V 1498cc Ford engine - £590; 4/4 Series V Competition Model - £650; Plus 4 two seater - £715; Plus 4 four seater - £725; Plus 4 Drop Head Coupé - £780; Plus 4 Super Sports - £950; all plus tax. Price list headed "Prices for full range of cars 1966/7". UK agents and overseas distributors are listed on pages 14 and 15. Specifications for the Super Sports model and the 4/4

Series V Competition Model. No printer listed, but price sheet "Printed in England".

1967 **Plus 4** and **4/4 Series V** Catalogue Pages Variation. As previous entry but no UK agents and overseas distributors are listed. No "extras when ordered new with car" and no page with "Guarantee". Specifications for the Super Sports model and the 4/4 Series V Competition Model. No printer listed, but price sheet "Printed in England".

1967 **Plus 4** and **4/4 Series V** Sheet. Black and white with blue highlights (sheet has same design as previous entry). Two sides. The front depicts the number 3 Morgan racer. The reverse shows the Plus 4 Drop Head Coupé (with 2138cc TR4A engine) at £960 9s. 5d. including tax; 4/4 two seater Tourer Series V (with Ford 1498cc engine) at £726 18s. 7d. including tax and 4/4 Competition Model at £800 13s. 7d. including tax; Plus 4 two seater (with 2138cc TR4A engine) at £880 11s. 6d including tax; and the Plus 4 four seater (with 2138cc TR4A engine) at £892 17s. 4d. including tax. UK agents are listed at the top of the reverse side. Photograph of worker hammering a shaping dolly on the metal cowl. Printed in England.

1968 **Plus 4** and **4/4 1600** Catalogue. Black and white, with light purple highlights. 16 pages. Cover shows the front nearside wheel area of a Morgan with small pink dots on the black and black dots on the pink. Cars illustrated are: 4/4 1600 two seater; Plus 4 Drop Head Coupé; Plus 4 two seater; and the Plus 4 four seater; also has a "cutaway" drawing of a Super Sports. UK agents and overseas distributors listed on pages 14 and 15. Specifications for the Super Sports model and the 4/4 1600 Competition Model. Prices listed on small sheet, black/white with purple highlights located between pages 14 and 15, not glued. Basic prices only listed: 4/4 1600 - £670; 4/4 1600 Competition Model - £695; Plus 4 two seater - £715; Plus 4 four seater - £725; Plus 4 Drop Head Coupé - £780; Plus 4 Super Sports - £950; all plus tax. Price list headed "Prices for full range of cars 1967/8". No printer listed.

1968 **Plus 8** Road Test Catalogue. 12 pages. Entitled "Vee - 8 Morgan (powerful Rover engine in traditional Morgan), and Autotest number 2204 Morgan Plus 8". Reprinted from *Autocar* 12th September 1968. Contains two articles from same issue of *Autocar*, the first details the production features of the Plus 8, while the second is a road test reporting driving impressions. Both articles contain photographs of MMC 11 as the test car. Printed in England by Newgate Press Ltd., 18-20 Laystall Street, London, EC1. Number RP5604/10.

1968 **Plus 4** and **4/4 1600** Sheet. Black and white with light purple highlights (sheet has same design as 1968 catalogue (two entries previously). Two sides. The front shows the nearside front wheel area of a Morgan as on the front of 1968 catalogue. The reverse side

shows the Plus 4 Drop Head Coupé (with 2138cc TR4A engine) at £960 9s. 5d. including tax; 4/4 1600 two seater Tourer Standard Model at £825 5s. 2d. including tax and 4/4 1600 Competition Model at £855 19s. 9d. including tax; Plus 4 two seater (with 2138cc TR4A engine) at £880 11s. 6d. including tax; and the Plus 4 four seater (with 2138cc TR4A engine) at £892 17s. 4d. including tax. UK agents are listed at top of the reverse side. Photograph of worker hammering a shaping dolly on the metal cowl. Printed in England.

1969 **Plus 8** and **4/4 1600** Catalogue. Black and white, with orange highlights. 8 pages. Cover illustrates dashboard of right hand drive Morgan with a view looking down the louvered bonnet at 5300rpm. Cars illustrated are: Plus 8 Roadster, 4/4 1600 two seater; 4/4 1600 four seater. UK agents and overseas distributors are listed on rear cover. This is the first Morgan catalogue to show the Plus 8. Printed by Adams and Sons (Printers) Ltd., East Street, Hereford, England.

1969 **Plus 8** Folder. 4 folds (concertina type). Black and white with pink highlights. This is the first Plus 8 folder, and is illustrated with a photograph of MMC 11. Five standard colours are listed, one is new for Morgan; i.e. Orange Chrome. UK and overseas agents are listed on the back page. No printer listed.

1969 **Plus 8** Folder with Print Variation. As for previous entry but no UK and overseas agents are listed on the back page.

1969 **4/4 1600** Folder. 4 folds (concertina type). Black and white with orange highlights. Both the two seater and four seater models of the 4/4 1600 are pictured. Specifications given for both 4/4 1600 standard and competition models. Five standard colours are listed, and includes the new Orange Chrome. UK and overseas agents are listed on the back page. No printer listed.

1969 **4/4 1600** Folder with Print Variation. As previous entry but with orange highlights and no UK and Overseas agents are listed on the back page. No printer listed.

1969 **Plus 8** and **4/4 1600** Sheet. Black and white with orange highlights. Front printed 'Morgan' in orange letters on black background, with a small photograph of Plus 8 at speed. UK agents are listed on front. Reverse side shows Plus 8 priced at £1647 5s. 10d. tax included; 4/4 1600 two seater at £1085 18s. 1d. tax included (standard model), Competition Model listed at £1125 1s. 5d. including tax; and the 4/4 1600 four seater priced at £1164 4s. 9d. tax included. Printer - Adams, Hereford.

1970 **Plus 8** and **4/4 1600** Catalogue. Black and white, with pink highlights. 8 pages. Cover printed with black background and the word "MORGAN" in big pink letters. Also a Morgan with the number plate "Morgan 1910-1970". Cars illustrated are: Plus 8 roadster; 4/

4 1600 two seater; 4/4 1600 four seater. UK agents and overseas distributors are listed on rear cover. Printed by Adams and Sons (Printers) Ltd., East Street, Hereford.

1971 **Plus 8** and **4/4 1600** Catalogue. Black and white, with orange highlights. 8 pages. Cover illustrated with number 49 racing Morgan with black car and orange background and covered with a large number of "dots". Cars illustrated are: Plus 8 roadster; 4/4 1600 two seater; 4/4 1600 four seater. UK agents and overseas distributors are listed on rear cover. Printed by Adams and Sons (Printers) Ltd., East Street, Hereford.

1971 **Plus 8** and **4/4 1600** Sheet. Black and white with orange highlights. Front shows word "MORGAN" in orange letters on black background. Small photograph of Plus 8 spinning wheels. UK agents are listed on front. Reverse shows Plus 8 priced at £1699.51 tax included; 4/4 1600 two seater at £1196.87 tax included; and the 4/4 1600 four seater was priced at £1236.04 tax included. Printer - Adams, Hereford.

1971 **Plus 8** and **4/4 1600** Sheet with Price and Colour Variation. As previous entry but with darker orange highlights. Reverse shows Plus 8 priced at £1789.37 tax included; 4/4 1600 two seater at £1369.37 tax included; and the 4/4 1600 four seater was priced at £1411.87 tax included. Printer - Adams, Hereford.

1972 **Plus 8** and **4/4 1600** Catalogue. Black and white, with gold highlights. 8 pages. Cover shows Morgan in the woods with a young lady leaning against a tree. Cars illustrated are: Plus 8; 4/4 1600 two seater; 4/4 1600 four seater. Specifications include the 4-speed Rover gear box for the Plus 8. UK agents and overseas distributors are listed on back cover. Printed by Adams and Sons (Printers) Ltd., East Street, Hereford.

1972 **Plus 8** and **4/4 1600** Sheet. Black and white with gold highlights. Front shows Morgan in the woods with a young lady leaning against a tree. UK agents are listed on front. Reverse shows Plus 8 priced at £1995.31 tax included; 4/4 1600 two seater at £1447.94 tax included; and the 4/4 1600 four seater priced at £1563.94 tax included. Printer - Adams, Hereford.

1973-74 **Plus 8** and **4/4 1600** Catalogue. Full colour catalogue. 12 pages. Cover illustrates a "psychedelic" Morgan on blue and white background with gold rays behind the car. Inside contains colourful psychedelic drawings. Cars pictured are: Plus 8; 4/4 1600 two seater; 4/4 1600 four seater. UK agents and overseas distributors are listed on page 9. Page 10 and 11 show 18 black and white photographs that illustrate old Morgan racing and factory scenes. Designed by Charles Morgan and printed by Adams and Sons (Printers) Ltd., Hereford.

1973-74 **Plus 8** and **4/4 1600** Sheet. Black and white with blue-green highlights. Front has a small photograph of white 4/4 next to jet plane. UK agents are listed on front. Reverse shows Plus 8 priced at £2162.86 tax included; 4/4 1600 two seater at £1569.43 tax included; and the 4/4 four seater was priced at £1694.43 tax included. Printer - Adams, Hereford.

1973-74 Morgan Paint Colour Chart. One sheet. Printed on gloss card. Has Morgan Motor Co. Ltd. topped by Plus 8 Wings. Five standard colours listed: Dark Blue, Light Orange, etc. With "Belco ICI Dulux" at bottom.

1975 **Plus 8** and **4/4 1600** Catalogue. Black and white with blue highlights. 12 pages. Cover (in full colour) shows street scene in London with two young men admiring a maroon Plus 8 with stone interior and side screens. Cars illustrated are: Plus 8; 4/4 1600 two seater; 4/4 1600 four seater. UK agents and overseas distributors are listed on page 10. Page 11 shows five black and white photographs that illustrate Morgan factory scenes. Printed by Adams and Sons (Printers) Ltd., East Street, Hereford.

1975 **Plus 8** and **4/4 1600** Sheet. Black and white. Front shows photograph of street scene in London with two young men admiring a Plus 8. UK agents are listed on front. Reverse shows Plus 8 priced at £2683 tax included; 4/4 1600 two seater at £1930 tax included; and 4/4 1600 four seater was priced at £2072 tax included. Printed by Adams and Sons (Printers) Ltd., East Street, Hereford.

1976 **Plus 8** and **4/4** Folder. 2 folds. Full colour. Cover depicts a yellow Plus 8 and small photograph of maroon Plus 8 at speed. Inside illustrates "The Big Beefy Plus 8", 4/4 two seater and 4/4 four seater. Black and white with yellow highlights. The back lists UK agents and overseas distributors, and Plus 8 and 4/4 extras. No printer listed. Separate price list sheet insert.

1976 **Plus 8** and **4/4** Folder with Print Variation. As previous entry but back page lists Plus 8 and 4/4 extras. No agents or distributors listed. No printer listed.

1977 **Plus 8** and **4/4** Folder. 2 folds. Full colour. Cover depicts blue Plus 8 on a white background. Inside depicts "Exciting Plus 8" and "Fantastic 4/4" two seater and "Four seat fun 4/4" four seater. Black and white with yellow highlights. The back lists UK agents and overseas distributors, and Plus 8 and 4/4 extras. No printer listed. Separate price list sheet insert.

1977 Morgan Paint Colour Chart. Details as for 1973/4 chart but with "Nut Brown 118" now included. Other colours: Indigo 88, Royal Ivory 44, Deep Brunswick Green 427, Signal Red 437. Bottom printed "ICI Logo Autocolor".

1978-79-80 **Plus 8** and **4/4** Folder. 2 folds. Full colour. Cover printed "Morgan", First of the Real Sports Cars" in white outline on a black background. Two small photographs of the factory and a larger photograph of a red Plus 8 on the front cover. A red Plus 8 is illustrated at the first opening of the folder. When fully opened the folder illustrates large colour photographs of a blue 4/4 two seater and a Deep Brunswick Green 4/4 four seater; also two colour photographs of the factory plus six black and white photographs of past Morgans (from a 1913 Morgan Grand Prix Three- wheeler to a 1967 Plus 4 two seater). The back page lists UK agents and overseas distributors and Plus 8 and 4/4 extras. No printer listed. Separate price list sheet insert.

1978 **Plus 8** and **4/4 1600** Sheet. Black and white with red highlights. Front illustrated with a photograph of white Plus 8 driving along a rain covered street. "It's Worth It!" is in big red letters. British agents are listed on front. Reverse illustrates Plus 8, 4/4 1600 two seater; and the 4/4 1600 four seater. No printer listed.

1980 **Plus 8** and **4/4 1600** Sheet. Black and white with light blue highlights. Front depicts red racing Plus 8; with Morris Stapleton stickers, in action. Heading reads "The sports car that goes on", in black letters. British agents listed on the front. The reverse illustrates the 4/4 two seater, the 4/4 four seater and the Plus 8 with Green highlight colour. No printer is listed.

1980 **Plus 8** and **4/4 1600** Sheet Variation. Black and white. As previous entry but under Plus 8 photograph caption reads "Willhire Snetterton 24-hour race for production cars. Winner of the Commanders Cup for the greatest distance by a single car entry Plus 8, entered by Morris Stapleton Motors, Order your Morgan from Morris Stapleton" with address under. No other agents listed. Bottom reverse "The Car, Hand Built by Craftsman ..."

1981 **Plus 8** and **4/4** Folder. 2 folds. Full colour. Cover printed "Morgan, First of the Real Sports Cars" in white outline on a black background. Two small photographs of the factory and one large photograph of a country scene with a green Plus 8, blue 4/4 two seater, and white 4/4 four seater illustrated on the front cover. A red Plus 8 is illustrated at the first opening of the folder. When fully opened the folder illustrates a large colour photograph of a blue 4/4 two seater and a Deep Brunswick Green 4/4 four seater. Plus two colour photographs of the factory plus six black and white photographs of past Morgans (from a 1913 Morgan Grand Prix Three-wheeler to a 1967 Plus 4 two seater). The back page lists UK agents and overseas distributors, and Plus 8 and 4/4 extras. The back cover is different from that of 1978-79-80. Several dealers and options are listed differently. No printer listed. Separate price list sheet insert.

1982-83-84 **Plus 8** and **4/4** Folder. 2 folds. Full colour. Cover shows a young couple in a red 4/4 two seater below the Morgan wings emblem and a Union Jack flag and a chequered flag. A black Plus 8 with stone leather interior is illustrated on the first opening of the folder. When fully opened the folder has colour photographs of a blue 4/4 two seater and a Deep Brunswick Green 4/4 four seater. Plus two colour photographs of the Fiat 1600 T/C engine and the Ford CVH (XR3) 1600 engine, and six black and white photographs of past Morgans (from a 1911 Morgan two seater runabout to a 1965 Plus 4 Plus). The back page lists UK agents and overseas distributors, and Plus 8 and 4/4 extras. No printer listed. Separate price list sheet insert.

1982 **Plus 8** and **4/4** 1600 Sheet. Black and white with red highlights. "The Professional Choice". Front shows photograph of Plus 8 on a mountain road in front of tall trees. Specifications for the Plus 8 and British agents also listed on front. Reverse shows 4/4 1600 two seater, and the 4/4 1600 four seater with a choice of the Fiat T/C engine or the Ford CVH engine. No printer listed.

1982 **Plus 8** Road Test Folder. Reprinted from *Motor*, 15th May 1982. Black and white. Six pages. Opens to large photograph of Plus 8 BUY 600M. Five other photographs. Specifications and test performance lists page 4 with a comparison of performance against five rivals. Bottom of back page "IPC Business Press Ltd. Printed by Weston Press Ltd., St. Bernards Works, Stoney Lane, London, SE19.

1984 Morgan Paint Colour Chart. Printed black on white card with Morgan wings at top and "Morgan Motor Co. Ltd. and 75th Anniversary". Shows six colours which includes a new colour, 'Jubilee Blue - Special Anniversary Colour', other colours are: Nut Brown 118; Deep Brunswick Green 427; Royal Ivory 44; Indigo 88; Signal Red 437. Printed in black at bottom, the ICI logo and Autocolour match colour with science.

1984-85-86 **Plus 8** and **4/4** Folder. 2 folds. Full colour. Cover shows a close-up of a Morgan grille with a gold tint to grille bars. The first fold opens to illustrate a red 4/4 two seater and a red 4/4 four seater with specifications. Fully opened the folder reveals a large colour photograph of a citron green Plus 8 with specifications for the Plus 8, both the carburettor and injection engines. The back page lists UK agents and overseas distributors. No printer listed.

1984-85-86 **Plus 8** and **4/4** Folder with Colour Variation. As two previous entries but cover shows a close-up of a Morgan grille with a blue tint to grille bars.

1985 **Plus 8** and **4/4 1600** Sheet. Black and white with light blue highlights. "Morgan, the Real Sports Car". Front shows photograph of white Plus 8 in a field in front of tall trees. Specifications for the Plus 8 (including those for both the carburettor engine and the new

FOUR SEAT
FUN

injection engine) and British agents are listed on front. Reverse shows 4/4 1600 two seater, and the 4/4 1600 four seater with the Ford CVH engine. No printer listed.

1985 **Plus 4** Sheet. Full colour. Front shows photograph of blue Plus 4 in a field. Specifications for the Plus 4 (with specifications for the 2000 Fiat engine with petrol injection listed on the reverse. This sheet was an insert in the 1985-86 folder as a supplement to the catalogue. This is the first Morgan sales literature for the Plus 4 since 1968 catalogue. Print number CG/1216/3.85/C.

1986-87-88 **Plus 8** and **4/4** Folder. 2 folds. Full colour, on glossy paper. Cover has a close-up of a dark green 4/4 two seater in a leaf covered country lane. The first fold opens to reveal a green 4/4 two seater, a red 4/4 four seater (complete with family of four), and a red Plus 8 being inspected by three firemen. Specifications are listed for all models. Fully opened the folder reveals a large colour painting (by Michael English) of a Plus 4 driven by a young woman. The back shows UK agents and overseas distributors, with two U.S.A. agents now listed, Isis Motors and Cantab Motors Ltd. No printer listed. Separate price list sheet insert.

1986-87-88 **Plus 8** and **4/4** Folder with Variation. As previous entry but uses lighter weight, unglossed paper. Separate price list sheet insert.

1988 **Plus 4** General Specification Sheet. Black and white with green highlights. Front shows Morgan Motor Company letterhead with printed specifications of the body/chassis. Reverse shows Rover M-16 engine specifications, clutch, gearbox, and rear axle specifications. Also included are: performance figures (top speed of approx. 115mph). Prices listed as: two seater Plus 4 - £13498.61; and the Plus 4 four seater - £14526.41 total prices including taxes. No printer listed.

1988-89-90-91 **Plus 8** and **4/4** Catalogue. 12 pages. Full colour, heavy "dimpled" paper used for the cover, which has illustration of a close-up of the Morgan wings emblem covered in frost. Catalogue opens to reveal a "silhouette" of a Plus 8. The new Plus 4 with the Rover M-16 engine is illustrated on pages 6 and 7. Specifications listed for all models. Page 11 shows UK agents and overseas distributors. The rear cover shows an old photograph (from 1951)

of a young lady leaning on the door of a 1951 Plus 4 in Paris. No printer listed. Separate price list sheet insert.

1988-89-90-91 **Plus 8** and **4/4** Catalogue with Variation on Cover. As previous entry but with smooth paper being used for the cover, the same paper as the inside pages.

1990 **Plus 8** (3.9-litre) Sheet. Full colour front, black and white back. Front shows photograph of a red Plus 8 in the Malvern hills. Specifications for the Plus 8 (3.9-litre) are on reverse. "Now equipped with twin catalysts and an evaporative control system to comply with California emission legislation, the most stringent in the world". No printer listed, but photograph is courtesy of Michael Bailie, Performance Car. This sheet is a supplement to 1990-91 catalogue.

1992-93-94 **Plus 8** and **4/4** Catalogue. 16 pages. Full colour. The cover has a reproduction of an original painting by Charles Morgan. Opens to reveal photographs of factory workers similar to those seen in the April 1990 issue of Esquire. Pictured are the Morgan 4/4, the Morgan Plus 4, and the Morgan Plus 8. Specifications are listed for all models. Pages 14 and 15 lists the UK agents and overseas distributors using a world map and flags from each country that Morgans are sold in. The back cover (page 16) shows a photograph of Tony Barry, who worked his whole life at the factory, then retired to die shortly thereafter. No printer listed, but photographs courtesy of Neil Miller, Richard Tipping, Richard J. Sowers. Separate price list insers for 1991, 1992, 1993 and 1994.

1993-94 4/4 **Ford 1800** Sheet. Full colour front shows dark green 4/4 with stone interior and chrome wire wheels on a country road. Reverse gives specifications for the 4/4 1800 (Zetec Ford engine) and his pictures (5) of U.S. "Racers", a Series I (the Prototype) and RNP 504 along the lower reverse part. No printer. This is a catalogue addendum for 1994.

Many of the main agents worldwide produced their own catalogues, folders, etc. For example, Worldwide Import Inc., and Fergus Imported Cars Inc., of the USA produced several in the 1960s. Also, Isis Imports Ltd. (USA) in the 1980s and 1990s. Earlier, in the late 1930s, many Far East importers produced sheets and a few folders. These have not been included as they did not originate from the Morgan factory.

This catalogue of Morgan sales literature was compiled from the private collections of the author, John Worrall and other Morgan enthusiasts, plus various articles in club magazines worldwide.
The author and publishers would be pleased to learn of any factory sales literature not included in the above list.

APPENDIX VIII

SAFETY, JACKING & WORKING PROCEDURES & GLOSSARY OF TERMS

Safety, jacking & working procedures

This book contains considerable advice concerned with practical aspects of maintenance, repair, renovation and modification. This information is intended for the use of qualified engineers and mechanics. You must not undertake any such practical work unless you are suitably qualified and confident of your ability to carry out the work safely and competently. We must draw your attention to the following - **IMPORTANT NOTE**. *While the author has prepared the practical information in this book with diligence and care, it is possible that it contains errors or omissions. It is not possible to foresee every possible area of personal danger or possibility of mechanical damage and warn readers accordingly. The author, publisher and retailers therefore accept no responsibility for personal injury or mechanical damage which is in any way related to the use of this publication. If you use the practical information contained within this book, you accept full personal responsibility for the consequences.*

• SAFETY

You must work responsibly at all times and always take appropriate precautions to avoid damage or personal injury. Always be aware of potential dangers whenever working on or around your car. Don't think just in terms of the obvious, go a little deeper. Here are just five examples of the level of awareness you should maintain. 1) Remember that most fluids used by the car or for maintenance/cleaning are in some way dangerous - so read the maker's instructions and don't make assumptions. 2) Old engine oil has been proved to cause skin cancer in mice - so protect your skin with gloves or barrier cream and wash contaminated areas quickly. 3) If you're working on the car's fuel system in your garage, remember that if the garage contains a house heating boiler the ignition sequence may occur while there are gas (petrol) fumes in the air - it's also possible the boiler has a constant pilot flame. 4) Slipping on spilled oil, or other fluids, could put you in hospital for a long time. 5) A metal watch strap, bracelet or even a ring could cause a short between a live terminal and earth (ground).

• JACKING AND SUPPORTING THE CAR

There are a number of maintenance, repair and restoration operations which require work under the car, and you will need to make some provision for this. In an ideal world, we would all have vehicle lifts, but most of us must make do with less exotic equipment.

Unless you happen to have an access pit in the floor of your garage, you'll need to raise the car high enough to permit good working access below the body, while preserving a good level of safety. A normal small wheeled hydraulic jack and two large axle (safety) stands are a minimum requirement . You can purchase a suitable jack from tool or auto parts stores, or from mail order sources. We recommend that you avoid the smallest of the jacks supplied for home use. These have a capacity of 1500kg/1.5 tons, which is adequate, but have a restrictive lift range of only around 200mm/8inches. The type with a capacity of 2000kg/2 tons and a lift range of just under 300mm/12 inches is more useful. You'll find that the lift range is significant when you need to raise the car high enough to work underneath. The further the jack can lift, the less you will need to jack in stages, which will save you a lot of time. As rule of thumb, buy the biggest lift capacity you can afford.

Axle stands come in various sizes too, and again, the rule is the bigger the better. These are not only stronger than the smaller types, they allow you to raise the vehicle much higher, and every extra inch helps. There are a few operations on the car which will require around 460mm/18inches clearance underneath, and in all cases, more space means more comfortable working conditions. Remember that if you use a crawler board, you lose a little clearance.

Warning! Don't forget that a car is heavy - if it collapses while you're under it, you will be killed or badly injured, so don't take chances. **Never work beneath a car that is not supported by at least two axle (safety) stands.**

Warning! Never use jacks or axle stands on sloping ground and always ensure that the jack and axle stand pads are bearing on suitably strong structures such as the car's front cross-axle, rear axle or reinforced sections of the chassis.

Warning! If you are only jacking

one end or side of the car, you must chock all those wheels which remain on the ground (back and front of the tyre).

Warning! If the vehicle has to be raised in stages, don't be tempted to jack too much at each stage: the vehicle will become unstable.

• WORKING PROCEDURES

Before you start any practical work on your car, read through the relevant details carefully. Check any drawings or photographs relating to the task, and compare this information with your own car. If necessary re-read the section until you are confident that you know what you will be doing. Not only does confident familiarity minimise mistakes, it will actually save you time when you do the job for real - you won't need to constantly refer back to the book for procedural details.

While working in the open is fine for minor jobs if a major repair or overhaul is envisaged you should make strenuous efforts to find somewhere under cover to work. If absolutely unavoidable, you could remove major assemblies outside, but any dismantling work should take place under some sort of roof.

Most of us will be working inside a normal domestic garage with restricted floor area and ceiling height. Before you start work, make sure that you have sufficient room to work comfortably. If you have the same kind of garage that most of us have to use, clear out as much junk as you can (especially on or around the bench area), and arrange your garden tools, bicycles, ski equip-ment or whatever neatly, and well away from your work area. Try to keep at least one side of the garage clear of domestic items.

You will need plenty of light as well. Make sure you have adequate general lighting, with extra lighting over the workbench, plus one or two inspection lights for use around and under the car and a flashlight for use in confined spaces.

Don't forget that you will need somewhere to store removed parts safely, and this requirement will vary according to what you intend to do. In most cases, you can lay out the parts on shelves or in boxes, though some of the bigger assemblies, especially things like the dash panel, seats or the hood will obviously require much more space.

If you are going to undertake a major overhaul which entails removal of the engine and transmission, you will need around twice the area required to park the car, plus adequate access to allow the engine/transmission assembly to be removed. You will need to assess the likely space requirement and make suitable arrangements before you start work.

Set aside an area where you can leave major parts or assemblies safely, with no risk of accidental damage. You will know best how you can arrange this according to your own circumstances. You may be planning to carry out major work over an extended period, maybe over the winter months. If so, plan some kind of long-term storage for removed parts, with dust sheets to cover removed major assemblies or body parts until they are needed again.

The seasoned mechanic will instinctively collect handy containers - plastic tubs and resealable plastic bags are great for tiny, easily lost parts, and cardboard cartons are good for bigger parts. If money is no object, get some stackable plastic bins. Avoid using glass jars for storage - they break too easily.

Use PVC electrical tape or masking tape to identify parts, hose and wiring connections, etc as they are removed - you can write on the tape or on the part itself with a fine-point indelible marker pen. You can also use card or paper labels for this. Have a notepad handy for making simple sketches of how specific parts fit together or how wiring or hoses are routed. Avoid pens that use water-based inks which will rub off easily. If you have the time and the equipment, a photographic record of your work can be very useful.

The value of marking things cannot be overstressed - you will be surprised how easily it is to get confused about which wire or bolt goes where, just a few hours after you disconnected them. In many cases you can make life easier for yourself by refitting bolts and screws as you remove them, either screwing them loosely back into position after removing the component they retain, or in the case of covers, pushing the screw back through the cover and through a piece of corrugated card. When you get round to installing the part, the fasteners will be in the correct relative positions - this is especially important where you have similar screws or bolts of varying length.

American/English glossary of automotive terms

American	English	American	English
A-arm	Wishbone (suspension)	Curve	Corner
Antenna	Aerial	Dashboard	Facia
Axleshaft	Halfshaft	Denatured alcohol	Methylated spirit
		Dome lamp	Interior light
Back-up	Reverse	Driveaxle	Driveshaft
Barrel	Choke/venturi	Driveshaft	Propeller shaft
Block	Chock/wedge		
Box end wrench	Ring spanner	Fender	Wing/mudguard
Bushing	Bush	Firewall	Bulkhead
		Flashlight	Torch
Clutch hub	Synchro hub	Float bowl	Float chamber
Coast	Freewheel	Freeway,	
Convertible	Drop head	turnpike, etc.	Motorway
Cotter pin	Split pin	Frozen	Seized
Counterclockwise	Anti-clockwise		
Countershaft	Layshaft (of gearbox)	Gas tank	Petrol tank
Crescent wrench	Open-ended spanner	Gas pedal	Accelerator pedal

American	English	American	English
Gasoline (gas)	Petrol	Quarter window	Quarterlight
Gearshift	Gearchange		
Generator (DC)	Dynamo	Recap	Retread
Ground	Earth (electrical)	Release cylinder	Slave cylinder
		Repair shop	Garage
		Replacement	Renewal
Header/manifold	Manifold (exhaust)	Ring gear	
Heat riser	Hot spot	(of differential)	Crownwheel
High	Top gear	Rocker panel	Sill panel
Hood	Bonnet (engine cover)	Rod bearing	Big-end bearing
		Rotor/disk	Disc (brake)
Idle	Tickover		
Intake	Inlet	Secondary shoe	Trailing shoe (of brake)
		Sedan	Saloon
Jackstands		Setscrew,	
/Safety stands	Axle stands	Allen screw	Grub screw
Jumper cable	Jump lead	Shift fork	Selector fork
		Shift lever	Gearlever/gearstick
Keeper	Collet	Shift rod	Selector rod
Kerosene	Paraffin	Shock absorber,	
Knock pin	Roll pin	shock	Damper/shocker
		Snap-ring	Circlip
Lash	Freeplay/Clearance	Soft top	Hood
Latch	Catch	Spacer	Distance piece
Latches	Locks	Spare tire	Spare wheel
License plate		Spark plug wires	HT leads
/tag plate	Number plate	Spindle arm	Steering arm
Light	Lamp	Stablizer	
Lock (for valve		or sway bar	Anti-roll bar
spring retainer)	Split cotter (for valve cap)	Station wagon	Estate car
Lopes	Hunts	Stumbles	Hesitates
Lug nut	Wheel nut		
		Tang or lock	Tab
Metal chips		Taper pin	Cotter pin
or debris	Swarf	Teardown	Strip(down)/dismantle
Misses	Misfires	Throw-out bearing	Thrust bearing
Muffler	Silencer	Tie-rod	
		(or connecting rod)	Trackrod (of steering)
Oil pan	Sump	Transmission	Gearbox
Open flame	Naked flame	Troubleshooting	Fault finding/diagnosis
		Trunk	Boot
Panel wagon/van	Van	Tube wrench	Box spanner
Parking light	Sidelight	Turn signal	Indicator
Parking brake	Handbrake		
Piston pin or wrist		Valve lifter	Tappet
pin bearing/bush	Small (little) end bearing	Valve lifter or tappet	Cam follower or tappet
Piston pin		Valve cover	Rocker cover
or wrist pin	Gudgeon pin	VOM (volt ohmmeter)	Multimeter
Pitman arm	Drop arm		
Power brake booster	Servo unit	Wheel cover	Roadwheel trim
Primary shoe	Leading shoe (of brake)	Wheel well	Wheelarch
Prussian blue	Engineer's blue	Whole drive line	Transmission
Pry	Prise (force apart)	Windshield	Windscreen
Prybar	Crowbar	Wrench	Spanner
Prying	Levering		

INDEX

Dear Reader,
We hope you enjoyed this Veloce Publishing
production. If you have ideas for books on
Morgan or other marques, please write and tell us.
Meantime, Happy Motoring!

THE END